# Lecture Notes in Artificial Intelligence 10928

Subseries of Lecture Notes in Computer Science

## LNAI Series Editors

Randy Goebel
*University of Alberta, Edmonton, Canada*
Yuzuru Tanaka
*Hokkaido University, Sapporo, Japan*
Wolfgang Wahlster
*DFKI and Saarland University, Saarbrücken, Germany*

## LNAI Founding Series Editor

Joerg Siekmann
*DFKI and Saarland University, Saarbrücken, Germany*

More information about this series at http://www.springer.com/series/1244

Vasiliki Vouloutsi · José Halloy
Anna Mura · Michael Mangan
Nathan Lepora · Tony J. Prescott
Paul F. M. J. Verschure (Eds.)

# Biomimetic and Biohybrid Systems

7th International Conference, Living Machines 2018
Paris, France, July 17–20, 2018
Proceedings

 Springer

*Editors*
Vasiliki Vouloutsi
SPECS, Institute for Bioengineering
 of Catalonia
Barcelona
Spain

José Halloy
Laboratoire Interdisciplinaire des
Université Paris Diderot
Paris Cedex 13
France

Anna Mura
SPECS, Institute for Bioengineering
 of Catalonia
Barcelona
Spain

Michael Mangan
University of Sheffield
Sheffield
UK

Nathan Lepora
Bristol University
Bristol
UK

Tony J. Prescott
University of Sheffield
Sheffield
UK

Paul F. M. J. Verschure
SPECS, Institute for Bioengineering
 of Catalonia
Barcelona
Spain

ISSN 0302-9743            ISSN 1611-3349  (electronic)
Lecture Notes in Artificial Intelligence
ISBN 978-3-319-95971-9        ISBN 978-3-319-95972-6  (eBook)
https://doi.org/10.1007/978-3-319-95972-6

Library of Congress Control Number: 2018948143

LNCS Sublibrary: SL7 – Artificial Intelligence

Printed on acid-free paper

This Springer imprint is published by the registered company Springer Nature Switzerland AG
The registered company address is: Gewerbestrasse 11, 6330 Cham, Switzerland

# Preface

These proceedings contain the papers presented at Living Machines 2018: the 7th International Conference on Biomimetic and Biohybrid Systems, held in Paris, France, July 17–20, 2018. The international conferences in the Living Machines series are targeted at the intersection of research on novel life-like technologies inspired by the scientific investigation of biological systems, *biomimetics*, and research that seeks to interface biological and artificial systems to create biohybrid systems. The conference aim is to highlight the most exciting international research in both of these fields united by the theme of "Living Machines."

The Living Machines conference series was first organized by the Convergent Science Network (CSN) of biomimetic and biohybrid systems to provide a focal point for the gathering of world-leading researchers and the presentation and discussion of cutting-edge research in this rapidly emerging field. The modern definition of biomimetics is the development of novel technologies through the distillation of principles from the study of biological systems. The investigation of biomimetic systems can serve two complementary goals. First, a suitably designed and configured biomimetic artifact can be used to test theories about the natural system of interest. Second, biomimetic technologies can provide useful, elegant, and efficient solutions to unsolved challenges in science and engineering. Biohybrid systems are formed by combining at least one biological component — an existing living system — and at least one artificial, newly engineered component. By passing information in one or both directions, such a system forms a new hybrid bio-artificial entity.

Although one may consider this approach to be modern, the underlying principles are centuries old. More specifically, after the European Renaissance, we observe the usage of automata to imitate the functionality of both animals and humans. Such endeavors not only served to entertain but can also be considered as philosophical experiments that allowed for the reproduction of aspects of living organisms in machines, while revealing important information regarding their nature. What initially started as a philosophical idea turned into a mechanical revolution as most of the automata of the 18th century were not only imitating the external appearance of an organism but also simulated the organism's functionalities or behaviors. An example of linking human kinesiology and anatomy is Leonardo da Vinci's "Knight" in 1495, where an elaborate system of pulleys and cables moved the knight's armor to produce various human-like independent motions. This compelling artifact has endowed modern robotics with scaffolds for kinematics and structural design.

A way to appreciate the early simulation of living beings is the central idea of "moving anatomy" in the creations of Jacques de Vaucanson (1709–1782), a French inventor and artist. One of his first biomechanical automata was the "Flute Player," a life-sized wooden statue of a man who played the flute by emitting air through its mouth. This design resulted from the extensive study of human flute players and was used to validate Vaucanson's hypothesis that the consequent pitch of a note was affected by the blowing pressure, aperture, and sounding length. Notably, his most famous creation was the "Digesting Duck" (1739) a mechanical artifact modeled upon thorough studies of real ducks that was conceptualized to teach the animal's anatomy. Both the "Flute Player" and the "Digesting Duck," although used for entertainment, are good examples that intended to approximate their biological counterparts.

Attention to anatomical, physiological, and behavioral simulations started with Vaucanson and climaxed with the creations of Pierre Jaquet-Droz (1721–1790). The father-and-son team of Pierre and Henri-Louis Jaquet-Droz produced three automata: "the Writer," "the Draughtsman," and "the Musician." Their hands were modeled after real human hands that later constituted the basis for constructing prosthetic limbs. The tendency of that period was to use mechanical artifacts to approximate nature and, through modeling, experimentation, and observation, draw conclusions about their biological counterparts. Nowadays, the study and modeling of biological systems has led to the acquisition of insights into a plethora of domains ranging from architecture to materials, sensors, and control systems and even robotics. Advances in each of these areas were presented in detail at the conference.

The main conference, July 18–20, took the form of a three-day single-track oral and poster presentation program that included five plenary lectures from leading international researchers in biomimetic and biohybrid systems: Jérôme Casas (University of Tours) on insect-inspired mechatronics; Metin Sitti (Max Planck Institute) on bio-inspired and bio-hybrid miniature mobile robots; Stéphane Viollet (Aix-Marseille University) on the application of insect perception models to robots; Simon Thorpe (University of Toulouse) on memory storage and retrieval in both humans and machines; and Pascal Brioist (University of Tours) on the machines of Leonardo Da Vinci. There were also 22 regular talks and one poster session and poster spotlight (featuring approximately 36 posters). Session themes included: advances in soft robotics; 3D-printed bio-machines; robots and society; biomimetic vision and control; utility and limits of deep learning for bio-robotics; collective and emergent behaviors in animals and robots; and bioinspired flight. The conference was complemented by workshops on July 17, 2018, held at the École Normale Superieure in Paris. More specifically, "Sapiens 5.0: Augmenting Humanity to Overcome the Challenges of the Anthropocene" was organized by professor Paul F. M. J. Verschure and Tony Prescott.

The main conference was hosted at the Muséum national d'Histoire Naturelle, MNHN (Paris, France), a place built initially for medicinal and educational purposes. Surrounded by the botanical garden and next to the Seine, for more than four centuries, the MNHN hosted revolutionary discoveries in the field of natural sciences held by prodigious minds, such as Buffon, Lamarck, or Cuvier. Today, the MNHN is one of the most highly considered places in Europe with regard to scientific dissemination, education, and integration of multiple areas of expertise, ranging from molecular biology to applied technology. Hosting the Living Machines conference in such a place reinforces the aim of MNHN in the exploration and promotion of nature to protect it and understand it. This year, Living Machines was held in Paris after successful previous editions in Stanford, USA in 2017; Edinburgh, UK in 2016; Barcelona, Spain in 2015; Milan Italy in 2014; London, UK in 2013; and Barcelona, Spain in 2012.

We would like to thank our hosts at the National History Museum of Paris, Emmanuelle Pouydebat DR CNRS, and Vincent Bels, our hosts for the poster session that was held at the Pierre and Marie Curie University, on the Jussieu Campus, in collaboration with Stéphane Doncieux UMPC, ISIR, and Benoît Girard DR CNRS, UPMC, ISIR.

We also wish to thank the many people that were involved in making the seventh edition of Living Machines possible: José Halloy and Paul Verschure co-chaired the meeting; Vasiliki Vouloutsi and Michael Mangan chaired the Program Committee and edited the conference proceedings; Tony Prescott chaired the international Steering Committee; Nathan Lepora was involved in the conference communication; Anna Mura was the general organization chair and also coordinated the website and communications; José Halloy and his group provided administrative and local organizational support in Paris. We are grateful to the SPECS lab and the Communication Unit at the Institute for Bioengineering of Catalonia (IBEC) in Barcelona for the assistance in the organization and for technical support. We would also like to thank the authors and speakers who contributed their work, and the members of the Program Committee for their detailed and considered reviews. We are grateful to the five keynote speakers who shared with us their vision of the future.

Finally, we wish to thank the organizers and sponsors of LM 2018: The Convergence Science Network for Biomimetic and Neurotechnology (CSNII; ICT-601167); the Institute for Bioengineering of Catalonia IBEC, and the Catalan Institution for Research and Advanced Studies (ICREA). Additional support was also provided by Springer. Living Machines 2018 was further supported by: the IOP physics journal *Bioinspiration & Biomimetics*, which will publish a special issue of articles based on the best conference papers, and *Biomimetics*, an Open Access journal, which will publish a special issue of articles based on the best conference posters, and by Eodyne SL (neuro-rehabilitation solutions) with an award for best paper with a social impact.

July 2018

Vasiliki Vouloutsi
José Halloy
Anna Mura
Michael Mangan
Nathan Lepora
Tony J. Prescott
Paul F. M. J. Verschure

# Organization

## Conference Chairs

José Halloy               Université Paris Diderot, France
Tony J. Prescott        University of Sheffield, UK
Paul F. M. J. Verschure    Institute for Bioengineering of Catalonia (IBEC),
                                  Barcelona
                                  Institute of Science and Technology (BIST), Catalan
                                  Institution for Research and Advanced Studies
                                  (ICREA), Barcelona, Spain

## Program Chairs

Vasiliki Vouloutsi       Institute for Bioengineering of Catalonia (IBEC),
                                  Barcelona
                                  Institute of Science and Technology (BIST), Barcelona,
                                  Spain
Michael Mangan       University of Lincoln, UK

## Local Organizers

José Halloy              Université Paris Diderot, France
Stéphane Doncieux     UMPC, ISIR, France
Benoît Girard          DR CNRS, UPMC, ISIR, France
Emmanuelle Pouydebat   DR CNRS, Muséum d'Histoire Naturelle, France
Vincent Bels           Muséum d'Histoire Naturelle, France

## Communications

Anna Mura             Institute for Bioengineering of Catalonia (IBEC),
                                  Barcelona
                                  Institute of Science and Technology (BIST), Barcelona,
                                  Spain
Nathan Lepora         University of Bristol, UK

## Conference Website

Anna Mura             Institute for Bioengineering of Catalonia (IBEC),
                                  Barcelona
                                  Institute of Science and Technology (BIST), Barcelona,
                                  Spain

## Workshop Organizers

| | |
|---|---|
| Tony J. Prescott | University of Sheffield, UK |
| Paul F. M. J. Verschure | Institute for Bioengineering of Catalonia (IBEC), Barcelona |
| | Institute of Science and Technology (BIST), Catalan Institution for Research and Advanced Studies (ICREA), Barcelona, Spain |

## International Steering Committee

| | |
|---|---|
| Joseph Ayers | Northeastern University, USA |
| Mark Cutkosky | Stanford University, USA |
| Marc Desmulliez | Heriot-Watt University, UK |
| José Halloy | Université Paris Diderot, France |
| Nathan Lepora | University of Bristol, UK |
| Barbara Mazzolai | Istituto Italiano di Tecnologia, Italy |
| Anna Mura | Catalan Institution for Research and Advanced Studies (IBEC-BIST), Barcelona, Spain |
| Tony Prescott | University of Sheffield, UK |
| Roger Quinn Case | Western Reserve University, USA |
| Paul Verschure | Catalan Institution for Research and Advanced Studies (IBEC-BIST) and Catalan Institution for Research and Advanced Studies, Barcelona, Spain |
| Vasiliki Vouloutsi | Catalan Institution for Research and Advanced Studies (IBEC-BIST), Barcelona, Spain |
| Stuart Wilson | University of Sheffield, UK |

## Program Committee

| | |
|---|---|
| Andrew Adamatzky | UWE, Bristol, UK |
| Xerxes Arsiwalla | Institute for Bioengineering of Catalonia (IBEC), Spain |
| Farshad Arvin | University of Manchester, UK |
| Farshad Arvin Tareq Assaf | BRL, UK |
| Pankaja Bagul | Symbiosis School of Architecture, Urban Development, and Planning, India |
| Yoseph Bar-Cohen | JPL, USA |
| Josh Bongard | University of Vermont, USA |
| Jorg Conradt | TU München, Germany |
| Federico Corradi | University of Zurich and ETH, Switzerland |
| Heriberto Cuayáhuitl | University of Lincoln, UK |
| Mark Cutkosky | Stanford University, USA |
| Vassilis Cutsuridis | University of Lincoln, UK |
| Kathryn Daltorio | Case Western Reserve University, USA |

| | |
|---|---|
| Marc Desmulliez | Heriot-Watt University, UK |
| Alex Dewar | University of Sussex, UK |
| Christian Dondrup | Heriot-Watt University, UK |
| Volker Dürr | Bielefeld University, Germany |
| Wolfgang Eberle | IMEC, Belgium |
| Benoît Girard | Sorbonne Université, CNRS, France |
| José Halloy | Université Paris Diderot, France |
| Helmut Hauser | University of Bristol, UK |
| Ivan Herreros | Universitat Pompeu Fabra, Spain |
| J. Michael Herrmann | University of Edinburgh, UK |
| Toby Howison | University of Cambridge, UK |
| David Hu | Gatech, USA |
| Ioannis Ieropoulos | University of the West of England, Bristol, UK |
| Jesung Koh | Ajou University, South Korea |
| Nathan Lepora | University of Bristol, UK |
| Alexis Lussier Desbiens | University of Sherbrooke, Canada |
| Michael Mangan | University of Sheffield, UK |
| Uriel Martinez-Hernandez | University of Bath, UK |
| Stefano Mintchev | EPFL, Switzerland |
| Ben Mitchinson | TUOS, UK |
| Vishwanathan Mohan | University of Essex, UK |
| Clément Moulin-Frier | Universitat Pompeu Fabra, Spain |
| Anna Mura | Institute for Bioengineering of Catalonia (IBEC), Spain |
| John Murray | University of Lincoln, UK |
| Iordanka Panayotova | Christopher Newport University, USA |
| Diogo Pata | Institute for Bioengineering of Catalonia (IBEC), Spain |
| Martin Pearson | Bristol Robotics Laboratory, UK |
| Andrew Philippides | University of Sussex, UK |
| Tony Prescott | University of Sheffield, UK |
| Roger Quinn | Case Western Reserve University, USA |
| Guillaume Rieucau | LUMCON, USA |
| Hannes Saal | University of Sheffield, UK |
| Sebastian Schneider | Bielefeld University, CITEC, Applied Informatics, Germany |
| Charlie Sullivan | University of the West of England, UK |
| Nicholas Szczecinski | Case Western Reserve University, USA |
| Pablo Varona | Universidad Autonoma de Madrid, Spain |
| Paul Verschure | ICREA, Institute for Bioengineering of Catalonia (IBEC), Spain |
| Vasiliki Vouloutsi | Institute for Bioengineering of Catalonia (IBEC), Spain |
| Benjamin Ward-Cherrier | University of Bristol, UK |
| Victoria Webster-Wood | Case Western Reserve University, USA |

| Stuart Wilson | University of Sheffield, UK |
| Daniel Withey | Council for Scientific and Industrial Research, South Africa |
| Hartmut Witte | Technische Universität Ilmenau, Germany |
| Jiawei Xu | University of Newcastle, UK |
| Shigang Yue | University of Lincoln, UK |
| Ketao Zhang | Imperial College London, UK |
| Riccardo Zucca | Institute for Bioengineering of Catalonia (IBEC), Spain |

# Contents

Undulatory Swimming Locomotion Driven by CPG with Multimodal
Local Sensory Feedback .......................................... 1
   *Kyoichi Akiyama, Kotaro Yasui, Jonathan Arreguit,*
   *Laura Paez, Kamilo Melo, Takeshi Kano,*
   *Auke Jan Ijspeert, and Akio Ishiguro*

A Nitinol-Actuated Worm Robot Bends for Turning
and Climbing Obstacles ......................................... 6
   *Kayla B. Andersen, Akhil Kandhari, Hillel J. Chiel,*
   *Roger D. Quinn, and Kathryn A. Daltorio*

Are Brains Computers, Emulators or Simulators? .................... 11
   *Xerxes D. Arsiwalla, Camilo M. Signorelli,*
   *Jordi-Ysard Puigbo, Ismael T. Freire, and Paul F. M. J. Verschure*

Prioritized Sweeping Neural DynaQ with Multiple Predecessors,
and Hippocampal Replays ....................................... 16
   *Lise Aubin, Mehdi Khamassi, and Benoît Girard*

Should Mobile Robots Have a Head? A Rationale Based
on Behavior, Automatic Control and Signal Processing .............. 28
   *François Bailly, Emmanuelle Pouydebat, Bruno Watier,*
   *Vincent Bels, and Philippe Souères*

The Neck of Pinobo, A Low-Cost Compliant Robot ................. 40
   *Arnaud Blanchard and Djamel Mebarki*

Artificial Compound Eye and Synthetic Neural System
for Motion Recognition ......................................... 52
   *Drago Bračun, Nicholas S. Szczecinski, Gašper Škulj,*
   *Alexander J. Hunt, and Roger D. Quinn*

Living in a Machine: Experiencing the World Through
a Robotic Avatar ............................................... 64
   *Daniel Camilleri and Tony Prescott*

How to Blend a Robot Within a Group of Zebrafish:
Achieving Social Acceptance Through Real-Time
Calibration of a Multi-level Behavioural Model .................... 73
   *Leo Cazenille, Yohann Chemtob, Frank Bonnet,*
   *Alexey Gribovskiy, Francesco Mondada,*
   *Nicolas Bredeche, and José Halloy*

Evolutionary Optimisation of Neural Network Models for Fish
Collective Behaviours in Mixed Groups of Robots and Zebrafish . . . . . . . . .      85
    *Leo Cazenille, Nicolas Bredeche, and José Halloy*

The Impact of Nature Inspired Algorithms on Biomimetic
Approach in Architectural and Urban Design . . . . . . . . . . . . . . . . . . . . .      97
    *Natasha Chayaamor-Heil*

Spiders' Ballooning Flight as a Model for the Exploration
of Hazardous Atmospheric Weather Conditions. . . . . . . . . . . . . . . . . . . .      110
    *Moonsung Cho, Klaus Affeld, Peter Neubauer,*
    *and Ingo Rechenberg*

Insect-Inspired Elementary Motion Detection Embracing Resistive
Memory and Spiking Neural Networks . . . . . . . . . . . . . . . . . . . . . . . . .      115
    *Thomas Dalgaty, Elisa Vianello, Denys Ly, Giacomo Indiveri,*
    *Barbara De Salvo, Etienne Nowak, and Jerome Casas*

Understanding Interstate Competitiveness and International
Security in European Dual-Use Research . . . . . . . . . . . . . . . . . . . . . . .      129
    *Saheli Datta Burton, Christine Aicardi, Tara Mahfoud,*
    *and Nikolas Rose*

Neuromechanical Model of Rat Hind Limb Walking
with Two Layer CPGs and Muscle Synergies . . . . . . . . . . . . . . . . . . . . .      134
    *Kaiyu Deng, Nicholas S. Szczecinski, Dirk Arnold,*
    *Emanuel Andrada, Martin Fischer, Roger D. Quinn,*
    *and Alexander J. Hunt*

A Hexapod Walking Robot Mimicking Navigation Strategies
of Desert Ants Cataglyphis. . . . . . . . . . . . . . . . . . . . . . . . . . . . . . .      145
    *Julien Dupeyroux, Julien Serres, and Stéphane Viollet*

Development and Characterization of a Novel Biomimetic Peristaltic
Pumping System with Flexible Silicone-Based Soft
Robotic Ring Actuators . . . . . . . . . . . . . . . . . . . . . . . . . . . . . . . . .      157
    *Falk Esser, Friederike Krüger, Tom Masselter,*
    *and Thomas Speck*

Artificial System Inspired by Climbing Mechanism of Galium
Aparine Fabricated via 3D Laser Lithography . . . . . . . . . . . . . . . . . . . .      168
    *Isabella Fiorello, Omar Tricinci, Anand Kumar Mishra,*
    *Francesca Tramacere, Carlo Filippeschi, and Barbara Mazzolai*

Modeling the Opponent's Action Using Control-Based
Reinforcement Learning . . . . . . . . . . . . . . . . . . . . . . . . . . . . . . . . .      179
    *Ismael T. Freire, Jordi-Ysard Puigbò, Xerxes D. Arsiwalla,*
    *and Paul F. M. J. Verschure*

Estimating Body Pitch from Distributed Proprioception in a Hexapod . . . . . .   187
  Arne Gollin and Volker Dürr

Emulating Balance Control Observed in Human Test Subjects
with a Neural Network . . . . . . . . . . . . . . . . . . . . . . . . . . . . . . . . . . .   200
  Wade W. Hilts, Nicholas S. Szczecinski, Roger D. Quinn,
  and Alexander J. Hunt

Active Collision Free Closed-Loop Control of a Biohybrid
Fly-Robot Interface . . . . . . . . . . . . . . . . . . . . . . . . . . . . . . . . . . . . . .   213
  Jiaqi V. Huang, Yiran Wei,
  and Holger G. Krapp

Cognitive Architectures on Discourse . . . . . . . . . . . . . . . . . . . . . . . . . .   223
  M. Iza

Slip Detection on Natural Objects with a Biomimetic Tactile Sensor . . . . . . .   232
  Jasper W. James and Nathan F. Lepora

Distributed Sensing for Soft Worm Robot Reduces Slip
for Locomotion in Confined Environments . . . . . . . . . . . . . . . . . . . . . . .   236
  Akhil Kandhari, Matthew C. Stover, Prithvi R. Jayachandran,
  Alexander Rollins, Hillel J. Chiel, Roger D. Quinn,
  and Kathryn A. Daltorio

Snake-Like Robot that Can Generate Versatile Gait Patterns
by Using Tegotae-Based Control. . . . . . . . . . . . . . . . . . . . . . . . . . . . . .   249
  Takeshi Kano, Ryo Yoshizawa, and Akio Ishiguro

Observation of Calcium Wave on Physical Stimulus
for Realizing Cell Tactile Sensor. . . . . . . . . . . . . . . . . . . . . . . . . . . . . .   255
  Hiroki Kawashima, Umakshi Sajnani, Masahiro Shimizu,
  and Koh Hosoda

Active Touch with a Biomimetic 3D-Printed Whiskered Robot. . . . . . . . . . .   263
  Nathan F. Lepora, Niels Burnus, Yilin Tao,
  and Luke Cramphorn

Implementation of Deep Deterministic Policy Gradients
for Controlling Dynamic Bipedal Walking . . . . . . . . . . . . . . . . . . . . . . .   276
  Chújun Liu, Andrew G. Lonsberry, Mark J. Nandor,
  Musa L. Audu, and Roger D. Quinn

Investigation of Tip Extrusion as an Additive Manufacturing
Strategy for Growing Robots . . . . . . . . . . . . . . . . . . . . . . . . . . . . . . . .   288
  Dario Lunni, Emanuela Del Dottore, Ali Sadeghi,
  Matteo Cianchetti, Edoardo Sinibaldi,
  and Barbara Mazzolai

Platform Selection of a Manta-Inspired Robot for Mitigating
Near-Shore Harmful Algal Blooms . . . . . . . . . . . . . . . . . . . . . . . . . . . . .    300
    Lauren Marshall, Adam Schroeder, and Brian Trease

Weak DC Motors Generate Earthworm Locomotion
Without a Brain . . . . . . . . . . . . . . . . . . . . . . . . . . . . . . . . . . . . . . . . . . .    304
    Yoichi Masuda, Masato Ishikawa, and Akio Ishiguro

3D Bioprinted Muscle-Based Bio-Actuators: Force Adaptability
Due to Training . . . . . . . . . . . . . . . . . . . . . . . . . . . . . . . . . . . . . . . . . . .    316
    Rafael Mestre, Tania Patiño, Xavier Barceló,
    and Samuel Sanchez

A System to Provide Oculomotor Functions to the User to Control
Direction of Gaze and Optical Zoom for both Eyes Independently . . . . . . . .    321
    Fumio Mizuno, Tomoaki Hayasaka, and Takami Yamaguchi

Simulating Flapping Wing Mechanisms Inspired
by the Manduca sexta Hawkmoth . . . . . . . . . . . . . . . . . . . . . . . . . . . . .    326
    Kenneth C. Moses, David Prigg, Matthias Weisfeld,
    Richard J. Bachmann, Mark Willis, and Roger D. Quinn

A Survival Task for the Design and the Assessment
of an Autonomous Agent . . . . . . . . . . . . . . . . . . . . . . . . . . . . . . . . . . . .    338
    Bhargav Teja Nallapu and Frédéric Alexandre

Moment Arm Analysis of the Biarticular Actuators
in Compliant Robotic Leg CARL . . . . . . . . . . . . . . . . . . . . . . . . . . . . . .    348
    Atabak Nejadfard, Steffen Schütz, Krzysztof Mianowski,
    Patrick Vonwirth, and Karsten Berns

An Adaptive Frequency Central Pattern Generator for Synthetic
Nervous Systems . . . . . . . . . . . . . . . . . . . . . . . . . . . . . . . . . . . . . . . . . .    361
    William Nourse, Roger D. Quinn, and Nicholas S. Szczecinski

Texture Perception with a Biomimetic Optical Tactile Sensor . . . . . . . . . . . .    365
    Nicholas Pestell and Nathan F. Lepora

Simulation of the Arthropod Central Complex: Moving Towards
Bioinspired Robotic Navigation Control . . . . . . . . . . . . . . . . . . . . . . . . . .    370
    Shanel C. Pickard, Roger D. Quinn,
    and Nicholas S. Szczecinski

Challenges of Machine Learning for Living Machines . . . . . . . . . . . . . . . . .    382
    Jordi-Ysard Puigbò, Xerxes D. Arsiwalla,
    and Paul F. M. J. Verschure

Quad-Morphing: Towards a New Bio-inspired Autonomous Platform
for Obstacle Avoidance at High Speed. . . . . . . . . . . . . . . . . . . . . . . . .   387
    *Valentin Riviere and Stephane Viollet*

Toward Computing with Spider Webs: Computational Setup Realization . . . .   391
    *S. M. Hadi Sadati and Thomas Williams*

Whisker-RatSLAM Applied to 6D Object Identification
and Spatial Localisation. . . . . . . . . . . . . . . . . . . . . . . . . . . . . . . . . .   403
    *Mohammed Salman and Martin J. Pearson*

Insect Behavioral Evidence of Spatial Memories During
Environmental Reconfiguration. . . . . . . . . . . . . . . . . . . . . . . . . . . . . .   415
    *Diogo Santos-Pata, Alex Escuredo, Zenon Mathews,
    and Paul F. M. J. Verschure*

Object Localisation with a Highly Compliant Tactile Sensory
Probe via Distributed Strain Sensors . . . . . . . . . . . . . . . . . . . . . . . . . .   428
    *Marco Schultz and Volker Dürr*

How the Sandfish Lizard Filters Particles and What We
May Learn from It . . . . . . . . . . . . . . . . . . . . . . . . . . . . . . . . . . . . . .   439
    *Anna Theresia Stadler, Michael Krieger,
    and Werner Baumgartner*

Braided Pneumatic Actuators as a Variable Stiffness
Approximation of Synovial Joints. . . . . . . . . . . . . . . . . . . . . . . . . . . .   450
    *Alexander G. Steele and Alexander J. Hunt*

An Analysis of a Ring Attractor Model for Cue Integration . . . . . . . . . . . .   459
    *Xuelong Sun, Michael Mangan, and Shigang Yue*

Hide and Seek: Knowledge Search in Biomimicry. . . . . . . . . . . . . . . . . .   471
    *Sun-Joong Kim*

Direction-Specific Footpaths Can Be Predicted by the Motion
of a Single Point on the Body of the Fruit Fly
*Drosophila Melanogaster*. . . . . . . . . . . . . . . . . . . . . . . . . . . . . . . . .   477
    *Nicholas S. Szczecinski, Ansgar Büschges,
    and Till Bockemühl*

A Novel Spatially Resolved 3D Force Sensor for Animal Biomechanics
and Robotic Grasping Hands . . . . . . . . . . . . . . . . . . . . . . . . . . . . . . .   490
    *Séverine Toussaint and Artémis Llamosi*

Aquatic Swimming of a Multi-functional Pedundulatory
Bio-Robotic Locomotor . . . . . . . . . . . . . . . . . . . . . . . . . . . . . . . . . . . . .   494
    Dimitris P. Tsakiris, Theodoros Evdaimon,
    and Emmanouil Papadakis

Evolution of Neural Networks for Physically Simulated Evolved
Virtual Quadruped Creatures . . . . . . . . . . . . . . . . . . . . . . . . . . . . . . . .   507
    Neil Vaughan

Evolutionary Robot Swarm Cooperative Retrieval . . . . . . . . . . . . . . . . . . . .   517
    Neil Vaughan

Multi-agent Reinforcement Learning for Swarm Retrieval
with Evolving Neural Network . . . . . . . . . . . . . . . . . . . . . . . . . . . . . . . .   522
    Neil Vaughan

A Neuromechanical Rat Model with a Complete Set
of Hind Limb Muscles. . . . . . . . . . . . . . . . . . . . . . . . . . . . . . . . . . . . . .   527
    Fletcher Young, Alexander J. Hunt, and Roger D. Quinn

Guided Growth of Bacterial Cellulose Biofilms. . . . . . . . . . . . . . . . . . . . . .   538
    Katia Zolotovsky, Merav Gazit, and Christine Ortiz

Author Index . . . . . . . . . . . . . . . . . . . . . . . . . . . . . . . . . . . . . . . . . . .   549

# Undulatory Swimming Locomotion Driven by CPG with Multimodal Local Sensory Feedback

Kyoichi Akiyama[1]([✉]), Kotaro Yasui[1], Jonathan Arreguit[2], Laura Paez[2], Kamilo Melo[2], Takeshi Kano[1], Auke Jan Ijspeert[2], and Akio Ishiguro[1]

[1] Research Institute of Electrical Communication, Tohoku University, 2-1-1 Katahira, Aoba-ku, Sendai 980-8577, Japan
{k-aki,k.yasui,tkano,ishiguro}@riec.tohoku.ac.jp
[2] EPFL STI BioRob, ME D1 1226, Station 9, 1015 Lausanne, Switzerland
{jonathan.arreguitoneill,laura.paez,kamilo.melo,auke.ijspeert}@epfl.ch
http://www.cmplx.riec.tohoku.ac.jp
https://biorob.epfl.ch/page-36354.html

**Abstract.** Many species such as eels, lampreys and leeches generate undulatory swimming locomotion adaptively. It is said that this coordinated locomotive patterns are produced by central pattern generators (CPGs) which generate rhythmic activities without any rhythmic inputs. Additionally, there are some local sensors underlying in their bodies (e.g. lampreys:stretch receptors, larval zebra-fish:lateral organs). We assumed that such several sensors likely cooperate and influence their adaptive locomotion with CPGs. However, there is still very little understanding how CPGs and multimodal local sensors interact for adaptive locomotive patterns. In this study, we aim to design a minimal CPG model for a swimming robot with multimodal local sensory feedback which can produce an adaptive undulatory swimming locomotion. Finally, we validated it under different conditions via 2D simulation.

**Keywords:** Undulatory swimming locomotion
Central pattern generators · Multimodal local sensory feedback

## 1 Introduction

Undulatory swimming locomotion, which propagates waves of body bending from head to tail along the body axis, is one of the highest energy-efficient locomotion for many species such as eels, lampreys and leeches. Furthermore, these animals can change their propagating patterns adaptively in response to variable environments. For instance, nematodes *Caenorhabditis elegans* increase wave numbers along the body axis as viscosity of environments increases [1,2].

From previous studies, it is well-known that the coordinated locomotive patterns are generated by central pattern generators (CPGs) which can produce rhythmic activities without any rhythmic inputs [3]. Additionally, the adaptive

© Springer International Publishing AG, part of Springer Nature 2018
V. Vouloutsi et al. (Eds.): Living Machines 2018, LNAI 10928, pp. 1–5, 2018.
https://doi.org/10.1007/978-3-319-95972-6_1

locomotion in variable environments is likely influenced by various types of local sensors in animal's bodies. For example, lampreys have stretch receptors (*proprioceptive* sensors) to detect muscle stretches [4]. Larval zebra-fish have the lateral organ (*exteroceptive* sensors) in the lateral line to sense pressure forces from water [5]. Thus, these findings suggest that how multimodal (proprioceptive and exteroceptive) local sensory information are integrated and fed back to CPGs is an important key for their adaptive undulatory swimming locomotion.

Although many types of CPG models have been designed including local sensory feedback mechanisms for producing the undulatory swimming locomotion for many years [6,7], it is not understood well how CPGs and multimodal local sensors are coupled. In this study, we proposed a minimal CPG model based on multimodal local sensory feedback to extract an essence of the relation between them. Finally, we evaluated the model in different conditions via 2D simulation.

## 2  Method

### 2.1  Simulation Model

As shown in Fig. 1(A), we designed a minimal CPG model for the undulatory swimming locomotion. The mechanical system is based on a 2D mass-spring-damper system for simplicity. The body is constructed of mass points and rigid links. Additionally, we use phase oscillators as CPGs in order to produce the

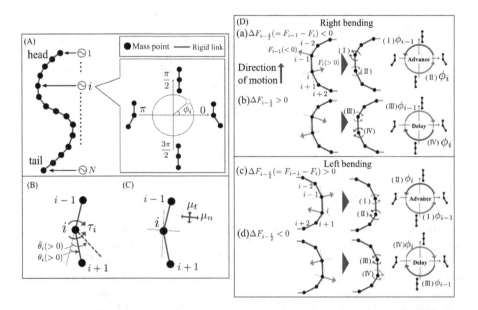

**Fig. 1.** The schematic of the model. (A) The CPG model based on phase oscillators, (B) Torque generated by rotary actuator, (C) The viscous coefficient and (D) Control scheme with multimodal local sensory feedback ($n = 1$).

periodic movement. One phase oscillator is implemented in each mass point. As shown in Fig. 1(B), the torque generation of rotary actuator $\tau_i$ is described as follows:

$$\tau_i = A^{tor}\bar{\theta}_i - K^{tor}\theta_i - D^{tor}\dot{\theta}_i, \tag{1}$$

where $\bar{\theta}_i$ and $\theta_i$ are command angle and actual angle of the $i$-th segment. Furthermore, $A^{tor}$, $K^{tor}$ and $D^{tor}$ indicate positive constants. The command angle $\bar{\theta}_i$ is decided by a oscillator phase $\phi_i$ as shown in Eq. (2):

$$\bar{\theta}_i = C_1 \cos \phi_i, \tag{2}$$

where $C_1$ is a positive constant. As shown in Fig. 1(A), it can generate the bending of joint periodically.

In this study, we included only viscous friction forces into the 2D simulation as the external forces. The viscous coefficient $\mu_t$ and $\mu_n$ which denote vectors tangential and normal to body axis, respectively. Considering the body characteristics of real fish, $\mu_t$ is smaller than $\mu_n$ as shown in Fig. 1(C).

## 2.2   Control Scheme

The multimodal local sensory feedback mechanism is described as follows:

$$\dot{\phi}_i = \omega + \sum_{j=1}^{n} a_j(|\tilde{\theta}_{i-j+\frac{1}{2}}|\Delta F_{i-j+\frac{1}{2}} - |\tilde{\theta}_{i+j-\frac{1}{2}}|\Delta F_{i+j-\frac{1}{2}}) \sin \phi_i, \qquad . \tag{3}$$

where

$$\tilde{\theta}_{i-\frac{1}{2}} = \frac{\theta_{i-1} + \theta_i}{2}, \tag{4}$$

$$\Delta F_{i-\frac{1}{2}} = F_{i-1} - F_i. \tag{5}$$

Here, $\omega$ is the intrinsic angular frequency of the phase oscillator and $F_i$ is the viscous friction force whose direction is normal to the body axis in $i$-th segment. The value of $F_i$ is positive when it denotes the viscous friction force from left side of the body. In Eq.(3), the second term of the right side indicates the multimodal feedback mechanism. The strength of the feedback towards the other segments becomes less and less as they are far from the segment $i$ and $i-1$. Thus, $a_j$ is described as follows:

$$a_j = max[-pj + q, 0], \tag{6}$$

where $p$ and $q$ are positive constants. Furthermore, the curvature of body part $\tilde{\theta}$ and the difference of viscous friction forces between segments $\Delta F$ indicate proprioceptive and exteroceptive local sensory information, respectively. Figure 1(D) represents how the feedback information are fed back to the phase oscillators by dividing the situation into 4 parts when $n=1$. The most right figures in Fig. 1(D) indicate how the phase oscillator of $i$-1-th and $i$-th segment modulates phases. In Fig. 1(D)(a) and (D)(b), the multimodal feedback advances $\phi_{i-1}$ and $\phi_i$. On the other hand, it delays each phase $\phi_{i-1}$ and $\phi_i$ in Fig. 1(D)(c) and (D)(d).

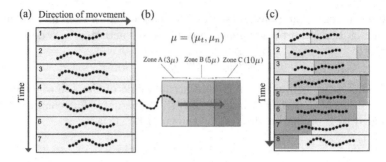

**Fig. 2.** (a) Undulatory swimming locomotion, (b) Experimental environment which has various types of viscous coefficient and (c) Adaptive undulatory swimming locomotion.

## 3   Simulation

We validated the CPG model via 2D simulation with the following parameters: $A^{tor} = 10.5$, $K^{tor} = 0.1$, $D^{tor} = 0.1$, $C_1 = 0.3$, $N = 15$, $n = 3$, $\omega = 1.0$, $\mu_t = 0.3$, $\mu_n = 3.0$, $p = 2.0$ and $q = 7.0$. We can observe that the CPG model generates undulatory swimming locomotion with multimodal local sensory feedback without any central coupling between phase oscillators as shown in Fig. 2(a).

Furthermore, in order to evaluate the adaptiveness of this CPG model, we conducted the experiment in the environments as shown in Fig. 2(b). As moving to right, the constant of viscous friction increases (zone A:3 times, zone B:5 times, zone C:10 times). In each environment, the adaptive undulatory swimming locomotion is produced by changing its wave numbers along the body as shown in Fig. 2(c).

## 4   Conclusion

We presented the minimal CPG model based on multimodal local sensory feedback systems via 2D simulation. Specifically, the CPG model is able to detect proprioceptive local sensory information and exteroceptive one. We could reproduce the adaptive locomotive patterns in variable conditions by changing the viscosity. We believe that our model extracts the essence how CPGs and multimodal local feedback sensors interact in response to environments. As future works, we plan to validate the CPG model with a real robot.

**Acknowledgement.** This work was supported by Human Frontier Science Program (RGP0027/2017) and Japan Science and Technology Agency, CREST (JPMJCR14D5).

## References

1. Boyle, J.H., Berri, S., Cohen, N.: Gait modulation in C. elegans: an integrated neuromechanical model. Front. Comput. Neurosci. **6**, 10 (1974)
2. Brenner, S.: The genetics of Caenorhabditis elegans. Genetics **77**, 71–94 (1974)

3. Grillner, S.: Biological pattern generation: the cellular and computational logic of networks in motion. Neuron **52**(5), 751–766 (2006)
4. Grillner, S., Degliana, T., El Marina, A., Hill, R.H., Orlovsky, G.N., Wallen, P., Ekeberg, O., Lansner, A.: Neural networks that co-ordinate locomotion and body orientation in lamprey. Trends Neurosci. **18**(6), 270–279 (1995)
5. Haehnel-Taguchi, M., Akanyeti, O., Liao, C.J.: Afferent and motoneuron activity in response to single neuromast stimulation in the posterior lateral line of larval zebrafish. J. Neurophysiol. **112**(6), 1329–1339 (2014)
6. Ijspeert, A.J.: Central pattern generators for locomotion control in animals and robots: a review. Neural Netw. **21**, 361–376 (2008)
7. Iwasaki, T., Chen, J., Friesen, W.O.: Biological clockwork underlying adaptive rhythmic movements. Proc. Natl. Acad. Sci. USA **111**, 978–983 (2014)

# A Nitinol-Actuated Worm Robot Bends for Turning and Climbing Obstacles

Kayla B. Andersen[1], Akhil Kandhari[2(✉)], Hillel J. Chiel[3],
Roger D. Quinn[2], and Kathryn A. Daltorio[2]

[1] NASA Jet Propulsion Lab, Pasadena, CA, USA
[2] Department of Mechanical and Aerospace Engineering,
Case Western Reserve University, Cleveland, OH 44106, USA
{axk751,kam37}@case.edu
[3] Departments of Biology, Neurosciences, and Biomedical Engineering,
Case Western Reserve University, Cleveland, OH 44106, USA

**Abstract.** Earthworms, *Lumbricus terrestris*, are multi-segmented invertebrate animals that have the ability to crawl over land, burrow beneath the soil, and bend their bodies to turn and coil. Each of these motions can be performed while maintaining a small form factor. The low profile locomotion is made possible via peristalsis, a locomotion method in which waves of circumferential and longitudinal contraction propagate in a retrograde manner (opposite to the direction of motion) down the length of the animal's many-segmented body. We have previously tested peristaltic locomotion on planar surfaces, but here we explore additional actuators in a smaller form factor for bending a pre-fabricated mesh body with nitinol shape memory alloy springs. This new robot, MiniWorm, has a minimum diameter of 1.7 cm, is capable of moving forward at a speed of 0.88 cm/min and can lift its front segment 1.5 times its diameter. We show that without lifting, the robot cannot cross even very small obstacles (14% of diameter), but that a head-lifting gait enables this motion. Future work will enable the robot to move farther with better integrated electronics.

**Keywords:** Earthworm-like robot · Peristalsis · Shape memory alloy

## 1 Introduction

Soft robots have the potential to reduce the computational complexity necessary to perform intricate motions and increase safety in human-robot interactions [1]. Many soft robots take inspiration from biology because animals use soft structures effectively. Hydrostatic-invertebrates are of particular interest because their structure enables them to uniquely conform to the terrain, perform multi-degree of freedom movements, and fit through small apertures [1]. This structure is comprised of a compliant body wall surrounding incompressible fluid or tissue, which couples longitudinal and circumferential motion by maintaining a constant internal volume [2].

Within the subset of hydrostatic invertebrates, worms have been used often as inspiration for robots because of their ability to burrow and move in confined spaces [3].

© Springer International Publishing AG, part of Springer Nature 2018
V. Vouloutsi et al. (Eds.): Living Machines 2018, LNAI 10928, pp. 6–10, 2018.
https://doi.org/10.1007/978-3-319-95972-6_2

With these abilities worm-inspired robots are uniquely suited for pipe inspection, endoscopy, search and rescue, and exploration [4, 5]. Multiple worm-inspired robots have been developed, with many able to travel through horizontal, vertical, curved, or compliant pipes [6–8]. Of those that travel on the ground, several have been able to steer [3, 6, 8]. However, most of these robots lack the ability to climb over obstacles or change the plane of their motion and would therefore be unable to climb into a pipe at a higher level during pipe inspection, or effectively traverse rubble during search and rescue. Thus, there exists a need to develop and test actuator arrangements to enable worm-inspired robots to climb over obstacles and uneven ground. This is especially critical at the smaller diameter scales because even small obstacles will be large relative to the body diameter.

## 2   Robot Design

MiniWorm uses a premade braided mesh tubing of diameter 1.7 cm. The braided mesh has diameter-length coupling which achieves motion similar to the segments of an earthworm due to hydrostatic coupling, i.e., circumferential expansion causes a longitudinal contraction and vice-versa. Nitinol spring actuators are used to extend the braided mesh's diameter. Three spring shaped nitinol actuators are placed around the circumference of the braided mesh at 120° (Fig. 1). Presence of three actuators for each segment allows the robot to move forward, turn and lift to climb over obstacles. Meshworm [6] uses a braided mesh tubing along with nitinol actuators wrapped around in a spiral pattern around the circumference. Presence of longitudinal springs on MiniWorm in discrete segment configuration allows us to try different waveforms. Rather than spacing actuators uniformly around each segment, left and right springs are mounted just under center and the dorsal actuator is mounted along the top of the segment. When the wires supplying current to the SMA actuators were placed within the robot, they often interfered with motion. Therefore, we moved these wires outside the body for testing.

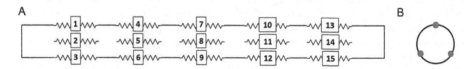

**Fig. 1.** Schematic of MiniWorm from the (A) top view and (B) front view shows the positioning of the nitinol spring shaped actuators for the five segment robot placed around the circumference at 120°.

MiniWorm uses an Arduino mega board in tandem with a custom circuit board containing logic-level MOSFETs and an external power supply. The logic-level MOSFETs allow the output from the Arduino pins to control the voltage supplied and enable supply of a sufficient amount of current to the springs for actuation.

## 3   Robot Performance

First, we consider locomotion across flat ground. With 3 DOF per segment, many different control policies are possible. We start with considering policies in which all actuators per segment are controlled together. Four promising waveforms were tried and evaluated for their effectiveness and speed: 2S3C, 2S4C, 2S3C-B4, and 2S4C-B4 (Fig. 2). The number preceding the letter "S" refers to the number of support (radially expanded) segments, and the number preceding the letter "C" refers to the maximum number of cantilevered segments. The – B4 indicates a modified version of the 2S3C and 2S4C waveforms with only the back four segments actuated. The back-four-only waveforms were tested to ensure the robot would be able to move forward with its front segment lifted off of the ground (as was expected to be necessary for surmounting obstacles).

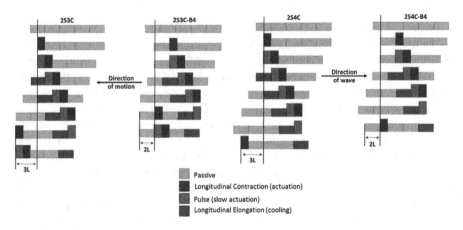

**Fig. 2.** The 2S3C and 2S4C waveforms both begin with circumferential expansion of the first segment, followed by circumferential expansion of the second segment while the first segment is held at the maximum diameter. Next, the third segment circumferentially expands while the second segment is held at the maximum diameter and the first segment is allowed to relax. This occurs twice more for the circumferential expansion of the fourth and fifth segments. For the 2S3C waveform, the first segment expands circumferentially while the fourth segment relaxes. For the 2S4C waveform no other segments expand while the fourth segment relaxes.

Overall, the most effective waveform was 2S4C or 2S4C-B4, which resulted in a speed of 0.8 cm/sec. While using the back segments resulted in slightly higher average speeds, the difference was not significant. 2S3C waveforms resulted in about 50% of the speed with a small but significant increase for 2S3C-B4.

In addition to being able to move forward, MiniWorm has the capacity to turn both left and right. In order to execute a turn, the actuators on only one side of the robot were contracted in a modified 2S4C-B4 waveform.

MiniWorm is also capable of motions that do not involve locomotion. By contracting just the actuators on the top of the robot, the robot can lift its front segments into the air (Fig. 3). Actuating both the first and second segment's top actuators allows the robot to lift its front segment 1.5 times its diameter into the air. Combining MiniWorm's ability to lift its front segment with its locomotion capabilities was hypothesized to enable the robot to climb (or at least begin to climb) obstacles in its path.

**Fig. 3.** (Left) The robot lifting up its first two segments by actuating top springs of segment one and two. Progress of the worm robot with an obstacle (ruler) in its path, the blue line shows the starting position of the front of the robot. Normal 2S4C (center). 2S4C with lifting front segment (right) shows progress when the front segment lifts.

To determine if this hypothesis was true, an experiment was conducted to evaluate whether lifting the front segment while moving forward was uniquely effective in climbing an obstacle. In this experiment, two different configuration/waveform combinations were tried: normal 2S4C-B4 and 2S4C-B4-Lift (Fig. 2). In the new waveform 2SC4-B4-Lift, the top actuator of segment one was contracted in conjunction with the second segment's contraction, and pulsed to remain in a raised position for the duration of the 24SC wave; as shown in the figure, this led to forward progress.

## 4   Conclusion and Future Work

This article presents a small scale (<2.5 cm diameter) worm inspired robot that is able to move forward, turn left and right, lift up its front segments, and surmount a small obstacle 14% of its diameter using an open-loop controller.

In future work, we will examine ways to increase segment strain, better enable complex motions, and integrate the electronics for trials with extended range.

## References

1. Kim, S., Laschi, C., Trimmer, B.: Soft robotics: a bioinspired evolution in robotics. Trends Biotechnol. **31**(5), 287–294 (2013). https://doi.org/10.1016/j.tibtech.2013.03.002
2. Quillin, K.J.: Kinematic scaling of locomotion by hydrostatic animals: ontogeny of peristaltic crawling by the earthworm lumbricus terrestris. J. Exp. Biol. **202**, 661–674 (1999)
3. Omori, H., Nakamura, T., Yada, T.: An underground explorer robot based on peristaltic crawling of earthworms. Ind. Robot Int. J. **36**(4), 358–364 (2009)
4. Tanaka, T., Harigaya, K., Nakamura, T.: Development of a peristaltic crawling. In: IEEE/ASME International Conference on Advanced Intelligent Mechatronics (AIM), pp. 1552–1557, Besançon, France (2014)
5. Manwell, T., Vitek, T., Ranzani, T., Menciassi, A., Althoefer, K., Liu, H.: Elastic mesh braided worm robot for locomotive endoscopy. In: IEEE Engineering in Medicine and Biology Society, pp. 848–851 (2014)

6. Seok, S., Onal, C.D., Cho, K., Wood, R.J., Rus, D., Kim, S.: Meshworm: a peristaltic soft robot with antagonistic nickel titanium coil actuators. IEEE/ASME Trans. Mechantron. **18**(5), 1485–1496 (2013)
7. Zarrouk, D., Shoham, M.: Analysis and design of one degree of freedom worm. J. Mech. Des. **134**(2), 021010 (2012). https://doi.org/10.1115/1.4005656
8. Kandhari, A., Huang, Y., Daltorio, K.A., Chiel, H.J., Quinn, R.D.: Body stiffness in orthogonal directions oppositely affects worm-like robot turning and straight-line locomotion. Bioinspiration Biomim. **13**(2), 026003 (2018)

# Are Brains Computers, Emulators or Simulators?

Xerxes D. Arsiwalla[1,2,5]($\boxtimes$), Camilo M. Signorelli[1,3,4], Jordi-Ysard Puigbo[1,2], Ismael T. Freire[2], and Paul F. M. J. Verschure[2,5,6]

[1] Universitat Pompeu Fabra, Barcelona, Spain
x.d.arsiwalla@gmail.com
[2] Institute for BioEngineering of Catalonia, Barcelona, Spain
[3] Department of Computer Science, University of Oxford, Oxford, UK
[4] Cognitive Neuroimaging Unit, INSERM, Gif-sur-Yvette, France
[5] Barcelona Institue of Science and Technology, Barcelona, Spain
[6] Institució Catalana de Recerca i Estudis Avançats (ICREA), Barcelona, Spain

**Abstract.** There has been intense debate on the question of whether the brain is a computer. If so, that challenge is to show that all cognitive processes can be described by algorithms running on a universal Turing machine. By extension that implies consciousness is a computational process. Both Penrose and Searle have vehemently argued against this view, proposing that consciousness is a fundamentally non-computational process [10]. Even proponents of the brain as a computer metaphor such a Dennett agree that the organizational architecture of the brain is unlike any computing system ever conceived, possibly alluding to non-classical computational processes [6]. The latter class of processes veer away from any program that can be encoded by Church's lambda calculus. In fact, such a program would have to be based on non-classical logic (either semi-classical or quantum). But quantum logic or machines that might implement them typically are not meant for solving the same type of problems that a classical computer solves (nor are they necessarily faster for any given problem). We will argue that machines implementing non-classical logic might be better suited for simulation rather than computation (a la Turing). It is thus reasonable to pit simulation as an alternative to computation and ask whether the brain, rather than computing, is simulating a model of the world in order to make predictions and guide behavior. If so, this suggests a hardware supporting dynamics more akin to a quantum many-body field theory.

**Keywords:** Consciousness · Godel's theorems · Computation
Non-classical logic

## 1 Computationalism

Proponents of the computationalist view in brain and mind theory claim that all mental processes can be encoded algorithmically. In this case, strict computationalism would mean all mental processes can be expressed as programs that

© Springer International Publishing AG, part of Springer Nature 2018
V. Vouloutsi et al. (Eds.): Living Machines 2018, LNAI 10928, pp. 11–15, 2018.
https://doi.org/10.1007/978-3-319-95972-6_3

can be implemented on a Turing machine. Following the Curry-Howard correspondence, programs are proofs in a formal logical system (the Church-Turing thesis can be thought of as a specific realization of this correspondence). This implies all mental processes, and by extension consciousness, follow from an underlying logical axiomatization. One may think of this as a top-down processing hierarchy. Alternatively, there is also a bottom-up processing hierarchy, one instance of which could be realized as a weaker form of computationalism. Artificial neural networks, when implemented on a computer, fall in this category (following the arguments below, other implementations of neural networks go beyond computationalism). A direct consequence of computationalistic thinking is that cognition and consciousness are by and large independent of the substrate or hardware performing the computation and hence can be embodied in various forms, including being simulated on a computer. This is one of the motivations for the so-called simulation theory or simulated reality hypothesis.

## 2    Limits of the Computationalist View

On the other hand, those opposed to a pure computationalist view of mental processes argue that Godel's incompleteness theorems set limits to any formal axiomatic system. More specifically, these theorems state that any formal axiomatic system (encoded in terms of the natural number system) will either be incomplete or inconsistent. In fact, the Peano axioms, which form the set theoretic foundations of natural number adheres to Godel's theorems. Peano arithmetic is incomplete within itself and so also are the set-theoretic ZFC axioms not consistent within itself. The Church lambda calculus is a formal system based on first-order logic and Peano arithmetic. An example of a Godelian sentence in this system leads to the well-known Halting problem which states that there does not exist a program that can decide whether any program on a Turing machine will finish running or continue forever. This was proved in 1936 by Alan Turing himself. These arguments imply that there are problems whose proofs are non-computational in the Church-Turing sense and hence cannot be implemented algorithmically on any classical computer. Penrose points to three such examples. The first example is the proof of the Goodstein theorem, which cannot be proven using the Peano axioms. The proof requires transfinite induction. The second example is the Penrose tiling problem, which requires determining whether multiple copies of a given tile motif can be arranged into a configuration that covers the entire plane. The third example of a non-computable problem is the collapse of the wave-function or the measurement problem in quantum physics, which evades an algorithmic description. Despite the complex nature of the first two problems, human do seem to have a "mathematical understanding" of these problems are able to provide mathematical proofs for some of them. According to Penrose, this reflects a fundamentally non-computational aspect of the human thought process and consciousness [10]. Furthermore, he argues that physics underlying non-computable processes is inherently non-classical. Though there are several proposals on how this might be realized, it remains an open problem. In this spirit, it has even been suggested that the "coming to being" aspect of consciousness has parallels to the wave-function collapse problem in quantum theory and consequently the qualia of consciousness are presumably akin to "be-ables" of a fundamental quantum description. If machines that may be able to realize mental processes culminating in consciousness are not classical computers, what are they?

# 3  What are Emulators?

The hypothesis of this paper is to argue that conscious machines for the most part, are not computers, but simulators. But before making that argument, for the sake of completeness, let us discuss the role of emulators. As such an emulator can be defined as any machine that can be used to specify dynamical states transitions of another system (ignoring the trivial case of a system specifying its own dynamics). Typically, a computer program can be used to encode generative models that output state transitions of the system being emulated. Commonly, that would be referred to as a computer simulation. By this construction, one may also use machines other than computers to simulate specific systems. Emulators, as defined here, generalize the notion of simulation to include both computer-based simulations as well as dynamical systems-based simulations (which are discussed in the next section). A logical consequence of this definition of emulators is that any systemic limitations that an emulating machine might have with regard to its own processing or operational hierarchies will inadvertently carry forward to the simulation. This implies Godel's theorems for computer-based simulations and suggests that for allowing non-computable processes in brain functions requires looking for other types of simulators.

# 4  The Simulation Argument

This brings us to the question: what are the type of problems where generating a simulation is a more viable strategy than performing a detailed computation? And if so, what are the kind of simulators that might be relevant for consciousness? The answer to the first question has to do with the difference of say computing an explicit solution of a differential equation in order to determine the trajectory of a system in phase space versus mechanistically mimicking the given vector field of the equation within which an entity denoting the system is simply allowed to evolve thereby reconstructing its trajectory in phase space. The former involves explicit computational operations, whereas the latter simply mimics the dynamics of the system being simulated on a customized hardware. For complex problems involving a large number of variables and/or model uncertainly, the cost of inference by computation may scale very fast, whereas simulations generating outcomes of models or counterfactual models may be far more efficient. In fact, in control theory, the method of eigenvalue assignment is used precisely to implement the dynamics of a given system on a standardized hardware. In the context of neuroscience, evidence for this phenomenon in the motor system has recently been demonstrated as a forward model of the motor system, implemented in the synapses of cerebellar Purkinje neurons [8]. Beyond this example of the motor system, if the brain is indeed tasked with estimating the dynamics of a complex world filled with uncertainties, including hidden psychological states of other agents (for a game-theoretic discussion on this see [1–4,9]), then in order to act and achieve its goals, relying on pure computational inference would arguably be extremely costly and slow, whereas implementing simulations of world models as described above, on its cellular and molecular hardware would be a more viable alternative. These simulation engines are customized during the process of learning and development to acquire models of the world. The simulated dynamics of these models lead to predictions as well as counterfactual hypotheses, which can then be passed through feedback control loops to correct for prediction errors. Note that these dynamics-based simulations differ from computer simulations. In the former, no specific function is being computed. Instead, as in control engineering, a model of the process is encoded (or learnt) in the network's connectivity and is used to generate subsequent state transitions. More complex models require more complex network architectures and multi-scale biophysical dynamics, rather than heavy computational algorithms, which is presumably not what we see the brain to be designed for.

# 5   Outlook

Given that these dynamical simulators implement physical models which will inevitably be endowed with an underlying logic, one may ask whether they face the same formal limitations as per Godel's theorem for any formal logical system? Indeed, so long as the implemented mechanics is based on classical logic, the answer will be yes. On the other hand, if the physics of the simulator involves semi-classical considerations involving non-classical logic, then there's a possibility to go beyond computable functions (Godel's theorem still applies, but the realm of problems that can be addressed is larger including some non-computable problems). As an explicit example, the validity of quantum logic has already been demonstrated in several cognitive paradigms [5]. The crucial physical property that classical systems often lack are long-range order. These properties are typical in any macroscopic condensed matter system (such as lasers, phonon propagation in crystals, the Josephson junction, etc.) and therefore simulators harnessing non-classical or semi-classical properties offer more than classical dynamics can offer. At what level might the brain possibly implement this is of course an open question. Whether molecular signaling at the synaptic scale might invoke such long-range order or spontaneous symmetry breaking of the electric dipole field turn out to be plausible candidates remains to be seen [7].

**Acknowledgments.** This work is supported by the European Research Council's CDAC project: "The Role of Consciousness in Adaptive Behavior: A Combined Empirical, Computational and Robot based Approach", (ERC-2013- ADG 341196).

# References

1. Arsiwalla, X.D., Herreros, I., Moulin-Frier, C., Sanchez, M., Verschure, P.F.: Is consciousness a control process?, pp. 233–238. IOS Press, Amsterdam (2016)
2. Arsiwalla, X.D., Herreros, I., Moulin-Frier, C., Verschure, P.: Consciousness as an evolutionary game-theoretic strategy. In: Mangan, M., Cutkosky, M., Mura, A., Verschure, P.F.M.J., Prescott, T., Lepora, N. (eds.) Living Machines 2017. LNCS (LNAI), vol. 10384, pp. 509–514. Springer, Cham (2017). https://doi.org/10.1007/978-3-319-63537-8_43
3. Arsiwalla, X.D., Herreros, I., Verschure, P.: On three categories of conscious machines. In: Lepora, N.F.F., Mura, A., Mangan, M., Verschure, P.F.M.J.F.M.J., Desmulliez, M., Prescott, T.J.J. (eds.) Living Machines 2016. LNCS (LNAI), vol. 9793, pp. 389–392. Springer, Cham (2016). https://doi.org/10.1007/978-3-319-42417-0_35
4. Arsiwalla, X.D., Moulin-Frier, C., Herreros, I., Sanchez-Fibla, M., Verschure, P.F.: The morphospace of consciousness. arXiv preprint arXiv:1705.11190 (2017)
5. Busemeyer, J.R., Bruza, P.D.: Quantum Models of Cognition and Decision. Cambridge University Press, Cambridge (2012)
6. Dennett, D.C.: From Bacteria to Bach and Back: The Evolution of Minds. WW Norton & Company, New York City (2017)
7. Freeman, W.J., Vitiello, G.: Dissipation and spontaneous symmetry breaking in brain dynamics. J. Phys.: Math. Theor. $41(30)$, 304042 (2008)
8. Herreros, I., Arsiwalla, X., Verschure, P.: A forward model at Purkinje cell synapses facilitates cerebellar anticipatory control. In: Advances in Neural Information Processing Systems, pp. 3828–3836 (2016)
9. Moulin-Frier, C., Puigbò, J.Y., Arsiwalla, X.D., Sanchez-Fibla, M., Verschure, P.F.: Embodied artificial intelligence through distributed adaptive control: an integrated framework. arXiv preprint arXiv:1704.01407 (2017)
10. Penrose, R.: Shadows of the Mind, vol. 4. Oxford University Press, Oxford (1994)

# Prioritized Sweeping Neural DynaQ with Multiple Predecessors, and Hippocampal Replays

Lise Aubin, Mehdi Khamassi, and Benoît Girard[✉]

Institut des Systèmes Intelligents et de Robotique (ISIR),
Sorbonne Université, CNRS, 75005 Paris, France
benoit.girard@sorbonne-universite.fr

**Abstract.** During sleep and wakeful rest, the hippocampus replays sequences of place cells that have been activated during prior experiences. These replays have been interpreted as a memory consolidation process, but recent results suggest a possible interpretation in terms of reinforcement learning. The *Dyna* reinforcement learning algorithms use off-line replays to improve learning. Under limited replay budget, *prioritized sweeping*, which requires a model of the transitions to the predecessors, can be used to improve performance. We investigate if such algorithms can explain the experimentally observed replays. We propose a neural network version of prioritized sweeping Q-learning, for which we developed a growing multiple expert algorithm, able to cope with multiple predecessors. The resulting architecture is able to improve the learning of simulated agents confronted to a navigation task. We predict that, in animals, learning the transition and reward models should occur during rest periods, and that the corresponding replays should be shuffled.

**Keywords:** Reinforcement learning · Replays · DynaQ
Prioritized sweeping · Neural networks · Hippocampus · Navigation

## 1 Introduction

The hippocampus hosts a population of cells responsive to the current position of the animal within the environment, the place cells (PCs), a key component of the brain navigation system [1]. Since the seminal work of Wilson et al. [2], it has been shown that PCs are reactivated during sleep – obviously in the absence of locomotor activity – and that these reactivations are functionally linked with improvement of the learning performance of a navigation task [3]. Similar reactivations have been observed in the a wakeful state [4], while the animal is immobile, either consuming food at a reward site, waiting at the departure site for the beginning of the next trial or stopped at a decision point. These reactivations contain sequences of PCs' activations experienced in the wakeful state

© Springer International Publishing AG, part of Springer Nature 2018
V. Vouloutsi et al. (Eds.): Living Machines 2018, LNAI 10928, pp. 16–27, 2018.
https://doi.org/10.1007/978-3-319-95972-6_4

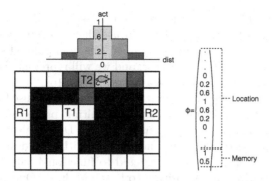

**Fig. 1. Model of the rat experiment used in** [6]**.** The maze is discretized into 32 positions (squares). The agent can use 4 discrete actions (N, E, S, W). The input state $\phi$ is the concatenation of 32 location components and two reward memory components. The location part of $\phi$ represents the activation of 32 place cells co-located with the maze discrete positions, their activity *act* depends on the Manhattan distance of the agent to the cell. Figures 1 to 5 by Aubin & Girard, 2018; available at https://doi.org/10.6084/m9.figshare.5822112.v2 under a CC-BY4.0 license.

(forward reactivations) [5], sequences played in the reverse order (backward reactivations) [4], and sometimes novel sequences (resulting from the concatenation of experienced sequences) [6]. These reactivations have been interpreted in the light of the memory consolidation theory [7]: they would have the role of copying volatile hippocampal memories into the cortex [8] for reorganization and longer-term storage [9]. However, recent results have shown that these reactivations also have a causal effect on reinforcement learning processes [3,10].

A number of reinforcement learning (RL) algorithms make use of input reactivations, reminiscent of hippocampal reactivations. These algorithms are thus candidates to explain the replay phenomenon [11]. Among them, the Dyna family of algorithms [12] is of special interest because it was specifically designed to make the best possible use of alternation between on-line and off-line learning phases (i.e. phases during which the agent acts in the real world or in simulation). We concentrate here on the Q-learning version of Dyna (Dyna-Q). When operating on-line, Dyna-Q is indistinguishable from the original *model-free* Q-learning algorithm: it computes reward prediction error signals, and uses them to update the estimated values of the (state, action) couples, $Q(s,a)$. In its original version [12], when off-line, the Dyna algorithm reactivates randomly chosen quadruplets composed of an initial state, a chosen action, and the predicted resulting state and reward (produced by a learned world-model, this phase being thus *model-based*), in order to refine the on-line estimated values. However, when the number of reactivations is under a strict budget constraint, it is more efficient to select those that will provide more information, which are those that effectively generated a large reward prediction error in the last on-line phase, and those that are predicted to do so by the world model, a principle called *prioritized sweeping* [13,14].

We are interested here in mimicking the process by which the basal ganglia, which is central for RL processes [15], can use the state representations of the world that are provided by the hippocampus. The manipulated state descriptor will thus be a population activity vector, and we will represent the Q-values and the world model with neural network approximators [16].

In the following, we describe the rat experimental setup used in [6], and how we simulated it. In this task, a state can have multiple predecessor states resulting from a single action, we thus present a modified Dyna-Q learning algorithm, with a special emphasis on the neural-network algorithm we designed to learn to approximate binary relations (not restricted to functions) with a *growing* approach: GALMO for Growing Algorithm to Learn Multiple Outputs. Our results successively illustrate three main points. First, because of interferences between consecutively observed states during maze experience, themselves due to the use of a neural-network function approximator, the world model had to be learned with shuffled states during off-line replay. Second, GALMO allows to efficiently solve the multiple predecessor problem. Third, the resulting system, when faced with a training schedule similar to [6], generates a lot of disordered state replays, but also a non-negligible set of varied backward and forward replay sequences, without explicitly storing and replaying sequences.

## 2   Methods

### 2.1   Experimental Task

We aim at modeling the navigation task used in [6]: two successive T-mazes (T1 and T2 on Fig. 1), with lateral return corridors. The left and right rewarding sites deliver food pellets with different flavors. The training involves daily changing contingencies, forcing rats to adapt their choice to turn either left or right at the final choice (T2) based on the recent history of reward. These contingencies are: (1) always turn right, while the left side of the maze is blocked; (2) always turn left, while the right side of the maze is blocked; (3) always turn right; (4) always turn left; (5) alternate between left and right on a lap-by-lap basis.

Rats attempting to run backward in the maze were prevented from doing so by the experimenter. The first day, they were exposed to task 1 (40 trials), and the next day, to task 2 (40 trials also). Then, depending on their individual learning speed, rats had between seventeen and twenty days to learn tasks 3, 4 and 5 (a single condition being presented each day). Once they had reached at least 80% success rate on all tasks, rats were implanted with electrodes; after recovery, recording sessions during task performance lasted for six days.

During the six recording sessions, the reward contingency was changed approximately midway through the session and hippocampal replays were analyzed when rats paused at reward locations. Original analyses of replayed sequences [6] revealed that: during same-side replays (i.e., replays representing sequences of previously visited locations on the same arm of the maze as the current rat position) forward and backward replays started from the current position; during opposite-side replays (i.e., representing locations on the opposite arm of the maze) forward replays occurred mainly on the segment leading up to reward sites, and backward replays covered trajectories ending near reward sites. In general, the replay content did not seem to only reflect recently experienced trajectories, since trajectories experienced 10 to 15 min before were replayed as well. Indeed, there were more opposite-side replays during task 3 and 4 than during the alternation task. Finally, among all replays, a few were shortcuts never experienced before which crossed a straight path on the top or bottom of the maze between the reward sites.

## 2.2   Simulation

We have reproduced the T-maze configuration with a discrete environment composed of 32 squares (Fig. 1, left), each of them representing a $10 \times 10$ cm area. States are represented by a vector $\phi$, concatenating place cells activity and a memory of past rewards (Fig. 1, right). The modeled place cells are centered on the discrete positions and their activity (color-coded on Fig. 1) decreases with the Manhattan distance between the simulated rat position to the position they encode (top of Fig. 1). When a path is blocked (contingencies 1 and 2), the activity field does not expand beyond walls and will thus shrink, as is the case for real place cells [17]. To represent the temporal dimension, which is essential during the alternation task, we have added two more components in the state's vector representation (Fig. 1, right): the left side reward memory (L) and the right side reward memory (R). They take a value of 1 if the last reward was obtained on that side, 0.5 if the penultimate reward was on that side, and 0 if that side has not been rewarded during the last two reward events. Therefore, after two successful laps, the task at hand can be identified by the agent based on the value of this memory (Table 1). This ability to remember the side of the rewards is supposed to be anchored both on the different position and flavor cues that characterize each side. Since it has been shown that, beyond purely spatial information, the hippocampus contains contextual information important for the task at hand [18], we hypothesize that this memory is also encoded within the hippocampus, along with the estimation of the agent's current position.

The agent can choose between four actions: North, South, East and West. As in the real experiment, the agent cannot run backward.

**Table 1.** State of the L and R memory components of $\phi$ and corresponding meaning in terms of task at hand, after two successful laps.

| L | R | Task identification (after 2 laps) |
|---|---|---|
| 1 | 0 | Always turn right (Tasks 1 & 3) |
| 0 | 1 | Always turn left (Tasks 2 & 4) |
| 0.5 | 1 | Alternation (Task 5), go left next time |
| 1 | 0.5 | Alternation (Task 5), go right next time |

## 2.3   Neural DynaQ with a Prioritized Sweeping Algorithm

Our algorithm is based on a Dyna architecture [12] which means that, as in model-based architectures, a world model composed of a reward and a transition model has to be learned [19]. *Prioritized sweeping* [13,14] requires the transition model to allow the prediction of the predecessors of a state $s$ given an action $a$, because this information will be needed to back-propagate the reward prediction computed in state $s$ to its predecessors. Hence, our architecture is composed of two distinct parts: one dedicated to learning the world model, and the other one to learning the Q-values.

---

**Algorithm 1.** LearnWM: learn the world model

---

collect $\mathcal{S}$ // a set of $(\phi^t, \phi^{t-1}, a, r)$ quadruplets
**for** $k \in \{N, S, E, W\}$ **do**
$\quad \mathcal{S}_P^k \leftarrow \{(\phi^t, \phi^{t-1}) : (\phi^t, \phi^{t-1}, a, r) \in \mathcal{S} \text{ and } a = k\}$
$\quad \mathcal{S}_R^k \leftarrow \{(\phi^t, r) : (\phi^t, \phi^{t-1}, a, r) \in \mathcal{S} \text{ and } a = k\}$
$\quad$ **for** $f \in \{P, R\}$ **do**
$\quad\quad$ // P,R: Predecessor and Reward types of networks
$\quad\quad \mathcal{N}_f^k \leftarrow$ null // list of networks (outputs)
$\quad\quad \mathcal{G}_f^k \leftarrow$ null // list of networks (gates)
$\quad\quad$ create $N_{new}^k$; append $N_{new}^k$ to $\mathcal{N}_f^k$
$\quad\quad$ create $G_{new}^k$; append $G_{new}^k$ to $\mathcal{G}_f^k$
$\quad\quad$ GALMO($\mathcal{S}_f^k, \mathcal{N}_f^k, \mathcal{G}_f^k$) // refer to Algo 2 for this specific training procedure
$\quad$ **end for**
**end for**

---

**Learning the World Model.** Two sets of neural networks compose the world model. Four reward networks $N_R^a$, one for each action $a$, learn the association between (state, action) couples and rewards ($N_R^a : s \rightarrow r(s,a)$). Four other networks $N_P^a$ learn the states for which a transition to a given state $s$ is produced after execution of action $a$, i.e., the predecessors of $s$ ($N_P^a : s \rightarrow \{s'\}$).

Owing to the nature of the task (navigation constrained by corridors) and the states' representation, the data that must be learned are not independent. Indeed, successive state vectors are very similar due to the overlap between place-fields, and are always encountered in the same order during tasks execution (because the agent always performs the same stereotyped trajectories along the different corridors). However, it is well known that the training of a neural network is guaranteed to converge only if there is no correlation in the sequence of samples submitted during learning, a condition that is often not respected when performing on-line reinforcement learning [20]. We indeed observed that in the task at hand, despite its simplicity, it was necessary to store the successive observations and to train the world model off-line with a shuffled presentation of the training samples (for the general scheme of the off-line training, see Algorithm 1). For that reason, we created a dataset $\mathcal{S}$ compiling all transitions, i.e ($\phi^t$, $\phi^{t-1}$, a, r) quadruplets from all tasks. When there is no predecessor of $\phi^t$

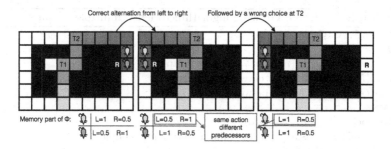

**Fig. 2. Example of multiple predecessors in the alternation task.** The agent first correctly goes to the right (left). It then goes to the left (middle) where, at the reward site, its predecessor state has a $(L = 0.5, R = 1)$ memory component. It then makes a wrong decision and goes to the left again (right), but is not rewarded: at this last position, the location component of the predecessor state (white mouse) is identical but the memory component is different $(L = 1, R = 0.5)$ from the previous lap. Violet gradient: past trajectory; white mouse: previous position; gray mouse: current position; white R: agent rewarded; black R: current position of the reward.

by action $a$ (as can be the case when this action would require to come through a wall), the transition is represented as $(\phi^t, \mathbf{0}, a, r)$: those "null" transitions allow $N_P^a$ networks to represent the fact that the transition does not exist.

Despite its simplicity, the navigation task modeled here has some specificities: during task 5 (alternation), some states have more than one predecessor for a given action (see an example on Fig. 2), the algorithm must thus be capable of producing more than one output for the same input. To do that, we have created a growing type of algorithm inspired by *mixture of expert* algorithms [21] (which we call here the *GALMO* algorithm, see Algorithm 2), based on the following principles:

– The algorithm should allow the creation of multiple $N_i$ networks (if needed) so that a single input can generate multiple outputs. Each of these networks is coupled with a gating network $G_i$, used after training to know if the output of $N_i$ has to be taken into account when a given sample is presented.
– When a sample is presented, the algorithm should only train the $N_i$ network that generates the minimal error (to enforce network specialization), and remember this training event by training $G_i$ to produce 1 and the other $G_{k \neq i}$ to produce 0.
– The algorithm should track the statistics of the minimal training errors of each sample during an epoch, so as to detect samples whose error is much higher than the others'. GALMO assumes that these outliers are caused by inputs which should predict multiple outputs and which are stuck in predicting the barycenter of the expected outputs. A sample is considered an outlier when its error is larger than a threshold $\theta$, equal to the median of the current error distribution, plus $w$ times the amplitude of the third quartile $(Q3 - median)$. When such a detection occurs, a new network is created on the fly, based on

**Algorithm 2.** GALMO: Growing algorithm to learn multiple outputs

---

**INPUT:** $\mathcal{S}, \mathcal{N}, \mathcal{G}$
**OUTPUT:** $\mathcal{N}, \mathcal{G}$
// $\mathcal{S} = \langle(in_0, out_0), ..., (in_n, out_n)\rangle$: list of samples
// $\mathcal{N} = \langle N_0\rangle$: lists of neural networks (outputs)
// $\mathcal{G} = \langle G_0\rangle$: lists of neural networks (gates)
$\theta \leftarrow +\infty$
**for** nbepoch $\in \{1, maxepoch\}$ **do**
   $\mathcal{M} \leftarrow$ null // $\mathcal{M}$ is a list of the minimal error per sample
   **for** each (in,out)$\in \mathcal{S}$ **do**
      $\mathcal{E} \leftarrow$ null // $\mathcal{E}$ is a list of errors for a sample
      **for** each $N \in \mathcal{N}$ **do**
         append $\|N(in) - out\|_{L_1}$ to $\mathcal{E}$
      **end for**
      **if** $\min(\mathcal{E}) < \theta$ **then**
         backprop($N_{argmin(\mathcal{E})}, in, out$)
         backprop($G_{argmin(\mathcal{E})}, in, 1$)
         **for** each $G \in \mathcal{G}$ with $G \neq G_{argmin(\mathcal{E})}$ **do**
            backprop($G, in, 0$)
         **end for**
      **else**
         create $N_{new}$; append $N_{new}$ to $\mathcal{N}$
         $N_{new} \leftarrow$ copy($N_{argmin(\mathcal{E})}$)
         backprop($N_{new}, input =$in, $target =$out)
         create $G_{new}$; append $G_{new}$ to $\mathcal{G}$
         backprop($G_{new}, in, 1$)
      **end if**
   **end for**
   $\theta \leftarrow median(\mathcal{M}) + w * (Q3(\mathcal{M}) - median(\mathcal{M}))$
**end for**

---

a copy of the network that produced the minimal error for the sample. The new network is then trained once on the sample at hand.

In principle, the algorithm could be modified to limit the maximal number of created networks, or to remove the networks that are not used anymore, but these additions were not necessary here.

**Neural Dyna-Q.** The second part of the algorithm works as a classical neural network-based Dyna-Q [16] with *prioritized sweeping* [13,14]. As in [16], the Q-values are represented by four 2-layer feedforward neural networks $N_Q^a$ (one per action). During on-line phases, the agent makes decisions that drive its movements within the maze, and stores the samples in a priority queue. Their priority is the absolute value of the reward prediction error, i.e., $|\delta|$. Every time the agent receives a reward, similarly to rats, it stops and replays are simulated with a budget B (Algorithm 3): the samples with the highest priority are replayed first, their potential predecessors are then estimated and placed in the queue with their respective priorities, and so on until the replay budget is exhausted.

---

**Algorithm 3.** Neural Dyna-Q with *prioritized sweeping* & multiple predecessors

---

**INPUT:** $\phi^{t=0}$, $\mathcal{N_P}$, $\mathcal{G_P}$, $\mathcal{N_R}$, $\mathcal{G_R}$
**OUTPUT:** $N_Q^{a \in \{N,S,E,W\}}$
PQueue $\leftarrow$ {} // PQueue: empty priority queue
nbTrials $\leftarrow$ 0
**repeat**
    a $\leftarrow$ softmax($N_Q(\phi^t)$)
    take action a, receive r, $\phi^{t+1}$
    backprop($N_Q^a$, *input* $= \phi^t$, *target* $= r + \gamma max_a(N_Q(\phi^{t+1}))$
    Put $\phi^t$ in PQueue with priority $|N_Q^a(\phi^t) - (r + \gamma max_a(N_Q(\phi^{t+1})))|$
    **if** r> 0 **then**
        nbReplays $\leftarrow$ 0
        Pr $= \langle\rangle$ // empty list of predecessors
        **repeat**
            $\phi \leftarrow$ pop(PQueue)
            **for** each $G_P \in \mathcal{G}_P$ **do**
                **if** $G_P(\phi) > 0$ **then**
                    $k \leftarrow$ index($G_P$)
                    append $N_P^k(\phi)$ to Pr
                **end if**
            **end for**
            **for** each $p \in$ Pr s.t norm(p) $> \epsilon$ **do**
                **for** each $a \in \{N, S, E, W\}$ **do**
                    backprop($N_Q^a$, *input* $=$ p, *target* $= N_R^a(p) + \gamma max_a(N_Q^a(\phi)))$
                    Put p in PQueue with priority $|N_Q^a(p) - (N_R^a(p) + \gamma max_a(N_Q^a(\phi)))|$
                    nbReplays $\leftarrow$ nbReplays + 1
                **end for**
            **end for**
        **until** PQueue empty **OR** nbReplays $\geq$ B
    **end if**
    $\phi^t \leftarrow \phi^{t+1}$
    nbTrials $\leftarrow$ nbTrials +1
**until** nbTrials $=$ maxNbTrials

---

The various parameters used in the simulations are summarized in Table 2.

# 3 Results

## 3.1 Learning the World Model

Because of correlations in sample sequences, the world model is learned off-line: the samples are presented in random order, so as to break temporal correlations. We illustrate this necessity with the learning of the reward networks $N_R$: when trained on-line (Fig. 3, left), the reward networks make a lot of erroneous predictions for each possible task, while when trained off-line with samples presented in randomized order, the predictions are correct (Fig. 3, right).

Table 2. Parameter values.

| Value | Parameter |
|---|---|
| 4000 | $maxepch$: Number of epoch replays to train the world model |
| 3 | $w$: Gain of the outlier detector threshold in GALMO |
| 20 | B: Replay budget per stop at reward sites |
| 2 | Number of layers in $N_P$, $N_R$ and $N_Q$ |
| 10, 16, 26 | Size of the hidden layers in $N_Q$, $N_R$ and $N_P$ (respectively) |
| ±0.05, ±0.0045, ±0.1 | Weight initialization bound in $N_Q$, $N_R$ and $N_P$ (resp.) |
| 0.5, 0.1, 0.1 | Learning rate in $N_Q$, $N_R$ and $N_P$ (resp.) |
| 0.9, 1, 1 | Sigmoid slope in $N_P$, $N_R$ and $N_Q$ (resp.) (hidden layer) |
| 0.5, 0.4, 0.4 | Sigmoid slope in $N_P$, $N_R$ and $N_Q$ (resp.) (output layer) |

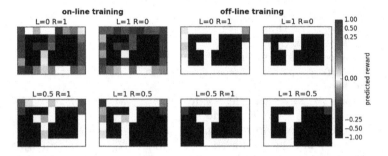

Fig. 3. **Reward predictions** are inaccurate when the model is trained on-line (Left panel) and accurate when it is trained off-line (Right panel). L, R: memory configuration. Note the use of a logarithmic scale, so as to make visible errors of small amplitude.

With a single set of $N_P$ networks, the error of the whole set of states decreases steadily with learning, except for four states which have multiple predecessors (Fig. 4, top left). With the GALMO algorithm, when the error of these states reaches the threshold $\theta$ (in red on Fig. 4, top right), networks are duplicated and specialized for each of the possible predecessors. We repeated the experiment 10 times. It always converged, with a number of final networks comprised between 2 and 5 (3 times 2 networks, 1 time 3, 5 times 4, and 1 time 5).

## 3.2   Reinforcement Learning with Multiple Predecessors

We compare the efficiency of the Dyna-Q model we developed with the corresponding Q-learning (i.e. the same architecture without replays with the world model). As expected, Q-learning is able to learn the task, as evidenced by the proportion of erroneous choices at the decision point T2 (Fig. 4, bottom left) . On average it does not fully converge before 1000 epochs of training, whereas the Dyna-Q learns much faster, thanks to the replay mechanism (Fig. 4, bottom right), converging on average after 200 trials.

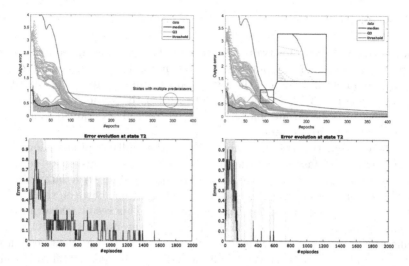

Fig. 4. **Top: Learning error dynamics without (left) and with (right) GALMO.** Errors of all samples (gray) during epochs of training. GALMO allows for the creation of multiple prediction networks to handle the states where multiple outputs have to be generated. **Bottom: Learning without (left) and with (right) replays.** Evolution of the proportion of decision errors at point T2 during the alternation task. Blue: 10 run mean, light blue: standard deviation.

## 3.3    Preliminary Analysis of Generated Replays

We analyze a posteriori the state reactivations caused by the prioritized sweeping DynaQ algorithm in always turn right, always turn left and alternate tasks. Prioritized sweeping does not rely on explicit replay of sequences, but it does favors them. We considered sequences or replays involving three or more consecutive steps; with 128 possible states, a 3-state sequence has a chance level of 0.01% of being produced by a uniform random selection process. We observed in all cases (Fig. 5) that a bit more than 80% of the state reactivations did not correspond to actual sequences. Most of the sequences are backward, except for the alternate task, which also generated 4.5% of forward ones. As in [6], we classified these sequences as being on the same side as the current agent location, on the opposite side, or in the central part of the maze. There is no clear pattern here, except that central reactivations were observed in the alternate task only.

Fig. 5. **Type of replays.** B: backward, F: forward, RND: random.

# 4   Discussion

We proposed a new neural network architecture (GALMO) designed to associate multiple outputs to a single input, based on the multiple expert principle [21]. We implemented a neural version of the DynaQ algorithm [16], using the prioritized sweeping principle [13,14], using GALMO to learn the world model. This was necessary because the evaluation task, adapted from [6], contained some states that have multiple predecessors.

We showed that this system is able to learn the multiple predecessors cases, and to solve the task faster than the corresponding Q-learning system (i.e., without replays). This required learning the world-model off-line, with data presented in shuffled order, so as to break the sequential correlations between them, which prevented the convergence of the learning process. This result makes an interesting neuroscientific prediction (independently of the use of GALMO): if the learning principles of the rat brain are similar to those of the gradient descent for artificial neural network, then the world model has to be learned off-line, which would be compatible with non-sequential hippocampal replays. Besides, the part of the DynaQ algorithm that uses the world model to update the Q-values predicts a majority of non-sequential replays, but also 15 to 20% of sequential reactivations, both backward and forward.

Concerning GALMO, it has been tested with a quite limited set of data, and should thus be evaluated against larger sets in future work. In our specific case, the reward networks $N_R^a$ did not require the use of GALMO; a single network could learn the full $(s, a) \rightarrow r$ mapping as rewards were deterministic. But should they be stochastic, GALMO could be used to learn the multiple possible outcomes. Note that, while it has been developed in order to learn a predecessor model in a DynaQ architecture, GALMO is much more general, and would in principle be able to learn any one-to-many mapping. Finally, in the model-based and dyna reinforcement learning contexts, having multiple predecessors or successors is not an exceptional situation, especially in a robotic paradigm. The proposed approach is thus of interest beyond the task used here.

**Acknowledgements.** The authors thank O. Sigaud for fruitful discussions, and F. Cinotti for proofreading. This work has received funding from the European Union's Horizon 2020 research and innovation programme under grant agreement No 640891 (DREAM Project). This work was performed within the Labex SMART (ANR-11-LABX-65) supported by French state funds managed by the ANR within the Investissements d'Avenir programme under reference ANR-11-IDEX-0004-02.

# References

1. O'Keefe, J., Dostrovsky, J.: The hippocampus as a spatial map. Preliminary evidence from unit activity in the freely-moving rat. Brain Res. **34**(1), 171–175 (1971)
2. Wilson, M.A., McNaughton, B.L., et al.: Reactivation of hippocampal ensemble memories during sleep. Science **265**(5172), 676–679 (1994)

3. Girardeau, G., Benchenane, K., Wiener, S.I., Buzsáki, G., Zugaro, M.B.: Selective suppression of hippocampal ripples impairs spatial memory. Nat. Neurosci. **12**(10), 1222–1223 (2009)
4. Foster, D.J., Wilson, M.A.: Reverse replay of behavioural sequences in hippocampal place cells during the awake state. Nature **440**(7084), 680–683 (2006)
5. Lee, A.K., Wilson, M.A.: Memory of sequential experience in the hippocampus during slow wave sleep. Neuron **36**(6), 1183–1194 (2002)
6. Gupta, A.S., van der Meer, M.A.A., Touretzky, D.S., Redish, A.D.: Hippocampal replay is not a simple function of experience. Neuron **65**(5), 695–705 (2010)
7. Chen, Z., Wilson, M.A.: Deciphering neural codes of memory during sleep. Trends Neurosci. **40**(5), 260–275 (2017)
8. Peyrache, A., Khamassi, M., Benchenane, K., Wiener, S.I., Battaglia, F.P.: Replay of rule-learning related neural patterns in the prefrontal cortex during sleep. Nat. Neurosci. **12**(7), 919–926 (2009)
9. McClelland, J.L., McNaughton, B.L., O'reilly, R.C.: Why there are complementary learning systems in the hippocampus and neocortex: insights from the successes and failures of connectionist models of learning and memory. Psychol. Rev. **102**(3), 419 (1995)
10. De Lavilléon, G., Lacroix, M.M., Rondi-Reig, L., Benchenane, K.: Explicit memory creation during sleep demonstrates a causal role of place cells in navigation. Nat. Neurosci. **18**(4), 493–495 (2015)
11. Cazé, R., Khamassi, M., Aubin, L., Girard, B.: Hippocampal replays under the scrutiny of reinforcement learning models (2018, submitted)
12. Sutton, R.S.: Integrated architectures for learning, planning, and reacting based on approximating dynamic programming. In: Proceedings of the Seventh International Conference on Machine Learning, pp. 216–224 (1990)
13. Moore, A.W., Atkeson, C.G.: Prioritized sweeping: reinforcement learning with less data and less time. Mach. Learn. **13**(1), 103–130 (1993)
14. Peng, J., Williams, R.J.: Efficient learning and planning within the Dyna framework. Adapt. Behav. **1**(4), 437–454 (1993)
15. Khamassi, M., Lacheze, L., Girard, B., Berthoz, A., Guillot, A.: Actor-critic models of reinforcement learning in the basal ganglia: from natural to arificial rats. Adapt. Behav. **13**, 131–148 (2005)
16. Lin, L.H.: Self-improving reactive agents based on reinforcement learning, planning and teaching. Mach. Learn. **8**(3/4), 69–97 (1992)
17. Paz-Villagrán, V., Save, E., Poucet, B.: Independent coding of connected environments by place cells. Eur. J. Neurosci. **20**(5), 1379–1390 (2004)
18. Eichenbaum, H.: Prefrontal-hippocampal interactions in episodic memory. Nat. Rev. Neurosci. **18**(9), 547 (2017)
19. Sutton, R., Barto, A.: Reinforcement Learning: An Introduction. MIT Press, Cambridge (1998)
20. Tsitsiklis, J.N., Van Roy, B.: Analysis of temporal-diffference learning with function approximation. In: Advances in Neural Information Processing Systems, pp. 1075–1081 (1997)
21. Jacobs, R.A., Jordan, M.I., Nowlan, S.J., Hinton, G.E.: Adaptive mixtures of local experts. Neural Comput. **3**(1), 79–87 (1991)

# Should Mobile Robots Have a Head?
## A Rationale Based on Behavior, Automatic Control and Signal Processing

François Bailly[1]([✉]), Emmanuelle Pouydebat[2], Bruno Watier[1], Vincent Bels[3], and Philippe Souères[1]

[1] LAAS-CNRS, Université de Toulouse, CNRS, Toulouse, France
fbailly@laas.fr
[2] UMR 7179, Mécanismes Adaptatifs: Des Organismes aux Communautés, CNRS, Muséum National d'Histoire Naturelle, Paris, France
[3] Institut de Systématique Evolution Biodiversité (ISYEB), Muséum National d'Histoire Naturelle, CNRS, Sorbonne Université, EPHE, Paris, France

**Abstract.** This paper presents an interdisciplinary study of the role of the head in multisensory integration and motor-control organization for the production of voluntary spatial actions. It combines elements from biology and engineering. First, morphological and behavioral characteristics of animals able to perform voluntary spatial actions through evolution are examined. The complexity of state-space representation and observation of multi-joint mobile robots is then described in the context of automatic control, and perception-related characteristics brought by the presence of a head are presented from the perspective of signal processing. Finally, the role of the head in locomotion and manipulation for animals and robots is discussed, paving the way for future robot design.

**Keywords:** Head · Voluntary action · Behavior · Mobile robot Sensory integration · Biomimetics

## 1 Introduction

A robot is a machine equipped with sensors, which provide it with information about its internal state and about the environment, computers that enable it to process sensory data and elaborate motor orders, and actuators that make it able to execute movements. Robots should then be able to perceive, process information and act in the physical world. In order to endow robots with such capabilities, roboticists are free to use the most advanced methodologies and techniques as well as the best adapted materials. A priori, their work should not be constrained by biomimicry concerns as only performance objectives should guide it. However, in the quest of designing systems that are able to sense and drive their movement consistently, animals appear as living models of efficiency. For this reason, roboticists sometimes try to design bio-inspired robots. However, in most cases, the bio-inspiration focuses on a particular functionality

© Springer International Publishing AG, part of Springer Nature 2018
V. Vouloutsi et al. (Eds.): Living Machines 2018, LNAI 10928, pp. 28–39, 2018.
https://doi.org/10.1007/978-3-319-95972-6_5

that engineers attempt to reproduce. In this perspective, various bio-inspired systems have been designed. Among the most remarkable are the salamander robot in [10] that demonstrates locomotion modes based on central pattern generators, the use of insect optical flow for navigation in [22], the gecko robot in [16] whose leg coating texture reproduces adhesion abilities, the eel robot in [4] endowed with an electric sense, and, more generally, humanoids robots designed to reproduce bipedal walking [17]. Despite these encouraging achievements, a lot of work remains to be done to understand the key principles that endow living beings with such autonomous navigation capabilities and transfer them to robots. Developing research in this direction is possible only through interdisciplinary studies involving biology and engineering.

With this objective in mind, the present article aims at gathering a set of arguments from life sciences and robotics to demonstrate that the existence of the head under the process of cephalization [14] is linked to animals ability to perform voluntary spatial actions and simplifies the integration process of sensory and motor functions for navigation. First, morphological and behavioral characteristics of animals capable of voluntary spatial action through evolution are examined. Then, the complexity of state-space representation and observation of multi-joints mobile robots is presented in the context of automatic control. After that, perception related features brought by the presence of a head are presented in the light of signal processing. Finally, the role of the head in locomotion and manipulation in animals and robots is discussed, paving the way for future robot design.

## 2    The Head in Animals

The evolution of organisms is related to a large number of external (environmental) and internal (phylogenetic or historical) pressures [3]. Every organism has to perform a series of motor actions to ensure its fitness at any time of its life. These actions are produced by functional structures in response to environmental stimuli. The process of natural selection has governed the shape of these structures and their functioning under different but complimentary proximate and ultimate causes through the evolutionary time [28]. Therefore, each individual has to optimize various motor strategies to respond to the diverse constraints of its environment (abiotic and biotic) and to its physiological needs (i.e., feed and cover the physiological demands, find mates and cover the reproductive effort, find partners for social interactions, etc.). This ability to perform different motor actions through various integrated systems, such as limbs or jaws, necessarily relies on appropriate decision mechanisms initiated and controlled by complex releasing factors [12]. Anatomy and functional morphology associated with developmental research make it possible to empirically categorize the structures and the motor patterns involved in these motor actions. Behavioral ecology and other disciplines (i.e., cognitive phenotypes studies) provide an understanding of their sensory-motor bases. Some of them are determined as taxes (animals simply heading towards or away from sources of stimulation), some other as fixed action patterns (FAPs, or activities with a relative fixed pattern of coordination [13,24]).

The evolutionary and ecological pressures involved into a trophic web can be considered as playing a primary role (though not the only one) to explain the diversity of these actions in organisms. In such a web, individuals are either predators and/or preys at one time of their life and thus have to select actions within contrasting contexts to gain food and energy while avoiding being injured or killed. A rough review of all metazoan organisms into extinct and extant food web shows that they can be divided into three major categories, according to their primary feeding behaviors [5,8]: fixed organisms with no voluntary exploratory movements, organisms whose movements follow any type of gradient (e.g., chemical), and organisms capable of voluntary movements. This difference remains in the diversification of all taxa, although our understanding of the earliest evolution of metazoans is still a controversial problem.

The earliest traces of voluntary motor actions seem to appear at the Ediacaran-Cambrian boundary (560-555 Mya). Within this context, ecosystem engineering attempts to explain how voluntary activities have affected the biological diversity of organisms through their ecological and evolutionary implications (i.e., nutriments flow modification, sediments transformation). Although faunas of both eras were probably temporally separated by a mass extinction, some forms of moving bilaterian animals that are characteristics of the Cambrian fauna are suggested to be present since the late Ediacara [5,8]. Although their evolution is not discussed here, paleontological evidences (organisms and traces) suggest that bilateral organisms developed voluntary tasks associated with two main strategies in aquatic environment: movement on and in the substratum, and navigation at benthic and pelagic levels in the water column. From anatomical descriptions, these actions were associated with a structural anterior-posterior organization. Notably, some authors suggested that hydraulic burrowing was performed by bilaterian animals with a frontal organ that can be called *head* [19]. Thus, the earliest traces of voluntary motor actions appear to have been produced by bilaterian animals. From these geological times (Cambrian explosion) they have developed elaborate strategies such as active hunting and escaping from predators, suggesting a possible causal relationship between the spatial abilities and the morphotypes of these animals.

Most of the major groups of bilaterian animals show rather similar morphotypes with two successive anterior-posterior regions of the body: an anterior region, called *head*, cumulating a series of sensory systems (visual, olfactory, vomerolfactory, auditory, etc.) with specialized trophic systems, and a posterior region comprising morphological devices permitting body deformations in order to move in determined directions. The head comprises a series of symmetrical complex structures (e.g., eyes, ears, whiskers, antennae) and the exteroceptive sensory organs (ESOs), that sense exteroceptive stimuli for actively interacting with the environment and generating voluntary spatially related actions (see Fig. 1). The head can be either fixed or mobile, probably to improve the success of actions implying the integration of sensory information or recruiting the

**Fig. 1.** Examples of anterior structures in different bilateral animals highlighting their heads, sensory and trophic systems. From left to right: Zygoptera, Sepiida, Felidae (*Panthera* lineage), Callitrichinae, Gekkota, Tetraodontidae, Culicidae, Casuarius.

trophic structure. This morphotype with accumulated morphological and sensory systems into the anterior region includes a central nervous system (CNS) to integrate the sensory information and produce coordinated motor orders for the body and the head (move towards a prey and catch it). Studying the evolution of such organisms through their centralized nervous system shows two alternative possibilities from the analysis of the brain–body complexity among extant Bilateria. The first one, a diffuse nerve plexus with ganglionated systems, probably existed in Ediacaran organisms that were not able to produce voluntary coordinated actions. The second one, an anterior cephalic nerve system (brain or a series of nervous ganglions) arose in the common Bilateria ancestor. From this point, ecological pressures could have triggered the evolutionary pattern of complex actions, in the context of two body regions with highly different morphological and functional traits. Indeed, within trophic webs, the predatory-prey strategies involved into an escalatory "arms race" can be as complex as needed to produce highly diversified morphological systems and FAPs under the control of the nervous system. Along the evolutionary process of the various phyla, these FAPs have been modulated by a series of traits such as learning or cognitive abilities. As soon as animals are able to voluntarily control their actions at any stage from initiation, they can exploit diverse ecological niches.

In conclusion, one of the main characteristics of all organisms that developed the ability to produce complex voluntary spatial actions along their evolution is the morphological, developmental and functional dichotomy of the body regions into a head, mobile or not, integrating the majority of sensory systems and the rest of the body.

## 3    A Head for State Observation in Mobile Robotics

Although robots are not subjects to physiological needs, we show in the following that the morphological solutions that arose in animals capable of voluntary spatial actions are relevant for state estimation in mobile robotics. Consider the problem of endowing a multi-joint mobile robot with the capacity to autonomously drive its motion in space. The theoretical frameworks that allows engineers to formalize this problem is the one of automatic control, the science of modeling, analysis and control of dynamic systems.

**Basics in Automatic Control.** Three fundamental notions are used to describe the system to be controlled: the state, the control input, and the output. The state $\mathbf{x} \in \mathbb{R}^n$ is a minimum-dimension vector which fully describes the

**Fig. 2.** Three different multi-joint mobile robots at LAAS: the flying manipulator Aeroarm (left), the mobile manipulator Jido (center), and the humanoid robot Talos (right). The usual choices for their root frame placement are displayed.

system configuration at each time. The state-space representation is not unique but its dimension is imposed by the nature of the system. The control input $\mathbf{u} \in \mathbb{R}^m$ describes the rudders thanks to which the system can be driven and the output $\mathbf{y} \in \mathbb{R}^p$ is the vector of data provided by sensors. Using this formalism, the state-space representation of the system is given by:

$$\dot{\mathbf{x}} = f(\mathbf{x}, \mathbf{u}), \tag{1a}$$
$$\mathbf{y} = g(\mathbf{x}, \mathbf{u}), \tag{1b}$$

where Eq. (1a) is a differential equation that describes the system dynamics and Eq. (1b) expresses the output as a function of the state and the control. Making the robot able to control its movement consistently as a function of its current state amounts to synthesizing a feedback control law $\mathbf{u}(\mathbf{x})$ that, injected in Eq. (1a), yields a closed-loop equation of the type $\dot{\mathbf{x}} = f(\mathbf{x}, \mathbf{u}(\mathbf{x})) = \tilde{f}(\mathbf{x})$, uniquely determining the behavior of the robot as a function of its state. However, usually the value of the state is unknown as it cannot be directly measured. In order to implement such a closed-loop controller, one needs to estimate the state of the robot from the sensory data that are measured at the output, a fundamental problem in automatic control, known as the observation problem. **State Space Representation and Control of a Multi-joint Mobile Robot.** Contrary to manipulator robots, which are rigidly fixed to the ground by their basis, mobile robots can move freely in their environment. Depending on their locomotion mode they can strongly differ as shown in Fig. 2.

Let us first focus on the kinematics of multi-joint mobile robots by neglecting the dynamic effects induced by the acceleration of masses. The kinematic state of these systems must include a parameterization $\mathbf{q}$ of their polyarticulated structure, hereinafter called *internal state*, and a parameterization of their pose $\mathbf{p}$, i.e. position and orientation with respect to the external world, that will be referred to as *external state*. In order to simply illustrate these definitions, let us consider the case of mobile robot made of three bodies linked by two rotational joints, as depicted in Fig. 3a. Each joint is actuated by a motor and thanks to the combination of both rotations this worm-like system is supposed to be able

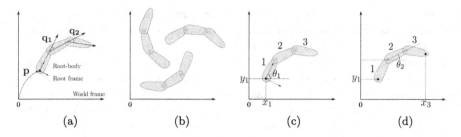

**Fig. 3.** Illustrations of the internal and external states of a simple polyarticulated mobile robot. (a): Absolute parameterization of the system in the plane. (b): Between the three cases depicted, only the external state of the system is changed. (c): The external state is parametrized by fully positioning the first body. (d): The parameterization of the external state is distributed on the three bodies of the robot.

move in the plane. The internal state of the robot is defined by two angles $q_1$ and $q_2$. Once both angles are fixed, the pose of the robot in the plane depends on two degrees of freedom in translation and one in rotation as shown in Fig. 3b. Hence, five scalar parameters are necessary to fully describe the kinematic configuration of the robot in the plane. Though the parameterization of the internal state by means of $q_1$ and $q_2$ appears to be quite natural, many parametrization can be used to describe the external state. Figure 3c and d depict two of them, encoded with respect to a world frame. In the first one, the pose of the first body is fully determined by its orientation $\theta_1$ and the coordinates $(x_1, y_1)$ of a point attached to it. Whereas in the second case, the parametrization is distributed over the three bodies, including the ordinate $y_1$ of a point on the first body, the orientation $\theta_2$ of the second body, and the abscissa $x_3$ of a point on the third body. From a mathematical point of view, if all variables can be determined with the same accuracy, both parameterizations are equivalent. In practice, we will demonstrate in the sequel that, as the measurement relies on sensors, these two parameterization cannot be implemented with the same level of accuracy.

Extending this reasoning to the kinematic modeling of a tri-dimensional multi-joint robot with $n$ rotational joints, the state representation must include $n + 6$ parameters: $n$ to describe the internal state plus 6 for the external state. In kinematic modeling the control inputs are joint velocities. As soon as the dynamic effects induced by the acceleration of the robot bodies are no more negligible, kinematics modeling becomes insufficient. One needs then to consider a model of the robot dynamics in consistency with Euler-Newton's laws of mechanics [23]. In that case, the dimension of the robot state is doubled. The internal state includes $2n$ parameters which encode the joint position and velocities, whereas the external state includes 12 parameters: 6 to parameterize the pose of the robot plus 6 to express its velocity. In dynamic modeling the control input is the vector of joint torques.

**The Observation Problem.** As previously explained the state variables cannot be directly measured and must be reconstructed from data provided by sensors at the output. Ideally, the sensors should be installed in such a way as to limit geometrical transformations and data processing. Usually the internal state of robots can be easily reconstructed from encoders located at the joints. It is then possible, modulo proprioceptives biases and flexibilities, to have a good knowledge of the internal structure of the robot and its variation. However, as previously explained, several parametrizations can be used to represent the external state. These parametrizations fall into two main categories as illustrated by the worm-like mobile robot example (see Fig. 3(c) and (d)). In the first one, the exteroceptive sensors are used to fully measure the pose and the velocity of one of its bodies, called *root-body*, whereas in the second, the exteroceptive sensors are distributed on different bodies of the robot providing partial measurements of their pose and velocity. In view of the inherent proprioceptive biases and the flexibility of the structure these two strategies are not equivalent. Indeed, with the first strategy, the quality of the estimation of the pose and velocity of the root-body only depends on the accuracy of exteroceptive sensors mounted on it. Whereas, using the second strategy, the estimation of the complete pose and velocity of any one of these bodies is degraded by proprioception inaccuracy. In sum, for the sake of accuracy, it is preferable to attach all exteroceptive sensors to one root-body in order to fully reconstruct its pose and velocity, and then deduce the relative configuration of other bodies from proprioception, rather than distributing the exteroceptive measurement on different bodies and then integrating them through proprioception. Furthermore, this strategy offers a natural way to decouple the exteroceptive anchoring of the robot in its environment and the estimation of its internal state. In practice, the 12 state variables describing the pose and the velocity of the root-body can be reconstructed from the measurement provided by an inertial central unit, combined with exteroceptive sensors such as cameras, laser, microphones, sonars, etc.

**Head Morphology and Exteroceptive Sensors.** Considering the analogy with the notion of root-body in robotics, it is interesting to remark that, in animals, the anatomic symmetries of the head and the positioning of the ESOs on it offer natural spatial references. Whether they are eyes, ears, whiskers, antennae, or of any other sort, exteroceptive sensors are symmetrically placed on the head and turned outward, making the "center of the head" as a common virtual origin for multi-sensory perception. This organization provides a natural and simple way of defining right, left, up and down direction for the animal, playing exactly the same role as a reference frame in geometry. Following this idea, interesting works have been carried out in humans based on the perception of visual and auditory target alignment [2, 18, 27]. They reported the existence of a similar origin for vision and hearing in humans strongly linked to the position of the ESOs. The sagittal plane of the head and the direction of gravity provided by the vestibular system constitute two fundamental geometrical references which, combined with visual and auditory data, provide all the necessary kinematic information to fully localize the head pose and estimate its velocity with respect to its environment.

In summary, the accuracy of state estimation and the ability to discriminate space is improved and simplified by symmetrically gathering exteroceptive sensors on a single body. It is worth stressing that this is also one of the features provided by the head in bilaterian animals, which might be strongly linked to their ability to generate voluntary movements requiring state observation.

## 4   A Head for Signal Processing and Cognition

**Centralizing Exteroceptive Perception and Its Processing.** The purpose of exteroceptive multisensory fusion is to combine a variety of sensory signals to mutually enrich them in order to make the perception as complete as possible. The fusion of these different signals can only be accomplished by collecting and matching information, a solution provided by the brain. For instance, the McGurk effect [15] and other experiences of sensory enrichment [6,7,9] are evidences that the addition or the removal of a sensory modality makes it possible to change the overall interpretation of a phenomenon. Alongside, the spatial proximity of the ESOs resulting from their attachment to a head, enables a spatially and temporally coherent acquisition of the different exteroceptive sensory modalities involved in multisensory perception. This seems essential since most of the physical processes living beings have to measure vary in space and time. Thus, if the ESOs were dispersed over the body, it would be necessary to estimate the measurement that they would have provided from a same spot and at the same time, in order to coherently enrich each other. For example, picture an imaginary creature with its ears placed on its hands and its eyes placed on its head. The spatial matching of the two resulting signals would require to estimate what the ears would have acquired if they had been located near the eyes, or vice versa. It goes without saying that this problem is of such mathematical complexity (equations of propagation, diffusion, diffraction, dynamics, etc.) that the centralization of ESOs on the head considerably simplifies the problem of coherent multisensory fusion. Cephalization, the evolutionary trend in which the concentration of the nervous system along with the migration of the ESOs result in a head, thus provides an efficient solution with regard to both acquisition and processing of multisensory signals.

**Shortening of the Brain-ESO Transmission Channel.** A second feature provided by cephalization is the proximity of the ESOs with regard to the CNS. This observation relates to the fields of information theory and data transmission, which attest that shortening a transmission channel limits a large number of undesirable effects, such as attenuation, phase distortion, delays and different noises that depend on the type of transmission and on the environment. According to Shannon [25], who connected the bandwidth of a communication channel to its signal-to-noise ratio introducing the notion of channel capacity, the less distorted the signal, the higher the admissible bitrate. In the context of visual, auditive and inertial data transmission, shortening the connections between the brain and the ESOs is one way of increasing the capacity of this transmission channel in order to increase the admissible flow rates which contribute to the richness of animal perception.

**Stiffening the Exteroceptive Kinematics.** Another interesting character-istic of the head is the kinematic limits that it imposes between the ESOs, especially in the clade of craniates. These animals are chordates with a cartilagi-nous or bony skull protecting the anterior part of the CNS. This rigid support strongly constrains the mobility between the ESOs which are fixed on it, limiting it to voluntary and very well calibrated displacements (eye saccades, ear and nose inflections, etc.). These kinematic constraints simplify the mathematical relation-ship between the signals acquired by different sensory modalities, enabling simple implementation of intermodal processes. For instance, the vestibulo-ocular reflex relies on simplified and very well calibrated transformations between the inner ear and the eyes. Moreover, these kinematic constraints make it easier to esti-mate the relative placement of the various ESOs, by reducing the number of parameters to be estimated. For instance, the distances between the two eyes, the two ears, the inner ears and the eyes, etc., are constant in most craniates. Thus, the estimation of the extrinsic calibration of the ESOs, which is necessary for multi-sensory fusion (see [30]), is simplified.

**Head Mobility for Enhanced Perception.** As the ESOs are gathered on it, endowing the head with sufficient mobility and proprioception is a way of mechanically filtering and stabilizing perception. Indeed, as the head is attached to the body, dynamic effects of the body moving during locomotion may induce disturbance on exteroceptive measurements. Notably, in legged organisms, foot contacts with the ground generate strong undesirable accelerations that are transmitted throughout the body via its musculo-skeletal structure. Decoupling the movement of the head from the one of the body is an efficient mean of compensating for these disturbances. Such a decoupling has been observed in humans during walking, based on vestibular data [21] and thanks to the vestibu-locollic reflex that stabilizes visual and auditory perception [29]. In [11], it was explored how this stabilization of the head could mechanically contribute to the balance of bipedal walking. In addition, the mobility of the head allows for an efficient implementation of active exploration strategies that are essential to perception [1]. Indeed, moving the head alone is more precise and requires less energy than performing whole-body exploration. This mobility however must be supported by a rich proprioception at the neck level, as observed in many animals and in humans [20].

# 5   The Role of the Head in Locomotion and Manipulation

**The Head at the Front-End of the Movement for Locomotion.** Address-ing the question of the head position with regard to the body is highly relevant in the context of locomotion. Animals whose morphology is bilateral are struc-tured along a mouth-anus axis and, except for bipeds in which this axis is ver-ticalized, their locomotion is directed along this axis. Whatever the mode of bilateral locomotion (flight, swimming, legged locomotion,...), the head of these animals precedes the rest of their body. The ESOs placed on the head sense the part of the environment ahead and the motor system is specialized to produce this forward movement. A very wide range of species including fishes, worms, insects, birds and mammals follow this model for locomotion. Interestingly, in engineering, such a model of locomotion directed along a main axis with specialized thrust and control has guided the conception of many vehicles. Wheeled vehicles are certainly the most representative ones among them. Thanks to the rolling-without-slipping constraint, which prevents instantaneous lateral movement, the control is greatly simplified. It boils down to two control gears, one for steering the wheels and the other one for controlling the acceleration. One can imagine how complex would be the control to stay the course and avoid drift if the wheels were spherical instead of circular. The same phenomenon applies to boats equipped with a centerboard, to planes, etc. In general, all of these systems are differentially flat, and the cascade structure of their dynamics can be controlled from a small number of variables [26]. It is thus possible to easily control the movement of a truck pulling several trailers by controlling only the leading vehicle. As for the head, the steering center of such vehicle is placed ahead to enable the pilot to perceive the part of space towards which the motion is directed.

**One Head for Supervising Manipulation.** Though many animals possess their mouth as only gripper (worms, fishes, snakes, etc.), and others are equipped with several end-effectors (paws, claws, hands, tentacles) as in mammals, birds or cephalopods, in either case they only have one head. In the second group, the existence of additional effectors enables manipulation behaviors. Each end-effector could be equipped with exteroceptive sensors, although this would lead to a redundant state observation, but having a unique head makes it possible to decouple exteroceptive perception from other motor tasks. Indeed, in these animals, the head is an easily steerable multi-sensory perception platform that can use exteroceptive feedback to coordinate manipulation while providing an independent anchoring with the environment.

## 6 Conclusion

Though the head is a key structure in animals able to perform voluntary spatial actions (see Fig. 1) and despite the numerous computational arguments presented in this paper, today few robots are supplied with a head that actually plays a functional role in their navigation. The main reason is that robotics is still a very young science and few works really attempt to integrate multisensory perception and motor control in a robust way that would emphasize the need for such a centralizing structure. In humanoid robots for instance, the presence of the head is mostly motivated by the sake of anthropomorphism. But the root-body that is usually taken into account for modeling their external state is the waist. The reason for this choice is that most walking pattern generators are based on the dynamical link between the center of mass located near the waist in standing position and the center of pressure on the ground. As a consequence, the pose and the velocity of the root-frame are usually not reconstructed from exteroceptive data but rely on proprioceptive measurements along the leg, plus inertial data provided by an IMU located in the trunk. Clearly, in such a scheme, the control and the observation problems appear not to be optimally connected, contrary to what could be obtained by using a head as a pivot body between exteroceptive measurement and internal motor control. In many other robots, as illustrated in Fig. 2, the root-frame used for modeling the external state is usually located along the main axis of the robot basis, in order to simplify the expression of the robot dynamics, but without real concerns of exteroceptive perception. So far, no theory exists to specify where exteroceptive sensors should be placed on a robot in order to optimize the execution of navigation tasks. If today's robots do not appear to suffer from the lack of a head, it is reasonable to assume that this structure will appear necessary as soon as tasks will require deeper multisensory and sensorimotor integration. Finally, the structural role played by the head in sensory data acquisition and processing could be involved in the emergence of higher cognitive capacities related to the representation of space, the construction of motor plans and the ability to learn and generalize.

**Acknowledgments.** Authors thank Drs. André Nel and Romain Garrouste (Sorbonne Université, ISYEB, France) for courteously providing pictures of Fig. 1. This work was partially funded by the FLAG-ERA JTC project ROBOCOM++.

# References

1. Bajcsy, R.: Active perception. Proc. IEEE **76**(8), 966–1005 (1988)
2. Barbeito, R., Ono, H.: Four methods of locating the egocenter: a comparison of their predictive validities and reliabilities. Behav. Res. Methods Instrum. **11**(1), 31–36 (1979)
3. Bateson, P., Laland, K.N.: Tinbergen's four questions: an appreciation and an update. Trends Ecol. Evol. **28**(12), 712–718 (2013)
4. Boyer, F., Porez, M., Leroyer, A., Visonneau, M.: Fast dynamics of an eel-like robot: comparisons with Navier-Stokes simulation. IEEE Trans. Robot. **24**(6), 1274–1288 (2008)
5. Budd, G.E., Jensen, S.: The origin of the animals and a 'savannah' hypothesis for early bilaterian evolution. Biol. Rev. **92**(1), 446–473 (2017)
6. Clark, J.J., Yuille, A.L.: Data Fusion for Sensory Information Processing Systems, vol. 105. Springer, New York (2013)
7. Ernst, M.O., Banks, M.S.: Humans integrate visual and haptic information in a statistically optimal fashion. Nature **415**(6870), 429–433 (2002)
8. Erwin, D.H., Laflamme, M., Tweedt, S.M., Sperling, E.A., Pisani, D., Peterson, K.J.: The cambrian conundrum: early divergence and later ecological success in the early history of animals. Science **334**(6059), 1091–1097 (2011)
9. Hillis, J.M., Ernst, M.O., Banks, M.S., Landy, M.S.: Combining sensory information: mandatory fusion within, but not between, senses. Science **298**(5598), 1627–1630 (2002)
10. Ijspeert, A.J., Crespi, A., Ryczko, D., Cabelguen, J.M.: From swimming to walking with a salamander robot driven by a spinal cord model. Science **315**(5817), 1416–1420 (2007)
11. Laumond, J.P., Benallegue, M., Carpentier, J., Berthoz, A.: The yoyo-man. Int. J. Robot. Res. **36**(13–14), 1508–1520 (2017)

12. Legreneur, P., Laurin, M., Bels, V.: Predator-prey interactions paradigm: a new tool for artificial intelligence. Adapt. Behav. **20**(1), 3–9 (2012)
13. Lorenz, K.: The foundations of ethology. Springer, New York (2013)
14. Manzanares, M., Wada, H., Itasaki, N., Trainor, P.A., Krumlauf, R., Holland, P.W.: Conservation and elaboration of hox gene regulation during evolution of the vertebrate head. Nature **408**(6814), 854–857 (2000)
15. McGurk, H., MacDonald, J.: Hearing lips and seeing voices. Nature **264**(5588), 746–748 (1976)
16. Menon, C., Murphy, M., Sitti, M.: Gecko inspired surface climbing robots. In: IEEE International Conference on Robotics and Biomimetics. IEEE (2004)
17. Naveau, M., Kudruss, M., Stasse, O., Kirches, C., Mombaur, K., Souères, P.: A reactive walking pattern generator based on nonlinear model predictive control. IEEE Robot. Autom. Lett. **2**(1), 10–17 (2017)
18. Neelon, M.F., Brungart, D.S., Simpson, B.D.: The isoazimuthal perception of sounds across distance: a preliminary investigation into the location of the audio egocenter. J. Neurosci. **24**(35), 7640–7647 (2004)
19. Pecoits, E., Konhauser, K.O., Aubet, N.R., Heaman, L.M., Veroslavsky, G., Stern, R.A., Gingras, M.K.: Bilaterian burrows and grazing behavior at >585 million years ago. Science **336**(6089), 1693–1696 (2012)
20. Pettorossi, V.E., Schieppati, M.: Neck proprioception shapes body orientation and perception of motion. Front. Hum. Neurosci. **8**, 895 (2014)
21. Pozzo, T., Berthoz, A., Lefort, L.: Head stabilization during various locomotor tasks in humans. Exp. Brain Res. **82**(1), 97–106 (1990)
22. Ruffier, F., Viollet, S., Amic, S., Franceschini, N.: Bio-inspired optical flow circuits for the visual guidance of micro air vehicles. In: Proceedings of the International Symposium on Circuits and Systems. IEEE (2003)
23. Saab, L., Ramos, O.E., Keith, F., Mansard, N., Soueres, P., Fourquet, J.Y.: Dynamic whole-body motion generation under rigid contacts and other unilateral constraints. IEEE Trans. Robot. **29**(2), 346–362 (2013)
24. Schleidt, W.M.: How "fixed" is the fixed action pattern? Ethology **36**(1–5), 184–211 (1974)
25. Shannon, C.E.: Communication in the presence of noise. Proc. IRE **37**(1), 10–21 (1949)
26. Sira-Ramirez, H., Agrawal, S.K.: Differentially Flat Systems. CRC Press, Boca Raton (2004)
27. Sukemiya, H., Nakamizo, S., Ono, H.: Location of the auditory egocentre in the blind and normally sighted. Perception **37**(10), 1587–1595 (2008)
28. Tinbergen, N.: On aims and methods of ethology. Ethology **20**(4), 410–433 (1963)
29. Wilson, V., Boyle, R., Fukushima, K., Rose, P., Shinoda, Y., Sugiuchi, Y., Uchino, Y.: The vestibulocollic reflex. J. Vestib. Res. Equilibr. Orient. **5**(3), 147–170 (1995)
30. Zhang, Q., Pless, R.: Extrinsic calibration of a camera and laser range finder (improves camera calibration). In: IEEE/RSJ International Conference on Intelligent Robots and Systems (2004)

# The Neck of Pinobo, A Low-Cost Compliant Robot

Arnaud Blanchard[✉] and Djamel Mebarki

ETIS Laboratory, 95000 Cergy-Pontoise, France
{arnaud.blanchard,djamel.mebarki}@ensea.fr
http://www-etis.ensea.fr

**Abstract.** We introduce in this paper a robotic neck with 3° of freedom. The Pinobo's neck has three important features: open source software, solid, and easy to made. This early prototype is light, fast and compliant. After explaining how to build the Pinobo's neck, we analyze the different properties of this system in order to obtain a robust controller. Pinobo is equipped with several sensors such as accelerometers, gyrometers and voltage of its motors. The robot is designed for students and researchers for scanning environment, stabilizing a head or interacting with humans.

## 1 Introduction

### 1.1 The Interest of a Minimalist Approach

A robotic neck has several advantages. First of all, it allows any sensors such as camera, microphone or even artificial nose to scan the environment. Usually, this is made through pan tilt supports (yaw and pitch movements). Secondly, it allows the stabilization of these sensors even when the support is moving — typically on the top of a rolling or walking robot. Thirdly, movement of the head improves human-robot interaction by helping humans to perceive what robots pay attention to. For example, a robot can express facial expressions toward an object to share emotional states [1]. A moving neck gives the robot a lifelike behavior.

Several contributions have been done in this area with high performances. However, they are often complex or fragile [2–5] and some are still in simulation [6–8].

The consequences of this complexity are that researchers and students avoid to working directly on robots. It is not a problem of financial cost but of time, personal resources to maintain the platforms and risks for the platform and the user. In this context, the simulation allows the development of efficient algorithms (optimization) by testing a huge number of times the simulated robot in different environments. Afterward, the optimized algorithm can be successfully applied to a real robot.

However fitting simulations with real robots implies very accurate simulators and very precise realization of the mechanical parts of the robots. Otherwise, even though the simulator is accurate it would be based on a slightly

© Springer International Publishing AG, part of Springer Nature 2018
V. Vouloutsi et al. (Eds.): Living Machines 2018, LNAI 10928, pp. 40–51, 2018.
https://doi.org/10.1007/978-3-319-95972-6_6

different robot than the reality. Moreover, to keep the simulation valid, the environment must be perfectly modeled and therefore it constraints the place where the robot can evolve. An important consequence is that the robots are used as illustrations or proofs of concept but rarely for an everyday tool of research or a final usable industrial product.

In this article, we present a robotic neck which can be used and modified in everyday research work by students and researchers. The robotic platform must be affordable, easy to use and maintain. A minimalist approach is used to provide useful features. The goal is to provide open source hardware and software in order to spread the approach (see also [3,9,10]).

## 1.2   Features for Scanning, Stabilizing and Interacting

In the introduction we claim that a robotic neck has three main advantages:

**Scanning.** The neck must allow moving sensors in order to scan the environment. This is one of the first use of a robotic neck in robotics as it was used to orient a sonar, a laser, a camera, a microphone... This implies that the robot must be able to move fast in yaw and pitch directions it also has to be quiet if we want to use a microphone.

**Stabilizing.** The neck can be used to compensate the movement of the body.

**Interacting.** The neck must improve interaction with humans, the control must be smooth and reproduce a natural dynamic. The way the robot is perceived and its own dynamics should look lifelike [11]. We consider that several degrees of freedom and a structure close to humans can improve the interaction. Moreover, the compliance is an important property allowing to interact physically with the robot.

Moreover if possible (this is a loose constraint as we want to keep a minimalist approach) we would like to approach a model of the real neck. This would allow to improve human likeness and to model bio-mechanic phenomenon.

## 1.3   Bio-inspiration

Even though bio-inspiration is not the main constraint, we study the biomechanics of the neck. We can notice that human neck has complex distributed joints spread over seven vertebrae but that the first two (C1 and C2) are very special. They are the main actors of the head's rotations. C1 implements a ball joint with the skull and C2 implements a pivot joint with C1 [12]. We neglect for now the other vertebrae (see Fig. 1).

There are eighteen groups of muscles in the neck with very complex configurations. However, we do not need to manage the jaw, the esophagus or the trachea. We consider only the $3°$ of freedom of the first two vertebrae in our model. The simplest way (in term of mechanics) to move a device is to use a motor directly with a cable and a pulley. This avoids gears, rods, or other costly material and this is also quiet allowing to place the motors away from the joints.

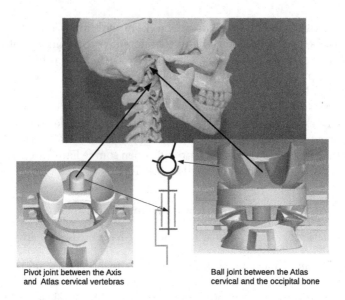

Pivot joint between the Axis
and Atlas cervical vertebras

Ball joint between the Atlas
cervical and the occipital bone

**Fig. 1.** Scheme of the two first vertebrae of the neck. 3D models extracted from the online video [13] with the authorization of the author.

The effect of a motor with a cable and a pulley is quite similar to a muscle and we use it. Some robots mimic biology in a more realistic way [10,14] but they are too complex for this study.

We follow the kinematics of these vertebrae as reviewed in [12].

## 2   Hardware

### 2.1   Mechanics

Important issues for robustness are the quality of the joints. Low quality of joints leads to fast deterioration and mechanical backlash of any robot. We use simple but high-quality gimball and ball bearing. Serial structures are simpler to control but have several flaws such as the accumulation of backslash and the fact that the first joints have to carry all the weight including the motors [6,8].

We propose a 3° of freedom joint pulled by cables with pulleys and motors. In theory we only need 3 motors and a pulling spring because the movement of the cable cannot be reversible (see an example [15]). We do not use a pulling spring but 4 motors which over actuate the system. The redundancy can be used to set the stiffness. Another advantage is that for each motion, two motors are working at the same time which divides the required power. The fact that we do not use servo-motors but simple DC motors improves the reversibility and helps us to get access to low level control which is important for learning algorithms. It also increases power for the same size and cost. Moreover it is more robust as we avoid problems with the reducer. The reduction is done by using small pulleys

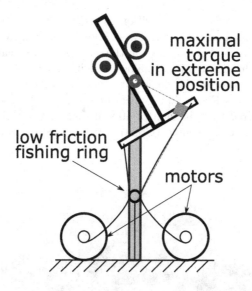

**Fig. 2.** Attachment of the cables

attaching cables far from the center of rotation. We optimize the phenomenon by maximizing the torque when the head reaches extreme positions (see Fig. 2).

## 2.2 Motors' Driver

In order to drive the speed or force of these motors we need an electric chopper. We chose a Grove I2C motor driver which is simple and robust. However the chopping frequency is low (30 Hz) thus we add a 4700μF capacitor on each motor in order to smooth the signal. This value is a compromise between a too low value which does not filter enough and a high one which makes the driver heat. We also add a radiator on the circuit to cool it down. In order to access to the compliance, we need to detect the current passing through the motors. This can be indirectly done by accessing the voltage on the motor — the motor driver as an internal resistance, if the intensity increases, the voltage decreases. We use an analog to digital converter (MCP3800) to access to these values. We use four classical €4 DC motors (6V, 1.34A, 46.2gcm and 6 effective watts). Due to the limits of the driver it is not useful to use bigger motors. We started with smaller motors (€1.5), it was working but we were most of the time working outside the limits of these motors.

## 2.3 Sensors

The minimum requirement to control the head is to know its position all the time. To keep the system simple we avoid to use coder on each motor or joint, therefore we use the values of an accelerometer giving the pitch and roll positions. Trough this sensor we cannot get the yaw position as the gravity does not change when we are turning the head on the vertical axis. Thus we include a potentiometer—implanted inside the wood structure—on the axis of the vertical pivot joint and access the voltage through another analog to digital converter.

You can get a picture of the device at a very prototypical stage Fig. 3, the electric scheme appears Fig. 4. The typical power is 5 v, but the drivers of the motor can be powered by a tension of 10 V if you want to increase force and speed. The design is open source (Creative Commons Attribution-ShareAlike 4.0 International).

**Fig. 3.** Prototype of the neck.

For the software, we use the open source Basic Libraries And Applications for Robotics [16] and we publish the specific code in [17].

The principle is simple: if you need a pitch movement toward the front, turn on the two front motors. For a roll movement on the left, turn on the two motors on the left and for a yaw movement, turn on the two diagonal motors. For each axis, turn on the two opposite motors to get an opposite movement. You can combine any movement by summing the activation on the motors. The result is not linear but we plan anyway to use learning systems to learn the non-linearity.

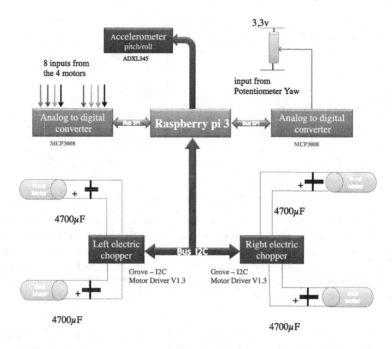

**Fig. 4.** Full electrical scheme of the robot. The input power is typically 5V.

## 3    Results

**Dynamics of the Motors and Drivers.** Now that we have a mechanical neck, we want to analyze its properties. This is fundamental as one of our main target are students and researchers. Even if the mechanics is not optimal we need to know the limits and potentials. First of all, we analyze the driver to check if we are able to have the quality we need (i.e. speed, force control and compliance or reversibility). We send the command to the motors at different force (25%, 50%, 75%, 100%). We check if the voltage varies properly and if we can detect the variation of force on the motor. We run two tests each time one with the motor running freely and one with the motor externally forced to stop. You can see the results Fig. 5.

We can definitely change the force and the speed of the motor. You can notice the defect of the driver chopping at 30 Hz in the right graph.

### 3.1    Compliance

As we mention earlier, it is important for us to make the robot compliant. To do so we avoid gearboxes to prevent any passive frictions. This reduces complexity, cost and size but the main advantage is that an effect on the head induces a direct effect on the motors. We check how sensitive the detection of external forces on the motors can be. To apply a controlled and variant force on a cable,

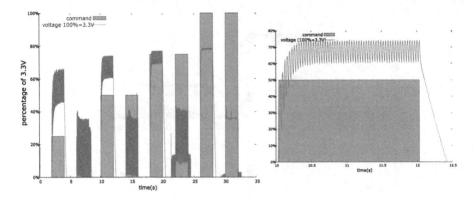

**Fig. 5.** Voltage applied on the motor depending on the command. In the second try of each set of twice the same command, the motor is externally blocked. This demonstrates the effect of the consumption of the motor on the voltage. The right side of the figure shows a zoom presenting the effect of the chopper and the capacitor on the voltage applied to the motor. We can notice that the delay between the command and the effect on the voltage is short (1 ms).

we use a second motor pulling the cable at different voltages with the following protocol. First, we wound the cable on the first motor (the one we want to test). Then a second motor winds the cable at different speeds. We repeat this test

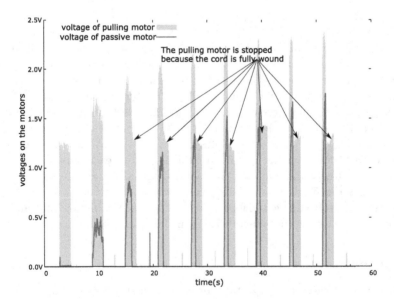

**Fig. 6.** A pulling motor wound the cable from the passive motor at different speeds. We can detect that the passive motor is moved because of the tension that it generates. Note that between each try, the passive motor actively rewinds the cable. It does not appear here because it is a negative voltage.

for 9 different speeds. You can see the results Fig. 6. We observe tensions on
the passive motor due to the fact that the second motor makes it move. We
can check that the speed increases at each try because the time to fully wind
the cord decreases. The acquisition is achieved by the system itself through the
circuit MCP3008.

## 3.2    Actual Movements

We have shown the property of an individual motor, now we validate the overall
behavior of the system. We first test a single axis. The pitch and roll movements
are blocked (we block the gimbals in fact) and we the yaw rotation is activated.
To do so we activate either the front left motor with the back right one or the
front right motor with the back left one for the opposite direction. We present
Fig. 7 the resulting dynamics of a sequence of commands.

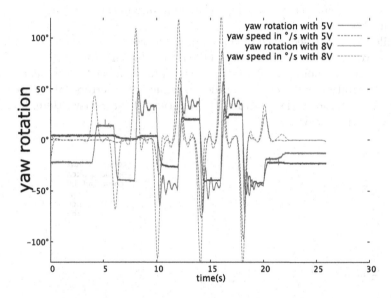

**Fig. 7.** Yaw rotation when the power is 5 or 8 V. We can see that the range of movement
is over ±40° and the maximal speed is over 100°/s. Oscillations are due to the fact we
send a square signal. This reveals the mechanical properties as the controller is only
proportional. The software part will be elaborated in the future.

## 3.3    Controller

This article is mainly focused on the hardware part of the system because we
want to use it as a tool to test and implement control and learning algorithms.
However, in order to show that this neck can be used and controlled, we implement simple movements. We apply a proportional controller on smoothed data
from the normalized sensors. It is especially important to smooth the data from

the accelerometers as they are sensitive to noise and vibrations. A low pass filter
is applied with $\epsilon$ as the parameter of the filtering for each axis. See Eq. 1.

$$\begin{cases} \overline{yaw} = & \overline{yaw} + \epsilon_y.(\overline{yaw} - yaw\_sensor), \epsilon_y = 0.9 \\ \overline{pitch} = & \overline{pitch} + \epsilon_p.(\overline{pitch} - pitch\_accelerometer), \epsilon_p = 0.075 \\ \overline{roll} = & \overline{roll} + \epsilon_r.(\overline{roll} - roll\_accelerometer), \epsilon_r = 0.075 \end{cases} \quad (1)$$

The differences between the commands and the smoothed sensors are amplified and used to activate the corresponding motors. However, as we explained,
for each axis two motors are pulling which may lead to contradictory pulling.
Therefore we subtract the activity of the second weakest motor to the activity
of the others motors. As a result, only the two most activated motors pull the
cables. On our raspberry pi 3, the algorithm was working at a refresh rate of
1 kHz. The gains from yaw, pitch, and roll axes are respectively 10, 8 and 8.

We test this algorithm successfully for different tasks (driving with the key-
board, using a sequence, stabilizing a change in orientation ...). You can see the
videos in [17].

While we send a sequence of commands, we record the result that you can
see Fig. 8 you can download the data (100 Hz resolution) from [17].

The results are not optimal because we need to use a better controller with at
least an integration of the errors in order to reduce static errors. There are many
other ways to improve the control [7,18] or see [8] for a review. Here, however,
we focus on the hardware.

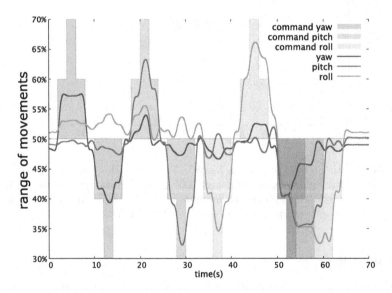

**Fig. 8.** Real normalized movements are compared to the commands. After 50 s, we
combine the commands. For the readability of the graph, the values of the sensors have
been smoothed. The extreme commands are never reached because we need a better
controller to at least integrate the errors.

Another important feature we have tested (see in the videos [17]) is the compliance. Actually, the neck of Pinobo is very compliant and resilient. It does not resist much as the motors are small but it quickly comes back to its desired position after perturbation. It looks like it is on a spring but there is no spring at all and the cable are very stiff. All this compliance comes from the reversibility of the motors.

## 4   Conclusion

We have introduced a prototypical robotic neck with modest properties but strong potential. It is easy to build (few hours), cheap (about €100) and more importantly: it is robust. It is easy to add or try different elements. The motor drivers are not efficient (heating, chopping at only 30 Hz) but simple to use. We were satisfied of their robustness and solidity (we will be still replaced by more efficient systems). The cables as well are reliable and we did not need to change one despite the fact we did some bad and difficult tests.

We have few intermediate elements to maximize the understanding and control of the overall system. No servo means no external controller. No spring and no gearbox, means a full control of the mechanics. The neck also includes many sensors like the voltage of the motors (and indirectly the intensity), accelerometers, gyrometers, and position of the yaw rotation.

This, combined with the fact that we use simple libraries [16] with the same philosophy (direct control, few abstractions), makes Pinobo an ideal platform for testing and prototyping new ideas.

In the future, the first thing we will do is to improve the motor drivers. We will apply learning algorithms to make the robot able to predict its dynamic and improve its control. Then we will add eyes with embedded cameras and ears with microphones. We may develop several versions improving either speed, life-likeness, force, or amplitude of movements depending on the need of each studied task. Knowing the environment and problems encountered in the field of robotics, which often exceed the skills of researchers (especially due to logistics, mechanical problems, constraints of physical or logical interfaces), the results we have obtained, the number of available inputs and, the simplicity of the interfaces (electronic and software), we hope to bring an asset to students and researchers in the field of humanoid robots to focus on their research.

**Acknowledgment.** We would like to thank Alexandre Pitti for useful advises, Artem Melnyk for the pulleys and Patrice Thiriet for useful pointers.

# References

1. Boucenna, S., Gaussier, P., Hafemeister, L.: Development of first social referencing skills: emotional interaction as a way to regulate robot behavior. IEEE Trans. Auton. Ment. Dev. **6**, 42–55 (2014)
2. Alfayad, S., El Asswad, M., Abdellatif, A., Ouezdou, F.B., Blanchard, A., Beaussé, N., Gaussier, P.: Hydroïd humanoid robot head with perception and emotion capabilities: modeling, design, and experimental results. Front. Robot. AI **3**, 15 (2016)
3. Metta, G., Natale, L., Nori, F., Sandini, G., Vernon, D., Fadiga, L., von Hofsten, C., Rosander, K., Lopes, M., Santos-Victor, J., et al.: The iCub humanoid robot: an open-systems platform for research in cognitive development. Neural Netw. **23**(8–9), 1125–1134 (2010)
4. Asfour, T., Regenstein, K., Azad, P., Schroder, J., Bierbaum, A., Vahrenkamp, N., Dillmann, R.: ARMAR-III: an integrated humanoid platform for sensory-motor control. In: 2006 6th IEEE-RAS International Conference on Humanoid Robots, pp. 169–175. IEEE (2006)
5. Zollo, L., Guglielmelli, E., Teti, G., Laschi, C., Eskiizmirliler, S., Carenzi, F., Bendahan, P., Gorce, P., Maier, M.A., Burnod, Y., et al.: A bio-inspired neuro-controller for an anthropomorphic head-arm robotic system. In: Proceedings of the 2005 IEEE International Conference on Robotics and Automation, ICRA 2005, pp. 12–17. IEEE (2005)
6. Hoang, N.P., Pham, H.T.: Design of a compliant bio-inspired camera-positioning mechanism for autonomous mobile robots. In: 2017 International Conference on System Science and Engineering (ICSSE), pp. 325–329, July 2017
7. Gao, B., Zhu, Z., Zhao, J., Jiang, L.: Inverse kinematics and workspace analysis of a 3 DOF flexible parallel humanoid neck robot. J. Intell. Robot. Syst. **87**(2), 211–229 (2017)
8. Lingampally, P.K., Selvakumar, A.A.: A humanoid neck using parallel manipulators. In: 2016 International Conference on Robotics and Automation for Humanitarian Applications (RAHA), December 2016
9. Lapeyre, M.: Poppy: open-source, 3D printed and fully-modular robotic platform for science, art and education. Theses, Université de Bordeaux, November 2014
10. Marques, H.G., Jäntsch, M., Wittmeier, S., Holland, O., Alessandro, C., Diamond, A., Lungarella, M., Knight, R.: ECCE1: the first of a series of anthropomimetic musculoskeletal upper torsos. In: 2010 10th IEEE-RAS International Conference on Humanoid Robots, pp. 391–396, December 2010
11. Złotowski, J., Proudfoot, D., Yogeeswaran, K., Bartneck, C.: Anthropomorphism: opportunities and challenges in human–robot interaction. Int. J. Soc. Robot. **7**(3), 347–360 (2014)
12. Bogduk, N., Mercer, S.: Biomechanics of the cervical spine. I: Normal kinematics. Clin. Biomech. **15**(9), 633–648 (2000)
13. Thiriet, P.: La colonne cervicale haute atlas et axis (2015). https://www.youtube.com/watch?v=OP924h2bc-w
14. Asano, Y., Okada, K., Inaba, M.: Design principles of a human mimetic humanoid: humanoid platform to study human intelligence and internal body system. Sci. Robot. **2**(13), eaaq0899 (2017)
15. Nori, F., Jamone, L., Sandini, G., Metta, G.: Accurate control of a human-like tendon-driven neck. In: 2007 7th IEEE-RAS International Conference on Humanoid Robots, pp. 371–378. IEEE (2007)

16. Blanchard, A.: BLAAR: Basic Libraries And Application for Robotics (2014–2018). http://blaar.org

17. Blanchard, A.: Pinobo: a bio-inspired compliant robot (2018). http://blaar.org/pinobo.html

18. Falotico, E., Cauli, N., Kryczka, P., Hashimoto, K., Berthoz, A., Takanishi, A., Dario, P., Laschi, C.: Head stabilization in a humanoid robot: models and implementations. Auton. Robot. **41**(2), 349–365 (2016)

# Artificial Compound Eye and Synthetic Neural System for Motion Recognition

Drago Bračun[1]([✉]), Nicholas S. Szczecinski[2], Gašper Škulj[1],
Alexander J. Hunt[3], and Roger D. Quinn[2]

[1] Faculty of Mechanical Engineering, University of Ljubljana,
Aškerčeva 6, 1000 Ljubljana, Slovenia
drago.bracun@fs.uni-lj.si
[2] Department of Mechanical and Aerospace Engineering, Case Western Reserve
University, 10900 Euclid Ave., Cleveland, OH 44106, USA
[3] Department of Mechanical and Materials Engineering, Portland State University,
1930 SW 4th Ave., Portland, OR 97201, USA

**Abstract.** This paper presents modelling of a fruit fly's visual neural system for motion recognition employing non-spiking Hodgkin-Huxley neurons. Motion detection operates based on the Hassenstein-Reichardt correlator principle. An array of motion detectors reveals the velocity field pattern, and an additional summation layer allows calculation of the vanishing point. The synthetic nervous system is successfully designed using the functional subnetwork approach. This allows the model to be scaled up to several hundred motion detectors according to the number of ommatidia. The output provides the abstraction of motion on a couple of exit neurons, which can be used in further implementation of control for the mobile robot. The simulation of operation on artificially generated input signals for different types of motion, and a summary of neuronal activities are given.

**Keywords:** Compound eye · Recognition of motion
Hassenstein-Reichardt correlator · Synthetic nervous system
Hodgkin-Huxley neurons

## 1 Introduction

The development of vision systems has always been to some extent biologically inspired, and the resulting solutions were conditioned by the current state of the art and the imagination of the developers. Neuroscience and the development of hardware with exceptional computational capabilities are greatly accelerating biologically inspired visual processing. From the perspective of neuroscience, a common fruit fly or *Drosophila melanogaster* is particularly interesting. It is much used in genetic research and is a common model organism in developmental biology [1]. Neuroscientists are making a great effort to explore internal relationships between neurons in the fly's visual neural structures. The fly's response

© Springer International Publishing AG, part of Springer Nature 2018
V. Vouloutsi et al. (Eds.): Living Machines 2018, LNAI 10928, pp. 52–63, 2018.
https://doi.org/10.1007/978-3-319-95972-6_7

to a moving visual stimulus is particularly well researched. The studies provide evidence on how the change in an observed pattern is detected, which neurons are involved and what their function is (e.g. edge detection, motion direction detection, etc.) [2–4].

A fly has two compound eyes that are the dominant features on its head and cover a wide field of view (approximately 180°). Each contains a few hundred ommatidia with eight photoreceptor cells that form a retina. An ommatidium typically has an acceptance angle of only a few degrees. Spatial resolution of the fly's eyes is therefore low in comparison to the human eye, but the temporal resolution is several times better. The fly's visual neural system consists of lamina, medulla and lobula. The retina connects to the lamina where large monopolar cells produce the effect of a temporal high pass filter. The lamina is connected to the medulla where key processes of motion detection take place. The lobula then uses the signals from the medula in higher level function, such as wide field motion detection.

Motion detection is usually modelled by the Hassenstein-Reichardt correlator [5,6]. The basic Hassenstein-Reichardt correlator has two input channels with fixed angular separation. The signal from each channel is passed through a delay filter. A delayed signal from one channel is then multiplied with a non-delayed signal from the other channel. This interaction between both channels forms an elementary motion detector (EMD). A strong response is provided only if the visual stimulus motion occurs in a preferred direction of EMD. To detect a bidirectional motion, two EMDs in the correlator are oriented in opposite directions. The final output of the correlator is a subtraction of both multiplications. In order to enhance the basic correlator, an additional spatial and temporal pre-filtering can be added before the delay filter. Some motion detectors and an artificial neural networks for collision detection and object tracking are presented in [7–9].

Modelling the EMDs and neural system for motion recognition could lead to a large synthetic nervous systems (SNS) with thousands of neurons when considering a compound eye with several hundred ommatidia. It is not an easy task to design and optimize parameters of a large pool of neurons. However, we know that motion recognition is built from basic, approximate mathematical operations e.g. multiplication, addition, subtraction etc. that are interconnected in some functional objects, e.g. EMDs, and those are replicated many times in dependence on the size of the compound eye. Such repeatable structure works to our advantage and can contribute to an easier design and optimization of the SNS parameters. Design can start with basic math operations to build a single EMD, and complete the eye by duplicating this network as many times as needed. Support for this approach comes from the functional subnetwork approach to designing SNS [10]. Described analytical methods enable direct construction of functional subnetworks that perform arithmetic and dynamical calculations. The designer can test their behavior and assemble them into larger SNS models.

This research builds upon a biological experiment regarding the fruit fly's visual neural system [11] and an idea to develop a visual system whose optics and computation are similar to that of a fly. Our previous work [12] presents possible designs of lensless artificial compound eyes. This paper demonstrates modelling of a fly's neural system for motion recognition employing non-spiking Hodgkin-Huxley neurons. The resulting motion detection SNS should recognize wide field motion in different directions and at the output should provide the abstraction of motion on a couple of exit neurons. A functional subnetwork approach is applied to the design of the SNS for two main reasons, the first being the previously described repeatable structure and underlying math operators, and the second the possibility of arbitrary scaling of the model according to the chosen number of ommatidia. The scaling of the model is important mainly from the aspect of model adaptation to different designs of an artificial compound eye.

## 2    Artificial Compound Eye

Our previous work [12] presents possible designs of the lensless artificial compound eye (ACE). The first approach to create a lensless ACE is to use long tubes or deep holes to limit the acceptance angle or view field of the individual light sensor. The long tube in combination with a light sensor forms an artificial ommatidium. An ACE model for a case of 12 ommatidia in a row is presented in Fig. 1. The long tubes or deep holes that form walls of ommatidium are depicted with red lines and the view field of ommatidia is indicated by black lines.

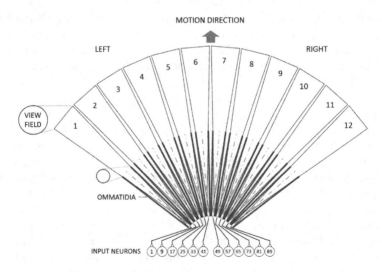

**Fig. 1.** Artificial compound eye (ACE) model for a case of 12 ommatidia in a row (red lines); View field of ommatidia is indicated by black lines. (Color figure online)

The light sensor at the bottom of the tube transforms the incident light into the electric stimulus (current). The model assumes that each ommatidium has one light sensor which is connected to the corresponding neuron, as shown in Fig. 1. When a light-blocking object moves past the ACE, the light pattern activates the ommatidia sequentially. For example, when a bright object moves from left to right, it is first detected by the extreme left ommatidium. Consequently, neuron 1 on the left side is excited. When the light pattern travels forward towards the center of the ACE, further neurons 17, 25, 33, etc. in this sequence are excited. At the same time, neurons 1 and 9 on the extreme left are not excited anymore.

## 3   Motion Detection

The synthetic nervous system detects motion based on the multiplication of the time delayed signals of adjacent ommatidia. Figure 2a shows the minimum combination of neurons for detecting the movement of the light pattern from the left to the right, for example from the first to the second ommatidium. Let us assume that ommatidia 1 and 2 are associated with neurons 1 and 9 (in red color). The first chart (Stimulus) in Fig. 3 helps to understand how ommatidia detect the movement of the bright object and what the time course of the external stimuli for the neurons 1 and 9 looks like. At time $t_1$ (20 ms) ommatidium 1 detects a bright object and light sensor with external stimulus $ES_{t1}$ excites neuron 1. At time $t_2 = t_1 + dt$ (30 ms), the bright object moves within the view field of ommatidium 2, and excites neuron 9. At time (35 ms) the first ommatidium does not see the bright object any more and ES to neuron 1 disappears.

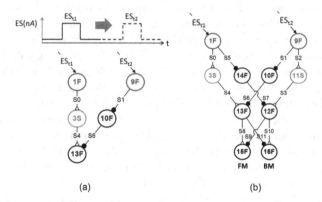

(a)                                   (b)

**Fig. 2.** (a) Minimum combination of neurons for detecting movement from the left to right. (b) Bidirectional motion detector. (Color figure online)

If the signals from neurons 1 and 9 are multiplied, their product will be almost zero, as they are time delayed. To detect movement from the left to the right, the output from neuron 1 must be delayed in time, so that at the moment of multiplication, at $t_2$, it will occur simultaneously with the output of the neuron 2. Their product will be larger than zero, depending on the speed of movement and amplitude of the ES. The time delay is achieved through neuron

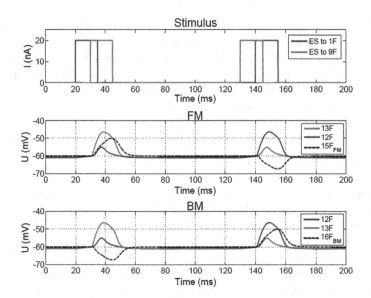

**Fig. 3.** Sample signals from motion detector on the Fig. 2b for forward and back motion. (Color figure online)

3 (in green color) with a capacitance substantially larger (slow response neuron - S) than the capacitance of the neurons 1 and 9 (fast response neurons - F). The outputs from the neurons 3 and 9 are multiplied by additional neurons 10 and 13 (in blue color). The second chart for forward motion (FM) in Fig. 3 shows with red line (at time 30 ms) the resulting product on neuron 13. When the light pattern moves in the opposite direction (see Stimulus chart at 130 ms), neuron 9 is initially excited, followed by neuron 1, with their product close to 0 (see red line in FM chart at 130 ms). Therefore, motion to the left is barely noticed.

Motion detection from right to left is performed with a similar arrangement of neurons in the opposite direction. The output from neuron 9 is delayed with a slow response from neuron 11 and multiplied by output from neuron 1. There are two additional neurons 15 and 16 that calculate the difference of products on neurons 12 and 13. Neuron 15 is excited when moving forward (FM), and 16 when moving backwards (BM). Their signals are displayed with a black line on the charts for FM and BM in Fig. 3. They represent the actual outputs from the motion detector to the rest of the brain.

All neurons in our network are modelled as non-spiking Hodgkin-Huxley compartments [13]. Each neuron's voltage, V, changes with the following dynamics:

$$C_m \cdot \frac{dV}{dt} = G_m \cdot (E_{rest} - V) + \sum_{i=1}^{n} G_{syn,i} \cdot (E_{syn,i} - V),$$

where $C_m$ is the neuron's membrane capacitance, $G_m$ is the neuron's membrane conductance, and $E_{rest}$ is the neuron's resting potential. Each $i^{th}$ synapse has a conductance $G_{syn}$, which is a function of the presynaptic (i.e. sending) neuron's voltage. Each $i^{th}$ synapse also has a potential $E_{syn}$. Therefore, the neuron's steady-state voltage is the sum of potentials $E$, weighted by the conductances $G$. The function of the network was designed directly using our functional subnetwork approach to network design [10]. By exploiting neural and synaptic dynamics, we can directly assemble networks that perform specific computations. For example, the membrane voltage of neuron 13 is proportional to the product of neurons 1 and 9 voltages, because the pathway from neuron 9 to neuron 13 increases the sensitivity of neuron 13 to inputs as the voltage of neuron 9 increases.

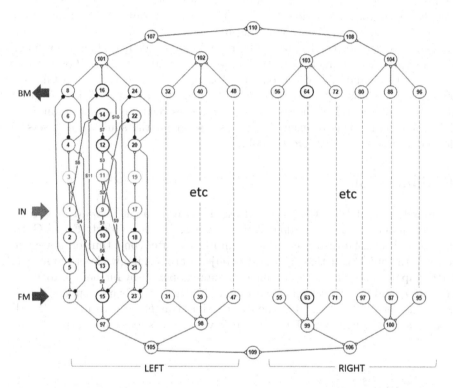

**Fig. 4.** Stack of motion detectors including summation neurons. External stimulus from the light sensors is applied in red colored neurons 1, 9, 17, etc. Forward motion is signalled on bottom neurons 7, 15, 13, etc. and backward motion is signalled on top neurons 8, 16, 14 etc. (Color figure online)

The synthetic nervous system model in Fig. 4 shows 12 motion detectors. Only the first three are drawn in detail, because all columns are identical, and the numbering of neurons in a column increases by 8. Motion detectors are interconnected with synapses $S_m$ and $S_n$, where $m = 4+i\cdot8$ and $n = 5+i\cdot8$ and $i = 0$ to 11 (number of motion detectors - 1). The light sensors in ommatidia are connected with the input neurons (1, 9, ... 89). Forward motion (FM) is signaled on the bottom neurons (7, 15, 23, ... 95) and backward motion (BM) on the top neurons (8, 16, 24, ... 96). This layout is for visual representation only; in the insect brain, the top and bottom neurons would run in parallel from the eyes to the central brain.

Each motion detector shows the direction of motion with output on FM or BM side and the speed of motion with signal amplitude. Consequently, a stack of motion detectors reveals the velocity field pattern known as optical flow. The type of motion (forward, backward or turning) can be identified from the properties of this velocity field. To find the vanishing point, the outputs from the detectors are firstly added together locally. In the model shown, the outputs from the three neighbouring motion detectors are added together. This way the complete stack of motion detectors is subdivided into quarters. Motion on the left or right half is obtained by adding up the quarters on the side of interest. Global movement to the left or to the right is obtained by adding all outputs. For example, any FM motion on the left side ommatidia is signalled on neurons 97, 98, and 105, and BM on neurons 101, 102 and 107. Similarly, any FM motion on the right side is signaled on neurons 99, 100 and 106, and BM on neurons 103, 104 and 108. When the compound eye moves relative to its surroundings, different combinations of excited neurons appear on the summation layers in dependence of the velocity vector field.

## 4    Simulation

If we assume that the ACE shown in Fig. 1 moves straight forward relative to its surroundings and also assume that at the time $t_1$, two objects E and G are in front of it at a far distance, as shown in Fig. 5a, after some time of movement towards the objects, at time $t_2 > t_1$, the objects are seemingly closer, larger and farther apart. This effect is becoming even more apparent by further approaching at times $t_3$ and $t_4$. The velocity vector field that theoretically corresponds to this motion is depicted in Fig. 5b in the top row for straight forward motion (SFM) case. When the objects are far away, their velocity is small (short arrows), and

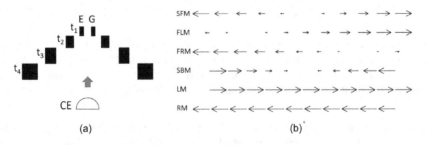

**Fig. 5.** (a) Simulated scene: an ACE is moving toward the two objects E and G. (b) Theoretical velocity vector field for different motion directions. (SFM - straight forward motion, FLM - forward left motion, FRM - forward right motion, SBM - straight back motion, LM - left motion, RM - right motion)

when they are close, they move fast (long arrows). In case of turning, the vanishing point of this pattern moves out of center as is depicted in the second row for forward left motion (FLM) and third row for forward right motion (FRM). If the motion is straight back (SBM), the pattern is opposite to SFM, and if the motion is lateral to the left or right, all velocities have the same direction as is demonstrated in the fifth and sixth rows for left (LM) and right motion (RM).

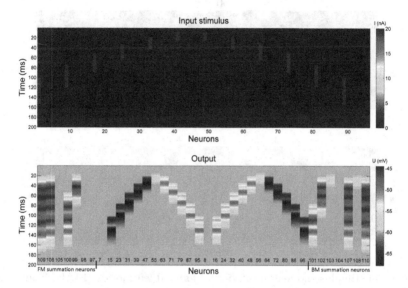

**Fig. 6.** Input stimulus and neural activity for straight forward motion (FM). Neurons 99, 100, 106 and 101, 102, 107 are excited.

The simulation of the previously described movement is shown in Figs. 6, 7 and 8. The top chart in each figure shows the input stimulus, and the lower chart shows neuron output versus time. For the first case of SFM motion, the input to the network is shown in the top chart of Fig. 6. Objects E and G are initially visible by ommatidia 6 and 7. Consequently, input neurons 41 and 49 receive the input stimulus (20 nA, rectangular function from time $t_1 = 10$ ms to 30 ms). By approaching the objects, their visibility moves from the middle ommatidia 6 and 7 towards the extreme left ommatidia 1 and right 12 and the input stimulus also moves from input neuron 41 to neuron 1 and from input neuron 49 to 89.

The lower chart shows neuron activity. First the summation layer for forward motion (109, 106, 105, 100-97), then FM outputs from motion detectors (7–95), BM outputs from motion detectors (8–96) and BM summation layer (101–104, 107, 108, 110). In case of straight forward motion (SFM), the neurons 99, 100, 101, 102 on the first summation layer and 106 and 107 on the second summation layer are excited (see Fig. 6 Output). These neurons are in a diagonally symmetric pattern. If the motion is straight backward (SBM), the pattern is symmetrically switched to neurons 97, 98, 103, 104, 105 and 108 (see Fig. 8). For identifying only SFM and SBM motion, the first layer neurons 99, 100, 101, 102 and 97, 98, 103, 104 can be omitted and FM and BM output neurons from motion detectors connected directly to the second layer; for example 7, 15, 23, 31, 39, 47 can be connected directly to the 105.

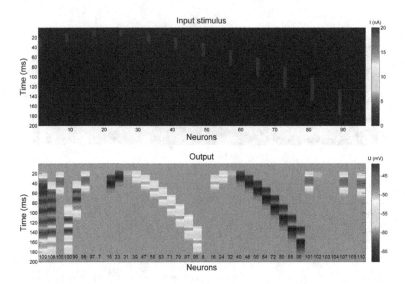

**Fig. 7.** Input stimulus and neural activity for forward left motion (FLM). Neurons 98, 99, 100 and 101 are excited on the first summation layer. Between neurons 98 and 101 the motion direction is changed indicating the vanishing point between the first and second quarter of the motion detector stack.

In case of turning to the left or to the right, the vanishing point is not in the middle of the eye (see Fig. 7). To estimate the vanishing point and direction of motion, the neurons on the first summation layer 97–104 are required. In case of forward left motion (FLM) in Fig. 7, neurons 98, 99 and 100 are excited on the FM side and neuron 101 on the BM side. Between summation neurons 98 and 101 the motion direction is changed indicating the vanishing point between the first and second quarter of the motion detector stack.

With the four neurons on the first summation layer the motion detector stack is split into quarters. Consequently, the vanishing point is predicted only between quarters 1/4, 1/2, 3/4 of the motion detector stack. By introducing more summation neurons to the first layer, the vanishing point can be predicted more accurately. On the other hand, the larger the output of summation neurons, the more complex the realization of further motion control would be.

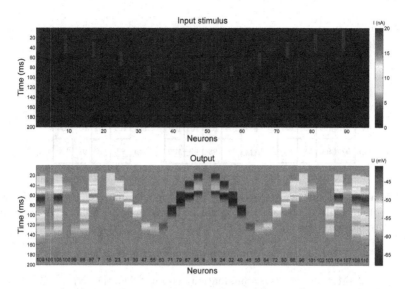

**Fig. 8.** Input stimulus and neural activity for straight back motion (SBM). Neurons 97, 98, 103 and 104 are excited on the first summation layer.

# 5    Discussion

Figure 9 shows a summary of the neuron activities at the first summation layer for different types of motion. When moving forward or backward, the activity patterns are symmetrical in relation to the FM and BM outputs. With the four summation neurons on the first layer, the vanishing point (VP) is identified only at the boundaries between the quarters, where activity is switched from the FM to BM outputs. These combinations of activities can be used in further implementation of control for the mobile robot. The second and third summation layers are in principle not needed to carry out the control. The vanishing point could be determined more precisely by adding more summation neurons in the first layer. However, the implementation of the robot control would become more demanding due to several inputs.

For this model with 12 ommatidia in one row, 110 neurons are required to identify the type of motion. The estimate of the number of neurons N is given by the equation $N = i \cdot 8 + n_{sum}$, where $i$ equals the number of motion detectors, for each motion detector 8 neurons are required, and $n_{sum}$ is the number of summation neurons in the first layer. For example, the compound eye with 120 ommatidia in a row and 12 summation neurons on each side has $N = 120 \cdot 8 + 2 \cdot 12 = 984$ neurons (see Table 1). For a two dimensional compound eye with an array of $12 \times 12$ ommatidia this leads to 1168 neurons. Table 1 reveals how the number of neurons exponentially increases in case of larger composite eyes. With the experiments that will follow this simulation, we will try to find what is the sufficient number of ommatidia for reliable detection of the direction of movement in practice, while the network is computable in real time.

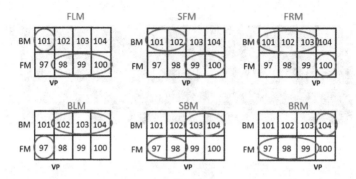

**Fig. 9.** Summary of the neuron activities on the first summation layer for different types of motion. Output neurons that would be active in each case are circled in red. (Color figure online)

**Table 1.** The estimate of the number of neurons.

| Motion detectors | Summation neurons | Neurons (N) |
| --- | --- | --- |
| 12 | $2 \times 4$ | 104 |
| 120 | $2 \times 12$ | 984 |
| $12 \times 12$ (2D) | $4 \times 4$ | 1168 |
| $120 \times 120$ (2D) | $12 \times 12$ | 115344 |

## 6   Conclusions

The synthetic nervous system for visual motion recognition is successfully designed using the functional subnetwork approach. The basic subnetwork is an elementary motion detector that is replicated many times depending on the number of ommatidia. The motion detector employs basic mathematical operations with non-spiking Hodgkin-Huxley neurons. It works on the principle of multiplication of the time-delayed signals from the adjacent ommatidia. The direction of motion is shown with the output on the forward or backward motion side and the speed of motion with the signal amplitude.

An array of motion detectors reveals the velocity field pattern. The outputs from the motion detectors are added together with additional neurons on summation layers. With the four neurons on the first summation layer the row of motion detectors is subdivided into quarters. This is already sufficient to identify the direction of motion e.g. forward, backward and rotation to the left or right by observing the location of the vanishing point.

As a simplified demonstration, a model with only 12 motion detectors in a row is shown. The simulation of operation on artificially generated input signals for different types of motion, and a summary of neuronal activities are given. In the case of 12 motion detectors, 110 neurons are required. However, the model can be simply scaled to several hundred motion detectors. In that case, the number of neurons exponentially increases and requires high performance hardware for real-time calculations of the network dynamics. The output from the network provides the abstraction of motion on a couple of exit neurons, which can be used in further implementation of control for the mobile robot.

# References

1. Guo, A., Gong, Z., Li, H., Li, Y., Liu, L., Liu, Q., Lu, H., Pan, Y., Ren, Q., Wu, Z., Zhang, K., Zhu, Y.: Vision, memory, and cognition in drosophila. In: Learning and Memory: A Comprehensive Reference, 2nd edn., pp. 483–503 (2017)
2. Serbe, E., Meier, M., Leonhardt, A., Borst, A.: Comprehensive characterization of the major presynaptic elements to the Drosophila OFF motion detector. Neuron 89(4), 829–841 (2016)
3. Ammer, G., Leonhardt, A., Bahl, A., Dickson, B.J., Borst, A.: Functional specialization of neural input elements to the Drosophila ON motion detector. Curr. Biol. 25(17), 2247–2253 (2015)
4. Ngo, K.T., Andrade, I., Hartenstein, V.: Spatio-temporal pattern of neuronal differentiation in the Drosophila visual system: a user's guide to the dynamic morphology of the developing optic lobe. Dev. Biol. 428(1), 1–24 (2017)
5. Hassenstein, B., Reichardt, W.: Structure of a mechanism of perception of optical movement. In: Proceedings of the 1st International Conference on Cybernetics, pp. 797–801 (1956)
6. Rajesh, S., O'Carroll, D.C., Abbott, D.: Elaborated reichardt correlators for velocity estimation tasks. Biomedical Applications of Micro-and Nanoengineering, International Society for Optics and Photonics 4937, 241–254 (2002)
7. Zhang, Z., Yue, S., Zhang, G.: Fly visual system inspired artificial neural network for collision detection. Neurocomputing 153, 221–234 (2015)
8. Stafford, R., Santer, R.D., Rind, F.C.: A bio-inspired visual collision detection mechanism for cars: combining insect inspired neurons to create a robust system. BioSystems 87(2–3), 164–171 (2007)
9. Missler, J.M., Kamangar, F.A.: A neural network for pursuit tracking inspired by the fly visual system. Neural Networks 8(3), 463–480 (1995)
10. Szczecinski, N.S., Hunt, A.J., Quinn, R.D.: A functional subnetwork approach to designing synthetic nervous systems that control legged robot locomotion. Front. Neurorobotics 11(37), 1–19 (2017)
11. Borst, A.: Fly visual course control: behaviour, algorithms and circuits. Nat. Rev. Neurosci. 15(9), 590–599 (2014)
12. Škulj, G., Bračun, D.: Research of a lensless artificial compound eye. In: Mangan, M., Cutkosky, M., Mura, A., Verschure, P., Prescott, T., Lepora, N. (eds.) Living Machines 2017, vol. 10384, pp. 406–417. Springer, Cham (2017). https://doi.org/10.1007/978-3-319-63537-8_34
13. Cofer, D., Cymbalyuk, G., Reid, J., Zhu, Y., Heitler, W.J., Edwards, D.H.: AnimatLab: a 3D graphics environment for neuromechanical simulations. J. Neurosci. Methods 187(2), 280–288 (2010)

# Living in a Machine: Experiencing the World Through a Robotic Avatar

Daniel Camilleri$^{(\boxtimes)}$ and Tony Prescott

Computer Science Department, University of Sheffield,
Western Bank, Sheffield, UK
d.camilleri@sheffield.ac.uk
http://www.sheffield.ac.uk

**Abstract.** Telepresence has become a main focus of research fuelled by the technological advancements in virtual reality hardware. In this paper we approach telepresence as a collection of sensory modalities and identify what the current state of the art allows with respect to user devices, robotic hardware and the mapping from one to the other.

**Keywords:** Telepresence · Teleoperation · Virtual Reality

## 1 Introduction

The idea of one day being able to control a physical body over long distances with the possibility of simultaneously enhancing the capabilities of our body, has captured the imagination of researchers since as early as 1980 [1,2] and even that of the public with films like Surrogates [3]. In essence, telepresence is the teleportation of your sense of presence [4] to a different location than your physical body; with your presence being contained within either an inanimate or an animate body. Moreover, recent advances in commercially available Virtual Reality (VR) hardware provide an ideal technological platform for the development of such a telepresence system.

This paper deals with the design of such a system. We are developing a telepresence application that is adaptable to the functionality of multiple VR hardware setups on the user side, as well as being able to control a wide variety of robots. Figure 1 shows the system diagram of the telepresence application with two principal components: the Client Application and the Robot Server.

Our aim for the telepresence system is not only to achieve a high level of immersion by combining multiple sensory input modalities and output modalities but also provide this experience with minimum lag and with a minimum training requirement for the user. In our paper we take a human-centric view of telepresence and for each sensory and output modality present in the human body we ask the following:

1. Which methods are technologically available to record or apply the modality to the human body

© Springer International Publishing AG, part of Springer Nature 2018
V. Vouloutsi et al. (Eds.): Living Machines 2018, LNAI 10928, pp. 64–72, 2018.
https://doi.org/10.1007/978-3-319-95972-6_8

2. Which analogues exist within robotic hardware, if any
3. What sensory mapping is required from robot to client and vice versa to retain the experience of being a robot whilst allowing for natural user interaction and control

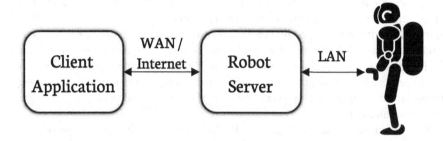

**Fig. 1.** System diagram of a telepresence system

Following the practical considerations outlined for each modality in the following section, we describe the current state of our system followed by our vision for its future development.

## 2 Components of a Telepresence System

### 2.1 Vision

Vision is one of the most important sensory input modalities in the human body and thus places stringent requirements on the quality of the visual apparatus used in VR applications. The main consideration for comfortable use is the frame rate. Low frame rates in VR result in discomfort and motion sickness as vision and head motion become decoupled at frame rates below at minimum 40 frames per second (FPS) with the recommended frame rate being 90 fps [5]. Furthermore the field of view (FOV) of vision is also an important component that significantly impacts user immersion [6]. Peak stereo immersion for the human eyes is at around 120° horizontal FOV and 135° vertical FOV.

The analogue to vision in robots is cameras. However different robot systems have different camera arrangements, camera types (RGB/Depth/RGBD), framerates and often times multiple cameras per robot. Therefore in mapping the visual input of the robot to that of a human, the primary consideration, as with the user application, is that the frame rate must not fall below the 25 fps threshold. The second consideration is that of camera arrangement.

In the case of stereo cameras with an adjustable vergence such as those in the iCub robot [7], one can map these cameras directly to the left and right eye as long as the vergence of the cameras is soft controlled to keep the object in the middle of the camera FOV, in focus, independent of distance.

Conversely if vergence control for stereo cameras is not possible or in the case of arbitrary RGB camera arrangements, the best immersion is achieved via stitching all the cameras together and providing this image to both eyes simultaneously. In this case it is important to equalise the colour responses of the cameras to provide a unified experience of all the camera inputs. This approach however removes any depth perception but provides better immersion when stereo cameras with vergence control are not available. Furthermore, by taking into consideration the respective translation, orientation and scaling of all cameras with respect to the head joint of the robot, one can present a scaled, stitched image to the user that is at the correct scale. Applying the correct scaling in turn provides a substitute mode of depth perception through previous experiences. The disadvantage of scaling images to correspond with user experience however, is that the user's field of view could be sparsely filled which reduces immersion.

Finally in the case of Depth or RGBD cameras, the best approach is to visualise the point cloud to scale within the user application providing the best possible perception of depth. This can however be computationally expensive so care must be taken not to drastically affect the frame rate.

## 2.2  Audition

Audition is another one of the primary senses. This can be stimulated by stereo headphones and the design of its experience has 2 factors: continuity and lag. Intermittent audio results in a loss of immersion but even worse is the presence of lag with respect to the visual input. The human brain allows up to 150 mms of lag for audio with respect to vision but can only tolerate a lag of 30 ms for vision with respect to audio [8,9]. Thus care must be taken in designing the throughput lag of the two systems.

On the robot side, similar to vision, a robot can also have multiple microphone inputs rather than a more simple binaural input. Thus in order to provide the complete range of auditory inputs to the user, one needs to also get the translation and orientation of the microphones with respect to the head and then compute the binaural equivalent of the spatialised auditory input.

## 2.3  Gustation and Olfaction

In the user space there is research being undertaken for the emulation of olfaction and gustation however with the exception of a single consumer device for a limited olfactory sense [10] the availability and usability of these devices is still poor. This turns out not to be an issue because the state of the technology for robots is also very far off and while specialised devices exist for olfaction [11,12] and gustation [13,14], their adoption in humanoid robots is virtually non-existent. Furthermore the impact of these senses on telepresence immersion is of yet unknown.

## 2.4    Somatosensation

Somatosensation is the last of the primary senses and just like gustation and olfaction, the artificial stimulation of touch is still an emerging technology with available commercial products using vibrating motors [15–17] to replicate the sensation of touch. These products are however limited in their resolution and coverage, thus the second generation tactile simulation products [18, 19] are using micro-fluidics to overcome this limitation and provide a much higher tactile resolution, possibly allowing for the sensation of texture, as well as higher body coverage.

The importance of somatosensation as an input modality cannot be overstated in the pursuit of high levels of immersion and minimal user training. This is because together with vision, studies regarding the rubber hand illusion [20, 21] and the Pinocchio illusion [22] have shown that vision and touch combined, significantly accelerate the construction of and adaptation to different body schemas [23, 24]. We hypothesize that this accelerated learning means that users can more naturally control their synthetic body.

On the robot side, somatosensation is oftenly overlooked with very few commercial systems providing a significant level of coverage with the exception of iCub and ... There is however a shift towards providing increased somatosensory coverage in robots such as Pepper [25] and Nao [26].

## 2.5    Thermoception

Keeping on the subject of the skin, thermoception is an essential sense for human survival because the operation of our bodies is only viable within a restricted range of temperatures. This is however different in the case of robots which can withstand a larger temperature range and is thus an example of surpassing our physical limitations with the use of synthetic avatars. Its importance for telepresence has not yet been demonstrated and thus is possibly low. That being said, most of the companies investigating the use of micro-fluidics for second generation somatosensation are also investigating its use for thermoception with individual micro-fluidic circuits being able to heat up or cool down [18, 19].

## 2.6    Proprioception

Compared with most other sensory modalities, proprioception is an interoceptive rather than an exteroceptive sense. This means that the feeling is contained within the body and cannot therefore be externally emulated. Thus in the user space this sense can only be replicated through technologies such as hand tracking in order to preserve the mapping learnt for hand-eye coordination. This is another crucial piece of the immersion puzzle, as without the preservation of hand-eye coordination, the experience feels unnatural and quickly discourages the user. This is evident from the incredible jump in immersion available with the latest generation VR devices that allow for hand control which preserves the visual-proprioceptive loop.

Conservation of this sense between the user and the robot space is however complex because of three principal factors. These are: different body scales, different joint configurations and improper visual scaling between the robot and the user.

## 2.7  Force Perception

Complementary to proprioception, the perception of force or force feedback is another aspect that ties in with proprioception and somatosensation. Consider a user that only has somatosensory feedback from the robot. In the presence of an obstacle, the robot's hand stops however that of the user is still free thus breaking the visual-proprioceptive loop. Thus the perception of force is also very important for a highly immersive telepresence application. Solutions for applying force-feedback in the user space resort to the use of actuated exoskeletons [27] with varying degrees of complexity.

On the other hand, force perception within the robot space can be acquired via the motor torque readings at the various joints after multiplying with the respective robot link lengths.

## 2.8  Equilibrioception

This sense, much like proprioception, is also interoceptive and thus difficult to trick without moving the whole body. Different solutions for the user space exist [28–30] but none of which allow for a standing experience except for the one being currently developed by HaptX [19] which is akin to a hoisted exoskeleton.

Equilibrioception in the robot space is provided via a gyroscope and accelerometer which indicate the current orientation of the robot with respect to gravity. This sense is present in all robots however its usefulness for telepresence is low except in the case of the teleoperation of bipedal robots.

## 2.9  Nociception

Starting from the robot space, the sensation of pain can be engineered by assigning different failure modes of the robot to localised sensations of pain. In the user space, pain cannot be simulated because it is another interoceptive sense and furthermore some may argue that the simulation of pain is unethical. However, setting aside the ethical implications, low levels of nociception would provide the user with a means of adapting behaviour to limitations arising due to malfunctions within the robot's body.

This could be especially crucial in the case of sensitive telepresence scenarios where a malfunctioning robot is inaccessible and thus a replacement is either impossible such as the case of a robot within a hazardous environment or outside of the time frame of a time sensitive operation such as search and rescue.

## 2.10   Motor Control

Motor control in the case of telepresence looks at maintaining the visual-proprioceptive loop between the robot and the user and thus is concerned with the same hardware as proprioception in both the user and robot space. The key consideration here is the lag between user movement and the visual feedback of that movement, which can break immersion, if above as little as 30 ms [31].

## 2.11   Speech

Speech is easy to replicate by streaming microphone input in the user space to a speaker in the robot space. The main consideration here, much like auditory input, is continuity and lag. Furthermore it has been shown that listening to an echo of yourself talking results in an unnatural feeling [32] and thus speech needs to be cancelled out from auditory input [33] in the robot space as is the case with most video conferencing applications.

## 2.12   Emotions

Emotions are something we can also replicate within the robot space by using colours, sounds or affective faces that allow for the expression of emotion. In the user space, one could either follow the route of Facebook Spaces [34] which assigns combinations of buttons on VR controllers to different emotions or something more involved like reading emotive states from EEG signals [35]. The latter would allow for a more natural expression of emotion by the user as the button combination route is more difficult to learn. However, much like gustation and olfaction the impact of this modality on immersion is yet unclear.

## 2.13   Approach

In the previous section we have laid out most of the theoretical framework required to build a wholly immersive telepresence application and in this section we will describe our approach and the results we have achieved so far in developing this application.

**Client Application.** Starting with the Client Application, in our approach we make use of the Unity 3D game engine [36] around which we design our user experience. This game engine was chosen because of its versatility in being cross compiled to multiple operating system platforms. As well as for the presence of the Virtual Reality ToolKit (VRTK) [37] addon which allows the client VR application to be run with multiple hardware setups like Oculus Rift, HTC Vive as well as Android Daydream (formerly Cardboard). This allows us to cater the available sensory modalities based on the type of hardware being used. We've also created a C# Yarp [38] plugin for Unity 3D which is used as the communication layer.

**Robot Server.** On the server side we are developing a universal driver in Python that is capable of interfacing with a variety of robots through the same set of functions allowing for research into the effect of robot morphology on the immersion of the user. Furthermore due to Yarp being an open protocol we employ the use of a VPN to protect sensory transmissions over the internet.

### 2.14  Results

So far of the 10 sensory modalities and 3 output modalities mentioned in Sect. 2 we have implemented vision, audition, proprioception + motor control, speech and emotion for the Pepper robot and soon for the iCub robot as well.

While we do not have a setup to measure and validate the lag in the different modalities of our application, we do have some preliminary user feedback for the current state of the system. The lag of audition with respect to vision is such that it is comfortable to watch a video via the telepresence application. As such it must be between the $-30$ and $+150$ ms range. Furthermore the lag between head movement and its visual feedback has been shown to be very responsive. This responsiveness however starts to decrease as locomotion and arm control are added to the mix requiring better implementation and tuning of our motor control system. In the case of speech, the lag in transmission is currently small but has a noticeable echo.

## 3  Unresolved Questions and Future Work

The implementation in its current state makes use of a mainstream VR setup based on the Oculus Rift Consumer Edition with Touch Controllers [39]. This will be the topic of future work on the client side as we expand our VR hardware setup to include further sensory modalities. Some of the most important items requiring future work are:

1. Developing methods for conserving user hand-eye coordination in the robot
2. Augmenting the current user VR setup with somatosensation and force-feedback
3. Exploring the mapping of robot somatosensation to that of the user and how this affects immersion
4. Assessing the importance of emotion for telepresence
5. Investigating the difference robot morphology has on the user experience
6. Conducting user studies to analyse the immersion of the full telepresence system and how different sensory modality sets affect the overall experience.

## 4  Conclusion

In summary, this paper has reviewed the current state of the art in virtual reality devices for the user space, the analogous devices that currently exist in the robot space and has also explored the mapping of one to the other with the aim of high levels of immersion and natural use. Furthermore we have outlined our initial approach and results in the pursuit of putting the theory into action and identified areas which require further theoretical and practical research.

# References

1. Minsky, M.: Telepresence (1980)
2. Slater, M., Sanchez-Vives, M.V.: Enhancing our lives with immersive virtual reality. Front. Robot. AI **3**, 74 (2016)
3. Mostow, J.: Surrogates - movie starring bruce willis. Movie (2009)
4. Steuer, J.: Defining virtual reality: dimensions determining telepresence. J. Commun. **42**(4), 73–93 (1992)
5. Murray, J.W.: Building Virtual Reality with Unity and Steam Vr. CRC Press, Boca Raton (2017)
6. Abrash, M.: What vr could, should, and almost certainly will be within two years. Steam Dev Days, Seattle, p. 4 (2014)
7. Metta, G., Sandini, G., Vernon, D., Natale, L., Nori, F.: The iCub humanoid robot: an open platform for research in embodied cognition. In: Proceedings of the 8th Workshop on Performance Metrics for Intelligent Systems, pp. 50–56. ACM (2008)
8. Van Wassenhove, V., Grant, K.W., Poeppel, D.: Temporal window of integration in auditory-visual speech perception. Neuropsychologia **45**(3), 598–607 (2007)
9. Conrey, B., Pisoni, D.B.: Auditory-visual speech perception and synchrony detection for speech and nonspeech signals. J. Acoust. Soc. Am. **119**(6), 4065–4073 (2006)
10. Feelreal, I.: Feel Real (2014). https://feelreal.com/. Accessed 30 Mar 2018
11. Trivino, R., Gaibor, D., Mediavilla, J., Guarnan, A.V.: Challenges to embed an electronic nose on a mobile robot. In: 2016 IEEE ANDESCON, pp. 1–4. IEEE (2016)
12. Zhang, X., Zhang, M., Sun, J., He, C.: Design of a bionic electronic nose for robot. In: ISECS International Colloquium on Computing, Communication, Control, and Management, CCCM 2008, vol. 2, pp. 18–23. IEEE (2008)
13. Latha, R.S., Lakshmi, P.: Electronic tongue: an analytical gustatory tool. J. Adv. Pharm. Technol. Res. **3**(1), 3 (2012)
14. Ha, D., Sun, Q., Su, K., Wan, H., Li, H., Xu, N., Sun, F., Zhuang, L., Hu, N., Wang, P.: Recent achievements in electronic tongue and bioelectronic tongue as taste sensors. Sens. Actuators B Chem. **207**, 1136–1146 (2015)
15. bHaptics: bHaptics - Tactsuit. https://www.bhaptics.com/. Accessed 30 Mar 2018
16. Hardlight VR (2017). http://www.hardlightvr.com/. Accessed 30 Mar 2018
17. Immerz, I.: KOR-FX (2014). http://www.korfx.com/. Accessed 30 Mar 2018
18. Teslasuit: Teslasuit. https://teslasuit.io/. Accessed 30 Mar 2018
19. HaptX Gloves. https://haptx.com/. Accessed 30 Mar 2018
20. Tsakiris, M., Haggard, P.: The rubber hand illusion revisited: visuotactile integration and self-attribution. J. Exp. Psychol. Hum. Percept. Perform. **31**(1), 80 (2005)
21. Costantini, M., Haggard, P.: The rubber hand illusion: sensitivity and reference frame for body ownership. Conscious. Cogn. **16**(2), 229–240 (2007)
22. Conson, M., Mazzarella, E., Trojano, L.: Self-touch affects motor imagery: a study on posture interference effect. Exp. Brain Res. **215**(2), 115 (2011)
23. Liu, Y., Medina, J.: Influence of the body schema on multisensory integration: evidence from the mirror box illusion. Sci. Rep. **7**(1), 5060 (2017)
24. Medina, J., Coslett, H.B.: From maps to form to space: touch and the body schema. Neuropsychologia **48**(3), 645–654 (2010)
25. Pepper. Softbank Robotics (2016)
26. Nao. Last accessed 20 (2017)

27. Frisoli, A., Rocchi, F., Marcheschi, S., Dettori, A., Salsedo, F., Bergamasco, M.: A new force-feedback arm exoskeleton for haptic interaction in virtual environments. In: Eurohaptics Conference, 2005 and Symposium on Haptic Interfaces for Virtual Environment and Teleoperator Systems, 2005. World Haptics 2005. First Joint, IEEE, pp. 195–201 (2005)
28. MMOne Project. http://mm-company.com/. Accessed 30 Mar 2018
29. Roto. http://www.rotovr.com/. Accessed 30 Mar 2018
30. Intelligent Counting Ltd. YawVR. https://www.yawvr.com/. Accessed 30 Mar 2018
31. Allison, R.S., Harris, L.R., Jenkin, M., Jasiobedzka, U., Zacher, J.E.: Tolerance of temporal delay in virtual environments. In: Proceedings of the IEEE Virtual Reality, pp. 247–254. IEEE (2001)
32. Kurihara, K., Tsukada, K.: Speechjammer: A system utilizing artificial speech disturbance with delayed auditory feedback. arXiv preprint arXiv:1202.6106 (2012)
33. Stenger, A., Trautmann, L., Rabenstein, R.: Nonlinear acoustic echo cancellation with 2nd order adaptive volterra filters. In: Proceedings of the 1999 IEEE International Conference on Acoustics, Speech, and Signal Processing, vol. 2, pp. 877–880. IEEE (1999)
34. Facebook: facebook Spaces. https://www.facebook.com/spaces Accessed 30 Mar 2018
35. Ramirez, R., Vamvakousis, Z.: Detecting emotion from EEG signals using the emotive epoc device. In: Zanzotto, F.M., Tsumoto, S., Taatgen, N., Yao, Y. (eds.) BI 2012. LNCS (LNAI), vol. 7670, pp. 175–184. Springer, Heidelberg (2012). https://doi.org/10.1007/978-3-642-35139-6_17
36. Technologies, U.: Unity 3D Game Engine. https://unity3d.com/. Accessed 30 Mar 2018
37. VRTK: VRTK. https://github.com/thestonefox/VRTK. Accessed 30 Mar 2018
38. Metta, G., Fitzpatrick, P., Natale, L.: YARP: yet another robot platform. Int. J. Adv. Rob. Syst. **3**(1), 8 (2006)
39. Oculus, V., et al.: Oculus rift (2015). http://www.oculusvr.com/rift

# How to Blend a Robot Within a Group of Zebrafish: Achieving Social Acceptance Through Real-Time Calibration of a Multi-level Behavioural Model

Leo Cazenille[1,2]([✉]), Yohann Chemtob[1], Frank Bonnet[3], Alexey Gribovskiy[3], Francesco Mondada[3], Nicolas Bredeche[2], and José Halloy[1]

[1] Univ Paris Diderot, LIED, UMR 8236, 75013 Paris, France
leo.cazenille@univ-paris-diderot.fr
[2] Sorbonne Université, CNRS, ISIR, 75005 Paris, France
[3] Robotic Systems Laboratory, School of Engineering, Ecole Polytechnique Fédérale de Lausanne, ME B3 30, Station 9, 1015 Lausanne, Switzerland

**Abstract.** We have previously shown how to socially integrate a fish robot into a group of zebrafish thanks to biomimetic behavioural models. The models have to be calibrated on experimental data to present correct behavioural features. This calibration is essential to enhance the social integration of the robot into the group. When calibrated, the behavioural model of fish behaviour is implemented to drive a robot with closed-loop control of social interactions into a group of zebrafish. This approach can be useful to form mixed-groups, and study animal individual and collective behaviour by using biomimetic autonomous robots capable of responding to the animals in long-standing experiments. Here, we show a methodology for continuous real-time calibration and refinement of multi-level behavioural model. The real-time calibration, by an evolutionary algorithm, is based on simulation of the model to correspond to the observed fish behaviour in real-time. The calibrated model is updated on the robot and tested during the experiments. This method allows to cope with changes of dynamics in fish behaviour. Moreover, each fish presents individual behavioural differences. Thus, each trial is done with naive fish groups that display behavioural variability. This real-time calibration methodology can optimise the robot behaviours during the experiments. Our implementation of this methodology runs on three different computers that perform individual tracking, data-analysis, multi-objective evolutionary algorithms, simulation of the fish robot and adaptation of the robot behavioural models, all in real-time.

**Keywords:** Collective behaviour · Real-time model fitting
Evolutionary algorithms · Decision-making · Multilevel model
Zebrafish · Robot · Biohybrid system

© Springer International Publishing AG, part of Springer Nature 2018
V. Vouloutsi et al. (Eds.): Living Machines 2018, LNAI 10928, pp. 73–84, 2018.
https://doi.org/10.1007/978-3-319-95972-6_9

# 1  Introduction

The study of animal collective behaviour involves the search for the relevant signals and mechanisms used by the animals for social interactions [26,33]. Robots can help ethologists to test various hypothesis on the nature of these signals by inducing specific and controlled stimuli to assess animal response.

Autonomous robots are capable to interact with animals and can serve as tools to study social dynamics [31]. This approach has already been used in studies to analyse the behaviour of ducks [41], drosophila [42], cockroaches [21], fish [2,6,10,24,25,27,28], bees [20,29,38] and birds [14,19,23].

Here, we socially integrate a behavioural biomimetic robotic lure into a group of four zebrafish (*Danio rerio*) moving in a structured environment and validate its acceptance by the animals. This problem is difficult because the robotic lure must be designed to be perceived as a social companion by the animals: it must, to a certain extent look like a fish, behave like a fish, be able to respond appropriately to environmental and social cues to close the loop of social interactions with the fish. Closing the loop of social interactions requires real-time individual perception and a decision-making algorithm to control the robot behaviours [10].

These aspects were investigated in [9,10] through the use of biomimetic robotic fish lures driven by a calibrated biomimetic model to make the robot mimics expected fish behaviour. An evolutionary algorithm (NSGA-II [15]) was used to optimise the parameters of this model so that the resulting collective dynamics corresponded to those observed in biological experiments. This type of controller allowed the robot to be a real group-member making its own decisions rather than a passive follower.

However, the model calibration was done off-line and not during the ongoing experiments. As such, it could not take into account the changes in animal behaviour across experiments and the intrinsic behavioural differences between groups used in experiments.

Here, we tackle this problem by continuously refining and calibrating the biomimetic model driving the robot behaviours in real-time during the experiment by using on-line evolutionary algorithm (NSGA-II [15]). This task is computationally-intensive and requires three computers to deal with agent real-time tracking, robot control, real-time data-analysis, and model calibration. We test this methodology in a set of 10 experiments with four fish and one robot. In each case, the robot closed-loop behaviour becomes progressively socially integrated into the group of fish. This is the first step towards evolving mixed-group of animals and robot [10].

# 2  Materials and Methods

## 2.1  Experimental Set-Up

We use the experimental set-up from [4,9,10,12,35] (Fig. 2, "Control & tracking" part) with a white plexiglass arena (Fig. 1A) of $1000 \times 1000 \times 100$ mm composed of two rooms linked by a corridor. We use the FishBot robot [3–5], powered by

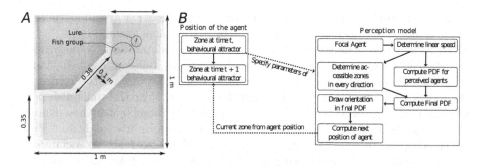

**Fig. 1. A.** Experimental setup: a tank with two square rooms ($350 \times 350$ mm at floor level) connected by a corridor ($380 \times 100$ mm). This set-up is used to study zebrafish collective behaviours [9–11,34,35]. It is composed of three zones (corridor, center of the rooms, close to room walls) that correspond to three different behavioural attractors. **B.** Multilevel model for fish behaviour [9,10]. The agents behave differently depending on the zone where they are situated.

two conductive plates under the aquarium, to interact with fish. An overhead camera captures frames (15 FPS, $500 \times 500$ px), that are then tracked to find the fish positions. A complementary fish-eye camera (15 FPS, $640 \times 480$ px) placed under the fish tank is used to track the position of the robot.

We used 10 groups of 4 adults wild-type AB zebrafish (*Danio rerio*) in ten 30-min experiments as in [9,10,35]: 30 min is sufficient to capture the behaviour and dynamics of groups of 4 zebrafish. Fish are released in the aquarium after the lure is placed in the aquarium.

To ensure real-time adaptation, our methodology is computationally intensive, and uses three networked 32-core computers (Fig. 2). Computer 1 is used to track the agents in real-time and control the robot according to the behavioural model of Sect. 2.2. Computer 2 performs every 60 s data-analysis on the tracked positions of agents from Computer 1, and estimates the biomimetism of robot behaviour (which, in our case, can be viewed as a metric of social integration as defined in [10]). Computer 3 re-calibrates every 60 s the behavioural model to correspond as close as possible to the behaviour of experimental fish (measured by Computer 2). The resulting calibrated parameter set is then sent to Computer 1 to serve as parameters of the robot controller model. It allows the robot to progressively mimics the behaviour of the fish and be socially accepted.

The experiments performed in this study were conducted under the authorisation of the Buffon Ethical Committee (registered to the French National Ethical Committee for Animal Experiments #40) after submission to the French state ethical board for animal experiments.

## 2.2 Behavioural Model

We use the multi-level model from [9,10] (inspired from [11]) that describes the individual and collective behaviours of fish (Fig. 1B). This model takes into account both social interactions and environmental cues (*i.e.* walls and structure of the tanks). It is stochastic, multi-level and context-dependent.

Fish behave differently depending on their spatial position. Namely, this model identify three zones of the structured set-up with different fish behaviours (Fig. 1A): when they are close to the walls, when they are in the centre of the rooms, and when they pass through the corridor. Near the walls, fish perform mainly thigmotactism (wall following) while in room centre they exhibit exploratory behaviour. In the corridor, they tend to go in a straight line with increased speed to reach the subsequent room. Fish also react to social cues leading to collective behaviour such as collective departures from the rooms [12]. Very few models of fish collective behaviours take into account the presence of walls [8, 11].

The agents update their position vector $X_i$ with a velocity vector $V_i$:

$$X_i(t + \delta t) = X_i(t) + V_i(t)\delta t \tag{1}$$

$$V_i(t + \delta t) = v_i(t + \delta t)\Theta_i(t + \delta t) \tag{2}$$

with $v_i$ the linear speed of the $i^{th}$ agent and $\Theta_i$ its orientation. The linear speed $v_i$ of the agent is randomly drawn from the experimentally measured instantaneous speed distribution.

The orientation $\Theta_i$ is drawn from probability density function (PDF) computed as a mixture distribution of von Mises distributions centred on the stimuli perceived by the focal agent. It takes into account the influence of other agents and of the walls of the experimental arena. The resulting PDF is composed of the weighted sum of (i) a PDF taking into account the effect of the walls and (ii) a PDF describing the response to other agents. The parameter $\gamma_{z_1,z_2}$, used as a multiplicative term of the final PDF, modulates the attraction of agents towards target zones.

We numerically compute the cumulative distribution function (CDF) corresponding to this final PDF by performing a cumulative trapezoidal numerical integration of the PDF in the interval $[-\pi, \pi]$. Then, the model draws a random direction $\Theta_i$ in this distribution by inverse transform sampling. The position of the fish is then updated according to this direction and his velocity.

## 2.3    Communication Between Computer Nodes

We connect the three computers (Fig. 2) using the ZeroMQ distributed messaging protocol [22]: computers receiving messages act as ZeroMQ subscribers, and computers sending messages act as ZeroMQ publishers.

The tracked agent trajectories are compiled in the form of trajectory files, and sent every 60 s from Computer 1 to Computer 2 through the `rsync` [1] command line application (a process which usually only need 2 s to 3 s that is sufficient because the parameter update is every 60 s). Then, Computer 1 send a ZeroMQ message to Computer 2 to acknowledge that the transfer is completed. Data-analysis scores from Computer 2 to Computer 3, and model parameters from Computer 3 to Computer 1 are sent every 60 s through ZeroMQ messages.

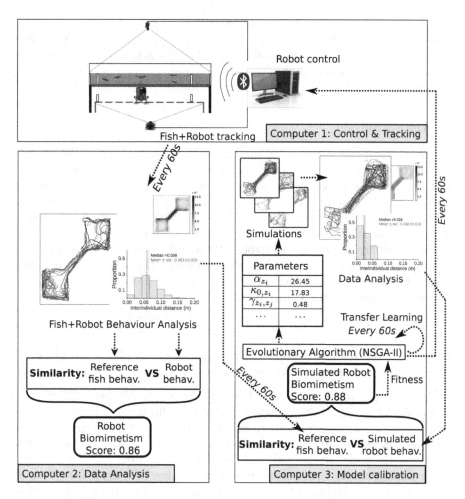

**Fig. 2.** Workflow of our real-time calibration methodology. It involves extensive computation to be able to function in real-time, and thus is implemented over three 32-core computers. Computer 1 tracks the positions of fish and robot and is also running the robot controller. Computer 2 performs data-analysis of the fish and the robot behaviour using the data gathered by Computer 1 during 60 s. Computer 3 calibrates the behavioural model (presented in Sect. 2.2) to be as close as possible to the observed behaviour of the fish as assessed by the data-analysis performed by Computer 2. It also uses the knowledge acquired during the previous calibration processes. The calibrated model is sent every 60 s to Computer 1 to be used to drive the robot. The social acceptation of the robot behaviour is measured by Computer 2 with a distance metric of collective features.

## 2.4   Real-Time Tracking

We use the CATS framework [4] to track agents (fish and robot) in real-time, on Computer 1. Fish are tracked (but not identified) by using frames captured by the overhead camera (Fig. 2) through the Shi-Tomasi method [36] implemented in the OpenCV library [7]. In parallel, the robot is tracked through the video frames from the camera below the fish-tank by colour and contours detection [39]. Every 60 s the positions of the agents are sent to Computer 2 for data-analysis.

## 2.5   Data-Analysis

Every 60 s, Computer 2 calculates the behavioural statistics using the tracked positions of agents (from computer 1) over the last 120 s of the running experiment, for all three zones of the arena. For a zone $e$, these statistics are: the distribution of inter-individual distances between agents ($D_e$), the distribution of distances of agents to their nearest wall ($W_e$), the distribution of zones occupation ($O_e$), the transition probabilities from zone $e$ to others ($Te$).

These statistics are computed either only on fish agents (**Control** case: $e_c$) or on fish and robotic agents (**Robot Social Integration** case: $e_r$). We define a similarity score (ranging from 0.0 to 1.0) to measure the biomimetism of robot behaviour compared to the **Control** case:

$$S(e_r, e_c) = \sqrt[4]{I(D_{e_r}, D_{e_c})I(W_{e_r}, W_{e_c})I(O_{e_r}, O_{e_c})I(T_{e_r}, T_{e_c})} \qquad (3)$$

The function $I(P,Q)$ is defined as such: $I(P,Q) = 1 - H(P,Q)$. The $H(P,Q)$ function is the Hellinger distance between two histograms [16]. It is defined as: $H(P,Q) = \frac{1}{\sqrt{2}}\sqrt{\sum_{i=1}^{d}(\sqrt{P_i} - \sqrt{Q_i})^2}$ where $P_i$ and $Q_i$ are the bin frequencies.

Cazenille et al. [9,10] demonstrated that robotic lures with biomimetic morphology and behaviour are be more socially integrated into the group of fish than non-biomimetic lures. As such, the biomimetism score defined earlier corresponds to the social acceptatation of the robot by the fish.

When this statistics and scores are computed, they are dispatched to Computer 3 (by the ZeroMQ system described in Sect. 2.3) to guide the optimisation process.

## 2.6   Real-Time Optimisation of Model Parameters

We design a calibration methodology (Fig. 2) capable of optimising in real-time the parameters of the behavioural model from Sect. 2.2 to mimic as close as possible to the behaviour of experimental fish. The behavioural similarity is quantified as described in Sect. 2.5.

It is inspired from the off-line calibration methodology in [9] and uses the NSGA-II [15] multi-objective global optimiser (population of 60 individuals, 300 generations) with three objectives to maximise. We define a fitness with three objectives: the first objective is a performance objective corresponding to the

$S_{(e_1, e_2)}$ function. Two other objectives are considered to guide the evolutionary process: one that promotes genotypic diversity [32] (defined by the mean euclidean distance of the genome of an individual to the genomes of the other individuals of the current population), the other encouraging behavioural diversity (defined by the euclidean distance between the $D_e$, $W_e$, $O_e$ and $T_e$ scores of an individual).

This process is performed and restarted every 60 s on Computer 3 (starting 120 s after the beginning of the experiment to gather data, Fig. 2) using data gathered during the last 120 s. Every restart of the evolutionary algorithm keeps the last generation of individuals evolved during the previous round of evolution to bootstrap the current round of evolution, a system akin to transfer learning. On our 32-core computer, one generation is computed approximately every 4 s, so around 15 generations are computed at every evolutionary round.

We do not optimise the linear speed $v_i$ of the agents. It is randomly drawn from the experimental speed distribution. We use the NSGA-II implementation provided by the DEAP python library [17].

## 2.7  Robot Implementation and Control

The robot is driven by the model presented in Sect. 2.2 thanks to the CATS framework [4]. The model is calibrated every 60 s using the methodology of Sect. 2.6, in experiments involving four fish and one robot. Every 200 ms, the tracked positions of the four fish are integrated into the model to compute the target position of a fifth agent. The robot is programmed to follow this target position by using the biomimetic movement patterns as in [5,10].

# 3  Results

We assessed the evolution of the similarity scores (defined in Sect. 2.5) between robot behaviour and fish behaviour, across sliding windows of 120 s intervals of a set of 10 trials each one lasting 30 min, starting in each trial from the second time interval (120 s to 180 s) to gather enough experimental data. These scores are compiled in Fig. 3. The variance for the 10 trials is plotted as a grey area around the curves and remains rather small.

From its initial value of about 0.610 (second time interval: 120 s to 180 s), the average fitness (mean scores) fastly converges to values around 0.850 starting from the fourth time interval (0.827 on 240 s to 300 s). This is also observed for similarity scores of transitions and of distances to nearest wall. This shows that both of these behavioural features can be effectively optimised through an online evolutionary algorithm process, and remain stables during the experiment.

The similarity score of zone occupation is particularly high at the beginning of the experiment, and is only slightly improved by our calibration methodology; this would suggests that room occupation is only slightly dependent of model parameters. This could be explained by a strong effect of room geometry (room size, and the general room configuration of the arena) over room occupation:

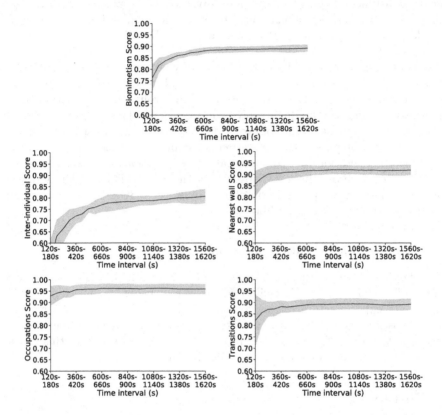

**Fig. 3.** Similarity scores between the behaviour of the experimental fish and the behaviour of the best-performing individuals of the calibrated model at different time intervals of 10 different experiments. These scores are computed using data over 120 s, and starting from the third time interval (120 s to 180 s) to ensure gathering enough experimental data. In these plots, lines correspond to the mean scores across the 10 experiments, and the grey translucent areas correspond to the standard deviation. We consider four behavioural features to characterise the behaviour exhibited in each time interval. **Inter-individual distances** corresponds to the similarity in distribution of inter-individual distances between all agents in a specific zone and measures the capabilities of the agents to aggregate. **Distances to nearest wall** corresponds to the similarity in distribution of agent distance to their nearest wall, and assess their capability to follow the walls. **Occupations** corresponds to the similarity in probability of presence of the agent in each zone. **Transitions** corresponds to the similarity in probabilities of an agent to transition from one zone to another. The **Biomimetic score** corresponds to the geometric mean of the other scores.

rooms cover a larger area than the corridor. This could also be an effect of the aggregative behaviour exhibited by fish and by the model: the robot would follow the fish, which would tend to follow walls, thus explaining the relative invariance of the occupation score with respect to parameter values.

The variations in similarity score of inter-individual distances suggests changes of fish aggregative behaviour during the experiment. This could be explained by the fact that, while zebrafish tend to remain cohesive most of the time, they have the tendency of forming short-lived (a few seconds to a few minutes) sub-groups, especially when confronted to a fragmented environment [10].

## 4   Discussion and Conclusion

Animal-robot interaction studies employ simple robot behavioural model that are not adaptive or updated during the experiments. Often they are not biomimetic and do not close the interaction loop between the animals and the robots [10]. Here we present a methodology to calibrate in real-time a multi-level context-dependent biomimetic model of fish behaviour to drive the behaviour of a biomimetic robot into a group of zebrafish. The model parameters are continuously refined to accurately correspond to the collective dynamics exhibited by fish during the experiments. The real-time nature of this calibration process allows the robot to react to changes in observed fish dynamics and cope with uncertainties.

Animals can present significant inter-individual behavioural differences. They can present significant differences in terms of personalities typically bold and shy types [40]. In most of the experiments individuals are selected randomly from a stock. Consequently, each group trial present differences depending on the characteristics of the individuals. Currently, the models are calibrated on a set of averaged experimental data and are not optimised to take into account inter-individuals differences. We present here a method to adapt in real-time the models and that is thus capable to cope with this issue. This method can reduce significantly the number of experimental trials necessary to calibrate the model.

Our approach is computationally intensive and use three networked computers to handle in real-time the tracking, the robot control, the data analysis and the model calibration tasks.

Our methodology builds on the work presented in [9] by adding real-time capabilities to the calibration process. However, it also suffers from the same limitations. Namely, the model we calibrate must still be structurally defined empirically (*i.e.* defining behavioural attractors, zones of the environment, etc.) with ethological *a-priori* knowledge about fish dynamics. The calibration process could also still be improved by taking into account additional behavioural metrics in the computation of similarity scores, either in term of collective dynamics (*e.g.* agent groups aspects, residence time in a zone), individual behaviours (*e.g.* agent trajectory aspects, curvature of trajectories). This could possibly be bypassed through the use of a calibration process without explicit similarity measure (e.g. GAN [18] or Turing Learning [30]). Our behavioural model could be revised to account for collective departures of agents from one room to the other, as described in biological studies [12].

Additionally, our methodology could make use of global optimisation techniques designed to minimise the number of evaluations before reaching convergence, like Bayesian Optimisation [13,37]. This would reduce calibration computation costs, and possibly reduce the time needed to accurately calibrate the models.

**Acknowledgement.** This work was funded by EU-ICT project 'ASSISIbf', no. 601074.

# References

1. rsync(1) Linux User's Manual
2. Bierbach, D., Landgraf, T., Romanczuk, P., Lukas, J., Nguyen, H., Wolf, M., Krause, J.: Using a robotic fish to investigate individual differences in social responsiveness in the guppy. bioRxiv (2018). https://doi.org/10.1101/304501
3. Bonnet, F., Binder, S., de Oliveria, M., Halloy, J., Mondada, F.: A miniature mobile robot developed to be socially integrated with species of small fish. In: IEEE International Conference on Robotics and Biomimetics (ROBIO), pp. 747–752. IEEE (2014)
4. Bonnet, F., Cazenille, L., Gribovskiy, A., Halloy, J., Mondada, F.: Multi-robots control and tracking framework for bio-hybrid systems with closed-loop interaction. In: IEEE International Conference on Robotics and Automation (ICRA). IEEE (2017)
5. Bonnet, F., Cazenille, L., Seguret, A., Gribovskiy, A., Collignon, B., Halloy, J., Mondada, F.: Design of a modular robotic system that mimics small fish locomotion and body movements for ethological studies. Int. J. Adv. Robot. Syst. **14**(3) (2017). https://doi.org/10.1177/1729881417706628
6. Bonnet, F., Gribovskiy, A., Halloy, J., Mondada, F.: Closed-loop interactions between a shoal of zebrafish and a group of robotic fish in a circular corridor. Swarm Intell. 1–18 (2018)
7. Bradski, G.: The OpenCV library. Dr. Dobb's J. Softw. Tools **25**, 120–126 (2000)
8. Calovi, D.S., Litchinko, A., Lecheval, V., Lopez, U., Escudero, A.P., Chaté, H., Sire, C., Theraulaz, G.: Disentangling and modeling interactions in fish with burst-and-coast swimming reveal distinct alignment and attraction behaviors. PLoS Comput. Biol. **14**(1), e1005933 (2018)
9. Cazenille, L., et al.: Automated calibration of a biomimetic space-dependent model for zebrafish and robot collective behaviour in a structured environment. In: Mangan, M., et al. (eds.) Living Machines 2017. LNCS (LNAI), vol. 10384, pp. 107–118. Springer, Cham (2017). https://doi.org/10.1007/978-3-319-63537-8_10
10. Cazenille, L., Collignon, B., Bonnet, F., Gribovskiy, A., Mondada, F., Bredeche, N., Halloy, J.: How mimetic should a robotic fish be to socially integrate into zebrafish groups? Bioinspiration Biomim. (2017)
11. Collignon, B., Séguret, A., Halloy, J.: A stochastic vision-based model inspired by zebrafish collective behaviour in heterogeneous environments. R. Soc. Open Sci. **3**(1) (2016). https://doi.org/10.1098/rsos.150473
12. Collignon, B., Séguret, A., Chemtob, Y., Cazenille, L., Halloy, J.: Collective departures in zebrafish: profiling the initiators. arXiv preprint arXiv:1701.03611 (2017)

13. Cully, A., Clune, J., Tarapore, D., Mouret, J.B.: Robots that can adapt like animals. Nature **521**(7553), 503 (2015)
14. De Margerie, E., Lumineau, S., Houdelier, C., Yris, M.R.: Influence of a mobile robot on the spatial behaviour of quail chicks. Bioinspiration Biomim. **6**(3), 034001 (2011)
15. Deb, K., Pratap, A., Agarwal, S., Meyarivan, T.: A fast and elitist multiobjective genetic algorithm: NSGA-II. IEEE Trans. Evol. Comput. **6**(2), 182–197 (2002)
16. Deza, M., Deza, E.: Dictionary of Distances. Elsevier, Amsterdam (2006)
17. Fortin, F.A., Rainville, F.M.D., Gardner, M.A., Parizeau, M., Gagné, C.: DEAP: evolutionary algorithms made easy. J. Mach. Learn. Res. **13**, 2171–2175 (2012)
18. Goodfellow, I., Pouget-Abadie, J., Mirza, M., Xu, B., Warde-Farley, D., Ozair, S., Courville, A., Bengio, Y.: Generative adversarial nets. In: Advances in Neural Information Processing Systems, pp. 2672–2680 (2014)
19. Gribovskiy, A., Halloy, J., Deneubourg, J., Mondada, F.: Designing a socially integrated mobile robot for ethological research. Robot. Autonom. Syst. **103**, 42–55 (2018)
20. Griparić, K., Haus, T., Miklić, D., Polić, M., Bogdan, S.: A robotic system for researching social integration in honeybees. PLoS ONE **12**(8), e0181977 (2017)
21. Halloy, J., Sempo, G., Caprari, G., Rivault, C., Asadpour, M., Tâche, F., Said, I., Durier, V., Canonge, S., Amé, J.: Social integration of robots into groups of cockroaches to control self-organized choices. Science **318**(5853), 1155–1158 (2007)
22. Hintjens, P.: ZeroMQ: Messaging for Many Applications. O'Reilly Media Inc., Sebastopol (2013)
23. Jolly, L., Pittet, F., Caudal, J.P., Mouret, J.B., Houdelier, C., Lumineau, S., De Margerie, E.: Animal-to-robot social attachment: initial requisites in a gallinaceous bird. Bioinspiration Biomim. **11**(1) (2016). https://doi.org/10.1088/1748-3190/11/1/016007
24. Katzschmann, R.K., DelPreto, J., MacCurdy, R., Rus, D.: Exploration of underwater life with an acoustically controlled soft robotic fish. Sci. Robot. **3**(16) (2018). http://robotics.sciencemag.org/content/3/16/eaar3449
25. Kim, C., Ruberto, T., Phamduy, P., Porfiri, M.: Closed-loop control of zebrafish behaviour in three dimensions using a robotic stimulus. Sci. Rep. **8**(1), 657 (2018)
26. Knight, J.: Animal behaviour: when robots go wild. Nature **434**(7036), 954–955 (2005)
27. Landgraf, T., et al.: Blending in with the shoal: robotic fish swarms for investigating strategies of group formation in guppies. In: Duff, A., Lepora, N.F., Mura, A., Prescott, T.J., Verschure, P.F.M.J. (eds.) Living Machines 2014. LNCS (LNAI), vol. 8608, pp. 178–189. Springer, Cham (2014). https://doi.org/10.1007/978-3-319-09435-9_16
28. Landgraf, T., Bierbach, D., Nguyen, H., Muggelberg, N., Romanczuk, P., Krause, J.: Robofish: increased acceptance of interactive robotic fish with realistic eyes and natural motion patterns by live trinidadian guppies. Bioinspiration Biomim. **11**(1) (2016). https://doi.org/10.1088/1748-3190/11/1/015001
29. Landgraf, T., Oertel, M., Kirbach, A., Menzel, R., Rojas, R.: Imitation of the honeybee dance communication system by means of a biomimetic robot. In: Prescott, T.J., Lepora, N.F., Mura, A., Verschure, P.F.M.J. (eds.) Living Machines 2012. LNCS (LNAI), vol. 7375, pp. 132–143. Springer, Heidelberg (2012). https://doi.org/10.1007/978-3-642-31525-1_12
30. Li, W., Gauci, M., Groß, R.: Turing learning: a metric-free approach to inferring behavior and its application to swarms. Swarm Intell. **10**(3), 211–243 (2016)

31. Mondada, F., Halloy, J., Martinoli, A., Correll, N., Gribovskiy, A., Sempo, G., Siegwart, R., Deneubourg, J.: A general methodology for the control of mixed natural-artificial societies. In: Kernbach, S. (ed.) Handbook of Collective Robotics: Fundamentals and Challenges, pp. 547–585. Pan Stanford, Singapore (2013). Chapter 15
32. Mouret, J., Doncieux, S.: Encouraging behavioral diversity in evolutionary robotics: an empirical study. Evol. Comput. **20**(1), 91–133 (2012)
33. Patricelli, G.: Robotics in the study of animal behavior. In: Breed, M., Moore, J. (eds.) Encyclopedia of Animal Behavior, pp. 91–99. Greenwood Press, Westport (2010)
34. Séguret, A., Collignon, B., Halloy, J.: Strain differences in the collective behaviour of zebrafish (danio rerio) in heterogeneous environment. R. Soc. Open Sci. **3**(10) (2016). https://doi.org/10.1098/rsos.160451
35. Séguret, A., Collignon, B., Cazenille, L., Chemtob, Y., Halloy, J.: Loose social organisation of AB strain zebrafish groups in a two-patch environment. arXiv preprint arXiv:1701.02572 (2017)
36. Shi, J., Tomasi, C.: Good features to track. In: Proceedings of the Computer Vision and Pattern Recognition, CVPR (1994)
37. Snoek, J., Larochelle, H., Adams, R.P.: Practical Bayesian optimization of machine learning algorithms. In: Advances in Neural Information Processing Systems, pp. 2951–2959 (2012)
38. Stefanec, M., Szopek, M., Schmickl, T., Mills, R.: Governing the swarm: controlling a bio-hybrid society of bees & robots with computational feedback loops. In: IEEE Symposium Series on Computational Intelligence (SSCI), pp. 1–8. IEEE (2017)
39. Suzuki, S., Abe, K.: Topological structural analysis of digitized binary images by border following. Comput. Vis. Graph. Image Process. **30**(1), 32–46 (1985)
40. Toms, C.N., Echevarria, D.J.: Back to basics: searching for a comprehensive framework for exploring individual differences in zebrafish (danio rerio) behavior. Zebrafish **11**(4), 325–340 (2014)
41. Vaughan, R., Sumpter, N., Henderson, J., Frost, A., Cameron, S.: Experiments in automatic flock control. Robot. Autonom. Syst. **31**(1), 109–117 (2000)
42. Zabala, F., Polidoro, P., Robie, A., Branson, K., Perona, P., Dickinson, M.: A simple strategy for detecting moving objects during locomotion revealed by animal-robot interactions. Current Biol. **22**(14), 1344–1350 (2012)

# Evolutionary Optimisation of Neural Network Models for Fish Collective Behaviours in Mixed Groups of Robots and Zebrafish

Leo Cazenille[1,2(✉)], Nicolas Bredeche[2], and José Halloy[1]

[1] Univ Paris Diderot, Sorbonne Paris Cité, LIED, UMR 8236, 75013 Paris, France
leo.cazenille@univ-paris-diderot.fr
[2] Sorbonne Université, CNRS, ISIR, 75005 Paris, France

**Abstract.** Animal and robot social interactions are interesting both for ethological studies and robotics. On the one hand, the robots can be tools and models to analyse animal collective behaviours, on the other hand the robots and their artificial intelligence are directly confronted and compared to the natural animal collective intelligence. The first step is to design robots and their behavioural controllers that are capable of socially interact with animals. Designing such behavioural bio-mimetic controllers remains an important challenge as they have to reproduce the animal behaviours and have to be calibrated on experimental data. Most animal collective behavioural models are designed by modellers based on experimental data. This process is long and costly because it is difficult to identify the relevant behavioural features that are then used as *a priori* knowledge in model building. Here, we want to model the fish individual and collective behaviours in order to develop robot controllers. We explore the use of optimised black-box models based on artificial neural networks (ANN) to model fish behaviours. While the ANN may not be biomimetic but rather bio-inspired, they can be used to link perception to motor responses. These models are designed to be implementable as robot controllers to form mixed-groups of fish and robots, using few *a priori* knowledge of the fish behaviours. We present a methodology with multilayer perceptron or echo state networks that are optimised through evolutionary algorithms to model accurately the fish individual and collective behaviours in a bounded rectangular arena. We assess the biomimetism of the generated models and compare them to the fish experimental behaviours.

**Keywords:** Collective behaviour · Neural networks
Echo state network · Multi-objective neuro-evolution
Bio-hybrid systems · Biomimetic · Robot · Zebrafish · Fish

## 1 Introduction

Autonomous, biomimetic robots can serve as tools in animal behavioural studies. Robots are used in ethology and behavioural studies to untangle the multimodal

© Springer International Publishing AG, part of Springer Nature 2018
V. Vouloutsi et al. (Eds.): Living Machines 2018, LNAI 10928, pp. 85–96, 2018.
https://doi.org/10.1007/978-3-319-95972-6_10

modes of interactions and communication between animals [23]. When they are socially integrated in a group of animals, they are capable of sending calibrated stimuli to test the animal responses in a social context [17]. Moreover, animal and autonomous robot interactions represent an interesting challenge for robotics. Confronting robots to animals is a difficult task because specific behavioural models have to be designed and the robots have to be socially accepted by the animals. The robots have to engage in social behaviour and convince somehow the animal that they can be social companions. In this context, the capabilities of the robots and their intelligence are put in harsh conditions and often demonstrate the huge gap that still exists between autonomous robots and animals not only considering motion and coping with the environment but also in terms of intelligence. It is a direct comparison of artificial and natural collective intelligence. Moreover, the design of such social robots is challenging as it involves both a luring capability including appropriate robot behaviours, and the social acceptation of the robots by the animals. We have shown that the social integration of robots into groups of fish can be improved by refining the behavioural models used to build their controllers [8]. The models have also to be calibrated to replicate accurately the animal collective behaviours in complex environments [8].

Research on animal and robot interactions need also bio-mimetic formal models as behavioural controllers of the robots if the robots have to behave as congeners [2,3]. Robots controllers have to deal with a whole range of behaviours to allow them to take into account not only the other individuals but also the environment and in particular the walls [7,8]. However, most of biological collective behaviour models deal only with one sub-part at a time of fish behaviours in unbounded environments. Controllers based on neural networks, such as multilayer perceptron (MLP) [22] or echo state networks (ESN) [20] have the advantage to be easier to implement and could deal with a larger range of events.

## Objectives

We aim at building models that generate accurately zebrafish trajectories of one individual within a small group of 5 agents. The trajectories are the result of social interactions in a bounded environment. Zebrafish are a classic animal model in the research fields of genetics and neurosciences of individual and collective behaviours. Building models that correctly reproduce the individual trajectories of fish within a group is still an open question [18]. We explore MLP and ESN models, optimised by evolutionary computation, to generate individual trajectories. MLP and ESN are black-box models that need few *a priori* information provided by the modeller. They are optimised on the experimental data and as such represent a model of the complex experimental collective trajectories. However, they are difficult to calibrate on the zebrafish experimental data due to the complexity of the fish trajectories. Here, we consider the design and calibration by evolutionary computation of neural network models, MLP and ESN, that can become robot controllers. We test two evolutionary optimisation methods, CMA-ES [1] and NSGA-III [33] and show that the latter gives better results. We show that such MLP and ESN behavioural models could be useful in animal robot interactions and could make the robots accepted by the animals by reproducing their behaviours and trajectories as in [8].

## 2   Materials and Methods

### 2.1   Experimental Set-Up

We use the same experimental procedure, fish handling, and set-up as in [2, 4,6,8,10,28]. The experimental arena is a square white plexiglass aquarium of $1000 \times 1000 \times 100$ mm. An overhead camera captures frames at 15 FPS, with a $500 \times 500$ px resolution, that are then tracked to find the fish positions. We use 10 groups of 5 adults wild-type AB zebrafish (*Danio rerio*) in 10 trials lasting each one for 30-min as in [2,4,6,8,10,28]. The experiments performed in this study were conducted under the authorisation of the Buffon Ethical Committee (registered to the French National Ethical Committee for Animal Experiments #40) after submission to the French state ethical board for animal experiments.

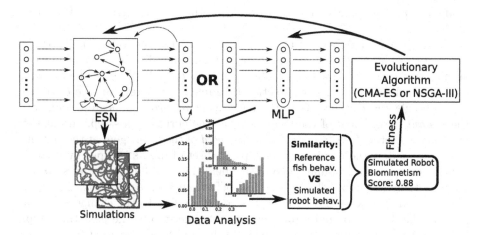

**Fig. 1.** Methodology workflow. An evolutionary algorithm is used to evolve the weight of a MLP (1 hidden layer, 100 neurons) or an ESN (100 reservoir neurons) neural networks that serves as the controller of a simulated robot interacting with 4 fish described by the experimental data. Only the connections represented by dotted arrows are evolved (for MLP: all connections; for ESN: connections from inputs to reservoir, from reservoir to outputs and from outputs to outputs and to reservoir). The fitness function is computed through data-analysis of these simulations and represent the biomimetism metric of the simulated robot behaviour compared to the behaviour exhibited by real fish in experiments. Two evolutionary algorithms are tested: CMA-ES (mono-objective) and NSGA-III (multi-objective).

## 2.2  Artificial Neural Network Model

Black-box models, like artificial neural networks (ANN), can be used to model phenomena with few *a priori* information. Although they are not used yet to model fish collective behaviours based on experimental data, here we show that they are relevant to model zebrafish collective behaviour. We propose a methodology (Fig. 1) where either a multilayer perceptron (MLP) [22] artificial neural network, or an echo state network (ESN) [20], is calibrated through the use of evolutionary algorithms to model the behaviour of a simulated fish in a group of 5 individuals. The 4 other individuals are described by the experimental data obtained with 10 different groups of 5 fish for trials lasting 30 min.

MLP are a type of feedforward artificial neural networks that are very popular in artificial intelligence to solve a large variety of real-world problems [25]. Their capability to universally approximate functions [11] makes them suitable to model control and robotic problems [25]. We consider MLP with only one hidden layer of 100 neurons (using a hyperbolic tangent function as activation function).

ESN are recurrent neural networks often used to model temporal processes, like time-series, or robot control tasks [26]. They are sufficiently expressive to model complex non-linear temporal problems, that non-recurrent MLP cannot model.

For the considered focal agent, the neural network model takes the following parameters as input: (i) the *direction vector* (angle and distance) from the focal agent towards each other agent; (ii) the *angular distance* between the focal agent direction and each other agent direction (alignment measure); (iii) the *direction vector* (angle and distance) from the focal agent towards the nearest wall; (iv) the *instant linear speed* of the focal agent at the current time-step, and at the previous time-step; (v) the *instant angular speed* of the focal agent at the current time-step, and at the previous time-step. This set of inputs is typically used in multi-agent modelling of animal collective behaviour [13,30]. As a first step, we consider that it is sufficient to model fish behaviour with neural networks.

The neural network has two outputs corresponding to the change in linear and angular speeds to apply from the current time-step to the next time-step. Here, we limit our approach to modelling fish trajectories resulting from social interactions in a homogeneous environment but bounded by walls. Very few models of fish collective behaviours take into account the presence of walls [5,9].

## 2.3  Data Analysis

For each trial, $e$, and simulations, we compute several behavioural metrics using the tracked positions of agents: (i) the distribution of *inter-individual distances* between agents ($D_e$); (ii) the distributions of *instant linear speeds* ($L_e$); (iii) the distributions of *instant angular speeds* ($A_e$); (iv) the distribution of *polarisation* of the agents in the group ($P_e$) and (v) the distribution of *distances of agents to their nearest wall* ($W_e$). The polarisation of an agent group measures how aligned the agents in a group are, and is defined as the absolute value of the mean agent heading: $P = \frac{1}{N}\left|\sum_{i=1}^{N} u_i\right|$ where $u_i$ is the unit direction of agent $i$ and $N = 5$ is the number of agents [32].

We define a similarity measure (ranging from 0.0 to 1.0) to measure the biomimetism of the simulated robot behaviour by comparing the behaviour of the group of agents in simulations where the robot is present (experiment $e_r$: four fish and one robot) to the behaviour of the experimental fish groups (experiment $e_c$: five fish):

$$S(e_r, e_c) = \sqrt[5]{I(D_{e_r}, D_{e_c})I(L_{e_r}, W_{e_c})I(A_{e_r}, O_{e_c})I(P_{e_r}, T_{e_c})I(W_{e_r}, T_{e_c})} \quad (1)$$

The function $I(X, Y)$ is defined as such: $I(X, Y) = 1 - H(X, Y)$. The $H(X, Y)$ function is the Hellinger distance between two histograms [14]. It is defined as: $H(X, Y) = \frac{1}{\sqrt{2}}\sqrt{\sum_{i=1}^{d}(\sqrt{X_i} - \sqrt{Y_i})^2}$ where $X_i$ and $Y_i$ are the bin frequencies.

This score measures the social acceptation of the robot by the fish, as defined in [7,8]. Compared to the similarity measure defined in these articles, we added a measure of the polarisation of the agents. This was motivated by the tendency of our evolved neural models, without a polarisation factor, to generate agents with unnatural looping behaviour to catch up with the group.

## 2.4   Optimisation

We calibrate the ANN models presented here to match as close as possible the behaviour of one fish in a group of 5 individuals in 30-min simulations (at 15 time-steps per seconds, *i.e.* 27000 steps per simulation). This is achieved by optimising the connection weights of the ANN through evolutionary computation that iteratively perform global optimisation (inspired by biological evolution) on a defined fitness function so as to find its maxima [21,27].

We consider two optimisation methods (as in [7]), for MLP and ESN networks. In the **Sim-MonoObj-MLP** case, we use the CMA-ES [1] monoobjective evolutionary algorithm to optimise an MLP, with the task of maximising the $S_{(e_1, e_2)}$ function. In the **Sim-MultiObj-MLP** and **Sim-MultiObj-ESN** cases, we use the NSGA-III [33] multi-objective algorithm with three objectives to maximise. The first objective is a performance objective corresponding to the $S_{(e_1, e_2)}$ function. We also consider two other objectives used to guide the evolutionary process: one that promotes genotypic diversity [24] (defined by the mean euclidean distance of the genome of an individual to the genomes of the other individuals of the current population), the other encouraging behavioural diversity (defined by the euclidean distance between the $D_e$, $L_e$, $A_e$, $P_e$ and $W_e$ scores of an individual). The NSGA-III algorithm was used with a 0.80% probability of crossovers and a 0.20% probability of mutations (we also tested this algorithm with only mutations and obtained similar results). The NSGA-III algorithm [33] is considered instead of the NSGA-II algorithm [12] employed in [7] because it is known to converge faster than NSGA-II on problems with more than two objectives [19].

In both methods, we use populations of 60 individuals and 300 generations. Each case is repeated in 10 different trials. We use a NSGA-III implementation based on the DEAP python library [16].

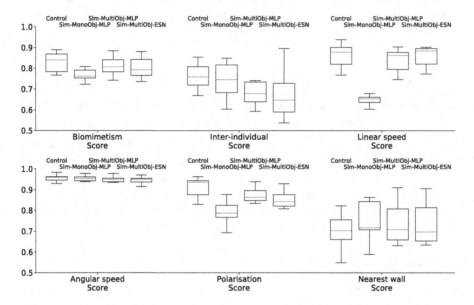

**Fig. 2.** Similarity scores between the behaviour of the experimental fish groups (control) and the behaviour of the best-performing simulated individuals of the MLP models optimised by CMA-ES or NSGA-III. Results are obtained over 10 different trials (experiments for fish-only groups, and simulations for NN models). We consider five behavioural features to characterise exhibited behaviours. **Inter-individual distances** corresponds to the similarity in distribution of inter-individual distances between all agents and measures the capabilities of the agents to aggregate. **Linear and Angular speeds distributions** correspond to the distributions of linear and angular speeds of the agents. **Polarisation** measures how aligned the agents are in the group. **Distances to nearest wall** corresponds to the similarity in distribution of agent distance to their nearest wall, and assess their capability to follow the walls. The **Biomimetic score** corresponds to the geometric mean of the other scores.

## 3   Results

We analyse the behaviour of one simulated robot in a group of 4 fish. The robots are driven by ANN (either MLP or ESN) evolved with CMA-ES (**Sim-MonoObj-MLP** case) or with NSGA-III (**Sim-MultiObj-MLP** and **Sim-MultiObj-ESN** cases) and compare it to the behaviour of fish-only groups (**Control** case). We only consider the best-evolved ANN controllers. In the simulations, the simulated robot does not influence the fish because the fish are described by their experimental data that is replayed.

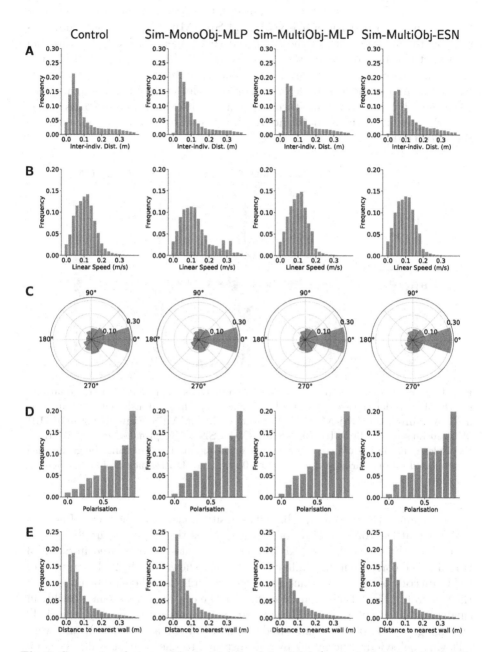

**Fig. 3.** Comparison between 30-min trials involving 5 fish (control, biological data) and simulations involving 4 fish and 1 robot, over 10 trials and across 5 behavioural features: inter-individual distances (**A**), linear (**B**) and angular (**C**) speeds distributions, polarisation (**D**), and distances to nearest wall (**E**).

Examples of agent trajectories obtained in the three tested cases are found in Fig. 4A. In the **Sim-MonoObj-MLP** and **Sim-MultiObj-\*** cases, they correspond to the trajectory of the simulated robot agent. In both case, we can see that the robot follow the walls like the fish, and are often part of the fish group as natural fish do. However, the robot trajectories can incorporate patterns not found in the fish trajectories. For example, small circular loop are done when the robot performs an U-turn to catch up with the fish group. This is particularly present in the **Sim-MonoObj-MLP** case, and seldom appear in the **Sim-MultiObj-\*** cases.

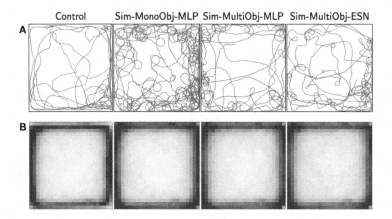

**Fig. 4.** Agent trajectories observed after 30-min trials in a square (1 m) aquarium, for the 4 considered cases: **Control** reference experimental fish data obtained as in [9, 28], **Sim-MonoObj-MLP** MLP optimised by CMA-ES, **Sim-MultiObj-MLP** MLP optimised by NSGA-III, **Sim-MultiObj-ESN** ESN optimised by NSGA-III. **A** Examples of an individual trajectory of one agent among the 5 making the group (fish or simulated robot) during 1-min out of a 30-min trial. **B** Presence probability density of agents in the arena.

We compute the presence probability density of agents in the arena (Fig. 4B): it shows that the robot tend to follow the walls as the fish do naturally.

For the three tested cases, we compute the statistics presented in Sect. 2.3 (Fig. 3). The corresponding similarity scores are shown in Fig. 2. The results of the **Control** case shows sustained aggregative and wall-following behaviours of the fish group. Fish also seldom pass through the centre of the arena, possibly in small short-lived sub-groups. There is group behavioural variability, especially on aggregative tendencies (measured by inter-individual distances), and wall-following behaviour (measured by the distance to the nearest wall), because each one of the 10 groups is composed of different fish *i.e.* 50 fish in total.

The similarity scores of the **Sim-MultiObj-\*** cases are often within the variance domain of the **Control** case, except for the inter-individual score. It suggests that groups incorporating the robot driven by an MLP evolved by NSGA-III exhibit relatively similar dynamics as a fish-only group, at least according to our proposed measures. However, it is still perfectible: the robot is some-times at the tail of the group, possibly because of gap created between the robot and the fish group by small trajectories errors (*e.g.* small loops shown in robot trajectories in Fig. 4A).

The **Sim-MonoObj-MLP** case sacrifices biomimetism to focus mainly on group-following behaviour: this translated into a higher inter-individual score than in the **Sim-MultiObj-\*** cases, and robot tend to follow closely the fish group. With **Sim-MonoObj-MLP**, the robot is going faster than the fish, and will fastly go back towards the centroid of the group if it is too far ahead of the group: this explains the large presence of loops in Fig. 4A. The **Sim-MonoObj-MLP** does not take into account behavioural diversity like the **Sim-MultiObj-\***, but focus on the one that is easier to find (namely the group-following behaviour) and stays stuck in this local optimum.

There are few differences between the results of the **Sim-MultiObj-MLP** and the **Sim-MultiObj-ESN** cases, the latter showing often slightly lower scores than the former. However, the **Sim-MultiObj-ESN** displays a large vari-ability of inter-individual scores, which could suggest that its expressivity could be sufficient to model agents with more biomimetic behaviours if the correct connection weights were found by the optimiser.

# 4  Discussion and Conclusion

We evolved artificial neural networks (ANN) to model the behaviour of a sin-gle fish in a group of 5 individuals. This ANN controller was used to drive the behaviour of a robot agent in simulations to integrate the group of fish by exhibiting biomimetic behavioural capabilities. Our methodology is similar to the calibration methodology developed in [7], but employs artificial neural networks instead of an expert-designed behavioural model. Artificial neural networks are black-box models that require few *a-priori* information about the target tasks.

We design a biomimetism score from behavioural measures to assess the biomimetism of robot behaviour. In particular, we measure the aggregative ten-dencies of the agents (inter-individual distances), their disposition to follow walls, to be aligned with the rest of the group (polarisation), and their distribution of linear and angular speeds.

However, finding ANN displaying behaviours of appropriate levels of biomimetism is a challenging issue, as fish behaviour is inherently multi-level (tail-beats as motor response vs individual trajectories vs collective dynam-ics), multi-modal (several kinds of behavioural patterns, and input/output sources), context-dependent (different behaviours depending on the spatial posi-tion and proximity to other agents) and stochastic (leading to individual and collectives choices and action selection) [9,29]. More specifically, fish dynamics involve trade-offs between social tendencies (aggregation, group formation), and response to the environment (wall-following, zone occupation); they also follow distinct movement patterns that allow them to move in a polarised group and react collectively to environmental and social cues.

We show that this artificial neural models can be optimised by using evolutionary algorithms, using the biomimetism score of robot behaviour as a fitness function. The best-performing evolved ANN controllers show competitive biomimetism scores compared to fish group behavioural variability. We demonstrate that taking into account genotypic and behavioural diversity in the optimisation process (through the use of the global multi-objective optimiser NSGA-III) improve the biomimetic scores of the evolved best-performing controllers. The ANN models evolved through mono-objective optimisation tend to focus more on evolving a group-following behaviour rather than a biomimetic agent.

Our approach is still perfectible, in particular, we only evolve the behaviour of a single agent in a group, rather than all agents of the group. This choice was motivated by the large increase in difficulty in evolving ANN models for the entire group, which would also involve additional behavioural trade-offs: *e.g.* individual free-will and autonomous dynamics, individuals leaving or re-joining the group. However, it also means that here the fish do not react to the robot in simulations because the fish behaviour is a replay of fish experimental trajectories recorded without robot.

Additionally, it may be possible to improve the performance (in term of biomimetism) of the multi-objective optimisation process by combining additional selection pressures as objectives (*i.e.* not just genotypic and behavioural diversity) [15]. We already include behavioural and phenotypic diversities as selection pressures to guide the optimisation process; however, taking into account phenotypic diversity can bias the optimisation algorithm to explore rather than exploit, which can prevent some desired phenotypes to be considered by the optimisation algorithm. An alternative would be to use angular diversity instead [31].

This study shows that ANN are good candidates to model individual and collective fish behaviours, in particular in the context of social bio-hybrid systems composed of animals and robots. By evolutionary computation, they can be calibrated on experimental data. This approach requires less *a priori* knowledge than equations or agent based modelling techniques. Although they are black box model, they could also produce interesting results from a biological point of view. Thus, ANN collective behaviour models can be an interesting approach to design animal and robot social interactions.

**Acknowledgement.** This work was funded by EU-ICT project 'ASSISIbf', no. 601074.

# References

1. Auger, A., Hansen, N.: A restart CMA evolution strategy with increasing population size. In: The 2005 IEEE Congress on Evolutionary Computation, vol. 2, pp. 1769–1776. IEEE (2005)
2. Bonnet, F., Cazenille, L., Gribovskiy, A., Halloy, J., Mondada, F.: Multi-robots control and tracking framework for bio-hybrid systems with closed-loop interaction. In: IEEE International Conference on Robotics and Automation (ICRA). IEEE (2017)

3. Bonnet, F., Cazenille, L., Seguret, A., Gribovskiy, A., Collignon, B., Halloy, J., Mondada, F.: Design of a modular robotic system that mimics small fish locomotion and body movements for ethological studies. Int. J. Adv. Robot. Syst. **14**(3) (2017). https://doi.org/10.1177/1729881417706628

4. Bonnet, F., Gribovskiy, A., Halloy, J., Mondada, F.: Closed-loop interactions between a shoal of zebrafish and a group of robotic fish in a circular corridor. Swarm Intell. 1–18 (2018)

5. Calovi, D.S., Litchinko, A., Lecheval, V., Lopez, U., Escudero, A.P., Chaté, H., Sire, C., Theraulaz, G.: Disentangling and modeling interactions in fish with burst-and-coast swimming reveal distinct alignment and attraction behaviors. PLoS Comput. Biol. **14**(1), e1005933 (2018)

6. Cazenille, L., Bredeche, N., Halloy, J.: Automated optimisation of multi-level models of collective behaviour in a mixed society of animals and robots. arXiv preprint arXiv:1602.05830 (2016)

7. Cazenille, L., et al.: Automated calibration of a biomimetic space-dependent model for zebrafish and robot collective behaviour in a structured environment. In: Mangan, M., Cutkosky, M., Mura, A., Verschure, P.F.M.J., Prescott, T., Lepora, N. (eds.) Living Machines 2017. LNCS (LNAI), vol. 10384, pp. 107–118. Springer, Cham (2017). https://doi.org/10.1007/978-3-319-63537-8_10

8. Cazenille, L., Collignon, B., Bonnet, F., Gribovskiy, A., Mondada, F., Bredeche, N., Halloy, J.: How mimetic should a robotic fish be to socially integrate into zebrafish groups? Bioinspiration Biomim. (2017)

9. Collignon, B., Séguret, A., Halloy, J.: A stochastic vision-based model inspired by zebrafish collective behaviour in heterogeneous environments. R. Soc. Open Sci. **3**(1) (2016). https://doi.org/10.1098/rsos.150473

10. Collignon, B., Séguret, A., Chemtob, Y., Cazenille, L., Halloy, J.: Collective departures in zebrafish: profiling the initiators. arXiv preprint arXiv:1701.03611 (2017)

11. Cybenko, G.: Approximation by superpositions of a sigmoidal function. Math. Control Signals Syst. **2**(4), 303–314 (1989)

12. Deb, K., Pratap, A., Agarwal, S., Meyarivan, T.: A fast and elitist multiobjective genetic algorithm: NSGA-II. IEEE Trans. Evol. Comput. **6**(2), 182–197 (2002)

13. Deutsch, A., Theraulaz, G., Vicsek, T.: Collective motion in biological systems. Interface Focus **2**(6), 689 (2012)

14. Deza, M., Deza, E.: Dictionary of Distances. Elsevier, Amsterdam (2006)

15. Doncieux, S., Mouret, J.B.: Beyond black-box optimization: a review of selective pressures for evolutionary robotics. Evol. Intell. **7**(2), 71–93 (2014)

16. Fortin, F.A., De Rainville, F.M., Gardner, M.A., Parizeau, M., Gagné, C.: DEAP: evolutionary algorithms made easy. J. Mach. Learn. Res. **13**, 2171–2175 (2012)

17. Halloy, J., Sempo, G., Caprari, G., Rivault, C., Asadpour, M., Tâche, F., Said, I., Durier, V., Canonge, S., Amé, J.: Social integration of robots into groups of cockroaches to control self-organized choices. Science **318**(5853), 1155–1158 (2007)

18. Herbert-Read, J.E., Romenskyy, M., Sumpter, D.J.: A turing test for collective motion. Biol. Lett. **11**(12), 20150674 (2015)

19. Ishibuchi, H., Imada, R., Setoguchi, Y., Nojima, Y.: Performance comparison of NSGA-II and NSGA-III on various many-objective test problems. In: IEEE Congress on Evolutionary Computation (CEC), pp. 3045–3052. IEEE (2016)

20. Jaeger, H.: Echo state network. Scholarpedia **2**(9), 2330 (2007)

21. Jiang, F., Berry, H., Schoenauer, M.: Supervised and evolutionary learning of echo state networks. In: Rudolph, G., Jansen, T., Beume, N., Lucas, S., Poloni, C. (eds.) PPSN 2008. LNCS, vol. 5199, pp. 215–224. Springer, Heidelberg (2008). https://doi.org/10.1007/978-3-540-87700-4_22

22. King, S.Y., Hwang, J.N.: Neural network architectures for robotic applications. IEEE Trans. Robot. Autom. **5**(5), 641–657 (1989)
23. Mondada, F., Halloy, J., Martinoli, A., Correll, N., Gribovskiy, A., Sempo, G., Siegwart, R., Deneubourg, J.: A general methodology for the control of mixed natural-artificial societies. In: Kernbach, S. (ed.) Handbook of Collective Robotics: Fundamentals and Challenges, pp. 547–585. Pan Stanford, Singapore (2013). Chapter 15
24. Mouret, J.B., Doncieux, S.: Encouraging behavioral diversity in evolutionary robotics: an empirical study. Evol. Comput. **20**(1), 91–133 (2012)
25. Norgaard, M., Ravn, O., Poulsen, N., Hansen, L.: Neural Networks for Modelling and Control of Dynamic Systems: A Practitioner's Handbook. Advanced Textbooks in Control and Signal Processing. Springer, Berlin (2000)
26. Polydoros, A., Nalpantidis, L., Krüger, V.: Advantages and limitations of reservoir computing on model learning for robot control. In: IROS Workshop on Machine Learning in Planning and Control of Robot Motion, Hamburg (2015)
27. Salimans, T., Ho, J., Chen, X., Sutskever, I.: Evolution strategies as a scalable alternative to reinforcement learning. arXiv preprint arXiv:1703.03864 (2017)
28. Séguret, A., Collignon, B., Cazenille, L., Chemtob, Y., Halloy, J.: Loose social organisation of AB strain zebrafish groups in a two-patch environment. arXiv preprint arXiv:1701.02572 (2017)
29. Sumpter, D.J.T., Szorkovszky, A., Kotrschal, A., Kolm, N., Herbert-Read, J.E.: Using activity and sociability to characterize collective motion. Philos. Trans. R. Soc. B **373**(1746) (2018). https://doi.org/10.1098/rstb.2017.0015
30. Sumpter, D.J., Mann, R.P., Perna, A.: The modelling cycle for collective animal behaviour. Interface Focus **2**(6), 764–773 (2012)
31. Szubert, M., Kodali, A., Ganguly, S., Das, K., Bongard, J.C.: Reducing antagonism between behavioral diversity and fitness in semantic genetic programming. In: Proceedings of the Genetic and Evolutionary Computation Conference, pp. 797–804. ACM (2016)
32. Turnstrøm, K., Katz, Y., Ioannou, C.C., Huepe, C., Lutz, M.J., Couzin, I.D.: Collective states, multistability and transitional behavior in schooling fish. PLoS Comput. Biol. **9**(2), e1002915 (2013)
33. Yuan, Y., Xu, H., Wang, B.: An improved NSGA-III procedure for evolutionary many-objective optimization. In: Proceedings of the 2014 Annual Conference on Genetic and Evolutionary Computation, pp. 661–668. ACM (2014)

# The Impact of Nature Inspired Algorithms on Biomimetic Approach in Architectural and Urban Design

Natasha Chayaamor-Heil[(✉)] [iD]

MAP-Maacc, CNRS-MCC, UMR 3495, ENSA PARIS-La-Villette, Paris, France
natasha.heil@paris-lavillette.archi.fr

**Abstract.** At the time when the value of architecture no longer results from creating shapes in space, but rather fostering relationships within it. A concept of architectural design becomes a strategic process rather than an object. Biological inspiration is dominating the era, and has its impact in diverse domains, including architecture and urbanism. The study of biomimetics bridges the biological functions, processes and organizational principles found in nature with our designs and technologies. Recently there are numerous mathematical algorithms have been developed along with the knowledge transferring process from the life forms to solve the design problems. Output of biomimetics study includes not only physical applications, but also various computation methods that can be applied in different areas. We can learn from biological processes and principles to design and develop a number of different kinds of optimisation algorithms that have been widely used in both theoretical study and practical applications. In this paper, we discuss and present the impact of nature inspired algorithms and digital advanced on biomimetic approach in architectural and urban design. We demonstrate how architects reuse bio-inspired computing to solve complex problem or optimise their designs, and nonetheless, how architects use algorithmic architecture software to directly transpose the complexity of nature's principles into their design process.

**Keywords:** Biomimetics · Biological process · Nature inspired algorithms
Architectural and urban design

## 1  Introduction

Nature has always been an inspirational source for architects and designers. This inspiration has given highly efficient designs in various fields. One of the best concept in which, we see nature as the influential source of inspiration. Biomimetics means imitating of biological processes. Biomimetics is a new science and design discipline that studies nature's models and then emulates these forms, processes, systems and strategies to solve the problems of our time [1]. In September 2015, the Economic, Social and Environmental Council of Paris issued a noticed entitled '*Biomimicry: taking inspiration from nature to innovate sustainably*' [2]. Architecture is presented as one of the promising areas of application and there is evidence of an emerging of biomimetics in

© Springer International Publishing AG, part of Springer Nature 2018
V. Vouloutsi et al. (Eds.): Living Machines 2018, LNAI 10928, pp. 97–109, 2018.
https://doi.org/10.1007/978-3-319-95972-6_11

architectural design activity capable of responding to current environmental issues. Undoubtedly, architects have been inspired by nature to stimulate a novelty in their designs, but beyond the appearance of a tree, a branch or a simple leaf, there are mathematical patterns at play in nature. Understanding nature's basic algorithms allows architects and designers to explore natural systems that can be translated into efficient designs and awe-inspiring architecture. In fact, nature as inspiration is often combined with mathematics in order to move beyond the superficial inspiration and realize a design [3]. The fluid order in nature is characterized by repetition, growth and change with the fundamental rules that generate order in nature not being absolute but relative, flexible and soft [4]. In contemporary architecture design, digital media is increasingly being used not as a representational tool for visualization but as a generative tool for the derivation of form and its transformation [5]. The use of computational techniques increasingly saturates development biology, from the acquisition, processing and analysis of experimental data to the construction of models of organisms. Similar to the biological processes, it is a process of shape/pattern development enabled by computation but in digital environment. However when it comes to algorithms it is not just about software's and computers, they describe a process of logical thinking [6]. Yet beyond this, a computational approach to architecture enables the generation of the previously unseen forms that can longer be conceived of through traditional methods become possible, thus opening up new realms.

## 2   The Overview of Biomimetics

### 2.1   The Emergence of Biomimetics

In the 1950s biophysicist and engineer Otto H. Schmitt established the field of biomedical engineering and proposed the term 'biomimetics' for this new science of the emerging engineer. The term 'bionics' in the United States, invented by the neurologist Jack E. Steel, and 'bionik' in Germany, originating from the work of the biologist Werner Nachtigall, appeared in the late 1950s. These terms referred to the study of the structures and functions of biological systems as models for the design and engineering of materials and machines. This field of investigation developed during the 1960s and remained mainly for robotics. During the 1970s, the concept of bionics became widespread among engineers and designers within companies. Nachtigall describes the concept as: 'Bionics is the process of taking nature as a source of inspiration for independent technical design' [7]. The term 'biomimicry' appeared in 1980 and was popularized by the biologist and environmentalist Janine Benyus, author of the book *Biomimicry: Innovation Inspired by Nature* [8]. Biomimicry is defined in her book as a new science that studies nature in order to imitate it or to draw inspiration from it to solve human problems. The concept of biomimicry, as supported by J. Benyus, proposes to draw inspiration from the brilliant ideas developed in nature to design our innovations from a perspective of sustainability. Benyus suggests looking at nature as a model, measure or mentor.

## 2.2   The Process Sequences in Biomimetic Research

If we consider the biomimetic design process as a whole, from the initial idea to the final product, two approaches have been identified [9]. The first approach starts from a human need or a design problem then examines the ways in which organisms or ecosystems found in nature solve this problem. This is a *problem-oriented approach* (Top-down or design looking to biology). This approach is actually carried out by designers who, after identifying initial objectives and design parameters, seek solutions in the nature world.

The second approach is to identify a particular characteristic, behavior, or function in an organism or ecosystem, and then look for the design problem that could be addressed. It is a *solution-oriented approach* (Bottom-up or biology influencing design). This approach is where knowledge in biology influences human design. It is conducted by biologists or scientists who are looking for possible applications relevant to the design.

## 2.3   The Levels of Biomimetics

Biomimetics inspires architecture in different levels as biology does in the nature and these levels can be summarized under three categories: form, process and ecosystem. Form and processes can mimic in an ecosystem. This approach is methodized by Zari [10] to specifically apply to a design or an architectural problem. The three levels mentioned above are rearranged and separated into five sub-levels (Fig. 1), and explained how biomimetics is considered for a design problem.

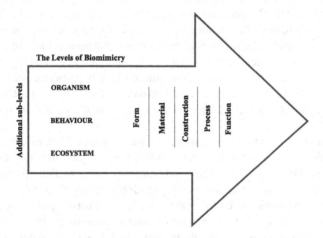

**Fig. 1.** Theoretical framework for the levels and additional sub-levels of biomimetics in architecture, adapted from [10]

*The organism level* refers to a specific organism like a plant or an animal and may involve mimicking part of or the whole organism, solutions related to efficient energy usage and materials, which are established already. In brief, it is mimicking an organism's physical attributes.

*The behavior level* refers to mimicking organism's behavior, to explore and understand how an organism relates and behaves to a larger context. It is possible to understand this level with observing how an organism tends to operate in its environmental capacity and within limits of energy and material availability.

*The ecosystem level* of biomimetics intends to create a whole ecosystem, which incorporates the other two levels to achieve a sustainable environment. This means a deep comprehension of ecology and the regenerative process of the nature, which may begin from a small scale and tends to lead to a bigger scale of thinking like green cities or eco-cities.

Within each of the three levels, a further five possible dimensions to the mimicry exist. The design may be biomimetic for example in terms of what it looks like (form), what it is made out of (material), how it is made (construction), how it works (process) or what it is able to do (function) [10].

## 3   Algorithms in Nature

The real beauty of nature inspired algorithms lies in the fact that it receives its sole inspiration from nature. They have the ability to describe and resolve complex relationships from intrinsically very simple initial conditions and rules with little or no knowledge of the search space. Nature is the perfect example for optimization, because if we closely examine each and every features or phenomenon in nature it always find the optimal strategy, still addressing complex interaction among organisms ranging from microorganism to fully fledged human beings, balancing the ecosystem, maintaining diversity, adaptation, physical phenomenon like river formation, forest fire, cloud, rain etc. [12]. Nature inspired algorithms is meta-heuristics that mimics the nature for solving optimization problems opening a new era in computation [11]. For the past decades, numerous research efforts have been concentrated in this particular area. Still being young and the results being very amazing, broadens the scope and viability of Bio Inspired Algorithms (BIAs) exploring new areas of application and more opportunities in computing.

Optimization is a commonly encountered mathematical problem in architectural and engineering disciplines. It literally means finding the best possible/desirable solution. Optimization problems are wide ranging and numerous, hence methods for solving these problems ought to be, an active research topic. Optimization algorithms can be either deterministic or stochastic in nature. Former methods to solve optimization problems require enormous computational efforts, which tend to fail as the problem size increases. This is the motivation for employing bio-inspired stochastic optimization algorithms as computationally efficient alternatives to deterministic approach. Meta-heuristics are based on the iterative improvement of either a population of solutions (as in Evolutionary algorithms, Swarm based algorithms) or a single solution (eg. Tabu Search) and mostly employ randomization and local search to solve a given optimization problem.

### 3.1    A Multidisciplinary Approach

Interdisciplinary collaboration is necessarily essential in biomimetic design process where the knowledge from different fields converges, which leads to innovation and increase the novelty of design ideas. Nature is providing a tremendous amount of information implemented into these scientific fields, assisting contemporary investigations that vary from the analysis of the human body's structural element: bone's micro-mechanical configuration [13], to the effect of the micro-fibril orientation into plant growth. However it must also be understood that as these design processes requires the collaboration between the architect and the biologist, a similar collaboration might be required between an architect and a computer programmer or mathematician to create the complex algorithms that are used in nature. As the architect though can create the concept and workflow may not be skilled enough in making the algorithm. In nature, the development of the life form and structure is complex; it is a kind of free-from, free-edge and non-linear structure, which can sometimes be modeled mathematically. There is a mathematics lies behind numerical pattern in nature, thus it is not a simple task for an architect to understand and demonstrate more advanced programming techniques with processing that focus on algorithms and simulation of natural formations. There are some distinct collaboration between computer programmers and architects for an advanced research in architectural project that produce a free-from and complex structure as in nature. One known is the work of Prof. Helmut Pottmann, who has collaborated with a number of architects (an example of a project, Fig. 2) [15]. He is also the author of a notable book 'Architectural Geometry' [14]. The book demonstrates some cutting-edge of complex geometrical modeling that needs a mathematically well trained to be able to produces such a models. These include central concepts on freeform curves and surfaces, differential geometry, kinematic geometry, mesh processing, digital reconstruction, and optimization of shapes [14]. Likewise, these concepts appear in nature.

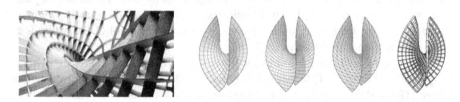

**Fig. 2.** Project designing grid structures using asymptotic curve networks, humanizing digital reality: design modeling symposium Paris 2017 [15]

Today, there are few known examples of architectural construction that are completely generated from scratch by algorithms based on biomimetic approach, for example, The algorithm developed by Chris Bosse for the design of the National Aquatics Centre in Beijing, the 'Water cube' [16], the building's form is inspired by natural formation of soap bubbles, crystals, cells and molecular structures, these are the most efficient subdivision of 3dimensional space with equally sized cells. In this design, it moves the algorithmic process one step further where a single material system produces structure and at the same time defines space. Structural stability is a priori assured by the design choice itself, the formation of a stable configuration of the geometry of bubble packing that also occurs spontaneously in many natural systems (Fig. 3).

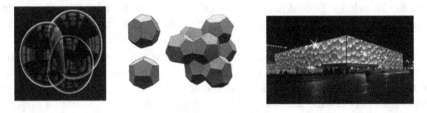

**Fig. 3.** (Left) The efficiency of soap-bubble structures is exploited with Weaire–Phelan geometrical principle, (Right) National Aquatics Centre in Beijing, the Watercube by Chris Bosse, 2008, [17]

The next chapter, we will present some case studies on the utilization of nature inspired algorithms within a framework of biomimetic design process in architecture along with the use of computational design and the relevant applications in architectural and urban domain.

## 4    The Biomimetic Framework in Architecture

*Biomimetic architecture* is a contemporary approach of architecture that seeks innovative and sustainable solutions in nature [18], without attempting to replicate its forms, but by seeking to understand the rules that govern them. The objective of biomimetic architecture no longer consists solely in giving form and measurement to space but also in developing synergistic relationships between the construct and its environment. The heuristic approach to biomimetics consists in bringing architecture to '*vitalism*' beyond the mechanistic view of life [19]. The biomimetic architecture could be at the origin of a transformation of the role of architects evolving from the control of the nature to a lasting participation with the nature.

Original method of biomimetic architecture is a cross-disciplinary approach between biology and architecture. This method is initially called '*Bau-Bionik*', coined by an architect, Göran Pohl and a biologist, Nachtigall [20]. As a result of a combined effort by the two disciplines describes the principles which can be used to compare nature, design and technology, how biology can be used as a source of inspiration and 'translated' in building and architectural solutions along with current advanced technology. However, it is not a trivial task to understand the principles that govern the living, especially for architects who need to search for an elegant biological analogy and transfer it to solve problem in architectural designs. One must only then be cautious of too direct interpretation [20]. Inspirations from nature for architecture will not function if they do not well abstract within the context of an interdisciplinary analogue.

In the book '*Bionik als Wissenschaft*' [21], which applies the theory of cognition to biomimetics, signified this process in three-step: *Research → Abstraction → Implementation.* By observing a cognitive biomimetic design process within the context of an interdisciplinary, '*identification*' and '*abstraction*' often proves to be one of the most important as well as most difficult steps in a biomimetic project [9]. Thus, we have found two common difficulties for an architect to apply biomimetic methodology into their design process, we define the difficulties in two transitions; *1. What to look for in nature? 2. How to interpret natures' principles and transfer into design phase?* (Fig. 4)

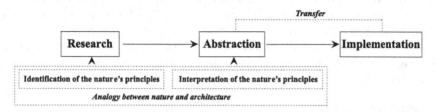

**Fig. 4.** The two transitions of a cognitive biomimetic design process within the context of an interdisciplinary, adapt from [21]

In view of these two transitions, it is possible to distinguish two postures of the use of biomimetic approach in architecture: *an indirect posture* where the architects explore biologically inspired computing as a tool derived from biomimetic interdisciplinary collaboration between biologists and computer scientists, and *a direct posture* where the architect integrates directly an interdisciplinary biomimetic activity and use computational algorithms to transpose biological knowledge in its architectural design process.

### 4.1  An Indirect Biomimetic Methodology in Architectural Design Activity

In many bio-inspired architectural design activity, architects construct design methods but the form and technical processes of their projects can be completely different from what is found in nature. These design methods generally rely on computer techniques such as particle systems, genetic algorithms or multi-agent systems whose functioning is bio-inspired. Bio-inspired computing, short for biologically inspired computing, is a field of research that breaks down into subfields including connectionism, social behavior and emergence. It is close to artificial intelligence or artificial life. It is related to the fields of biology, computer science and mathematics. Briefly, it is a matter of creating innovative algorithms to solve known problems, such as optimization problems, for example, based on phenomena observed in nature. The following case study presents the use of a biomimetic algorithm capable of designing an optimized transport network between different cities while taking into account a certain number of characteristics (population, points of interest, possible breakdowns on the network, etc.).

**Case study: Biomimetic Algorithms: Slime Mold Inspired Network Design**
It all began in the early 2000s when a team of Japanese and Hungarian researchers discovered that a kind of slime mold called *Physarum Polycephal* is able to find its way in a labyrinth [22]. This mold appears to be intelligent and capable of exploring its environment to find the shortest paths to food sources [23]. Based on these observations, an algorithm was constructed; mimicking the behavior of *Physarum Polycephal* called

the *Physarum Solver* [24]. This algorithm is able to find an optimal path in a network and proves to be more efficient than the classical algorithms when the number of nodes of the network is very important. This stunning algorithm can for example solve problems of optimization of a transport network. How to connect cities in a minimum of lines with maximum efficiency, that is to say taking into account population density, geography, possible breakdowns or accidents that may occur on the network and etc. It has been tested in several cities and countries: the New York City street network, the railway network in Japan and other transportation networks in Mexico and China [25]. It is clear that this type of algorithm can be used by urban planners or architects to design, for example, optimized and resilient distribution networks (for example, energy, water and etc.) (Fig. 5).

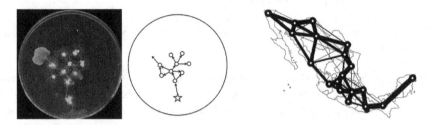

**Fig. 5.** (Left) The behavior of the *Physarum Polycephal* observed in a petri dish and the bio-inspired mathematical model of the exploratory behavior of *Physarum Polycephal* [26], (Right) the transportation network in Mexico City developed by the *Physarum Solver* [25]

The following figure describes a possible architectural design process resulting from collaboration between biologists, computer scientists and architects (Fig. 6).

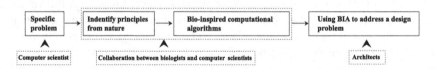

**Fig. 6.** The steps of an indirect biomimetic design process in architectural activity, [27]

This framework of an indirect biomimetic methodology does not directly concern the architectural field. It produces innovation (optimization) in the field of computing.

It is clear that in such a process, it is the algorithm used that is innovative because it is designed in a biomimetic approach between computer scientists and biologists. The architect, by reusing these algorithms, produces an optimized architectural and urban design but not necessarily innovative. That's why we called this process an indirect biomimetic methodology.

### 4.2 A Direct Biomimetic Methodology in Architectural Design Activity

In the case study presented below and unlike the previous one, there is direct collaboration between the architect and the biologist and the use of computational algorithms to support the transfer of nature's principles into the design process. The collaborative design activity consists of the initial phase *'specific design problem'* that architect specify, then the architects themselves observe in nature and collaborate with biologists to identify the strategy and abstract the design principles from nature to solve the problem in architectural and urban design.

**Case study: District 11 – Skolkovo Innovation Center and Thermal Regulation System of Emperor Penguins, 2017**
Inspired by the complex social behaviour of group organization of emperor penguins that protects from the cold and save energy. *Agence d'Architecture A. Bechu & Associés* collaborates with biologists to study the thermal regulation system of emperor penguins on how a penguin colony works as a system to allow all penguins a chance to be warm. The architects use the computational algorithm to transpose this principle into a complex town planning, which will be housing researchers and their families in single-family homes as well as providing them with a living environment that encourages social inter-action. Much like penguins on an ice shelf forming a circle to share their heat, a hundred villas are grouped ten by ten in a vast clearing surrounded by a waterway able to drain away the melting snow. Each of the villas will be unique, giving occupants their own identity within the urban ensemble, but will all feature a modular concrete frame, green roof, and use of renewable energy and water recycling. Public functions and common shared services will be located in a central area, in order to create a social link between residents [28] (Fig. 7).

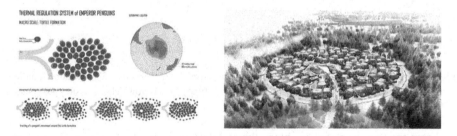

**Fig. 7.** (Left) Thermal regulation system of Emperor penguins [29], (Right) District 11, Skolkovo innovation center, Russian [28]

**Case study: AEOMIUM: A Fog Sensor Dome to Produce Drinking Water in Arid Area. Site Study: Burkina Faso, Africa, 2017**
This architectural project 'AEONIUM' [30] proposes a fog sensor built near a typical rural village of Burkina Fuso. The operation of the dome is inspired by the metabolism of Xerophile plants (for example, succulents) and their different strategies developed to capture and store the water contained in the ambient air. By bringing the source of drinking water to the villages, the installation is a tribute to the tradition of the water carriers since it facilitates the activity while creating a pleasant meeting place. The project is realized by the groups of students within the program of Biomimetic project applied algorithmic and digital method for architectural design and fabrication at the Laval University in Canada [31]. The project was entirely realized with the help of an

algorithmic software Grasshopper [32] and algorithmic families (fractals, AC, AG, complexity, etc.) while adopting a biomimetic approach. The architects have made an analogy between the principles of the plant and the design concept and once the biological principles are understood as a design task, the architect transcript them in Grasshopper. This new way of reasoning allows the architects to better understand the functioning of the biological models studied, since they respond to an algorithmic logic like Grasshopper. In this project, the algorithms in grasshopper first and foremost helped the architects to develop all the kinematics of opening and closing of their protective envelope, the principle of which stemmed from the in-depth study of the functioning of stomata in Xerophile plants (Fig. 8).

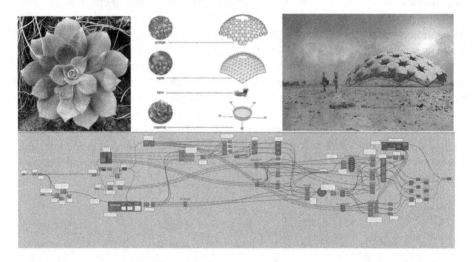

**Fig. 8.** (From top left to right) The succulent plant *Aeonium percarneum* [33], the functionality of the fog sensor dome, the rendering of the dome prototype [30], (Below) The Grasshopper canvas of the AEONIUM design process [30]

From the two case studies above, the architect seeks to understand application of algorithm based on biomimetic principles to the architectural context. The architects involve directly in biomimetic activity, from the initial to the final phase. Additionally, at present, the algorithm scripting in Grasshopper tool [32] are being used to transpose nature's principles towards biomimetic approach within the architectural domain. Grasshopper is an extremely powerful tool but unfortunately it's still little known specially in bio-inspired architectural field. In somehow, any natural principle can be retransmitted as lines of code to determine a sequence of actions composing the biological system, but this way requires strong knowledge in computer science and code, which is not necessarily the case in an architect. With Grasshopper it is now possible to simplify all this procedure through clusters. Indeed thanks to these small 'boxes' closing actions predefined by the software, it is possible to design sequences of operations so as to reproduce the biological system explicitly and visualize the result in real time.

The following figure describes a possible architectural design process resulting from direct collaboration between architects and biologists and the use of computational algorithms to transpose nature's principles into design phase (Fig. 9).

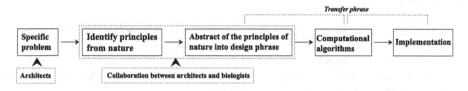

**Fig. 9.** The steps of a direct biomimetic design process in architectural activity, [27]

The unique framework of biomimetic design is directly related to the architectural field. It produces innovation directly in the field of architecture. This is a direct biomimetic design process because there is an effective interdisciplinary collaboration between architects, biologists and computer programmer, the latter welcoming with great interest the idea of developing this type of collaboration.

## 5   Conclusion

This paper is an investigation into the development of design method based on biological principles that are applied and correlated with nature inspired algorithm and computational design in the field of architecture. It is important to materialize the architectural output based on application of biomimetics. It can be concluded that the stated methodological frameworks enable the designer to produce an efficient architecture in terms of innovation and sustainability. But at the same time this approach relies on very specific knowledge, skills and tools. Architects have been searching for answers from nature to their complex questions about different kinds of structures, and they have mimicked a lot of forms from nature to create better and more efficient structures for different architectural purposes. Without computers these complex ways and forms of structures couldn't been mimicked and thus using computers had risen the way of mimicking and taking inspiration from nature because it is considered a very sophisticated and accurate tool for simulation and computing, as a result designers can imitate different nature's models in spite of its complexity. Bio-inspired algorithms are going to be a new revolution in computer science. Nevertheless, nature-inspired algorithms are among the most powerful algorithms for optimization, which is going to have a wide impact on future generation computing. Though these algorithms are becoming widespread in many design and fabrication industries, perhaps their best use is in architectural design, where they can enable architects to work in intuitive and nondeterministic ways. Thus new and innovative designs can be produced that achieve structural and environmental performances that were once considered to be post-design optimization processes.

**Acknowledgements.** This article is part of an extended research of Biomimicry in Architecture: State, methods and tools, which is published in les Cahiers la recherche architecturale, urbaine et paysagère, issue Innover 2018 (https://journals.openedition.org/craup/309). I would like to thank

François Guéna, the director of Map-maacc UMR 3495, Paris, France and Pierre Côté, Professor at Laval University, Canada who provided expertise that greatly assisted on this subject.

# References

1. Biomimicry Guild: Innovation Inspired by Nature Work Book, Biomimicry Guild (2007)
2. Ricard, P.: Le biomimétisme: s'inspirer de la nature pour innover durablement, Les projet d'avis du Conseil économique, social et environnemental (CESE), Paris, Septembre 2015
3. Toyo, I.: Algorithms are Nothing More than an Opportunity to Create Architecture that Respires, pp. 36–45. The Japan Architect, Japan (2010)
4. Rian, I.M.: Tree - inspired dendriforms and fractal like branching structures in architecture: a brief historical overview. Front. Archit. Res. **3**(3), 298–323 (2014)
5. Kolarevic, B.: Architecture in the Digital Age – Design and Manufacturing. Spon Press/ Taylor & Francis Group, London/New York (2003)
6. Bagul, P., Uke, N.: Algorithms in Architectural Design. Int. J. Electron. Commun. Comput. Eng. **6**(4), 126–130 (2014)
7. Wahl, D.C.: Bionics vs. biomimicry: from control of nature. WIT Trans. Ecol. Environ. **87**, 289–298 (2006). W. Press, Éd.
8. Benyus, J.: Biomimicry: Innovation Inspired by Nature. Harper Collins Publishers, New York (1997)
9. Speck, T.: Process sequences in biomimetic research. Des. Nat. IV **114**, 3–11 (2008). Brebbia (ed.) WIT Press
10. Zari, M.P.: Biomimetic approaches to architectural design for increased sustainability. In: Sustainable Building Conference, Auckland (2007)
11. Siva Sathya, B.: A survey of bio-inspired optimization algorithms. Int. J. Soft Comput. Eng. **2**(2), 137–151 (2012)
12. Sidhu, T., Samarabandu, J., Premaratne, U.: A new biologically inspired optimization algorithm. In: Fourth International Conference on Industrial and Information Systems, ICIIS, Sri Lanka, pp. 28–31, (2009)
13. Huiskes, R.: If bone is the answer, then what is the question. J. Anat. **197**, 145–156 (2000)
14. Pottmann, H., Asperl, A., Hofer, M., Kilian, A.: Architectural Geometry, Bentley Institute Press, Exton (2007)
15. Schling, E., Hitrec, D., Barthel, R.: Designing grid structures using asymptotic curve networks. In: De Rycke, K., Gengnagel, C., Baverel, O., Burry, J., Mueller, C., Nguyen, M.M., Rahm, P., Ramsgaard Thomsen, M. (eds.) Humanizing Digital Reality, pp. 125–140. Springer, Singapore (2018). https://doi.org/10.1007/978-981-10-6611-5_12
16. Water cube. http://www.chrisbosse.de/watercube/. Accessed 29 May 2018
17. https://en.wikipedia.org/wiki/Beijing_National_Aquatics_Center. Accessed 29 May 2018
18. Pawlyn, M.: Biomimicry in Architecture. RIBA Publishing, London (2011)
19. Gruber, P.: The signs of life in architecture. Bioinspir. Biomim. **3**, 023001 (2008)
20. Nachtigall, W.: Bau-Bionik: Natur ← Analogien → Technik. Springer, Berlin (2003). https://doi.org/10.1007/978-3-662-05991-3
21. Nachtigall, W.: Bionik als Wissenschaft: Erkennen-Abstrahieren-Umsetzen. Springer, Berlin (2010). https://doi.org/10.1007/978-3-642-10320-9
22. Nakagaki, T., et al.: Intelligence: maze-solving by amoeboid organism. Nature **407**, 470 (2000)
23. Nakagaki, T., et al.: Otaining multiple separate food sources: behavioural intelligence in the Physarum plamodium. R. Soc. **271**, 2305–2310 (2004)

24. Tero, A., et al.: Physarum solver: a biologically inspired method of road-network navigation. Phys. A: Stat. Mech. Appl. **363**, 1 (2005)
25. Mahadevan, S.: A biologically inspired network design model. Sci. Rep. **5**, 10794 (2015)
26. Adamatzky, A.: Slime mould processors, logic gates and sensors. Philos. Trans. R. Soc. Math. Phys. Eng. Sci. **373**(2046) (2005)
27. Chayaamor-Heil, N., Guéna, F., Hannachi-Belkadi, N.: Biomimicry in Architecture: State, methods and tools, Les Cahiers de la recherché Architecturale Urbaine et Paysagère (2017). http://journals.openedition.org/craup/
28. Agence d'architecture A.Bechu. http://www.anthonybechu.com/fr. Accessed 1 Feb 2018
29. Asknature. https://asknature.org. Accessed 15 Mar 2018
30. AEONIUM. https://aeonium.wixsite.com/project. Accessed 29 May 2018
31. AENIUM project is part of the program Méthodes en Architecture en Fabrication numériques ARC-6046, Automne 2017, University Laval, by Prof. Pierre Côté, Marie-Jeanne Allaire-Côté, Théo Jarrand, Marc-Antoine Juneau and Josianne Ouellet-Daudelin
32. Grasshopper: Algorithmic modeling for Rhino. http://www.grasshopper3d.com. Accessed 15 Jan 2018
33. Wikipedia Aeonium. https://fr.wikipedia.org/wiki/Aeonium. Accessed 29 May 2018

# Spiders' Ballooning Flight as a Model for the Exploration of Hazardous Atmospheric Weather Conditions

Moonsung Cho[1,2(✉)], Klaus Affeld[3], Peter Neubauer[1], and Ingo Rechenberg[2]

[1] Technical University of Berlin, Institute of Biotechnology,
Ackerstraße 76/ACK 24, 13355 Berlin, Germany
m.cho@campus.tu-berlin.de
[2] Technical University of Berlin, Institute of Bionics and Evolution Technique,
Ackerstraße 76/ACK 1, 13355 Berlin, Germany
[3] Charité – Universitätsmedizin Berlin, Biofluid Mechanics Lab,
Augustenburger Platz 1, 13353 Berlin, Germany

**Abstract.** Passive flight in living things, such as in maple or dandelion seeds, is one of the most primitive methods of aerial dispersal. This mechanism is robust and efficient, as it utilizes the present wind conditions. Passive flight is used not only by plant seeds but also by some animals. Spiders use fine, flexible silk filaments to fly, a behavior known as ballooning. This capability is distinct from that of other winged insects, as some ballooning spiders can travel hundreds of kilometers, reaching as high as 4.5 km above sea level. Various hypotheses explain the physical mechanism of ballooning flight. Some studies have shown that turbulent flow in the atmospheric boundary layer enhances spiders' flight endurance. This mechanism may be usefully applied in the exploration of hazardous weather conditions, such as severe storms, tornadoes, and clear-air turbulence, in the atmosphere, if we scale them up. In this paper, the authors briefly introduce the flight characteristics of the ballooning structure (i.e., the spider body and silk filaments), which were revealed in a simulation using a bead-spring model, and examine the possibility of scaling up ballooning flight from 25 mg to 1–2.5 kg for the exploration of hazardous weather conditions in the atmosphere.

**Keywords:** Ballooning spider · Passive flight · Hurricane · Clear-air turbulence
Atmospheric boundary layer

## 1 Introduction

The study of hazardous weather conditions in the atmosphere is important for public safety. Hurricanes, typhoons, tornadoes, and severe storms can threaten life and property [1]. Clear-air turbulence may cause unsafety in aircraft operation [2]. These hazardous phenomena have been studied and measured via radar, satellite, and stationary instruments. Recently, more direct methods have been employed, such as the National Oceanic and Atmospheric Administration's (NOAA's) deployment of dropsondes from a highly

© Springer International Publishing AG, part of Springer Nature 2018
V. Vouloutsi et al. (Eds.): Living Machines 2018, LNAI 10928, pp. 110–114, 2018.
https://doi.org/10.1007/978-3-319-95972-6_12

instrumented aircraft and the Taiwan Aerosonde Team's (TAT's) operation of an aerosonde (unmanned air vehicle) to acquire more accurate data [3, 4]. However, these methods are risky and relatively expensive and require highly experienced personnel [4].

In researching severe and unknown weather conditions, the passive flight mechanism may be useful due to its adaptability and high robustness [5]. For many years, the authors have studied passive flight in spiders utilizing fine, flexible silk filaments for aerial dispersal. The authors hypothesized that shear flow and vorticity (i.e., coherent structure) in atmospheric turbulence enhance the spiders' buoyancy and allow them to achieve long-range dispersal [6]. In this paper, we propose a macroscopic model for ballooning flight at the kilogram scale. This model can be used to research clear-air turbulence, hurricanes, typhoons, and tornadoes.

## 2    Characteristics of a Spider's Ballooning Structure

In a recent study, Cho et al. [6] showed how spiders use abundant nanoscale multi-fibers for aerial dispersal. These flexible silk filaments adapt to turbulent airflow, enhancing the buoyancy of the spider [6–8] (Fig. 1). Cho et al. explained that low-Reynolds-number fluid dynamics—in which the viscous force of the air is much more dominant than the inertial force of the air, —plays a vital role in ballooning flight. The low-Reynolds-number fluid dynamics in spider ballooning is characterized firstly by the large drag coefficient of a filament, because of the dominant viscous flow, and secondly by the anisotropic drag of a filament, which means that the drag of a filament changes according to the direction of the fluid flow [9, 10].

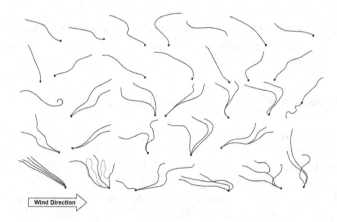

**Fig. 1.** Sketches of the ballooning structure (i.e., spider body and silk filaments) affected by turbulence in the atmospheric boundary layer [6].

The characteristics of a spider's ballooning structure can be summarized as follows:

1. The filament should generate enough aerodynamic drag to counteract its weight.
2. The ratio of normal drag to tangential drag should be about 2:1.

3. The filament should be highly flexible.
4. Most of the weight should be located at one end of the filament.

Our simulation used a bead-spring model, which is frequently employed in investigating the dynamics of microswimmers and in polymer physics [11]; it revealed that the settling speed of the ballooning structure in low-Reynolds-number shear flow decreases as the shear rate increases (Fig. 2). This reduction in the settling speed is caused firstly by the geometrical shape of the ballooning structure and secondly by the generation of fluid-dynamic forces in nonuniform flows. Additionally, we found that the ballooning structure could become trapped in a vortex flow.

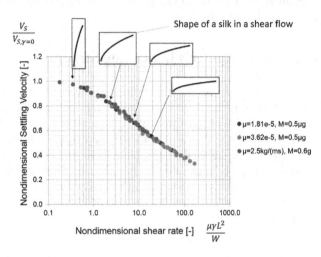

**Fig. 2.** Influence of shear flow on the ballooning structure simulated using a bead-spring model. $V_S$: settling speed, $V_{S,\gamma=0}$: settling speed at a shear rate of zero, $\mu$: dynamic viscosity of the fluid, $L$: length of the filament, $W$: weight of the body.

## 3   Design and Fabrication of the Ballooning Structure

Spiders' ballooning flight is dominated by low-Reynolds-number flow (i.e., Stokes flow, which has a Reynolds number lower than 1) due to their extremely thin ballooning filaments (about 200 nm wide). In this flow regime, the drag coefficient of a certain object is tens to hundreds of times greater than that of objects in high-Reynolds-number flow [10]. The scaling up of this mechanism is problematic because the structure loses the characteristics of low-Reynolds-number flow as it becomes large. There is an over $10^4$-scale difference in weight between the spider system and a payload system; the weight of *Xysticus* spp. is 25 mg, while the weight of a payload is about 1–2.5 kg. To mimic the ballooning dynamics of spiders, we designed an ultralight membranous structure. The basic unit of the structure is a three-dimensional quasi-isotropic membrane structure, the drag of which is quasi-independent of the flow direction (Fig. 3A). This single structure is called an isotropic kite, and it is possible to create a chain of kites.

The drag of the chain then becomes anisotropic, similar to that of a thin filament in low-Reynolds-number flow (Fig. 3B, C). Large ballooning spiders utilize multiple fine fibers; however, here, we use the single-silk case to experimentally identify the characteristics of the structure. In the experimental stage, the structure will first be launched with the help of a weather balloon and then released at a suitable altitude. If this chain-like structure is positioned within suitable turbulent flows, we expect that it will maintain buoyancy for long periods.

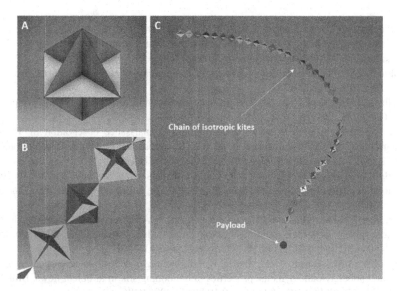

**Fig. 3.** (A) An isotropic kite. (B) A chain of isotropic kites. (C) A ballooning structure for weather-monitoring missions. The payload can transmit data (e.g., GPS, triple-axis acceleration, pressure, temperature, relative humidity, wind speed, wind direction, etc.) back to the operator directly or via satellites.

Each isotropic kite is designed to be constructed from polyethylene film and a 1-mm-thick carbon rod, and the kites can be connected to one another. At first, the diameter of each isotropic kite will be assumed to be about 40 cm. For a prototype of the ballooning structure, the length of the chain and the maximum weight of the payload will be determined based on wind-tunnel test results.

## 4    Conclusions and Future Work

To explore severe weather phenomena such as hurricanes, typhoons, tornadoes, and clear-air turbulence, we propose a passive flight structure inspired by spiders' ballooning flight. The structure consists of a chain of multiple quasi-isotropic, membranous kites and a payload at the end of the chain. The chain is highly flexible so that it can adapt to turbulent flow. Passive flight reduces the aerodynamic load on the structure due to its adaptability, decreasing the cost of stabilizing the flying object in turbulence. As the optimum dimensions for the prototype have not yet been determined, future research will implement wind-tunnel and drop testing.

**Acknowledgments.** MS.C. was supported by the state of Berlin's Elsa Neumann Scholarship (T61004) during this study.

# References

1. Pielke, R.A., Gratz, J., Landsea, C.W., Collins, D., Saunders, M.A., Musulin, R.: Normalized hurricane damage in the United States: 1900–2005. Nat. Hazards Rev. **9**(1), 29–42 (2008). https://doi.org/10.1061/(asce)1527-6988(2008)9:1(29)
2. Golding, W.L.: Turbulence and its impact on commercial aviation. J. Aviat./Aerosp. Educ. Res. **11**(2), 19–29 (2000)
3. Collins, J., Flaherty, P.: The NOAA hurricane hunters: a historical and mission perspective. Fla. Geogr. **45**, 14–27 (2014)
4. Lin, P.H., Lee, C.S.: The eyewall-penetration reconnaissance observation of Typhoon Longwang (2005) with unmanned aerial vehicle, aerosonde. J. Atmos. Oceanic Technol. **25**(1), 15–25 (2008). https://doi.org/10.1175/2007JTECHA914.1
5. Pandolfi, C., Izzo, D.: Biomimetics on seed dispersal: survey and insights for space exploration. Bioinspir. Biomim. **8**(2), 25003 (2013). https://doi.org/10.1088/1748-3182/8/2/025003
6. Cho, M.S., Neubauer, P., Fahrenson, C., Rechenberg, I.: An observational study of ballooning in large spiders: nanoscale multifibers enable large spiders' soaring flight. PLoS bio. **16**(6), e2004405 (2018). http://doi.org/10.1371/journal.pbio.2004405
7. Reynolds, A.M., Bohan, D.A., Bell, J.R.: Ballooning dispersal in arthropod taxa with convergent behaviours: dynamic properties of ballooning silk in turbulent flows. Biol. Lett. **2**(3), 371–373 (2006). https://doi.org/10.1098/rsbl.2006.0486
8. Zhao, L., et al.: Flying spiders: simulating and modeling the dynamics of ballooning. In: Layton, A., Miller, L. (eds.) Women in Mathematical Biology. AWMS, vol. 8, pp. 179–210. Springer, Cham (2017). https://doi.org/10.1007/978-3-319-60304-9_10
9. Childress, S.: Mechanics of Swimming and Flying (Cambridge Studies in Mathematical Biology, 2). Cambridge University Press, Cambridge (1981). https://doi.org/10.1017/cbo9780511569593
10. Tritton, D.J.: Experiments on the flow past a circular cylinder at low Reynolds numbers. J. Fluid Mech. **6**(4), 547 (1959). https://doi.org/10.1017/S0022112059000829
11. Gauger, E., Stark, H.: Numerical study of a microscopic artificial swimmer. Phys. Rev. E. Stat. Nonlin. Soft Matter Phys. **74(2 Pt. 1)**(2), 21907 (2006)

# Insect-Inspired Elementary Motion Detection Embracing Resistive Memory and Spiking Neural Networks

Thomas Dalgaty[1]([✉]), Elisa Vianello[1], Denys Ly[1], Giacomo Indiveri[2], Barbara De Salvo[1], Etienne Nowak[1], and Jerome Casas[3]

[1] CEA-leti, MINATEC Campus, 38054 Grenoble, France
{Thomas.DALGATY,Elisa.VIANELLO}@cea.fr
[2] University of Zurich and ETH Zurich, 8092 Zurich, Switzerland
[3] Insect Biology Research Institute, UMR CNRS 7261, University of Tours, 37200 Tours, France

**Abstract.** Computation of the direction of motion and the detection of collisions are important features of autonomous robotic systems for course steering and avoidance manoeuvres. Current approaches typically rely on computing these features in software using algorithms implemented on a microprocessor. However, the power consumption, computational latency and form factor limit their applicability. In this work we take inspiration from motion detection studied in the Drosophila visual system to implement an alternative. The nervous system of the Drosophila contains 150000 neurons [1] and computes information in a parallel fashion. We propose a topology comprising a dynamic vision sensor (DVS) which provides input to spiking neural networks (SNN). The network is realised through interconnecting leaky-integrate and fire (LIF) complementary metal oxide semiconductor (CMOS) neurons with hafnium dioxide ($HfO_2$) based resistive random access memories (RRAM) acting as the synaptic connections between them. A genetic algorithm (GA) is used to optimize the parameters of the network, within an experimentally determined range of RRAM conductance values, and through simulation it is demonstrated that the system can compute the direction of motion of a grating. Finally, we demonstrate that by modulating RRAM conductances and adjusting network component time constants the range of grating velocities to which it is most sensitive can be adapted. It is also shown that this allows for the system to reduce power consumption when sensitive to lower velocity stimulus. This mimics the behavior observed in Drosophila whereby the neuromodulator octopamine adjusts the response of the motion detection system when the insect is resting or flying.

**Keywords:** Neuromorphic computing · Elementary Motion Detection Resistive memories · Spiking Neural Network · Biomimicry

© Springer International Publishing AG, part of Springer Nature 2018
V. Vouloutsi et al. (Eds.): Living Machines 2018, LNAI 10928, pp. 115–128, 2018.
https://doi.org/10.1007/978-3-319-95972-6_13

# 1   Introduction

In recent years detailed partial connectomes of insect neural networks have been produced. An example is the elementary motion detection (EMD) network of Drosophila's visual system [2–4]. The insect has two large eyes composed of repeating hexagonal columns called ommatidia. Each ommatidia has an identical structure which processes visual information from a small region of the full visual field. It is composed of four distinct layers of neuropil - the retina, lamina, medulla and the lobula as shown in Fig. 1(a). The neural pathway for detecting elementary motion within this structure is depicted schematically in Fig. 1(b). It begins at the retina where cells transduce light into electrical signals. These then synapse onto L1 and L2 cells in the lamina. At this stage the information is rectified into ON and OFF pathways - ON pathways carry information on luminescence increments and the OFF pathways luminescence decrements. The L1 and L2 cells in the lamina synapse predominantly onto the Mi1, Tm3 and Tm2, Tm1 cells in the medulla. These cells are implicated in implementing temporal delays between adjacent activity in spatial regions in the visual field [5]. The pairs of cells in the medulla synapse onto T4 and T5 cells in the lobula which are then excited if a spatiotemporal correlation exists between it's presynaptic cells indicating motion. Subsets of T4 and T5 cells are sensitive to motion in one of the four cardinal directions up, down, left and right and terminate independently in one of four distinct layers in the lobula plate (LP). Groups of lobula plate tangential cells (LPTC) are excited by activity in one layer of the LP and fire to indicate motion in a specific direction. Another group of lobula plate/lobula columnar type two (LPLC2) cells are excited only by diverging motion in each layer of the LP such that they indicate a looming stimulus on a collision course [6]. Furthermore, it has also been found that the neuromodulator octopamine tunes dynamics of the EMDs in the Drosophila visual system as a function of whether the insect is resting or flying [7–9]. This allows the insect to adapt its sensitivity to different velocities of stimulus as well as reduce power consumption whilst in a resting state. In Fig. 1(c) tshe response of an LTPC cell is reported for Drosophila stimulated with a moving grating when it is in resting and flying states. The area under the curve for the insect in its resting state is greatly reduced relative to that of its flying state which is thought to be an evolutionary adaptation to optimize its consumption of energy. The Hassenstein-Reichardt EMD (HR-EMD) is a popular model which reproduces experimental observations of Drosophila's EMDs [10]. Photoexcitation at adjacent regions in the visual field propogates signals through crossing low pass filters before being recombined at a multiplication unit to detect spatiotemporal correlations. The output of the unit can be either positive or negative indicating motion in one of two directions as in Fig. 1(d). A number of previous works have implemented the HR-EMD in analogue very large scale integrated (aVLSI) systems for point [11], 1D [12], 2D [13] and rotational motion [14] detection but the platform is yet to be adopted for applications. Another perspective on hardware based motion detection are token and feature based EMDs [15–18]. Here we propose an alternative approach which stays true to the guiding principle of detecting

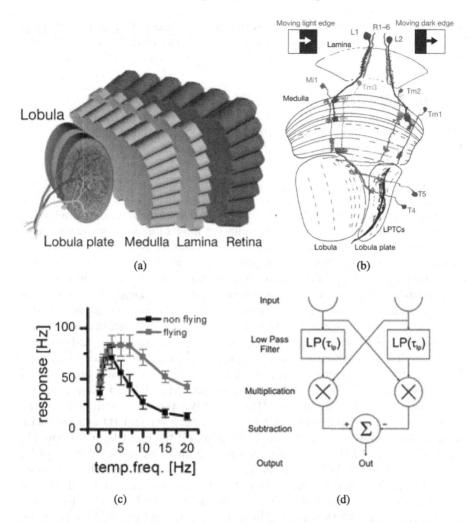

**Fig. 1.** The architectural layout of the Drosophila visual system and its detection of motion. (a) The four layers of neuropil in the Drosophila visual system [3]. (b) The specific cells identified in the pathway from the retina to the lobula plate involved in elementary motion detection [5]. (c) Temporal frequency sensitivity tuning curve of the mean response of LPTC neuron in Drosophila in resting and flying states as modulated by octopamine. [7]. (d) A schematic of the HR-EMD model often implemented in hardware motion detectors [14].

spatiotemporal correlations but takes advantage of the ability to integrate resistive memory with CMOS technology and recent insights into the structural organization of Drosophila's elementary motion detection neural network. We use a dynamic vision sensor (DVS) to provide input for a SNN composed of CMOS LIF neurons interconnected by RRAM synapses to perform direction detection and detect collisions. First we present the network topology followed by relevant electrical measurements of RRAM matrices and finally demonstrate through simulation the ability of the network to compute the direction of motion of a grating.

## 2    The Network

This section introduces the sub-units of the full system individually before outlining how they fit together.

### 2.1    Delay and Correlate Network

To detect motion in one direction along a single dimension a temporal delay can be implemented between two spatially adjacent inputs followed by a downstream mechanism for detecting spatiotemporal correlations. In Drosophila this delay is thought to be implemented between pairs of neurons in the medulla [5] and the correlation performed by the postsynaptic neurons in the lobula. Delay can be implemented in a LIF CMOS neuron through controlling the input time constant of the neuron and a correlation operation can be performed by parameterizing a neuron to fire only when two presynaptic spikes arrive within a short time window. These features are captured by the one dimensional delay and correlate spiking neural network shown in Fig. 2(a). Neurons in the input layer fire to denote spatial activity and synapse with excitatory connections onto a second delay layer. In this layer the input time constant of the B1 and B3 neurons are larger than the central B2 neuron. B1 and B2 synapse with excitatory connections onto the correlator neuron C1 in the output layer and B3 synapses with an inhibitory connection. As depicted in Fig. 2(b) if the input layer is excited in the sequence A1, A2 then A3 along its preferred direction the firing times of B1 and B2 should be similar and the firing time of B3 will be delayed. This allows for the two excitatory spikes from B1 and B2 to arrive at C1 within a short time window such that it fires. For motion against the preferred direction, excitation in the sequence A3, A2 then A1, the firing times of B3 and B2 will be similar and that of B1 will be delayed. Consequently C1 will not be sufficiently excited given the combination of inhibition and temporal separation of the excitatory input. In a third case where all input elements are excited simultaneously B1 and B3 will fire at the same time, negating each others contribution, such that C1 does not receive sufficient excitation from B2 alone to fire. For detection of motion in two dimensions four identical 1D delay and correlate SNNs, sharing the same central low input time constant node, can be arranged orthogonally. If the input neurons are spatially arranged in a cross then spatiotemporal correlations can be detected corresponding to UP, DOWN, LEFT and RIGHT motion within a small region of the visual field. A 2D delay and correlate SNN and the spatial organization of its input is shown in Fig. 3. To extract information from an entire visual field it then follows that an array of 2D delay and correlate SNNs can be connected to an input such that they receive spatially corresponding excitation from across the visual field.

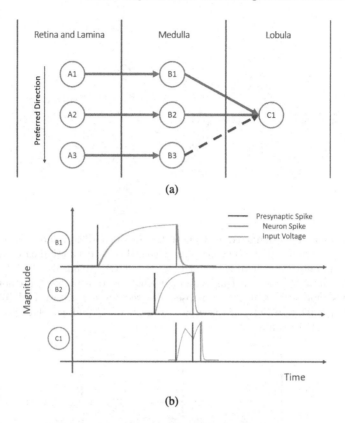

**Fig. 2.** The one dimensional delay and correlate spiking neural network and its functional basis. (a) A 1D delay and correlate SNN. Open blue circles represent LIF CMOS neurons, green arrows excitatory synapses and red dashed arrows inhibitory synapses. Vertical lines separate the three layers of the network into the abstracted functions as performed by the different layers of neuropil in the elementary motion detection system. (b) A time domain plot for the three neurons involved in detection of motion - B1 and B2 being excited in sequence and their resulting signals meeting at C3. Red spikes correspond to the activity of a presynaptic neuron, blue spikes to the activity of the neuron associated with the plot and the green trace is the neuron input voltage resulting from the incoming presynaptic spikes. (Color figure online)

## 2.2   Readout Network

Inspired by the connectivity pattern observed in Drosophila which allows for motion and collision detection we connect the 2D delay and correlate SNN array to a readout network of five neurons in a similar manner. The connection pattern between the 2D delay and correlate SNNs across the visual field and the readout network is depicted in Fig. 4. To readout the direction of motion four neurons, modelling the LPTCs, corresponding to UP, DOWN, LEFT and RIGHT motion are excited by the corresponding directional output of each of the 2D delay and correlate SNNs across the visual field. Additionally, one further neuron,

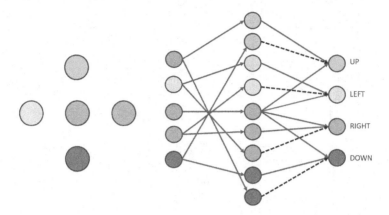

**Fig. 3.** The two dimensional equivalent of the delay and correlate network. Blue filled circles represent LIF CMOS neurons where the fill colour indicates the pathway involved in detecting the directions UP (green), DOWN (purple), LEFT (yellow), and RIGHT (blue) while the central shared low time constant pathway is coloured red. Green arrows represent excitatory synapses and red dashed arrows inhibitory ones. The spatial organization (left) of the inputs to a 2D delay and correlate SNN (right) is shown. (Color figure online)

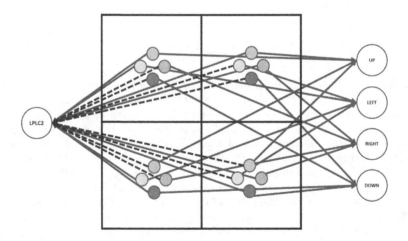

**Fig. 4.** The connection pattern required between the 2D delay and correlate SNNs within the four quadrants of the visual field and the five readout network neurons for motion detection and detecting collisions. The coloured blue circles correspond to the output layer neurons from Fig. 3 with their spatial organization indicating which direction they detect. From all four quadrants excitatory (green) connections project to the corresponding readout neuron per direction. Diverging directions in the four quadrants provide excitation (green) to the LPLC2 neuron on the left hand side of the figure while directions converging towards the centre make inhibitory (red dashed) connections. Therefore, four readout neurons denote motion and one is excited during an expanding edge denoting impending collision. (Color figure online)

modelling the LPLC2 neuron is included. This neuron splits the visual field into four quadrants. From each quadrant excitatory connections are made between the 2D delay and correlate SNN directions which diverge from the centre of the visual field and inhibitory connections from directions corresponding to movement converging towards the centre. A looming stimulus on a collision course is defined as an expanding dark edge from the centre to the edges of the visual field and therefore this neuron will fire to denote looming.

### 2.3   System Architecture

Activity in the visual field excites a DVS camera [19, 20] which propagates spikes presynaptically to spatially corresponding 2D delay and correlate SNNs using the address event representation (AER) protocol [21]. Two dimensional spatiotemporal correlations of the input data are detected by the 2D delay and correlate SNNs before their outputs are integrated together in a readout layer which computes the direction of motion and detects impending collisions.

## 3   Relevant Properties of RRAM Synapses

In oxide based resistive random access memories (RRAM) the storage element consists of a transition metal oxide (TMO) material - sandwiched between metal electrodes - which can be switched to two distinct stable conductance values. The low resistance state (LRS) or the high resistance state (HRS) can be achieved through SET or RESET operations respectively by applying electric fields of opposite polarities between the electrodes. RRAM devices can be integrated in matrices [22] whereby each device in the matrix is connected in series at the drain of a transistor (1T1R). This allows for each memory device to be read from and written to individually. Each 1T1R structure in the matrix is addressed using the bit line (BL) and source line (SL) which connect to the top electrode of the device and the source of the transistor respectively and a wordline (WL) which connects to the gate of the transistor. The WL voltage therefore regulates the transistor drain source current, in this case termed the programming current ($I_{CC}$), which determines device conductance and variability in this value after a SET operation. The method of connecting LIF CMOS neurons together through a RRAM matrix is depicted in Fig. 5. Connections between neurons are defined by a device in LRS whereas non-connections are defined by a device in HRS and specific devices can be programmed individually. In this manner specific feed-forward network topologies can be realised. The data plotted in Fig. 6 corresponds to measurements from a 4kbit matrix of $HfO_2$ based TMO RRAM devices with titanium nitride (TiN) electrodes integrated in a 130 nm CMOS technology node [23]. In Fig. 6(a) the cumulative distribution function (CDF) of the conductance values per RRAM device state in the matrix is plotted whereby the LRS and HRS conductance value of each device is shown. Additionally, in Fig. 6(b) the effect of varying the gate voltage of the transistor, therefore the programming current, on the mean value of the LRS conductance CDF is shown.

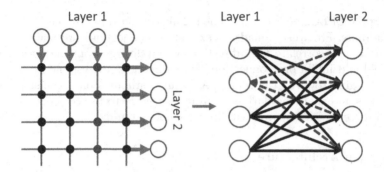

**Fig. 5.** The method of networking neurons with RRAM matrices. CMOS LIF neurons arranged as such around a RRAM matrix (left) implements a two layer feed forward network (right). Open blue circles correspond to LIF CMOS neurons while filled navy and red circles correspond to RRAM memories in different conductance states. Arrows indicate the direction of spike prorogation between the output of one layer of neurons and the input of the following. (Color figure online)

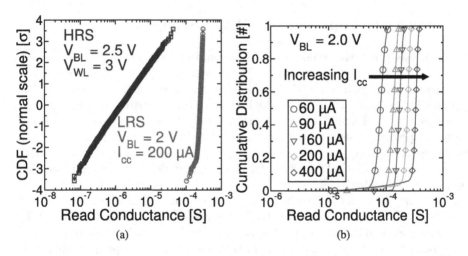

**Fig. 6.** Data from electrical measurement of a 4kbit RRAM matrix relevant for the application. (a) The cumulative distribution function of LRS (red) and HRS (blue) of HfO$_2$-based RRAM devices integrated in a 4kbit matrix. A SET operation is performed with $V_{BL} = 2$ V, $V_{WL} = 1.3$ (corresponding to $I_{CC} = 200\,\mu A$) and $T_{pulse} = 100$ ns, whereas RESET is performed with $V_{SL} = 2.5$ V, $V_{WL} = 3.5$ V and $T_{pulse} = 100$ ns. (b) The cumulative distribution function of the LRS with a range of programming currents when performing a SET operation over the 4kbit matrix. (Color figure online)

Crucially, the ability to modulate RRAM device conductance allows emulation of neural plasticity [24] - an essential property of neural networks for learning, adapting and maintaining homeostasis.

## 4    Simulation Results

A simulated DVS of resolution $10 \times 10$ is stimulated with a horizontal grating moving upwards vertically over its input in time providing OFF pathway spikes for the network topology. Noise is also simulated through setting each DVS pixel to spike with a probability of 0.025 per step of the grating. The frequency of the grating is defined as pixels crossed per second of simulation time. Twenty 2D delay and correlate SNNs are used to span the visual field each containing thirteen neurons and twenty one synapses. In total the topology requires 256 neurons and 580 synapses for a DVS of resolution $10 \times 10$. The simulation advances in discrete time steps at which the synaptic currents and neuron input and output voltages are updated with respect to their values at the previous timestep in accordance with the LIF neuron model and the first order dynamic synapse model [25]. The desired outcome is for the readout layer neuron denoting upward motion to fire at an elevated rate relative to the others. UP, DOWN, LEFT and RIGHT correspond to the number of times each readout neuron fires within one vertical sweep of the grating. The $F_1$ score corresponding to correctly identified upward motion, defined in Eq. 1, is used to assess the network performance. $F_1$ score ranges from a minimum value of zero to a maximum value of one. The grating is swept over the input at a range of frequencies and the $F_1$ score is calculated per frequency. We refer to the plot of $F_1$ score with grating frequency as the sensitivity tuning curve (STC).

$$F_1 = \frac{2UP}{2UP + (DOWN + LEFT + RIGHT)} \tag{1}$$

Genetic algorithms (GA) are bio-inspired approaches to multi-parameter optimization problems simulating the process of natural selection to arrive at a near optimal solution [26] and are readily applied to optimize neural networks [27]. Here a GA is used to set the free parameters of the network. Therein, the conductances and time constants of the synapses and the threshold voltage and the input time constants of the neurons for the repeating 2D delay and correlate SNN and the readout network. The parameters for each of the four orthogonal 1D delay and correlate SNNs are the same such that each EMD is composed of four identical rotations of the same network sharing a common central node. Similarly, parameters for all readout layer neurons and synapses are set equal such that the full parameter space has twenty-four dimensions. The values for RRAM conductance are bounded between $5 \times 10^{-5}$S and $3 \times 10^{-4}$S corresponding to the range of values obtained through measurement of RRAM LRS with different values of $I_{CC}$ as in Fig. 6(b). Sixty networks are created per generation. First generation parameters are assigned by sampling from a uniform distribution between a lower and upper bound per parameter. A STC is produced for each of the sixty networks and the ten with the largest area under the curve (AUC) in addition to two randomly selected ones are recombined in pairs to produce the next generation. Parameters are assigned with a certain probability of mutation. Hard mutations occur with a probability of 0.05 whereby the parameter is randomly assigned a value from a uniform distribution between an upper and lower bound. A soft mutation occurs with a probability of 0.5 whereby the parameter is reassigned from a normal distribution around the value inherited from the parent with a standard deviation of 1%. The optimization terminates when the $F_1$ score plateaus. Using the parameters of the best performing network after termination of the genetic optimization ten sensitivity tuning curves were obtained with ten instances of the topology and the means were plotted since the performance of each instance differs slightly due to the modelled inherent RRAM variability and simulated DVS noise. In total two network configurations were found inspired by Drosophila using octopamine to adapt its elementary motion detection neural network between a flying and resting state. One configuration is optimized to detect lower frequency gratings and the other to detect higher frequency gratings - they are referred to as the Slow and Fast network states respectively. The Slow and Fast configurations are plotted with a red dashed and green trace in Fig. 7(a) which shows that the Slow state accurately detects the direction of motion within a range of grating frequencies of 0.7–3 Hz while the Fast state does so within a range between 2–20 Hz. Further, with greater correspondence to experimental results reported in Fig. 1(c), a firing-rate tuning curve (FTC) is plotted in Fig. 7(b) corresponding to the frequency at which the UP neuron fires in the Slow and Fast network states. Since the area under the FTCs of Fig. 7(b) is greater over the range of grating frequencies when the network is in the Fast

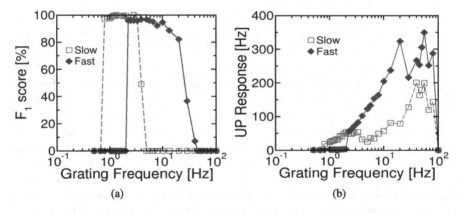

(a)                                    (b)

**Fig. 7.** Results of the spiking network simulation demonstrating the performance and power consumption of the two network configurations over a range of grating frequencies. (a) The sensitivity tuning curve corresponding to the performance of the topology in detecting the correct direction of motion over a range of grating frequencies. The red points correspond to the Slow network configuration and the green points to the Fast network configuration using the parameters from the genetic optimizations. (b) The firing-rate tuning curve corresponding to the response frequency of the neuron defined as the number of times the UP neuron fires per second over the same range of grating frequencies. It can be seen that resulting from the reduced response in the Slow configuration the power consumption is reduced in this state relative to that of the Fast configuration. (Color figure online)

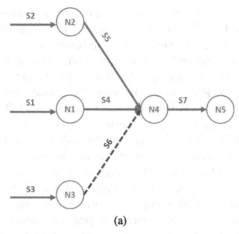

(a)

| | Time Constant Slow (s⁻¹) | Time Constant Fast (s⁻¹) | Conductance Slow (S) | Conductance Fast (S) |
|---|---|---|---|---|
| | Time Constant Slow $(s^{-1})$ | Time Constant Fast $(s^{-1})$ | Conductance Slow (S) | Conductance Fast (S) |
| S1 | $8.0\times10^{-2}$ | $5.0\times10^{-2}$ | $2.0\times10^{-4}$ | $3.0\times10^{-4}$ |
| S2 | $1.1$ | $9.0\times10^{-2}$ | $1.4\times10^{-4}$ | $2.1\times10^{-4}$ |
| S3 | $1.0$ | $9.0\times10^{-2}$ | $2.0\times10^{-4}$ | $3.0\times10^{-4}$ |
| S4 | $5.0\times10^{-1}$ | $2.0\times10^{-1}$ | $1.0\times10^{-4}$ | $1.5\times10^{-4}$ |
| S5 | $8.5\times10^{-1}$ | $3.0\times10^{-1}$ | $1.0\times10^{-4}$ | $1.5\times10^{-4}$ |
| S6 | $1.3$ | $3.0\times10^{-1}$ | $1.0\times10^{-4}$ | $1.5\times10^{-4}$ |
| S7 | $5.0\times10^{-2}$ | $5.0\times10^{-2}$ | $2.0\times10^{-4}$ | $2.0\times10^{-4}$ |

(b)

| | Time Constant Slow $(s^{-1})$ | Time Constant Fast $(s^{-1})$ | Threshold Voltage Slow (V) | Threshold Voltage Fast (V) |
|---|---|---|---|---|
| N1 | $4.0\times10^{-3}$ | $1.3\times10^{-3}$ | 0.8 | 0.8 |
| N2 | $5.9\times10^{-1}$ | $2.1\times10^{-1}$ | 0.35 | 0.35 |
| N3 | $5.9\times10^{-1}$ | $2.1\times10^{-1}$ | 0.38 | 0.38 |
| N4 | $1.6\times10^{-1}$ | $1.2\times10^{-1}$ | 0.8 | 0.8 |
| N5 | $2.0\times10^{-2}$ | $2.0\times10^{-2}$ | 0.6 | 0.6 |

(c)

**Fig. 8.** The network parameters used to produce the plots in Fig. 7. (a) The blue open circles represent LIF CMOS neurons, the green arrows excitatory synapses and the red dashed arrows inhibitory synapses. (b) The RRAM synapse time constants and conductances resulting from the genetic optimization for the Slow and Fast configurations. The colours of the conductance values refer to the colour of the trace in Fig. 6(b) which correspond to the value of $I_{CC}$ required to obtain the conductance value. (c) The LIF CMOS neuron time constants and threshold voltages resulting from the genetic optimization for the Slow and Fast configurations. Since the threshold voltages and readout synapse and neuron values are fixed they are the same for both configurations and are written in bold. The value of RRAM conductance variability for both configurations was set to 10% as observed in Fig. 6 for SET operations. (Color figure online)

state than the Slow state the power consumed by the readout network in the Slow state is reduced by 42% relative to that of the Fast state. In Fig. 8(a) the schematic of the repeating structure across the topology is depicted. Figure 8(b) and (c) report the synapse and neuron parameters used to achieve the results of Fig. 7. To arrive at these values for the Slow state the network was optimized with the described genetic algorithm to have the greatest area under the STC within the range of 1–3 Hz. On this occasion values of the RRAM conductances were multiplied by one and a half times and a second genetic optimization to maximize the area under the STC between 10–25 Hz was performed with only the synapse and neuron input time constants as free parameters. The result of Fig. 7 shows that, like Drosophila, the range of velocities of stimulus to which the system is most sensitive to can be adapted by tuning the RRAM synapse conductances and the network component time constants. Additionally when the network is switched to the Slow state the power consumption of the system is reduced since it no longer responds to non-relevant higher velocity stimulus.

## 5    Conclusions

Making use of resistive memory and spiking neural networks an alternative approach to elementary motion detection was proposed. A DVS camera provided input on the visual field to an array of delay and correlate spiking neural networks composed of simulated LIF CMOS neurons and RRAM synapses based on HfO$_2$ technology to compute the direction of motion and to detect collisions. The network was parameterized using a genetic algorithm and then through simulation sensitivity tuning curves demonstrated that it was able to detect the motion of a grating over a range of frequencies. As observed in Drosophila through tuning RRAM conductances and network component time constants the range of grating frequencies to which it is most sensitive to can be adapted. In addition it was seen that, like Drosophila, when the topology was parameterized such that it was sensitive to lower velocity stimulus the power consumption was reduced relative to the configuration for higher velocity stimulus.

**Acknowledgments.** The authors would like to acknowledge the support of J. Casas through the CARNOT chair of excellency in bio-inspired technologies. In addition this work was also partially supported by the h2020 NeuRAM3 project.

## References

1. Chiang, A.S., Lin, C.Y., Chuang, C.C., Chang, H.M., Hsieh, C.H., Yeh, C.W., Shih, C.T., Wu, J.J., Wang, G.T., Chen, Y.C., Wu, C.C., Chen, G.Y., Ching, Y.T., Lee, P.C., Lin, C.Y., Lin, H.H., Wu, C.C., Hsu, H.W., Huang, Y.A., Chen, J.Y., Chiang, H.J., Lu, C.F., Ni, R.F., Yeh, C.Y., Hwang, J.K.: Three-dimensional reconstruction of brain-wide wiring networks in drosophila at single-cell resolution. Curr. Biol. **21**(1), 1–11 (2011)

2. Takemura, S., Bharioke, A., Lu, Z., Nern, A., Vitaladevuni, S., Rivlin, P.K., Katz, W.T., Olbris, D.J., Plaza, S.M., Winston, P., Zhao, T., Horne, J.A., Fetter, R.D., Takemura, S., Blazek, K., Chang, L.A., Ogundeyi, O., Saunders, M.A., Shapiro, V., Sigmund, C., Rubin, G.M., Scheffer, L.K., Meinertzhagen, I.A., Chklovskii, D.B.: A visual motion detection circuit suggested by drosophila connectomics. Nature **500**, 175 (2013)
3. Maisak, M.S., Haag, J., Ammer, G., Serbe, E., Meier, M., Leonhardt, A., Schilling, T., Bahl, A., Rubin, G.M., Nern, A., Dickson, B.J., Reiff, D.F., Hopp, E., Borst, A.: A directional tuning map of drosophila elementary motion detectors. Nature **500**, 212 (2013)
4. Haag, J., Arenz, A., Serbe, E., Gabbiani, F., Borst, A.: Complementary mechanisms create direction selectivity in the fly. eLife **5**, e17421 (2016)
5. Behnia, R., Clark, D.A., Carter, A.G., Clandinin, T.R., Desplan, C.: Processing properties of ON and OFF pathways for drosophila motion detection. Nature **512**, 427 (2014)
6. Klapoetke, N.C., Nern, A., Peek, M.Y., Rogers, E.M., Breads, P., Rubin, G.M., Reiser, M.B., Card, G.M.: Ultra-selective looming detection from radial motion opponency. Nature **551**, 237 (2017)
7. Jung, S.N., Borst, A., Haag, J.: Flight activity alters velocity tuning of fly motion-sensitive neurons. J. Neurosci. **31**(25), 9231–9237 (2011)
8. Suver, M., Mamiya, A., Dickinson, M.: Octopamine neurons mediate flight-induced modulation of visual processing in drosophila. Curr. Biol. **22**(24), 2294–2302 (2012)
9. Arenz, A., Drews, M.S., Richter, F.G., Ammer, G., Borst, A.: The temporal tuning of the drosophila motion detectors is determined by the dynamics of their input elements. Curr. Biol. **27**(7), 929–944 (2017)
10. Hassenstein, V., Reichardt, W.: Systemtheoretische Analyse der Zeit-, Reihenfolgen- und Vorzeichenauswertung bei der Bewegungsperzeption des Rüsselkäfers Chlorophanus. Z. Naturforsch. B **11**, 513 (1956)
11. Harrison, R.R., Koch, C.: An analog VLSI model of the fly elementary motion detector. In: Jordan, M.I., Kearns, M.J., Solla, S.A. (eds.) Advances in Neural Information Processing Systems 10, pp. 880–886. MIT Press, Cambridge (1998)
12. Liu, S.C.: A neuromorphic a VLSI model of global motion processing in the fly. IEEE Trans. Circ. Syst. II Analog Digital Signal Proces. **47**(12), 1458–1467 (2000)
13. Harrison, R.R.: A biologically inspired analog IC for visual collision detection. IEEE Trans. Circ. Syst. I Regul. Pap. **52**(11), 2308–2318 (2005)
14. Plett, J., Bahl, A., Buss, M., Kühnlenz, K., Borst, A.: Bio-inspired visual ego-rotation sensor for MAVs. Biol. Cybern. **106**(1), 51–63 (2012)
15. Krammer, J.: Compact integrated motion sensor with three-pixel interaction. IEEE Trans. Pattern Anal. Mach. Intell. **44**(2), 86–101 (1996)
16. Krammer, J., Koch, C.: Pulse-based analog VLSI velocity sensors. IEEE Trans. Cir. Syst. II Analog Digit. Signal Process. **44**(2), 86–101 (1997). https://doi.org/10.1109/82.554431
17. Sarpeshkar, R., Kramer, J., Indiveri, G., Koch, C.: Analog VLSI architectures for motion processing: from fundamental limits to system applications. Proc. IEEE **84**(7), 969–987 (1996). https://doi.org/10.1109/5.503298
18. Shoemaker, P.A.: Implementation of Visual motion detection in analog neuromorphic circuitry - a case study of the issue of circuit precision. Proc. IEEE **102**(10), 1557–1570 (2014)
19. Lichtsteiner, P., Posch, C., Delbruck, T.: A 128 × 128 120 dB 15 µs latency asynchronous temporal contrast vision sensor. IEEE J. Solid-State Circ. **43**(2), 566–576 (2008)

20. Serrano-Gotarredona, T., Linares-Barranco, B.: A 128 ×128 1.5% contrast sensitivity 0.9% FPN 3 μs latency 4 mW asynchronous frame-free dynamic vision sensor using transimpedance preamplifiers. IEEE J. Solid-State Circ. **48**(3), 827–838 (2013)
21. Chan, V., Liu, S.C., van Schaik, A.: AER EAR: a matched silicon cochlea pair with address event representation interface. IEEE Trans. Circ. Syst. I Regul. Pap. **54**(1), 48–59 (2007). https://doi.org/10.1109/TCSI.2006.887979
22. Grossi, A., Vianello, E., Zambelli, C., Royer, P., Noel, J.P., Giraud, B., Perniola, L., Olivo, P., Nowak, E.: Experimental investigation of 4kbit RRAM arrays programming conditions suitable for TCAM. IEEE Trans. Very Large Scale Integr. (VLSI) Syst. **PP**(99), 1–9 (2018)
23. Grossi, A., Nowak, E., Zambelli, C., Pellissier, C., Bernasconi, S., Cibrario, G., Hajjam, K.E., Crochemore, R., Nodin, J.F., Olivo, P., Perniola, L.: Fundamental variability limits of filament-based RRAM. In: 2016 IEEE International Electron Devices Meeting (IEDM), pp. 4.7.1–4.7.4, December 2016. https://doi.org/10.1109/IEDM.2016.7838348
24. Garbin, D., Vianello, E., Bichler, O., Rafhay, Q., Gamrat, C., Ghibaudo, G., DeSalvo, B., Perniola, L.: HfO$_2$-based OxRAM devices as synapses for convolutional neural networks. IEEE Trans. Electron Devices **62**(8), 2494–2501 (2015). https://doi.org/10.1109/TED.2015.2440102
25. Brette, R., Rudolph, M., Carnevale, T., Hines, M., Beeman, D., Bower, J.M., Diesmann, M., Morrison, A., Goodman, P.H., Harris, F.C., Zirpe, M., Natschläger, T., Pecevski, D., Ermentrout, B., Djurfeldt, M., Lansner, A., Rochel, O., Vieville, T., Muller, E., Davison, A.P., El Boustani, S., Destexhe, A.: Simulation of networks of spiking neurons: a review of toolsand strategies. J. Comput. Neurosci. **23**(3), 349–398 (2007)
26. Simon, D.: Evolutionary Optimization Algorithms. Wiley, Hoboken (2013)
27. Montana, D.J., Davis, L.: Training feedforward neural networks using genetic algorithms. In: IJCAI 1989 Proceedings of the 11th International Joint Conference on Artificial Intelligence - Volume 1, pp. 762–767. Morgan Kaufmann Publishers Inc., San Francisco (1989)

# Understanding Interstate Competitiveness and International Security in European Dual-Use Research

Saheli Datta Burton[✉] [iD], Christine Aicardi, Tara Mahfoud, and Nikolas Rose

Global Health and Social Medicine, King's College London,
London WC2R2LS, UK
{saheli.1.datta,christine.aicardi,tara.mahfoud,
nikolas.rose}@kcl.ac.uk

**Abstract.** Dual-use (DU) technologies are both a threat to human security and an opportunity to generate economic value. This article reflects on tensions between state preferences for greater competitiveness in DU technologies and its implications for human security. These tensions are analysed through the lens of the Ethics Issues Checklists (EIC) used by the European Commission (EC) to implement upstream controls on European DU research. We show that the shift towards an economistic framing of DU in the EICs privileges competitiveness at the expense of security imperatives and thereby undermines Europe's commitments to human security as agreed in multilateral treaties. Furthermore, findings show a nuanced understanding of the EC's preference for economic considerations as it combines economic growth expectations from a more competitive DU industry with a strengthening of Europe's hard power capacities via a strengthened domestic security industry.

**Keywords:** Dual use · Competitiveness · Human security

## 1 Introduction

Dual-use technologies are both a threat to human security and an opportunity to generate economic value. As such, 'dual-use' (DU) refers to the possibility that research and technological developments designed to generate benefits for civilians can also be used for military or other purposes with non-peaceful intents. These include emerging technologies of immense promissory socioeconomic significance like artificial intelligence and genetics which can be easily weaponised into autonomous warfighters, agents of bioterrorism, etc. Indeed, neuromorphic computing and other biologically-inspired systems are increasingly recognized as DU areas of concern to researchers and regulators [1].

The European Commission (EC) [2] defines 'dual-use items' as:

> …goods, software and technology that can be used for both civilian and military applications and/or can contribute to the proliferation of Weapons of Mass Destruction (WMD) [and thus] …subject to **controls** to prevent the risks that these items may pose for **international security**.
> 1 [bold added for emphasis]

© Springer International Publishing AG, part of Springer Nature 2018
V. Vouloutsi et al. (Eds.): Living Machines 2018, LNAI 10928, pp. 129–133, 2018.
https://doi.org/10.1007/978-3-319-95972-6_14

As the term *international security* suggests, the risks of DUIs are viewed by the EC as global (beyond the confines of national borders). DUI risks are governed by multi-lateral treaties like the 1972 *Biological Weapons Convention* (BWC), the 1993 *Chemical Weapons Conventions* (CWC) and the 2004 *UN Security Council Resolution 1540* (amended in 2016). In turn, the *problem* of security risks posed by DUIs – according to the above definition - is resolved through *controls*. Within Europe, as in other nations, *controls* in the DUI context derive from state obligations to multilateral treaties. These typically refer to policies aimed at controlling "the export, transit and brokering of dual-use items as a key instrument contributing to international peace and human security" [2] (hereafter referred as *human security*). As a result, this trade-based approach to managing the security risks posed by DUIs - or what the EC calls a "security-related trade instrument" [2] - casts DUIs as tradable goods with all the concomitant pros and cons of trade and commerce, such as interstate competitiveness and profit-driven micro interests.

This article takes a closer look at policies for upstream control of European DU research. The aim is to understand the human security implications of policy shifts towards greater competitiveness between 2009 and 2016 in Europe's international trade in DUIs. We present an inward-looking analysis of security-trade dynamics within the European Union (EU) from the perspective of international relations theory instead of the standard cross-national comparative studies [3]. Notably, for the purposes of this paper, we consider the EU as one analytical unit (interchangeably referred to as *national*). This is because the EC's DUI Export Control policies - primarily Regulation ECR428/2009 - are centralised with the explicit aim of controlling the "export, transit and brokering" of dual-use items within the EU's *Common Commercial Policy* regu-lating the European single market (Article 207 in *Treaty on the Functioning of the European Union* in [2]).

## 1.1 DUIs and the EU Economy

International trade in DUIs makes a substantial contribution to Europe's economy. In the period 2008-2014, 20% of Europe's exports (worth €900 billion) fell within the DUI export control domain[1] [4]. In approximately the same period (2008-2012), DUI and DUI-related sectors were estimated to have employed between 7 to 8.5 million people thus accounting for 14% of all export-based employment within the EU [4, p. 19]. Given the immense socioeconomic value of trade in DUIs to the European economy, sustaining the DUI sector's international competitiveness is important for Europe's long-term growth objectives [2]. A review of the existing DUI export control regime has been underway since 2011 to make the DUI sector more competitive by optimising the balance between "ensuring security and competitiveness in a changing world" [2, p. 5]. However, Stewart and Bauer [6, p. 23] have suggested that it was the USA's review and reform of its DUI export regime in 2009 (to make it more competitive) that escalated Europe's competitive concerns. This triggered the EC's DUI review process, which was

---

[1] Including trade within EU and re-export [6], although Stewart [13] estimates the value of EU's DUI production substantially lower between €26 and €37 billion.

backed by the European DUI industry's calls for relaxing the EU's stricter standards as compared to the USA and emerging competitors like China and India [see e.g. *European Commission's Impact Assessment Report* of 2016 in [5, p. 7], [6]. The question is: does the framing of the European DUI review process with competitiveness as a policy target (at par with security risks) suggest a state preference for economic goals at the expense of human security goals?

## 2    Method and Methodology

To understand the co-existence of state preferences for specific economic (i.e. trade) and security goals [7], we draw on the specific case of upstream DU controls imposed on European research via the mechanism of *Ethics Issue Checklists*. According to Europe's key dual-use regulation ECR 428/2009, applicants for EC research funding are required to self-assess the dual use and potential misuses of their proposed research by completing an *Ethics Issues Checklist* (EIC). Informed by concepts from international relations theory [7–11], we conducted discourse and content analysis of (a) the changes to the EIC over the period 2009-2016; (b) accompanying guidance notes for EIC applicants; and (c) related policy documents to understand the tensions between state preferences for competitiveness and human security in the European DU domain.

## 3    Findings

Findings showed considerable variances in the content and intent of EICs issued between 2009 and 2016 towards an economistic framing of DU regulations. This privileges the EC's unitary economic considerations at the expense of Europe's commitment to human and international security as agreed in multilateral treaties like the BWC and CWC. Furthermore, our analysis suggests a nuanced understanding of the EU's preference for economic considerations as it combines economic growth expectations from a stronger European DU innovation and industry along with a strengthening of the EU's hard power capacities via a strengthened domestic security industry.

## 4    Discussion

Findings showed that the shift towards economic considerations between the 2014 and 2016 EICs was underpinned by the EC's strategic shift towards incentivising the defence sector to diversify into the civilian sector. This is done via the quick innovation route of adapting DU defence technologies to civilian-use products aimed at creating wealth, jobs and growth for the aggregate European economy. The notion that this shift was motivated by, and in the interests of, a few industry and private actors rather than the aggregate was unfounded. However, the 2016 EIC's silence on the questions of human rights and military ethics were concerning. One reason for these lack of human rights and ethics protections may have been motivated by the desire to smooth the defence sector's foray into the civilian sector; to bolster European DU innovation and industry with the expectation that it would contribute both to the EU's economic growth as well as its hard power via a strong European security industry.

Furthermore, findings showed that the 2014 EIC's strategy of discursively fragmenting the DU domain into good and bad to commercialise the *good DU* (like trade in DUIs) and prohibit *bad DU* or *misuses* like terrorist abuse, created ambiguous outcomes in the 2016 EIC. In the 2016 EIC, *good* DU was expected to bolster research collaboration between defence-civilian sectors, eventually leading to a strong indigenous defence-security sector. In reality, the economistic framing of DUs weakened the 2016 EIC to a tokenistic exercise of checking boxes about human security without "clear and enforceable safeguards" to ensure it [12].

## 5   Conclusion

The discursive fragmentation of the DU domain into *good* and *bad* DU to serve economic goals, - although understandable from the perspective of the relative benefits for the imagined aggregate European society - casts the EIC as a transaction cost or 'Administrative burden' [according to DU review clause 1.1.5 & 6 in 4]. This is challenging for international security, for it hollows out the intent and content of security and rights protections agreed with other states and enshrined in multilateral agreements towards greater competitiveness in international trade in DUIs. As history has shown, if other nations choose to enhance competitiveness following the example of the EC, it would suggest a global weakening of the protections against bioterrorism - especially in emerging biologically-inspired dual use technologies such as artificial intelligence and robotics. To avoid this global race to the bottom, it is thus imperative that the EIC – as a basic tool for controlling DUIs – should be strengthened, beginning with a re-reframing of its purpose as a protective mechanism.

**Acknowledgements.** This work was supported by the European Union's Horizon 2020 Research and Innovation Programme (European Commission) [grant number 720270 (HBP SGA1)].

## References

1. Mahfoud, T., Aicardi, C., Datta, S., Rose, N.: Beyond dual use: exploring the limits of dual use as a guiding concept for ethical research. Issues in Science and Technology (Forthcoming)
2. European-Commission Dual-use trade controls Homepage. http://ec.europa.eu/trade/import-and-export-rules/export-from-eu/dual-use-controls/index_en.htm. Accessed 22 Jan 2018
3. Fuhrmann, M.: Exporting mass destruction? The determinants of dual-use trade. J. Peace Res. **45**(5), 633–652 (2008)
4. European-Commission. Report From The Commission To The European Parliament And The Council on the implementation of Regulation (EC) No 428/2009 setting up a Community regime for the control of exports, transfer, brokering and transit of dual-use items. COM (2016) 521 final., (428) (2016)

5. European-Commission. Commission Staff Working Document Impact assessment Report on the EU Export Control Policy Review. Proposal for a Regulation of the European Parliament and of the Council Setting up a Union Regime for the Control of Exports, Transfer, Brokering, Technical Assistance and Transit of Dual-Use Items (2016)
6. Stewart, I., Bauer, S.: Directorate-General for External Policies. Policy Department. Workshop Dual use export controls. European Union. In EP/EXPO/B/INTA/FWC/2013-08/Lot7/11 (2015)
7. Moravcsik, A.: Taking preferences seriously: a liberal theory of international politics. Int. Organ. **51**(4), 513–553 (1997)
8. Gowa, J.: Bipolarity, multipolarity, and free trade. Am. Polit. Sci. Rev. **83**(4), 1245–1256 (1989)
9. Moravcsik, A.: Liberal international relations theory: A social scientific assessment. Weatherhead Center for International Affairs Working Paper (2001)
10. Keohane, R., Nye, J.: Power and Interdependence, pp. 17–19. Little, Brown, Boston (1977)
11. Waltz, K.N.: Theory of International Politics. Addison-Wesley, Reading (1979)
12. Liberties.eu. Shared statement on the update of the EU dual-use regulation May 2017. Access Now (May), 1–5. https://www.accessnow.org/cms/assets/uploads/2017/05/NGO_Shared statement_dualuse_May2017.pdf. Accessed 18 Jan 2018
13. Stewart, I.: EU Production of Dual-use Goods. Project Alpha (2015)

# Neuromechanical Model of Rat Hind Limb Walking with Two Layer CPGs and Muscle Synergies

Kaiyu Deng[1]([⊠]), Nicholas S. Szczecinski[1], Dirk Arnold[2], Emanuel Andrada[2], Martin Fischer[2], Roger D. Quinn[1], and Alexander J. Hunt[3]

[1] Case Western Reserve University, Cleveland, OH, USA
kxd194@case.edu
[2] Friederich-Schiller-University, Jena, Germany
[3] Portland State University, Portland, OR, USA

**Abstract.** We present a synthetic nervous system modeling mammalian loco-motion using separate central pattern generator and pattern formation layers. The central pattern generator defines the rhythm of locomotion and the timing of extensor and flexor phase. We also investigated the capability of the pattern formation network to operate using muscle synergies instead of single muscle pairs. The result is that this model is capable of adjusting rhythm and muscle forces independently, and stepping is successfully produced using two synergies, one with the hip, and the other with the knee and ankle combined. This work demonstrates that pattern formation networks can activate multiple muscles in a coordinated way to produce steady walking. It encourages the use of more complex synergies activating more muscles in the legs for 3D limb motion.

**Keywords:** Synthetic nervous system · Rat · Rhythm generator
Muscle synergies

## 1 Introduction

There are many parallels between robotic and neurobiological walking controllers [1]. However, there are still many questions about how neurobiological systems produce dynamic and robust walking. For example, little is known about the details of neuron activity when animals perform steady walking, as it is difficult to record from individual neurons of live, intact animals as they move freely. Modeling is a useful tool to test how these circuits can give rise to walking [10].

Previously, we developed a synthetic nervous system (SNS) that applies the neuro-biological hypothesis of Central Pattern Generators (CPGs) [7] as the main controller for walking [5, 6]. We successfully showed that the reduced pattern generating circuit is sufficient for performing forward walking in a rat model and a dog robot. However, in the CPG model we implemented in our network, the "half-center" oscillators are directly connected to motoneurons. Thus, any excitation of the CPGs altered step cycle timing and motoneuron activation amplitude simultaneously [9]. This makes it difficult to modify rhythm timing and muscle force independently. Additionally, experiments on animal spinal cords have indicated an additional layer in the organization. Rhythmic

© Springer International Publishing AG, part of Springer Nature 2018
V. Vouloutsi et al. (Eds.): Living Machines 2018, LNAI 10928, pp. 134–144, 2018.
https://doi.org/10.1007/978-3-319-95972-6_15

bursts of motoneurons can be absent for a few cycles and reappear without phase shifting in the locomotor cycle during cat fictive locomotion [4, 8]. These so-called "non-resetting deletions" were also found in intracellular studies of scratch reflex activity in turtles [11]. To answer these questions, Rybak and others [9, 12–14] have proposed two-level CPGs that separate rhythm control from motoneuron activation levels. One goal for this paper is to test whether our rat model simulation could match biological findings by adding a rhythm generator structure to our CPGs.

Additionally, the exact method in which the multitude of muscles in the body are activated during walking is still unknown. By separating rhythm generation and motoneuron activation, we also enable the ability to activate muscle synergies instead of just antagonistic muscle pairs. If we were to implement our current pattern formation layer network (developed for antagonistic pairs of muscles) with the many more muscles actually in the rat leg, our neurobiological controller would grow significantly in complexity. Muscle synergies are considered a plausible way to simplify this control problem [3, 9, 15, 16]. It is theorized that the Central Nervous System produces a wide range of motor behaviors by co-activating groups of muscles with similar activation patterns in space or time [3, 15]. There are two types of muscle synergies [16]: (1) "synchronous synergies," which activate all muscles at the same time with no temporal delay, and (2) "time-varying synergies," which produce patterns with a temporal profile of weighting coefficient for each muscles.

This paper presents several improvements to our neural model of rat hind limbs. (1) We reconstructed our network hierarchically and implemented a rhythm generator to test new biological findings concerning the organization of a central pattern generator. (2) We removed one pattern formation network, making knee and ankle share a single pattern formation network to test the capabilities of the pattern formation network to activate muscle synergies instead of just single muscle pairs.

## 2   Knee and Ankle Synergy

We collected kinematic and dynamic data of rats running on a treadmill. Frame by frame tracking of x-ray video of these animals reveals coordination between joints. Figure 1 presents some of the frames. By applying red marks on the mid spine and all joints of the rat's left hind legs, we digitally tracked the joint motions.

During normal walking, the knee and ankle joint motions are similar while the hip joint motion follows its own pattern. Frame 4 to frame 5 of Fig. 1 show that the hip joint is still performing flexion while the ankle and the knee begin extension. Moreover, from frame 6 to frame 7, the hip extends while the ankle and the knee flex. These observations are verified by the resulting joint rotation data extracted from the frames (Fig. 2). The similarity of knee and ankle motion patterns in kinematic analysis motivates us to consider the possibility of applying the same rhythm control for both the knee and ankle joints.

Our previous SNS successfully reproduced rat forward walking in simulations. All three joints were properly coordinated by feedback to match the desired timing between stance and swing phase [5]. Comparing the pattern formation neuron activities of the

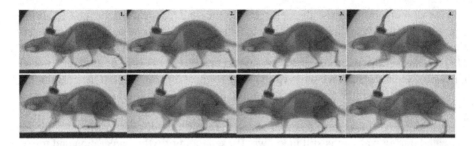

**Fig. 1.** Pictures from X-ray video of rat walking on the treadmill. We apply red marks on mid spinal cord and all joints of rat left hind leg to makes it easier to observe the joint motion. (Color figure online)

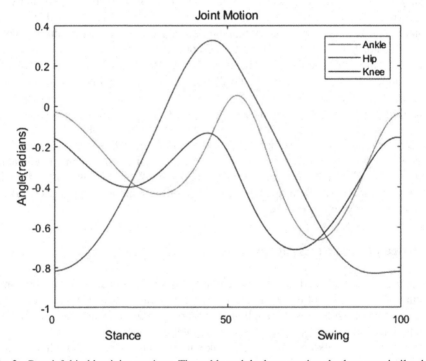

**Fig. 2.** Rats left hind leg joint motions. The ankle and the knee motion rhythms are similar, but the timing and the magnitude are different.

knee and ankle joint in that model also verify our hypothesis that the knee and the ankle can share the same pattern formation network to generate steady walking behavior (Fig. 3). The shape of neuron activations above −60 mV is similar for the knee and the ankle joint, and the active timing is nearly identical, while the hip joint MN activity operates with different phase timing.

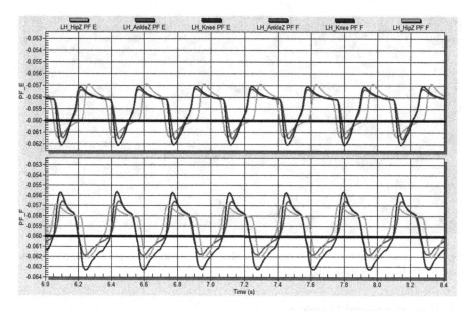

**Fig. 3.** The pattern formation neuron activity of our previous synthetic nervous system. The operation range of the excitatory synapses project pattern formation network activities to motoneuron is −60 mV to −50 mV.

## 3   Method

### 3.1   Biomechanical Modeling

All the modeling and simulation is done in Animatlab [2]. To improve simulation and calculation speed, we simplified the biomechanical model (Fig. 4). The biomechanical model reconstruction is limited to motion in the sagittal plane for the rat hind limb, resulting in a total of 6 degrees of freedom, three for each hind leg (hip, knee, and ankle). Instead of loading rat bones files scanned from x-ray images as was done in our previous work [5], we reconstructed the pelvis (red), femur (green), tibia (yellow), and foot (purple) with simple box models to speed up the simulation by 4 times. The length, weight, and density of the bones, and the insertion points and properties of muscle are the same as in our previous biomechanical model. Similar to previous work, we used two bars to support the front of the body and the tail while walking on the ground in the simulation.

**Fig. 4.** Biomechanical model of rat hind limb. Motion is constrained in the sagittal plane with hinge joints. (Color figure online)

## 3.2 Synthetic Neural Modeling

The previous version of our rat model used a neural controller for each limb with a CPG-pattern formation network that was coordinated by afferent feedback [5]. The new network adds a rhythm generator and removes one pattern formation network - the knee and the ankle now share a single pattern formation network. A hierarchical representation of the resulting network is shown in Fig. 5A.

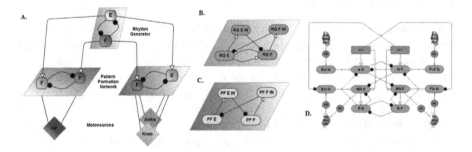

**Fig. 5.** Neural network. (A) Single Limb control hierarchy. (B) Rhythm Generator configuration. (C) Pattern Formation network. (D) Motoneuron.

The new neural network is composed of three hierarchies. The top layer is the Rhythm Generator layer (Fig. 5B), which is biologically located in the spinal cord. We modeled our rhythm generator similar to the one found in Zhang et al. [17], with two interacting neurons coupled by mutual excitation (weak connection) and inhibition (via inhibitory interneurons). The endogenous rhythmogenic properties of rhythm generator neurons are generated using persistent sodium channels [12]. The rhythm generator defines the rhythm of locomotion and the general timing of extensor and flexor phase.

The second layer is the Pattern Formation network (Fig. 5C) found in the distal regions of the spinal cord. It directs the rhythms from the rhythm generator to motoneurons and distributes the synergies to motoneuron pools. The knee and ankle share one pattern formation network. The last layer is Motoneuron Layer (Fig. 5D); this layer mediates the magnitude of motoneuron activation with feedback and it is connected to muscles and responsible for generating muscle force.

To test our hypothesis that by implementing the rhythm generator, our new SNS is capable of the different modes of sensory control and non-resetting deletions, we ran tests to investigate if our simulations matched the observed animal behaviors. To better observe the rhythm maintenance and phase shifting, we tuned the network to make the rat produce hopping motion in simulation, in which the behavior and neuron actives of the left and right hind legs are mirrored.

The first test inhibits the extensor neuron of the pattern formation layer (PF E in Fig. 5C). We expected to observe non phase-shifting on the post-inhibition rhythm. The second test inhibits the extensor neuron of the rhythm generator layer (RG E in Fig. 5B), which should result in permanent alteration of the walking rhythm. To eliminate other influences, we apply each stimulus with the same intensity and activation timing. Experimental results of longer deletions on the pattern formation layer is presented in the appendix.

## 4   Results

### 4.1   Non-resetting Deletions Test

We applied $-10$ nA tonic stimulus to inhibit the left hip pattern formation extensor neuron from 2s to 2.1s. Figure 6 presents the joint motion corresponding to this stimulus. The rat hind leg produced hopping motions until 2s, before the inhibitory stimulus was applied. At that moment, the hip joint was still in its flexion phase, but a short time after that while the right hip joint starts extension, the stimulus prolonged the flexion phase, causing the left leg to lag behind the master phase of the pattern generation level. The left hip restarts extension after the stimulus ends, and generates a fast step to compensate for the delay. There is a small phase shift after the stimulus ends, but a short time later, the motion rhythm quickly returned to the original motion rhythm. This brief phase shifting is caused by feedback coordinating the joint as shown in Fig. 6, the knee and the ankle joint also shift their phase accordingly to produce steady steps.

To better understand this rhythm behavior, we inspected the neuron activities of the left hind leg. As Fig. 7 depicts, the extensor neuron in the pattern formation network is inhibited by the stimulus, reducing the activation time of the extensor motoneuron. The cycle timing generated by the rhythm generator is not influenced by the stimulus. So after the stimulus ends, the extension phase is still ongoing. The pattern formation extensor neuron, driven by the rhythm generator, undergoes a swift hyper-polarization and produces more neuron activation than normal, compensating for the delay, which leads to an overshoot of extension in the hip joint as observed on Fig. 6. However, the rhythm generator is affected by afferent feedback for the following few cycles, which results in some phase shifting. However, the influence of the feedback is reduced by the intrinsic rhythmogenic properties of the rhythm generator, so the step cycle rhythm recovers.

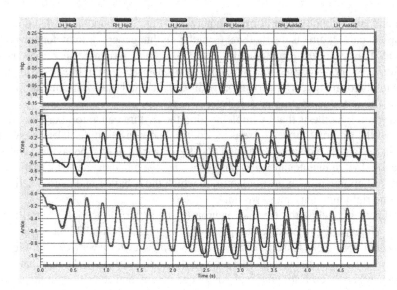

**Fig. 6.** Joint motion for non-resetting test. The stimulus was applied from 2s to 2.1s at left hip pattern formation extensor neuron.

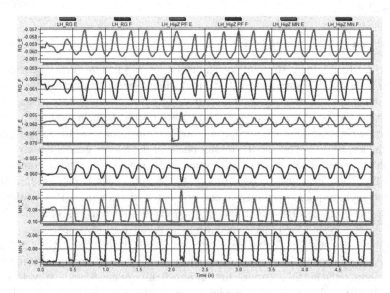

**Fig. 7.** Neuron actives of non-resetting deletions. The inhibitory stimuli applied at Pattern Formation extensor neuron from 2s to 2.1s.

## 4.2    Resetting Deletions Test

We also tested the resetting-deletion by inhibiting the left Rhythm Generator extensor neuron with the same stimulus. When the inhibiting stimulus is applied to the extensor neuron of the Rhythm Generator, the walking rhythm is permanently altered, as the rat produces a prolonged stance phase in the left leg (Fig. 8, t = 2). This switches the gait from hopping to alternating stepping, but without neural connections between the legs.

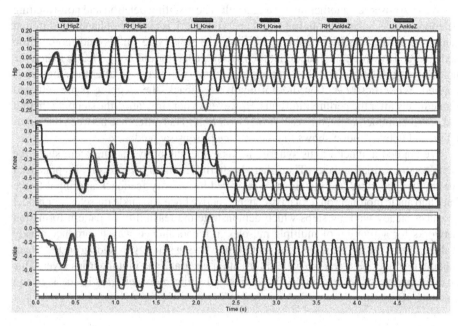

**Fig. 8.** Joint motion for resetting test. The stimulus was applied at left hip rhythm generator extensor neuron from 2s to 2.1s.

## 5    Discussion

In this work, we present improvements to our previous neural model of rat locomotion [5]. We made two primary improvements. First, we implemented a two-layer CPG structure, which enables our network to exhibit both phase-nonresetting and phase-resetting deletions. This is an important improvement for two reasons. First, our model is more biologically accurate in that it captures more phenomena observed in the animal. Second, this new model can more robustly control its stepping phase, which would be advantageous for a legged robot controlled by such a system, such as in Hunt et al. [6]. The second improvement was the establishment of a simple muscle synergy, coordinating the ankle and knee motion by using the same pattern formation layer for both joints. This is an important first step towards synergy-based control, which is an increasingly common idea in motor control [15, 16].

Our synthetic nervous system successfully produces steady hopping (Fig. 6) and alternating stepping (Fig. 8) and the hip and knee joint motion patterns for walking match the animal data. However, the ankle does not. This is possibly the result of simplifications we made in our biomechanical model. However, the advantage of these simplifications is much greater simulation speed which enables more rapid tuning of parameters in the neural network using our Matlab toolbox SIMSCAN [18]. More detailed modeling will be needed to match the ankle data.

We also observed another interesting result. The resetting deletion and non-resetting deletion tests revealed that our improved neural network is capable of handling different sensory control tasks by separately adjusting the step cycle timing and motoneuron activations. However, we found that the rhythm generator did not perfectly match the non-resetting deletions and the joint angle performs an overshoot after the stimulus is applied. While fictive motion did not involve feedback, the stepping phase returned immediately after the perturbation ends. However, in our simulation the stepping rhythm did not reset immediately, but reset slowly over time. This difference between our simulation and fictive motion shows the importance of sensory feedback.

We applied a synchronous synergy to knee and ankle, by making them share the same pattern formation layer. Their shared pattern formation layer receives inputs from the rhythm generator and the signal is reshaped by sensory feedback and input to the knee and ankle motoneuron pools. By coherent active knee and ankle muscles, our model produces steady walking steps which demonstrate the feasibility of pattern formation networks for activation of multiple muscles in a coordinated way to produce steady walking. In the future, we will implement a time-varying synergy by adding an additional modulation layer between the pattern formation layer and the motoneurons layer. This enables the use of more complex synergies activating more muscles in the legs and enabling 3D motion.

**Acknowledgements.** This work was supported by grants from the US-German CRCNS program including NSF IIS160811.

# Appendix

See Fig. 9.

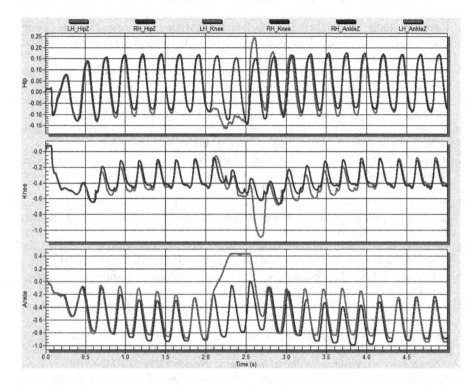

**Fig. 9.** Joint motion for non-resetting test. The stimulus was applied from 2s to 2.5s at left hip pattern formation extensor neuron.

# References

1. Buschmann, T., Ewald, A., von Twickel, A., Bueschges, A.: Controlling legs for locomotion —insights from robotics and neurobiology. Bioinspiration & Biomim. **10**(4), 041001 (2015)
2. Cofer, D., Cymbalyuk, G., Reid, J., Zhu, Y., Heitler, W.J., Edwards, D.H.: AnimatLab: a 3D graphics environment for neuromechanical simulations. J. Neurosci. Methods **187**(2), 280–288 (2010)
3. d'Avella, A., Saltiel, P., Bizzi, E.: Combinations of muscle synergies in the construction of a natural motor behavior. Nat. Neurosci. **6**(3), 300 (2003)
4. Grillner, S., Zangger, P.: On the central generation of locomotion in the low spinal cat. Exp. Brain Res. **34**(2), 241–261 (1979)
5. Hunt, A.J., Szczecinski, N.S., Andrada, E., Fischer, M., Quinn, R.D.: Using animal data and neural dynamics to reverse engineer a neuromechanical rat model. In: Wilson, S.P., Verschure, P.F.M.J., Mura, A., Prescott, T.J. (eds.) LIVINGMACHINES 2015. LNCS (LNAI), vol. 9222, pp. 211–222. Springer, Cham (2015). https://doi.org/10.1007/978-3-319-22979-9_21

6. Hunt, A., Szczecinski, N., Quinn, R.: Development and training of a neural controller for hind leg walking in a dog robot. Front. Neurorobotics **11**, 18 (2017)
7. Ivashko, D.G., Prilutsky, B.I., Markin, S.N., Chapin, J.K., Rybak, I.A.: Modeling the spinal cord neural circuitry controlling cat hindlimb movement during locomotion. Neurocomputing **52**, 621–629 (2003)
8. Lafreniere-Roula, M., McCrea, D.A.: Deletions of rhythmic motoneuron activity during fictive locomotion and scratch provide clues to the organization of the mammalian central pattern generator. J. Neurophysiol. **94**(2), 1120–1132 (2005)
9. McCrea, D.A., Rybak, I.A.: Organization of mammalian locomotor rhythm and pattern generation. Brain Res. Rev. **57**(1), 134–146 (2008)
10. Pearson, K., Ekeberg, Ö., Büschges, A.: Assessing sensory function in locomotor systems using neuro-mechanical simulations. Trends Neurosci. **29**(11), 625–631 (2006)
11. Robertson, G.A., Stein, P.S.: Synaptic control of hindlimb motoneurones during three forms of the fictive scratch reflex in the turtle. J. Physiol. **404**(1), 101–128 (1988)
12. Rybak, I.A., Shevtsova, N.A., Lafreniere-Roula, M., McCrea, D.A.: Modelling spinal circuitry involved in locomotor pattern generation: insights from deletions during fictive locomotion. J. Physiol. **577**(2), 617–639 (2006)
13. Rybak, I.A., Stecina, K., Shevtsova, N.A., McCrea, D.A.: Modelling spinal circuitry involved in locomotor pattern generation: insights from the effects of afferent stimulation. J. Physiol. **577**(2), 641–658 (2006)
14. Shevtsova, N.A., Rybak, I.A.: Organization of flexor–extensor interactions in the mammalian spinal cord: insights from computational modelling. J. Physiol. **594**(21), 6117–6131 (2016)
15. Ting, L.H., McKay, J.L.: Neuromechanics of muscle synergies for posture and movement. Curr. Opin. Neurobiol. **17**(6), 622–628 (2007)
16. Tresch, M.C., Jarc, A.: The case for and against muscle synergies. Curr. Opin. Neurobiol. **19**(6), 601–607 (2009)
17. Zhang, J., Lanuza, G.M., Britz, O., Wang, Z., Siembab, V.C., Zhang, Y., Velasquez, T., Alvarez, F.J., Goulding, M.: V1 and v2b interneurons secure the alternating flexor-extensor motor activity mice require for limbed locomotion. Neuron **82**(1), 138–150 (2014)
18. Szczecinski, N.S., Hunt, A.J., Quinn, R.D.: Design process and tools for dynamic neuromechanical models and robot controllers. Biol. Cybern. **111**(1), 105–127 (2017)

# A Hexapod Walking Robot Mimicking Navigation Strategies of Desert Ants Cataglyphis

Julien Dupeyroux, Julien Serres, and Stéphane Viollet$^{(\boxtimes)}$

Aix Marseille Univ., CNRS, ISM UMR 7287, Marseille, France
stephane.viollet@univ-amu.fr,
http://www.biorobotics.eu/

**Abstract.** In this study, a desert ant-inspired celestial compass and a bio-inspired minimalist optic flow sensor named M$^2$APix (which stands for Michaelis Menten Auto-adaptive Pixels), were embedded onboard our 2 kg-hexapod walking robot called AntBot, in order to reproduce the homing behavior observed in desert ants *Cataglyphis fortis*. The robotic challenge here was to make the robot come back home autonomously after being displaced from its initial location. The navigation toolkit of AntBot comprises the celestial-based heading direction, and both stride- and ventral optic flow-based odometry, as observed in desert ants. Experimental results show that our bio-inspired approach can be useful for autonomous outdoor navigation robotics in case of GPS or magnetometer failure, but also to compensate for a drift of the inertial measurement unit. In addition, our strategy requires few computational resources due to the small number of pixels (only 14 here), and a high robustness and precision (mean error of 4.8 cm for an overall path ranging from 2 m to 5 m). Finally, this work presents highly interesting field results of ant-based theoretical models for homing tasks that have not been tested yet in insectoid robots.

**Keywords:** Celestial compass · Polarized light · Optic flow
Outdoor navigation · Homing · Odometry · Path integration
Legged robot · Biorobotics

## 1 Introduction

Most insects, especially desert ants *Cataglyphis*, are experts in daily long-range navigation, reaching highly robust precision in locating significant areas (nest, food). Due to the extreme heat, desert ants cannot use pheromones to track their navigating path. However, they are equipped with a useful navigation toolkit comprising: (i) a path integration (PI) routine relying on celestial cues, and both stride and ventral optic flow integration, and (ii) a view-based landmark guidance where panoramic snapshots are memorized to retrieve and follow routes established in cluttered environments [1–3]. It has been shown that desert ants

V. Vouloutsi et al. (Eds.): Living Machines 2018, LNAI 10928, pp. 145–156, 2018.
https://doi.org/10.1007/978-3-319-95972-6_16

keep their PI updated whenever they follow familiar routes or not. However, as PI is prone to accumulative errors, desert ants will opt for landmark-based navigation when visual cues are available [4].

The sensory modalities involved in desert ants *Cataglyphis* PI strategy are combined to compute a homing vector, namely a vector (distance and heading direction) constantly pointing toward the nest when foraging. The heading direction information is computed based on celestial cues: the sun position in the sky and the direction of linearly polarized skylight (e-vectors) in the zenith part of the sky [5]. The acquisition of the polarized cues is found in the insect's dorsal rim area (DRA) where photoreceptors are sensitive to the direction of polarization [6], mostly in the ultraviolet (UV) range [5]. Then, desert ants estimate their distance from both stride [7] and ventral optic flow [8] integration, though *Cataglyphis* are known to correct the estimated distance in the absence of any optic flow information.

Former implementations of the desert ants navigational toolkit have led to very interesting results. The Sahabot 1 and 2 projects [9,10] experimented celestial compass on board wheeled robots in an ant-like homing navigation task with average error of 13.5 cm. The sensor was composed of three polarization units, each of them combining two visible polarized light sensors with orthogonal polarization selectivity. According to the Labhart's polarization opponent model [6], they computed the direction of polarization of the moving robot. More recently, a miniaturization of this celestial compass was proposed by [11,12], embedded onboard a small rover in [13] and tested in ant-like homing navigation tasks. The average error in these experiments was equal to 42 cm, and their odometer used wheel encoders. Interesting investigations have been conducted on polarization vision [14,15]. Yet, it seems no other full robotic implementation of polarization vision has been used as an input for autonomous outdoor navigation tasks.

In this paper, we propose to test our ant-inspired 2-pixel UV-polarized light celestial compass and our 12-pixels $M^2$APix bio-inspired ventral optic flow sensor on board our hexapod walking robot called AntBot. The challenge was to make the robot autonomously come back to its initial location after being randomly displaced, with outbound trajectories ranging from 4 m to 8 m. The AntBot insectoid robot is fully described in Sect. 2. The homing procedure is outlined in Sect. 3, and field results are displayed and discussed in Sect. 4.

## 2    AntBot, the Robotic Ant

### 2.1    Designing the Hexapod Walking Robot

AntBot is a six-legged walking robot designed to mimic desert ants *Cataglyphis fortis* (Fig. 1), first on the morphological and locomotive aspects, then on the sensory modalities and navigation skills. Each leg has three joints actuated by means of Dynamixel AX 18 servomotors, integrated in a fully 3D-printed structure (printing being made with polyactic acid (PLA) filament). The servos are all connected to an Arduino-like micro-controller (the OpenCM 9.04C board) through USART serial communication. An extra degree of freedom has been added to control the roll of the robot while walking, but in this study the roll actuation is only used for the heading estimation. The locomotion firmware of AntBot has been adapted from the one used for his predecessor Hexabot [16] and thus benefits from high walking stability. AntBot is mastered by a Raspberry Pi 2B micro-computer, which communicates with all sensors as described in the robot's electronic architecture shown in Fig. 1. A WiFi communication can be established between the robot's computer unit and the host computer. The robot is powered by a three cells 11.4 V 5300 mAh lithium polymer battery (Gens ACE), with a maximum autonomy of 30 min.

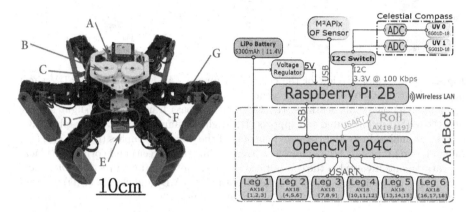

**Fig. 1.** Left: Photography of AntBot. (A) AntBots micro-computer Raspberry Pi 2B placed below its top shelf (in white). (B) The celestial compass with its two POL-units $UV_0$ and $UV_1$ looking at the zenith part of the sky dome. (C) Roll actuation of the top shelf. (D) Ventral optic flow sensor called $M^2$APix. (E) AntBot's powering battery (Gens ACE, 11.4V 5300 mAh). (F) AntBot's micro-controller OpenCM 9.04C, set on top of the battery. (G) Dynamixel AX18 servomotors. Right: Hardware architecture of AntBot. The robot's low-level electronics, including the micro-controller ant the 19 servomotors, are gathered within the dashed line.

## 2.2   The Celestial Compass

To compute its heading direction while navigating, AntBot makes use of its ant-inspired celestial compass embedded on its roll-actuated shelf. It is composed of two UV-light photodiodes SG01D18 (SgLux) topped with rotating linear sheet polarizers (HNP'B replacement), for a final spectral sensitivity from 270 nm to 400 nm with peak transmission at 330 nm (Fig. 2). Each polarization unit (POL-unit), namely $UV_0$ and $UV_1$, has a refreshing rate of 33 Hz and an angular field of view of approximately 100°. Former investigations showed that our celestial compass successfully worked under various weather conditions, even with very poor UV-index [17,18].

Let $x$ be the orientation of the linear sheet polarizers. According to the polarization pattern of the skylight at the zenith, $UV_0(x)$ and $UV_1(x)$ are expected to be $\pi$-periodic sine waves (see [17] for details). Consequently, these raw signals

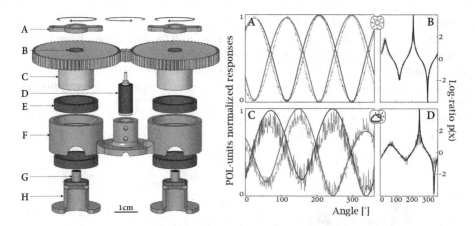

**Fig. 2.** Left: Exploded view of the celestial compass. (A) Fixation for the UV sheet polarizers (B), holded by rotating gears (C). (D) Stepper motor AM0820-A-0,225-7 (Faulhaber). (E) Ball bearings. (F) Celestial compass frame. (G) UV-light sensors SG01D-18 (SgLux) mounted on supports (H). Right: Examples of signals. Graphs (A,C) display normalized raw and corrected outputs of the celestial compass ($UV_0$ in red, $UV_1$ in blue), and graphs (B,D) display the corresponding raw (green) and corrected (black) log-ratio signals involved in the computation of the robot's heading direction. Data were collected in Marseille in April, 2017, under both clear (A,B) and cloudy (C,D) weather conditions (UV-index equal to 7). (Color figure online)

are first low-pass filtered and then normalized between $\epsilon$ and 1 as described in Fig. 2 ($\epsilon \sim 10^{-6}$ is set to prevent from logarithm computation failure). We then compute the log-ratio $p(x)$ of the two normalized and corrected signals $UV_0^{nc}(x)$ and $UV_1^{nc}(x)$, therefore:

$$p(x) = \log_{10}\left(\frac{UV_1^{nc}(x)}{UV_0^{nc}(x)}\right) \qquad (1)$$

In a $[0; \pi]$ interval, the angle of polarization corresponds to the fiber angle for the maximum value of the $p$-function, while the angle direction $\Psi$ of the solar meridian is depicted by the fiber angle for the minimum value. At this stage of the heading direction computation, $\Psi$ is considered between $0°$ and $180°$. Consequently, we have:

$$\Psi = \frac{1}{4}\left(\underset{x\in[0;\pi]}{\arg\min}\, p(x) + \underset{x\in[0;\pi]}{\arg\max}\, p(x) + \underset{x\in[\pi;2\pi]}{\arg\min}\, p(x) + \underset{x\in[\pi;2\pi]}{\arg\max}\, p(x) - \pi\right) \qquad (2)$$

Due to the physical properties of the Rayleigh's scattering of sunlight, it is not possible to determine the absolute orientation of AntBot from the polarized light celestial compass. In their project Sahabot, Lambrinos *et al.* used 8 photodiodes to detect the angular sector corresponding to the highest illumination (e.g. the sun location) [9]. Here, the solar/anti-solar ambiguity is treated as follows: the top shelf is rolled left and right to get the sun position which corresponds to the highest UV level measured by the two POL-units. The final decision is taken based on the algorithm depicted by Fig. 3 on the basis of the initial heading direction measured $\Psi_{INIT}$ when the robot is placed with the sun exactly aligned with its longitudinal axis.

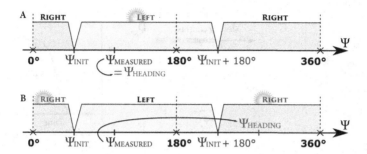

**Fig. 3.** Principle of solar-based ambiguity resolution of the heading direction computation. (A) The measured heading direction $\Psi_{MEASURED}$ is located in the LEFT angular sector as the sun is located on the left of the robot. Consequently, $\Psi_{HEADING} = \Psi_{MEASURED}$. (B) In this case, the measured heading direction is still located in the LEFT angular sector but the robot detects the sun on its right: $\Psi_{HEADING} = \Psi_{MEASURED} + 180°$.

When the rolling procedure leads to very similar left and right UV-levels, then the robot decides whether $\Psi = \Psi_{INIT}$ or $\Psi = \Psi_{INIT} + 180°$ just by integrating its stride-based orientation. Indeed, despite this estimation is poor due to cumulative drift, it is good enough to be used as a cue for disambiguation. Last, the sun deviation was corrected using a solar ephemeris table with respect to the time and location of each experiments.

## 2.3    The Ventral Optic Flow Sensor

Our hexapod AntBot also integrates a 12-pixel ventral optic flow sensor called $M^2APix$ (Michaelis-Menten Auto-adaptive Pixels, Fig. 4, [19]) which main advantage consists in auto-adaptability in a 7-decade light range, with appropriate responses when measuring signals that change up to $\pm 3$ decades. This attribute makes $M^2APix$ suitable for outdoor experiments where light variations occur randomly.

The ventral optic flow $\omega$ (in $rad/s$) is defined as follows:

$$\omega = \frac{\Delta\varphi}{\Delta T} = \frac{V}{D} \tag{3}$$

with $\Delta\varphi$ the inter-pixel angle between two adjacent pixels in a row (Fig. 4), $\Delta T$ the time delay measured between two adjacent pixels, $V$ the robot's speed and $D$ the height-to-the-ground of the $M^2APix$ sensor. Former characterization of the sensor used in AntBot showed that $\Delta\varphi$ is equal to $3.57°$ with standard deviation of 0.027° (see [20] for details). $\Delta T$ is computed using the cross-correlation method described in [21]. The height variation of AntBot does not exceed 1 cm while walking. On average, these small variations do not disturb $M^2$APix measurements enough to cause navigation failure. In particular, this property is guaranteed by a threshold process ahead the cross-correlation computation.

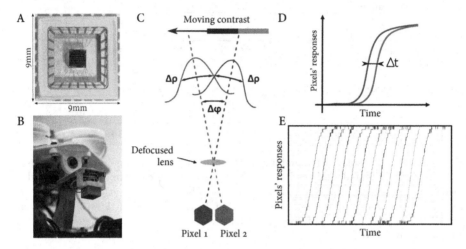

**Fig. 4.** (A) The $M^2$APix silicon retina. Adapted from [19]. (B) Photography of the $M^2$APix sensor topped with the optics of a Raspberry Pi NoIR Camera and connected to the Teensy 3.2 micro-controller. (C) Optics geometry explaining how the optic flow detection is operated. $\Delta\varphi$ is the inter-pixel angle between two adjacent pixels forming a local motion sensor (LMS). $\Delta\rho$ is the acceptance angle given by the width of the Gaussian angular sensitivity at half height. Adapted from [21]. (D) Theoretical signals obtained for pixels 1 and 2 from (C) according to the moving contrast. Adapted from [21]. $\Delta T$ is the time delay between the two pixels and is used for optic flow computation. (E) Real signals obtained for the 12 pixels when detecting a moving edge.

## 3    The Ant-Inspired Navigation Model

Let $\Psi_{ROBOT}$ be the orientation of the robot relative to the ground horizontal X-axis, $\Psi_{COMP}$ its orientation according to the solar azimuth obtained with the celestial compass, $\Psi_{INIT}$ the initial orientation given by the celestial compass, and $\Psi_{RELEASE}$ the orientation of the robot after being released on the ground, also given by the celestial compass. Every angle value is given in degrees. The location of the robot is given for each homing checkpoint $C_i$ by its $(X[i], Y[i])$ position. The initial position is set at $(0,0)$ and the release position is provided by the operator and denoted as $(X_{release}, Y_{release})$. All Cartesian coordinates are given in centimeters. When the robot is released on a random place on the ground, the homing distance $Dist_{HOMING}$ and orientation $\Psi_{HOMING}$ are computed using Eqs. 4 and 5 respectively. The combination of the homing distance and direction forms the robot's homing vector, as described in desert ants.

$$Dist_{HOMING} = \sqrt{X_{release}^2 + Y_{release}^2} \qquad (4)$$

$$\Psi_{HOMING} = \begin{cases} atan\left(\frac{Y_{release}}{X_{release}}\right), & \text{if } X_{release} < 0 \\ 180 + atan\left(\frac{Y_{release}}{X_{release}}\right), & \text{if } X_{release} > 0 \end{cases} \qquad (5)$$

In case the position along the X-axis is equal to 0.00 (with float precision), the heading direction is chosen between 0° and 180° on the basis of turning stride integration. The homing rotation order to be applied $R_H$ is given by:

$$R_H = \Psi_{HOMING} - \Psi_{RELEASE} \qquad (6)$$

The stride order is computed as the Euclid division of $Dist_{HOMING}$ by the average stride length $d_{Stride}$, then equally split into the $N_H$ homing checkpoints. For each checkpoint $C_i$, $i \in [1..10]$, the current orientation of the robot $\Psi_{ROBOT}[i]$ is computed as follows:

$$\Psi_{ROBOT}[i] = \Psi_{COMP}[i] - \Psi_{INIT} \qquad (7)$$

The walked distance $Dist[i]$, estimated from the robot's sensors and stride, from checkpoint $C_{i-1}$ to checkpoint $C_i$ is computed as the mean between the static estimate of distance provided by the stride integrator, and the dynamic estimate of distance provided by the ventral optic flow sensor as given in Eq. 3:

$$Dist[i] = \frac{1}{2}\left( Stride[i] \cdot d_{Stride} + \beta \cdot \frac{D \cdot \Delta\varphi \cdot T_{STRIDE}[i]}{\Delta T[i]} \right) \qquad (8)$$

where $Stride[i]$ is the number of strides executed, $\beta$ is an empiric gain, $D$ is the distance to the ground of the $M^2$APix sensor, $\Delta\varphi$ is the inter-pixel angle of the $M^2$APix, $T_{STRIDE}[i]$ is the walking time, and $\Delta T[i]$ is the time delay between two adjacent pixels which detect the same light variation. The robot then computes its current location $\big(X[i], Y[i]\big)$ relative to its release point:

$$\begin{cases} X[i] = X[i-1] + Dist[i] \cdot \cos\big(\Psi_{ROBOT}[i]\big) \\ Y[i] = Y[i-1] + Dist[i] \cdot \sin\big(\Psi_{ROBOT}[i]\big) \end{cases} \qquad (9)$$

The homing procedure is divided into $N_H$ checkpoints separated by steady distances. For each checkpoint $C_i$, $i \in [1.. N_H]$, AntBot acquires its new heading, and computes a new homing angle (Eq. 5, using the new $(X[i], Y[i])$ coordinates) which is compared to the current one. If the two homing angles differs by more than one turning stride, then AntBot updates its homing vector. The same test is made on the homing distance (using Eq. 4 with the correct coordinates). These $N_H$ homeward checkpoints therefore make the robot able to precisely estimate its drift and correct its ballistic trajectory toward the goal location.

*Choice of the Parameter $\beta$ in Eq. 8.* The Dynamixel servos used in AntBot exhibit varying dynamic behavior in accordance with the ambient temperature.

Consequently, the estimated average distance traveled may differ between morning and afternoon experiments. Besides, the first and last strides are prone to highly variable length as the robot is stepping from null to maximum speed, and vice versa, which involves high optic flow measurements. Therefore, if the number of strides to be applied is low, the optic flow disturbances will inevitably cause wrong distance estimate. To solve these issues, a set of empiric gains $\beta$ has been used to correct the optic flow measurements (Table 1).

**Table 1.** Empiric gain $\beta$ used for the outdoor experiments. $\beta_M$ stands for the morning value of $\beta$, and $\beta_A$ is for the afternoon value.

| Number of strides | $\beta_M$ | $\beta_A$ |
|---|---|---|
| 1 or 2 | 0.667 | 0.500 |
| 3 | 0.850 | 0.750 |
| More than 3 | 0.980 | 0.980 |

## 4   Experimental Results

According to its firmware, several parameters can be adjusted in order to set AntBot's walking tripod gait (Table 2). The values used for the experiments led to the following gait characteristics: AntBot's straight forward walking speed was approximately 10 cm/s with an average stride length $d_{Stride}$ equal to 8.2 cm, and its average turning angle per turning stride is equal to 10.9°. These characteristics highly depend on the environmental conditions, especially in terms of temperature. Finally, the height of the M²APix sensor $D$ in the experimental conditions is constant and equal to 17 cm.

**Table 2.** Description of the walking gait parameters of AntBot's firmware.

| Parameters | Description | Min | Max | AntBot |
|---|---|---|---|---|
| FREQ | Frequency of execution of the walking strides | 0.2 Hz | 3 Hz | 1.0 Hz |
| DX | Amplitude of a straight forward stride length | - | - | 8.2 cm |
| TURN | Amplitude of a turning stride | - | - | 10.9° |
| ALT | Height of the legs' end during the transfer phase | 10 mm | 50 mm | 20 mm |
| H | Height of the robot's center of mass | 55 mm | 145 mm | 75 mm |

Each experiment is organized as follows: the operator first places the robot onto its departure location $(0, 0)$. AntBot then computes its initial heading angle $\Psi_{INIT}$, before being displaced to a random location $(X_{release}, Y_{release})$ with a random heading angle $\Psi_{RELEASE}$. This angle is acquired by AntBot before computing its homing vector. Then the homing procedure is executed until AntBot

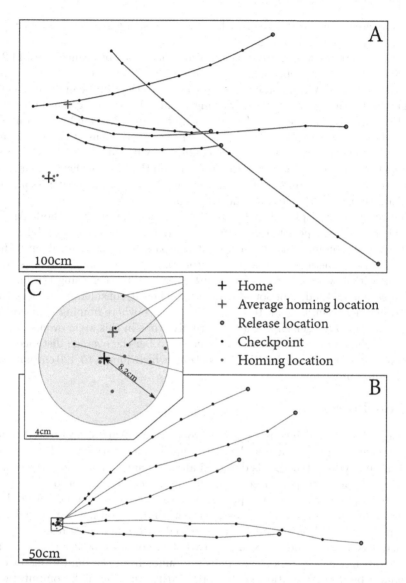

**Fig. 5.** Overall results of the homing experiments. Black cross: initial location to be reached. Red cross: average final position. Red dots: where the robot believes to be at the end of the homing procedure. Black circles: release locations. (A) Homing trajectories according to the blind method (both distance and orientation are computed by stride integration). (B) Homing trajectories when the robot uses the celestial compass to compute its heading direction, and merges both ventral optic flow and stride integration to estimate its travel distance. (C) Magnified view of the homing results in (B); the circle depicts the positions that are less than one stride away from the goal. (Color figure online)

reaches its goal with a distance error less than one stride length (*ie* 8.2 cm). The number of checkpoints $N_H$ was set at 8.

The experiments were performed in Marseille, south of France (43°14'02.1" N, 5°26'37.4" E), from February 15 to February 25, 2018, under clear sky conditions without any day-time preference. According to the European Space Agency (ESA), the UV-index was slightly varying around 1.6 (index given under clear sky). Five experiments were conducted, each of them corresponding to a unique and random release location. To show how precise and robust this ant-inspired strategy is, the same experiments were conducted without using any sensor: the homing vector was computed and updated only on the basis of the stride integrator. Consequently, this blind approach prevents AntBot from getting its angular and distance drifts along its inbound trajectory.

The results are displayed in Fig. 5. When using the blind method, AntBot resulted in an mean position error equal to 124 cm with high variability (sd: 59 cm). When homing with the celestial compass and the ventral optic flow sensor, AntBot drastically reduced its error: the average homing error is equal to 4.8 cm with low variability (sd: 1.8 cm). Besides, whether using the blind or the full sensor method, AntBot always stops when it considers to be less than one stride away from its goal. In the particular case where homing is performed with the ant-inspired sensors, AntBot actually stops in this area, even if its real location slightly differs from where it believes to be: the average distance error between real and believed locations is 5.4 cm, which jumps to 120 cm with the blind homing procedure.

## 5    Conclusion

We designed a new ant-inspired hexapod robot called AntBot and tested in real homing navigation experiments. AntBot is ant-like at every level of its conception: first, its overall structure is designed after the ants' thorax and legs (6 legs, hexagonal shape); the poor resolution of the insect vision is also reproduced with only 14 pixels (the vision of polarization, as observed in the DRA, and the perception of ventral optic flow); last, the path integration navigation behavior of desert ants *Cataglyphis* has been reproduced with remarkable results.

AntBot is an outstanding example of what biorobotics means: this is a fully autonomous navigating robot that does not suffer from the limitations of conventional tools (low-resolution GPS, IMUs' drift, and the high computational cost of SLAM methods, for example), and we hope it will give rise to some interesting discussions among the members of the biologists' community, on topics such as navigation. In that sense, AntBot could be considered in testing neural models of the insects' path integrator like those proposed in [22,23].

Future work will focus on the robustness and precision of the presented method with respect to variable meteorological conditions, and will be compared to gradual integration of the sensors in the path integration model. The odometry will also be investigated to reduce the stride-based distance estimation error [24]. Soon, AntBot will be asked to travel random trajectories before coming back to its departure location.

**Acknowledgments.** The authors would like to thank Marc Boyron and Julien Diperi for their technical support in the conception of the celestial compass.

**Funding**
This work was supported by the French Direction Générale de l'Armement (DGA), CNRS, Aix-Marseille University, the Provence-Alpes-Côte d'Azur region, and the French National Research Agency for Research (ANR) with the Equipex/Robotex project.

# References

1. Muller, M., Wehner, R.: Path integration in desert ants, cataglyphis fortis. Proc. Nat. Acad. Sci. **85**(14), 5287–5290 (1988)
2. Collett, M., Collett, T.S., Bisch, S., Wehner, R.: Local and global vectors in desert ant navigation. Nature **394**(6690), 269 (1998)
3. Wehner, R.: Desert ant navigation: how miniature brains solve complex tasks. J. Comp. Physiol. A. **189**(8), 579–588 (2003)
4. Wehner, R.: The desert ant's navigational toolkit: procedural rather than positional knowledge. Navigation **55**(2), 101–114 (2008)
5. Labhart, T., Meyer, E.P.: Detectors for polarized skylight in insects: a survey of ommatidial specializations in the dorsal rim area of the compound eye. Microsc. Res. Tech. **47**(6), 368–379 (1999)
6. Labhart, T.: Polarization-opponent interneurons in the insect visual system. Nature **331**(6155), 435 (1988)
7. Wittlinger, M., Wehner, R., Wolf, H.: The desert ant odometer: a stride integrator that accounts for stride length and walking speed. J. Exp. Biol. **210**(2), 198–207 (2007)
8. Ronacher, B., Gallizzi, K., Wohlgemuth, S., Wehner, R.: Lateral optic flow does not influence distance estimation in the desert ant Cataglyphis fortis. J. Exp. Biol. **203**(7), 1113–1121 (2000)
9. Lambrinos, D., Kobayashi, H., Pfeifer, R., Maris, M., Labhart, T., Wehner, R.: An autonomous agent navigating with a polarized light compass. Adapt. Behav. **6**(1), 131–161 (1997)
10. Moller, R., Lambrinos, D., Roggendorf, T., Pfeifer, R., Wehner, R.: Insect strategies of visual homing in mobile robots. In: Proceedings of the Computer Vision and Mobile Robotics Workshop CVMR, vol. 98 (2001)
11. Chu, J., Zhao, K., Zhang, Q., Wang, T.: Construction and performance test of a novel polarization sensor for navigation. Sens. Actuators A: Phys. **148**(1), 75–82 (2008)
12. Chu, J.K., Wang, Z.W., Guan, L., Liu, Z., Wang, Y.L., Zhang, R.: Integrated polarization dependent photodetector and its application for polarization navigation. IEEE Photonics Technol. Lett. **26**(5), 469–472 (2014)
13. Chu, J., Wang, H., Chen, W., Li, R.: Application of a novel polarization sensor to mobile robot navigation. In: 2009 International Conference on Mechatronics and Automation, ICMA 2009, pp. 3763–3768. IEEE (2009)
14. Stürzl, W., Carey, N.: A fisheye camera system for polarisation detection on UAVs. In: Fusiello, A., Murino, V., Cucchiara, R. (eds.) ECCV 2012, Part II. LNCS, vol. 7584, pp. 431–440. Springer, Heidelberg (2012). https://doi.org/10.1007/978-3-642-33868-7_43

15. Stürzl, W.: A lightweight single-camera polarization compass with covariance estimation. In: IEEE International Conference on Computer Vision (2017)
16. Dupeyroux, J., Passault, G., Ruffier, F., Viollet, S., Serres, J.: Hexabot: a small 3D-printed six-legged walking robot designed for desert ant-like navigation tasks. In: 2017 20th IFAC Word Congress, Toulouse, France, pp. 16628–16631 (2017)
17. Dupeyroux, J., Diperi, J., Boyron, M., Viollet, S., Serres, J.: A novel insect-inspired optical compass sensor for a hexapod walking robot. In: IROS 2017-IEEE/RSJ International Conference on Intelligent Robots and Systems, Vancouver, Canada, pp. 3439–3445 (2017)
18. Dupeyroux, J., Diperi, J., Boyron, M., Viollet, S., Serres, J.: A bio-inspired celestial compass applied to an ant-inspired robot for autonomous navigation. In: ECMR-European Conference on Mobile Robotics, Paris, France (2017)
19. Mafrica, S., Godiot, S., Menouni, M., Boyron, M., Expert, F., Juston, R., Marchand, N., Ruffier, F., Viollet, S.: A bio-inspired analog silicon retina with Michaelis-Menten auto-adaptive pixels sensitive to small and large changes in light. Opt. Express $23(5)$, 5614–5635 (2015)
20. Dupeyroux, J., Boutin, V., Serres, J., Perrinet, L., Viollet, S.: $M^2$APix: a bio-inspired auto-adaptive visual sensor for robust ground height estimation. In: 2018 IEEE International Symposium on Circuits and Systems (ISCAS), Florence, Italy (2018, Accepted)
21. Vanhoutte, E., Mafrica, S., Ruffier, F., Bootsma, R.J., Serres, J.: Time-of-travel methods for measuring optical flow on board a micro flying robot. Sensors $17(3)$, 571 (2017)
22. Haferlach, T., Wessnitzer, J., Mangan, M., Webb, B.: Evolving a neural model of insect path integration. Adapt. Behav. $15(3)$, 273–287 (2007)
23. Stone, T., Webb, B., Adden, A., Weddig, N.B., Honkanen, A., Templin, R., Wcislo, W., Scimeca, L., Warrant, E., Heinze, S.: An anatomically constrained model for path integration in the bee brain. Current Biol. $27(20)$, 3069–3085 (2017)
24. Lin, P.C., Komsuoglu, H., Koditschek, D.E.: A leg configuration measurement system for full-body pose estimates in a hexapod robot. IEEE Trans. Robot. $21(3)$, 411–422 (2005)

# Development and Characterization of a Novel Biomimetic Peristaltic Pumping System with Flexible Silicone-Based Soft Robotic Ring Actuators

Falk Esser[1,2(✉)], Friederike Krüger[1], Tom Masselter[1], and Thomas Speck[1,2]

[1] Plant Biomechanics Group, Faculty of Biology, Botanic Garden University Freiburg, Freiburg im Breisgau, Germany
`Falk.esser@biologie.uni-freiburg.de`
[2] FMF – Freiburg Materials Research Center, Freiburg im Breisgau, Germany

**Abstract.** In nature and technology peristaltic pumping systems can be found transporting various media in a simple and secure way. In the field of soft robotics different types of peristaltic pumping systems exist, most with rigid framing and complex actuators like pneumatic network (pneu-net) fluidic elastomer actuators or artificial muscles. The novel biomimetic peristaltic pumping system presented in this study is actuated by silicone-based, flexible, compliant, lightweight pneumatic ring actuators with an elliptical inner conduit. Single actuators as well as the whole peristaltic pumping system are characterized in terms of occlusion rate and volume flow rate. The characterization indicates that the developed flexible and elastic silicone-based peristaltic pump achieves sufficient flow rates and can be an alternative to conventional technical pumps.

**Keywords:** Silicone-based ring actuators · Elliptical conduit · Soft robotics Peristaltic pumping system · Biomimetics

## 1 Introduction

Directional transport of various fluidic media is achieved in nature and technology via the utilization of pumping systems. Natural pumping systems comprise muscular contracting chambers with valves, as found e.g. in hearts, different types of lungs, open circulatory systems of arthropods, ciliated surfaces and peristaltic contractions of hollow organs [1–4]. Technical pumping systems like rotary and positive displacement pumps, e.g. centrifugal pumps, rotary vane pumps and gear pumps are the technological state-of-the-art with flow rates from 100 to 1000 l/h for automotive coolant pumps depending on engine conditions [5, 6].

In the present study, we focus on the implementation of peristalsis into a novel biomimetic pumping system based on a flexible silicone material. In preliminary studies, we identified and characterized biological pumping systems and their biomimetic potential [4, 7]. The peristaltic principle was identified as very promising for a biomimetic implementation in terms of technical feasibility and innovation depth. Consequently, for a prior study, we developed a novel foam-based peristalsis pump (FBPP) with soft

© Springer International Publishing AG, part of Springer Nature 2018
V. Vouloutsi et al. (Eds.): Living Machines 2018, LNAI 10928, pp. 157–167, 2018.
https://doi.org/10.1007/978-3-319-95972-6_17

robotic ring actuators (FSRA) [8]. The FSRAs consisted of flexible open celled PU-foam coated with PU rubber and were capable of inward directed occlusion ratios up to 60%, which is in the range of their biological role model, i.e., the esophagus. The peristalsis occlusion ratio of the esophagus is in the range of 60 to 100% [3, 9–11] with an esophageal diameter of 20 mm [12].The occlusion rate describes to what percentage the cross-sectional area of the conduit is reduced by contraction. The characterization of the FBPP in terms of volume flow rate, pressure and actuation frequency showed that the FSRAs could not reach an occlusion rate over 60%, which prohibits a high volume displacement and necessitate check valves in the circuit to prevent back flow. The foam and the coating were not durable and flexible enough to withstand higher pressures which are necessary to achieve higher occlusion rates. After 500 actuations the coating began to crack and fluid could flow into the foam material. To overcome these problems, we radically changed the actuator geometry and base material and developed a flexible silicone-based soft robotic ring actuator (SSRAs) based peristaltic pumping system.

Soft robotic peristaltic systems have been well covered in recent literature [9, 12–21]. In 2017 Dirven *et al.* presented a prototype of a biomimetic swallowing robot as a medical, rheological instrument for characterization of different bolus viscosities [18]. It consists of twelve silicone ring actuators each with a four air chamber system in a stiff frame. The actuators are based on pneumatic network (pneu-net) fluidic elastomer actuators (FEAs) with an inner network of channels and chambers that are deformed by pressurized inflation [22].

In this study, we propose an elliptical inner conduit radius to ensure full closure of the system, which could not be achieved by a circular conduit [8]. The outer side of the actuators is jacketed with a strain-limiting layer similar to the FSRAs in order to direct the expansion of the fully flexible SSRAs inwards.

The main goal of this study is the biomimetic implementation of peristalsis into a flexible, silent, robust, energy efficient, space-saving and low cost technical application for the usage in combustion engines, electric engines and cooling systems.

## 2   Material and Methods

### 2.1   Development of the Soft Robotic Silicone-Based Biomimetic Peristalsis Pump (SBPP)

The soft robotic silicone-based biomimetic peristalsis pump (SBPP) consists of a serial arrangement of eight silicone-based actuators (Fig. 1). Three specific actuation patterns of the ring actuators (see below) were chosen to ensure a peristaltic transport of fluid. The smaller diameter of the actuator units matches the inner conduit diameter of ca. 20 mm of the biological role model (esophagus). The octagonal ring actuator units were fabricated using mold casting. After casting the units were bonded together to achieve a water-proof and oil resistant inner conduit. The elliptical geometry of the inner conduit was chosen to achieve higher occlusion rates. Furthermore, only two pneumatic chambers were integrated into each actuator, which proved enough to ensure full closure and accelerated the production process. Free space was subtracted at both ends of the long axis of the inner ellipse (Fig. 1) for stabilizing the expansion of the pneumatic chambers and minimizing dead volume.

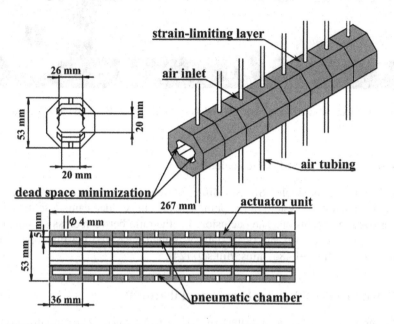

**Fig. 1.** Technical drawing of the soft robotic silicone-based biomimetic peristalsis pump (SBPP).

For improving the durability of the system a flexible silicone rubber material Ecoflex™ 00-50 (EF50; KauPo Plankenhorn, e.K.) was used as base material for actuator production. EF50 is a two component platinum-catalyzed addition cure silicone that is easy to mix and exhibits a short curing time (≈3 h) at room temperature. EF50 was selected due to its high elongation at break (980%) and for its sufficient water and oil resistance [23].

For batch production, 3.5 cm high 3D printed casting molds were used to fabricate actuators. After curing, eight actuators were bonded together in order to form the SBPP (Fig. 2(A)), or furnished with a cover plate to act as single actuators for individual testing (Fig. 2(B)). For pressurization, the actuators were outfitted with silicone air tubing and a strain-limiting layer, which consisted of polypropylene tape (curling ribbon). The tape was wound around the actuators and glued into place with a layer of EF50. This setup prevents outer expansion, so that only the inner diameter is decreased when air pressure is applied.

The SBPP was operated with a specifically designed and custom-built pump test bench, which is described in detail in [8]. A square wave like opening and closing pattern of valves allowed for the formation of a peristaltic wave and pumping in the SBPP. The diameter of inlet and outlet tubing of the pump was set to 8 mm.

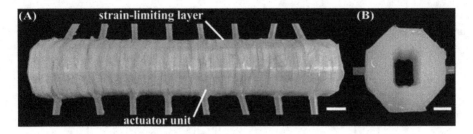

**Fig. 2.** (A) Silicone-based biomimetic peristalsis pump (SBPP). (B) Single SSRA in top view. Scale bars: 20 mm.

## 2.2   Determination of SSRA Occlusion Rate

The occlusion rates of single SSRAs at different frequencies and pressures were tested by using the pneumatic system of the pump test bench. A video camera setup allowed for measuring the occlusion. The occlusion, i.e. the ratio between cross-sectional area of the conduit in occluded and open state, was then measured via Fiji (open-source software, version ImageJ.48q, https://fiji.sc/) [24].

## 2.3   Determination of Volume Flow Rate of the SBPP

The volume flow rates produced by the SBPP were investigated using a modified version of the test bench for the biomimetic pumping system, described in detail in [8]. In the tests the influence of check valves on the flow rate was also investigated. The flow rate produced by the SBPP at different actuation frequencies and pressures was measured by transported volume over time. The transported volume was measured after 50 actuation sequences for the SBPP. The measured volume was then extrapolated to liters per hour [l/h]. Based on the results of the single actuator characterization, actuation frequencies of 1 Hz, 3 Hz and 5 Hz and an actuation pressure of 0.3 bar (system pressure) were used in the flow rate measurements of the SBPP.

Furthermore three different peristaltic actuation sequence patterns were investigated during the SBPP volume flow rate measurements, see Table 1. Pattern 1 represents a simple peristalsis motion pattern, in which a continuous square wave motion was used to pressurize the individual actuators consecutively. In pattern 2 two actuators are simultaneously active and in pattern 3 three actuators. The actuation moves along the conduit in a peristaltic motion, thereby displacing the fluid inside the conduit. The duration of SSRA actuations in the patterns is determined by the different frequencies, e.g. this means at 5 Hz the actuators were inflated for 200 ms.

**Table 1.** Peristaltic actuation patterns of the SBPP, O: open state, **X**: occluded state.

| Pattern 1 | Pattern 2 | Pattern 3 |
|-----------|-----------|-----------|
| **XOOOOOOO** | **XOOOOOOX** | **XOOOOOXX** |
| **OXOOOOOO** | **XXOOOOOO** | **XXOOOOOX** |
| **OOXOOOOO** | **OXXOOOOO** | **XXXOOOOO** |
| **OOOXOOOO** | **OOXXOOOO** | **OXXXOOOO** |
| **OOOOXOOO** | **OOOXXOOO** | **OOXXXOOO** |
| **OOOOOXOO** | **OOOOXXOO** | **OOOXXXOO** |
| **OOOOOOXO** | **OOOOOXXO** | **OOOOXXXO** |
| **OOOOOOOX** | **OOOOOOXX** | **OOOOOXXX** |

## 2.4   Statistics

The software GNU R 3.4.3 was used for statistical analyses (R Core Team, 2017) [25]. We performed a two-way ANOVA on ranked transformed data, having checked for normal distribution (Shapiro–Wilk test) and homoscedasticity of variances in advance (Levene test). This allowed for determining the significance of correlation between (1.1) varying actuation frequencies and (1.2) actuation pressures on (1.3) actuator occlusion rate, as also (2.1) different actuation frequencies and (2.2) the presence of check valves in the setup, on (2.3) the transported fluid volume of the SBPP pumping with different peristaltic patterns. Post-hoc tests were performed via multiple comparisons using Tukey's test.

# 3   Results

## 3.1   Characterization of Single SSRAs

The occlusion rate of the inner conduit of single SSRAs (silicone-based soft robotic ring actuators) was measured at different actuation pressures and frequencies. With the occlusion rate tests we were able to identify the ideal actuation frequencies and pressures to achieve high occlusion rates of the inner conduit. The measured occlusion rates at frequencies from 0.15 Hz to 1 Hz and 0.1 bar range from 74.5% to 89.5% (Fig. 3). At 3 Hz, occlusion rates decrease to values between 33% and 50%. The measured occlusion rates at 0.15 Hz to 1 Hz actuation frequency and 0.2 bar actuation pressure are in the range of 97 to 99.3%. At 3 Hz and 2 bar the achieved occlusion rates range from 79% to 88%. Utilizing 0.3 bar actuation pressure at frequencies from 0.15 Hz to 1 Hz occlusion rates from 99% to 99.8% and at 3 Hz occlusion rates from 65% to 92% are achieved.

The data shows that there is a significant difference between the investigated actuations pressures and frequencies, indicating that with an actuation pressure of 0.3 bar and up to 1 Hz frequency an occlusion rate of over 99% of the inner conduit can be achieved. For further characterization of the SBPP 0.3 bar was set as actuation pressure.

The silicone-based actuators showed a high durability with over 15,000 actuations, only bursting at the bonding surface, where the actuator body was bonded to its side-cover. This high durability was also observed in the entire SBPP (silicone-based

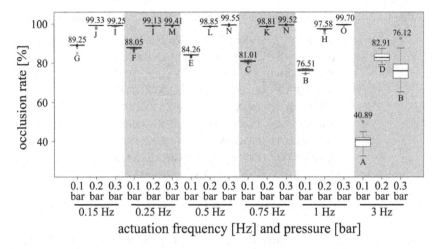

**Fig. 3.** Occlusion rates of single SSRAs at different frequencies and pressures. Highest occlusion rates over 99.4% were achieved with 0.3 bar actuation pressure at frequencies up to 1 Hz. Occlusion rates are shown above the box plots. The capital letters are significance level indicators, all actuators with different letters showed significant difference in achieved occlusion rate with $p$ values below 0.05. Sample size for each boxplot $n = 50$.

biomimetic peristaltic pumping system), failures were also only observed at the bonding surface on the inner conduit side.

## 3.2    Characterization of the SBPP (Silicone-Based Biomimetic Peristaltic Pumping System)

For the volume flow rate characterization of the SBPP (consisting of eight single SSRAs), the actuation frequencies over the whole SBPP of 1 Hz, 3 Hz and 5 Hz were chosen as these had proven to yield good occlusion rates in tests of single actuators (see above). The SBPP was characterized utilizing three different actuation patterns (see Table 1) at 0.3 bar. The influence of check valves was also investigated. To note here is that, other than the SBPP; the single actuator occlusion rates (Fig. 3) showed lesser occlusion at high actuation frequencies. In single actuators, at higher frequencies residual air remains inside the pneumatic chambers which cannot escape in between the pressurizations. In the SBPP this is not observed, as the eight single actuators are activated consecutively and have enough time to deflate fully in between pressurizations.

With the actuation pattern 1 (only 1 actuator is activated consecutively along the conduit) the highest volume flow rate of 21 l/h is achieved at 3 Hz with two check valves (Fig. 4(A)). Using pattern 3, the highest volume of 48 l/h is measured with one check valve at the SBPP outlet and 5 Hz actuation frequency (Fig. 4(C)). Pattern 2 reached overall the highest flow rates at any frequency (Fig. 4(B)), with the highest median flow rate over 52 l/h at 5 Hz with no check valves, which demonstrates that the SBPP is self-priming and able to produce high flow rates without check valves.

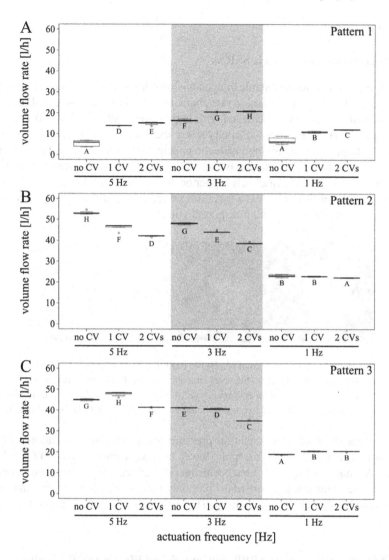

**Fig. 4.** Volume flow rate measurements of SBPP with and without check valves (CV) in the setup and three different actuation patterns. The three check valve setups are denoted as "no CV" (no check valve), "1 CV" (one check valve at SBPP outlet) and "2 CVs" (check vales at inlet and outlet of the SBPP). The flow rate produced by the SBPP at different actuation frequencies and pressures was measured by transported volume over time; the transported volume was measured after 50 pattern repetitions. The actuation pressure was 0.3 bar. The capital letters are significance level indicators, actuators with different letters showed significant difference in achieved volume flow rate with $p$ values below 0.05. The sample size for the boxplots was $n = 10$. (**A**) Volume flow rate measurements of actuation pattern 1, highest volume flow rates are achieved with 2 CVs setup at 3 Hz. (**B**) Volume flow rate measurements of actuation pattern 2, overall highest volume flow rates are achieved with no CVs setup at 5 Hz. (**C**) Volume flow rate measurements of actuation pattern 3, highest volume flow rates are achieved with 1 CV setup at 5 Hz.

# 4    Discussion

## 4.1    Characterization of Single SSRAs

The novel SSRAs can achieve stable high occlusion rates of 99% at specific frequencies and pressures (Fig. 3). The occlusion rate characterization of the SSRAs indicates that higher occlusion rates can be achieved with higher pressures and slower frequencies. The poor performance, i.e. low occlusion rates of the SSRAs at high frequencies (3 Hz) is caused by trapped air remaining inside the pneumatic chambers so that the actuators did not fully return to their relaxation state. The SSRAs, in direct comparison to the FSRAs [8] (Fig. 5), produce markedly higher occlusion rates with lower actuation pressure over all frequencies, which is a great advantage of the SSRA over the FSRAs in terms of energy consumption and transported volume.

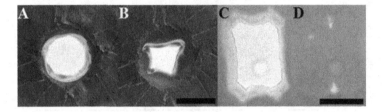

**Fig. 5.** Comparison of occlusion rates of (A, B) PU foam-based FSRAs and (C, D) silicone-based SSRAs with a strain-limiting layer on the outer ring surface. (A) FSRA in resting state (B) FSRA in actuated state with 0.8 bar and an occlusion rate of 55% at 0.4 Hz. (C) SSRA in resting state (D) SSRA in actuated state with 0.2 bar and an occlusion rate of 99% at 1 Hz. Scale bars: 20 mm.

The results show that the actuation pressure has a positive correlation with the occlusion rate, e.g. below 0.2 bar only lower occlusion rates below 90% could be achieved. As shown in Fig. 3 at 0.1 bar occlusion rates decrease with increasing actuation frequency. Due to the low pressure of 0.1 bar, only little air can flow into the pneumatic chambers during shorter activation times. This results in an insufficient inflation of the chambers.

## 4.2    Characterization of the SBPP (Silicone-Based Biomimetic Peristaltic Pumping System)

In contrast to the foam-based actuator pump (FBPP), the silicone-based actuator pump (SBPP) is self-priming (i.e. no check valves are needed) and able to produce a fluid flow rate of above 50 l/h, which is over 15 times that of the FBPPs (3.5 l/h) [8]. The results show that there is a significant difference between the flow rates of varying actuation frequency and the presence/absence of check valves.

In actuation pattern 1 (Fig. 4(A)) we observe lower flow rates than in the other patterns; this is due to the fact that only one actuator is active and may also not inflate fully. In addition, fluids inertia may have an effect on the flow rate as the fluid volume of the whole system has to be set into motion by the actuators. This is achieved faster in pattern 2 and 3 than in pattern 1, because more actuators are active at the same time, whereby a higher volume is displaced and more fluid indraught is achieved due to deflating actuators. The highest flow rates are achieved with pattern 2 and no check valves.

Results indicate the ambivalent influence of the check valves on the flow rate: they prevent back flow and thus increase the flow rates below 20 l/h at low frequencies. On the other hand, check valves are a hydrodynamic hindrance to flow, due to their structure reducing the conduit diameter and further compartmentalizing the transported volume, so thus tend to decrease flow rates above 40 l/h at higher frequencies.

Like the biological role models esophagus, gut and small intestines, the SBPP is self-priming and able to successfully produce valveless directional transport of fluid. The SBPP is in the lower range of flow rates of technical cooling pumps with about 50 l/h, but the results indicate that with higher frequencies we might be able to attain higher volume flow rates in the range of technical automotive cooling pumps (100 to 1000 l/h) [6].

## 5   Conclusion and Outlook

Our experiments show that the developed SSRAs represent suitable and good functioning actuators for a peristaltic pump (SBPP). The silicone-based ring actuators are able to expand and decrease their inner elliptical diameter into the conduit in function of the applied pressure and allow for fluid transport in the SBPP. Achieved occlusion rates of the SSRAs correspond to peristaltic occlusions found in natural hollow organs, being in the range of 60% to 100% [3, 9–11]. With the developed structure of the SSRAs and the SBPP, we were able to establish a new actuation platform for flexible self-priming biomimetic soft robotic pumping systems.

In future studies, we will analyze various peristaltic actuation patterns and characterize the SBPP with a higher system tubing diameter, which equals the diameter of the esophagus and automotive cooling tubing systems (20 mm). Furthermore we will characterize the SBPPs at higher actuation system pressures and frequencies with the goal to achieve high occlusion and flow rates.

Ultimately we would like to further develop the design into an advanced system, in which an electrically or magnetically driven actuation is incorporated in the silicone material. This holds the promising possibility to develop flexible, lightweight, quiet, space-saving and energy efficient pumping systems, detached from the rigid designs and room demand of modern pumps. This further enables an application of the pump in combustion engines, the growing field of electro mobility and fuel cell powered vehicles as well as a phantom gut or artificial esophagus in medical experiments, as in the system described by Dirven et al. [9, 12–16].

# References

1. Vogel, S.: Living in a physical world X. Pumping fluids through conduits. J. Biosci. **32**, 207–222 (2007). https://doi.org/10.1007/s12038-007-0021-4
2. Pass, G.: Accessory pulsatile organs: evolutionary innovations in insects. Ann. Rev. Entomol. **45**, 495–518 (2000). https://doi.org/10.1146/annurev.ento.45.1.495
3. Jaffrin, M.Y., Shapiro, A.H.: Peristaltic pumping. Ann. Rev. Fluid Mech. **3**, 13–37 (1971). https://doi.org/10.1146/annurev.fl.03.010171.000305
4. Bach, D., Schmich, F., Masselter, T., Speck, T.: A review of selected pumping systems in nature and engineering - potential biomimetic concepts for improving displacement pumps and pulsation damping. Bioinspir. Biomimetics **10**, 051001 (2015). https://doi.org/10.1088/1748-3190/10/5/051001
5. Krutzsch, W.C., Cooper, P.: Introduction: classification and selection of pumps. In: Karassik, I.J., Cooper, P., Messina, J.P., Heald, C.C. (eds) Pump Handbook, 4th edn. vol. 1, pp. 2–7. Mc Graw Hill (2008). https://doi.org/10.1002/aic.690220632
6. Pierburg Pump Technology GmbH: Water circulation pump – compact and versatile. Rheinmetall Automotive AG (2018). http://www.kspg.com
7. Esser, F., Bach, D., Masselter, T., Speck, T.: Nature as concept generator for novel biomimetic pumping systems. In: Bionik: Patente aus der Natur, Tagungsbeiträge zum 8. Bionik-Kongress in Bremen, vol. 8, pp. 116–122 (2017). ISBN 978-3-00-055030-0
8. Esser, F., Steger, T., Bach, D., Masselter, T., Speck, T.: Development of novel foam-based soft robotic ring actuators for a biomimetic peristaltic pumping system. In: Mangan, M., Cutkosky, M., Mura, A., Verschure, Paul F.M.J., Prescott, T., Lepora, N. (eds.) Living Machines 2017. LNCS (LNAI), vol. 10384, pp. 138–147. Springer, Cham (2017). https://doi.org/10.1007/978-3-319-63537-8_12
9. Chen, F.J., Dirven, S., Xu, W.L., Bronlund, J., Li, X.N., Pullan, A.: Review of the swallowing system and process for a biologically mimicking swallowing robot. Mechatronics **22**, 556–567 (2012). https://doi.org/10.1016/j.mechatronics.2012.02.005
10. Walsh, J.H., Leigh, M.S., Paduch, A., Maddison, K.J., Philippe, D.L., Armstrong, J.J., Sampson, D.D., Hillman, D.R., Eastwood, P.R.: Evaluation of pharyngeal shape and size using anatomical optical coherence tomography in individuals with and without obstructive sleep apnoea. J. Sleep Res. **17**, 230–238 (2008). https://doi.org/10.1111/j.1365-2869.2008.00647.x
11. Brasseur, J.G.: A fluid mechanical perspective on esophageal bolus transport. Dysphagia **2**, 32–39 (1987). https://doi.org/10.1007/BF02406976
12. Dirven, S., Xu, W., Cheng, L.K., Allen, J., Bronlund, J.: Biologically-inspired swallowing robot for investigation of texture modified foods. Int. J. Biomechatron. Biomed. Robot. **2**, 163–171 (2013). https://doi.org/10.1504/IJBBR.2013.058719
13. Chen, F.-J., Dirven, S., Xu, W., Li, X.-N., Bronlund, J.: Design and fabrication of a soft actuator for a swallowing robot. In: Kim, J.-H., Matson, E.T., Myung, H., Xu, P., Karray, F. (eds.) Robot Intelligence Technology and Applications 2. AISC, vol. 274, pp. 483–493. Springer, Cham (2014). https://doi.org/10.1007/978-3-319-05582-4_42
14. Dirven, S., Xu, W., Cheng, L.K.: Sinusoidal peristaltic waves in soft actuator for mimicry of esophageal swallowing. IEEE/ASME Trans. Mechatron. **20**, 1331–1337 (2015). https://doi.org/10.1109/TMECH.2014.2337291
15. Chen, F., Dirven, S., Xu, W., Li, X.: Large-deformation model of a soft-bodied esophageal actuator driven by distributed air pressure. IEEE/ASME Trans. Mechatron. **22**, 81–90 (2016). https://doi.org/10.1109/TMECH.2016.2612262

16. Zhu, M., Xu, W., Cheng, L.K.: Measuring and imaging of a soft-bodied swallowing robot conduit deformation and internal structural change using videofluoroscopy. In: 2016 23rd International Conference on Mechatronics and Machine Vision in Practice (M2VIP), pp. 1–6 (2016). https://doi.org/10.1109/m2vip.2016.7827312

17. Zhu, M., Xu, W., Cheng, L.K.: Esophageal peristaltic control of a soft-bodied swallowing robot by the central pattern generator. IEEE/ASME Trans. Mechatron. **22**, 91–98 (2016). https://doi.org/10.1109/TMECH.2016.2609465

18. Dirven, S., Allen, J., Xu, W., Cheng, L.K.: Soft-robotic esophageal swallowing as a clinically-inspired bolus rheometry technique. Meas. Sci. Technol. **28**, 035701 (2017). https://doi.org/10.1088/1361-6501/aa544f

19. Suzuki, K., Nakamura, T.: Development of a peristaltic pump based on bowel peristalsis using for artificial rubber muscle. In: 2010 IEEE/RSJ International Conference on Intelligent Robots and Systems (IROS), pp. 3085–3090 (2010). https://doi.org/10.1109/iros.2010.5653006

20. Kimura, Y., Saito, K., Nakamura, T.: Development of an exsufflation system for peristaltic pump based on bowel peristalsis. In: 2013 IEEE/ASME International Conference on Advanced Intelligent Mechatronics (AIM), pp. 235–1240 (2013). https://doi.org/10.1109/aim.2013.6584263

21. Yoshihama, S., Takano, S., Yamada, Y., Nakamura, T., Kato, K.: Powder conveyance experiments with peristaltic conveyor using a pneumatic artificial muscle. In: 2016 IEEE International Conference on Advanced Intelligent Mechatronics (AIM), pp. 539–1544 (2016). https://doi.org/10.1109/aim.2016.7576989

22. Ilievski, F., Mazzeo, A.D., Shepherd, R.F., Chen, X., Whitesides, G.M.: Soft robotics for chemists. Angew. Chem. **123**, 1930–1935 (2011). https://doi.org/10.1002/ange.201006464

23. Smooth-on safety data sheets. https://www.smooth-on.com

24. Schindelin, J., Arganda-Carreras, I., Frise, E., Kaynig, V., Longair, M., Pietzsch, T., Preibisch, S., Rueden, C., Saalfeld, S., Schmid, B., Tinevez, J.-Y., White, D.J., Hartenstein, V., Eliceiri, K., Tomancak, P., Cardona, A.: Fiji: an open-source platform for biological-image analysis. Nat. Methods **9**, 676–682 (2012). https://doi.org/10.1038/nmeth.2019

25. R Core Team.: R: A language and environment for statistical computing. R Foundation for Statistical Computing, Vienna, Austria (2017). https://www.R-project.org/

# Artificial System Inspired by Climbing Mechanism of Galium Aparine Fabricated via 3D Laser Lithography

Isabella Fiorello[1,2(✉)], Omar Tricinci[1], Anand Kumar Mishra[1,2], Francesca Tramacere[1], Carlo Filippeschi[1], and Barbara Mazzolai[1(✉)]

[1] Center for Micro-BioRobotics@SSSA, Istituto Italiano di Tecnologia, Pontedera, Italy
{isabella.fiorello,barbara.mazzolai}@iit.it
[2] The BioRobotics Institute, Scuola Superiore Sant'Anna, Pontedera, Italy

**Abstract.** In this work, we present an artificial dry adhesive system inspired by the leaf-climbing mechanisms in *Galium aparine*. Among the different species of climbing plants, *G. aparine* shows a unique capability of adhesion to a wide range of roughness and stiffness objects, mainly via its leaves, using microscopic hooks for the physical interlocking. The adaxial (upper) and abaxial (lower) leaf surfaces differ significantly in attachment properties, which depend on the direction of the applied force (ratchet-like mechanism). In order to mimic this adhesive behavior, we designed artificial abaxial and adaxial leaf hooks by extracting the morphological parameters from the natural structures. We fabricated artificial hooks at different scales (1:1, 1:2, 1:4) using Direct Laser Lithography (DLL), a technique that allows a rapid prototyping of 3D microstructures. The adhesion of the artificial systems was tested on a polyester tissue substrate, obtaining adhesive forces comparable or higher than the natural counterpart. This biomimetic approach can open new opportunities to understand nature through artificial investigations and lead to several applications in the fields of robotics and space technology.

**Keywords:** Biomimetics · Dry adhesion · Climbing plants · Leaf hooks
Direct laser lithography

## 1 Introduction

Climbing plants have unique capabilities to climb through a wide range of objects using different mechanisms, such as twining, coiling, adhesive disk pads, adventitious roots and hook-like thorns [1]. On the basis of the attachment mechanism exploited for clinging to their hosts, these plants are categorized into hook-climbers, twining plants, leaf-climbers, tendril-bearers, and root-climbers [2]. The morphological and biomechanical features of climbing plants have been objects of study [3–6]. This research is interesting from a robotics point of view and can lead to the conception of innovative smart attachment devices working in unstructured environments. Yet, despite their

---

O. Tricinci and A. K. Mishra—Contributed equally.

V. Vouloutsi et al. (Eds.): Living Machines 2018, LNAI 10928, pp. 168–178, 2018.
https://doi.org/10.1007/978-3-319-95972-6_18

exceptional evolutionary adaptation, a few examples of advanced adhesive materials and artificial systems inspired by climbing plants are available [7]. An example of the recent increasing interest in climbing plants as a model for designing artificial dry adhesion mechanisms is the cleavers *Galium aparine* (Fig. 1a) [8].

The cleavers *G. aparine* is able to climb up surfaces with various roughness and stiffness objects mainly via its leaves, which contain microscopic hooked trichomes (Fig. 1b) [6]. Although hooks are present on both leaf surfaces, adaxial (upper side) and abaxial (lower side) leaf surfaces differ significantly in attachment properties, due to their different morphology and mechanical characteristics (Fig. 1c–e). The result of these differences is a ratchet-like mechanism, in which the abaxial leaf surface provides strong adhesion upon the leaves of adjacent plants, while the adaxial hooks, curved in the opposite direction, can easily slide off the contact surface [6, 9].

Direct Laser Lithography (DLL) has recently demonstrated its potentiality for the fabrication of biomimetic surfaces patterns with three-dimensional features at the micro and nano-scale [10–12]. This technique allows high flexibility in mimicking bioinspired surfaces, especially for the change of scale dimension, while preserving high resolution. Thus, DLL represents a perfect tool for investigating how the attachment performance depends on size and shape, optimizing the adhesion for specific tasks.

In this work, we present the first prototype of an artificial dry adhesive system inspired by the natural morphology of abaxial and adaxial leaf hooks of *G. aparine* developed using DLL. In particular, adaxial and abaxial hooks are fabricated at a different dimensional sizes, such as 100% (1:1), 50% (1:2) and 25% (1:4) respect to the selected natural model. The adhesion force was tested on a polyester tissue by means of a dedicated setup to compare the performance of the natural structures and the artificial replicates.

**Fig. 1.** (a) Image of the herbaceous climbing plant *G. aparine*, in hedgerows; (b) Detail of a leaf; (c) Lateral view of a leaf with abaxial (AB) and adaxial (AD) hooks curved in the opposite direction; (d–e) Overview of AB and AD hook distributions (details of adaxial and abaxial hooks are shown in the inset).

## 2  Materials and Methods

### 2.1  Morphological Characterizations

Samples of *G. aparine* plants were collected in February from a garden in Pontedera (Pisa, Italy). A scanning electron microscope Zeiss EVO LS10 was used to characterize natural leaf hooks sample morphology in the environmental condition (ESEM). For the ESEM examinations, no samples preparation was required: hydrated samples were attached to a Peltier stage (temperature = 1 °C) after removal from the plant. ESEM images were collected in wet-mode (pressure 800 Pa), at an accelerating voltage of 20 kV with a working distance of about 8 mm. To characterize the morphology of the artificial samples, they were mounted onto aluminum stubs using adhesive carbon discs and coated with a 15 nm gold layer using a sputter coater (Quorum Q150R ES). Surface topography images were acquired using SEM (Zeiss EVO LS10) at an accelerating voltage of 5 kV, a vacuum of $2.6 \times 10^{-4}$ Pa and a working distance of about 12 mm. A digital microscope Hirox KH-7700 was used to characterize the structures of both natural and artificial samples.

### 2.2  Microfabrication via Direct Laser Lithography

For the 3D biomimetic hooks design, we extract the morphological parameters from the ESEM images, such as length, diameter and angle (Fig. 3a, e). This information was used to develop a 3D model in SolidWorks® 2010 (Fig. 3b, f). Artificial hooks were fabricated in IP-S photoresist (Nanoscribe GmbH) on a glass substrate, by means of Photonic Professional GT system (Nanoscribe GmbH). The IP-S photoresist was poured on the glass substrate and exposed to the laser beam with a center wavelength of 780 nm (Toptica laser source), using a scan speed of 50 mm/s with a power of 135 mW. The sample was developed for 20 min in SU-8 Developer (MicroChem Corp) and rinsed with isopropyl alcohol and deionized water.

### 2.3  Adhesion Measurements

Adhesion forces achieved by natural and artificial hooks were measured using a dedicated multi-axis measurement platform, equipped with a three-axis micrometric translation stage and a six-axis force/torque sensor (ATI, Nano17) (Fig. 2a) with a limit of resolution of 0.317 g/force. The adhesion test procedure consisted of four phases (Fig. 2b): (1) approaching; (2) perpendicular preloading; (3) parallel displacement in order to ensure the proper interaction of the hooks to the substrate; (4) perpendicular detachment. A sample was placed on the base plate and a piece of 1 $cm^2$ of polyester tissue substrate (100% textured polyester, PNHS Polynit Heatseal, Contec) was fixed to the top plate. The top plate was lowered, at a speed of 0.2 mm/s towards the sample till a preload of 1 N. When the preload reaches 0.7 N the moving stage is horizontally displaced of 500, 250 and 125 μm for abaxial and adaxial hooks at scale 1:1, 1:2 and 1.4, respectively, in the direction of the orientation of leaf hooks. Subsequently, the top plate was retracted at a speed of 0.2 mm/s until the final detachment occurred. The contact separation force was determined to be the maximum force measured before the final detachment. This procedure was repeated at least three times for each sample. The adhesion forces were normalized to the number of hooks both in natural and artificial samples. The density of natural adaxial hooks was determined as the number of hooks for the unit of area ($\sim 72$ hooks cm$^{-2}$), while the density of abaxial hooks was determined as the number of hooks for the unit of length ($\sim 12$ hooks cm$^{-1}$) similarly as described from [6]. The number of artificial hooks in a fixed area of 0.6 cm$^2$ is 36, 144 and 576 for the abaxial and adaxial hooks at scale 1:1, 1:2, 1:4, respectively.

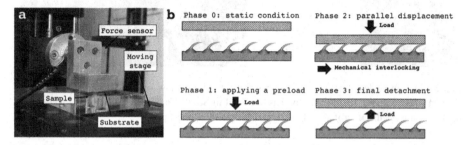

**Fig. 2.** (a) Experimental set up used to perform adhesion measurements; (b) Schematic summary of the adhesion test procedure.

## 3 Results and Discussion

### 3.1 Results of the Microfabrication of *G. aparine* Hooks

The structure of abaxial and adaxial hooks is variable in shape and size [6]. After the analysis of ESEM images, we observed that the height of abaxial and adaxial hooks is in the range of $\sim 150$–$400$ µm and $\sim 200$–$500$ µm, respectively. The abaxial hooks have a basal diameter of $\sim 200$–$400$ µm, which is larger respect to the adaxial ones, which is $\sim 100$–$200$ µm. Both leaf hooks are getting sharper - thinner as approaching the end portion. In particular, the diameter of the middle part of the hooks is $\sim 50$–$100$ µm for the abaxial hooks and $\sim 30$–$70$ µm for the adaxial hooks. The end portion of the adaxial hooks has a thin tip (d = 5–20 µm), whereas the abaxial hooks have a thicker tip structure (d = 5–30 µm). A representative example of the abaxial and adaxial leaf hooks morphology is reported in Figs. 3a and e, respectively. The microfabrication of the hooks (scale 1:1) by means of direct laser lithography gave satisfactory results in terms of resolution and reproducibility (Fig. 3c–d), even at the level of the tips (Fig. 3g–h).

The selected natural model (1:1) was downscaled to 50% (1:2) and 25% (1:4), in order to investigate how attachment performance depends on hooks size (Fig. 4), with outstanding fabrication results. *Galium aparine*-like artificial abaxial and adaxial hooks were fabricated in a fixed area of 0.6 cm$^2$, for a total of 6 different designs as summarized in Table 1 and illustrated in Fig. 4. For abaxial hooks, the 1:1 design consists of an array of $6 \times 6$ structures at a fixed distance of 1 mm, with a height of 300 µm, a basal diameter of 400 µm, a diameter of the middle part of 100 µm and an upper part with a tip of 10 µm (Fig. 4a–c); for the adaxial hooks, it consists of an array of $6 \times 6$

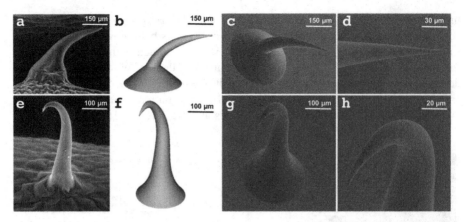

**Fig. 3.** Design of leaf hooks of *G. aparine*: (a, e) natural view of (a) AB and (e) AD hooks (ESEM micrographs), (b, f) CAD models obtained in SolidWorks of (b) AB and (f) AD hooks, (c, g) Results of the microfabrication and (d, h) detail of the tips.

structures at a fixed distance of 1 mm between hooks with a height of 350 μm, a basal diameter of 200 μm, a diameter of the middle part of 50 μm and an upper part with a tip of 5 μm (Fig. 4j–l). Since the area is fixed, when we scaled down hooks size and distance, the hooks density increases whereas the size and distance decreases (Fig. 4). All the geometrical details of the arrays are reported in Table 1.

### 3.2  Adhesion Force Measurements of *G. aparine* Hooks

Adhesion on a polyester tissue substrate was tested for both natural and artificial surfaces (Fig. 5a–d). The cyclic adhesion test for the artificial abaxial hooks (h = 300) is plotted in Fig. 5e as a representative example. The four phases of the test (Fig. 2b) are well deducible from the graph. In particular, the fall of the perpendicular force around 0.7 N is related to the concomitant application of the parallel preload in terms of parallel displacement that allows a rearrangement of the hooks interacting with the polyester fibers. Once the set preload (1 N) is reached, the tissue is moved far from the sample with the hooks anchored on it: this adhesive force corresponds to the negative peak in the graph.

The results of the adhesion tests by pulling the artificial hooks surfaces (contact area = 0.6 cm$^2$) to the substrate are summarized in Fig. 5f. The maximum forces of the hooks are 458 ± 54 and 406 ± 7 mN, which is achieved by the artificial abaxial hooks (artificial AB) at the scale 1:1 (N = 36) and 1:2 (N = 144), respectively. An adhesion force of 201 ± 29 mN was obtained by the smallest artificial abaxial hooks (N = 576). For the artificial adaxial surfaces (artificial AD), the best result is 151 ± 19 mN which is obtained testing the biggest one (scale 1:1, N = 36). When the size of artificial adaxial hooks decreases and the density increases, the adhesion force decreases to 28 ± 25 mN (N = 144). However, for the artificial AD hooks at 1:4 scale, the measured force was negligible (close to 0).

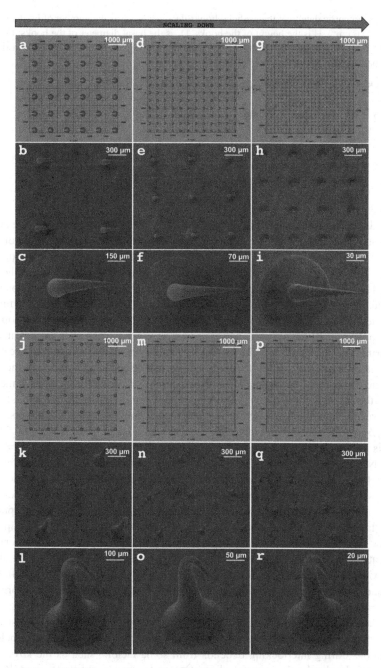

**Fig. 4.** Images of the results of the microfabrication of artificial abaxial and adaxial hooks at scale 1:1 (DeScribe pictures; a–c, AB; j–l, AD), 1:2 (SEM pictures; d–f, AB; m–o, AD) and 1:4 (SEM pictures; g–i, AB; p–r, AD).

**Table 1.** Geometric details of the artificial hooks designs: $N_{array}$ is the number of hooks for each fixed area (0.6 cm$^2$), H is the height of the hooks, $D_b$ is the basal diameter of the hooks, $D_m$ is the diameter of the middle part of the hook, $D_t$ is the diameter of the tip of the hook and d is the distance between hooks in the array.

| Design | Type | Size | $N_{array}$ | H (μm) | $D_b$ (μm) | $D_m$ (μm) | $D_t$ (μm) | d (μm) |
|--------|------|------|-------|--------|-------|-------|-------|-------|
| 1 | AB | 100% | 36 | 300 | 400 | 100 | 10 | 1000 |
| 2 | AB | 50% | 144 | 150 | 200 | 50 | 5 | 500 |
| 3 | AB | 25% | 576 | 75 | 100 | 25 | 2.5 | 250 |
| 4 | AD | 100% | 36 | 350 | 200 | 50 | 5 | 1000 |
| 5 | AD | 50% | 144 | 175 | 100 | 25 | 2.5 | 500 |
| 6 | AD | 25% | 576 | 87.5 | 50 | 12.5 | 1.25 | 250 |

In order to compare the performance of the artificial hooks with different size and the natural ones, the adhesion force was normalized by the total number of hooks. An overview of adhesion test results normalized for a single natural and artificial hooks are reported in Fig. 5g. The adhesion force of the single artificial abaxial hook is $12.7 \pm 1.37$, $2.8 \pm 0.12$ and $0.3 \pm 0.06$ mN, in correlation with its dimensional size (from the biggest to the smallest, Fig. 5g). In particular, the best results were obtained by testing the biggest artificial abaxial hooks, which seem to have a greater adhesion force respect to the natural ones (Force$_{natural\ AB}$ = $4.2 \pm 1$ mN). This could be explained by considering that the natural hooks on the leaf can more easily conform to the tissue, while it is moving, due to the flexibility of the leaf itself, gently releasing the fibers during the detachment. Moreover, the correlation of the force with the hook dimension is due to the higher amount of fibers that bigger hooks can catch. For this reason, the size of the structures could be selectively implemented according to specific targets.

The best adhesion force obtained in the artificial adaxial hook is $4.2 \pm 0.53$ mN, which is slightly more performing than the natural system (Force$_{natural\ AD}$ = $1.4 \pm 0.48$ mN). A small force of $0.2 \pm 0.17$ mN was obtained by scaling down the structure to 50%. As previously mentioned, no force was obtained by scaling down the structures to 75%. This can be explained due to stably trapped fibers for tiny hooks. In order to improve the adhesion force, a first attempt could be to change the morphology of the adaxial hook, such as modifying the angle and the dimensions of the tip.

After the adhesion testing, the morphology of the artificial hooks was observed to investigate if possible deformations occurred (Fig. 6). SEM microscopy of the abaxial and adaxial hooks at scale 1:1 showed that there was no damage to the hooks after tests (Fig. 6a, d), demonstrating that they can respond well to the load. A minor deformation was observed in hooks at scale 1:2, although most of them remained intact (Fig. 6b, e). We observed some deformation in the smallest abaxial hooks (Fig. 6c). Most of the smallest adaxial hooks were deformed during the test (Fig. 6f). The adhesive behavior of the hooks during interlocking depends from some factors, such as the size, shape, stiffness of the hook, the interfacial contact and type of substrate used [6, 13]. Decreased hooks size ($\leq$ 1:4) cannot easily interlock big tissue fibers and thus, in case of interlocking, could be damaged (in particular the adaxial hooks). For this reason, the smallest hooks can be useful for more suitable substrates, with dense and smaller fibers network.

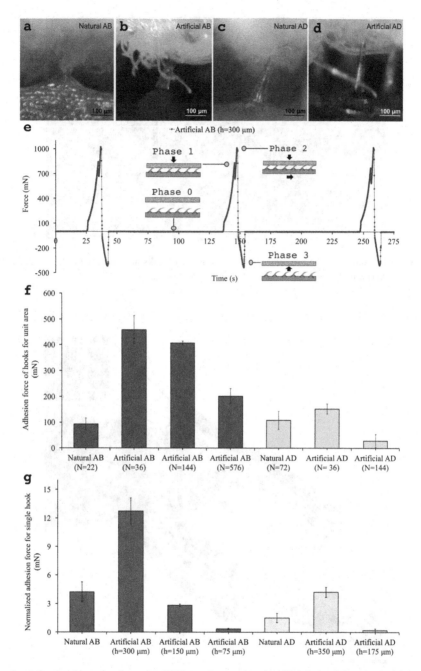

**Fig. 5.** Adhesion investigations: (a–d) View of natural and artificial abaxial and adaxial hooks attacked on a polyester substrate; (e) Typical adhesion force graph; the cyclic behavior of artificial abaxial hooks with a height of 300 μm it has been reported as example. (F) Overview of adhesion test results for the surfaces of artificial hooks (contact area = 0.6 cm²). N is the number of hooks. (G) Overview of adhesion test results normalized for one hook (h = height).

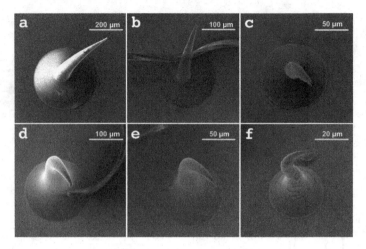

**Fig. 6.** SEM images of the artificial abaxial and adaxial hooks at scale 1:1 (a, AB; d, AD), 1:2 (b, AB; e, AD) and 1:4 (c, AB; f, AD) after adhesion testing.

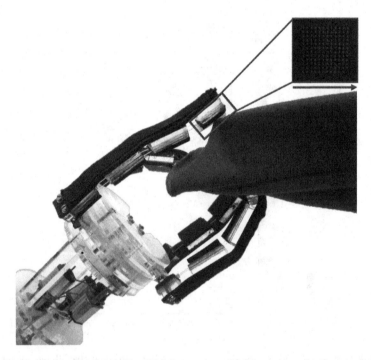

**Fig. 7.** Example of a plant-inspired artificial system useful for micromanipulators and grippers. Artificial hooks are glued to the finger of the manipulator (SIMBA, [17]) and they are visible in the inset. The red arrow indicates the direction of the load. (Color figure online)

# 4 Conclusions

In this work, we developed dry-adhesive artificial systems inspired by the leaf hooks of the *G. aparine* climbing plant in three different dimensional scales using 3D laser lithography. Overall, DLL has demonstrated to be a useful tool to mimic the *G. aparine*'s adhesive behavior. The adhesion tests of the artificial hooks on polyester tissue substrate provided encouraging results, in particular regarding the abaxial surface with a maximum adhesion force of $12.7 \pm 1.37$ mN for a single abaxial hook (h = 300 μm), three times higher than the natural counterpart. As future perspectives, adhesion measurements will be performed testing several others micro-rough substrates such as Velcro, wood, skin and rocks, in order to better characterize all types of hooks for different applications.

The goal will be to apply this technology in a wide variety of real-world unstructured environment: for example, dense arrays of micro-hooks with appropriate density and size could allow robots to climb on smooth surfaces or grasp objects, similarly to the micro-spines used in JPL RoboSimian, SpinyBot and LEMUR robots [14–16]. Therefore, these results represent a starting point to develop innovative plant-inspired dry adhesive systems useful for micromanipulator and grippers (Fig. 7) and micro-robot climbing inclined slopes, which could have several applications in the fields of space technology and robotics.

**Acknowledgments.** This work is supported by the European Commission under the FLAG-ERA JointTransnational Call (JTC) 2016, RoboCom++.

# References

1. Isnard, S., Silk, W.K.: Moving with climbing plants from Charles Darwin's time into the 21st century. Am. J. Bot. **96**(7), 1205–1221 (2009)
2. Darwin, C.: On the movements and habits of climbing plants. Bot. J. Linn. Soc. **9**(33–34), 1–118 (1865)
3. Gallenmüller, F., Feus, A., Fiedler, K., Speck, T.: Rose prickles and asparagus spines-different hook structures as attachment devices in climbing plants. PLoS ONE **10**(12), e0143850 (2015)
4. Melzer, B., Seidel, R., Steinbrecher, T., Speck, T.: Structure, attachment properties, and ecological importance of the attachment system of English ivy (Hedera helix). J. Exp. Bot. **63**(1), 191–201 (2011)
5. Seidelmann, K., Melzer, B., Speck, T.: The complex leaves of the monkey's comb (Amphilophium crucigerum, Bignoniaceae): a climbing strategy without glue. Am. J. Bot. **99**(11), 1737–1744 (2012)
6. Bauer, G., Klein, M.C., Gorb, S.N., Speck, T., Voigt, D., Gallenmuller, F.: Always on the bright side: the climbing mechanism of *Galium aparine*. Proc. Biol. Sci. **278**(1715), 2233–2239 (2011)
7. Burris, J.N., Lenaghan, S.C., Stewart, C.N.: Climbing plants: attachment adaptations and bioinspired innovations. Plant Cell Rep. **37**(1–10), 565–574 (2017)
8. Andrews, H.G.: Badyal, J.P.S.: Bioinspired hook surfaces based upon a ubiquitous weed (*Galium aparine*) for dry adhesion. J. Adhes. Sci. Technol. **28**(13), 1243–1255 (2014)

9. Niklas, J.K.: Climbing plants: attachment and the ascent for light. Curr. Biol. **21**(5), 199–201 (2011)
10. Tricinci, O., Terencio, T., Mazzolai, B., Pugno, N.M., Greco, F., Mattoli, V.: 3D micropatterned surface inspired by salvinia molesta via direct laser lithography. ACS Appl. Mater. Interfaces. **7**, 25560–25567 (2015)
11. Brodoceanu, D., Bauer, C.T., Kroner, E., Arzt, E., Kraus, T.: Hierarchical bioinspired adhesive surfaces—a review. Bioinspiration & Biomim. **11**, 051001 (2016)
12. Marino, A., Filippeschi, C., Mattoli, V., Mazzolai, B., Ciofani, G.: Biomimicry at the nanoscale: current research and perspectives of two-photon polymerization. Nanoscale **7**(46), 2841–2850 (2015)
13. Chen, Q., Gorb, S.N., Gorb, E., Pugno, N.: Mechanics of plant fruit hooks. J. R. Soc. Interface **10**(81) (2013). https://doi.org/10.1098/rsif.2012.0913
14. Wang, S., Jiang, H., Cutkosky, M.R.: A palm for rock climbing based on dense arrays of micro-spines. In: IEEE/RSJ International Conference on Intelligent Robots and Systems (IROS), Daejeon, Korea, pp. 52–59. IEEE (2016)
15. Asbeck, A.T., Kim, S., McClung, A., Parness, A., Cutkosky, M.R.: Climbing walls with microspines. In: IEEE/ICRA International Conference on Robotics and Automation, Orlando, Florida (2006)
16. Parness, A., Frost, M., Thatte, N., King, J.P., Witkoe, K., Nevarez, M., Garrett, M., Aghazarian, H., Kennedy, B.: Gravity-independent rock-climbing robot and a sample acquisition tool with microspine grippers. J. Field Robot. **30**(6), 897–915 (2013)
17. Mishra, A.K., Del Dottore, E., Sadeghi, A., Mondini, A., Mazzolai, B.: SIMBA: tendon driven modular continuum arm with soft reconfigurable gripper. Front. Robot. AI **4**, 4 (2017)

# Modeling the Opponent's Action Using Control-Based Reinforcement Learning

Ismael T. Freire[1,3]([✉]), Jordi-Ysard Puigbò[1,3], Xerxes D. Arsiwalla[1,2,3], and Paul F. M. J. Verschure[1,3,4]

[1] IBEC, Institute for BioEngineering of Catalonia, Barcelona, Spain
ismaeltito.freire@gmail.com
[2] UPF, Universitat Pompeu Fabra, Barcelona, Spain
[3] BIST, Barcelona Institue of Science and Technology, Barcelona, Spain
[4] ICREA, Catalan Institute for Research and Advanced Studies, Barcelona, Spain

**Abstract.** In this paper, we propose an alternative to model-free reinforcement learning approaches that recently have demonstrated Theory-of-Mind like behaviors. We propose a game theoretic approach to the problem in which pure RL has demonstrated to perform below the standards of human-human interaction. In this context, we propose alternative learning architectures that complement basic RL models with the ability to predict the other's actions. This architecture is tested in different scenarios where agents equipped with similar or varying capabilities compete in a social game. Our different interaction scenarios suggest that our model-based approaches are especially effective when competing against models of equivalent complexity, in contrast to our previous results with more basic predictive architectures. We conclude that the evolution of mechanisms that allow for the control of other agents provide different kinds of advantages that can become significant when interacting with different kinds of agents. We argue that no single proposed addition to the learning architecture is sufficient to optimize performance in these scenarios, but a combination of the different mechanisms suggested is required to achieve near-optimal performance in any case.

**Keywords:** Multi-agent models · Cognitive architectures
Theory of mind · Game theory · Social decision-making
Reinforcement learning

## 1  Introduction

Recent advances in Machine Learning (ML) have shown how model-free Reinforcement Learning (RL) algorithms can solve, apparently, any variety of tasks. This becomes more salient by works from Botvinick, Abeel and collaborators that show how RL agents can learn to collaborate in tasks, develop verbal and non-verbal communication mechanisms and develop Theory-of-Mind (ToM) like

ITF and JP have contributed equally to this work.

V. Vouloutsi et al. (Eds.): Living Machines 2018, LNAI 10928, pp. 179–186, 2018.
https://doi.org/10.1007/978-3-319-95972-6_19

behaviors [1,2]. Nonetheless, our ability to understand how these algorithms generate this set of behaviors is limited and doesn't provide a further understanding of the mechanisms underlying both biological or artificial agents cognitive abilities. To our knowledge, these algorithms behave as an optimization system that converges to a possible, reactive solution, whereas the adaptability to small changes in the environment takes substantially more time than in biological learning or adaptive systems.

In this paper, we propose a methodology to generate cognitive architectures with the objective to understand, particularly, what are the underlying mechanisms of ToM-related behavior. For this reason, we borrow from game theory the Battle of the Exes (BotE) game. We propose a variety of architectures that include the assumption of underlying ToM mechanisms and compare them in order to understand how collaboration and emergence in social interactions can occur. The following section describes the experimental setup and the architectures. We detail the comparative results between a pure RL algorithm and our architectures in Sect. 3. Finally, we discuss the results and provide insights for future advancement in social robot interactions.

## 2   Methods

### 2.1   Experimental Setup

To test the interaction between these models, we used as a benchmark the continuous-time version of *Battle of the Exes* [3]. In this version, two agents compete against each other to obtain one of the two possible rewards. One of them (high reward) gives a significantly better outcome than the other one (low reward), but if both agents reach for the same reward, none of them will obtain any. We created two conditions, *"High"* and *"Low"*, to see if the manipulation of the difference between both rewards affects the outcome. As shown in Fig. 1(A), the high reward gives 4 points in the *"High"* condition, and 2 in the *"Low"*.

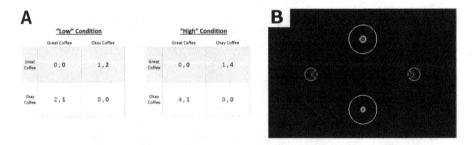

**Fig. 1.** (A) Payoff matrices of the *Low* (left) and *High* (right) reward conditions used in both experiments. (B) Snapshot of the experimental setup at the start of each round. In blue, two simulated *ePucks*; and in green, the reward spots. The high reward is represented by the bigger spot. The threshold that indicates the tie area is represented by the white circles.

In the two experiments carried out in this study, we perform 50 matches between different pairs of agents, with each match consisting of 200 rounds. In experiment one, for each of the three cognitive models described below (check *Control-based Reinforcement Learning Model*, *Opposing Model* and *Predictive Model* sections) we make both agents play against each other using both the same model for each of the payoff conditions, *High* and *Low*. In experiment two we test the new models against the original *Control-based Reinforcement Learning Model*. For that, we follow the same $3 \times 2$ experimental paradigm, but in this case, an agent of each pair is endowed with the original model in all conditions.

The experimental setup has been implemented in a 2D robot simulator, *PyRobot2DSim*, that is based on the *PyBox2D* and *PyGame* libraries (see Fig. 1(B) for a visual depiction of the game). All the agents used during the two experiments are embodied and situated in this 2D environment as virtual ePuck robots, so they all have the same number of sensors and actuators. More specifically, they have 3 pairs of sensors, each specialized in detecting one type of object (the high reward, the low reward, and the other agent); and two motors, to control the left and right wheels.

Regarding the rules of the Battle of the Exes, they are implemented as follows: Both agents start at equally distant positions of both rewards (see Fig. 1(B) to see the initial conditions of the game). A round ends at the moment that an agent touches a reward spot. A round ends in a tie if both agents are inside the same white circle that surrounds each reward. In any other case, the agent that first reaches a reward receives the points attached to it, and the other agent immediately receives the points of the opposite reward, as indicated by the payoff matrix. After the reward assignment is done, both agents are automatically transported to their initial positions and a new round starts.

## 2.2  Original Model

This model is building on the Control-based Reinforcement Learning (CRL) cognitive architecture presented in our previous work [4]. The CRL is a two-layered control architecture that follows the organizing principles of the biologically grounded Distributed Adaptive Control (DAC) theory of mind and brain. It features a low-level *Reactive Layer* for real-time sensorimotor control and an *Adaptive Layer* composed of an actor-critic reinforcement learning algorithm that can learn high-level discrete-time strategies. This hierarchical composition enables both top-down and bottom-up interactions between the reactive and adaptive components of the architecture, which helps to coordinate behavior between both layers.

The *Reactive Layer* is composed of two reactive behaviors: *"attraction towards rewards"* and *"escape from agents"*. The implementation is motivated by Valentino Braitenberg's *Vehicles* [7], where he demonstrates how to generate behavior by directly connecting the sensors and actuators of an agent. Following this approach, the *"attraction towards rewards"* is composed of a direct inhibitory connection and a crossed excitatory connection between the reward sensors of the agent and its motors. The resulting behavior will make the agent turn in the direction of a reward with a speed proportional to the activation of its reward sensors. Given that the agent has two sets of sensors, each special-ized in detecting one type of reward, this behavior is implemented twice, once for the high reward and once for the low reward. For the *"escape from agents"* behavior, the set of connections is the opposite; a crossed inhibitory connection and a direct excitatory connection. The effect of this configuration is an avoid-ance behavior whose speed is also linked to the level of activation of the sensors specialized to detecting other agents.

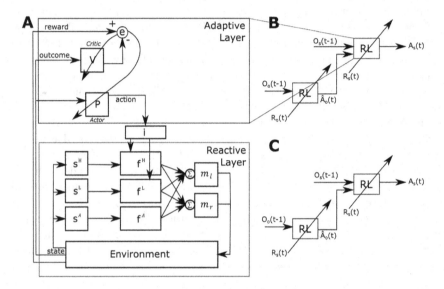

**Fig. 2.** (A) Schema of the Control-based Reinforcement Learning architecture. The Adaptive Layer (big red box, top) is implemented as a TD-learning algorithm, that in turn is composed of an Actor $(P)$ and a Critic $(V)$. The Critic predicts the expected value of a given state, and based on the outcome of the previous round, it calculates a temporal-difference error -or TD error- $(e)$ that serves to update itself and the Actor. The Actor is in charge of selecting which action to perform in each state. This action is sent down to the inhibitor $(i)$, that will shut down one of the reactive behavior depend-ing on the action chosen. The Reactive Layer (big green box, bottom) is integrated by three set of sensors to detect high and low rewards $(s^H, s^L)$ and other agents $(s^A)$, two motors $(m_l, m_r)$ and three functions that connect the sensors and the motors $(f^H, f^L, f^A)$ to create the reactive behaviors of reward attraction and agent avoidance. (B) Schematic description of the Other's Model. It's composed of two Reinforcement Learning algorithms (RL) such as the one described in A. The first one (left) predicts the action of the other agent based on its outcome, and its updated with the other agent's reward. The second one (right), uses that prediction and its own outcome to choose its own action. (C) Schematic description of the Self Model. It's made of two RL algorithms as in B. The first RL module its also used to predict an action based on the other agent's outcome, but then its updated according to the agent's own reward. (Color figure online)

The *Adaptive Layer* implements a Temporal-Difference reinforcement learning algorithm (TD-learning) [8] whose goal is to learn how to maximize the acquisition of reward. It does it by learning a policy that decides which action to perform for a given state of the environment. In this task, the state of the environment is the outcome of the previous round. When a new round starts, the TD-learning chooses an action based on the previous outcome, and when the round ends, it updates its policy according to the reward received (for a detailed explanation see Fig. 2(A)). In this implementation, there are three possible states - *"high"*, *"low"*, and *"tie"*- that correspond to agent's last result of the game (it got the high reward, the low reward or it tied, respectively). The available actions are: *"to the high"*, *"to the low"*, and *"none"*.

The interaction between the *Reactive* and *Adaptive* layers is modulated by the action selected in each round, and it serves to selectively inhibit those reactive behaviors that are not needed to execute the selected action. In the case that the *Adaptive Layer* has chosen the action *"to the high"*, the *"attraction towards low reward"* reactive behavior will be inhibited. On the contrary, if the *Adaptive Layer* selects *"to the low"*, then the inhibited behavior will be *"attraction towards high reward"*. However, when the selected action is *"none"*, none of the reactive behaviors is inhibited. This capacity to modulate the agent's attention according to its planned action, in combination with the intrinsic agent-avoidance behavior, has been shown crucial for achieving efficient multi-agent interactions in real-time scenarios [4].

### 2.3 Other's Model

The *Other's Model* architecture implements two RL algorithms in the Adaptive layer, such as the one described in the previous section (TD-learning). The first algorithm is in charge of predicting the action of the other agent. It receives the other agent's outcome to make the prediction, and it keeps track of the other agent's reward to update it's prediction, effectively creating an internal model of the other agent's policy. Then, the action predicted by the first RL serves as an input to the second one, along with the outcome of the previous round, to produce the agent's next action (see Fig. 2(B)). As in the original *Control-Based Reinforcement Learning* model, the second RL is updated according to its own reward.

### 2.4 Self Model

The *Self Model* architecture presents a subtle change compared to the *Other's Model* architecture. Conceptually, instead of trying to predict the action of the other agent based on an internal model of the other's strategy, this architecture allows an agent to predict what it would do if it were in the position of the other, and to use this information to chose its own action. Structurally, the first RL algorithm still uses the other agent outcome to make a prediction about the other's future action but is updated using the agent's own information regarding outcome and reward. The second RL functions in the same way as the second RL of the *Other's Model*. So, in this architecture, both RL algorithms are updated following the agent's own model, without taking into account any information about the other, except for the moment of making the prediction (see Fig. 2(C)).

## 3  Results

In order to assess performance of different models described above, we use the same metrics as in [4]: *Efficiency*, *Fairness* and *Stability*. *Efficiency* measures the cumulative sum of rewards that agents were able to earn collectively in each round, divided by the total amount of possible rewards. A value of 1 in efficiency is equivalent to both agents obtaining all rewards with no ties at all. *Fairness* quantifies the balance in reward distribution between the two agents. In this case, a fairness value of 1 means that both players earned the higher payoff the same amount of times or, equivalently, that the agents entered a turn-taking kind of convention that fairly distributed rewards among them. Finally, *Stability* measures how predictable the behavior was or, equivalently, whether the agents converged to a common strategy or alternated between non-deterministic states. In other words, stability quantifies how predictable are the outcomes of the following rounds based on previous results by using the information-theoretic measure of surprisal (also known as self-information), which Shannon defined as "the negative logarithm of the probability of an event". Analysis of variance and post-hoc tests were performed for each condition.

Our results compare the different architectures detailed in the previous section in the following manner. First, we compare the performance of each algorithm when interacting with itself (Fig. 3, top panels). Then we extend this comparison by making each architecture interact with the original RL model (Fig. 3, bottom panels). By doing this, we observe how models achieve similar levels of efficiency and fairness when competing against opponents of equal complexity (Fig. 3(A)). In contrast, when both predictive models are paired with the Original model, they tend to engage in more efficient interactions. Nonetheless, these interactions are not necessarily equally fair, observed by the reduced fairness in Fig. 3(B), where projecting self into the other agent tends to lead to more efficient and less fair interactions. We interpret that this behavior is derived from the added complexity in the predictive model, which allows to rapidly converge into dominant interactions.

Overall, we observed that when these models are faced with simpler models (i.e. the original RL model), the benefits of the ToM modules in the architecture provide a significant benefit, reflected by an increase in efficiency in both high (*Original*, $M = 0.88$; versus *Other's Model*, $M = 0.91$, $p < .001$; and versus *Self Model*, $M = 0.92$, $p < .001$) and low (*Original*, $M = 0.86$; versus *Other's Model*, $M = 0.88$, $p < .001$; and versus *Self Model*, $M = 0.89$, $p < .001$) conditions. Our previous work (IROS, under review), showed that Supervised Learning (SL) based predictive algorithms were having a similar effect when facing the Original model. However, in that case, they showed decreased efficiency when facing themselves. We suggest that the difference in the results between RL-based models and SL-models is in the nature of their learning paradigm: while SL algorithms can easily predict systems that are simpler than themselves, RL models seem to be able to improve performance even in the most adverse odds, as observed in [1,2].

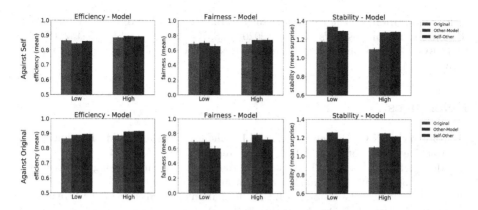

**Fig. 3.** Predictive models are generally more efficient. Top panel: Results of the models competing against themselves measured by *Efficiency*, *Fairness*, and *Stability*, both in *High* and *Low* payoff difference conditions. Note that *Stability* is measured by the level of surprisal, so a high value in surprisal means lower *Stability*. Bottom panel: Results of the models competing against the original (non-predictive) model, measured with the same metric as in the top panel.

## 4   Discussion

Our model proposes two alternatives to previous work, by either including a model of the other or a model of the self that are used to predict the other agent's potential actions. With this, we test the architectural properties of some of the underlying processes of Theory Of Mind. These models have demonstrated to be an advantage when tested in a social decision-making task as shown by the increased efficiency of the outcomes. More particularly, our results suggest that having such predictive models of the other benefits the global outcome of the interaction, whereas the model of the other vs. the model of one's self, differ significantly on their ability to collaborate (illustrated by the fairness measure).

We conclude that the evolution of mechanisms that allow for the control of other agents provide different kinds of advantages that can become significant when interacting with other kinds of agents. We argue that no single proposed addition to the learning architecture is sufficient to significantly optimize performance in these scenarios by its own, but a combination of the different mechanisms suggested may achieve near-optimal performance in any case.

Additionally, our framework provides an interesting possibility to model complex social behaviors using multi-agent robotic systems [9]. These behaviors have also been tied to evolutionary dynamics of biological life forms and conscious beings [10], [11], [12], [13]. The study of these social behaviors can also be of great interest for achieving a greater understanding of human social and cultural development and testing these ideas using multi-agent robot platforms.

**Acknowledgments.** The research leading to these results has received funding from the European Commission's Horizon 2020 socSMC project (socSMC-641321H2020-FETPROACT-2014) and by the European Research Council's CDAC project (ERC-2013-ADG341196).

# References

1. Rabinowitz, N.C., Perbet, F., Song, H.F., Zhang, C., Eslami, S.M., Botvinick, M.: Machine Theory of Mind (2018). arXiv preprint arXiv:1802.07740
2. Mordatch, I., Abbeel, P.: Emergence of grounded compositional language in multi-agent populations (2017). arXiv preprint arXiv:1703.04908
3. Hawkins, R.X.D., Goldstone, R.L.: The formation of social conventions in real-time environments. PLoS One **11**, e0151670 (2016)
4. Freire, I.T., Moulin-Frier, C., Sanchez-Fibla, M., Arsiwalla, X.D., Verschure, P.: Modeling the Formation of Social Conventions in Multi-Agent Populations (2018). arXiv preprint arXiv:1802.06108
5. Verschure, P.F.M.J., Voegtlin, T., Douglas, R.J.: Environmentally mediated synergy between perception and behaviour in mobile robots. Nature **425**, 620–624 (2003)
6. Moulin-Frier, C., Arsiwalla, X.D., Puigbo, J.Y., Sanchez-Fibla, M., Duff, A., Verschure, P.F.: Top-down and bottom-up interactions between low-level reactive control and symbolic rule learning in embodied agents. In: CoCo@ NIPS (2016)
7. Braitenberg, V.: Vehicles: Experiments in Synthetic Psychology. MIT Press, Cambridge (1986)
8. Sutton, R.S.: Learning to predict by the methods of temporal differences. Mach. Learn. **3**, 9–44 (1988)
9. Moulin-Frier, C., Puigbo, J.Y., Arsiwalla, X.D., Sanchez-Fibla, M., Verschure, P.F.: Embodied artificial intelligence through distributed adaptive control: An integrated framework (2017). arXiv preprint arXiv:1704.01407
10. Arsiwalla, X.D., Herreros, I., Moulin-Frier, C., Sanchez, M., Verschure, P.F.: Is consciousness a control process? Artificial Intelligence Research and Development, pp. 233–238. IOS Press, Amsterdam (2016)
11. Arsiwalla, X.D., Herreros, I., Verschure, P.: On three categories of conscious machines. In: Conference on Biomimetic and Biohybrid Systems, pp. 389–392 (2016)
12. Arsiwalla, X.D., Herreros, I., Moulin-Frier, C., Verschure, P.: Consciousness as an Evolutionary Game-Theoretic, Strategy, pp. 509–514 (2017)
13. Arsiwalla, X.D., Moulin-Frier, C., Herreros, I., Sanchez-Fibla, M., Verschure, P.: The Morphospace of Consciousness (2017). ArXiv preprint arXiv:1705.11190

# Estimating Body Pitch from Distributed Proprioception in a Hexapod

Arne Gollin[1,2(✉)] and Volker Dürr[1,2]

[1] Department of Biological Cybernetics, Faculty of Biology,
Bielefeld University, Bielefeld, Germany
`arne.gollin@uni-bielefeld.de`
[2] Cognitive Interaction Technology - Center of Excellence,
Bielefeld University, Bielefeld, Germany

**Abstract.** Adaptability of legged locomotion relies on distributed proprioceptive feedback from the legs. Apart from low-level control of leg movements, proprioceptive cues may also be integrated to estimate overall locomotion parameters relevant to high-level control of behavior. For example, this could be relevant for reliable estimates of body inclination relative to the substrate, particularly in animals that lack dedicated graviceptors such as statocycsts. With regard to robotic systems, distributed proprioception could exploit physical interaction with the substrate to improve the robustness of inclination estimates. In insect locomotion, it is unknown how overall parameters such as body inclination or forward velocity may be represented in the nervous system. If proprioceptive encoding was optimal, the afferent activity pattern of distributed proprioceptive cues from across the body should be a suitable representation in itself. However, given noisy encoding in multiple afferent spike trains, it is unknown (i) how reliable the parameter estimates can be, and (ii) which parts of a distributed proprioceptive code are most relevant.

Here we use a database on unrestrained whole-body kinematics of walking and climbing stick insects in conjunction with simple spiking proprioceptor models to transform sets of joint angle time courses into corresponding sets of spike trains. In total, we tested four different types of models: a reference model without proprioceptive encoding and three proprioception models with different filter properties and spike generators. Within each model, we compared $4 \times 4$ conditions that differed in number and combination of joints and legs. Our results show that the contribution of middle and hind legs is of similar relevance for the estimation of body pitch, whereas front legs contribute only very little. Furthermore, femoral levation proved to be the most relevant degree of freedom, whereas estimates based on protraction and extension angles were less accurate.

**Keywords:** Locomotion · Proprioceptor · Artificial neural network · Hair field
Stimulus encoding

© Springer International Publishing AG, part of Springer Nature 2018
V. Vouloutsi et al. (Eds.): Living Machines 2018, LNAI 10928, pp. 187–199, 2018.
https://doi.org/10.1007/978-3-319-95972-6_20

# 1   Introduction

For robust walking and climbing behavior, knowing about the own body orientation with respect to the substrate may be essential. Gravity provides a good reference frame to monitor relevant locomotion parameters such as absolute body inclination, since its direction and strength is constant. However, most invertebrates do not have dedicated graviceptors to monitor the gravity vector directly, such as statocysts do in crustaceans. Insects like ants [1] and stick insects [2] appear to use distributed proprioception by means of hair fields and chordotonal organs for implicit graviception. In their cases, the direction of gravity is inferred from passive variation of the joint angles as an effect of body weight. This suggests that body pitch relative to substrate could be estimated from joint angle variations of the legs that are in contact with the substrate.

In biomimetic robots, it is common to equip the main body with sensors such as IMUs in order to obtain information about absolute body orientation or changes in body pitch. However, IMUs are prone to drift and do not provide reliable estimates over longer time periods. In case of legged robots, distributed proprioception of leg posture and movement - as done in invertebrates - could provide a reliable additional source of information about body pitch relative to the substrate, which is not prone to drift, since information is integrated spatially not temporally.

To date, it is largely unknown whether the nervous system (NS) of insects use proprioception to form an internal representation of body pitch or other higher order parameters of locomotion, which kind of information is accessible and whether the NS is able to gate proprioceptive feedback only when the information is relevant. However, it is well known that insects use optic flow for distance estimates (e.g.: desert ant: [3]; and control of flight velocity in honey bees [4]), proving that the insect NS is capable of deriving higher-order information from low-level sensor data. Several lines of evidence suggest that spatial coordination of limbs in insects involves short-term memory of postural information (for review, see [5]). For example, stick insects can transfer spatial information about foot position from one leg to another, as revealed by spatial congruence of touch-down locations of neighboring legs [6]. Furthermore, a proprioceptive hair field on the base of the leg was shown to be involved in this coordinate transfer among legs. Ablation of the homologous hair field in cockroaches leads to an increase in overstepping due to lacking inhibitory feedback that is mediated by this hair field in intact animals [7]. Among other evidence, these studies show that proprioceptive hair fields provide relevant postural information for spatial coordination of body parts.

Given this evidence on the functional roles of proprioceptive hair fields, and the potential use of distributed postural information in both natural and biomimetic walking systems, the main objective of this study is to assess how well higher-order locomotion parameters can be estimated from a set of proprioceptive hair fields. Given the noisy encoding in multiple afferent spike trains, the major questions addressed in this study are (i) how reliable the body pitch estimate can be, in case of continuous integration of joint angles and (ii) which parts of the distributed code are most relevant.

## 2    Material and Methods

### 2.1    Dataset

We used a database on whole-body kinematics of unrestrained walking and climbing stick insects (*Carausius morosus*) that was originally acquired for the characterization of distinct step classes [8] and an inter-species comparison of whole-body kinematics of insect locomotion [9]. This dataset was particularly suitable to investigate body pitch, because the stairs of the setup required transient, large-amplitude adjustment of body pitch. Other parameters could either not be measured accurately (e.g., body roll) or did not vary very much (e.g., body height). The results presented in this study are based on a sample of in total 80 climbing trials from nine animals. Whole-body kinematics were recorded at 200 Hz with a marker-based motion-capture system. Markers were attached to the thorax and legs of the insect and tracked by infrared cameras (Vicon MX10 equipped with eight T10 cameras). The insects were walking freely on a horizontal walking path (40 mm × 490 mm, Fig. 1a). At the far end of the setup the animals had to climb two stairs of 48 mm height. The recorded marker trajectories (Fig. 1b, c) were used to reconstruct the trajectories of the thorax segments and the six legs, in order to calculate the joint angle time courses of three joints per leg and the time course of body pitch, i.e., the inclination of the metathorax relative to the horizontal plane of the setup (Fig. 2).

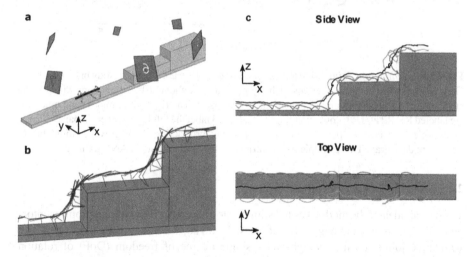

**Fig. 1.** *A representative single trial of unrestrained walking and climbing behavior of Caurausius morosus.* (a) Schematic of the Vicon setup, showing six viewing planes of the motion capture cameras (of eight in total). Gray circles show the marker positions on the thorax and legs. The setup has two stairs of 48 mm height each. (b) Movement of the body axis (gray lines) and hind legs (black lines) of one trial, illustrated by a superimposed stick figures every second. (c) Side and top view of trajectories of the tibia–tarsus joint of left (light gray) and right (dark gray) hind legs, and of the metathorax (black line).

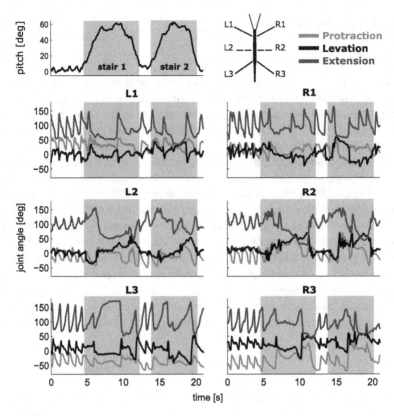

**Fig. 2.** *Body pitch and Joint angle time courses of a single trial.* Top left: Body pitch over time. Grey shading indicates the intervals of body pitch angles above 10°, which approximates the encounter of a stair. Top right: schematic of a stick insect. The right front, middle and hind legs are labeled R1, R2 and R3; correspondingly, L1, L2, L3 label the left legs. Lower six panels: Three joint angle time courses per leg (one panel per leg; protraction: light gray; levation: black; extension: dark gray. This example trial contributed 4672 data points to ANN training.

## 2.2 Model of Leg and Proprioceptors

The overall idea of the model was to estimate the afferent activity of joint proprioceptors given the recorded joint angle time courses. To do so, we used a simplified leg model with three joints, each of which had a single degree of freedom (DoF) of rotation (Fig. 3a). Accordingly, the thorax-coxa joint was assumed to protract/retract the leg by rotation around a slanted joint axis. The assumption of a slanted axis takes account of the strong correlation of protraction and supination of the leg plane (or retraction with pronation) as found by [9]. The coxa-trochanter joint accounts for levation/depression of the trochanterofemur relative to the coxa, and the femur-tibia joint accounts for extension/flexion of the tibia relative to the femur. Throughout this study, the functions of the three leg joints will be referred to as protraction, levation and extension, equivalent to the motion directions specified by increasing joint angles. The position and motion

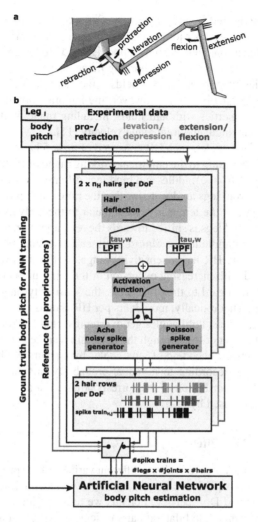

**Fig. 3.** *Model concept and variants.* (a) Schematic of the leg model. Each leg has three joints with one degree of freedom (DoF) of movement: protraction/retraction, levation/depression and extension/flexion. Joint position and motion are monitored by proprioceptors which, for simplicity, are modeled as one pair of hair rows per DoF. Individual hairs are getting deflected according to their position within the hair row. (b) Three proprioception model variants are compared against the reference condition without sensory encoding: Ache (2015), Ache (tuned), and Poisson. In all cases, an Artificial Neural Network (ANN) is trained to predict the body pitch angle (ground truth). In the reference model, joint angles are used to train the ANN directly. In the three proprioception models, joint angles are encoded by $2 \times 3$ hair rows per leg, each one containing N individual hairs. Encoding by individual hairs follows the model of [14], where each hair's deflection time course is transformed into an afferent activation by a set of parallel linear 1st order high- (HPF) and low-pass filters (LPF) with time constant, tau, and weight factor, w. Given this afferent activation, a spike train is generated, either by means of a Poisson point process (Poisson variant) or a noisy spike generator as used by [14]. $2 x n_H$ spike trains per DoF are then used to train the ANN.

of each joint was monitored by proprioceptors. For simplicity, they were modeled as two opposing hair rows (HR) per joint, i.e. linearly arranged proprioceptive hair fields. Each pair of HR acted as one unit, with the upper HR and the lower HR monitoring the upper and the lower half of the angular working range, respectively. Note that the real stick insect leg carries proprioceptive hair fields at the thorax-coxa and coxa-trochanter joint, but not at the femur-tibia joint. However, the femoral chordotonal organ shares important encoding properties with hair fields, including range fractionation [10] and sensitivity to both joint angle and joint angle velocity [11].

In the standard (full) model, each HR consisted of $n_H = 5$ hairs. For each HR, these hairs were arranged according to the empirical working range of each joint and each leg pair, as joint actions of front-, middle- and hind legs differ considerably. For example, protraction angles of front legs are located within the range of approximately $-20°$ and $70°$, with $0°$ meaning that the femur is perpendicular to the body axis. In contrast, the working range of the hind legs is shifted towards the rear, approximately between $-80°$ to $10°$, and that of the middle legs is almost symmetrical around $0°$ ($-45°$ to $45°$; see Fig. 2). Each hair of the HR has a sensitivity range. Within this range the hair gets increasingly deflected with increasing excursion of the joint, until complete deflection of the hair ($90°$). With regard to the joint angle, the sensitivity ranges of hairs within one HR may overlap. Theoretically, more hairs per HR should give better resolution of joint angle encoding, at least until angles get overrepresented and the information gain from an additional hair is not lost through the noise of its spike generator. In all model variants used here, optimal encoding of joint angles by $n_H$ hairs per HR was attempted by placing single hairs according to $n_H$ equal-probability quantiles of the empirical cumulative probability distribution of the corresponding joint and leg type, analogous to a coding scheme proposed by [12].

## 2.3    Estimation of Body Pitch

Since the goal of the study was to evaluate different variants of the proprioception model for the estimation of body pitch, we tested each model variant on different numbers and combinations of legs and DoF per leg. For this we took the joint angle time courses either of all legs or from single bilateral pairs of legs, i.e. front-, middle- or hind legs only (equivalent to R1/L1, R2/L2 or R3/L3 in Fig. 2). Each one of these four leg combinations were tested in four combinations of DoF per leg (full: all joints per leg; pro: protraction only; lev: levation only; ext: extension only).

Body pitch was estimated by means of an artificial neural network (ANN) with a single output (pitch) and $2 \times n_H \times n_L \times n_{DoF}$ inputs, i.e., one input per modelled afferent spike train, with $n_L$ being the number of legs (i.e., 2 or 6) and $n_{DoF}$ being the number of DoF per leg (i.e., 1 or 3).

In all proprioception model variants, the continuous joint angle time courses were first transformed into hair deflection angles, according to each hairs' sensitivity range (Fig. 3b). A lead-lag system of two parallel linear first-order low- and high-pass filters then converted the hair deflection into the activation function of the corresponding afferent, similar to the membrane potential of a mechanosensory neuron. Time constant *tau* and scaling weight *w* of the filters (Table 1) were hand-tuned to match single-unit recordings of single hair field afferents of the cockroach antenna [13]. The afferent activation was then transformed into a discrete spike train, using one of two spike generators (Ache model: noisy spike generator; Poisson model: Poisson spike generator). Accordingly, the output of a proprioception model was always a set of spike trains, with one spike train per proprioceptive hair.

**Table 1.** Linear filter parameters

| Model | Filter | tau [ms] | Weight w |
|-------|--------|----------|----------|
| Ache (2015) | HPF | 30 | 20 |
| Ache (tuned) | HPF | 1050 | 4.5 |
| Poisson | HPF | 1050 | 4.5 |
| Ache (2015) | LPF | 10 | 2 |
| Ache (tuned) | LPF | 1250 | 2.4 |
| Poisson | LPF | 1250 | 2.4 |

**Ache Models.** The hair field afferent model proposed by [14] was used to simulate afferent spike trains of antennal hair fields. Its noisy spike generator is a simple probabilistic model, where a spike is elicited at time, t, if the afferent activation at time t, act(t), exceeds a randomly generated number and no spike had occurred in the preceding time step (refractory period):

$$spike(t) = \begin{cases} 1 & if \quad act(t) \cdot 0.3 > rand \quad and \quad spike(t-1) = 0 \\ 0 & otherwise \end{cases}, \quad (1)$$

where *spike(t)* is a time series of zeros and ones, indicating whether or not a spike has been fired at time *t*, and *rand* is a random number between 0 and 1. In the present study, we used either the original parameter settings [14], or an alternative setting with much longer time constants and more equal weighting of the HPF and LPF (compare *Ache (2015)* and *Ache (tuned)* in Table 1).

**Poisson Model.** For comparison with the simplistic noisy spike generator of the Ache model variants, we used a non-stationary Poisson process. The theory of Poisson processes is well-studied and they are commonly used in computational neuroscience [15]. A Poisson process as implemented here is an offline method that uses a continuous function lambda to describe how the likelihood of a spike depends on the activation of the neuron. In our model, we used the Poisson thinning method according to [16]. Specifically, we used a third-order Gamma process, which can be viewed as a perfect integrator of the Poisson process with excitatory inputs only and a threshold of n spikes, with n corresponding to the order of the Gamma process. Since the Gamma process acts as an integrator, the lambda in the thinning process needs to be scaled by n. The gamma process generates discrete spike trains with more evenly spread spikes given constant activation. Due to the Poisson process, the refractory period is soft, i.e., the probability of two consecutive spikes is low but not zero.

**Artificial Neural Network.** Body pitch was estimated using a three-layered feed-forward ANN. The hidden and output layers contained ten and one neurons, respectively. In order to compare the performances of proprioception models with differing numbers of DoF, we adjusted the number of hairs per HR, $n_H$, so as to keep the number of input neurons of the ANN constant for the different numbers of DoF per leg (three DoF: $n_H = 5$; single DoF: $n_H = 15$). Nevertheless, the input layer size varied with the number of legs considered. For variants considering all six legs, the input layer size was 180. For variants with bilateral leg pairs it was 60. ANNs were trained separately for each animal, as the joint angle distributions and, therefore, the kinematic changes from walking to climbing varied among animals. Half of the trials were used for training (n = 41) and the other half for evaluation (n = 39). All calculations were done in MatLab 2014a (The Mathworks, Natick/MA) with custom-written scripts. The ANNs were generated and trained by use of the ANN toolbox of Matlab, using the Levenberg-Marquardt optimisation for supervised learning. ANN performance was evaluated by calculating the median $r^2$-value of all evaluation trials.

## 3    Results

### 3.1    Relevance of Particular Legs and Joint Types

By considering subsets of legs and single-DoF conditions, we aimed to identify the relevance of particular leg and proprioceptor subsets. To assess the performance of the distributed proprioception models, the reference model bypassed proprioceptive encoding to reveal how well body pitch could be estimated from correlations with joint angle time courses. By considering subsets of legs and single-DoF conditions of that reference model, we aimed to identify the relevance of particular legs and joint types for estimation of body pitch. We expected to obtain the most reliable estimates if all six legs and three DoF per leg were considered. Indeed, this was the case for almost all trials. In the reference model without proprioceptive encoding (Fig. 4a), the median goodness of fit reached almost 2/3 of the total variance explained $(r^2 = 0.64)$ in the "full" condition. For the same leg condition (all legs, black box plots in Fig. 4a), the next best estimates were obtained for "protraction only" and "levation only", both of which reached almost the same goodness of fit (pro: $r^2 = 0.47$, lev: $r^2 = 0.50$). The condition "extension only" resulted in lowest $r^2$-values ($r^2 = 0.34$), indicating that body pitch correlated least with changes in the femur-tibia joint angles. Accordingly, a ranking of "single-DoF relevance" within all legs considered is: full > lev ≥ pro > ext.

Considering the conditions "middle legs only" (medium grey box plots in Fig. 4a) and "hind legs only" (dark grey box plots in Fig. 4a), the variance explained dropped by at least 10% compared to the condition "all legs", irrespective of which DoF were considered. The ranking of single-DoF relevance described above was repeated here, with two notable exceptions: (i) For hind legs only, protraction explains less variance than extension (pro: $r^2 = 0.11$; ext: $r^2 = 0.24$); (ii) for middle legs the decrease in variance explained by femur-tibia extension was much more pronounced (ext: $r^2 = 0.06$, compared to the "all legs" condition: $r^2 = 0.34$), and also femoral levation produced much lower goodness of fit (lev: $r^2 = 0.25$) than protraction only (pro: $r^2 = 0.32$). In case of the hind legs

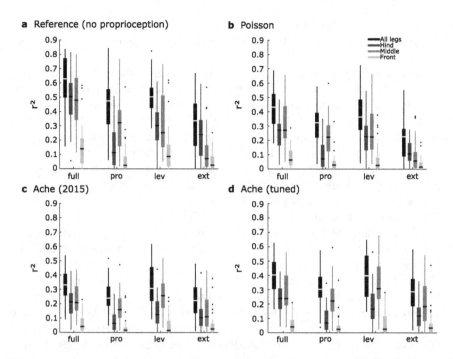

**Fig. 4.** *Model comparison and relevance of individual DoF.* The performance of each model was evaluated by correlating the ANN prediction with the ground truth body pitch. Box plots show distributions of $r^2$-values for all trials and animals. Boxes indicate inter-quartile ranges; horizontal lines in boxes show medians; whiskers show minimum and maximum values, with outliers shown as black dots. Each panel shows the results of one model, with 16 conditions that combined different sets of legs and DoF. DoF variants were: full: all joint angles per leg are used; pro: pro-/retraction only; lev: levation/depression only; ext: extension/flexion only. Leg variants were: All legs: all six legs included in black, Hind: hind legs only; Middle: middle legs only; Front: front legs only. For parameter settings, see Table 1.

only, the rankings of single-DoF relevance was: full > lev > ext > pro; for the middle legs only, it was: full > pro > lev >> ext.

The strongest decrease in variance explained was found if only the front legs were considered (light gray box plots in Fig. 4a), suggesting that front leg joint angles correlated least with body pitch. With front legs only, the median goodness of fit never exceeded the $r^2 = 0.14$ that was observed for the "full" condition. The single-DoF relevance ranking for front legs was: full > lev > pro = ext.

### 3.2 Comparison of Proprioception Models

The goodness for body pitch estimates of all four tested models are shown in Fig. 4. In general, we found lower $r^2$-values for proprioception models than for the reference model. For example, in the "all legs & full DoF" condition, i.e., with a total 18 DoF considered, the drops in performance for the proprioception models relative to the reference model ($r^2 = 0.64$) were: *Poisson*: $-21\%$ ($r^2 = 0.43$, Fig. 4b); *Ache (tuned)*: $-24\%$ ($r^2 = 0.40$, Fig. 4d); and *Ache (2015)*: $-31\%$ ($r^2 = 0.33$, Fig. 4c) less variance explained.

The rankings of single-DoF relevance looked similar to those described for the reference model but were shifted to lower values of variance explained. However, some notable differences from the reference model were observed. First, for the *Poisson* model (Fig. 4b), the gap between $r^2$-values of the "full DoF" and "levation only" conditions were smaller than for the reference model (Fig. 4a). Second, when only middle legs were considered in the *Ache (tuned)* model, the condition "extension only" produced much better estimates than any other model in that condition, though with fairly low goodness of fit ($r^2 = 0.23$). With regard to the different leg conditions, the ranking among leg pairs stayed the same as described for the reference model.

For an overall comparison of the four models, Fig. 5 shows the median $r^2$-values for all conditions examined, with the values of the propioception models plotted against their corresponding reference value. As mentioned above, the reference model typically yielded the highest $r^2$-values. As a result, all but four symbols in Fig. 5 are located below the diagonal. All four of these cases concern the lower range of model performances (with $r^2 < 0.3$), where the *Ache (2015)* and *Ache (tuned)* models yielded higher $r^2$-values than the reference model if only the middle legs were considered. Apart from these exceptions, the *Ache (tuned)* and *Poisson* models tended to produce estimates of similar goodness of fit, while the *Ache (2015)* model usually generated lowest values of goodness of fit, regardless of leg or joint condition.

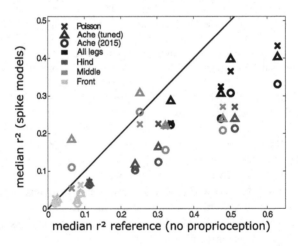

**Fig. 5.** *Overall performance of model.* Median performances of each model (symbols) and leg combinations (grey levels) plotted against the corresponding medians of the reference model. Note that the information about the set of DoF used is not displayed. However, for each leg combination, typically, $r^2$ values decreased in the order full > lev > pro > ext.

# 4 Discussion

## 4.1 Relevance of DoF and Leg Types

Despite we did not exclude the swing phases from the joint angle time courses, the changes in joint kinematics during climbing yield sufficient information to estimate body pitch (with a median of 64% of variance explained in the reference model, and 43% in a proprioception model, Fig. 4b). Furthermore, regardless of the model variant, femoral levation proved to be of greatest relevance to the estimation of body pitch (Fig. 4). This finding is in line with the results of [17], who analyzed the same data set to estimate the relevance of 36 parameters for successful classification of climbing steps as opposed to normal steps. They found that the femoral levation was most relevant, owing to its increased variability during climbing.

In our experiment, the condition "protraction only" usually reached similar $r^2$-values as the condition "levation only". A notable exception to this was found for the hind legs, where "protraction only" did not exceed $r^2$-values of 0.15, whereas the "extension only" condition yielded much better estimates than for the other leg types. This exception might be explained by the different function of the leg pairs. The hind legs' main function is to propel the body [18]. Owing to their posterior working range, the extension of a hind leg appears to vary more strongly during climbing than during straight walking, and correlate more strongly with body pitch.

Note that, because our database contained ascending climbs only, it is possible that the relevance of individual legs may turn out differently if descents were included. With this in mind, we found that middle and hind legs proved to be most relevant to the estimation of body pitch. This may be due to the fact that front legs step more irregularly, they execute more short steps and engage more in searching movements. Since all these aspects reduce the efficiency and fraction of time of stance movements in front legs, they contribute less efficiently and less frequently to the mechanical coupling of the body and the substrate, likely reducing their relevance for estimating body pitch. With regard to biomimetic robots, our results suggest that equipping all legs and joints with the same set of sensors might not be very efficient because morphology and type of application will render some DoF more relevant than others.

## 4.2 Proprioceptors

For all DoF per leg, hair fields were modeled as the only joint angle proprioceptors, despite the fact that the femur-tibia joint angle of insects is monitored by the femoral chordotonal organ (fCO). However, afferent neurons within an fCO share two important functional aspects with hair field afferents: the fractionation of the overall sensitivity range [10] and the velocity dependency (e.g., [11]). Accordingly, a conceptual model of an fCO would have similar computational properties as the hair field models used here (Fig. 3). In fact, the modeled computational properties probably apply to various other animal mechanoreceptors, too. The use of hair fields only enabled us to make a direct comparison of the contribution of the joint angles, given the same computational properties of the proprioceptive encoding among DoF and legs. Nevertheless, since information is ultimately conveyed via spike trains, an fCO might have a larger range of spike frequencies, particular filter properties, or simply more afferent neurons (100 afferents in an fCO, as opposed to 10 to 30 afferents here), specific tuning of the proprioception model used for the femur-tibia joint may improve its contribution to the estimation of body pitch. In future work, we will address (i) the gating of stance phases, (ii) how many proprioceptive afferents are optimal to encode the angular working range, and (iii) the optimal tuning of filter characteristics in afferents.

# References

1. Markl, H.: Borstenfelder an den Gelenken als Schweresinnesorgane bei Ameisen und anderen Hymenopteren. Z. Vergl. Physiol. **45**, 475–569 (1962)
2. Bässler, U.: Propriorezeptoren am Subcoxal- und Femur-Tibia-Gelenk der Stabheuschrecke *Carausius morosus* und ihre Rolle bei der Wahrnehmung der Schwerkraftrichtung. Kybernetik **2**, 168–193 (1965)
3. Ronacher, B., Wehner, R.: Desert ants *Cataglyphis fortis* use self-induced optic flow to measure distances travelled. J. Comp. Physiol. A **177**, 21–27 (1995)
4. Baird, E., Srinivasan, Mandyam V., Zhang, S., Lamont, R., Cowling, A.: Visual control of flight speed and height in the honeybee. In: Nolfi, S., Baldassarre, G., Calabretta, R., Hallam, John C.T., Marocco, D., Meyer, J.-A., Miglino, O., Parisi, D. (eds.) SAB 2006. LNCS (LNAI), vol. 4095, pp. 40–51. Springer, Heidelberg (2006). https://doi.org/10.1007/11840541_4
5. Dürr, V., Theunissen, L.M., Dallmann, C.J., Hoinville, T., Schmitz, J.: Motor flexibility in insects: Adaptive coordination of limbs in locomotion and near-range exploration. Behav. Ecol. Sociobiol. **72**, 15 (2018)
6. Theunissen, L.M., Vikram, S., Dürr, V.: Spatial co-ordination of foot contacts in unrestrained climbing insects. J. Exp. Biol. **217**, 3242–3253 (2014)
7. Wong, R.K.S., Pearson, K.G.: Properties of the trochanteral hair plate and its function in the control of walking in the cockroach. J. Exp. Biol. **64**, 233–249 (1976)
8. Theunissen, L.M., Dürr, V.: Insects use two distinct classes of steps during unrestrained locomotion. PLoS ONE **8**, e85321 (2013)
9. Theunissen, L.M., Bekemeier, H.H., Dürr, V.: Comparative whole-body kinematics of closely related insect species with different body morphology. J. Exp. Biol. **218**, 340–352 (2015)
10. Matheson, T.: Range fractionation in the locus metathoracic femoral chordotonal organ. J. Comp. Physiol. **170**, 509–520 (1992)
11. Hofmann, T., Koch, U.T., Bässler, U.: Physiology of the femoral chordotonal organ in the stick insect, *Cuniculina impigra*. J. Exp. Biol. **114**, 207–223 (1985)
12. Laughlin, S.B.: A simple coding procedure enhances a neuron's information capacity. Zeitschrift für Naturforschung C **36**, 910–912 (1981)
13. Okada, J., Toh, Y.: Peripheral representation of antennal orientation by the scapal hair plate of the cockroach *Periplaneta americana*. J. Exp. Biol. **204**, 4301–4309 (2001)
14. Ache, J.M., Dürr, V.: A computational model of a mechanoreceptive descending pathway involved in active tactile sensing. PLoS Comput. Biol. **11**, e1004263, 1–27 (2015)
15. Nawrot, M.P., Boucsein, C., Rodriguez Molina, V., Riehle, A., Aertsen, A., Rotter, S.: Measurement of variability dynamics in cortical spike trains. J. Neurosci. Meth. **169**, 374–390 (2008)
16. Lewis, P.A.W., Shedler, G.S.: Simulation of nonhomogeneous poisson processes by thinning. Naval Res. Logist. **26**, 403–413 (1979)

17. Schleif, F.-M., Mokbel, B., Gisbrecht, A., Theunissen, L., Dürr, V., Hammer, B.: Learning relevant time points for time-series data in the life sciences. In: Villa, Alessandro E.P., Duch, W., Érdi, P., Masulli, F., Palm, G. (eds.) ICANN 2012. LNCS, vol. 7553, pp. 531–539. Springer, Heidelberg (2012). https://doi.org/10.1007/978-3-642-33266-1_66
18. Dallmann, C.J., Dürr, V., Schmitz, J.: Joint torques in a freely walking insect reveal distinct functions of leg joints in propulsion and posture control. Proc. R. Soc. B **283**, 20151708 (2016)

# Emulating Balance Control Observed in Human Test Subjects with a Neural Network

Wade W. Hilts[1]([✉]), Nicholas S. Szczecinski[2], Roger D. Quinn[2], and Alexander J. Hunt[1]

[1] Department of Mechanical and Materials Engineering,
Portland State University, Portland, OR, USA
whilts@pdx.edu
[2] Department of Mechanical and Aerospace Engineering,
Case Western Reserve University, Cleveland, OH, USA

**Abstract.** Human balance is likely achieved using many concurrent control loops that combine to react to changes in environment, posture, center of mass and other factors affecting stability. Though numerous engineering models of human balance control have been tested, no models of how these controllers might operate within the nervous system have yet been established. We have developed such a neural model, focusing on a proprioceptive feedback loop. For this model, angular position is measured at the ankle and corrective torque is applied about the joint to maintain a vertical orientation. We built a physical model of an upright human maintaining balance with an inverted pendulum actuated by a torque-control motor. We used an engineering control model for human balance to calculate the control parameters that will cause our physical model to have the same dynamics as human test subject data collected on a tilting platform. We reconstruct this controller in a neural network and compare performance between the neural and classical engineering models in experiment, demonstrating that the design tools in this paper can be used to emulate a classical controller using a neural network with relatively few free parameters.

## 1 Introduction

In recent years, neuromorphic computing chips with promises to revolutionize computing technology have become available, however, there are few synthetic neural control algorithms that can utilize them. These chips effectively model neurons and synapses in a compact architecture that consumes orders of magnitude less power than a comparable digital system [1,2]. Most synthetic neural research has been focused around pattern recognition, image processing, or decision making [3–5]. Almost all of these systems do not require quick reactions to external changes or interaction with an unpredictable environment. A few neural controllers that must dynamically interact with their environment have been

© Springer International Publishing AG, part of Springer Nature 2018
V. Vouloutsi et al. (Eds.): Living Machines 2018, LNAI 10928, pp. 200–212, 2018.
https://doi.org/10.1007/978-3-319-95972-6_21

developed for legged systems [6–8]. These controllers quickly process sensory data and take action to maintain effective interaction with the surrounding environment [6–8]. However, these neural systems are built on individual case studies and though insights can be gathered from how the control systems worked, they are not easily portable to new problems or systems.

To this end, tools that assist in creating neural controllers for new systems have been developed. Nengo provides methods to set up spiking neural systems and then train them to produce specific desired outputs [9]. We have crafted methods in which parameters in small neural systems can be set analytically to perform mathematical operations such as addition, subtraction, multiplication, division, differentiation, and integration [10]. These different subnetworks can be developed independently and then added together to perform complex mathematical operations. We have also developed tools for analyzing and setting parameters in pattern generating circuits common in locomotion [11]. In 2017's Living Machines conference, we showed how elementary subnetworks could be assembled to emulate the function of a proportional-derivative (PD) controller [12], but this PD controller existed in simulation only. It is unclear how effective these methods are when applied to even more dynamic and unsteady control problems encountered in the robotics world.

It is our hypothesis that the analytical methods we have developed, combined with classical control techniques will provide a reasonable starting point for developing dynamic neural controllers. We test this hypothesis by developing a neural controller that is analogous to a classical control model fit to human test subject data [13,14]. In this system, a PD controller with time delay and low-passed positive feedback uses corrective torque to keep an inverted pendulum system upright. Parameters in the system are first calculated using classical control methods. Our analytical methods are then applied to the system to determine neural network connectivity and parameters needed to replicate the classical control results.

## 2 Methods for System Identification and Controller Design

### 2.1 A Linear Model for Human Balance

The human balance controller in this paper was based off a model proposed by Peterka derived from human test subject data collected on a tilting platform [13]. The test subjects in Peterka's experiment had profound vestibular loss, and the data was collected with their eyes closed. Additionally, the subjects were strapped to a fixture that allowed them to only use corrective torque at the ankle joint. This experiment effectively eliminated the contribution of vestibular and visual feedback while constraining the corrective output to torque at the ankle joint.

Frequency response data points were collected for these test subjects and Peterka proposed a control architecture to fit the test data. The plant model for the human body consisted of a simple inverted pendulum model, free of any damping effects. He also proposed a model for the control response that includes a time delay, positive force feedback with a low-pass filter, a PD controller in the standard controller position and a feedforward controller modeling the passive muscle dynamics (unaffected by the time delay) [13]. Peterka's results provide an engineering control model that has been tuned to match human test data in simulation on an inverted pendulum plant model. This engineering model was used as the basis for the neural control structure in this paper.

## 2.2   Identifying the Plant Model Used in the Experiment

The first step to implementing a control system that matches human balance characteristics is accurately identifying the plant's dynamic response to inputs, and fitting a model to this data. The system being controlled was a single-jointed inverted pendulum model with a motor placed at the base joint (Fig. 1) modeled by the time domain differential equation:

$$J\ddot{\theta} + b\dot{\theta} - mgh\theta = T_c. \tag{1}$$

Where $\theta$ is the angular position, $T_c$ is the commanded torque, $J$ is the moment of inertia, $b$ is the damping ratio and the $mgh$ term is the destabilizing torque due to gravity. We assume an ideal motor that produces the commanded torque instantly, the HEBI motor is capable of behaving as such according to manufacturer specifications. We also use the small-angle approximation, $sin(\theta) = \theta$, to linearize the model.

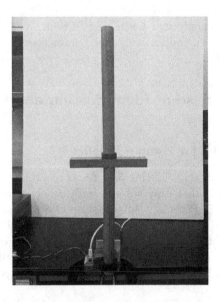

**Fig. 1.** Plant model used in this experiment. The model is comprised of a several pieces of steel rigidly fastened together, with torque controlled motor acting as the base joint.

System identification is performed using a closed loop controller because the inverted pendulum plant model is unstable for open-loop position control. A proportional controller was used to experimentally determine the gain and phase shift of the system output with a closed loop transfer function of the form:

$$\frac{\theta_{act}}{\theta_{des}} = \frac{K_p}{Js^2 + bs - mgh + K_p} = \frac{G_cG_p}{1 + G_cG_p}. \tag{2}$$

Where $G_c = K_p$ represents the proportional controller and $G_p$ is the plant model. An 8-degree peak to peak sinusoidal commanded position signal was used. The proportional gain, $K_p$, was set to 30 and the moment of inertia, destabilizing torque due to gravity of the system were measured before the experiment. These values were found to be $J = 0.44\,\mathrm{kg \cdot m^2}$, and $mgh = 9.5\,\mathrm{kg \cdot m^2/s^2}$.

The motor used to control the system had more complex dynamics at torque values near zero and introduced unknown damping to the system. A state space model of this system in MATLAB was constructed, and the theoretical form of the model enforced by using the *greyest* linear function fitting tool. This was done by setting the damping ratio parameter completely free and fixing the other known parameters. The *greyest* function was used to optimize the damping ratio value to closest match experimental results, by minimizing the error between the model prediction and the experimental data.

### 2.3 Designing a Controller that Will Produce a Closed Loop Response Similar to the Test Subject Data

After identifying a linear plant model for the inverted pendulum system, a controller that produces similar frequency response characteristics as the human test subjects was developed. The proposed control system takes a single input, the inverted pendulum's angular position, and outputs a corrective torque that is applied at the base joint. This control system can be represented by the block diagram in Fig. 2 and closed loop transfer function (3):

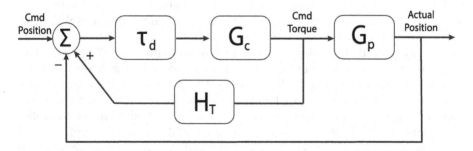

**Fig. 2.** Block diagram of human balance control engineering model. There are two nested feedback loops here. The inner feedback loop consists of a time delayed controller receiving a low-passed positive torque feedback signal. The outer loop is a negative angular position feedback loop, drawn from the output of the plant model's ($G_p$) response to the torque signal.

$$\frac{\theta_{act}}{\theta_{des}} = \frac{\tau_d G_c G_p}{1 - \tau_d G_c H_T + \tau_d G_c G_p} \tag{3}$$

$$G_p = \frac{1}{Js^2 + bs - mgh} \tag{4}$$

$$G_c = K_p + K_d s \tag{5}$$

$$H_T = \frac{K_t \omega_c}{s + \omega_c} \tag{6}$$

$$\tau_d = \frac{(-\tau s + 2)}{(\tau s + 2)} \approx e^{-\tau s} \tag{7}$$

Where $K_p$ is proportional gain, $K_d$ is derivative gain, $K_t$ is positive torque feedback gain, $\omega_c$ is low-pass filter cutoff frequency and $\tau$ is a time delay. A first order Padé approximant was used to linearize the time delay (7).

Using a similar method as in the plant model identification, the above transfer function can be converted into state space form and plugged into the MATLAB *greyest* function. We set the time delay, low-pass filter cutoff frequency, and the proportional, derivative and torque positive feedback gains as free parameters and used the *greyest* function to minimize the error between the test subject data and the controlled system's forecasted closed loop frequency response. This process produced a controller for our inverted pendulum plant model that would emulate the response of a blindfolded human with vestibular loss on a tilting platform using only corrective torque at the ankle joints.

The control loop was run at a sampling frequency of 150 Hz. As with many control system applications, high frequency noise is amplified by the derivative component of a controller, and frequencies higher than the Nyquist frequency must be filtered out. We included two second order Butterworth low-pass digital filters, each with cutoff frequencies of 50 Hz, to filter the incoming position feedback and outgoing torque command signals.

The controller was validated using MATLAB's system identification toolbox to derive the closed loop transfer function of the controlled system. Rather than fitting to frequency domain data, we used time domain experimental data to obtain a transfer function. Filtered Gaussian white noise was sent as an input, with a low-pass filter applied that removed frequencies above 2 Hz. The max amplitude was set at 8° peak to peak, which represented the majority of the operating space observed in the human data [13]. We took the input and output time domain data and fit it to a fourth order transfer function using the MATLAB System Identification toolbox. Based on the plant model and the controller design that was defined in (3), the resulting closed loop system should be well represented by a transfer function with 4 poles and 3 zeros. The transfer function fit to this data was then compared to the human data, theoretical prediction, and the classical controller.

## 3  Methods for Synthetic Neural Control System Design

The neural network, shown in Fig. 3, was created by connecting a series of sub-networks to create a PD controller with a time delay and low passed positive torque feedback. The neurons and synapses in each subnetwork are assigned specific characteristics and connections to approximate the mathematical operations of the classical controller. This work utilizes a leaky integrator non-spiking neuron model. Information is encoded in the neurons' membrane voltage, and is transmitted via synaptic connections. The membrane voltage of a neuron is governed by:

$$C_m \frac{dV}{dt} = I_{leak} + I_{syn} + I_{app}. \tag{8}$$

Where $C_m$ is the membrane capacitance, $V$ is membrane voltage, and $I_x$ are the various current sources and sinks. The leak current is:

$$I_{leak} = G_m(E_r - V). \tag{9}$$

Where $G_m$ is the membrane conductance. Neurons can transmit information via synapses, this input current, $I_{syn}$, is defined as:

$$I_{syn} = \sum_{i=1}^{n} G_{s,i}(E_{s,i} - V). \tag{10}$$

Where $G_{s,i}$ represents the synapse conductance of the $i$th synapse. The synapse conductance can be described by a piecewise function:

$$G_{s,i} = \begin{cases} 0 & V_{pre} < E_{lo} \\ g_{s,i} \frac{V_{pre} - E_{lo}}{E_{hi} - E_{lo}} & E_{lo} \leq V_{pre} \leq E_{hi}. \\ g_{s,i} & V_{pre} > E_{hi} \end{cases} \tag{11}$$

The above equation parametrizes the range over which postsynaptic neurons receive increasing current from presynaptic neurons, after which the synapse is saturated at its maximum conductance, $g(s,i)$. $E_{lo}$ and $E_{hi}$ are the lower and upper thresholds of this conductance activation range. $I_{app}$, is an external stimulus current. For the purpose of this simulation, the external stimulus current is injected into a neuron to represent outside information, such as the angular position of the inverted pendulum model.

To more easily describe neural arithmetic operations mathematically, we employ the simplifying definition:

$$\Delta E_{s,i} = E_{s,i} - E_{r,post}. \tag{12}$$

Where $\Delta E(s,i)$ is the potential difference between the synaptic equilibrium potential and the postsynaptic neuron's resting potential.

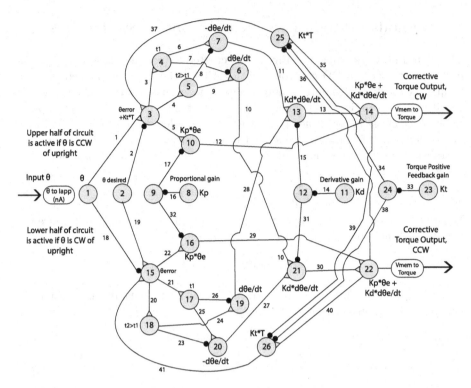

**Fig. 3.** A network of neurons and synapses that outputs a torque command based on a joint angle input signal. The circuit is a collection of interconnected addition, subtraction, multiplication and derivative subnetworks and is broken into two sections, each governing the clockwise and counterclockwise regions (about the marginally stable midpoint) of the pendulum system. CW and CCW torque response signals are manifest in the membrane potentials of neurons 14 and 22.

## 3.1    Subnetworks

A graphical representation of each subnetwork is shown in Fig. 4. The parameters for the neural network controller were calculated using Szczecinski's methods [10] and are for a network designed with an operating range of 20 mV. Since the selected control parameters called for large gain values that stretched the linear bounds of Szczecinski's multiplication subnetworks, we increased the synapse conductance to preamplify input signals to the multiplication network. This allows the multiplication subnetworks used in the proportional, derivative and positive feedback portions of the neural controller to function as modulating circuits, allowing a secondary gain adjustment between 0.1 and 1. Another tunable parameter in these subnetworks that is useful is the neuron time constant. In our model, neurons behave as an RC low-pass filter, the membrane capacitance determines the time constant of this filter. We used this property to filter out high frequency noise from the motor position feedback signal and the

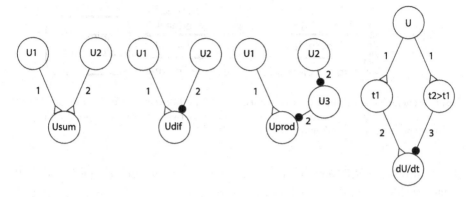

**Fig. 4.** Graphical representations of the neurons and synapses. From left to right: addition, subtraction, multiplication and derivative subnetworks. Synapses terminating in a triangle are excitatory, whereas the shaded circular terminals are inhibitory synapses.

commanded torque output signals. It also is used to filter the positive torque feedback signal. The neural network control parameters were matched to the classical control parameters by hand tuning synapse conductances and multiplication neuron stimulus currents, this was validated by sending a test signal to the network and observing the output.

## 3.2 Simulating the Network in Animatlab

The subnetworks outlined above were assembled into a larger network (Fig. 3) that emulates the classical controller design. The network was simulated in Animatlab [15], an open source neuromechanical simulation tool. It provides a powerful environment based in C++ that can perform neural network simulation in real-time. It simulates the same leaky integrator non-spiking neuron model as used in Szczecinski's subnetworks [10]. Animatlab also allows the user to construct a visual model of the network and graphically represent the signal at different points throughout the circuit.

Animatlab has the ability to interface with external devices or software via a serial connection. In order to control the HEBI motor in the inverted pendulum system, the HEBI MATLAB API is used to send torque commands and pull feedback information from the motor (Fig. 5).

A virtual serial port is used to provide communication between Animatlab and MATLAB. During each iteration of the control loop, MATLAB gets feedback from the motor and writes the current angular position to the serial port going to Animatlab. Animatlab then transforms this position value into an external stimulus current that is injected into Neuron 1. This stimulus current affects the membrane voltage of Neuron 1. The signal is processed by the subnetworks, resulting in the control signal being represented in Neurons 14 and 23's membrane voltages. Animatlab writes the membrane voltage of Neurons 14 (CCW torque) and 23 (CW torque) to the serial port going to MATLAB. This signal

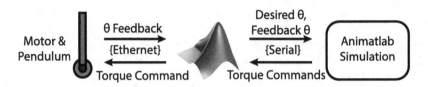

**Fig. 5.** Schematic representation of information flow between software and hardware platforms. MATLAB regulates the communication between the motor/pendulum system and the neural controller in Animatlab.

is read into MATLAB and summed to generate a commanded torque value that is sent to the motor.

# 4    Results

For the controllers designed to match human test data, we obtained time domain data on both the classical and neural closed loop control systems. Fitting a 4-poles, 3-zeros transfer function to the this input/output data resulted in the highest degree of accuracy compared to other transfer function forms for both the neural and classical controllers. The controller parameters that were found to be the best fit using the *greyest* function are $K_p = 11.69$, $K_d = 1.90$, $K_t = 0.0548$, $\omega_c = 0.209$ and $\tau = 0.0774$. Tables 1 and 2 display the neural network parameters selected to emulate the classical control performance.

The neural and classical controllers matched the classical simulation reasonably well (Fig. 6). All of the tested and simulated models agreed reasonably well with the phase and gain plots of the human test data, until they diverge near 0.4 Hz. The human data drops in gain and phase much quicker than the other models beyond this threshold. The neural network system response exhibits a slight swell in gain and phase in the higher frequencies between 0.5 and 1.5 Hz that the classical controller simulation and experimental data do not show.

**Table 1.** Neuron parameters used in the controller shown in Fig. 3

| Neuron number | Resting potential (mV) | Time const (ms) | Stim current, $I_{app}$ (nA) |
|---|---|---|---|
| 1, 2 | −50 | 20 | 0 |
| 3, 6–7, 10, 13, 15–16, 19–21 | −60 | 1 | 0 |
| 4, 17 | −60 | 0.1 | 0 |
| 5, 18 | −60 | 8 | 0 |
| 8 | −60 | 1 | 12.5 |
| 9, 12, 24 | −60 | 1 | 20 |
| 11 | −60 | 1 | 13.5 |
| 14, 22 | −60 | 20 | 0 |
| 23 | −60 | 1 | 0.8 |
| 25, 26 | −60 | 30, 000 | 0 |

**Table 2.** Synapse parameters used in the controller shown in Fig. 3

| Synapse number | $\Delta E$ (mV) | Conductance, $g_s$ ($\mu$S) | Notes |
|---|---|---|---|
| 1, 3–4, 6, 9, 12–13, 19–21, 24–25, 29–30, 35, 37, 40–41 | 194 | 0.115 | Addition |
| 2, 7–8, 18, 23, 26, 36, 39 | −40 | 0.55775 | Subtraction negative |
| 5, 22 | 194 | 2.2 | Mult. $K_p$ |
| 10–11, 27–28 | 194 | 54 | Mult. $K_d$ |
| 14–17, 31–34, 38 | 0 | 20 | Mult. Syn 2 |

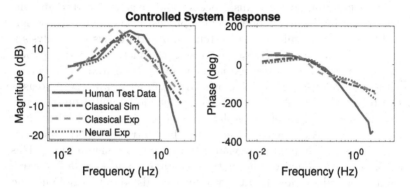

**Fig. 6.** Comparison of human test data with the responses of the classical controller design in both simulation and experiment, as well as the response of the neural controller in an experiment

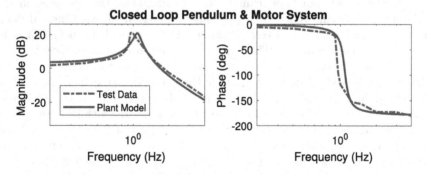

**Fig. 7.** Modeling the frequency response of the motor-pendulum system with commanded torque as input and angular position as output. A simple proportional controller was used with a gain of $K_p = 30$.

For the plant model identification part of this experiment outlined in Sect. 2.2, the theoretical model and experimental data are compared in Fig. 7. After running the optimization script, it was found that fixing the theoretical parameters for moment of inertia, $J$, and destabilizing torque, $mgh$, and only allowing the damping term, $b$, to be free placed the model closest to the experimental results. The plant parameters that were chosen are $J = 0.44$, $b = 0.40$ and $mgh = 9.50$.

## 5  Discussion

We hypothesized that the methods presented in this paper would produce a reasonable starting point for developing dynamic neural controllers. We demonstrated this by taking a classical control model fit to test subject data and reproducing this model's behavior using a simple network of neurons. Our experiment shows that neural networks are capable of emulating classical control for an inverted pendulum, however this process could be generalized to any physical system that can be linearly modeled. This process also enables the designer to specify the desired dynamics of the systems and perform system analysis in the well-mapped classical controls domain. Using the methods in this paper, any classical controller can be converted into an analogous neural controller.

For the controller experiments shown in Fig. 6, there are many areas where error can be introduced. Any errors in the plant model will propagate into the system including a controller. The plant model provided an excellent fit to the experimental data. As shown in Fig. 7, the best fitting second order transfer function has a small amount of deviance from the experimental data. This discrepancy can be explained by the motor's non-linear and non-ideal behavior at very low torque values (low frequency input signals) due to Coulomb friction, and by the $\sin(\theta) = \theta$ linearizing assumption becoming less accurate at high gain values near resonance. Also, the motor position sensor introduces high frequency noise, but this effect was diminished using low-pass filters. However, the sum of all error sources was not significant enough to invalidate the proposed model for the overall system. When fitting a transfer function to experimental data, it was found that a 4 poles, 3 zeros transfer function provided a better fit than other transfer function orders. This suggests that our overall theoretical transfer function (3) for the system model was an accurate representation.

The controllers simulated and tested in this paper deviated from human test data more significantly at higher frequencies. This stems from the lack of muscle dynamics as represented by a feedforward PD component, which increases phase lag and gain drop in this region. The feedforward part of Peterka's model was included to model passive muscle dynamics [13,16], and it was intentionally omitted as it is an artifact of the physical constraints of the human body - not a deliberate control calculation. Combining this neural control architecture with complaint actuators (Festo muscles), biologically inspired joints [17], and physical properties that maximize open loop stability [18], is an exciting path in the field of bio-inspired robotics. We intend to merge physical components and actuators that emulate biological systems into future robotic designs, so capturing these dynamics within our controller is not desirable.

This neural control design process can be used to build large models of balance control with a cascaded control model built off of many neural subnetworks. Centralized vestibular and visual information can be used to determine the desired stabilizing maneuvers that are necessary to achieve the optimal posture for quality sensory feedback and minimize the likelihood of falling over [16]. Engineering models of human balance control that include vestibular and visual feedback loops, with the reliance on each of these sensory signals varying with their quality, have already been postulated [13,14].

# References

1. Mead, C.: Neuromorphic electronic systems. Proc. IEEE **78**(10), 1629–1636 (1990)
2. Schuman, C.D., Potok, T.E., Patton, R.M., Birdwell, J.D., Dean, M.E., Rose, G.S., Plank, J.S.: A survey of neuromorphic computing and neural networks in hardware. arXiv:1705.06963 [cs], May 2017
3. Chu, M., Kim, B., Park, S., Hwang, H., Jeon, M., Lee, B.H., Lee, B.G.: Neuromorphic hardware system for visual pattern recognition with memristor array and CMOS neuron. IEEE Trans. Ind. Electron. **62**(4), 2410–2419 (2015)
4. Franco, J.A.G., Padilla, J.L.d.V., Cisneros, S.O.: Event-based image processing using a neuromorphic vision sensor. In: IEEE International Autumn Meeting on Power Electronics and Computing (ROPEC), pp. 1–6, November 2013
5. Corradi, F., You, H., Giulioni, M., Indiveri, G.: Decision making and perceptual bistability in spike-based neuromorphic VLSI systems. In: IEEE International Symposium on Circuits and Systems (ISCAS), pp. 2708–2711, May 2015
6. Hunt, A.J., Schmidt, M., Fischer, M.S., Quinn, R.D.: A biologically based neural system coordinates the joints and legs of a tetrapod. Bioinspiration Biomim. **10**(5), 055004 (2015). http://stacks.iop.org/1748-3190/10/i=5/a=055004?key=crossref. 20c5a9df87c65225ca5da5f729b912e6
7. Li, W., Szczecinski, N.S., Hunt, A.J., Quinn, R.D.: A neural network with central pattern generators entrained by sensory feedback controls walking of a bipedal model. In: Lepora, N.F.F., et al. (eds.) Living Machines 2016. LNCS (LNAI), vol. 9793, pp. 144–154. Springer, Cham (2016). https://doi.org/10.1007/978-3-319-42417-0_14
8. Hunt, A.J., Szczecinski, N.S., Andrada, E., Fischer, M., Quinn, R.D.: Using animal data and neural dynamics to reverse engineer a neuromechanical rat model. In: Wilson, S.P., Verschure, P.F.M.J., Mura, A., Prescott, T.J. (eds.) Living Machines 2015. LNCS (LNAI), vol. 9222, pp. 211–222. Springer, Cham (2015). https://doi.org/10.1007/978-3-319-22979-9_21
9. Bekolay, T., Bergstra, J., Hunsberger, E., DeWolf, T., Stewart, T.C., Rasmussen, D., Choo, X., Voelker, A.R., Eliasmith, C.: Nengo: a Python tool for building large-scale functional brain models. Front. Neuroinform. **7** (2014). https://www.ncbi.nlm.nih.gov/pmc/articles/PMC3880998/
10. Szczecinski, N.S., Hunt, A.J., Quinn, R.D.: A functional subnetwork approach to designing synthetic nervous systems that control legged robot locomotion. Front. Neurorobot. **11** (2017). https://www.ncbi.nlm.nih.gov/pmc/articles/PMC5552699/
11. Szczecinski, N.S., Hunt, A.J., Quinn, R.: Design process and tools for dynamic neuromechanical models and robot controllers. Biol. Cybern. **111**(1), 105–127 (2017)
12. Hilts, W.W., Szczecinski, N.S., Quinn, R.D., Hunt, A.J.: Simulation of human balance control using an inverted pendulum model. In: Mangan, M., et al. (eds.) Living Machines 2017. LNCS (LNAI), vol. 10384, pp. 170–180. Springer, Cham (2017). https://doi.org/10.1007/978-3-319-63537-8_15

13. Peterka, R.J.: Simplifying the complexities of maintaining balance. IEEE Eng. Med. Biol. Mag. **22**(2), 63–68 (2003)
14. Peterka, R.J., Loughlin, P.J.: Dynamic regulation of sensorimotor integration in human postural control. J. Neurophysiol. **91**(1), 410–423 (2004). http://jn.physiology.org/content/91/1/410
15. Cofer, D., Cymbalyuk, G., Reid, J., Zhu, Y., Heitler, W., Edwards, D.: AnimatLab: a 3D graphics environment for neuromechanical simulations. J. Neurosci. Methods **187**, 280–288 (2010)
16. Assländer, L., Peterka, R.J.: Sensory reweighting dynamics following removal and addition of visual and proprioceptive cues. J. Neurophysiol. **116**(2), 272–285 (2016). http://jn.physiology.org/content/116/2/272
17. Steele, A.G., Hunt, A., Etoundi, A.C.: Development of a bio-inspired knee joint mechanism for a bipedal robot. In: Mangan, M., et al. (eds.) Living Machines 2017. LNCS (LNAI), vol. 10384, pp. 418–427. Springer, Cham (2017). https://doi.org/10.1007/978-3-319-63537-8_35
18. Narioka, K., Tsugawa, S., Hosoda, K.: 3D limit cycle walking of musculoskeletal humanoid robot with flat feet. In: IEEE/RSJ International Conference on Intelligent Robots and Systems, pp. 4676–4681, October 2009

# Active Collision Free Closed-Loop Control of a Biohybrid Fly-Robot Interface

Jiaqi V. Huang[(✉)], Yiran Wei, and Holger G. Krapp

Department of Bioengineering, Imperial College London, London, SW7 2AZ, UK
j.huang09@imperial.ac.uk

**Abstract.** We implemented a closed-loop control algorithm that uses information on the turning radius of a biohybrid fly-robot interface (FRI) to interpret the spike rate of a motion sensitive interneuron, the H1-cell, as a function of distance from a patterned wall. The fly-robot interface repeatedly triggers collision avoidance manoeuvres during an oscillatory forward movement with bias towards the wall whenever the H1-cell spiking activity exceeds a certain threshold value. In addition, we further investigated the parameters which will ultimately enable the system to manoeuvre autonomously, and in an energy-efficient way within arbitrary visual environments.

**Keywords:** Motion vision · Brain machine interface · Blowfly · H1-cell
Collision avoidance

## 1 Introduction

Blowflies use a variety of sensory modalities to estimate attitude changes and control their locomotor behaviour [1]. But for methodological reasons, studies on the integration of signals from different modalities in flies that are actually moving in space are sparse. To partially overcome this problem, we have developed a Fly-Robot-Interface (FRI) where a fly is mounted on a 2-wheeled robot, the trajectory of which is controlled by the spiking activity of a directional-selective interneuron in the animal's motion vision pathway [2]. The FRI will ultimately serve as an experimental platform to study the interactions between visual and mechanosensory systems, in particular the signals provided by the compound eyes [3], the gyroscopic halteres [4] and the antennae, sensing air flow changes [5]. To achieve this objective the FRI has to move autonomously without colliding with any obstacles in its surroundings. Simultaneous monitoring of its trajectory and logging the neuronal activities for post hoc data analysis would then allow us to correlate kinematic parameters of the FRI with the spiking activity of individual visual interneurons – with and without other sensory modalities modulating its responses.

In most animals, collision avoidance is achieved by visual mechanisms either implemented in dedicated pathways [6] or involving wide-field visual interneurons that analyse optic flow. The latter strategy has been suggested for blowflies [1] where identified directional-selective lobula plate tangential cells (LPTCs) integrate local motion signals. A subset of LPTCs connects to the fly's motor systems supporting fundamental

© Springer International Publishing AG, part of Springer Nature 2018
V. Vouloutsi et al. (Eds.): Living Machines 2018, LNAI 10928, pp. 213–222, 2018.
https://doi.org/10.1007/978-3-319-95972-6_22

behaviours including gaze stabilization as well as the control of flight and walking [7]. One such LPTC is the well-characterized H1-cell. Its spiking activity can be measured comparatively easily at high signal-to-noise (SNR) ratios, even when using miniaturized electrophysiological recording equipment that can be mounted on a small robot [8]. This cell has been extensively studied regarding its directional motion preferences [9, 10], response dynamics [8, 11] and is part of a cellular network analysing visual motion during phases of yaw rotations and translations within the horizontal plane [12]. When not presented with visual motion, the H1-cell generates a spontaneous spike rate of 20–50 Hz, but can easily reach spike rates of >300 Hz during stimulation with a high contrast pattern moving in its preferred direction. Such high dynamic signal range, together with the fact that stable recordings can be established easily and maintained over several hours, make the H1-cell an ideal candidate neuron to serve as a visual sensor on the FRI [2, 8, 13–15].

A potential drawback is, however, that the H1-cell prefers horizontal back-to-front motion and is inhibited by motion in the opposite direction. Therefore, during forward translation of a robot the fly would be mounted on, the cell would be constantly inhibited and thus useless to control the robot's trajectory. The problem has been overcome by inducing an oscillatory trajectory of the robot which results in an alternating pattern of excitation and inhibition [13]. This strategy is reminiscent of active sensing mechanisms where a known actuation (or movement) of the sensor helps to extract and interpret its outputs ([15]; see below). In connection with the FRI, the active sensing turned out to be a critical prerequisite to establish a collision avoidance system. Previous work under open-loop conditions suggested that the spike-rate of the H1-cell could be interpreted as a distance-dependent signal given the turning radius of the robot, i.e. the ratio between translational and rotational components of its active movement is known [15]. At a small turning radius, which corresponds to a high rotational component, the H1-cell spiking activity is high when the robot is close to the wall of an experimental arena, while the activity decreases with increasing wall distance. At increasingly higher turning radii, corresponding to increasingly larger translational components, however, the dynamic output range indicating wall distance is reduced and may even be inverted if the turning radius exceeds a certain equilibrium value ([15] see discussion).

Building upon our previous studies, we have now designed and implemented a closed-loop collision avoidance system on the FRI that enables nearly perfect collision-free movements. The system includes an active component – an oscillatory trajectory at a small turning radius – combined with an estimate of the H1-cell's instantaneous spike rate which, if exceeding a distance-dependent threshold, triggers an avoidance manoeuvre away from the wall.

## 2  Methods

A new control algorithm was designed and implemented on the robot's on-board micro-processor (see below) to trigger collision avoidance based on the neuronal distance esti-mation of blowfly H1-cell [15]. Control performance was benchmarked by the success rate of the bio-hybrid robot passing a corridor without collision.

## 2.1  Experiment Setup

The robot was moving in a light-controlled corridor with dimensions of 1800 × 500 × 520 mm enclosed by black fabric (Fig. 2). A striped pattern (spatial wavelength = 30 mm, pattern contrast = 84%) was attached to the left corridor wall covering a height of 520 mm. LED light stripes (length: 1000 mm) were fixed at the top of the arena opposite to the striped pattern at a height of 540 mm. A GoPro fisheye camera (GoPro Hero 3+) was mounted above the arena at a height of 540 mm for recording the trajectory of the robot.

The interface firmware was programmed on a microprocessor (mbed NXP LPC1768), on-board of a two-wheeled robot (Pololu© m3pi), which also carried the extracellular recording platform. The H1-cell activity was recorded extracellularly from the lobula plate of a blowfly fixed in the centre of the recording platform, approximately 150 mm above the floor. On the platform, a tungsten electrode was used to record extracellularly H1-cell signals which were fed into a customised miniature preamplifier

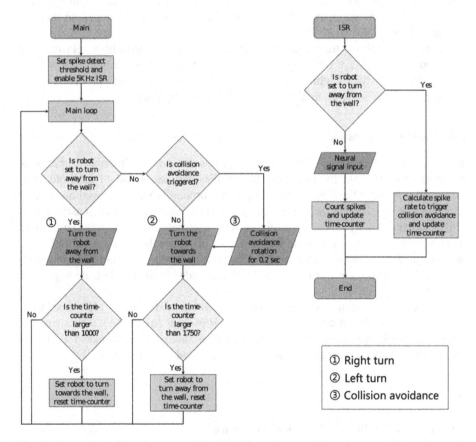

**Fig. 1.** Flow chart of the firmware of the FRI. The robot was driven in an oscillatory forward movement (with bias towards the wall), while the interrupt service routine (ISR) was running at the background, processing neural signals.

with a nominal gain of 10 k. The amplified signals were sent to an analog input pin of the microprocessor where the neural signals were processed and converted into command signals controlling the robot. A copy of the data was also recorded by a data acquisition board (NI USB-6215, National Instruments Corporation, Austin, TX, USA) at a rate of 20 k Hz, and stored on the hard disk of a PC for off-line analysis.

The firmware was programmed to generate an oscillating forward trajectory with a turning radius of 5 cm (see Fig. 1). At this turning radius a steep linear relationship between spike rate and wall distance was observed (Fig. 4. Right, Rt = 5). On top of the oscillating forward movement, the firmware added a bias towards the left wall (where the turning duration for motor driving the right wheel was larger than that of the left one). The bias gradually and repeatedly drove the robot towards the wall which allow us to test the reliability of the collision avoidance control. The sampling frequency of the neural signal was set to 5 kHz in the microprocessor on the robot. H1-cell spikes were sampled during each turn that caused preferred direction (PD) motion, and instantaneous spike rates were calculated during each turn causing motion in the opposite null direction (ND). A threshold spike rate was set which, when exceeded, did trigger a collision avoidance manoeuvre. During this manoeuvre, the robot rotated on the spot for approximately 90° away from the wall.

As mentioned above, the movements of the robot were recorded with a GoPro camera equipped with a fish-eye lens. The inevitable distortions in the resulting videos were corrected using "Adobe Lightroom" software. Robot trajectories were produced by the software "Tracker", tracing markers on the robot frame by frame.

## 2.2 Blowfly Preparation

The preparation of blowfly, *Calliphora vicina*, was the same as described in previous experiments (e.g. [15]). In brief: Female blowflies between 4 and 11 days old were chosen. Wings were fixed by bee wax. Legs and proboscis were removed and sealed with bee wax. The head of the blowfly was adjusted (according to the deep pseudopupil [16]) and fixed to a fly holder by using bee wax, together with the thorax. The cuticle was cut open and fat/muscle tissue were removed to expose the lobula plate. The preparation was done under optical magnification using a stereo microscope (Stemi 2000, Zeiss©). Ringer solution (for recipe see [17]) was added to the lobula plate to prevent desiccation.

Cells were extracellularly recorded by tungsten electrodes (of ~3 MΩ impedance, product code: UEWSHGSE3N1M, FHC Inc., Bowdoin, ME, USA). The signal-to-noise-ratio (SNR) was accepted only if the peak amplitude of the cell spikes was at least twice as high as the largest amplitude of the background noise (SNR > 2:1).

## 3    Results

### 3.1    Robot Tracking and Collision Avoidance

After switching the power on, the robot started to move forward with small oscillations. The bias added to the wheels gradually drove the robot towards the wall. As soon as the

H1-cell spike rate exceeded the threshold, the robot was triggered to perform a collision avoidance manoeuvre (shown in Fig. 2).

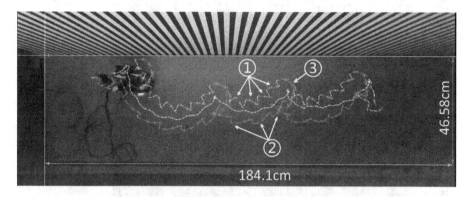

**Fig. 2.** The yellow line is the trajectory of the left tracking marker, the green line is the trajectory of the right tracking marker, and the white line is the trajectory of the fly (① Onset of Right Turn; ② Onset of Left Turn; ③ Onset of Collision Avoidance Turn. See also flow chart in Fig. 1). The video clip can be accessed from the link: https://youtu.be/g902ZEw_YcQ (Color figure online)

The instantaneous wall distances were directly exported from the trajectory coordinates obtained by Tracker. The instantaneous robot orientations with respect to the wall were calculated from the position data of the tracking markers in Matlab. Although the distortion caused by the fisheye lens was corrected, the perspective distortion in the far positions from the camera was not avoidable, so the last few data points were not considered during the data processing.

### 3.2 Spike Rate, Wall Distance and Robot Orientation

To investigate the relationship between H1-cell activity, wall distance and orientation of the robot we computed the average spike rate within all PD turns (duration: around 400 ms each) obtained in 10 sets of experiments. Figure 3 shows the resulting data plotted against the mean instantaneous wall distance and mean instantaneous robot orientations of the corresponding PD turns. A surface was fitted to the scatter plot and produced a heat map of mean spike rates.

In order to compare our data with the results obtained under open loop conditions in a previous study that revealed a linear relationship between spike rate and wall distance [15], we selected spike rates measured during robot orientations in range of −45 to 45°. Those data were binned into five distance ranges (0–10, 10–20, 20–30, 30–40, 40–50 cm) and then plotted as a function of wall distance. Figure 4 (left) shows the mean and standard deviation of the spike rates for the different wall distance bins.

The slope of the function obtained under closed loop conditions (Fig. 4. Left) was: $(280 − 160)/(35 − 5) = 4$, which – at a turning radius of $Rt = 5$ – was the same as we found in our previous open loop experiments: $(220 − 160)/(25 − 10) = 4$ (Fig. 4. Right, $Rt = 5$).

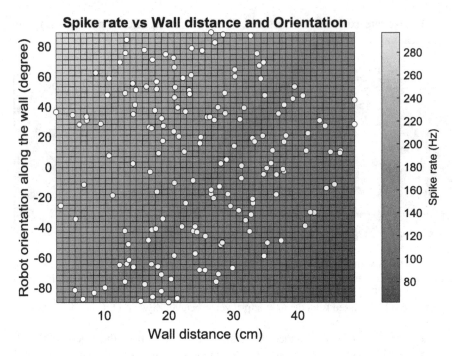

**Fig. 3.** The heatmap of H1-cell mean spike rates against wall distances and robot orientations among all PD turns. Each white point represents the mean spike rate during a PD turn measured at corresponding wall distance and robot orientation.

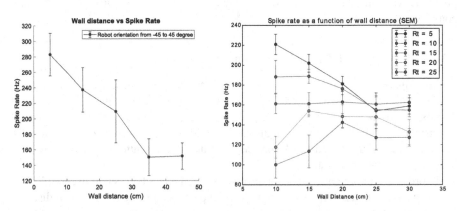

**Fig. 4.** (**Left**) The H1-cell spike rate as a function of wall distance obtained under closed loop condition where the turning radius is 5 cm. (n = 20). (**Right**) The H1-cell spike rate as functions of wall distances during open loop experiments [15]. Note the similarity of the slope and plateau of the blue curves, both were obtained for a turning radius of Rt = 5.

# 4 Discussion

## 4.1 Collision Avoidance Performance

The success rate of the collision avoidance system implemented on our FRI has been improved by a new control algorithm described in this paper. It takes advantage of a known turning radius of the platform to interpret the H1-cell spike rate as a function of wall distance. When a threshold spike rate is exceeded indicating close proximity to the wall, a collision avoidance manoeuvre is triggered, causing the robot to turn away from the wall. The success rate of the system was 9/10, defined by the robot reaching the end of a corridor-like experimental arena without running into the wall (the only failure was caused by the robot scratching the wall). As a comparison, the success rate of our previous control algorithm was 5/12, which was implemented by means of a "semi-closed-loop" structure (bang-bang control), that compares the period of spike counting (a continuously updated value in closed-loop control) with a timer (a fixed value in open loop control) to steer the robot either towards or away from the wall [14].

## 4.2 Spike Rates and Input Parameters

The relationship between spike rates and wall distance in the closed loop experiment presented here is very similar to that observed during open-loop experiments in a previous study [15]. In both cases, the spike rate was inversely proportional to wall distance (Fig. 4) up to a value of 25 and 35 cm for open-loop and closed-loop conditions, respectively. At further distances, no further change of the spike rate was observed in either case. The reason for this is probably related to limited spatial resolution of the compound eye which effectively acts as a low-pass filter that reduces image contrast with increasing distance [18]. Image contrast, in turn, is an important input parameter for elementary movement detectors (EMDs) which have been suggested to provide the insect visual system with local directional motion information that is integrated on the dendrites of LPTCs [19]. Due to its functional structure, the output of an EMD is proportional to the square of image contrast [20].

In addition, because of the inhomogeneous sensitivity in the receptive field of the H1-cell, the orientation of the blowfly will almost certainly affect the spike rate of the H1-cell during the oscillatory forward movements along a wall [10]. In our experiments, this feature increases the performance of the collision avoidance system, because any collision would be expected to occur frontally or frontolaterally (if nothing else is moving, but the fly). In this region, the H1-cell is highly sensitive to visual motion and any potential obstacles are likely to induce substantial spiking activity which trigger collision avoidance manoeuvres.

Another parameter is light intensity; we observed that the initiation of collision avoidance manoeuvres is delayed at the end of the corridor where the light intensity is less homogeneous. Because of the local light intensity adaptation at the photoreceptor and lamina monopolar cells [21], this parameter will probably not be the most crucial one as long as the time constants increase only at a moderate level.

A major drawback of the current FRI is the low (5 kHz) sampling frequency at which the robot microprocessor samples the H1-cell spikes. Such under sampling of the signals inevitably results in the loss of H1-spikes and such a reduction of the output dynamic range. In the future, by using a faster microprocessor to sample the spikes at 20 kHz, the collision avoidance performance is expected to improve to reach 100% success rate.

### 4.3   Active Control and Potential Energy Efficiency

Why choosing the H1-cell to close the loop for collision avoidance control? There are other horizontal LPTCs, such as: HSE [10], which receives inputs from the H1-cell [22] and is sensitive to front-to-back optic flow which might be more suitable for the forward movement [23].

One of the potential reasons might be explained by energy efficiency. At the behavioural level, it would save energy to use a straight thrust rather than an oscillatory forward movement as it uses less switching between acceleration and deceleration. At the cellular level, monitoring and controlling thrust costs more energy for a cell that responds preferentially to front-to-back optic flow (e.g. HSE-cell), which would be continuously stimulated during a straight thrust translation. On the other hand, a cell which is sensitive to back-to-front optic flow (e.g. H1-cell) saves energy during thrust movements, or movements along bigger turning radii, as it is inhibited by front-to-back optic flow. Is there an optimal balance? As previous studies suggest [24], a blowfly generates more thrust in open space, and perform a greater number of yaw body saccades in narrow space. A big turning radius generates a lower spike rate in the H1-cell, while a small turning radius generates a high spike rate (Fig. 4. Right) [15]. Switching between big and small turning radii actively, such as: a rapid saccade before collision, uses less energy for neuronal processing and muscular activity, while obtaining sufficient sensory information to avoid collisions.

We used a fixed turning radius of 5 cm to obtain a steep linear relationship between spike rate and wall distance, which results in comparatively high neuronal activity in the H1-cell and cost a significant amount of energy. In the future, we will test a bigger turning radius, e.g. 25 cm. The FRI could gradually switch the turning radius depending on the nature of the visual environment to minimize overall energy consumption.

## 5   Summary

We have successfully implemented a collision avoidance system on a biohybrid fly-robot-interface based on the spike rate of the identified H1-cell. For a given turning radius and up to a certain wall distance, the spike rate of the cell and there is linearly related to the distance between the robotic platform and the patterned wall of an experimental arena. Spike rates up to nearly 300 Hz indicate close distances which is decreasing at a slope of 4 spikes/cm up to a distance of about 25–35 cm. Beyond that distance – presumably because of the limited contrast sensitivity of compound eyes at larger distance – the cell's response stays at a comparatively high spike rate of about 150 Hz. The dynamic output range of the H1-cell that depends on wall distance is sufficiently broad to reliably trigger collision avoidance manoeuvres whenever the spike rate exceeds a give threshold value. In the future, the performance of the FRI may be improved by controlling the turning radius of the platform in an adaptive way to generate more energy-efficient trajectories. Increasing the costly active sensing component may be limited to the use in challenging visual environments.

**Acknowledgments.** The authors would like to thank Peter Swart for proofreading the manuscript. This work was partially supported by US AFOSR/EOARD grant FA8655-09-1-3083 (HGK).

# References

1. Taylor, G.K., Krapp, H.G.: Sensory systems and flight stability: what do insects measure and why? In: Casas, J., Simpson, S.J. (ed.) Advances in Insect Physiology, pp. 231–316. Academic Press (2007)
2. Huang, J.V., Krapp, H.G.: Closed-loop control in an autonomous bio-hybrid robot system based on binocular neuronal input. In: Wilson, S.P., Verschure, P.F.M.J., Mura, A., Prescott, T.J. (eds.) LIVINGMACHINES 2015. LNCS (LNAI), vol. 9222, pp. 164–174. Springer, Cham (2015). https://doi.org/10.1007/978-3-319-22979-9_17
3. Parsons, M.M., Krapp, H.G., Laughlin, S.B.: A motion-sensitive neurone responds to signals from the two visual systems of the blowfly, the compound eyes and ocelli. J. Exp. Biol. **209**, 4464–4474 (2006)
4. Huston, S.J., Krapp, H.G.: Nonlinear integration of visual and haltere inputs in fly neck motor neurons. J. Neurosci. **29**, 13097–13105 (2009)
5. Fuller, S.B., Straw, A.D., Peek, M.Y., Murray, R.M., Dickinson, M.H.: Flying Drosophila stabilize their vision-based velocity controller by sensing wind with their antennae. Proc. Natl. Acad. Sci. **111**, E1182–E1191 (2014)
6. Gabbiani, F., Krapp, H.G., Hatsopoulos, N., Mo, C.-H., Koch, C., Laurent, G.: Multiplication and stimulus invariance in a looming-sensitive neuron. J. Physiol.-Paris. **98**, 19–34 (2004)
7. Krapp, H.G., Taylor, G.K., Humbert, J.S.: The mode-sensing hypothesis: matching sensors, actuators and flight dynamics. In: Frontiers in Sensing. pp. 101–114. Springer, Vienna (2012). https://doi.org/10.1007/978-3-211-99749-9_7
8. Huang, J.V., Krapp, H.G.: Miniaturized electrophysiology platform for fly-robot interface to study multisensory integration. In: Lepora, N.F., Mura, A., Krapp, H.G., Verschure, P.F.M.J., Prescott, T.J. (eds.) Living Machines 2013. LNCS (LNAI), vol. 8064, pp. 119–130. Springer, Heidelberg (2013). https://doi.org/10.1007/978-3-642-39802-5_11
9. Hausen, K.: Functional characterization and anatomical identification of motion sensitive neurons in the lobula plate of the blowfly Calliphora erythrocephala. Z Naturforsch, pp. 629–633 (1976)
10. Krapp, H.G., Hengstenberg, R., Egelhaaf, M.: Binocular contributions to optic flow processing in the fly visual system. J. Neurophysiol. **85**, 724–734 (2001)
11. Maddess, T., Laughlin, S.B.: Adaptation of the motion-sensitive neuron H1 is generated locally and governed by contrast frequency. Proc. R. Soc. Lond. B Biol. Sci. **225**, 251–275 (1985)
12. Haag, J., Borst, A.: Recurrent network interactions underlying flow-field selectivity of visual interneurons. J. Neurosci. **21**, 5685–5692 (2001)

13. Huang, J.V., Krapp, H.G.: A predictive model for closed-loop collision avoidance in a fly-robotic interface. In: Duff, A., Lepora, N.F., Mura, A., Prescott, T.J., Verschure, P.F.M.J. (eds.) Living Machines 2014. LNCS (LNAI), vol. 8608, pp. 130–141. Springer, Cham (2014). https://doi.org/10.1007/978-3-319-09435-9_12

14. Huang, J.V., Wang, Y., Krapp, H.G.: Wall following in a semi-closed-loop fly-robotic interface. In: Lepora, N.F.F., et al. (eds.) Living Machines 2016. LNCS (LNAI), vol. 9793, pp. 85–96. Springer, Cham (2016). https://doi.org/10.1007/978-3-319-42417-0_9

15. Huang, J.V., Krapp, H.G.: Neuronal distance estimation by a fly-robot interface. In: Mangan, M., Cutkosky, M., Mura, A., Verschure, P.F.M.J., Prescott, T., Lepora, N. (eds.) Living Machines 2017. LNCS (LNAI), vol. 10384, pp. 204–215. Springer, Cham (2017). https://doi.org/10.1007/978-3-319-63537-8_18

16. Franceschini, N.: Pupil and pseudopupil in the compound eye of drosophila. In: Wehner, R. (ed.) Information Processing in the Visual Systems of Anthropods, pp. 75–82. Springer, Heidelberg (1972). https://doi.org/10.1007/978-3-642-65477-0_10

17. Karmeier, K., Tabor, R., Egelhaaf, M., Krapp, H.G.: Early visual experience and the receptive-field organization of optic flow processing interneurons in the fly motion pathway. Vis. Neurosci. **18**, 1–8 (2001)

18. Chahl, J.S.: Range and egomotion estimation from compound photodetector arrays with parallel optical axis using optical flow techniques. Appl. Opt. **53**, 368–375 (2014)

19. Krapp, H.G., Wicklein, M.: 1.06 - central processing of visual information in insects. In: Masland, R.H., Albright, T.D., Albright, T.D., Masland, R.H., Dallos, P., Oertel, D., Firestein, S., Beauchamp, G.K., Bushnell, M.C., Basbaum, A.I., Kaas, J.H., Gardner, E.P. (eds.) The Senses: A Comprehensive Reference, pp. 131–203. Academic Press, New York (2008)

20. Buchner, E.: Behavioural analysis of spatial vision in insects. In: Ali, M.A. (ed.) Photoreception and Vision in Invertebrates, pp. 561–621. Springer, US (1984)

21. De Ruyter Van Steveninck, R.R., Laughlin, S.B.: Light adaptation and reliability in blowfly photoreceptors. Int. J. Neural Syst. **07**, 437–444 (1996)

22. Borst, A., Weber, F.: Neural action fields for optic flow based navigation: a simulation study of the fly lobula plate network. PLoS ONE **6**, e16303 (2011)

23. Bertrand, O.J.N., Lindemann, J.P., Egelhaaf, M.: A bio-inspired collision avoidance model based on spatial information derived from motion detectors leads to common routes. PLoS Comput. Biol. **11**, e1004339 (2015)

24. Kern, R., Boeddeker, N., Dittmar, L., Egelhaaf, M.: Blowfly flight characteristics are shaped by environmental features and controlled by optic flow information. J. Exp. Biol. **215**, 2501–2514 (2012)

# Cognitive Architectures on Discourse

M. Iza[✉]

University of Málaga, Málaga, Spain
iza@uma.es

**Abstract.** In order to realize human-computer interface, the architecture specification should be based not only on the functional aspects of the cognitive processes but also on an emotional evaluation, such as the inferences gained from the language processing of the model. In this paper, we discuss the use of cognitive architectures in order to solve the problems that arise from rigid models based on AI.

**Keywords:** Human-computer interface · Dialogue · Emotion · Autonomous systems

## 1 Introduction

Recently, the notion of human-computer interface has become an important concept in various fields. However, the specification of systems designed for humans should be based not only on their internal functional aspects, such as representations and processes but also on emotional inferences in order to facilitate their social effectivity (see Vernon 2014; Clark 2016; Dodig-Crnkovic and Giovagnoli 2017; Lieto et al. 2018a, 2018b). The research in AI has tried to use rigid representations and processes in order to find solutions. Normally, the design of tasks and domains are well defined. That implies a narrow interaction between the human and the computer (Essau and Kleinjohann 2011; Kurup and Lebiere 2012; Ogi 2011; Watanabe 2011).

In contrast, more psychologically or biologically inspired architectures make assumptions about the necessary modules in order to focus on such tasks. More recent cognitive theories center on embodied and situated cognition (Anderson 2003; Anderson et al. 2004; Anderson and Lebiere 2003; Wilson and Myers 2000; Laird 2012; Langley et al. 2009). Within each module there are different kinds of representations and processes. These modules go from perception and action to language understanding, and high-level reasoning. Here the goal is to postulate different kind of architectures that can explain the interactions between modules. One example is the hybrid ones, where low level processes are performed by subsymbolic methods and high level processes are performed by AI symbolic methods (e.g., Sun 2002, 2006, 2016).

These architectures mainly refer to the problem of representation. The representations on memory are necessary for the activation of cognitive processes (Squire 2004). The problem of how activate representations on long term memory and bring them to working memory in order to operate cognitive processes (e.g., Baddeley's model of working memory).

© Springer International Publishing AG, part of Springer Nature 2018
V. Vouloutsi et al. (Eds.): Living Machines 2018, LNAI 10928, pp. 223–231, 2018.
https://doi.org/10.1007/978-3-319-95972-6_23

Here, the key issue is how we can deal with emotion with this kind of cognitive architectures. That is, if cognitive processes are previous to emotional processes; or vice versa. In this paper we will discuss this problem considering emotion as a key focus in order to control the extent of cognitive inferences.

## 2   Bases for Human-Computer Interface

There have been numerous approaches to detail a core set of bases for achieving a human-computer interface. While some of them are more directed to AI applications, others try to point out the design of a psychologically plausible architecture. Both share many similarities. For the purposes of this paper, we have recollected a list of points for a human-computer interaction where emotion can play an important role. Lately, we will discuss these prompts for comparing and contrasting different architectures.

Representation of knowledge. Inference performance and natural language processing need large and different knowledge representation to abroad many different domains and tasks. Here, it is essential if semantic knowledge and emotional knowledge are independent or strongly related in order to focus inference.

Learning trough experience. In the case of human-computer interaction, both agents are constantly learning about the communication and themselves through implicit versus automatic learning. These episodic instances are stored in memory in order to quickly identify and recognize similar situations.

Inference performance. Depending on the topic of the discourse and, in particular, on different emotional states, the conclusions of the inference processes can be different in similar situations. It is essential both agents embody such strategies.

Interaction cognition-emotion. In human-computer interaction, there is the necessity of design a way where cognition can interact with emotion. For instance, if cognition is before emotion or whether emotion can guide cognition performance. Several models take or other direction and this decision have important consequences in the design of the architecture and its performance.

Psychological and biological plausibility (Clark 2016; Dodig-Crnkovic and Giovagnoli 2017; Vernon et al. 2016).

## 3   Knowledge Representation

An important component of architecture is how knowledge is represented. Normally, each piece of knowledge is represented in different modules, such as semantic memory, procedural memory and episodic knowledge. This knowledge is compiled in order to perform different processes of language comprehension and of language production. In general, the architecture commits to some form of working memory where the selected knowledge from long-term memory is retrieved and used for different purposes. The others are some components for perceptual and motor processes.

In classical AI, these components are separated and knowledge representation is independent of the domain or task. At the architectural level, memories have been differentiated (Squire 2004) as: (i) memories of skill, represented using production rule systems, as condition-action pairs, to interact with the world.; (ii) memories of facts (semantic memories), represented using schemas/frames; (iii) memories of experience (episodic memories), using a combination of productions and semantic elements, adding temporal and self-referential information.

Normally, these architectures have used these different systems for reducing conflict and improving access and retrieval times. For instance, semantic memory (i.e., chunk knowledge made up of a number of propositions; see Anderson 1990) is less context-sensitive than production rules; it can be applied to a wider range of situations. They are neutral to the nature of the represented knowledge, for instance, if there is necessary a sort of ontology that can facilitate the of an agent's knowledge.

Apart from the classic ACT-R architecture (Anderson 1990), recent architectures have tried to introduce an episodic memory. This new module goes in association with semantic memory including activation values and learning mechanisms. For instance, CLARION (Sun 1992) facilitates links to other concepts/chunks in memory in order to get an explicit association network. Even, semantic memory can be hierarchically represented in order to provide inferential capabilities (e.g., emotion lexicon; Mohammad and Turney 2012).

The use of hybrid systems (symbolic and subsymbolic representations) allows capturing different aspects of the world. The symbolic representation use statistical regularities extracted from the context for focused performance. Symbolic representations are compositional, productive and required for learning discrete pieces of information very fast (Kurup and Lebiere 2012). Subsymbolic representations are very adaptive to different contexts but are opaque in relation to how the information is represented in the system.

One of the best examples of this kind of architecture is CLARION. Here, every part of the architecture is hybrid (symbolic and subsymbolic). The subsymbolic level represents information in a connectionist network, while the symbolic level uses predicate-symbolic representations. Both levels are distinct representational levels and come to different conclusions that are combined by the architecture. Learning occurs both at the levels themselves and between levels. This differs from previous approaches, such as ACT-R and SOAR, where the subsymbolic level is used to capture certain values that are associated to representational items at the higher level (productions or chunks).

Moreover, CLARION incorporates a two-module solution towards addressing meta-cognition. The Motivational Subsystem (MS) provides the drive for the agent. Drives are either low-level primary (e.g., get food), high-level primary (relationships) or secondary (e.g., conditioning). The difference between primary and secondary drives is that primary drives are hard-wired while secondary drives are derived or acquired. These drives provide the goals and reinforce the actions performed by the agent. The Meta-Cognitive Subsystem (MCS) monitors, controls and regulate cognitive processes via the setting of goals, setting of parameters, and interrupting or changing ongoing processes.

# 4  Learning

Apart from the initial or minimal knowledge represented on memory, the architecture needs to be constantly learning new knowledge. That is, new facts, skills and experiences. This new knowledge can be reused in similar situations. The representation on memory and the retrieval processes need to be generalized to new problems and situations of communication. It also has to be efficient to retrieve the required knowledge within the constraints of the focused inferencing process.

In order to know what is necessary and focused for inferencing, the agent needs to be constantly learning; in such a way that it allows for reuse across similar situations.

The processes of memory representation and retrieval need to be very flexible to access to the necessary knowledge within the constraints of the problem-solving process. This capacity makes possible an adaptive behavior in dynamic situations.

This goal is crucial in the emergent perspective. That is, to form the basis for the development of cognitive capabilities through ontogeny over extended periods of time (Langley et al. 2009; Thórison and Helgasson 2012).

# 5  Inferencing

Inference performance must responds appropriately to the limits of the situation. In several approaches, it is an emergent result that arises out of the interplay between several demands of the situation and the different constraints imposed by its design. Inference performance must be controlled or focused on optimal solutions according to the task at hand.

Human inferencing is limited and restricted by several factors such as decay and interference of information in working memory, attentional limitations and problems on the processes of retrieval and performance control.

These limitations imply a special factor of human inferencing, that is, it reacts in an appropriate way to the requirements of the situation. From the point of view of the architectural approach, these limitations are a consequence of the architecture. In this sense, inferencing arises out of the interrelationship between the competing demands of the situation and the restrictions imposed by the design of the architecture. Inferencing focuses on providing the best solution to a given problem, taking into account these temporal and computational constraints.

This is the main goal in the cognitivist perspective (Vernon 2014, 2017). That is, to capture, at the computational level, the invariant mechanisms of human cognition, including those underlying the functions of reasoning, control, learning, memory, adaptivity, perception and action (Oltramari and Lebiere 2012).

# 6  Interaction Cognition-Emotion

An interesting framework where simulate the interaction between cognition and emotion is the design and development of robots. Mainly, those that are to deal with real applications (for instance, Callejas et al. 2011; Zhanj and Barnden 2012).

For instance, Kushiro et al. (2013) presented a cognitive architecture that tries to measure the effects of emotional cognition on learning. That is, it uses emotional intelligence to learn new concepts from previously unknown kind of experiences.

The basic elements of the system are three subsystems based on recursive neural networks, which are combined to create a complex neural network. The goal is that this network structure can explain the function of human consciousness. They assume that the conscious system comprises these functional subsystems: reason subsystem, association subsystem and emotion-feelings subsystem.

The reason subsystem acquires information on external objects and, based on the derived recognition, generates actions. The emotion subsystem accepts information from the internal sensory receptors distributed throughout the body, and based on recognition, generates action or transmits information to the feelings subsystem. This one receives information from the reason and emotion subsystems and generates representations such as (un-)pleasantness. They pose a functional difference between emotional states and feelings, for instance, pain is derived from emotion and unpleasantness from feelings. Finally, the association subsystem plays the part of exchanging information between the reason and the emotion-feeling subsystem.

Their experiment demonstrated that a robot incorporating this conscious system can cognize and learn unknown information, because it represents information that is not yet learned as unpleasant. Based mainly on the emotion-feeling subsystem, these authors believe that this experiment could represent a kind of model or mechanism for cognizing and learning the unknown.

# 7 Psychological and Biological Plausibility

There have been several attempts for adding emotions to intelligent agents, to play a role in belief generation (Marsella and Gratch 2009), reasoning, attention and learning. The role of emotion has also been used in whole integrated cognitive architectures, like HCogAff (Sloman and Chrisley 2003) and tripartite framework (Larue et al. 2013).

Two theories have been proposed in order to deal with emotions. On the one hand, appraisal theories: the conceptualization of emotions normally is a constructionist approach that tries to characterize the psychological primitives involved in the emergence of emotions. Here, patterns of appraisal are formalize according to encoding devices (situational meaning structures) that derive the appraisal variables. On the other hand, dimensional theories: the dynamical mode of functioning is a neurodynamical approach. Here, emotions are not discrete events but emotions are situated in a continuous dimensional space (Russell 2003). Dimensional architectures reject previous discrete emotion categories. Even, they try to associate specific brain regions to specific emotions.

Appraisal theories have been dominant in computational models of emotions and have been applied extensively in symbolic architectures, because their theoretical structures can easily be translated into if-then rules.

Dimensional architectures use to reject symbolic representations or emotional labels. The implementation of emotional intelligence relies on cognitive features present in the architecture. Normally it does not implement other phenomena, like explicit learning or theory of mind (recognition and understanding of other's emotions).

New emotional hybrid architectures try to combine both the situated conceptualization approach and the dynamical mode of functioning approach. For instance, in the tripartite approach of Larue et al. (2013), three main dimensions are important to understand emotions: semantic, cognitive and neurophysiological. In the proposed architecture, each dimension emerges from the interaction and mechanisms taken from the two approaches.

# 8    Discussion

The cognitive architecture approach has a long history with different implementations for solving a huge variety of tasks. However, all these architectures maintain some key concepts and principles that reflect the philosophical presuppositions with the classical AI. We have discussed these conceptual principles and explained some examples of cognitive architectures.

These architectures have a number of limitations. While classical AI approach has evolved together with the serial-fast processor nature of available computing technology, the cognitive architecture approach claims for massively parallel data structures and processes. Implementing these structures and processes finishes in reduced performance along some dimensions. In this respect, we need a convergence among cognitive architectures from two points of view: (i) computational aspect, necessity to perform complex tasks in demanding contexts; (ii) implementational aspect, reflecting the exponentially increasing knowledge figure about the nature of brain processes.

The goal would be a significant implementation of cognitive architectures that takes the broad range of cognition and emotion, from perception to motor action to reasoning and problem solving. Most implementations are hard-wired in respect to the relation between emotion and cognition (Ezquerro and Iza 2015, 2017). Architectures need a more serious integration in order to be used in robotics.

Larue et al. (2013) present an architecture where three sets of processes can interact: processes responsible for fast context-sensitive behaviors (an autonomous mind), processes responsible for cognitive control (an algorithmic mind) and processes responsible for deliberative processing and rational behavior (a reflective mind). By reasoning on counterfactual situations, the system tries to link emotional semantic and cognition with neuromodulations. These ones, proposed as physiological components, act like an attentional focus on salient emotional aspects of environments.

To sum up, a possible way for evaluating the provided advancements of the different architectures, or the encountered problems that prevent to obtain psychological and biologically plausible advancements (Alshawi et al. 2014; Lieto et al. 2018a, 2018b), is that one of focusing on classes of problems that are easily manageable for humans but very hard to solve for machines. For example, these involve aspects concerning commonsense reasoning about space, action, change and language categorization (Bhatt et al. 2013; Lieto et al. 2017); selective attention; integration of multi-modal perception; the interaction between cognition and emotion (Zhanj and

Barnden 2012; Juvina et al. 2018); learning from few examples (Vanderelst and Winfield 2018); robust integration of mechanisms involving planning, acting, monitoring and goal reasoning (Clark 2016; Choi and Langley 2018).

# References

Alshawii, H., Chang, P.C., Ringgaard, M.: Deterministic statistical mapping of sentences to underspecified semantics. In: Bunt, H., et al. (eds.) Computing Meaning, Text, Speech and Language Technology, vol. 47. Springer, Dordrecht (2014). https://doi.org/10.1007/978-94-007-7284-7_2

Anderson, J.R.: The Adaptive Character of Thought. Erlbaum, Hillsdale (1990)

Anderson, J.R., Bothell, D., Byrne, M.D., Dougass, S., Lebiere, C., Qin, Y.: An integrated theory of the mind. Psychol. Rev. **111**(4), 10–36 (2004)

Anderson, J.R., Lebiere, C.: The Newell test for a theory of cognition. Behav. Brain Sci. **26**, 587–637 (2003)

Anderson, M.: Embodied cognition: a field guide. Artif. Intell. **149**, 91–130 (2003)

Arbib, M.A., Fellous, J.M.: Emotions; from brain to robot. Trends Cogn. Sci. **8**(12), 554–561 (2004)

Bhatt, M., Schultz, C., Freksa, C.: The 'Space' in spatial assistance systems: Conception, formalization, and computation. In: Representing Space in Cognition: Behaviour, Language, and Formal Models. Explorations in Language and Space, pp. 171–214. Oxford University Press (2013)

Callejas, Z., Griol, D., López-Cózar, R., Espejo, G., Abalos, N.: Merging intention and emotion to develop adaptive dialogue systems. In: Delgado, C., Kobayashi, T. (eds.) Advances in Speech and Language Technologies for Iberian Languages. CCIS, vol. 328, pp. 165–174. Springer, Heidelberg (2011). https://doi.org/10.1007/978-3-642-35292-8_18

Choi, D., Langley, P.: Evolution of the ICARUS cognitive architecture. Cogn. Syst. Res. **48**, 25–38 (2018)

Clark, A.: Surfing Uncertainty: Prediction. Action and the Embodied Mind. Oxford University Press, Oxford (2016)

Dodig-Crnkovic, G., Giovagnoli, R. (eds.): Representation and Reality in Humans, Other Living Organisms and Intelligent Machines. Springer (2017). https://doi.org/10.1007/978-3-319-43784-2

Essau, N., Kleinjohann, L.: Emotional robot competence and its use in robot behavior control. In: Fukuda, S. (ed.) Emotional Engineering, pp. 119–142. Springer, London (2011). https://doi.org/10.1007/978-1-84996-423-4_7

Ezquerro, J., Iza, M.: Computational emotions. In: Liljenström, H. (ed.) Advances in Cognitive Neurodynamics, pp. 9–13. Springer, Dordrecht (2015). https://doi.org/10.1007/978-94-017-9548-7_2

Ezquerro, J., Iza, M.: Language processing, computational representational theory of mind and embodiment: inferences on verbs. In: Dodig-Crnkovic, G., Giovagnoli, R. (eds.) Representation and Reality in Humans, Other Living Organisms and Intelligent Machines, pp. 51–68. Springer, Cham (2017). https://doi.org/10.1007/978-3-319-43784-2_4

Faghihi, U., McCall, R., Franklin, S.: A computational model of attentional learning in a cognitive agent. Biol. Inspired Cogn. Archit. **2**, 25–36 (2012)

Juvina, I., Larue, O., Hough, A.: Modeling valuation and core affect in a cognitive architecture: the impact of valence and arousal on memory and decision-making. Cogn. Syst. Res. **48**, 4–24 (2018)

Kushiro, K., Harada, Y., Takeno, J.: Robot uses emotions to detect and learn the unknown. Biol. Inspired Cogn. Archit. **4**, 69–78 (2013)

Kurup, U., Lebiere, C.: What can cognitive architectures do for robotics? Biol. Inspired Cogn. Archit. **2**, 88–99 (2012)

Laird, J.E.: The SOAR Cognitive Architecture. MIT Press, Cambridge (2012)

Langley, P., Laird, J.E., Rogers, S.: Cognitive architectures: research issues and challenges. Cogn. Syst. Res. **10**, 141–160 (2009)

Larue, O., Poirier, P., Nkambou, R.: The emergence of (artificial) emotions from cognitive and neurological processes. Biol. Inspired Cogn. Archit. **4**, 54–68 (2013)

Lieto, A., Bhatt, M., Oltramari, A., Vernon, D.: The role of cognitive architectures in general artificial intelligence. Cogn. Syst. Res. **48**, 1–3 (2018a)

Lieto, A., Lebiere, C., Oltramari, A.: The knowledge level in cognitive architectures: current limitations and possible developments. Cogn. Syst. Res. **48**, 39–55 (2018b)

Lieto, A., Radicioni, D.P., Rho, V.: Dual PECCS: a cognitive system for conceptual representation and categorization. J. Exp. Theor. Artif. Intell. **29**(2), 433–452 (2017)

Marsella, S., Gratch, J.: EMA: a process model of appraisal dynamics. J. Cogn. Syst. Res. **10**, 70–90 (2009)

Mohammad, S., Turney, P.: Crowdsourcing a word-emotion association lexicon. Computational Intelligence, 1467–8640 (2012)

Ogi, T.: Emotional design in the virtual environment. In: Fukuda, S. (ed.) Emotional Engineering, pp. 103–118. Springer, London (2011). https://doi.org/10.1007/978-1-84996-423-4_6

Oltramari, A., Lebiere, C.: Pursuing artificial general intelligence by leveraging the knowledge capabilities of ACT-R. In: Bach, J., Goertzel, B., Iklé, M. (eds.) AGI 2012. LNCS (LNAI), vol. 7716, pp. 199–208. Springer, Heidelberg (2012). https://doi.org/10.1007/978-3-642-35506-6_21

Russell, J.A.: Core affect and the psychological construction of emotion. Psychol. Rev. **110**, 145–172 (2003)

Sloman, A., Chrisley, R.L.: Virtual machines and consciousness. J. Conscious. Stud. **10**(4–5), 113–172 (2003)

Squire, L.R.: Memory systems of the brain: a brief history and current perspective. Neurobiol. Learn. Mem. **82**, 171–177 (2004)

Sun, R.: On variable binding in connectionist networks. Connection Sci.**4**(2), 93–124 (1992)

Sun, R.: Duality of the Mind: A Bottom-Up Approach to Ward Cognition. LEA, Mahwah (2002)

Sun, R.: The CLARION cognitive architecture: extending cognitive modeling to social simulation. Cognition and Multi-agent Interaction, 79–99 (2006)

Sun, R.: Anatomy of the Mind: Exploring Psychological Mechanisms and Processes with the Clarion Cognitive Architecture. Oxford University Press, Oxford (2016)

Thórison, K., Helgasson, H.: Cognitive architectures and autonomy: a comparative review. J. Artif. General Intell. **3**(2), 1–30 (2012)

Vanderelst, D., Winfoeld, A.: An architecture for ethical robots inspired by the simulation theory of cognition. Cogn. Syst. Res. **48**, 56–66 (2018)

Vernon, D.: Artificial Cognitive Systems: A Primer. MIT Press, Cambridge (2014)

Vernon, D.: Two ways (not) to design a cognitive architecture. Cogn. Robot Archit. **42** (2017)

Vernon, D., von Hofsten, C., Fadiga, L.: Desiderata for developmental cognitive architectures. Biol. Inspired Cogn. Archit. **18**, 116–127 (2016)

Watanabe, T.: Human-entrained embodied interaction and communication technology. In: Fukuda, S. (ed.) Emotional Engineering, pp. 161–178. Springer, London (2011). https://doi.org/10.1007/978-1-84996-423-4_9

Zhanj, L., Barnden, J.: Affect sensing using linguistic, semantic and cognitive cues in multi-threaded improvisational dialogue. Cogn. Comput. **4**(4), 436–459 (2012)

# Slip Detection on Natural Objects with a Biomimetic Tactile Sensor

Jasper W. James[1,2]([✉]) and Nathan F. Lepora[1,2]([✉])

[1] Bristol Robotics Laboratory, Bristol, BS16 1QY, UK
[2] Department of Engineering Mathematics, University of Bristol, Bristol, UK
{jj16883,n.lepora}@bristol.ac.uk

**Abstract.** Slip detection enables robotic hands to perform complex manipulation tasks by predicting when a held object is about to be dropped. Here we use a support vector machine classifier to detect slip with a biomimetic optical tactile sensor: the TacTip. Previously, this method has been shown to be effective on various artificial stimuli such as flat or curved surfaces. Here, we investigate whether this method generalises to novel, everyday objects. Five different objects are tested which vary in shape, weight, compliance and texture as well as being common objects that one might encounter day-to-day. Success of up to 90% is achieved which demonstrates the classifier's ability to generalise to a variety of previously unseen, natural objects.

**Keywords:** Slip detection · Tactile sensing · Machine learning

## 1 Introduction

Humans have highly effective slip detection mechanisms that are deployed when grasping an object. Humans continuously adjust the grasp to prevent an object from being dropped [1]. Meissner corpuscles respond to local skin movements that are present when slip occurs which initiates a reflexive response [2]. Meissner corpuscles are densely populated in the fingertip which is why the human hand is such an effective grasping mechanism. Mimicking the function of the Meissner corpuscles and subsequent response in a robotic hand will yield a more sophisticated sense of touch and enable complex object manipulation by reducing the likelihood of an object being dropped [3].

Slip detection has been a poplar area of research since the 1980s with many different sensors and methods used [4,5]. The aim of this study is to investigate whether a previously developed slip detection method generalises to novel objects. We use the TacTip biomimetic tactile sensor [6]. Previous work with the TacTip has focused mainly on object perception [7,8] so slip detection capabilities will further demonstrate the sensor's versatility.

Supported by the EPSRC Centre for Doctoral Training in Future Autonomous and Robotic Systems (FARSCOPE) and a Leadership Award from the Leverhulme Trust on 'A biomimetic forebrain for robot touch' (RL-2016-39).

© Springer International Publishing AG, part of Springer Nature 2018
V. Vouloutsi et al. (Eds.): Living Machines 2018, LNAI 10928, pp. 232–235, 2018.
https://doi.org/10.1007/978-3-319-95972-6_24

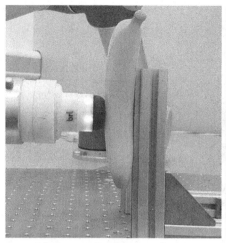 

(a) Banana held before slipping                (b) Banana caught after slipping

**Fig. 1.** The experimental setup. An object is secured above the ground by using the tactile sensor to press it against a vertical metal plate. When slip is detected the sensor moves in to prevent the object from falling. A clear drop in height of the plastic banana is evident.

## 2   Methods

The TacTip is a 3D-printed, biomimetic, optical tactile sensor containing 127 pins on the inside of a soft, compliant hemisphere. A camera is focused on the pins and records their positions when the TacTip contacts an object. The TacTip is mounted on a six degree-of-freedom robotic arm (UR5, Universal Robots).

For this work we use the same classification method described in James et al. [9]. This involves using the velocity of each pin in the TacTip as an input to a support vector machine (SVM). Image capture, processing and classification leads to the data being sampled at 100 FPS.

Being able to detect the velocity of each pin individually is analogous to the Meissner corpuscles which each contain a single nerve fiber capable of detecting slip in its receptive field. This will allow for slip to be detected in objects where contact area varies.

This work, presented by James et al. has already demonstrated a high degree of success at slip detection and preventing objects from being dropped. However, the objects used were regularly shaped, solid objects and a variety of common household objects was not tested. Here, we use the same classifier used to test those objects which is not modified or re-trained in any way.

**Fig. 2.** The five different objects that were tested for this study. The objects were chosen due to their different shapes, weights and compliances so that an indication of the slip detection method's ability to generalise to random objects can be tested.

## 3   Experiments

Each experiment proceeds as follows. The UR5 robotic arm - to which the Tac-Tip is attached - presses an object against a vertically mounted metal plate until it is securely held with no slipping. The arm then begins to slowly retract $(0.2 \text{ mms}^{-1})$ until the object slips (Fig. 1).

The data from the sensor is continually being passed through the SVM classifier and if slip is detected the arm moves forward to try to prevent the object from being dropped. The experiment is considered a success if the object is visually seen to start falling, the classifier detects the slip, the arm moved forward and the object is secured against the wall without further slippage. Any other outcomes such as slip being detected but the object still being dropped is classed as a failure.

The five objects chosen were; a paper box containing a plastic cube, a metal coffee container, a mustard bottle, a water bottle (approx. 1/3 full) and a plastic banana. Figure 2 shows each object that was tested. The objects were chosen as each has a different shape, weight, compliance and texture as well as being common objects and shapes that one might encounter day-to-day.

## 4   Results and Discussion

Each object was tested ten times in the manner described above and the results are summarised in Table 1. The results show that four of the five objects are stopped from falling with a high success of up to 90%. The only low scoring object is the banana which was only stopped 30% of the time. For this case the classifier was able to detect the onset of slip but the shape of the banana meant that moving to re-secure it mostly pushed the banana out of the way and onto the floor.

**Table 1.** Showing the success at the slip detection method at generalising to a variety of objects. Each object has a different shape, compliance and weight and the slip detection method still performs well.

| Object | Success (%) | Mass (g) |
|---|---|---|
| Box | 90 | 145 |
| Mustard | 80 | 47 |
| Water bottle | 90 | 186 |
| Coffee | 90 | 97 |
| Banana | 30 | 66 |

Each object used was novel to the classifier and no parameters of the object were known to the classifier prior to each experiment. This demonstrates the versatility of the classifier to generalise to previously unseen objects.

Having a single tactile sensor moving with a single degree of freedom means that the ability to handle complex objects is severely limited. However, the fact that slip was reliably detected, even on the banana, means that using a gripper with more degrees of freedom is likely to be successful at preventing slipping objects from being dropped.

# References

1. Johansson, R.S., Flanagan, J.R.: Coding and use of tactile signals from the fingertips in object manipulation tasks. Nat. Rev. Neurosci. **10**(5), 345 (2009)
2. Saal, H.P., Bensmaia, S.J.: Touch is a team effort: interplay of submodalities in cutaneous sensibility. Trends Neurosci. **37**(12), 689–697 (2014)
3. Yousef, H., Boukallel, M., Althoefer, K.: Tactile sensing for dexterous in-hand manipulation in robotics-a review. Sens. Actuators A Phys. **167**(2), 171–187 (2011)
4. Howe, R.D., Cutkosky, M.R.: Sensing skin acceleration for slip and texture perception. In: 1989 Proceedings of the IEEE International Conference on Robotics and Automation, pp. 145–150. IEEE (1989)
5. Veiga, F., Van Hoof, H., Peters, J., Hermans, T.: Stabilizing novel objects by learning to predict tactile slip. In: 2015 Proceedings of the IEEE/RSJ International Conference on Intelligent Robots and Systems (IROS), pp. 5065–5072. IEEE (2015)
6. Chorley, C., Melhuish, C., Pipe, T., Rossiter, J.: Development of a tactile sensor based on biologically inspired edge encoding. In: 2009 Proceedings of the International Conference on Advanced Robotics, ICAR 2009, pp. 1–6. IEEE (2009)
7. Lepora, N.F., Aquilina, K., Cramphorn, L.: Exploratory tactile servoing with active touch. IEEE Robot. Autom. Lett. **2**(2), 1156–1163 (2017)
8. Ward-Cherrier, B., Pestell, N., Cramphorn, L., Winstone, B., Giannaccini, M.E., Rossiter, J., Lepora, N.F.: The TacTip family: soft optical tactile sensors with 3D-printed biomimetic morphologies. Soft Robot. (2018)
9. James, J.W., Pestell, N., Lepora, N.F.: Slip detection with a biomimetic tactile sensor. IEEE Robotics and Automation Letters (2018, in press)

# Distributed Sensing for Soft Worm Robot Reduces Slip for Locomotion in Confined Environments

Akhil Kandhari[1]([✉]), Matthew C. Stover[1], Prithvi R. Jayachandran[1], Alexander Rollins[2], Hillel J. Chiel[3], Roger D. Quinn[1], and Kathryn A. Daltorio[1]

[1] Department of Mechanical and Aerospace Engineering,
Case Western Reserve University, Cleveland, OH 44106, USA
{axk751,kam37}@case.edu
[2] Mayfield High School, Cleveland, OH 44106, USA
[3] Departments of Biology, Neurosciences, and Biomedical Engineering,
Case Western Reserve University, Cleveland, OH 44106, USA

**Abstract.** Earthworms are soft-bodied animals with mechanosensory organs that allow them to bend and contort, and adapt to external perturbations. To mimic these attributes of the earthworm on a robotic platform, we designed and constructed a new robot: Distributed-Sensing Compliant Worm (DiSCo-Worm) Robot. DiSCo-Worm is equipped with 36 Force Sensing Resistors (6 per segment) that allow the robot to detect external constraints and 12 flexible stretch sensors (2 per segment) that allow for tracking the shape of the robot. We show the ability of the robot to navigate in constrained spaces using an open-loop, time-based controller and a closed-loop sensory feedback controller. The results indicate that the robot can sense external constraints and its internal state (longitudinal extension of each segment) and use this information to change its state of either expanding in diameter, contracting in diameter or anchoring. Sensory feedback reduces high forces that otherwise result in damage to the robot by stopping actuation shortly after contact. In this way, each segment applies forces 33% to 80% (based on the location of the sensor) of its weight, when locomoting between two parallel surfaces. Using a closed-loop controller, the robot is able to adapt to its environment and almost eliminates forward slip, which accounts for 58% of the total motion in case of open-loop control.

**Keywords:** Sensors · Earthworm-like robots · Soft-robotics

## 1 Introduction

Compliant or "soft" robots that can undergo large deformations are promising because of their ability to passively adapt their shape to the environment (for example in grasping an arbitrary object [1]), store collision energy (for example in running legs [2]), and recover from damage (for example bouncing back into shape after being compressed [3]). There are many instances where performance is improved by compliance, but often the cost of compliance is uncertainty.

© Springer International Publishing AG, part of Springer Nature 2018
V. Vouloutsi et al. (Eds.): Living Machines 2018, LNAI 10928, pp. 236–248, 2018.
https://doi.org/10.1007/978-3-319-95972-6_25

As sensor technology improves, it is possible to put tactile sensors in new places and with softer materials. However, the value of such sensors for soft-body locomotion is not yet established.

To assess the added value of such sensors, we have built a new worm-like robot with a total of 49 sensors and 12 actuators. Unlike our previous Compliant Modular Mesh Worm Robot which relied only on smart servomotors to control the diameter of each segment and infer ground contact [4], here each segment diameter is controlled independently on the left and right side, contact pressures are measured directly with force-resistive sensors, and stretch sensors assess body shape.

While there have been many other worm-like robots [3, 5–10], contact sensing has not been explored in most cases. Thus, this platform is valuable for (1) implementing closed-loop control for constrained environments, (2) better understanding mechanics of peristaltic locomotion in animals and robots, (3) determining critical requirements for sensor operation and placement, and (4) in future work, validating simulations [11] of modular soft bodies.

In this article we discover that (a) the forward progress under open loop control is largely due to slip, (b) the actuators work harder and longer in open loop, wasting energy and risking damage to structure and actuation cables, and (c) the movements of the closed loop robot incur less slip, which is a key cause of imprecision.

## 2  Background

Soft-bodied invertebrates such as earthworms can access constrained environments by contorting their bodies in order to comply with their surroundings. The multi-segmented body of an earthworm incorporates circumferential and longitudinal muscles. Due to hydrostatic coupling, activation of a segment's circumferential muscles causes it to contract in diameter while extending in length, whereas activation of longitudinal muscles causes the segment to shorten in length and expand in diameter [12]. Peristaltic waves of segment contractions and expansions along the length of the earthworm's body [13] cause the soft-bodied animal to locomote. This coupling between the length and diameter of a segment [12] allows the longer contracted segments to lift off the ground while the circumferentially expanded segments rest on the ground to anchor forward locomotion [14]. While complying with their surroundings, earthworms are also capable of exerting forces radially and laterally against their environment to break up compacted soil, create and enlarge burrows, and resist extraction from their burrows by predators.

During peristaltic locomotion, sensory feedback allows the animal to adapt to environmental perturbations [15]. Sensory feedback from various mechanosensory organs and stretch, touch, and pressure receptors [16] allow the animal to maintain rhythmic peristaltic locomotion by modulating motor patterns [13]. Setae, present on the body of the earthworm, serve as mechanoreceptors that allow it to adapt to its environment and crawl smoothly even on rough surfaces [15].

Soft-bodied robots have been shown to be mobile in constrained-space applications [5, 10, 17–20]. In simulation, we have shown that a worm-like robot can be more efficient in crawling through constrained environments with contact sensing [21]. Specifically, we have shown that a worm-like robot crawling through a narrowing in a pipe will exert more energy because the segments lose energy to friction and slip. However, if ground contact forces can be sensed, the Cost of Transport (COT) can be reduced. This paper is the first step in implementing such a controller on a physical robot.

## 3   Robot Design

Our Distributed-Sensing Compliant Worm robot (DiSCo-Worm) (Fig. 1) has a modularly assembled soft mesh body, like our previous robot CMMWorm [6]. The mesh of the robot consists of short "links" of flexible tubing connected via 3-D printed "vertex pieces", that allow relative rotation. Links of tubes and vertex pieces are assembled to form a rhombus, such that rotation of the vertex pieces will cause the aspect ratio of a rhombus to change. These rhombuses are connected in a ring-like structure to form a segment.

Each of the six modular segments has two actuators, one for each half of the segment [22]. Connected to each actuator spool, a cable travels halfway around the circumference of the segment, either controlling the left or the right half of the segment. The actuators spool in the cable causing the segment to contract in diameter, while extending in length, equivalent to the circumferential muscles in earthworms. The diameter of the segment is constrained by the amount of cable spooled in. Longitudinal springs placed along the length of each segment perform similarly to the longitudinal muscle of an earthworm's body. On removal of the circumferential actuation force that causes the robot to decrease in diameter, these longitudinal springs return the segment to the maximum diameter as the circumferential cable is spooled out. Sequential actuation of the segments causes a wave of circumferential contractions and expansions to travel down the length of the body. This results in peristaltic locomotion opposite to the direction of the wave's travel.

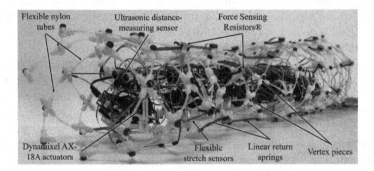

**Fig. 1.** Distributed-Sensing Compliant Worm robot (DiSCo-Worm) during a peristaltic wave on flat surface. The various components of the robot mesh including the sensors and actuators are labelled.

Unlike other worm robots, DiSCo-Worm incorporates a suite of pressure and stretch sensors along the surface of its body. This network of distributed sensors allows the robot to sense external perturbations and constraints, while keeping track of its own configuration. Each sensor works independently. Each segment incorporates six Force Sensing Resistors® (FSR-402) and two flexible stretch sensors. The FSR-402 sensors are placed on each vertex piece around the circumference of each segment (Fig. 2), in order to detect external loads that may act on the robot radially (for example, from the inner surface of a pipe). FSR sensors exhibit a decrease in resistance with increase in force applied to the 14.7 mm active area of the sensor. This decrease in resistance corresponds to external loads the robot experiences.

Because the readings from the FSR sensors are independent of segment position, we also added conductive stretch sensors that run along the length of the segments (one on each side). As the segment extends in length, the resistance of the stretch sensors increases, directly correlated to the extended length of the segment. Because the radius of a segment is kinematically constrained to decrease with length, these sensors indicate the shape of the segment.

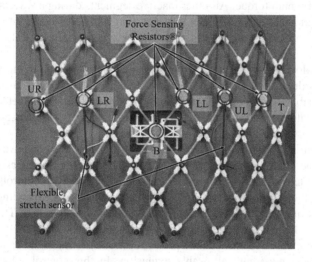

**Fig. 2.** Sensor configuration of a single segment placed flat on a surface. The FSR sensors are marked by circles around them. Stretch sensors are highlighted in red. UR: Upper Right, LR: Lower Right, UL: Upper Left, LL: Lower Left, T: Top, B: Bottom. Left and right vertex pieces join to form the ring-like structure and anterior and posterior segments are connected to the vertex pieces at the top and bottom of the figure.

To detect objects in the robot's path, the first segment is specialized with the addition of an HC-SR04 ultrasonic distance-measuring sensor. This allows the robot to respond to obstacles in the robot's path.

DiSCo-Worm thus has distributed sensing: Each of the six segments has eight sensors and the first segment has an ultrasonic sensor, for a total of forty-nine sensors to determine its configuration and environment.

## 4    Electronics and Control

DiSCo-Worm is actuated by twelve Dynamixel AX-18A actuators connected to an ArbotiX-M microcontroller. The actuators are powered using an off-board DC power supply at a constant voltage of 11.8 V. All forty-nine sensors are wired back to an off-board Mayhew Labs MUX Shield II connected to the ArbotiX-M microcontroller. The MUX Shield II allows the ArbotiX-M microcontroller to extend its total number of analog ports from 8 to 53.

A $3 \times 1$ waveform, where 3 represents the number of segments per wave (including inactive suspended segments) and 1 represents the number of waves along the body, was used for all tests throughout this paper. The $3 \times 1$ wave consists of an expanding segment, a contracting segment and an inactive suspended (contracted) segment between the two active segments. The active actuators are commanded to move at a specified speed with maximum torque. All other inactive segments during a wave are expanded to their maximum allowable diameter, for anchoring. An open-loop time-based control is compared to a closed-loop control scheme where both controllers always maintain this pattern.

With open-loop (time-based) control, actuators are configured to move for a fixed duration. This duration is based on the time it takes for a segment to contract to its minimum possible diameter of 13 cm from its maximum (initial) diameter of 22 cm at a constant actuator speed. The next set of actuators in the wave sequence are activated immediately after the previous duration terminates.

With closed-loop control, speeds are the same but the duration is limited by the forces measured at the FSRs (during radial expansion) and the extension measured with the conductive stretch sensors (during radial contraction). The microcontroller interprets the data from the sensors to control the actuators such that an expanding segment is commanded to move until a preset force threshold value is reached. The preset was established via single-segment testing to achieve a desired normal force. A contracting segment is commanded to move until a preset stretch sensor threshold value is reached, correlating to its maximum allowable extension. In this control scheme, the two segments are actuated independently. If a contracting or expanding segment reaches its threshold value first, the segment stops and waits for its corresponding active segment to stop. The next set of actuators are activated once both segments in the previous wave sequence stop. In case an external threshold is not reached (no external constraint), a time-based threshold is set in order to stop the expanding segment once it reaches its maximum diameter.

## 5    Experimental Methods and Results

### 5.1    Single Segment in Pipe

To demonstrate contact forces in a radially symmetric environment, a single segment of DiSCo-Worm was tested inside a pipe with inner diameter of 20.32 cm (92% of the nominal maximum diameter). The segment was first contracted and inserted in a pipe and then cycled between successive expansions and contractions. This allowed us to calibrate the force applied by FSR sensors on an external constraint. A video from the lateral view allowed us to map the stretch sensor data to segment length. Tracker (version 4.10) video analysis software was used to measure the length of the segment.

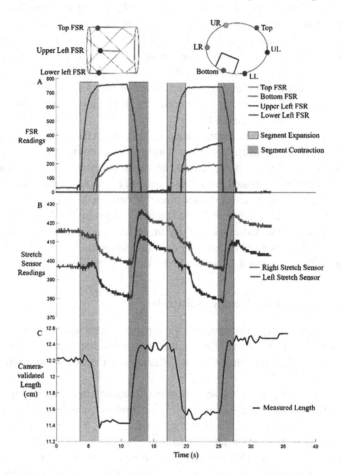

**Fig. 3.** Expansion of a single segment within a pipe of 20.32 cm inner diameter (orientation of the segment when placed within the pipe is shown on top). (A) FSR readings from four pressure sensors along the circumference of the segment indicate the segment encountering the inner wall of the pipe. The segment diagram on top shows the placement of the sensors around the circumference when viewed from a transverse view. Lower Left sensor shows large force readings on the onset of segment expansion. On completion of expansion, the three FSR readings (Bottom, Upper Left and Lower Left) indicate continuous contact with the inner wall of the pipe until contraction starts at which point no radial force is applied on these sensors. (B) Stretch sensor measurement from both right and left side of the segment shows an increase in resistance as the segment begins to extend in length. The offset between the two stretch sensors is due to the initial lengths of the sensors being different. During operation, we subtract the current reading from the reading obtained at maximum possible extension. (C) Measured side length of the segment using video analysis indicating the expansion and contraction cycle aligned with sensory data.

The placement of each FSR relative to gravity determines the order in which contact forces are sensed during radial expansion (Fig. 3). Consider the 4 sensors on the left side of the body: in this case, the Lower Left (LL) FSR was at the bottom of the pipe, so it measures contact forces first. Then the Upper Left FSR, and Bottom FSR also made contact. The positioning of the segment is such that these two sensors are placed on vertex pieces opposite each other. However, due to the weight of the segment, UL FSR experiences a larger force compared to the Bottom FSR. The Top (T) FSR sensor never records any force, as it never encountered the inner wall of the pipe because gravity keeps the soft structure in a non-circular, deformed shape. The LL FSR sensor experiences a total force of 2.9 N which is the entire weight of a segment, whereas UL and bottom FSR sensors experience 0.5 N.

Stretch sensors are more accurate during radial contraction than during extension, which suits our need to limit contraction. During radial contraction, as the segment length increases, the values recorded from these sensors also increase. Since the segment uniformly contracts and expands, both these sensors exhibit a similar trend. However, on segment expansion, the values do not directly correlate to segment length. This is because the sensors have a few resistive artifacts (i.e., hysteresis). When stretched into position and released, the resistance slightly increases upon release, and decays exponentially to its resting resistive values. Figure 3 shows that the stretch sensor values start to decay during the suspension phase while the length of the segment is still constant.

## 5.2   Locomotion Between Parallel Substrates

DiSCo-Worm with all six segments and 49 sensors locomoted between two parallel wooden surfaces set 16 cm apart (72% of initial maximum diameter (Fig. 4)), using both open-loop and closed-loop control schemes. Results from these tests are summarized in this section.

During closed loop control, the sensors stop expansion after contact (Fig. 5A). Note that between two parallel constraints, the figure shows that only the top and bottom sensors contact the ground. The threshold set (dashed lines, Fig. 5A) indicate when the top or bottom have sufficient normal force to stop further expansion and allow anchoring of the segment. The bottom FSR sensor placed directly underneath the actuator mount experiences a high normal force, due to the weight of the segment resting on it. During expansion, on coming in contact with the constraint, the normal force on the Top FSR sensor increases the set threshold, thereby stopping any further expansion of the segment. It can be observed that during contraction and the suspended phase of the wave, the sensor reading for the bottom sensor indicates no contact with the ground. In contrast, during the anchoring phase of the peristaltic cycle, the bottom sensor measures large values, indicating the anchoring phase.

The bottom FSR sensor exerts a force of 2.3 N (80% of segment weight); compliance between adjacent segments prevents the segment from exerting 100% of its weight on the surface. The top FSR sensor experiences a maximum force of 1.0 N which quickly decreases due to motion of the other segments.

Stretch receptors indicate increase in resistive values when the segment undergoes contraction (Fig. 5B). The threshold for the stretch sensors indicates when the segment reaches maximum longitudinal extension with some allowance. On reaching this preset threshold, the contraction phase of the actuation is stopped. During the expansion phase, the resistive values of the stretch sensors decay to their initial values, similar to the case of a single segment.

**Fig. 4.** DiSCO-Worm locomoting through two parallel horizontal wooden surfaces. The distance between the two surfaces was set at 16 cm. Both the open-loop controller and closed-loop controller were tested in the same constrained environment.

Actuator positions logged using the actuators encoder allow for tracking all four phases of the 3 × 1 peristaltic cycle (expansion, anchoring, contraction, suspension) and aligning with sensory feedback information.

How does limiting the duration of each step affect behavior? In 50 s, the closed loop control resulted in 5.04 cm progress over 7 peristaltic waves, whereas the open loop controller resulted in 10.43 cm over 5 peristaltic waves. Thus, as a result of the feedback control, the robot takes smaller steps adapting to its environment with an overall speed of 48% of the open loop speed. Although the open-loop movements are faster, they are less precise, as we describe below.

During open-loop control, there is a large amount of slip in both forward and backward directions. Slip occurs when segments move during anchoring phases. Slip is measured at the contact point using video analysis. For the open-loop controller, the segment slipped backward by 8.67 cm. If no backward slip had occurred, the total forward progress of the segment using an open-loop controller would have been 19.1 cm. Using the closed-loop controller, the robot experienced backward slip of 6.70 cm, so there is less backward slip. Most of the backward slip, in both cases, was experienced during the contraction and suspension phase of the peristaltic cycle. Although both control schemes have high backward slip, forward slip in the case of open-loop control is higher than that of closed-loop control. With open-loop control, the robot progressed by approximately 6.10 cm during its anchoring phase. In contrast, the closed-loop controller did not progress noticeably during its anchoring phase. The maximum longitudinal extension in both cases was similar, but due to forward slip, segments in open-loop control contribute to larger progress. For some applications, slip in any direction is undesirable as it leads to imprecise control. Out of the total progress made by the open-loop controller, 58% was due to slip in the forward direction (at a time that the segment should have been anchoring). During slip, the upper and bottom surface of the segment was in continuous contact with the external constraint. If there was no forward slip, the robot would have progressed by 4.3 cm for the open-loop controller.

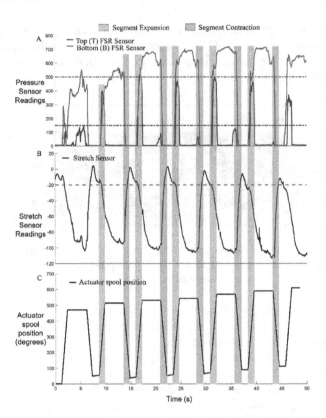

**Fig. 5.** Data recorded from the 2$^{nd}$ segment using the closed-loop controller as the robot was allowed to locomote between two parallel horizontal surfaces. (A) Sensory information from the Top and Bottom FSR indicating when the robot came in contact with the external constraint. The robot rests on ground so the bottom FSR reading is high when the segment is anchoring. The segment then contracts until it is completely lifted away from the ground (all FSR for that segment read zero). Then the segment expands causing the bottom and also the top FSR sensors to make contact with the substrates (both top and bottom FSR show contact forces). Due to the compliance of the structure, as the adjacent segments move, the top sensor loses contact, thus exhibiting no contact during the anchoring phase. The dashed orange and blue line indicates the preset force threshold for the closed-loop controller for the Bottom and Top FSR respectively. (B) Data from stretch sensor indicates longitudinal extension of the segment during contraction phase. Stretch sensor's resistance increases with an increase in length. The maximum extension that the stretch sensor experiences is set to zero. At zero, the contracting segment is at its minimum possible diameter. Negative values indicate the length of the stretch sensor is shorter than its maximum extension. Zero indicates that the segment has reached its maximum extension and any further extension can cause the robot to break. By setting the maximum extension, we eliminate any preexisting discrepancies between stretch sensors (the offset observed between the left and right side in Fig. 3). (C) Actuator position logged aligned with sensor data showing the four different phases of the peristaltic 3 × 1. The expansion and contraction phase are highlighted.

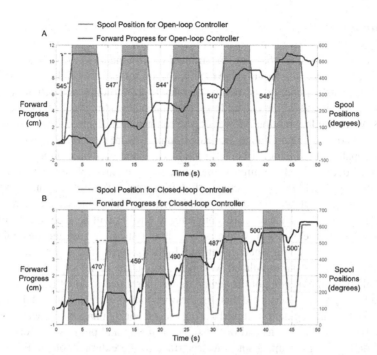

**Fig. 6.** Comparison between (A) open-loop and (B) closed-loop controller. On the left Y-axis is the forward progress, measured using video tracking software, of the second segment during peristaltic locomotion (Note the scale difference in both figures (A) and (B)). Right Y-axis indicates the spool position of the actuator of that segment. Gray boxes are aligned with the spool position indicating anchoring phase. The angle by which the actuators rotate from contraction phase to expansion phase is indicated beside the gray boxes. Overall, in a span of 50 s, the total forward progress achieved by the open-loop controller is 10.43 cm in 5 complete waves. In contrast, for the closed loop-controller, forward progress is 5.04 cm by the end of the anchor phase of the 7th peristaltic wave.

This soft robot shows the ability to alter its gait pattern in accordance to its environment using a closed-loop controller. With open loop control, the motors continue to rotate even after coming in contact with an external constraint. The actuators rotate for approximately 545° in the open-loop controller. For the closed-loop controller, on encountering an external constraint, the actuators stop rotating, thereby causing no further expansion. During this time, the actuators rotate between 459°–500°. The reduction in degrees rotated causes the peristaltic cycle to move faster, by shortening the time duration of each cycle. The adaptability of the closed-loop controller to its external environment leads to coordinated motion that wastes less energy.

# 6 Conclusions

In this article we discover that in a constrained environment (a) the forward progress under open-loop control is largely due to slip, (b) the actuators work harder and longer in open loop, wasting energy and risking damage to the structure and actuation cables, and (c) the movements of the closed loop robot incur less slip which is a key cause of imprecision during locomotion. However, the robot's overall speed is slowed relative to open loop control, in part due to the reduction in forward slip. With sensors, DiSCo-Worm is capable of reducing slip in both the forward and backward direction.

The FSR data will help to improve the closed loop control for soft robots in future work. From Fig. 5A, blue line, the contact forces decrease after initial contact. Whether this is due to structural interdependence of segments or multi-time scale dynamics, this work demonstrates that an anchoring-state force controller will be necessary to prevent early cut-off of soft expansion. Conversely, without such a controller, designing the segment structure for compliance might be a higher priority than developing sensors. On the other hand, in our simulated worm-like robot, the gains in performance were very small unless the phasing of the segments was permitted to adapt [21].

From Fig. 6, it can be observed that, for the open loop controller, most of the forward progress for the 2nd segment occurred during the anchoring phase of the wave (58% of the total 10.43 cm). Thus, instead of the segment lifting and progressing forward, the segment drags along the upper and lower surface of the external constraints. For the closed-loop controller, minimal slip was observed during the anchoring phase of peristaltic locomotion (~0). However, the segment did experience a large amount of backward slip during its contraction phase. An improved controller could solve this problem. In Fig. 6, a drift in actuator positions is observed in the closed-loop controller due to inaccuracies in stretch sensors during contraction. We can reduce these sensor inaccuracies using signal processing techniques. Furthermore, it may be valuable to be able to sense shear force in order to detect slip [23].

This work suggests the type of sensors that are valuable for reducing positional uncertainty in worm like motion. Sensory feedback can also protect the robot from damage. Due to continuous rotation, there have been instances where the excess actuation tangles the cable, causing the cable to break. The closed-loop control prevents this from happening. With the sensory feedback, we can develop control that is more precise and allows the robot to navigate through various constrained environments.

The next step is to develop more complex control algorithms for generating and maintaining friction against the ground with the goal of navigating more challenging constrained surfaces.

**Acknowledgments.** This material is based upon work supported by the National Science Foundation under Grant No. NSF #1743475.

# References

1. Rateni, G., Cianchetti, M., Ciuti, G., Menciassi, A., Laschi, C.: Design and development of a soft robotic gripper for manipulation in minimally invasive surgery: a proof of concept. Meccanica **50**(11), 2855–2863 (2015)
2. Altendorfer, R., Moore, N., Komsuoglu, H., Buehler, M., Brown, H.B., McMordie, D., Saranli, U., Full, R., Koditschek, D.E.: Rhex: a biologically inspired hexapod runner. Auton. Robots **11**(3), 207–213 (2001)
3. Seok, S., Onal, C.D., Cho, K.J., Wood, R.J., Rus, D., Kim, S.: Meshworm: a peristaltic soft robot with antagonistic nickel titanium coil actuators. IEEE/ASME Trans. Mechatron. **18**(5), 1485–1497 (2013)
4. Kandhari, A., et al.: Sensing contact constraints in a worm-like robot by detecting load anomalies. In: Lepora, N., Mura, A., Mangan, M., Verschure, P., Desmulliez, M., Prescott, T. (eds.) Living Machines 2016. LNCS (LNAI), vol. 9793, pp. 97–106. Springer, Cham (2016). https://doi.org/10.1007/978-3-319-42417-0_10
5. Mangan, E.V., Kingsley, D.A., Quinn, R.D., Chiel, H.J.: Development of a peristaltic endoscope. In: Proceedings of the IEEE International Conference on Robotics and Automation, pp. 347–52 (2002)
6. Horchler, A.D., Kandhari, A., Daltorio, K.A., Moses, K.C., Ryan, J.C., Stultz, K.A., Kanu, E.N., Andersen, K.B., Kershaw, J., Bachmann, R.J., Chiel, H.J., Quinn, R.D.: Peristaltic locomotion of a modular mesh-based worm robot: precision, compliance, and friction. Soft Robot. **2**(4), 135–145 (2015)
7. Vaidyanathan, R., Chiel, H.J., Quinn, R.D.: A hydrostatic robot for marine applications. Robot. Auton. Syst. **30**, 103–113 (2000)
8. Boxerbaum, A.S., Horchler, A.D., Shaw, K.M., Chiel, H.J., Quinn, R.D.: Worms, waves and robots. In: Proceedings of the IEEE International Conference on Robotics and Automation, pp. 3537–3538 (2012)
9. Trivedi, D., Rahn, C.D., Kier, W.M., Walker, I.D.: Soft robotics: biological inspiration, state of the art, and future research. Appl. Bionics Biomech. **5**(3), 99–117 (2008)
10. Dario, P., Ciarletta, P., Menciassi, A., Kim, B.: Modeling and experimental validation of the locomotion of endoscopic robots in the colon. Int. J. Robot. Res. **23**(4–5), 549–556 (2004)
11. Huang, Y., Kandhari, A., Chiel, H.J., Quinn, R.D., Daltorio, K.A.: Mathematical modeling to improve control of mesh body for peristaltic locomotion. In: Conference on Biomimetic and Biohybrid Systems, pp. 193–203 (2017)
12. Chiel, H.J., Crago, P., Mansour, J.M., Hathi, K.: Biomechanics of a muscular hydrostat: a model of lapping by a reptilian tongue. Biol. Cybern. **67**(5), 403–415 (1992)
13. Gray, J., Lissmann, H.W.: Studies in animal locomotion VII. Locomotory reflexes in the earthworm. J. Exp. Biol. **15**, 506–517 (1938)
14. Kanu, E.N., Daltorio, K.A., Quinn, R.D., Chiel, H.J.: Correlating kinetics and kinematics of earthworm peristaltic locomotion. Proc. Int. Conf. Biomim. Biohybrid Syst. **9222**, 92–96 (2015)
15. Mizutani, K., Shimoi, T., Ogawa, H., Kitamura, Y., Oka, K.: Modulation of motor patterns by sensory feedback during earthworm locomotion. Neurosci. Res. **48**(4), 457–462 (2004)
16. Mill, P.J.: Recent developments in earthworm neurobiology. Comp. Biochem. Physiol. **12**, 107–115 (1982)
17. Ikeuchi, M., Nakamura, T., Matsubara, D.: Development of an in-pipe inspection robot for narrow pipes and elbows using pneumatic artificial muscles. In: Proceedings of the IEEE/RSJ International Conference on Intelligent Robots and Systems, pp. 926–931 (2012)

18. Trimmer, B.A., Takesian, A.E., Sweet, B.M., Rogers, C.B., Hake, D.C., Rogers, D.J.: Caterpillar locomotion: a new model for soft-bodied climbing and burrowing robots. In: International Symposium on Technology and the Mine Problem, vol. 1, pp. 1–10 (2006)

19. Bertetto, A.M., Ruggiu, M.: In-pipe inch-worm pneumatic flexible robot. In: Proc. IEEE/ASME International Conference on Advanced Intelligent Mechatronics, vol. 2, pp. 1226–1231 (2001)

20. Tanaka, T., Harigaya, K., Nakamura, T.: Development of a peristaltic crawling robot for long-distance inspection of sewer pipes. In: Proc. IEEE/ASME International Conference on Advanced Intelligent Mechatronics, pp. 1552–1557 (2014)

21. Daltorio, K.A., Boxerbaum, A.S., Horchler, A.D., Shaw, K.M., Chiel, H.J., Quinn, R.D.: Efficient worm-like locomotion: slip and control of soft-bodied peristaltic robots. Bioinspir. Biomim. **8**(3), 035003 (2013)

22. Kandhari, A., Huang, Y., Daltorio, K.A., Chiel, H.J., Quinn, R.D.: Body stiffness in orthogonal directions oppositely affects worm-like robot turning and straight-line locomotion. Bioinspir. Biomim. **13**(2), 026003 (2018)

23. Umedachi, T., Kano, T., Ishiguro, A., Trimmer, B.A.: Gait control in a soft robot by sensing interactions with the environment using self-deformation. R. Soc. Open Sci. **3**(12), 160766 (2016)

# Snake-Like Robot that Can Generate Versatile Gait Patterns by Using *Tegotae*-Based Control

Takeshi Kano$^{(\boxtimes)}$, Ryo Yoshizawa, and Akio Ishiguro

Research Institute of Electrical Communication, Tohoku University,
2-1-1 Katahira, Aoba-ku, Sendai 980-8577, Japan
{tkano,r-yoshi,ishiguro}@riec.tohoku.ac.jp,
http://www.cmplx.riec.tohoku.ac.jp/

**Abstract.** Snakes exhibit versatile gait patterns to adapt to various environments. Implementing the underlying mechanism in snake-like robots will enable them to work well in unstructured real-world environments. We previously proposed a decentralized control scheme for snake-like robots based on *Tegotae*, a Japanese concept describing how well a perceived reaction matches an expectation. In this study, we developed a snake-like robot to demonstrate via real-world experiments that the proposed control scheme enables to produce versatile gait patterns such as scaffold-based locomotion on irregular terrain and concertina locomotion in narrow aisle without changing any parameter.

**Keywords:** Snake-like Robot · *tegotae*-based control,
Scaffold-based locomotion, Concertina locomotion

## 1 Introduction

Snakes possess versatile gait patterns and use them appropriately to adapt to various environments in real time [1–4]. For example, snakes exhibit scaffold-based locomotion on an unstructured terrain, wherein they actively utilize terrain irregularities and move effectively by actively pushing their bodies against 'scaffolds' that they encounter (Fig. 1(a)) [1]. Meanwhile, they exhibit concertina locomotion in a narrow aisle wherein the tail part of the body is first pulled forward with the head part anchored, followed by the extension of the head part with the tail part anchored (Fig. 1(b)) [2]. This remarkable ability of snakes is a source of inspiration for the development of snake-like robots. However, snake-like robots developed thus far [3,4] are less adaptive than real snakes because the previous studies concentrated on generating specific gait patterns individually.

To address this issue, we previously proposed an autonomous decentralized control scheme based on *Tegotae*, a Japanese concept describing how well a perceived reaction matches an expectation [5,6]. We demonstrated via simulations that versatile gait patterns such as scaffold-based and concertina locomotion

V. Vouloutsi et al. (Eds.): Living Machines 2018, LNAI 10928, pp. 249–254, 2018.
https://doi.org/10.1007/978-3-319-95972-6_26

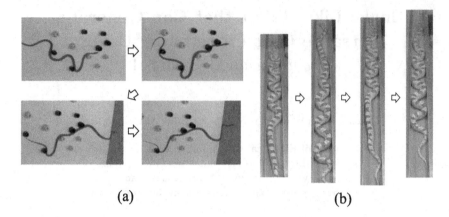

(a)                                              (b)

**Fig. 1.** Locomotion patterns of real snakes: (a) scaffold-based locomotion (*Elaphe cli-macophora*) and (b) concertina locomotion (*Elaphe guttata*).

emerged in response to the environment [5]. Further, we developed a snake-like robot and successfully reproduced scaffold-based locomotion in the real world [6].

However, our previous work [6] could not reproduce concertina locomotion owing to several technical issues such as shortage of motor torque and limited motion range of the joints. In this study, we developed a new snake-like robot HAUBOT VII with solving these technical issues. We demonstrate in the real world that the developed robot with the proposed control scheme can generate both scaffold-based and concertina locomotion in response to the environment without any parameter change.

## 2   Robot

### 2.1   Mechanical System

The overview of the developed robot HAUBOT VII is shown in Fig. 2(a). The robot consists of 30 identical body segments that are concatenated one-dimensionally. The total length and weight of the robot are 1.5 m and 3.3 kg, respectively. Passive wheels are attached to the bottom of the segments to enforce anisotropy in the frictional coefficient between the body and the ground. Such frictional anisotropy is also observed in real snakes [7].

Figure 2(b) shows the detailed structure of each segment. A servo motor (RS405CB, Futaba) is implemented in each segment, which can generate a torque up to 48.0 [kgf · cm] to drive the joint. The maximum bending angle of each joint is $\pi/4$ [rad]. The target joint angles, which are given by Eqs. (1)–(3) below, are calculated at control circuits with microcomputers implemented in each five segments.

The joint angles can be detected via communication commands with the servo motors. The joint torque can be estimated from the difference between

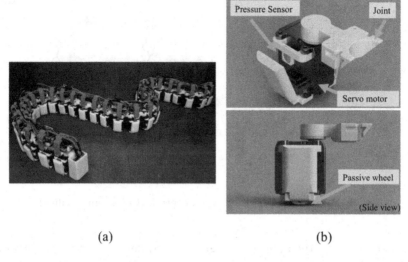

**Fig. 2.** Snake-like robot HAUBOT VII: (a) overview and (b) detailed structure of each segment.

the target and real joint angles. A pressure sensor is embedded on each side of a segment and covered by a body wall made from a hard material. When the body wall is pushed against external objects such as pegs, the sensor detects the corresponding pressure.

### 2.2 Control System

Each joint is controlled according to proportional control, and the target and real angles of the $i$th joint are denoted by $\bar{\phi}_i$ and $\phi_i$, respectively. The contact forces detected at the $i$th segment from the right- and left-hand side are denoted by $f_{r,i}$ and $f_{l,i}$, respectively.

The control scheme was designed based on [5,6]. The target joint angle $\bar{\phi}_i$ is updated each time step as follows:

$$\bar{\phi}_i(t+1) = 0 \qquad\qquad (0 \le i < n_\alpha), \tag{1}$$

$$\bar{\phi}_i(t+1) = h_d(t) \qquad\qquad (n_\alpha \le i < n_\beta), \tag{2}$$

$$\bar{\phi}_i(t+1) = \phi_{i-1}(t) + \sigma \tanh \left\{ \sum_{j=i-n_b}^{i+n_f} \tau_j(t)(f_{l,j}(t) + f_{r,j}(t)) \right\},$$

$$(n_\beta \le i < 30) \tag{3}$$

where $t$ is a time step, $h_d(t)$ is the motor command from a operator, $\sigma$ is a positive constant, $\tau_j(t)$ is a torque generated at the $j$th joint. Note that $\bar{\phi}_i(t+1)$ is updated to $\pm\pi/4$ when it exceeds $\pm\pi/4$, considering the maximum bending angle described above.

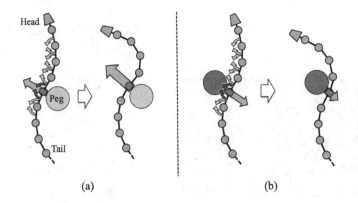

**Fig. 3.** Mechanism of *Tegotae*-based control. (Color figure online)

The first term on the right-hand side of Eq. (3) denotes curvature derivative control [8] wherein torques proportional to the curvature derivative of the body curve are generated so that bodily waves propagate from the head to the tail. The second term on the right-hand side of Eq. (3) denotes a sensory feedback based on *Tegotae*, which is described as the product of the torque, *i.e.*, intended action, and the contact forces, *i.e.*, reaction. This feedback works as shown in Fig. 3. When a torque generated to bend the body leftward (red arrow in Fig. 3(a)) resulted in receiving a contact force from the right (purple arrow in Fig. 3(a)), the contact force assists propulsion, and the feedback works to generate further torques (yellow arrow in Fig. 3(a)) so that the contact force increases. On the other hand, when a torque generated to bend the body leftward (red arrow in Fig. 3(b)) resulted in receiving a contact force from the left (purple arrow in Fig. 3(b)), the contact force impedes propulsion, and the feedback works to generate further torques (yellow arrow in Fig. 3(b)) so that the contact force decreases.

## 3    Experimental Result

We performed experiments by using the robot. We constructed an experimental environment wherein the robot passed through an aisle of 15 cm width and a terrain with pegs. The side walls of the aisle and the pegs were made of sponge and chloroethene pipes of 11 cm diameter, respectively. The parameter values, which were determined by trial-and-error and were not changed during the experiments, are as follows: $n_\alpha = 1$, $n_\beta = 2$, $n_f = 3$, $n_b = 1$, $\kappa = 2.5$, and $\sigma = 20.0$.

When the robot experienced the terrain with several pegs, it moved effectively by pushing itself against pegs that assist propulsion (Fig. 4(a)); this gait pattern was scaffold-based locomotion. When the robot experienced the aisle, it exhibited concertina locomotion in which the tail part of the body was first pulled forward with the head part anchored, and this was followed by the extension of the

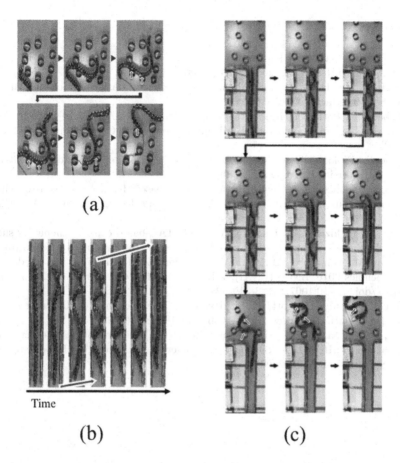

**Fig. 4.** Experimental results when the robot experienced (a) a terrain with several pegs, (b) an aisle of 15 cm width, and (c) an aisle of 15 cm width, followed by a terrain with pegs. Yellow areas and green arrows indicate the contact points. (Color figure online)

head part with the tail part anchored (Fig. 4(b)). Further, it could adapt by changing locomotion patterns from concertina to scaffold-based locomotion when the environment changed from the aisle to the terrain with pegs (Fig. 4(c)). Thus, the proposed control scheme enabled the robot to change locomotion patterns autonomously in response to the changes in the environment.

**Acknowledgments.** This work was supported by Japan Science and Technology Agency, CREST (JPMJCR14D5). The authors would like to thank Dr. Kosuke Inoue of Ibaraki University, and the late Dr. Michihisa Toriba, Dr. Atsushi Sakai and Dr. Hisashi Miho of the Japan Snake Institute for their cooperation.

# References

1. Moon, B.R., Gans, C.: Kinematics, muscular activity and propulsion in gopher snakes. J. Exp. Biol. **201**, 2669–2684 (1998)
2. Marvi, H., Hu, D.L.: Friction enhancement in concertina locomotion of snakes. J. Roy. Soc. Interface **9**, 3067–3080 (2012)
3. Liljebäck, P., Pettersen, K.Y., Stavdahl, Ø., Gravdahl, J.T.: Snake Robots - Modelling, Mechatronics, and Control: Advances in Industrial Control. Springer, London (2012)
4. Hirose, S.: Biologically Inspired Robots (Snake-Like Locomotor and Manipulator). Oxford University Press, Oxford (1993)
5. Kano, T., Yoshizawa, R., Ishiguro, A.: Tegotae-based decentralised control scheme for autonomous gait transition of snake-like robots. Bioinsp. Biomim. **12**, 046009 (2017)
6. Kano, T., Yoshizawa, R., Ishiguro, A.: TEGOTAE-based control scheme for snake-like robots that enables scaffold-based locomotion. In: Lepora, N.F.F., Mura, A., Mangan, M., Verschure, P.F.M.J.F.M.J., Desmulliez, M., Prescott, T.J.J. (eds.) Living Machines 2016. LNCS (LNAI), vol. 9793, pp. 454–458. Springer, Cham (2016). https://doi.org/10.1007/978-3-319-42417-0_46
7. Hu, D.L., Nirody, J., Scott, T., Shelley, M.J.: The mechanics of slithering locomotion. Proc. Natl. Acad. Sci. U.S.A. **106**, 10081–10085 (2009)
8. Date, H., Takita, Y.: Adaptive locomotion of a snake like robot based on curvature derivatives. In: IEEE/RSJ International Conference on Intelligent Robotic Systems (IROS), pp. 3554–3559 (2007)

# Observation of Calcium Wave on Physical Stimulus for Realizing Cell Tactile Sensor

Hiroki Kawashima[1]([✉]), Umakshi Sajnani[2], Masahiro Shimizu[1], and Koh Hosoda[1]

[1] Graduate School of Engineering Science, Osaka University,
1-3, Machikaneyama, Toyonaka 560-8531, Japan
{kawashima.hiroki,shimizu,hosoda}@arl.sys.es.osaka-u.ac.jp
[2] Cluster of Excellence Cognitive Interaction Technology, Bielefeld University,
Universitätsstraße 25, 33615 Bielefeld, Germany

**Abstract.** The biological cells maintain their life functions by responding to the stimulus from the external environment and even change their structure and function upon long-term mechanical stimulation. Such characteristics of the biological cells can be utilized for realizing cell tactile sensors. This report shows some preliminary observation how the calcium wave propagates when aligned cells are physically stimulated, which can be utilized for picking up tactile information from the living cells. The biological cells are aligned in one direction by utilizing self-organization process during cell growth. The observation shows that the direction of wave tends to be perpendicular to the direction of the aligned cells. This can be utilized for local information processing of the stimuli to the tactile sensor.

**Keywords:** Calcium wave · Cell tactile sensor
Mechanical stimulation

## 1 Introduction

Living organisms adapt to the environmental changes by their significant abilities such as self-repair, self-assembly, and self-organization. Bio-machine hybrid systems have been attracting a lot of attention since we can utilize such adaptation of the biological organisms to realize highly adaptive machines. The biological cells are the basic units of such systems, and it is crucial to investigate the nature of the cells so that we can synthesize a new type of bio-machine system.

This research aims to develop a tactile sensor using living cells. We utilize them as an engineering tool to accept mechanical stimulation from outside. Utilizing living cells for sensors have been studied in not only robotics but also biology. Misawa et al. [1] developed an odorant sensor with cell expressed pheromone receptors. Using the odorant sensor, they realized a robot mannequin that can accurately responded and turned its neck to chemical detection. Taniguchi [2]

© Springer International Publishing AG, part of Springer Nature 2018
V. Vouloutsi et al. (Eds.): Living Machines 2018, LNAI 10928, pp. 255–262, 2018.
https://doi.org/10.1007/978-3-319-95972-6_27

studied on utilization of cell cytotoxicity detection phenomenon. It leads to high-throughput cytotoxicity detection system for biomaterials, nanotoxicology, environmental assessment, and drug screening. As addressed in these studies, we can utilize living cells as engineering tools for embedding such significant abilities of living organisms directly to the bio-machine hybrid system.

Our research group has been focusing particularly on tactile sensors with living cells. To realize a tactile sensor with living cells, we have to solve (1) how we can align the cells so that we can determine the sensitivity of the sensor, and (2) how we can pick up information from the living cells. We have developed a cell tactile sensor [3] that selectively responds to the stimulus which is given in the growth phase. We applied physical stimuli to the cells and they aligned perpendicular to the stretch. For picking out the information, we cultured mouse myoblast C2C12 on elastic PDMS chamber and introduced G-CaMP into the cells in order to visualize calcium signal as fluorescence responding to mechanical stimulation.

By utilizing G-CaMP, we could observe the calcium signal of each cell, but actually, in the biological system, this leads to the diffusion of calcium ions into the neighboring cells. The propagation should be done mainly by gap junction between cells. Therefore, a pathway of calcium wave should be determined due to cell confluency, which is characterized by cell alignment. Balaji *et al.* [4] reported that calcium waves propagate in certain directions in epithelial cells. There still remains unclear about how the tactile information spread depending on the orientation of cells. The dynamics of the propagation contributes to some information processing, and as a result, the organism may be able to get richer information on the physical stimulus.

In this report, we shed light on calcium wave propagation after mechanical stimulation to the cells. We investigate the dependency of calcium wave propagation on the arrangement of cell group by taking methodology as follows: (1) we construct aligned cell aggregation in one direction by utilizing self-organization process in cell growth, which reflects mechanical stimulation; (2) we apply mechanical stimulation to several cells, and observe calcium wave propagation. Investigation of the relationship between cell group arrangement and calcium wave propagation will lead to the design of a novel tactile sensor device for a bio-machine hybrid system. A cellular mechanism of calcium wave propagation is activated upon application of a mechanical force to the cell. If we can intentionally control the propagation pathway of calcium wave using specifically designed cell group geometrical arrangement, we can develop a tactile sensor that responds to the stimuli selectively.

## 2   Development of Aligned Cell Aggregation as a Tactile Sensor

### 2.1   Cell Alignment Using Cyclic Mechanical Stimulation

Firstly, we introduce the development of aligned cell aggregation as a tactile sensor. Some previous work has been demonstrating that we can control the

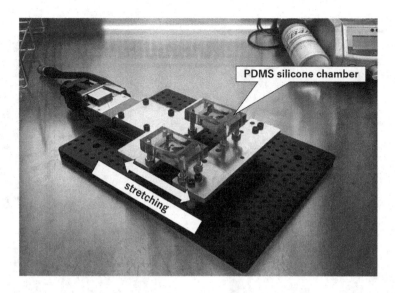

**Fig. 1.** A stretchable PDMS silicone chambers driven by motors

alignment of living cells by use of mechanical stimulation during cultivation of the cells. It has been reported that the cell can be oriented perpendicular to the stretching direction when cyclic stretch is continuously applied to the scaffold where the cell adheres [5–7]. By utilizing this feature, we can culture some pattern of aggregation by changing the type of mechanical stimulation such as poking [8,9].

We develop a device to apply cyclic stretching to the scaffold where the cell adheres (Fig. 1). It has a stretchable polydimethylsiloxane (PDMS) silicone chamber (STB-CH-04, STREX Inc. Japan) and the cells are cultured on it. The PDMS chamber can be stretched by an electric servo motor controlled by a microcomputer. By programming cyclic motion of the motor, we can apply precise cyclic stretch to the chamber. In the PDMS chamber, we add C2C12 that is a cell line derived from mouse skeletal muscles. When we seed the cells into the chamber, the cells can be fixed at the bottom of the chamber and are hard to peel off. In this experiment, the chamber containing C2C12 cells was stretched at a frequency of 0.5 Hz, 20% stretching for 6 h.

## 2.2   Estimation of Cell Alignment

Two samples cultured for 6 h with/without the cyclic stretch are shown in Fig. 2(a) and (b), respectively. In Fig. 2(a), the cells are oriented perpendicular to the direction of stretching as a result of cyclic stretch stimulation, whereas they are not aligned in Fig. 2(b).

The cell density is investigated in Fig. 3. From the samples (a) and (b), we pick 3 horizontal and 3 vertical lines randomly from each, and count number

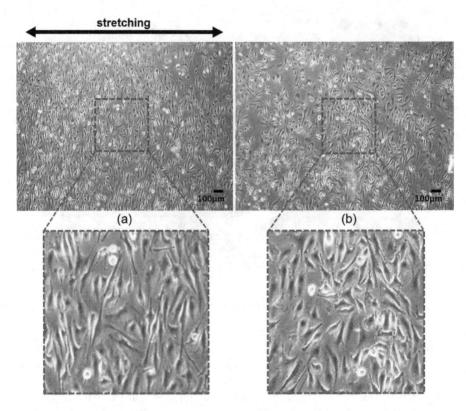

**Fig. 2.** Two samples cultured for 6 h with/without cyclic stretch: (a) a sample stretched at a frequency of 0.5 Hz, 20% stretching for 6 h, and (b) a sample without cyclic stretch.

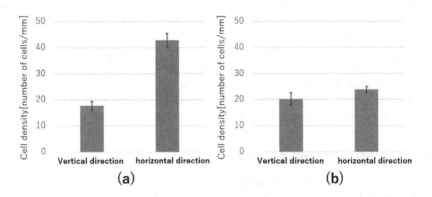

**Fig. 3.** From the samples (a) and (b), we pick 3 horizontal and 3 vertical lines randomly from each, and count number of cells in horizontal and vertical directions along the lines. This graph shows how many of these cells per unit length. It demonstrates that the cells are aligned perpendicular to the cyclic stretch stimulation, whereas they are not aligned when there is no stimulation.

of cells in horizontal and vertical directions along the lines. Figure 3 shows how many of these cells per unit length. The graphs demonstrate that the cells are aligned perpendicular to the cyclic stretch stimulation whereas they are not aligned when there is no stimulation.

# 3 Observing Calcium Wave Responding to Stimulation

## 3.1 Experimental Setup for Observing Calcium Wave

For observing fluorescence of calcium wave, cells on the PDMS chamber are administered with fluorescence probe Fluo-8. Fluo-8 changes the fluorescence spectrum depending on the intracellular calcium ion concentration, therefore, it is possible to observe changes in intracellular calcium ion concentration of each cell by calcium wave in real time. We adopt a fluorescence microscope FSX100 (OLYMPUS Co., Ltd.) for observing the fluorescence (Fig. 4). We mechanically poke the cells on the PDMS chamber by a glass needle shown in Fig. 4, and observe the propagation of the calcium wave by the fluorescence.

## 3.2 Observed Propagation of Calcium Wave

Snapshots of the fluorescence after poking are shown in Fig. 5. They are processed by image processing software ImageJ so that we can recognize the wave easily. This sample was cultured under the cyclic stretch along horizontal direction, which means the cells are aligned in the vertical direction.

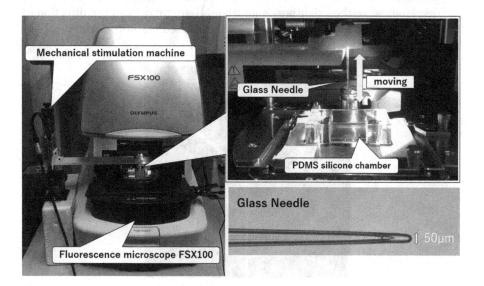

**Fig. 4.** Observing system

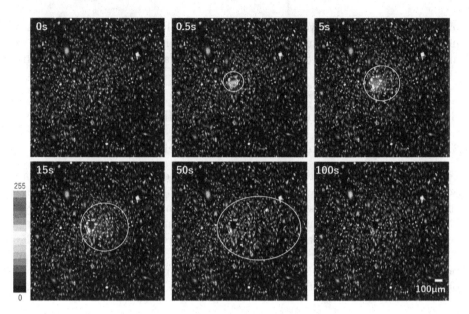

**Fig. 5.** Propagation of calcium wave

At 0.5 [s], the wave starts from the point poked by the needle. We can observe that the wave propagates from the point to the right direction (indicated by circles in the figures). In order to estimate pricisely the direction of the "calcium wave propagation", we translated the 2D images into an graph which indicates a time development of the brightness amplitude. Here, we defined the direction of the calcium wave propagation as Fig. 6. The translated graph is shown in Fig. 7.

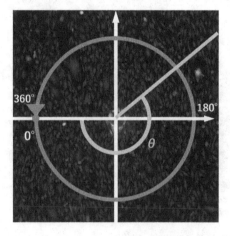

**Fig. 6.** Definition of the direction of the calcium wave propagation

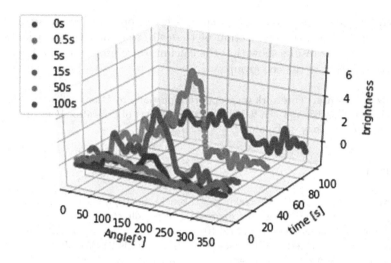

**Fig. 7.** Time development of the calcium wave propagation

Where, we converted each 2D snapshot indicated in Fig. 5 into a grayscale image. Next, we averaged the brightness values of pixels along the radial line of a certain angle $\theta$. Then, we obtained the direction distribution of the brightness values for each time step. Finally, we can take the time development of the cacalcium wave propagation as a 3D graph of brightness vs time vs direction graph. Since the cells are aligned in the vertical direction, this result demonstrate that the wave propagates perpendicular to the cell alignment.

## 4   Discussion

In this report, we developed a cell group structure that unifies the orientation of cells in one direction and investigated the propagation of calcium wave. The results showed that the direction of propagation of calcium wave is determined depending on the orientation of cell group.

It is difficult to infer the reason why the wave propagates perpendicular to the cell alignment. It can be explained by the difference in density of the cells in two directions. Also, it can be explained by the chemical diffusion through GAP junctions. In any case, we can control the direction of the wave by mechanical stimulation during cultivation.

We have developed a cell tactile sensor [3] that selectively responds to the stimulus which is given in the growth phase. If the mechanism of this experiment is properly modelled, we may be able to explain the selectivity. This may lead to the design issue, how we can design the selectivity to a particular stimulus of the tactile cell sensor.

Calcium signaling is a cell-specific property that cannot be found in engineering. Therefore, this sensor can not only detect the presence of a stimulus but also the propagation of tactile information. In this report, as a fundamental research for the development of cellular tactile sensor, we have investigated the relationship between the orientation of the cell group and the propagation of calcium wave. The results show that the calcium wave propagation is dependent on the orientation of the cell group.

**Acknowledgments.** This work was supported partially by Grant-in-Aid for Scientific Research on 15H02763, and 17K19978 from the Ministry of Education, Culture, Sports, Science and Technology of Japan.

# References

1. Misawa, N., Mitsuno, H., Kanzaki, R., Takeuchi, S.: Highly sensitive and selective odorant sensor using living cells expressing insect olfactory receptors. Proc. Natl. Acad. Sci. **107**(35), 15340–15344 (2010)
2. Taniguchi, A.: Live cell-based sensor cells. Biomaterials **31**(23), 5911–5915 (2010)
3. Minzan, K., Shimizu, M., Miyasaka, K., Ogura, T., Nakai, J., Ohkura, M., Hosoda, K.: Toward living tactile sensors. In: Lepora, N.F., Mura, A., Krapp, H.G., Verschure, P.F.M.J., Prescott, T.J. (eds.) Living Machines 2013. LNCS (LNAI), vol. 8064, pp. 409–411. Springer, Heidelberg (2013). https://doi.org/10.1007/978-3-642-39802-5_50
4. Balaji, R., Bielmeier, C., Harz, H., Bates, J., Stadler, C., Hildebrand, A., Classen, A.K.: Calcium spikes, waves and oscillations in a large, patterned epithelial tissue. Sci. Rep. **7**, 42786 (2017)
5. Engler, A.J., Sen, S., Sweeney, H.L., Discher, D.E.: Matrix elasticity directs stem cell lineage specification. Cell **126**(4), 677–689 (2006)
6. Hayakawa, K., Tatsumi, H., Sokabe, M.: Actin filaments function as a tension sensor by tension-dependent binding of cofilin to the filament. J. Cell Biol. **195**(5), 721–727 (2011)
7. Hayakawa, K., Tatsumi, H., Sokabe, M.: Mechano-sensing by actin filaments and focal adhesion proteins. Commun. Integr. Biol. **5**(6), 572–577 (2012)
8. Akiyama, Y., Hoshino, T., Hashimoto, M., Morishima, K.: Evaluation of mechanical stimulation effect on cellular orientation under confluence based on 2D-FFT and principal component analysis. J. Micro-Nano Mechatron. **7**(1–3), 69–77 (2012)
9. Shimizu, M., Yawata, S., Miyamoto, K., Miyasaka, K., Asano, T., Yoshinobu, T., Yawo, H., Ogura, T., Ishiguro, A.: Toward biorobotic systems with muscle cell actuators. In: The Proceedings of AMAM, pp. 87–88 (2011)

# Active Touch with a Biomimetic 3D-Printed Whiskered Robot

Nathan F. Lepora[1,2]([✉]), Niels Burnus[1,2], Yilin Tao[1,2], and Luke Cramphorn[1,2]

[1] Department of Engineering Mathematics, University of Bristol, Bristol, UK
n.lepora@bristol.ac.uk
[2] Bristol Robotics Laboratory, Bristol, UK
http://www.lepora.com

**Abstract.** We propose a new design of active tactile whiskered robot: the actuated TacWhisker array, analogous to motile tactile vibrissae such as the rodent macrovibrissae. The design is particularly simple, being completely 3D-printed, only having one motor to actuate all 10 whiskers, and utilizing optical tactile sensing to transduce whisker deflections into bending moments. This robot is used to investigate active touch on a simple localization task where the robot seeks to move the whisker array to centre on a stimulus while perceiving its location. Active localization with a threshold-crossing decision rule was found to rapidly improve the perceptual errors with successive whisks. Curiously, although the sensing is dominated by the whisker motion, this does not appreciably affect performance on this simple task. Overall, the robot promises to give a simple embodiment of whisker-based active touch to give insight into the mechanisms underlying perception in the mammalian brain.

**Keywords:** Tactile sensing · Active touch · Biomimetics · Whiskers

## 1 Introduction

Tactile whiskers (vibrissae) are a striking facial feature of almost all mammals except for humans [1]. Rodent whiskers have evolved into a primary sense organ for navigating, exploring and interacting with their surroundings. Whisker motion is controlled by the animal to direct its attention onto objects and other salient aspects of the environment [2]. In many behaviours, such as locomotion, these movements are based around a periodic protraction and retraction of the whiskers known as whisking [3]. Both the head/body movements and whisker motion are controlled to aid sensing in a process known as active touch, whereby sensing, perception and action are tightly coupled in a feedback loop. The mechanisms underlying active touch are of great interest to neuroscientists in giving a window to understand perception and action in the mammalian brain. A complementary approach to investigating active touch is to embody putative

N. F. Lepora—This research was supported in part by a grant from the Leverhulme Trust on 'A biomimetic forebrain for robot touch' (RL-2016-39).

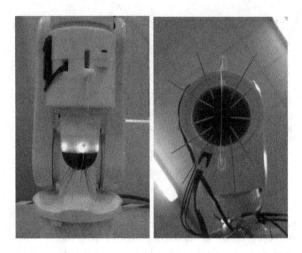

**Fig. 1.** Side (left image) and front (right image) views of the actuated TacWhisker array. The sensor is modular with actuation, body and whiskered tip components.

mechanisms in whiskered robots [4], so that one may test and formulate new biological theories based on how they perform in biomimetic systems.

In this paper we make two contributions to the biomimetics of active touch with robotic whiskers. First, we propose a new design of active tactile whiskered robot: the actuated TacWhisker array (Fig. 1), analogous to motile tactile vibrissae such as the rodent macrovibrissae. The design is particularly simple compared to state-of-the-art whiskered robots such as SHREWbot [5], being completely 3D-printed, only having one motor to actuate all whiskers (here arranged in 2 rows of 5 whiskers), and utilizing optical tactile sensing to transduce whisker deflections. Second, we investigate active touch with the actuated TacWhisker array on a simple localization task where the robot seeks to move the whisker array to centre on a rod stimulus while perceiving its location. We find that active localization is superior to passive localization, in having lower perceptual errors for a decision time, consistent with past work on active touch [6]. Curiously, although the sensing is dominated by the whisker motion, this does not affect performance on this simple task, as comparable localization is attained with and without self-motion compensation.

## 2  Background

Over the last decade, a succession of biomimetic tactile whiskered robots have been developed in collaboration between Sheffield Robotics and Bristol Robotics Laboratory [4]. The initial Whiskerbot mobile robot had an array of 6 glass-fibre moulded whiskers mounted on strain gauges to measure 2D deflections of the whisker shaft [7]. This was followed with the SCRATCHbot mobile platform, having 18 actuated 3D-printed whiskers with Hall effect sensors to measure deflections while actively whisking [8]. These single-actuated whiskers were modularized as part of the BIOTACT project, leading to another mobile whiskered platform called SHREWbot [5] and a robot arm-mounted whisker array [9].

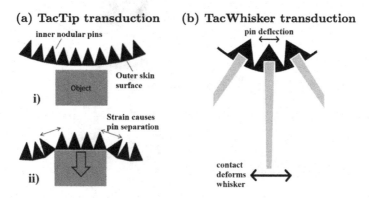

**Fig. 2.** Common transduction principle of the TacTip and TacWhisker. (a) For the TacTip, surface strain causes separation between the inner nodular pins. (b) For the TacWhisker, whisker shaft deflection causes pin movement. In both cases, the pin movement is tracked by an internally mounted camera.

This paper investigates a novel vibrissal tactile sensor based on modifying a 3D-printed biomimetic tactile fingertip called the TacTip (Fig. 2). The TacTip is based on the layered structure of human glabrous skin [10, 11], with an outer biomimetic epidermis made from a rubber-like material over an inner biomimetic dermis made from polymer gel, which interdigitate in a mesh of inner nodular pins. Local strain on the sensor surface is transduced into pin movements that are imaged with an internal camera (Fig. 3). The principle underlying the TacWhisker array is that this transduction mechanism can also be applied to tactile whiskers by attaching the whiskers into sockets protruding into the internal pins; moreover, this design combines with a simple actuation mechanism that actively protracts and retracts the whiskers akin to rodent whisking (Fig. 4). For the actuated TacWhisker array, there are two main contributions to the whisker sense: local shear of the sensor surface from the actuation mechanism; and rotational deflection of the pins when whiskers impinge on an object from the bending moment of the whisker at its base. Both contributions are apparent in the transduced whisker data (Figs. 5 and 6).

## 3    Methods

### 3.1    Actuated TacWhisker Robot

We call the whiskered version of the TacTip a *TacWhisker* array, emphasising it is based on tactile whiskers rather than tactile (finger)tips. The design comprises several modular components, described below.

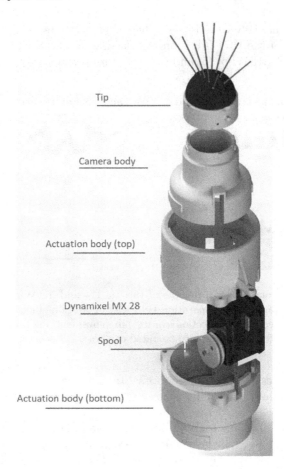

**Fig. 3.** Actuated TacWhisker array. The 3D-printed tip with mounted whiskers attaches to the base housing the camera, which attaches to the actuation module comprising the motor and housing. A tendon runs from the spool, through guides and across a groove in the compliant tip.

**TacWhisker Housing:** The underlying design of TacWhisker array modifies the standard TacTip tip to house whiskers (Fig. 3). There is no modification of the 3D-printed TacTip base (Fig. 3), which contains the USB camera (Lifecam, Microsoft) and an LED ring to illuminate the pin markers (see [10] for details). The tip is based on recent versions of the TacTip [10] that use multi-material 3D-printing. The compliant surface and inner pins printed in a rubber-like material (Tango Black+ 27) and the pin tips and mount in hard plastic (Vero White); this outer surface is filled with a soft clear silicone gel (Techsil RTV27905) held in place with a clear acrylic lens cap.

**TacWhisker Tip:** For housing whiskers that can be actuated, the tip is modified to: (i) reduce the number of pins to 10 (from 127) sited near the top of

**(a) Active protraction    (b) Passive retraction**

**Fig. 4.** Whisking motion. (a) The motor pulls on the tendon to actively protract (bring together) the two rows of whiskers. (b) Reversing the motor releases the tendon to passively retract (pull apart) the whiskers by elastic reformation of the tip.

the tip; (ii) arrange the pins in 2 rows of 5 in a bilaterally symmetric pattern; (iii) enlarge and extrude the solid markers through the compliant surface (2.2 mm dia. × 3.5 mm depth pins, increased from 1.2 mm × 2 mm); and (iv) include a hole (1 mm dia. × 3 mm depth) functioning as a socket for the whiskers. These design choices were chosen to give good pin movement upon deflection of the whiskers, and to site the whiskers appropriately for contacting objects.

The whiskers (Fig. 4) are modified versions of BIOTACT vibrissae [5] that are 3D printed using nanocure-25. The main change is to reduce the whisker size for the smaller scale of the TacTip (40 mm dia.) compared with the BIOTACT conical housing (100 mm dia.). Accordingly, we chose whiskers 40 mm long with a 0.98 mm dia. base tapering to 0.6 mm dia. at the tip, similar in scale to real rat whiskers. For simplicity, all whiskers had the same dimensions, but it would be straightforward to introduce size variations like those of rodent macrovibrissae.

**Actuation Body:** The actuated TacWhisker array is designed to be modular and re-use parts of the static TacWhisker array. Apart from the modified whiskered tip, the TacWhisker base housing the camera and LED lighting is the same as the conventional TacTip. The underside of the base has a bayonet fitting, which is used to connect to an actuation module for driving the tendon (Fig. 3). This actuation body houses a Dynamixel MX 28 servomotor and spool for the tendon, with outer guides to ensure the tendon runs smoothly from the spool, outside the actuation and body modules, and over the TacWhisker tip.

The actuation module moves the whiskers back and forth in a whisking motion (Fig. 4). A tendon runs through a groove between these rows and two guides in the tip mount. Forwards whisker motion (protraction) results from tensioning the tendon to compress the surface at the midline (Fig. 4a); backwards whisker motion (retraction) results from releasing the tendon to elastically reform the surface (Fig. 4b). The compliant surface and whisker mounts are shaped so that the whisker tips can meet under modest surface compression.

The actuated TacWhisker array can thus rhythmically protract and retract its whiskers together and apart in a motion akin to rodent whisking.

**Robotic Platform:** For testing, the static or actuated TacWhisker array is mounted as an end-effector on a 6-DOF robotic arm (IRB 120, ABB; Fig. 1). The arm is mounted on a table that also contains mounting stations for the stimuli. A custom 3D-printed mount is bolted to the rotating (wrist) section of the arm to which either sensor can be attached via a common bayonet fitting on the TacWhisker base and actuation module.

A modular software infrastructure is used in which MATLAB is the primary interface for running tests and analysing data. The ABB arm is controlled via an IronPython and RAPID interface, and data gathered from the USB camera within the TacWhisker sensor with Python OpenCV. Similarly, a Python interface controls the dynamixel motor of the actuated TacWhisker array. Communication between software modules is via TCP/IP ports and sockets.

### 3.2   Sensing, Perception and Active Touch

**Sensing:** Following recent studies with the TacTip [10,12], the sensor output is treated a time series of pin deflections extracted from the camera images. The transformation of the camera image to marker positions requires that the pin markers be detected, which is done via standard 'blob detection' methods in Python OpenCV. Overall, the data processing is a pipeline: camera image to pin detection to pin identification (nearest neighbour tracking) to give an ordered time series of pin deflections measured in pixels (Fig. 5).

The resulting tactile whisker data comprises a multi-dimensional time series of pin $(x, y)$ deflections, measured in pixels on the camera image. For visualization, the time series plots of the $x$- and $y$-deflections are labelled by colouring the tactile dimension by its pin location (Fig. 5, right plots).

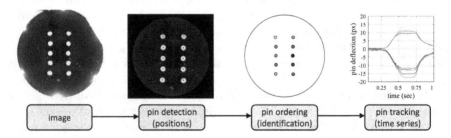

**Fig. 5.** Data processing pipeline. The internal camera captures an image of the pins attached to the shafts of the whiskers. The pins are detected and tracked from frame-to-frame (here coloured by their row) to produce a real-time output. (Color figure online)

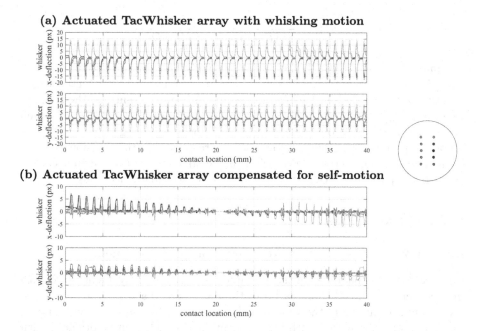

**Fig. 6.** Whisking data over a (40 mm) range of locations from the actuated TacWhisker array. The plot colour denotes the identity of the whiskers (right image). Both the raw whisker data (a) and self-motion compensated (b) data are shown. (Color figure online)

**Perception:** Tactile perception is the process of inferring the properties of a stimulus from data collected by contacting that stimulus. Here we use a likelihood model that transforms tactile data $D$ into a likelihood probability $P(D \mid H_i)$ for a set of perceptual hypotheses $\{H_1, ..., H_N\}$, which could be the labels (e.g. location in mm) for training data used to construct the model. The perceptual decision is then the hypothesis $H_j$ with $j = \arg\max_i P(D \mid H_i)$ that has the maximum likelihood for some sensed tactile data $D$.

Following recent studies with the TacTip, here we use a histogram likelihood model [6,13], which bins the sensor data into intervals and counts bin frequency to form sampling distributions that are multiplied over sensor dimension and time. While simple, this model is effective for the TacTip and other sensors [6,12], bears analogy with neural processing [6] and is fairly robust and efficient. That said, the likelihood model is not the focus of this study, and so any model that works reasonably well would have been sufficient.

**Active Touch:** In active perception, we assume that perceptual decisions are sequential over multiple tactile contacts $D(1), \cdots, D(T)$, with actions being made between contacts to improve the perception. As perception is over multiple contacts, we combine the likelihood model of each contact into a probability using Bayes rule applied recursively after the $t$th contact

$$P(H_i \mid D(t)) = \frac{P(D(t) \mid H_i)\, P(H_i \mid D(t-1))}{\sum_j P(D(t) \mid H_j)\, P(H_j \mid D(t-1))},$$

beginning from flat priors $P(H_i \mid D(0)) = P(H_i) = 1/N$. Here we use a very simple active perception policy, in which actions are taken to move the tactile sensor directly onto the object $x_{\text{fix}}$, which we assume to be in the centre of the training data range $x_{N/2}$. Thus, if the perceptual hypotheses are positions $H_i = x_i$, then the actions are translations $\Delta x(t) = x_{\text{fix}} - x_j(t)$ where $j = \arg\max_i P(D(t) \mid x_i)$. Following past work on biomimetic active perception [6], the decision is made when the probability crosses a decision threshold $P(H_i \mid D(t)) > \theta$ that can be set to give a particular decision time $\bar{T}$ averaged over many decisions.

## 4    Results

### 4.1    TacWhisker Data on a Rod Localization Experiment

The localization capabilities of the actuated TacWhisker array are assessed with an experiment where a (6 mm dia.) rod stimulus is sensed across a (40 mm) range of horizontal locations in the whisker field, motivated by similar experiments in rats examining the neural encoding of location [14]. The sensor oriented with its whiskers pointing vertically downwards with the rod oriented along the rows of the whiskers ($y$-direction in Fig. 5), and rod positions sampled every 1 mm moving from left to right (examples in Fig. 8a, b and c, d). The TacWhisker whisks onto and off the rod by protracting then retracting its whiskers.

In all experiments, good quality data were obtained from the TacWhisker array, as is evident in the smoothly varying sensor readings with signal apparently dominating over noise (Fig. 8).

The unprocessed sensor data is dominated by the whisking motion, visible as the large periodic signals in both the $x$- and $y$-deflection data (Fig. 8a).

**(a) Whisking motion**    **(b) Self-motion compensated**

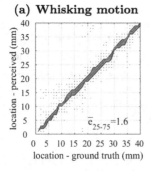
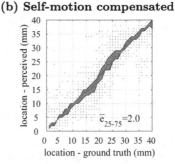

**Fig. 7.** Accuracy of location perception. Monte Carlo 10-fold cross validation (10000 samples), plotting the perceived against ground truth locations (red markers). Variability of location perception is shown between 25th and 75th percentiles (gray region). (Color figure online)

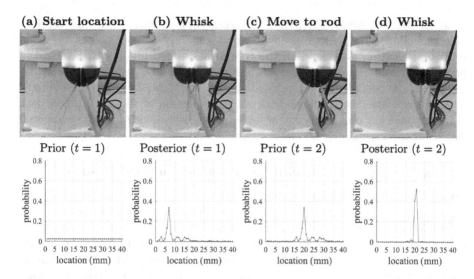

**Fig. 8.** Example of active touch. The TacWhisker array begins to the left of the rod (a), then whisks onto it (b); from an initial estimate of the rod location, the sensor then moves right to centre on the rod (c) and whisks again (d). The according probability distributions over location at each step are shown below. (Color figure online)

Overall, there are two main contributions to the sensor signals: (i) local shear of the sensor surface from the actuation mechanism, resulting in large periodic signals; and (ii) rotational deflection of the pins when whiskers impinge on an object, resulting in smaller perturbations of the whisking signal.

To compensate for the whisking self-motion, a reference signal is subtracted from the sensor data to leave the perturbations due to object contact (Fig. 8b). Whisking data from the centre of the range ($x_i = 20$ mm) is used for this reference, as the rod lies between the two whisker rows when they are fully protracted. This compensation makes a whisker contact more visually apparent, with a clear trend of the right row of whiskers (shown in red) being increasingly deflected as the rod moves to the left of the array, and likewise the left row of whiskers (shown in blue) being increasingly deflected in the negative direction as the rod moves to the right of the array (Fig. 8b).

### 4.2   Location Perception with the Actuated TacWhisker Array

The accuracy of location perception with the TacWhisker array is quantified with a probabilistic classifier that estimates the maximum likelihood of a location from the sensor data (Sec. 3.2). Examples of TacWhisker data at labelled locations $x_i = 1$–$40$ mm are used for training data, from which a histogram model of the data is constructed that used to estimate the likelihoods of an instance of test data. Overall, we collected 10 sets over this location range, using 10-fold cross validation to compare the perceived location with the ground truth.

Both the raw whisking data and the self-motion compensated whisking data appear similarly good for perceiving location (Fig. 7a, b): in both cases, the mean estimated location is centred on the true location (red line), with a spread in perceived locations (red markers) of which the central 50% percentiles are within 1–2 mm of the overall 40 mm range (1.6 mm for raw data; 2.0 mm compensated). These results are in accordance with visual inspection of the TacWhisker data (Fig. 6), which covaries with contact location, consistent with the data being well suited for perceiving location.

## 4.3    Active Localization with the Actuated TacWhisker Array

A simple example of active touch is to localize an object while using intermediate estimates of the object location to move the sensor to a better location on the object for perceiving its location. For a simple object, such as perceiving the location of a rod, a basic active touch strategy is to move the sensor to centre the object within its whisker field. Active touch can then be seen as implementing a control policy (centre the object of interest) while simultaneously perceiving the object, in this case the object's location.

An illustration of active touch for localization in action shows the TacWhisker array beginning off-centre to the left of the rod (Fig. 8a), then whisking (when the right whiskers are deflected in Fig. 8b); from an initial estimate of the rod location, the array then moves to the right to centre (Fig. 8c) and then whisk onto the rod (Fig. 8d). In accordance, before the whisker has contacted the probability of it being at any location is constant (Fig. 8a, prior), after contacting it is a fairly broad distribution peaked to the left of the rod (Fig. 8b, posterior); after moving, the location distribution has the same broad shape shifted to centre on the rod (Fig. 8c, prior), and then after whisking and using Bayes rule to combine the new likelihood distribution with that prior, the posterior distribution becomes more strongly peaked around the rod location (Fig. 8d, posterior).

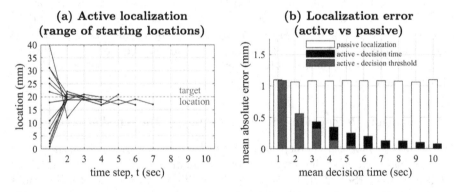

**Fig. 9.** Comparison of active and passive perception of location. Under active localization, the sensor centres itself on the stimulus while perceiving its location (panel a). Experimentally, active perception has a lower mean error at longer decision times (panel b), with a threshold-crossing stopping rule better than a fixed-time rule.

Repeating the active localization experiment over many trials with a range of starting locations, shows that the robot robustly localizes onto the rod (Fig. 9a). The overall decision time is stochastic, because a probability-threshold crossing decision rule is used (Sect. 3.2), in which the accumulated probability for a percept must cross a minimum value before making a decision. Mean location errors for active perception improve with mean decision time (Fig. 9b), reaching near perfect accuracy at a mean decision time of 5 contacts. Conversely mean errors for passive perception remain the same as at the first contact, because the robot then cannot move to gather new data (Fig. 9b, white histogram). Thus, overall, the mean location errors for active perception with a probability-threshold crossing decision rule improves faster with mean decision time than having a preset decision time.

## 5 Discussion

In this paper, we proposed a new design of active tactile whiskered robot, the actuated 'TacWhisker' array, and used the robot to investigate active touch on a simple localization task where the robot orients its array onto a stimulus while perceiving its location. The actuated TacWhisker array has a simple design in which a 3D-printed optical tactile fingertip (the TacTip [10,11]) is modified have whiskers protruding from the tactile surface, with an actuation module that pulls a tendon running through a surface groove to protract the whiskers together (Figs. 3 and 4). Here a morphology comprising two rows of five whiskers was used, although other (symmetric) layouts are readily attainable with this design. The use of a single motor to actuate all whiskers vastly simplifies the robot, and bears analogy with the principal component of rodent whisking which is to synchronously protract and retract all whiskers together.

The tactile robot successfully performed a simple active localization task, where a rod stimulus is placed randomly in the whisker field and the robot moves to whisk directly onto the rod while simultaneously perceiving the rod location (Fig. 8). The control is based on an action selection policy that tries to centre the rod in the middle of the whisker field, based on intermediate estimates of the rod location [6]. Several methods for perceiving location were compared (Fig. 9), and the active localization with a threshold-crossing decision rule found to be best, in that the perceptual errors improved most rapidly with successive whisks (unlike passive perception where the errors did not improve).

Curiously, although the sensing is dominated by the whisker motion, this does not affect performance on this simple task. Comparable localization acuity is attained with and without self-motion compensation (2.0 mm vs 1.6 mm), by subtracting a reference signal that leaves the perturbations due to object contact (Fig. 8b). This raises questions about how the brain solves this problem for rodent whisking, where a related issue of self-motion compensation occurs [15]. That said, this self-motion is likely less pronounced in other whiskered robots (for example, Shrewbot), where the effect appears due primarily to the whiskers' inertia rather than the actuation mechanism.

Our intention is to apply our actuated TacWhisker robot to other active perception tasks. Preliminary results have also shown the TacWhisker is effective on estimating object shape while localizing on the object, using an experiment like the 'where' and 'what' tasks described in Ref. [6]. Moreover, the whiskered robot can also be applied to navigation and exploration tasks, which are primary functions of the rodent whisker system [16]. Overall, the robot promises to give a simple embodiment of whisker-based active touch to give insight into the mechanisms underlying perception in the mammalian brain.

**Acknowledgments.** I thank members of the Tactile Robotics group, including Benjamin Ward-Cherrier, Nicholas Pestell, Kirsty Aquilina, Jasper James and John Lloyd, and also BRL colleagues Martin Pearson and Ben Mitchinson.

# References

1. Ahl, A.S.: The role of vibrissae in behavior: a status review. Vet. Res. Commun. **10**(1), 245–268 (1986)
2. Mitchinson, B., Prescott, T.J.: Whisker movements reveal spatial attention: a unified computational model of active sensing control in the rat. PLoS Comput. Biol. **9**(9), e1003236 (2013)
3. Sofroniew, N., Svoboda, K.: Whisking. Curr. Biol. **25**(4), R137–R140 (2015)
4. Prescott, T.J., Pearson, M.J., Mitchinson, B., Sullivan, J.C.W., Pipe, A.G.: Whisking with robots. IEEE Robot. Autom. Mag. **16**, 42–50 (2009)
5. Pearson, M.J., Mitchinson, B., Sullivan, J.C., Pipe, A.G., Prescott, T.J.: Biomimetic vibrissal sensing for robots. Philos. Trans. R. Soc. B Biol. Sci. **366**(1581), 3085–3096 (2011)
6. Lepora, N.F.: Biomimetic active touch with fingertips and whiskers. IEEE Trans. Haptics **9**(2), 170–183 (2016)
7. Pearson, M.J., Pipe, A.G., Melhuish, C., Mitchinson, B., Prescott, T.J.: Whiskerbot: a robotic active touch system modeled on the rat whisker sensory system. Adapt. Behav. **15**(3), 223–240 (2007)
8. Pearson, M.J., Mitchinson, B., Welsby, J., Pipe, T., Prescott, T.J.: SCRATCHbot: active tactile sensing in a whiskered mobile robot. In: Doncieux, S., Girard, B., Guillot, A., Hallam, J., Meyer, J.-A., Mouret, J.-B. (eds.) SAB 2010. LNCS (LNAI), vol. 6226, pp. 93–103. Springer, Heidelberg (2010). https://doi.org/10.1007/978-3-642-15193-4_9
9. Sullivan, J.C., Mitchinson, B., Pearson, M.J., Evans, M., Lepora, N.F., Fox, C.W., Melhuish, C., Prescott, T.J.: Tactile discrimination using active whisker sensors. IEEE Sens. J. **12**(2), 350–362 (2012)
10. Ward-Cherrier, B., Pestell, N., Cramphorn, L., Winstone, B., Giannaccini, M.E., Rossiter, J., Lepora, N.F.: The tactip family: soft optical tactile sensors with 3d-printed biomimetic morphologies. Soft Robot. **5**(2), 216–227 (2018)
11. Chorley, C., Melhuish, C., Pipe, T., Rossiter, J.: Development of a tactile sensor based on biologically inspired edge encoding. In: International Conference on Advanced Robotics (ICAR), pp. 1–6 (2009)
12. Lepora, N.F., Ward-Cherrier, B.: Superresolution with an optical tactile sensor. In: IEEE/RSJ International Conference on Intelligent Robots and Systems (IROS), pp. 2686–2691 (2015)

13. Lepora, N.F., Sullivan, J.C., Mitchinson, B., Pearson, M., Gurney, K., Prescott, T.J.: Brain-inspired Bayesian perception for biomimetic robot touch. In: IEEE International Conference on Robotics and Automation, pp. 5111–5116 (2012)
14. Diamond, M.E., Von Heimendahl, M., Knutsen, P.M., Kleinfeld, D., Ahissar, E.: 'Where' and 'what' in the whisker sensorimotor system. Nat. Rev. Neurosci. **9**(8), 601–612 (2008)
15. Anderson, S.R., Pearson, M.J., Pipe, A., Prescott, T., Dean, P., Porrill, J.: Adaptive cancelation of self-generated sensory signals in a whisking robot. IEEE Trans. Robot. **26**(6), 1065–1076 (2010)
16. Salman, M., Pearson, M.J.: Advancing whisker based navigation through the implementation of Bio-Inspired whisking strategies. In: IEEE International Conference on Robotics and Biomimetics (ROBIO), pp. 767–773 (2016)

# Implementation of Deep Deterministic Policy Gradients for Controlling Dynamic Bipedal Walking

Chujun Liu[✉], Andrew G. Lonsberry[✉], Mark J. Nandor[✉],
Musa L. Audu[✉], and Roger D. Quinn[✉]

Department of Mechanical and Aerospace Engineering, Case Western Reserve
University, 10900 Euclid Ave., Cleveland, OH 44106, USA
{cxl936,agl10,mjn18,mxa93,roger.quinn}@case.edu
http://biorobots.case.edu/

**Abstract.** A control system for simulated two-dimensional bipedal walking was developed. The biped model was built based on anthropometric data. At the core of the control is a Deep Deterministic Policy Gradients (DDPG) neural network that is trained in GAZEBO, a physics simulator, to predict the ideal foot location to maintain stable walking under external impulse load. Additional controllers for hip joint movement during stance phase, and ankle joint torque during toe-off, help to stabilize the robot during walking. The simulated robot can walk at a steady pace of approximately 1 m/s, and during locomotion it can maintain stability with a 30 N-s impulse applied at the torso. This work implement DDPG algorithm to solve biped walking control problem. The complexity of DDPG network is decreased through carefully selected state variables and distributed control system.

**Keywords:** Biped · DDPG neural network · Gait

## 1 Introduction

A robust control algorithm for biped locomotion is presented as a means to assist individuals with spinal cord injury (SCI). Using Functional Neuro-muscular Stimulation (FNS) and a powered lower limb exoskeleton, locomotion can be restored to such individuals [1,2]. The methods presented are designed to apply control to the powered lower limb exoskeleton. To make the system robust for any user, the control approach must be able to adapt to various sizes of humans [7]. It should thus function with limited information about the human. To accomplish this, exploratory reinforcement based optimization algorithms such as Deep Q-Networks (DQN) can be applied. As biped control is continuous, a variation of DQN called deep deterministic policy gradients (DDPG) [8] will be utilized. In total, three separate controllers are designed to operate together to produce stable walking control. The use of three separate controllers actually reduces the

© Springer International Publishing AG, part of Springer Nature 2018
V. Vouloutsi et al. (Eds.): Living Machines 2018, LNAI 10928, pp. 276–287, 2018.
https://doi.org/10.1007/978-3-319-95972-6_29

complexity of the control system, making the DDPG network easier to train. As degrees of freedom increase, neural networks can have certain issues such as covariate shift [5] and increased training time. Since the application at hand is time sensitive, the speed of learning is crucial [3]. Furthermore, using three separate controllers allows for easy parallelization of the processes and dedicated threading.

For this work, one of the three controllers is a trained DDPG network and the other two are conventional PID feedback controller and an open loop controller.

## 2    Methods

A DDPG network is trained to work in conjunction with two other PID feedback controllers. DDPG is a model free policy learning algorithm. It consists of an actor network that updates the policy parameters, and a critic network that estimates the action-value function. DDPG uses the expected gradient of the action-value function as a policy gradient instead of a stochastic policy gradient so as to estimate the correct gradient much more efficiently. [8] Below we introduce the model, the simulation environment, the target locomotion, and the controllers.

### 2.1    Biped Model

A biped model, based partially on anthropometric data, is used in simulation to both train and verify the effectiveness of the DDPG network. The model contains 7 rigid bodies: the torso as well as the left and right thigh, shank, and foot. Additionally, the model has the following 6 joints: left and right hip, knees, and ankles. The hip and ankle joints can rotate along both the x and y axises. Two frictionless walls are added in the simulation environment to constrain biped in two-dimension, so x axis rotation of the ankle is the major. There is a small gap between the biped and the wall which can cause the biped to slight tilt sideways. This gap is left intentionally, because this will reduce the impact generate by the imperfection collision model in ODE(open dynamic engine). So y axis rotation of the ankle is kept because so the foot can have a solid contact with ground when biped is tilting sideways. The knees are constrained to just the x axis, giving the system a total of 10 degrees of freedom. The proportion of mass and length of the biped's bodies are found from anthropometric data, while the shape and the rotary inertia of the bodies are simplified to a regular box shape to speed simulations. All the components are proportional to the height, thus making resizing of the simulated biped easier. In this work, the height is set at 1.8 m. A simulated IMU sensor is attached to the center of the torso to measure its velocity and acceleration. This replicates what might be implemented on a powered exoskeleton. Touch sensors are added on both the left and right feet to detect ground contact and contact force. All joint angles and joint velocities can be directly read from the simulation environment.

## 2.2  Simulation Environment

The biped is simulated using GAZEBO and controlled by ROS (Robot Operating System). GAZEBO is an open source simulator, while ROS is a set of software libraries and convenient tools used for robotic systems. ROS has become a popular platform for robotics research [4]. Joint movement is controlled in the simulation in two ways. Firstly, we can call an "ApplyJointEffort" ROS service directly to set a torque value for some duration. Secondly, we use GAZEBO's controller plug-in. The controller plug-in provides three different PID control methods: torque feedback, velocity feedback and position feedback. In this work, the plug-in's velocity feedback control is utilized. The PID parameters are tuned to react in a fast and stable manner. For the work here we focus on constrained locomotion. The 10 DOF biped is restricted by two frictionless walls to prevent any lateral movement, constraining the model to only move in sagittal plane.

## 2.3  Target Locomotion

Human gait is a complex process. [6,11] The target gait is simplified into 4 sections for each leg: early swing, terminal swing, stance, and toe-off as depicted in Fig. 1.

**Fig. 1.** Simplified gait cycle for right leg

**Early Swing.** Through this phase, the thigh will swing forward. The knee is bent to prevent the swing foot from hitting the ground. The swing angle of the hip joint and the duration of the swing is determined by the output of the reinforcement learning process.

**Terminal Swing.** Following early swing, the hip joint is locked for a short duration allowing the knee to straighten. This move is in preparation for making ground contact.

**Stance.** Once the foot touches the ground, the biped will rotate around the ankle joint like an inverted pendulum. The hip joint is then unlocked. A PID controller is tuned to control the torso pitch via control of hip joint velocity.

**Toe-Off.** The stance of the current leg will end when the opposite foot makes contact with the ground and enters its stance phase. The current leg will enter the toe-off phase. To do so, a torque is applied to the ankle joint to drive the foot to push off. This pushing action will propel the biped forward. The amount of the torque is determined by the current walking speed. Following the pushing action, a torque is applied on the ankle joint to quickly retract the foot from the ground.

### 2.4 Control

**DDPG.** In this work the DDPG network is used to control the step length and step duration in the forward swing phase.It was previously believed that the deterministic policy gradient of a model free network did not exist, but later it is proved that it does indeed exist [8] and is easier to compute than stochastic policy gradient for it only need to integrate in the state space. The deterministic policy gradient is:

$$\nabla_\theta J(\pi_\theta) = \int_S \rho^\pi(s) \nabla_\theta \pi_\theta(s) \nabla_a Q^\pi(s,a)|_{a=\pi_\theta(s)} ds \tag{1}$$

the deterministic policy gradient can be treated as two parts. One is the gradient of the action value to actions, and another is the gradient of the policy to the policy parameters. DDPG uses actor critic framework. The action value is approximate by critic using a DNN. The parameter of the network is update using temporal-difference method in the similar way as traditional actor-critic. The actor also uses a DNN as policy. The policy parameters are update by deterministic policy gradient $\nabla_\theta J(\pi_\theta)$. DDPG also uses replay buffer to store transitions to break correlation in the sample trajectory. When training the actor network, the policy will change constantly. So the temporal difference is calculated by a copy of the actor, critic network. It is called target network. These network only update after a period of time, or update at a very small changes. This off policy method allow the behavior to be more stochastic to explore the environment and keep the prediction deterministic. The target network is update by soft replacement method.

$$\theta' \leftarrow \tau\theta + (1-\tau)\theta' \tag{2}$$

The full biped system state, includes position, velocity, and acceleration terms for all 10 degrees of freedom. This many inputs can lead to network convergence issues and require the use of a very large network to sufficiently understand the interaction of the different state variables together. We simplify the input. As the biped will never leave the ground during normal operation, walking is limited to the sagittal plane by frictionless rails in the simulation, and lastly there exists a controller to stabilize torso pitch angle, we reduce the model to include only the following: $\phi$: torso pitch angle, $v$: torso forward speed, $l$: the actual step length and $d_{zmp}$: the distance between the ZMP and the foot. The input of the network, state $s$, is,

$$s = [v, \phi, d_{zmp}, l]. \tag{3}$$

Note that the "existing controller for torso pitch" is a PID that controls the torso pitch through the hip joint velocity. This controller will be explained in the next subsection (Fig. 2).

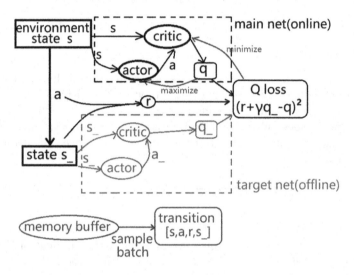

**Fig. 2.** The critic and actor network (evaluate/target) both have two hidden layers, the first layer has 400 neurons and the second layer has 300 neurons. The activation function is Relu. And the output of the actor network goes through a tanh activation function. The network has a memory of 70000 step. The learning rate of the actor and critic are set to be 1e-8 and 2e-8. The reward discount is set to 0.99. The training batch is 32 samples.

ZMP has been often used in biped control to evaluate the stability of the system and to drive control algorithms. If the ZMP is outside the support area, the biped can tip over and fall [9]. The state variables phi and v are measured by the IMU sensor attached to the torso. The step length l can be calculated from the forward kinematics in real robot, in simulation, it can be read directly from GAZEBO. ZMP is calculated after measuring the acceleration. From Cart-Table Model:

$$y_{zmp} = y_{com} - \frac{\ddot{y}_{com}}{g} z_{com}. \tag{4}$$

Although the biped is in a simulated environment, the acceleration measured by the IMU has noise due to the surface contact model from physics engine itself.

This noise must be filtered before the value can be used in any calculation. In this work, a mean value and Kalman filter is used on the acceleration data [10]. This is important because, in a physical system, the measurements of the acceleration are often extremely noisy as well. The state is updated at the moment when the front foot contacts the ground, then passed to the network which returns an action. Decaying noise is added to the action chosen to promote initial exploration but then allows refinement over time,

$$a' \sim (N, \sigma^2). \tag{5}$$

Once training is completed the system will run forward without additional noise added to the action selection (Fig. 3).

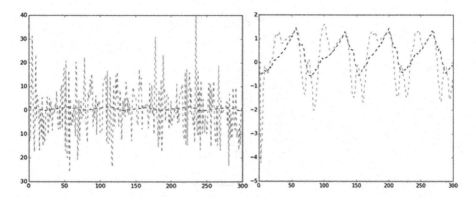

**Fig. 3.** Before and after the filter. Blue line is the acceleration. Red line is the velocity (Color figure online)

The trained network decides how far and how fast to put the next step based on the velocity, torso pitch angle, step length and ZMP position of the previous step. This way, the network requires less state input. It is noted the states are only sampled with every foot step. Consequently, if there is any major disturbance in between two foot steps, the network will not respond in time to compare with other more quickly updated systems. The network must wait until the foot touches the ground to update the state. But since the output of the network is the length and duration of the next step, as long as the biped won't fall between two steps, it can counter the disturbance by adjusting the output of the next step. To speed up the training, the output is initialized based on Height-to-Stride-Length Ratio. A better starting point makes the network converge more quickly.

In order to train the control network using a reinforcement learning approach, a reward function is created to indicate if the actions taken by the controller are either good or bad. The reward function used here takes into consideration the same variables as the state vector, where every element is normalized and weighted. The weights of every factor can change and the network will try to maximize the most weighted factor at first.

**Stance Controller.** When the foot touches the ground, the biped will start to rotate around the ankle joint. In this phase, the hip joint needs to move according to the ankle joint to keep the torso up straight and provide power to drive the torso forward. The output of the controller here deemed the "stance controller" is the angular velocity of the hip joint. The goal is to keep the torso upright without overshoot which would cause the torso to pitch back and forth jeopardizing stability. Ideally the torso is pitched slightly forward to maintain momentum and a smooth natural walking gait. To achieve this, a proportional controller is designed, and the residual error from the controller will allow the torso to slightly pitch away from the z axis (Fig. 4).

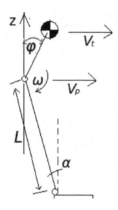

**Fig. 4.** Biped in stance phase

With the torso pitch remaining constant with respect to the z axis, the horizontal velocity of the hip will be the same as the horizontal velocity of the torso center. Given the following,

$$v_t = v_p, \tag{6}$$

and,

$$\omega = -\dot{\alpha}, \tag{7}$$

the angular velocity of the ankle can be read directly. The moment when the foot impacts the ground, noise will be introduced. So the angular velocity of the ankle is calculated by,

$$\dot{\alpha} = \frac{v_p}{\cos \alpha * L}. \tag{8}$$

We thus design a controller given that,

$$\omega = K * \phi = -\dot{\alpha}, \tag{9}$$

where if the pitch angle is larger than the target pitch,

$$\phi > \phi_0, \tag{10}$$

then,

$$|\omega| > |\dot{\alpha}|. \tag{11}$$

Thus the pitch angle will decrease and vice versa. The control gain K will be,

$$K = \frac{-\dot{\alpha}}{\phi_0} = \frac{-v_p}{\cos\alpha * L * \phi_0}, \tag{12}$$

where target pitch is chosen to be close to zero,

$$\phi_0 = 0.02. \tag{13}$$

it cannot be too close to zero, otherwise it will produce a very large gain, causing the system to be sensitive to noise.

**Ankle Torque Control.** The ankle joint is passive except in the toe-off phase. The advantages of setting the ankle to be a passive joint are as follows: (1) smoother ground contact for the foot; (2) dynamic property of the inverted pendulum is maintained; (3) minimal force is needed to drive the biped around the ankle when the foot is in contact with the ground; and (4) total noise of the system is reduced. The damping coefficient of the ankle is set to 1. This amount of damping helps to absorb the impact from the ground contact without hindering the swing motion (Fig. 5).

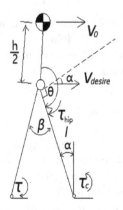

Fig. 5. Biped in toe-off phase

In the toe-off phase, a torque is applied on the ankle to propel the biped forward. The torque is determined by the current walking speed. The goal is to maintain the momentum of the biped within a certain range. If the desired walking speed is given then,

$$\Delta v = v_0 - v_{desire}, \tag{14}$$

and if the torso pitch remains constant, then the angular velocity of the torso is zero,

$$\omega_{torso} = 0. \tag{15}$$

Subsequently the velocity of the hip is equivalent to the velocity of the center of the torso,

$$\Delta v_{center} = \Delta v_{hip}. \tag{16}$$

assuming the toe-off phase is very short, the hip joint angle of the rear leg keeps the same during toe-off, and the momentum of the rear foot can be overlooked. To keep the torso angular velocity $\omega_{torso} = 0$, a torque$\tau_{hip}$ must act on the hip joint of the front leg.

$$\tau_{hip} * \Delta t = J_{torso} * \Delta \dot{\alpha}, \tag{17}$$

$$J_{torso} \approx \frac{1}{3}mh^2 \tag{18}$$

About the front foot ankle joint we have the following,

$$(\tau - \tau_c - \tau_{hip}) * \Delta t = J_{leg} * \Delta \dot{\alpha} \tag{19}$$

$$\Delta \dot{\alpha} = \frac{\Delta v_{hip}/\cos \alpha}{l} \tag{20}$$

$$J_{leg} \approx \frac{1}{12}m_l l^2 + m_l[l^2 sin^2\beta + (l \cos \beta - \frac{l}{2})^2] + \frac{1}{3}m_l l^2, \tag{21}$$

$$\tau_c = c * \dot{\alpha}, \tag{22}$$

$J_{leg}$ is the Moment of inertia of front and rear leg about front ankle joint. $c$ is the damping coefficient of the ankle joint.

This controller in the future could also be changed to a network trained using the reinforcement learning paradigm.

## 3    Results and Conclusion

The average walking speed of the biped was approximately 1 m/s. The maximum recorded speed occurs just before the front foot contacts the ground, when the stance leg is perpendicular to the ground. To test the stability of the biped while walking an impulse was applied to different locations on the robot. It was found that the biped was able to remain stable and continue walking after a maximum impulse of 30 N-s was applied to the back of the robot as well as after a maximum impulse of 40 N-s was applied to the front of the robot. During testing all impulses were applied for a duration of 0.1 s. It can be seen in Fig. 6, that after applying the impulse, the robot's velocity drastically increases or decreases, depending on the direction of the impulse, but then returns to a consistent oscillation in less than 5 s. Keeping the pitch of the torso below −0.15 rad during walking, keeps the oscillation less than 0.1 rad. It was found experimentally that the biped was able to resist larger disturbances when the robot was in the toe-off phase of the gait compared to the forward-swing. Increasing the target walking speed $v_{desire}$

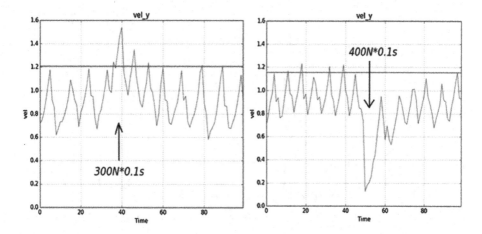

**Fig. 6.** Biped velocity response under impulse load

and lowering the damping coefficient of the ankle joint were shown to increase
the overall speed of the robot but reduced the robustness of the system causing
instability at lower impulses (Fig. 7).

In Fig. 8 it can be seen that a positive impulse disturbance applied to the
biped will cause an increase in torso speed. To recover from this disturbance the
DDPG network increases step length and decreases step duration accordingly
to regain stability. When a negative impulse is applied to the biped, the DDPG
network reduces step length and increases step duration to adapt to a lower
speed. All the adjustments made by the DDPG network to retain stability were

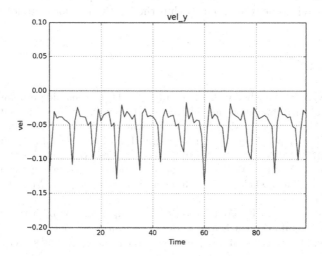

**Fig. 7.** Torso pitch angle during normal walking

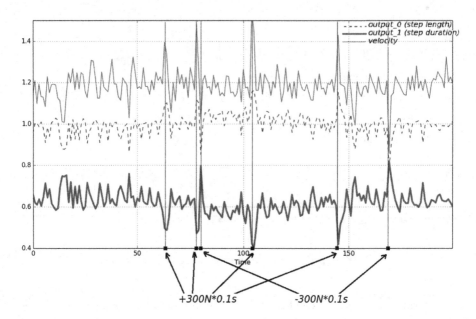

**Fig. 8.** DDPG network output at different torso speed

learned purely by experience without prior knowledge. When training the DDPG network, a large memory storage is necessary. The simplified input state proved to be sufficient to train a successful network.

An even further simplified state input $s = [d_{zmp}, \phi]$ was additionally used to train a network with the same parameters, but only but even after extended training period, it did not converge. The over-simplified state input cannot describe the environment adequately thus the DDPG network cannot make right decision.

## References

1. Lonsberry, A.G., Lonsberry, A.J., Quinn, R.D.: Deep dynamic programming: optimal control with continuous model learning of a nonlinear muscle actuated arm. In: Mangan, M., Cutkosky, M., Mura, A., Verschure, P.F.M.J., Prescott, T., Lepora, N. (eds.) Living Machines 2017. LNCS (LNAI), vol. 10384, pp. 255–266. Springer, Cham (2017). https://doi.org/10.1007/978-3-319-63537-8_22
2. Chang, S.R., Nandor, M.J., Li, L., et al.: A muscle-driven approach to restore stepping with an exoskeleton for individuals with paraplegia. J. NeuroEng. Rehabil. **14**, 48 (2017)
3. Morimoto, J., Doya, K.: Acquisition of stand-up behavior by a real robot using hierarchical reinforcement learning. Robot. Auton. Syst. **36**(1), 37–51 (2001)
4. Cashmore, M., et al.: ROSPlan: planning in the robot operating system. In: ICAPS (2015)
5. Ioffe, S., Szegedy, C.: Batch normalization: accelerating deep network training by reducing internal covariate shift. arXiv preprint arXiv:1502.03167 (2015)

6. Hausdorff, J.M., Peng, C.K., Ladin, Z.V.I., Wei, J.Y., Goldberger, A.L.: Is walking a random walk? Evidence for long-range correlations in stride interval of human gait. J. Appl. Physiol. **78**(1), 349–358 (1995)
7. Sepulveda, F., Wells, D.M., Vaughan, C.L.: A neural network representation of electromyography and joint dynamics in human gait. J. Biomech. **26**(2), 101–109 (1993)
8. Silver, D., Lever, G., Heess, N., Degris, T., Wierstra, D., Riedmiller, M.: Deterministic policy gradient algorithms. In: ICML, June 2014
9. Vukobratović, M., Borovac, B.: Zero-moment point-thirty five years of its life. Int. J. humanoid Robot. **1**(01), 157–173 (2004)
10. Grewal, M.S.: Kalman filtering. In: Lovric, M. (ed.) International Encyclopedia of Statistical Science, pp. 705–708. Springer, Heidelberg (2011). https://doi.org/10. 1007/978-3-642-04898-2
11. Song, S., Geyer, H.: Evaluation of a neuromechanical walking control model using disturbance experiments. Front. Comput. Neurosci. **11**, 15 (2017)

# Investigation of Tip Extrusion as an Additive Manufacturing Strategy for Growing Robots

Dario Lunni[1,2(✉)], Emanuela Del Dottore[1], Ali Sadeghi[1],
Matteo Cianchetti[2], Edoardo Sinibaldi[1], and Barbara Mazzolai[1(✉)]

[1] Center for Micro-BioRobotics, Istituto Italiano di Tecnologia,
Polo SantAnna Valdera, Via Rinaldo Piaggio 34, 56025 Pontedera, Pisa, Italy
{dario.lunni,barbara.mazzolai}@iit.it
[2] The BioRobotics Institute, Scuola Superiore Sant Anna,
Polo SantAnna Valdera, Via Rinaldo Piaggio 34, 56025 Pontedera, Pisa, Italy
d.lunni@santannapisa.it

**Abstract.** This paper presents a new design for material extrusion as embeddable additive manufacturing technology for growing robots inspired by plant roots. The conceptual design is proposed and based on the deposition of thermoplastic material a complete layer at a time. To guide the design of the system, we first studied the thermal properties through approximated models considering PLA (poly-lactic acid) as feeding material. The final shape and constituent materials are then accordingly selected. We obtained a simple design that allows miniaturization and a fast assembly of the system, and we demonstrate the feasibility of the design by testing the assembled system. We also show the accuracy of our thermal prediction by comparing the thermal distribution obtained from FEM simulations with experimental data, obtaining a maximal error of $\sim 8\ °C$. Preliminary experimental growth results are encouraging regarding the potentialities of this approach that can potentially achieve $0.15 \div 0.30$ mm/s of growth speed. Our results suggest that this strategy can be explored and exploited for enabling the growth from the tip of artificial systems enouncing robots' plasticity.

**Keywords:** Additive manufacturing · Growing robot · Bioinspiration

## 1 Introduction

To bring autonomous robots in our everyday life, we need flexible and intelligent solutions able to cope with unpredictable changes in the environment and to adapt to different task needs. This way, the new applications of robotics appears to radically diverge from the classical robotic approach, oriented to the optimization of a specific industrial process [1]. The advent of these emergent paradigms and rules in robotics requires new methodologies to engineer continuously adaptable artificial systems. Bioinspiration helps in rethinking robotics outside factories and in pushing towards the understanding of principles behind locomotion, adaptation or morphological change and aggregation of natural systems; as well as in using such natural principles as guidelines to build their artificial counterpart [2].

© Springer International Publishing AG, part of Springer Nature 2018
V. Vouloutsi et al. (Eds.): Living Machines 2018, LNAI 10928, pp. 288–299, 2018.
https://doi.org/10.1007/978-3-319-95972-6_30

Nature has endowed living systems with the ability to adapt their bodies, for instance, to pass through small apertures with soft and squeezing bodies (e.g. worms), evolve with different shapes (e.g. metamorphosis from worm to butterfly), or adapt dimensions and growing directions to environmental stimuli (e.g. plant roots), this suggests that a predefined and completely rigid structure can limit robot functionalities in unstructured environments [3].

Probably the first attempt to rethink the design of robots for enouncing their adaptability taking inspiration from Nature was made by Fukuda with the concept of a Dynamic Reconfigurable Robotic System [4], giving rise to the new field of cellular robotics, whose aim is to obtain robots with a non-predefined shape. Based on this concept, a single robot can be composed of multiple modules, resembling simple units like cells composing a tissue, each implementing simple functionalities, letting the intelligence of the system emerge from the interaction among the modules (or cells) [5] moreover, often the assembly is guided by rules extracted from organization strategies of living systems [6]. The robots developed in this field demonstrate to be highly adaptable thanks to self-assembly and self-reconfigurable properties [7–9]. By the rearrangement of the modules, the same robot modifies its shape for several purposes and to accomplish different tasks, for instance achieving different gaits of locomotion [10, 11], manipulation [12], or reproducing several kinds of furniture [13].

In this context, the system's functionality is not limited by an initial design; however, a limit is imposed on the possible configurations by the mechanical design and latching mechanisms. This issue was discussed by Lipson and Pollack in [14], who proposed the idea of a continuously self-designing reconfigurable robot. The authors implemented this concept by computationally evolving a design for the robot's body together with its control and by printing with a commercial 3D-printer the components of the robot's body, and then manually assembling it. Although this approach did not allow integrating additive manufacturing technology directly as part of the robot, additive manufacturing enables the fabrication of bodies otherwise potentially difficult to manufacture with classical techniques (e.g. molding or assembling).

The potential of additive manufacturing has been exploited in robotics for instance for the fabrication of the robots' body [15] or components (e.g., soft skin [16]), to assist and enhance robot functionalities allowing the robot to self-build its tools or grippers [17, 18], or enabling its locomotion [19, 20].

Specifically, in [20], taking inspiration by plant growth strategies, the authors implemented a root-like growing robot that directly embeds a 3D-printer based mechanism in its tip for the deposition of new material in the apical zone of the robot (Fig. 1). Analogously, plant roots move within the soil by adding material in the meristem zone [21]: the division and elongation of the cells behind the root apex allows the apex itself to penetrate through the soil reducing pressure [22], navigate the environment [23] and dynamically adapt the morphology of the root apparatus [24].

In the case of [20], additive manufacturing, specifically Fused Deposition Modeling (FDM), has enabled the robot to self-build its body (a tubular structure), while continuously pushing forward the exploratory tip. The obtained tubular structure can be used as a communication channel for the transmission of data from a sensorized tip, in environment monitoring tasks, or for the passing of food or oxygen, in rescue scenarios, considering also the coordinated movements of multiple roots.

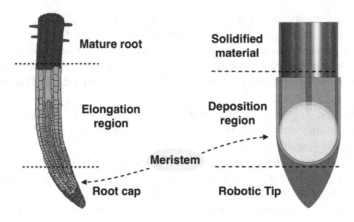

**Fig. 1.** Biological root system and artificial robotic system in comparison highlighting similarities between characteristic zones.

Following the idea of exploiting additive manufacturing technologies to enhance robotic solutions with growing capabilities, in this paper, we propose a simplified version of manufacturing approach with respect to [20] aimed at reducing the number of components to be assembled (e.g. number of motors), while at the same time allowing the miniaturization of the system. Differently from the classical FDM, where the melted material is deposited sequentially in a layer, here, we propose a shaping strategy similar to the extrusion technique, preserving the employment of thermoplastic material (specifically PLA - poly-lactic acid). In fact, every single layer is plotted and cooled all at once, allowing to speed up the movements of the robot.

The paper is organized as follow: Sect. 2.1 presents the conceptual design of the system, Sect. 2.2 describes the final design used as prototype, Sect. 2.3 shows the FEM model used to predict the temperature distribution and the experimental setup for validation, Sect. 3 presents the results of thermal validation, Sect. 4 discusses results and some improvements that should be implemented and Sect. 5 has conclusive remarks.

## 2   Materials and Methods

### 2.1   Conceptual Design of the Tip Extruder

To obtain the deposition of new material circularly all at once, a precise and well-localized control of the temperature is needed. Ideally, three different thermal zones should be present in the system to manage the transition of the material from solid, melted and solid state again. There are three main thermal regions that can be identified in the system (Fig. 2a): heating, melting and cooling zone. The thermoplastic material enters in the system through an axial channel; it passes through the heating zone and reaches the melting temperature allowing the material to change its shape in the melting region. Here, the material is radially pushed and then passes through a cooling region, where it cools down to reach the solid state again at the solidifying section and constitute a stable base for the next layer to be deposited. The working principle of the movement is depicted in Fig. 2b–d: the push of the feeding material ($F_{feed}$) pressurizes the material present in the melting zone, if the forces exerted by the pressurized melted material on the solidified extruded material ($F_{grow}$) are greater than the external forces exercised on the tip ($F_{ext}$) (e.g., friction if moving in a medium, or gravity if moving in air), the tip will move in the same direction of the feeding material.

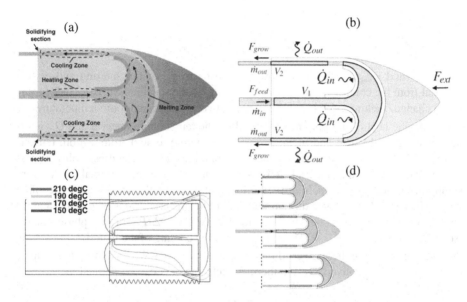

**Fig. 2.** Expected thermal distribution and conceptual design. In (a) it is depicted the conceptual design with the different desired thermal zones. In (b) the forces acting on the growing system and the heat fluxes acting on the control volumes are shown, in (c) the isothermal contours dividing these estimated thermal zones using the thermo-fluid-dynamics model are shown. While in (d) the growing principle and direction of movement are depicted.

In this perspective and with the aim to obtain a simple assembly of the system, an accurate design of each component is fundamental and tightly connected with the distribution of the temperature within the system. To predict the behavior of the material during the heat exchange, we developed mathematical models considering PLA (poly-lactic acid) as feeding material (melting temperature $\sim 180$ °C) and considering the heat exchange of the system with the environment at 25 °C. The PLA has been chosen because of its cheapness, availability and well known thermal properties since widely used as feeding material in commercial 3D printers. Firstly, an analytical analysis was carried out to understand preliminarily the general requirements of the design. To verify the temperature distribution and the behavior of an approximate geometry of the system, thermo-fluid-dynamics FEM simulations were carried out using COMSOL software (v5.0), considering as structural materials Aluminum (used for its conductivity) and PTFE (Polytetrafluoroethylene) (adopted for its resistance to high temperatures) as discussed in Sect. 2.2. In particular, these simulations allowed an approximate estimation of thermal source temperature, mass flow rate and power thermal consumption (Fig. 2c).

Analytically, we modeled the heating phase of the material considering an energy balance in the heating and melting zone $(V_1)$ of the system. Assuming, the heat exchange and a mass balance with constant density, the energy balance can be described by:

$$\dot{m}_{in} = \dot{m}_{out} = \dot{m} \tag{1}$$

$$\dot{Q}_{in} = \dot{m}\left(C_p \Delta T + \Delta H_m\right) \tag{2}$$

where $\dot{m}_{in}$ and $\dot{m}_{out}$ are the mass flow rates respectively of the entering and exiting material from the control volume, $\Delta H_m$ ($\sim 45$ J/g) is the specific heat necessary for the phase change (melting), $\Delta T$ is the difference between source and room temperature, $C_p$ is the specific heat of the polymer averaged on the temperature interval and $\dot{Q}_{in}$ is the heat entering in the heat and melting zone. Considering to start from a room temperature of 25 °C up to an internal source temperature of 230 °C, and assuming a mass rate of 0.04 g/s for the material, it is possible to estimate the minimal power consumption needed for the melting of the material as $\sim 12$ W. To design the cooling zone, which should guarantee the solidification of the material, we used Eqs. (1) and (2) applied on the cooling zone $(V_2)$ considering $\Delta H_s = -\Delta H_m$ for the phase change (solidification) and $\Delta T = -90$ °C to account for the cooling of the material. Preserving the same mass rate $\dot{m}$, the power to dissipate is $\dot{Q}_{out} = \sim 9$ W. Assuming to dissipate the heat by natural convection, the thermal exchange area can be defined as:

$$A = \frac{\dot{Q}_{out}}{h(T_c - T_{amb})} \tag{3}$$

where $h$ is the value of convective exchange parameter in free air ($h = 15$ W/(m$^2$K)), $\dot{Q}_{out}$ is the dissipated power, $T_c$ is the average temperature of the cooler component and $T_{amb}$ is the environment temperature. In order to be able to solidify the fused material, the exchange area can be estimated as A $= 6.04 \cdot 10^{-3}$ mm$^2$.

For this preliminary evaluation, we built an approximated axis symmetrical geometry in order to decrease the computational costs. The temperature of the source was kept at 230 °C and the speed of the feeding material at the entrance of the heater was imposed at 13 mm/s to allow obtaining the thermal distribution shown in Fig. 2c.

## 2.2   Design and Prototyping

The final design includes four principal components: base, heater, hat and cooler (Fig. 3a). We prototyped the proposed design using classical fabrication techniques and assembling it with six screws (Fig. 3b).

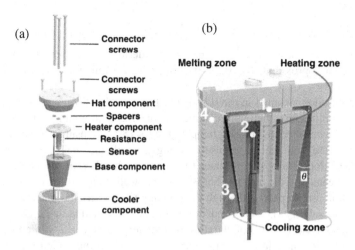

**Fig. 3.** Design of the system. In (a) a view of the assembled is shown; while in (b) the assembled design is presented highlighting the different thermal zones; the numbered with white dots localize the position of the sensors used to validate the thermal model.

The base component is used to receive the feeding material and to support the whole assembly. It should resist to compression at high temperature and it needs to have a good thermal insulation. For these reasons, PTFE (Polytetrafluoroethylene) was chosen as the constituent material for the base. The heating system was composed of a resistance (2.5 $\Omega$) made of NiCr alloy which was heated using Joule effect. The heating power was controlled through Pulse Width Modulation (PWM) managing the current of a 10 V power source. A temperature sensor (Negative Thermal Coefficient Thermistor) is integrated into the base to close the temperature control loop. An Arduino$^{TM}$ MEGA 2560 was used to control the heating mechanism and the temperature sensor value was used as feedback for the implemented PI temperature control. The parameters of the control system were tuned approximating the step response of the system with a first-order dynamic system ($\tau = 500$ s) and choosing the parameter to achieve the desired response time.

To define the geometry of the base, we considered the friction between the deposited material and the structural material. In fact, by preliminary experimental prototypes, we observed the shrinking of the solidifying material, inducing the deposited material and the base to get in contact increasing the friction. To minimize this source of dissipation, we used low friction material and geometrical precautions. In particular, the external part of the base was designed with a variable section in order to avoid this increment of friction. The dimension of the sections was chosen considering an approximated friction coefficient between the base component and the moving plastic material. Specifically, we defined the inclination of the lateral walls to exploit the shrinkage of the material and to obtain a sliding movement of the material itself. To obtain this sliding, the angle of inclination of the lateral wall $\theta$ (Fig. 3b) needs to be greater than the angle of the friction cone of the base:

$$\theta > \tan^{-1}(\mu). \tag{4}$$

The friction coefficient $\mu$ was evaluated considering the contact of PTFE and the sliding material approximated as static friction; thus, assuming a value of $\mu \cong 0.14$, it results $\theta > 8\,^\circ$.

A central hollow channel in the base is used to pass the raw material to the heater. The heater is built with a thermally conductive material (aluminum) and is activated to reach the PLA characteristic melting temperature ($\sim 180\,^\circ C$), using a resistance located between the base and the heater itself. Being pushed, the melted material moves, increases its temperature and reaches the melting chamber of the system, placed between the heater and the hat. The hat is used as a wall, to invert the movement of the melted material and to push it through the cooling zone where the material can finally cool down and solidify. The hat needs to be thermally insulating and characterized by low friction, so again PTFE (Polytetrafluoroethylene) was selected, while the cooler is made of conductive material (aluminum) and endowed with fins increasing the thermal exchanging area.

## 2.3  Thermal Behavior Validation

We performed FEM simulations using COMSOL software to verify the temperature distribution that can be obtained with the chosen design. The simulation results were compared with temperature measurements acquired experimentally on the prototype while heating without the passage of PLA.

A pure thermal 3D model was built up to accurately simulate the presence of the conductive connectors in the assembly. The accurate geometry of the proposed design (Fig. 3) was taken into account and the thermal and mechanical properties of the materials used for the fabrication were considered. The external boundary conditions were chosen considering the thermal environment in which the prototype is placed. So, in the external limits of the system we considered an outgoing thermal flux by natural convection of air at room temperature. Finally, the thermal source was simulated as heat power source generated in the dominion occupied by the component called heater, allowing in this way a time-dependent study.

On the prototype, the temperature was measured at different points: one along the external surface and three in the internal structure, one for each thermal zone, as depicted in Fig. 3b. Three experiments (each lasting $T_{exp} \sim 3500$ s) have been carried out and the temperature acquired every 0.5 s ($\Delta t$). For each sensor position, the experimental temperature, averaged over the repetitions, was calculated for each interval of time ($T_s(t)$). These values of $T_s(t)$ were then compared with the expected temperatures $T_e(t)$ in the system as obtained by the model to calculate the errors:

$$\varepsilon(t) = |T_s(t) - T_e(t)|. \tag{5}$$

For each sensor position, the final temperature error was averaged on the steady-state condition of the system reached approximately after 2500 s.

# 3   Results

As introduced in Sect. 2.3, the analysis of the thermal distribution was predicted using a time-dependent simulation, considering a heating flux as source (6 W) (Fig. 4b). After reaching the steady-state condition, we can observe a good agreement between the thermal distribution predicted by the FEM simulation (Fig. 4a) and the expected one (Fig. 2).

**Table 1.** The obtained final errors between expected and experimental temperature for each monitored location in the system, averaged over the region of steady state.

| Sensor | 1 | 2 | 3 | 4 |
|---|---|---|---|---|
| Averaged Error $\varepsilon_f$ (°C) | 8.3 | 5.6 | 2.4 | 3.2 |

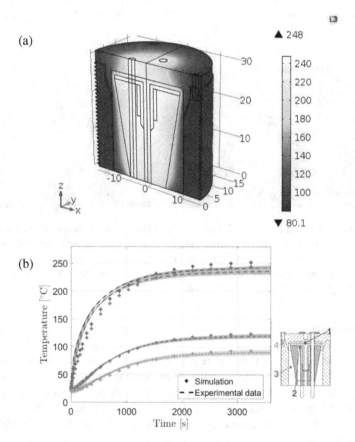

**Fig. 4.** Thermal simulation considering a 3D model of the real system. The screw connectors are considered in these simulations. In (a) the results of thermal prediction at steady state; in (b) the thermal simulation and experimental data obtained along time in four different positions of the system.

The thermal behavior in time predicted by the model is instead plotted in Fig. 4b (cross markers) for each of the four positions. Simulated results are then compared with experimental data (dashed lines), obtained on the assembled system (all the fabricated components are depicted in Fig. 5a and the assembled system in Fig. 5b). As observable in the plot, the temperature of the heating and cooling zone is lower than the melting temperature of the material ($\sim 180$ °C), while higher temperature is found in the melting zone, and for each location we obtained a good agreement between simulated and experimental results, with a maximal error of $\sim 8$ °C. The errors between expected and experimental temperatures are presented in Table 1.

Finally, we tested the assembled system with the PLA filament to verify the thermal distribution and usability of the system. The system with an extrusion of $\sim 4.5$ cm is presented in Fig. 5. Figure 5a depicts the real disassembled system used for the experimental tests. Figure 5b shows the complete system assembled with part of the obtained extrusion coming out from the cooling zone surrounded by the cooler. Figure 5c presents instead the same extrusion without the external cooler. The feeding material has melted and has reached the cooling zone becoming solid in the predicted part of the system.

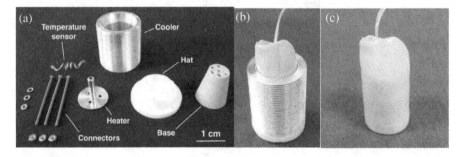

**Fig. 5.** The realized final design. In (a) the disassembled system is shown. In (b) the complete assembled system is shown after experimental tests. In (c) the complete extruded structure is presented without the cooling component of the system. The yellow material was extruded and solidified moving away from the cooler, above the extruded material it is possible to see the electrical connection of the temperature sensor.

## 4   Discussions

As already assessed in Sect. 3, the results predicted by the developed models are confirmed by the experimental results. Thus, demonstrating the effectiveness of embedding additive manufacturing techniques in the artificial system and use them as a strategy for self-growing robots. In particular, the results demonstrate the feasibility of a system that allows the simultaneous deposition of a thermoplastic material on the whole section.

The proposed design and implementation certainly present some issues. Firstly, to choose the direction of growth, and perform a bending, an accurate control on the viscosity of the extruded material should be achieved. A possible way to achieve this could be a differential control of the temperature distribution in the cooling zone, achieved by using, for instance, three different cooling chambers. Secondly, the energy efficiency still remains an issue, in fact the high temperatures used to extrude the thermoplastic material needs to be preserved constant during the whole operation. A possible solution reducing the impact of energy consumption could be the employment of a polymer with a lower melting temperature (e.g. polycaprolactone).

The use of a thermal field to induce the change of phase of the material turns out to be the most intuitive choice (also in view of the ease of availability of 3D printers), but certainly imposes important difficulties in terms of feasibility, controllability and energy efficiency of the system. However, we demonstrate in this paper, the feasibility of the conceptual design opening the way also for a different mechanism enabling the stiffness variation. In fact, the same strategy of depositing a single layer of material all at once could be used by exploiting other kinds of phenomenon, different from the thermal (e.g. chemical reaction), to induce the phase change of the material. It would be enough to construct a model describing the selected phenomenon and the movement of the feeding material, but the concept of everting or depositing some kind of raw material at the tip level would remain unchanged. Nevertheless, the use of a different physical field to induce phase change should certainly be assessed against the controllability, effectiveness and energy efficiency of the transformation itself.

Moreover, our design can potentially enable a faster growth speed, with respect for instance to the approach adopted in [20]. In fact, considering having the speed of the feeding material at the entrance of the heater imposed at 13 mm/s the growing speed could be chosen in the range $0.15 \div 0.30$ mm/s, having the approximation of a constant density of the feeding material and the control of the thermal outflow. In this perspective, the system would result $\sim 4.5$ times faster with respect to the FDM technique used in [20] (from 4 mm/min to 18 mm/min).

Another additional advantage of the proposed design is the simplicity. In fact, it accounts only for four components and a single motor for pulling the filament is envisaged. Also, this simple design allows for miniaturization and fast assembling of the complete system.

## 5  Conclusions

This paper investigates on material extrusion as an additive manufacturing strategy for enabling the growth from the tip of artificial systems. The proposed design allows the deposition of the material all at once on the whole section of deposition. This strategy can potentially enable a fast growth speed (up to 18 mm/min), while the simple design guarantees a fast assembling of the system. This investigation is of relevance for developing new embeddable techniques in robotic systems enabling the movement from the tip by addition of new material. Such systems, able to self-build their structure, can exploit this ability not only to explore the environment but also to configure their bodies on real time, without the need for a predefined design, thus enouncing conformability and adaptability of artificial systems to unpredictable conditions, such as after a disaster or in underground exploration activities.

# References

1. Ballard, L.A., Sabanovic, S., Kaur, J., Milojevic, S.: George Charles Devol, Jr. [history]. IEEE Robot. Autom. Mag. **19**(3), 114–119 (2012)
2. Kim, S., Laschi, C., Trimmer, B.: Soft robotics: a bioinspired evolution in robotics. Trends Biotechnol. **31**(5), 287–294 (2013)
3. Laschi, C., Mazzolai, B., Cianchetti, M.: Soft robotics: technologies and systems pushing the boundaries of robot abilities. Sci. Robot. **1**(1), eaah3690 (2016)
4. Fukuda, T., Nakagawa, S.: Dynamically reconfigurable robotic system. In: Proceedings of 1998 IEEE International Conference on Robotics and Automation, Philadelphia, PA, USA, pp. 1581–1586. IEEE (1988)
5. Fukuda, T., Ueyama, T.: Cellular Robotics and Micro Robotic Systems, vol. 10. World Scientific, Singapore (1994)
6. Beni, G., Wang, J.: Swarm intelligence in cellular robotic systems. In: Dario, P., Sandini, G., Aebischer, P. (eds.) Robots and Biological Systems: Towards a New Bionics?. NATO ASI Series (Series F: Computer and Systems Sciences), vol. 102, pp. 703–712. Springer, Heidelberg (1993). https://doi.org/10.1007/978-3-642-58069-7_38
7. Gilpin, K., Rus, D.: Modular robot systems. IEEE Robot. Autom. Mag. **17**(3), 38–55 (2010)
8. Groß, R., Dorigo, M.: Self-assembly at the macroscopic scale. Proc. IEEE **96**(9), 1490–1508 (2008)
9. Yim, M., White, P., Park, M., Sastra, J.: Modular self-reconfigurable robots. In: Meyers, R. (ed.) Encyclopedia of Complexity and Systems Science, pp. 5618–5631. Springer, New York (2009). https://doi.org/10.1007/978-0-387-30440-3
10. Wei, H., Chen, Y., Tan, J., Wang, T.: Sambot: a self-assembly modular robot system. IEEE/ASME Trans. Mechatron. **16**(4), 745–757 (2011)
11. Murata, S., Yoshida, E., Kamimura, A., Kurokawa, H., Tomita, K., Kokaji, S.: M-TRAN: self-reconfigurable modular robotic system. IEEE/ASME Trans. Mechatron. **7**(4), 431–441 (2002)
12. Wang, T., Li, H., Meng, C.: Collective grasping for non-cooperative objects using modular self-reconfigurable robots. In: 2015 IEEE/RSJ International Conference on Intelligent Robots and Systems (IROS), Hamburg, pp. 3296–3301. IEEE (2015)
13. Spröwitz, A., Moeckel, R., Vespignani, M., Bonardi, S., Ijspeert, A.J.: Roombots: A hardware perspective on 3D self-reconfiguration and locomotion with a homogeneous modular robot. Robot. Auton. Syst. **62**(7), 1016–1033 (2014)
14. Lipson, H., Pollack, J.B.: Automatic design and manufacture of robotic lifeforms. Nature **406**(6799), 974 (2000)
15. Bartlett, N.W., Tolley, M.T., Overvelde, J.T., Weaver, J.C., Mosadegh, B., Bertoldi, K., Whitesides, G.M., Wood, R.J.: A 3D-printed, functionally graded soft robot powered by combustion. Science **349**(6244), 161–165 (2015)
16. Kim, J., Alspach, A., Yamane, K.: 3D printed soft skin for safe human-robot interaction. In: 2015 IEEE/RSJ International Conference on Intelligent Robots and Systems (IROS), Hamburg, Germany, pp. 2419–2425. IEEE (2015)
17. Brodbeck, L., Wang, L., Iida, F.: Robotic body extension based on hot melt adhesives. In: 2012 IEEE International Conference on Robotics and Automation (ICRA), Saint Paul, MN, USA, pp. 4322–4327. IEEE (2012)
18. Wang, L., Brodbeck, L., Iida, F.: Mechanics and energetics in tool manufacture and use: a synthetic approach. J. R. Soc. Interface **11**(100), 20140827 (2014)
19. Wang, L., Culha, U., Iida, F.: A dragline-forming mobile robot inspired by spiders. Bioinspir. Biomim. **9**(1), 016006 (2014)

20. Sadeghi, A., Mondini, A., Mazzolai, B.: Toward self-growing soft robots inspired by plant roots and based on additive manufacturing technologies. Soft Robot. **4**(3), 211–223 (2017)
21. Baluška, F., Mancuso, S., Volkmann, D., Barlow, P.W.: Root apex transition zone: a signalling–response nexus in the root. Trends Plant Sci. **15**(7), 402–408 (2010)
22. Sadeghi, A., Tonazzini, A., Popova, L., Mazzolai, B.: A novel growing device inspired by plant root soil penetration behaviors. PloS ONE **9**(2), e90139 (2014)
23. Hart, J.W.: Plant Tropisms: and Other Growth Movements. Springer Science & Business Media, Amsterdam (1990)
24. Hodge, A.: The plastic plant: root responses to heterogeneous supplies of nutrients. New Phytol. **162**(1), 9–24 (2004)

# Platform Selection of a Manta-Inspired Robot for Mitigating Near-Shore Harmful Algal Blooms

Lauren Marshall$^{(\boxtimes)}$, Adam Schroeder, and Brian Trease

University of Toledo, Toledo, OH 43606-3390, USA
lauren.marshall@rockets.utoledo.edu

**Abstract.** Anthropologic impacts on freshwater have created toxic algal blooms that are challenging to address due to scale and shallow conditions along the shore. Mimicking a manta ray's motion and structure offers a platform for an environmental service robot that can thrive under such constraints. The structure of the manta enables slow-gliding high-maneuverability in shallow conditions. The fin placement allows periods of gliding through the water, reducing actuation frequency and its disruption to the surrounding environment. This report analyzes various ray inspired robotics and their features, to determine the optimal design for an environmental service robot. By integrating a bioinspired algal filter with a manta-inspired robotic platform, near-shore blooms could be reduced without introducing a new threat to the struggling ecosystem.

## 1 The Robotic Platform

Aquatic robotic platforms in the field vary in almost every detail. Design goals range from influencing fish behavior [1] to increasing speed and agility [2]. Certain characteristics better lend themselves to shallow water low-speed applications, especially the mode of propulsion. Fish exploit many modes of propulsion, making them a valuable source of inspiration for aquatic robots. To better understand which mode is ideal, an array of propulsive modes from angilliform (undulation across entire body) to rajiform (undulation across large, pectoral fins) [3] were analyzed. A rajiform- or mobuliform-inspired structure was determined as the optimal mode for an algal collection platform.

Manta rays utilize mobuliform motion and have been inspiring aquatic robotics for over a decade (see Table 1). Mobuliform motion employs large pectoral fins to generate thrust via oscillatory motion, where less than one wave would be present in the fin instead of undulating motion, which displays more than one wave [2]. The design offers a smooth gliding platform, ideal for mapping or surveillance. The form offers the possibility for increased payloads, such as sensors for environmental data [4]. Several ray-inspired robotic projects focus on increasing maneuverability in difficult conditions such as shallow water. Existing designs aim to optimize the propulsion-to-energy ratio by adjusting fin frequency, improve stability, decrease cost, or reduce noise.

The details of each ray-inspired platform vary depending on their intended application. Some designs enable a more robust collection structure while others have negative impacts on the effectiveness of a collection platform. For example, each of the ray-inspired platforms in Table 1 uses a fin-driven mode of propulsion. How the fins are actuated varies

© Springer International Publishing AG, part of Springer Nature 2018
V. Vouloutsi et al. (Eds.): Living Machines 2018, LNAI 10928, pp. 300–303, 2018.
https://doi.org/10.1007/978-3-319-95972-6_31

**Table 1.** Manta Ray Robot Comparison (https://docs.google.com/spreadsheets/d/144X5_jmRtn_iOCDN05-cR6UUiM5Hrh-i5IhUmUIB3u8/edit#gid=0)

Review of Mobile Aquatic Manta Robotics

| | | | | | | | | | |
|---|---|---|---|---|---|---|---|---|---|
| Date of publication | 2006-2009 | 2009 | 2010 | 2010 | Apr. 2012 | 2012 | Jan. 2015 | May. 2016 | 2017 |
| Institution | Festo | Harbin Institute of Technology | Nanyang Technological University | Beihang University | University of Virginia | University of Virginia | Taizhou Vocational & Technical Colleg | Worcester Polytechnic Institute | National University of Singapore |
| Name | Aqua_ray | N/A: Micro-Robot | RoMan-II | N/A: Robotic Manta | N/A: IPMC Manta Robot | MantaBot | N/A: Robotic Ray | N/A: Prototype | MantaDroid |
| Fin Motion | Oscillatory | Oscillatory | Oscillatory | Oscillatory | Oscillatory | Oscillatory | Undulation | Oscillatory | Oscillatory |
| Proposed Goal/ Application | Marine Research | Light weight design | Inspection or Investigation | Shallow water applications | Mimic swim behavior | Military/Environme ntal | Stability & Maneuvering | Improve UAV efficiency | Search and Resc |
| Buoyancy | N/A | Net | Negative | Net after weight | Positively | N/A | Adjustable | Control in Tier 2 | N/A |
| Type of Propulsion | Brushless motor t power pump & 2 servos | SMA actuator: Nc noise propulsion option | Servo-motor | McKibben pneumatic muscles | Ionic polymer-metal composite | Expandable cable: and rods in fins | 8 Evenly spaced servomotors | MG200 gear pump | 2 Electric motors |
| Swimming Efficiency | Poor | 0.43 BL/s | 1 BL/s | -0.5 BL/s | 0.067 BL/s | Poor | 0.38 BL/s | N/A | ~2 BL/s |
| Power Source/ Consumption | 24 V, 10 Ah. 30 mins at max load | 1500 mAh, 12 C L polymer bat. | 10.8 W | External Tether | Under 2.5 W | Battery | 3200mAh provide 30 min | 12V LiFePo4 battery | 10 hours |
| Maneuverability | High, nearly mimics living ray | Turning adjusted by flapping pulse | Gliding, Pivot, Backward | Focused on linea swimming | Focused on linea 100% tip deflection & 40 degree twist | forward, turn, glide and maintain position | Forward and turning bias-oscillating | 60 Degree tip deflection | "Good": forward, turn, diving |
| Payload Capacity | None | Minimal, Lightweight | 4 kg | N/A | Minimal, Lightweight | Goal: Various | Minimal, suitable add. accessory | Additional payload possible | N/A |
| Manufacturability | High Difficulty | Medium Difficulty: Embedded SMA custom machining | High Difficulty: custom machining | Low Difficulty: Part Mold | Low Difficulty: 2- electroplating | Medium Difficulty: Tensegrity structure | Low Difficulty: uniform cantilever | Low Difficulty: 2- Part Mold | Low Difficulty: 3D printed |
| Weblink | Link | Link | Link | Link | Link | Link | Link | Link | Link |

significantly. Servomotors are the simplest option, however, the sound emitted may draw fish to the device, which adds hazards to the operating environment. Shape memory alloys (SMA) have been used with positive results. The aquatic environment provides a rapid cooling mechanism for the alloys, increasing actuation potential and providing quiet actuation [5], but uneven actuation may reduce control. Pneumatic and hydraulic systems are another form of actuation utilized to drive the fins. The actuator structure requires more space than an SMA, while providing consistent motion, but pose an environmental risk, unless the fluids are inert or can be safely contained.

Our implementation is markedly different than these previous examples because it is (i) actively interacting with the environment using a bioinspired filter, not only passively sensing, and (ii) applied to the novel problem of mitigating near-shore harmful algal blooms (HABs). Integration of a filter, whose performance is impacted by the robot's propulsion and flow across the robot's body, is a unique design challenge. Only one design above focuses on operation in shallow conditions, and while several of the ray-inspired robotics focus on environmental applications, they are only used as a monitoring platform. Also, our prototype is designed to carry collected algae, eliminating the light-weight designs, and to be neutrally or positively buoyant as the collection would increase weight, eliminating heavier designs. Finally, smaller, non-manta-inspired platforms have addressed algal reduction (e.g., EcoBot and Row-Bot), converting algae to a fuel source using microbial fuel cells (MFC) [6]. They successfully remove algae but do not focus on the rough conditions produced by shallow water nor a large-scale implementation.

HABs accumulate in areas where water remains warmer and less disrupted. Under these conditions, the high maneuverability of a ray platform at low speeds [5] is critical for algal collection. The application requires the robot to often be near the surface of the water, exposing it to wave action. The design must be resistant to rolling, which is accomplished better by the wide footprint of the manta shape than in narrow-bodied fish [3]. Buoyancy control must prevent the robot from lodging in the lake bed or operating at an incorrect depth, preventing it from collecting algae. All of these factors were considered along with materials, filter design, filter space, algal storage, payload capacity, and manufacturability in the design phase for this application.

## 2  Designing a Filter and Moving Forward

Several fish species filter feed; the shape of their mouths and internal structures aid capture or redirection of food, such as algae. These biological processes are looked to for inspiration to develop a filter that would be integrated into this manta robot platform. Specifically, a filter that mimics the unique geometry of a manta's mouth, 1:2.6 height to width [5] (see Fig. 1), was tested by counting particles collected by the filter. Details on the methodology and results are reported by the authors in [7]. The particles collected were chosen to emulate algal colonies' size, shape, and neutral buoyancy.

A skeleton version of the manta platform is under construction. The design mimics the fin and body cavity dimensions of a manta ray, making the fins slightly larger than the body cavity [5]. The fins will be molded from a flexible material, and some

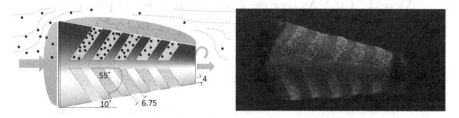

**Fig. 1.** (Left) Flow through and around a manta-inspired filter with basic dimensions. Elements shown: external flow (dotted lines), bow wave at the inlet and slow flow along gill slots (gray hemispherical shapes), bulk flow at the inlet and outlet (bold arrows), induced turbulence at each gill slot exit and the outlet (curved arrows), and particles used to represent algae (black dots). Image adapted from previous work. [7], (Right) Image from particle collection experiments. (Color figure online)

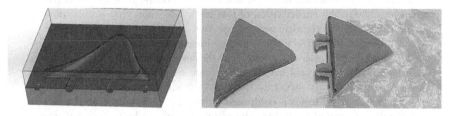

**Fig. 2.** (Left) Manta-inspired fin mold for soft-body prototypes. (Right) Silicone fin prototypes; the left is solid silicone and the right has fiberglass woven mesh embedded, which provides a means to tradeoff strength and durability for flexibility.

development has begun of the fin shape and molding materials (See Fig. 2). The completed platform will house the algal filter in the 'mouth' of the robot. All power will initially be externally-provided via a tether system. For later iterations, we are investigating an onboard power supply and a microbial fuel cell to utilize the captured algae for supplemental energy, enabling longer operating cycles.

## References

1. Polverino, G., Abaid, N., Kopman, V., Macrì, S., Porfiri, M.: Zebrafish response to robotic fish : preference experiments on isolated individuals and small shoals. Bioinspir. Biomim. **7**(7), 36019-13 (2012)
2. He, J., Zhang, Y.: Development and Motion Testing of a Robotic Ray. J. Robot. (2015)
3. Lauder, G.V., Madden, P.G.A.: Learning from fish: kinematics and experimental hydrodynamics for roboticists. Int. J. Autom. Comput. **4**, 325–335 (2006)
4. Zhou, C., Low, K.H.: Better endurance and load capacity: an improved design of manta ray robot (RoMan-II). J. Bionic Eng. **7**, S137–S144 (2010)
5. Chu, W.S., et al.: Review of biomimetic underwater robots using smart actuators. Int. J. Precis. Eng. Manuf. **13**(7), 1281–1292 (2012)
6. Ieropoulos, I., Greenman, J., Melhuish, C.: Imitating Metabolism: Energy Autonomy in Biologically Inspired Robots, pp. 191–194 (2003)
7. Marshall, L., Schroeder, A., Trease, B.: Comparing Fish-Inspired Ram Filters for Collection of Harmful Algae. In: ASME IMECE (2018, submitted)

# Weak DC Motors Generate Earthworm Locomotion Without a Brain

Yoichi Masuda[1]($\boxtimes$), Masato Ishikawa[1], and Akio Ishiguro[2]

[1] Osaka University, 2-1, Yamadaoka, Suita, Osaka 565–0871, Japan
masuda@eom.mech.eng.osaka-u.ac.jp, ishikawa@mech.eng.osaka-u.ac.jp
[2] Tohoku University, 2-1-1 Katahira, Aoba-ku, Sendai 980–8577, Japan
ishiguro@riec.tohoku.ac.jp

**Abstract.** In this paper, we develop an extremely simple earthworm-like robot as a minimal model of the wave generation principle of earthworms. The major contribution of this work is to show that autonomous and distributed peristaltic wave generation is possible without a sensor, controller, or microprocessor. The key idea behind this brainless robot is to exploit the passivity intrinsic to the low-torque DC motor in each linear joint as a control law of a rhythmic oscillator. To reproduce an earthworm-like body structure that allows body contraction and expansion, the proposed robot is composed of multiple body segments that are mutually connected by linear joints. Inflation of the body segment was reproduced by a flexible plate that connects two adjacent segments. The experiments show that the brainless robot generates peristaltic locomotion similar to that of real earthworms.

**Keywords:** Decentralized autonomous control · Brainless control
Earthworm-like robot · Peristaltic motion · Crawling

## 1 Introduction

The underlying mechanisms that enable animals in nature to adapt to uncertain environments remains an open question. A factor in this issue is the complex interactions between the brain–nervous system, body, and environment. To address this issue, we attempted to extract the principle of environmental adaptation based on a constructive minimal modeling approach. We constructed a minimal model by scraping away the functional elements that do not contribute to adaptive motions. By implementing the model as simple robots, we aim to identify the sufficient conditions for the reproduction of animal adaptability.

In our previous study, we presented a series of extremely simple robots, called *Brainless*, which are capable of exhibiting typical animal locomotion despite having no sensor, brain, or controller. Our quasi-passive legged robots [1,2] generate typical quadruped gaits and can select one of them automatically

Supported by funding from the Tateisi Science and Technology Foundation, Grant-in-Aid for JSPS Research Fellow JP17J00601, and CREST.

(walk → gallop), whereas a snake-like robot [3] reproduces serpentine locomotion with a retrograde wave. The key to these adaptabilities is a "weakness" intrinsic to the low-torque DC motor. When a disturbance force from the body and environment is applied to the rotating "weak" motor, followed by a load torque applied to the motor, a delay corresponding to the load torque occurs in the motor phase. In this method, we do not consider this delay as a disturbance but exploit it as a control law to adjust the phase differences between multiple motors. In other words, the dynamics of an actuator behaves as an oscillator that follows a kind of sensory feedback law. The basic characteristics of this method, called *Compliant Oscillator*, is reported in [4]. The study showed that fundamental systems with the *Compliant Oscillator* generate resonance modes autonomously and achieve transitions between modes that correspond to the applied voltage. These results suggest that a large part of the source of adaptive animal locomotion exists in the body and actuator dynamics, not only in the brain–nervous system.

The *Compliant Oscillator* can generate versatile motions depending on body morphology, material, flexibility, and environmental constraints. In this study, we develop an earthworm-like robot with a different body structure from conventional *Brainless robots*. Numerous earthworm-inspired robots have been developed previously with various drive systems, electric motors [5,6], solenoid [7], SMA [8–13], DEA [14], magnetic field [15], and pneumatic [16]. For these artificial earthworms, some controllers have been proposed, for adaptive control [17,18], gait generation [19–21]. However, these previous crawling robots and controllers employed predesigned gaits (phase differences) or heuristic and complicated algorithms to generate waves; thus, the source of the wave locomotion of earthworms is still unclear. An distributed adaptive controller in a simulation of earthworms was proposed in articles [22,23], and we achieve a similar control law mechanistically by exploiting the "weakness" intrinsic to motors.

The major contribution of this work is to show that autonomous peristaltic wave generation is possible without any explicit controller. Actual earthworms generate waves of contraction and expansion from head to tail, and the contracted segment inflates to generate friction with the ground [24]. To reproduce an earthworm-like body structure, the proposed robot is composed of multiple body segments, with each segment mutually connected by a linear joint that contracts and expands its own body. Inflation of the body segment is reproduced by a flexible plate that connects two adjacent segments. Each linear joint is connected to a low-torque DC motor through a slider-crank mechanism, and produces periodic contraction and expansion motions under a constant voltage. Each motor, which drives the corresponding linear joint, adjusts its own phase depending on the load torque applied from adjacent segments and the ground through the link mechanism. As a result, phase differences between multiple motors converge, and the robot generates peristaltic motions automatically and adaptively corresponding to different input voltages.

## 2    Earthworm-Like Robot Without a Brain

### 2.1    Structure of the Earthworm-Like Robot

In this paper, we develop a brainless earthworm-like robot that generates a peristaltic motion autonomously without a sensor, controller, or microprocessor. The proposed robot is composed of six body segments, and each segment has one low-torque DC motor (Pololu 75:1 Micro Metal Gearmotor HP). Figure 1 shows the overview of the proposed earthworm-like robot. The total weight of the robot is 409 g. The deformation length of each joint is 20 mm, and the total length during contraction and expansion are 430 mm and 510 mm, respectively. The total height during contraction and expansion are 125 mm and 120 mm, respectively.

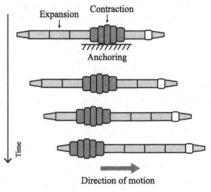

**Fig. 1.** Overview of the brainless earthworm-like robot.

**Fig. 2.** Schematic of an earthworm. Real earthworms generate waves of contraction and expansion from head to tail, and the contracted segment inflates to generate friction with the ground [24].

Real earthworms generate waves of contraction and expansion from head to tail, and the contracted segment inflates to generate friction with the ground [24] (Fig. 2). To reproduce an earthworm-like structure, each segment is mutually connected by a linear joint that contracts and expands its own body. Each linear joint is connected to a low-torque DC motor through a slider-crank mechanism (Fig. 3). This linkage is composed of a crank that connects the motor to the shaft, and a slider that connects the crank to the linear joint. The crank in continuous rotation produces periodic contraction and expansion motions. Inflation of the body segment is reproduced by a flexible plate that connects two adjacent segments; we attached anti-slip sheets (PVC foam sheets) to the bottom surfaces of the plate. In Fig. 4, when the crank is rotated by the motor (red arrow), it produces periodic contraction and expansion motions under a constant voltage (blue arrow); at the same time, the bottom surface is pushed up and pulled down (green arrow).

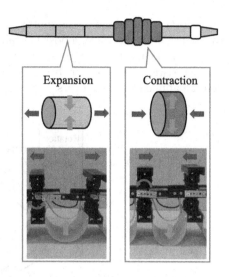

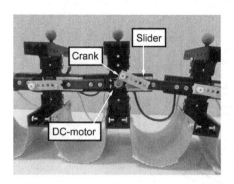

**Fig. 3.** Structure of the contraction and expansion mechanism that is composed of the slider-crank.

**Fig. 4.** Movement of the earthworm-like robot. When the crank is rotated by the motor (red arrow), it produces periodic contraction and expansion motions under a constant voltage (blue arrow); at the same time, the bottom surface is pushed up and pulled down (green arrow). (Color figure online)

## 2.2 Modeling of the Contraction and Expansion Mechanism with a Weak DC-motor

This robot has no sensor, controller, or microprocessor. The key idea behind this brainless robot is to exploit the passivity intrinsic to the low-torque DC motor in each linear joint as a control law of a rhythmic oscillator. Each motor rotates continuously under a constant voltage from a stabilized power source, and adjusts its own phase by exploiting the "weak" dynamics intrinsic to the motor itself.

Figure 5 shows a model of the contraction and expansion mechanism. First, we assume that the flexible plate at the bottom can be approximated as a linkage in Fig. 5 (link OABC, orange link), and that the link lengths $\overline{OA}$ and $\overline{AB}$, $\overline{DE}$ and $\overline{EF}$ are equal, respectively.

Suppose that a constant voltage is supplied to the motor that is proportional to the angular velocity $\omega > 0$ of the motor shaft under the no-load running condition. When a disturbance torque $\tau$ is applied to the motor shaft, the angular velocity of the motor is given by

$$\dot{\theta}(t) = \omega + \varepsilon\tau(t), \tag{1}$$

where $\theta(t)$ is the phase of the motor and $\varepsilon > 0$ is the sensitivity of the motor to the external torque. Here, a positive value for $\tau$ indicates that the torque is in the counterclockwise direction. $\varepsilon$ is determined by the crank length $\overline{OA}$ and electric characteristics of the motor. In this case, we can only change $\omega$ by adjusting the voltage applied to the motors.

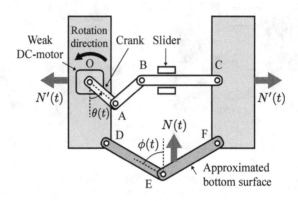

**Fig. 5.** Model of the contraction and expansion mechanism. (Color figure online)

When the ground reaction force $N(t)$ is applied to the bottom link, a force $N'(t)$ to expand the body segment is generated as follows:

$$N'(t) = \frac{N(t)}{2}\tan\phi(t), \tag{2}$$

where $0 < \phi(t) < \pi/2$ is the angle of the bottom linkage. The force $N'(t)$ is transmitted through the linkage OABC and causes a disturbance torque $\tau$ that is applied to the motor shaft

$$\tau(t) = 2\overline{AO}N'(t)\cos\theta. \tag{3}$$

Finally, by substituting Eq. (2) and Eq. (3) for Eq. (1), we get the entire model:

$$\dot{\theta}(t) = \omega + a(t)N(t)\cos\theta, \tag{4}$$

where $a(t) = \varepsilon\overline{AO}\tan\phi(t)$ is a function that changes the transmission rate of the ground reaction force. From Eq. (4), when a ground reaction force $N(t) > 0$ is applied to the bottom surface, the low-torque DC motor adjusts its own phase through the linkage mechanism. In other words, the passivity of the DC motor for the purely physical mechanism Eq. (4) makes it function like a state feedback controller.

We call this effect the *compliant oscillator* [4]. Despite having no sensor, brain, or controller, the *compliant oscillator* is capable of synching multiple motors through physical interaction. A similar phenomenon is the *Huygens synchronization* [25], which syncs multiple pendulum clocks. It is considered that the same principle also works in this method. Furthermore, the formulation of Eq. (4) is closely related to a previous oscillator model that generates quadruped gaits [26], earthworm gaits [22], and caterpillar gaits [23]. The relationship between these similar phenomena will be investigated in future work.

## 3 Experiment

In this section, we conduct fundamental experiments to investigate the generated motion patterns.

Figure 6 shows the experimental setup. All of the motors were connected to a power source in parallel. The initial state of all linear joints was set to contract (all of the motor phases are $\theta = 3\pi/2$ in Fig. 5 ). The trial was conducted once for each input voltage of 2 V and 3 V. The horizontal displacement of the robot was captured by a motion capture system, and the markers were attached above the each motor shaft.

Figures 7 and 8 show the locomotion of the robot with 2 V. In the figures, the motors generate periodic motions with in-phase pattern temporarily, and stays while adjusting the motor phases. However, after approximately 15 s, the linear joints generate waves from right to left; as a result, the robot moves to the right (retrograde wave). Figure 9 shows the spatiotemporal plots of the motor phase with 2 V. From the figure, in motor1, motor2, and motor3, a steady peristaltic wave is generated as

$$Motor1 \rightarrow Motor2 \rightarrow Motor3 \rightarrow Motor1 \rightarrow Motor2 \rightarrow ... \tag{5}$$

This manner of locomotion is the same as the locomotion of real earthworms. This result is attributed to the interaction between the body segments and the ground contact conditions through physical forces. The movement of each motor

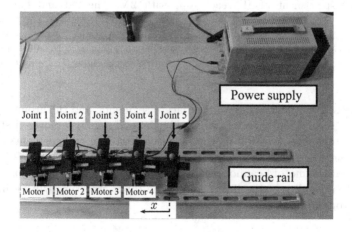

**Fig. 6.** Experimental setup.

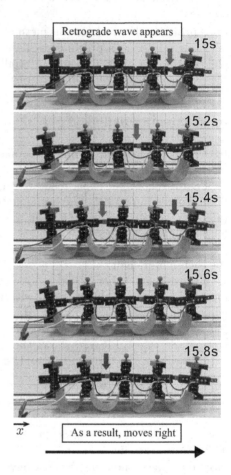

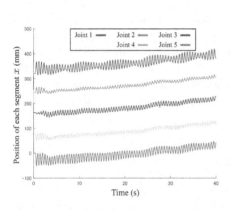

**Fig. 7.** Experimental result with 2 V: horizontal displacement of the each joint.

**Fig. 8.** Snapshot of the locomotion with 2 V. The red and blue arrows denote extended joints. The robot generates retrograde waves (waves from right to left); as a result, the robot moves to the right. (Color figure online)

was suppressed by the left and right adjacent segments, and the ground reaction and friction forces. For these reasons, only the end segment moves first, and it seems that a chain expansion motion starting from the end segment occurred. However, there is a slow drift of the motor4 phase at $t = [15, 40]s$. This result assumed that the motor4 cannot receive a sufficient ground reaction forces owing to the lack of rigidity of the linear joint. The robot structure will be improved in future work.

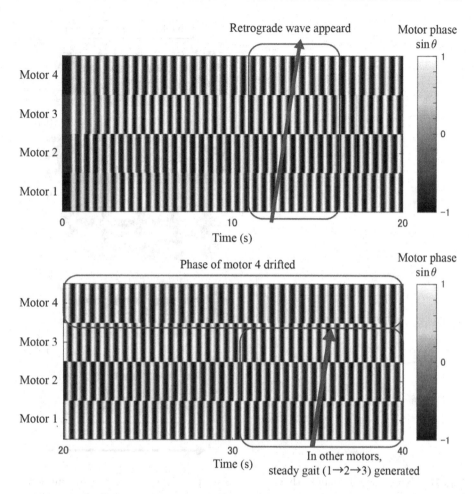

**Fig. 9.** Spatiotemporal plot of the motor phase with 2 V. From the figure, in motor1, motor2, and motor3, a steady peristaltic wave is generated. However, there is a slow drift of the motor4 phase at $t = [15, 40]s$.

Figure 10 and Fig. 11 show the locomotion of the robot with 3 V. In the figure, the motors generate a steady in-phase pattern from beginning to end; as a result, the robot moves to the left. Figure 12 shows the spatiotemporal plots the motor phase with 3 V. The movement, in which all the motors contract and expand at the same time, is the 1st resonance mode of the robot body. It is assumed

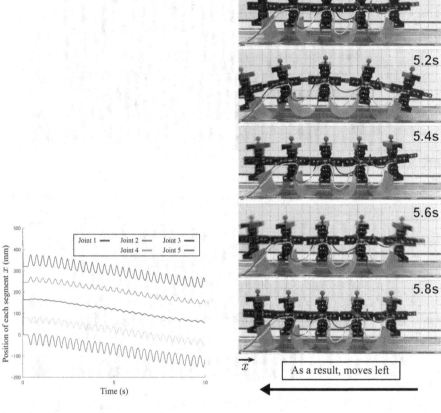

**Fig. 10.** Experimental result with 3 V: horizontal displacement of the each joint.

**Fig. 11.** Snapshot of the locomotion with 3 V. The robot generates in-phase pattern; as a result, the robot moves to the left.

that this movement is caused by the inertial force between the body modules becoming greater than the frictional force. In our previous study [4], we showed that systems affected by the inertia with *Compliant Oscillator* converge in the resonance modes.

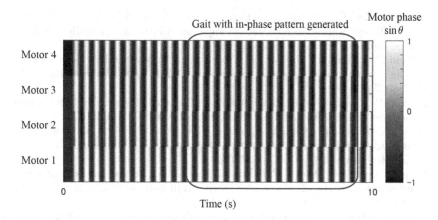

**Fig. 12.** Spatiotemporal plot of the motor phase with 3 V. The movement, in which all the motors contract and expand at the same time, is the 1st resonance mode of the robot body.

## 4 Conclusion

In this paper, we reported an extremely simple earthworm-like robot as a minimal model of the wave generation principle of earthworms. This robot generated the peristaltic locomotion of actual earthworms autonomously without a sensor, controller, or microprocessor. The results suggest the contribution of the forces interacting between the body segments. Moreover, the robot generated different locomotion that adaptively corresponds to the input voltage. We expect that comparison of these two different phenomena will provide critical clues to understanding the contributions of friction and inertial force to peristaltic locomotion.

## References

1. Masuda, Y., Naniwa, K., Ishikawa, M., Osuka, K.: Weak actuators generate adaptive animal gaits without a brain. In: IEEE International Conference on Robotics and Biomimetics (ROBIO2017), China, Macau SAR (2017)
2. Naniwa, K., Masuda, Y., Ishikawa, M., Osuka, K.: Weak actuators generate versatile locomotion patterns without a brain. In: IEEE International Conference on Robotics and Biomimetics (ROBIO2017), China, Macau SAR (2017)
3. Masuda, Y., Ishikawa, M., Ishiguro, A.: Adaptive motion generation of a snake robot without a brain. In: 15th SICE Symposium on Decentralized Autonomous Systems (domestic) (2018)
4. Masuda, Y., Minami, Y., Ishikawa, M.: Actuator synchronization for adaptive motion generation without any sensor or microprocessor. In: Asian Control Conference (ASCC2017), Australia, Goald Coast (2017)

5. Daltorio, K.A., Boxerbaum, A.S., Horchler, A.D., Shaw, K.M., Chiel, H.J., Quinn, R.D.: Efficient worm-like locomotion: slip and control of soft-bodied peristaltic robots. Bioinspir. Biomim. **8**(3), 035003 (2013)
6. Zarrouk, D., Sharf, I., Shoham, M.: Conditions for worm-robot locomotion in a flexible environment: theory and experiments. IEEE Trans. Biomed. Eng. **59**(4), 1057–1067 (2012)
7. Song, C.W., Lee, D.J., Lee, S.Y.: Bioinspired segment robot with earthworm-like plane locomotion. J. Bionic Eng. **13**(2), 292–302 (2016)
8. Seok, S., Onal, C.D., Cho, K.J., Wood, R.J., Rus, D., Kim, S.: Meshworm: a peristaltic soft robot with antagonistic nickel titanium coil actuators. IEEE/ASME Trans. Mechatron. **18**(5), 1485–1497 (2013)
9. Kim, B., Lee, M.G., Lee, Y.P., Kim, Y., Lee, G.: An earthworm-like micro robot using shape memory alloy actuator. Sens. Actuators A Phys. **125**(2), 429–437 (2006)
10. Gu, D.Q., Zhou, Y.: An approach to the capsule endoscopic robot with active drive motion. J. Zhejiang Univ.-Sci. A **12**(3), 223–231 (2011)
11. Menciassi, A., Gorini, S., Pernorio, G., Dario, P.: A SMA actuated artificial earthworm. In: IEEE International Conference on Robotics and Automation (ICRA), vol. 4, pp. 3282–3287. IEEE (2004)
12. Trimmer, B.A., Lin, H.T.: Bone-free: Soft mechanics for adaptive locomotion (2014)
13. Fang, H., Zhang, Y., Wang, K.W.: Origami-based earthworm-like locomotion robots. Bioinspir. Biomim. **12**(6), 065003 (2017)
14. Jung, K., Koo, J.C., Lee, Y.K., Choi, H.R.: Artificial annelid robot driven by soft actuators. Bioinspir. Biomim. **2**(2), S42 (2007)
15. Saga, N., Nakamura, T.: Development of a peristaltic crawling robot using magnetic fluid on the basis of the locomotion mechanism of the earthworm. Smart Mater. Struct. **13**(3), 566 (2004)
16. Calderón, A.A., Ugalde, J.C., Zagal, J.C., Pérez-Arancibia, N.O.: Design, fabrication and control of a multi-material-multi-actuator soft robot inspired by burrowing worms. In: IEEE International Conference on Robotics and Biomimetics (ROBIO), pp. 31–38. IEEE (2016)
17. Schwebke, S., Behn, C.: Worm-like robotic systems: generation, analysis and shift of gaits using adaptive control. Artif. Intell. Res. **2**(1), 12 (2012)
18. Behn, C.: Adaptive control of straight worms without derivative measurement. Multibody Syst. Dyn. **26**(3), 213–243 (2011)
19. Fang, H., Wang, C., Li, S., Wang, K.W., Xu, J.: A comprehensive study on the locomotion characteristics of a metameric earthworm-like robot. Multibody Syst. Dyn. **35**(2), 153–177 (2015)
20. Fang, H., Li, S., Wang, K.W., Xu, J.: Phase coordination and phasevelocity relationship in metameric robot locomotion. Bioinspir. Biomim. **10**(6), 066006 (2015)
21. Chen, I.M., Yeo, S.H., Gao, Y.: Locomotive gait generation for inchworm-like robots using finite state approach. Robotica **19**(5), 535–542 (2001)
22. Kano, T., Ishiguro, A.: Decentralized control of earthworm-like robot based on tegotae function. In: The 8th International Symposium on Adaptive Motion of Animals and Machines (AMAM2017), pp. 92–93 (2017)
23. Umedachi, T., Kano, T., Ishiguro, A., Trimmer, B.A.: Gait control in a soft robot by sensing interactions with the environment using self-deformation. R. Soc. Open Sci. **3**(12), 160766 (2016)
24. Gray, J., Lissmann, H.W.: Studies in animal locomotion: VII. locomotory reflexes in the earthworm. J. Exp. Biol. **15**(4), 506–517 (1938)

25. Bennett, M., Schatz, M.F., Rockwood, H., Wiesenfeld, K.: Huygens's clocks. Proc. Math. Phys. Eng. Sci. **458**, 563–579 (2002)
26. Owaki, D., Kano, T., Nagasawa, K., Tero, A., Ishiguro, A.: Simple robot suggests physical interlimb communication is essential for quadruped walking. J. R. Soc. Interface **10**(78), 20120669 (2013)

# 3D Bioprinted Muscle-Based Bio-Actuators: Force Adaptability Due to Training

Rafael Mestre[1], Tania Patiño[1], Xavier Barceló[1],
and Samuel Sanchez[1,2(✉)]

[1] Institute for Bioengineering of Catalonia (IBEC), The Barcelona Institute
of Science and Technology, Baldiri Reixac 10-12, 08028 Barcelona, Spain
{rmestre,tpatino,ssanchez}@ibecbarcelona.eu
[2] Institució Catalana de Recerca i Estudis Avancats (ICREA), Barcelona, Spain

**Abstract.** The integration of biological tissue and artificial materials plays a fundamental role in the development of biohybrid soft robotics, a subfield in the field of soft robotics trying to achieve a higher degree of complexity by taking advantage of the exceptional capabilities of biological systems, like self-healing or responsiveness to external stimuli. In this work, we present a proof-of-concept 3D bioprinted bio-actuator made of skeletal muscle tissue and PDMS, which can act as a force measuring platform. The 3D bioprinting technique, which has not been used for the development of bio-actuators, offers unique versatility by allowing a simple, biocompatible and fast fabrication of hybrid multi-component systems. Furthermore, we prove controllability of contractions and functionality of the bio-actuator after applying electric pulses by measuring the exerted forces. We observe an increased force output in time, suggesting improved maturation of the tissue, opening up possibilities for force adaptability or modulation due to prolonged electrical stimuli.

**Keywords:** Biohybrid systems · Bio-bots · Bio-actuators · 3D bioprinting

## 1 Introduction

Biohybrid soft robotics is a discipline that aims at integrating biological entities and artificial materials to form hybrid systems capable of performing different tasks [1]. The integration of living muscle cells with other materials has already been successfully implemented in simple bio-bots or bio-actuators that can crawl [2], swim [3] or perform simple actuations [4] by taking advantage of the force produced by muscle cell contractions. Interested reader should refer to recent reviews for additional information [5, 6]. Mainly cardiac and skeletal muscle cells have been used for this purpose. Cardiac cells have the ability of contract and synchronize spontaneously and produce very robust contractions. However, the former characteristic can also be a disadvantage, as they are less controllable. Skeletal muscle cells do not produce such strong contractions, but they are more suitable for 3D cultures and can be more easily controlled.

Most of the examples of bio-actuators or bio-bots rely on the fabrication of molds to obtain the desired shape, biochemical or mechanical cues to obtain muscle fiber alignment or the use complex microfabrication techniques. Although 3D bioprinted has

© Springer International Publishing AG, part of Springer Nature 2018
V. Vouloutsi et al. (Eds.): Living Machines 2018, LNAI 10928, pp. 316–320, 2018.
https://doi.org/10.1007/978-3-319-95972-6_33

been presented as a powerful tool for the creation of functional three-dimensional tissues [7], the versatility of this technique to parallelly print various artificial or biological materials has not been exploited in the field of biohybrid robotics.

In this work, we present the use of 3D bioprinting for the fabrication of custom-made, process-integrated and functional bio-actuators made of a hydrogel containing skeletal muscle cells and polydimethylsiloxane (PDMS) as skeleton. As a proof-of-concept, we present the creation of a simple bio-actuator composed of two posts and a tissue ring which can act as a force measuring platform. We prove the controllability of the actuation and we show how prolonged electrical stimulation can increase the force output.

## 2    3D Bioprinting and Maturation of Skeletal Muscle Tissue

An extrusion-based bioprinter was used to 3D bioprint a cell-laden hydrogel with skeletal muscle myoblasts. In order to mimic the extracellular matrix of these cells and the optimal 3D bioprinting conditions, we chose a hydrogel made of bio-polymers readily available: fibrinogen (20 mg/mL) hyaluronic acid (3 mg/mL) and gelatin (35 mg/mL) (Fig. 1a). Both fibrinogen and gelatin contain cell attachment sites, providing a suitable environment for a 3D culture as well as cell proliferation and differentiation. Furthermore, the combination of these three hydrogels gave rise to a non-Newtonian fluid with high shear-thinning and yield stress, making it suitable for 3D bioprinting. Shear-thinning behavior protects cells from high stresses and decreases the necessary pressure for printing and high yield stress avoids dripping of the hydrogel when no pressure is applied. We found 18 °C to be an adequate temperature for the process, since gelatin is gelled at this temperature and the 3D bioprinted constructs do not lose their shape. After the structure was printed (Figure b), a solution of 20 U/mL of thrombin was added. Thrombin is an enzyme that catalyzes the cross-linking of fibrinogen to fibrin, and therefore maintaining the structure of the construct during incubation at 37 °C, when gelatin dissolves.

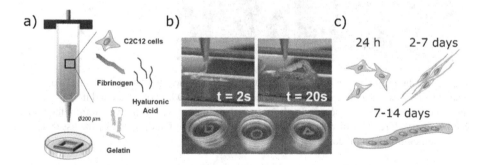

**Fig. 1.** Extrusion-based 3D bioprinting of skeletal muscle tissue. (a) C2C12 mouse myoblasts are encapsulated in a hydrogel made of fibrinogen, hyaluronic acid and gelatin. (b) Then, they are loaded in a syringe and 3D bioprinted with a 200 μm nozzle. (c) After switching to differentiation medium, several days are needed to obtain mature myotube fibers.

Skeletal muscle myoblasts can differentiate into myotubes, complex cellular structures composed of several fused myoblasts with contractile abilities (Fig. 1c). After 3D bioprinting, the construct was incubated in differentiation medium, which promotes cell differentiation intro myotubes. Up to seven days are considered sufficient time for differentiation but, usually, more days are necessary to achieve full maturation [8]. Furthermore, myotubes were aligned in the direction of the 3D bioprinted fibers, which is a necessary condition for maximum force generation.

## 3    Actuation and Training

The versatility of 3D bioprinting to print different materials was exploited to develop a 3D bioprinted bio-actuator that could be used as a force measuring platform. The bio-actuator consisted of a ring of cell-laden hydrogel surrounding two posts made of a highly viscous PDMS. Both objects were 3D printed during the same process in two different syringes and the PDMS was left to slowly cure at 37 °C in a cell incubator along with the tissue during the differentiation process.

Even though the cell-laden hydrogel and the posts were separated by some millimeters during the fabrication, cell reorganization and differentiation in the interior of the hydrogel caused compaction of the tissue (Fig. 2a). During differentiation, cell reorganization shrunk the tissue until it met the posts and started pulling from it. This mechanical stretching of the tissue has been proven to be beneficial for cell differentiation [2]. An inverted microscope was used to calculate the bending of the posts (Fig. 2b). By using Euler-Bernoulli's beam bending theory, we could correlate the displacement of the post to the force exerted by the cells (Fig. 2c).

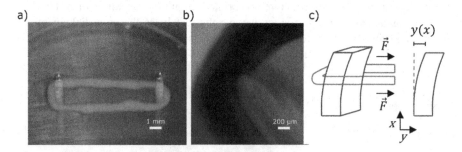

**Fig. 2.** 3D bioprinting of a biological actuator as a force-measuring platform. (a) Two posts made of PDMS are 3D printed and a cell-laden hydrogel is 3D bioprinted around it. (b) Under a microscope, after applying electrical pulses at a certain frequency, a displacement from the posts can be observed. (c) This displacement can be correlated to the force applied by the tissue using Euler-Bernoulli bending theory.

Electrical pulses of 1 Hz with an electric field of 1 V/mm and 1 ms of pulse width were applied. In any case, the bio-actuator faithfully responded to the applied frequencies and the contractions were powerful enough to bend the posts. Figure 3a shows the generated force during a 10 s interval of stimulation. The red dotted line represents the passive force due to tissue compaction, that is, the initial bending of the post before stimulation. The blue line displays the active force due to the electrical stimulation at 1 Hz, reaching values of approximately 15 µN per contraction.

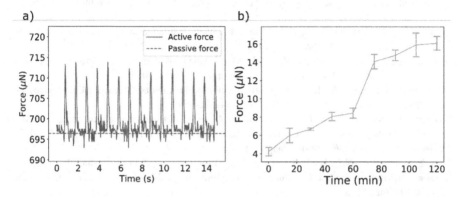

**Fig. 3.** Effect of stimulation protocol. (a) By applying electrical pulses at 1 Hz, the bio-actuator moves the posts according to this frequency, and the applied force can be calculated. Red dotted line represents the passive pre-bending state due to tissue compaction. (b) After applying a stimulation protocol of 1 Hz for 2 h, the force exerted by the tissue increased, indicating an increased force output due to training (Color figure online).

The maturation and force production capabilities of skeletal muscle cells improve with continuous stimulation [9]. The prove the possibility of fabricating custom 3D bioprinted bio-actuators with training capabilities, we applied a continuous 1 Hz stimulation for a period of 2 h. We observed a four-fold force increase from 4 µN to 16 µN during the 2 h period, reaching a plateau after 1 h of stimulation (Fig. 3b).

## 4  Conclusions and Outlook

Biohybrid soft robots based on skeletal or cardiac muscle cells could produce a boost in performance and capabilities in future robots by taking advantage of characteristics of biological systems like self-healing, adaptation, damage tolerance or responsiveness to external stimuli. In this work, we demonstrated how 3D bioprinting can become a powerful tool for the development of bio-bots and bio-actuators due to the simplicity of designing and fabricating structures of different materials in a fast, biocompatible and process-integrated manner. We built a bio-actuator that acted as a force measuring platform as a proof-of-concept and we demonstrated external control of contractions and an increase of force output.

# References

1. Patino, T., Mestre, R., Sánchez, S.: Miniaturized soft bio-hybrid robotics: a step forward into healthcare applications. Lab Chip 16 (2016). https://doi.org/10.1039/c6lc90088g
2. Raman, R., Cvetkovic, C., Uzel, S.G.M., et al.: Optogenetic skeletal muscle-powered adaptive biological machines. Proc. Natl. Acad. Sci. USA **113**, 3497–3502 (2016). https://doi.org/10.1073/pnas.1516139113
3. Park, S.-J., Gazzola, M., Park, K.S., et al.: Phototactic guidance of a tissue-engineered soft-robotic ray. Science **353**, 158–162 (2016). https://doi.org/10.1126/science.aaf4292
4. Chan, V., Park, K., Collens, M.B., et al.: Development of miniaturized walking biological machines. Sci. Rep. **2**, 857 (2012). https://doi.org/10.1038/srep00857
5. Ricotti, L., Menciassi, A.: Bio-hybrid muscle cell-based actuators. Biomed. Microdevices **14**, 987–998 (2012). https://doi.org/10.1007/s10544-012-9697-9
6. Webster-Wood, V.A., Akkus, O., Gurkan, U.A., et al.: Organismal engineering toward a robotic taxonomic key for devices using organic materials. Sci. Robot., 2, eaap9281 (2017). https://doi.org/10.1126/scirobotics.aap9281
7. Kang, H.-W., Lee, S.J., Ko, I.K., et al.: A 3D bioprinting system to produce human-scale tissue constructs with structural integrity. Nat. Biotechnol. **34**, 312–319 (2016). https://doi.org/10.1038/nbt.3413
8. Raman, R., Cvetkovic, C., Bashir, R.: A modular approach to the design, fabrication, and characterization of muscle-powered biological machines. Nat. Protoc. **12**, 519–533 (2017). https://doi.org/10.1038/nprot.2016.185
9. Fujita, H., Nedachi, T., Kanzaki, M.: Accelerated de novo sarcomere assembly by electric pulse stimulation in C2C12 myotubes. Exp. Cell Res. **313**, 1853–1865 (2007). https://doi.org/10.1016/j.yexcr.2007.03.002

# A System to Provide Oculomotor Functions to the User to Control Direction of Gaze and Optical Zoom for both Eyes Independently

Fumio Mizuno[1](✉), Tomoaki Hayasaka[2], and Takami Yamaguchi[2]

[1] Department of Electrical and Electronic Engineering,
Tohoku Institute of Technology, 35-1, Yagiyama Kasumi-cho,
Taihaku-ku, Sendai, Miyagi, Japan
fumio@tohtech.ac.jp
[2] Department of Biomedical Engineering, Graduate School
of Biomedical Engineering, Tohoku University, Sendai, Miyagi, Japan

**Abstract.** In our previous work, we developed a system named Virtual Chameleon, which provides the user with independent views for both the eyes. Visual stimuli affect the durations of alternation between dominance and suppression of cognition induced by binocular rivalry. Visual motion, spatial resolution, and visual contrast are considered as representative visual stimuli that affect the cognitive conditions induced by binocular rivalry. Therefore, we implemented a function to generate artificial saccade. In this work, we focused on visual motion for radial direction and spatial resolution. We further implemented a function to control optical zoom in the Virtual Chameleon.

**Keywords:** Binocular rivalry · Chameleon · Natural user interface
Eye movement · Optical zoom

## 1 Introduction

In our previous work, we derived a method from the characteristics of visual behaviors of chameleons when they move their eyes independently. We further developed a wearable system, named "Virtual Chameleon" to give independent fields of view to both eyes of a human user [1]. The system is a robotic system to control postures of two CCD cameras and a head-mounted display (HMD). The user can get two independent fields of view by controlling the two cameras with two sensors set on each of their hands. The HMD projects two images captured by each camera onto each eye independently in real time.

To evaluate human performance, we conducted experiments to find out targets set on both sides of the user [2]. The results showed that the response

Supported by the Ministry of Education, Culture, Sports, Science and Technology (MEXT) in Japan, Grant-in-Aid for Scientists (C) 26330227.

times of the users in cognitive behavior were delayed up to 134.9%, although they could look around and distinguish between the independent views. We confirmed that binocular rivalry [3] happened to the users while using the Virtual Chameleon. During the experiments, images captured when the user moved quickly were dominantly visible for a longer period of time than images from stationary positions. Fluctuations in dominance and suppression with binocular rivalry are irregular; however, it is possible to bias these fluctuations by boosting the strength of one rival image over the other. In this case, strong visual stimulation has an advantage in predominance. Moving visual stimulations have an advantage over stationary ones; they also strongly influence dominance. We suppose that users who could effectively use the Virtual Chameleon used the dominance of moving visual stimuli in practice. This advantage is one of the most important factors in perceiving independent fields of view and controlling visual axes using the Virtual Chameleon. We focused on the quick motion of a captured image and implemented functions to control postures of the two cameras quickly in the system [4]. The implementation of these function improved the response time by 32.4% as seen in the experiments.

The perceptual alternation is affected by visual stimuli such as motion, spatial resolution, and contrast and color of images projected onto both eyes. In this work, we focused on visual stimuli induced by change of spatial resolution such as zoom-in/out.

Further, we developed a system to provide independent fields of view by installing cameras equipped with electronic controllable zoom lenses (Fig. 1).

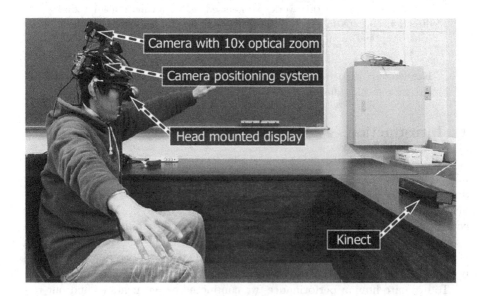

**Fig. 1.** Exterior view of Virtual Chameleon with a function to control optical zoom

## 2    System Configuration

A schematic of the system configuration is shown in Fig. 2. This device is composed of a natural user interface (NUI), camera positioning system, camera control system, and HMD system. Adding a new function in the system requires a new manipulation device which causes an increase in the complexity of operation. It is assumed that an increase in complexity of the manipulation affects human performance during use of the system. In this work, we introduced a NUI (Microsoft Kinect v2), equipped with motion capture, gesture interface, and speech recognition, to the system. The Microsoft Kinect v2 detects 25 points of skeletal joints at 1 [mm] distance resolution in the range from 500 [mm] to 4500 [mm]. In this system, wrist positions and gestures of both hands and shoulder positions are extracted and sent to the camera positioning and camera control systems.

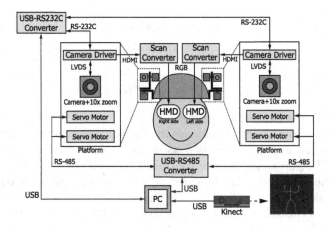

**Fig. 2.** System architecture of Virtual Chameleon

The camera positioning system controls the postures of each CCD camera (TAMRON, MP1010M-VC, Signal system: 1080p/60, Lens: 10x optical zoom) independently to follow individual positions of the wrist in relation to the shoulder. The wrist and shoulder positions and camera are shown in Fig. 3. The desired angles, $\theta_n$ and $\varphi_n$ ($n = 0, 1$), needed to control the posture of the camera are computed from the coordinates of three dimensional positions sampled by the NUI. The origin of configuration space of each wrist was based on each of the shoulders of the user. $^O\mathbf{p_n}$ is a vector from a joint of a shoulder to the position of the wrist and is described as follows:

$$^O\mathbf{p_n} = \begin{bmatrix} x_n & y_n & z_n \end{bmatrix}^T \tag{1}$$

**Fig. 3.** Posture of the camera and joints of the user

$\theta_n$ and $\varphi_n$ are computed as follows:

$$\|^O\mathbf{p}_n\|_2 = \sqrt{x_n^2 + y_n^2 + z_n^2} \qquad (2)$$

$$\theta_n = \tan^{-1} \frac{y_n}{x_n} \qquad (3)$$

$$\varphi_n = \tan^{-1} \frac{z_n}{\|^O\mathbf{p}_n\|_2} \qquad (4)$$

In this system, the relationship between vector $^{C_n}\mathbf{p}_n$ with respect to the coordinate system of the camera $n$ and vector $^O\mathbf{p}_n$ was assumed to be parallel.

Therefore, $\theta_n$ and $\varphi_n$ were used as desired angles of the camera $n$. The postures of the two cameras were controlled by servo motors. The maximum velocity of the servo motor is 545.5 [deg/s], which is approximately equal to the human saccade.

The camera control system is composed of USB-RS232C converters and camera drivers. The optical zoom of each camera is controlled by hand gesture. In this work, when the right hand is closed, the images captured by the right camera are zoomed in, whereas the image was opened and zoomed out when the hand was opened. Each image from the corresponding camera is trimmed and converted from FHD (1920) to SVGA (800 × 600) RGA signal and projected onto the HMD (SVGA resolution in natural color, PC analog RGB display signal) in real time. The HMD is specialized for this device, which consists of two independent monocular display modules set in front of the right and left eye.

Therefore, the user can control the tracking directions and optical zoom of the two cameras with corresponding positions of the wrists and hand gesture so that the user can control independent arbitrary fields of view for each eye.

## 3   Conclusion

In this work, we developed a system to provide independent fields of view by installing each camera equipped with an electronically controllable zoom lens.

The user can control optical zoom in addition to the posture of the two cameras independently. The scaling up and down of the field view by the zoom lens provides the user not only the visual stimuli induced by the control of spatial resolution of the view but also the visual stimuli induced by the motion of images in zoom.

In future work, we will conduct experiments to investigate effects of the change of spatial resolution and motion of images in zoom induced by zoom lens on human performance of the user during the use of Virtual Chameleon.

# References

1. Mizuno, F., Hayasaka, T., Yamaguchi, T.: Virtual chameleon - a system to provide different views to both eyes. IFMBE Proc. **25**, 169–172 (2009)
2. Mizuno, F., Hayasaka, T., Yamaguchi, T.: A fundamental evaluation of human performance with use of a device to present different two-eyesight both eyes. IFMBE Proc. **37**, 1176–1179 (2011)
3. Blake, R., Logothetis, N.K.: Visual Competition. Nature Re-views Neuroscience, vol. 3, pp. 1–11 (2002)
4. Mizuno, F., Hayasaka, T., Yamaguchi, T.: Development of a system to provide different fields of view to eyes with a function to generate rapid movements. In: Proceedings of the 35th IEEE EMBC, pp. 5311–5314 (2013)

# Simulating Flapping Wing Mechanisms Inspired by the *Manduca sexta* Hawkmoth

Kenneth C. Moses[1(✉)], David Prigg[1], Matthias Weisfeld[1],
Richard J. Bachmann[1], Mark Willis[2], and Roger D. Quinn[1]

[1] Department of Mechanical and Aerospace Engineering,
Case Western Reserve University, Cleveland, OH 44106-7222, USA
kcm7@case.edu
[2] Department of Biology, Case Western Reserve University,
Cleveland, OH 44106-7080, USA

**Abstract.** Several flapping wing mechanisms have been designed from studying the *Manduca sexta* hawkmoth. Simulations of these mechanisms have advanced our understanding of the multiple underlying and interconnected (coupled) mechanical principles at work. Kinematic models are created and indicate that a Scotch yoke inspired mechanism more closely mimics the wing-tip motions observed in *M. sexta* as compared to a slider-crank type mechanism. Subsequently, a kinetic simulation of the Scotch yoke actuator is developed utilizing Lagrange multipliers and solving the system of equations with a Runge-Kutta Fehlberg numerical method. Inspired by analysis of the *M. sexta* hawkmoth thorax muscles, spring-like components are introduced into this system that engage as the wings enter stroke reversal and disengage prior to midstroke. Results of the kinetic simulation indicate areas in which improvements can be made to reduce energy losses due to friction. These simulations serve as a tool for tuning the components of the multibody dynamic system and therefore aid in future designs of the flapping wing mechanism. Establishing the mechanism and associated power requirements is a prerequisite to the development of a fully functional flight-worthy hawkmoth inspired drone.

**Keywords:** Flapping-wing · Simulation · Multibody dynamic modelling

## 1 Introduction

Biologically inspired flapping wing micro air vehicles (FWMAVs) are of great interest due to their potential for overcoming persistent difficulties associated with the use of conventional fixed wing and rotary wing vehicles [1–5]. Their development is driven by a desire to navigate confined spaces, requiring them to be able to fly at relatively low speeds, while being exceptionally maneuverable and having the capability to hover efficiently. In this work, the *Manduca sexta* hawkmoth serves as the model organism for FWMAV development. Their flight kinematics along with flexible wing membrane, flight musculature and completely passive wing structure gives them simple but highly efficient dynamic flight capabilities [6–12]. They exhibit advance flight maneuvers such as rapid pitching and side slipping.

© Springer International Publishing AG, part of Springer Nature 2018
V. Vouloutsi et al. (Eds.): Living Machines 2018, LNAI 10928, pp. 326–337, 2018.
https://doi.org/10.1007/978-3-319-95972-6_35

Previous work has been presented in the design and fabrication of wings that closely mimic the form, shape and structure, and flexibility of the *M. sexta* hawkmoth forewing [13]. While wing design is important for efficient flight, the mechanical mechanism used to drive the wing motion is also a critical component. The efficiency of a flapping wing mechanism is determined by its effectiveness to convert a power source to oscillatory flapping motion, thereby driving the wings to generate lift for the FWMAV. The design of this mechanism is particularly challenging. Further work was completed more recently in which an insect-scale flapping wing mechanism was developed [22]. This work was based on the common approach found in literature that applies empirical methods to examine the insect and its biological components, select and assemble matching man-made components, test to verify performance, and iterate to optimize. However, developing a simulation as a tool to aid in the process would allow for quick component manipulation and thereby reduce the number of hardware iterations. The purpose of this paper is to present the approach and benefits of developing simulation tools to evaluate designs of mechanical flapping mechanisms at *M. sexta* scales.

This paper is organized in the following way; Sect. 2 describes two fundamental types of flapping wing mechanisms investigated for simulation. In Sect. 3, you will find details of the kinematic and dynamic models and their governing equations for each type of mechanism. Section 4 presents the results of the simulations on the flapping wing mechanisms investigated, and Sect. 5 offers our overall findings and conclusions.

## 2   Flapping Wing Mechanisms

An extensive literature review reveals that researchers have designed numerous types of flapping wing mechanisms for biologically inspired MAV development. Often, rotary electric motors are used as a means of propulsion for these actuators due to their efficiencies; however, this means that a device is needed that converts rotary motion into flapping motion. Of the various possible mechanisms, we will discuss four-bar linkages in the form of slider-crank and crank-rocker mechanisms, and Scotch yoke actuators as these cover the majority of current designs.

### 2.1   Four-Bar Linkages, Crank-Rocker and Slider-Crank Mechanisms

Four-bar linkages are prevalent in the design of flapping wing mechanisms [14–19]. In 2005, Zbikowski, Galinski, and Pedersen constructed an insect-like flapping mechanism on a 150 mm scale based on a four-bar linkage combined with spatial articulation [14]. They considered both Bernoulli's lemniscate and Watt's sextic in order to recreate the popular figure eight wingtip trajectory seen in hovering insects and determined that the latter was more feasible for this application. They verified the kinematics of their mechanism through empirical observations using a high-speed digital camera. Another four-bar linkage for studying the structural dynamics of insect wings was conceived by Norris, Palazotto and Cobb [15]. They attempted to account for the aeroelastic response of the wing by designing the mechanism to undershoot and lead their kinematic data thereby allowing the wing to flex and achieve the desired wingtip trajectories.

Several of these four-bar linkages have four revolute joints; therefore, they can also be classified as crank-rocker mechanisms. Furthermore, in a number of these examples a flexible member is realized for energy cost savings. Sahai, Galloway, and Wood successfully improved the performance of their FWMAV by introducing rubber-based flexures into a four-bar mechanism [18]. They were able to produce similar amounts of thrust for a given system with 20% less power using latex rubber strips. Moreover, incorporating these elastic elements in their mechanism only added a cost of 0.02 g in weight but generated 0.3 g of additional thrust while consuming a comparable amount of power.

Unlike crank-rockers, slider-crank linkages have three revolute joints and one prismatic joint. Modeled after dragonflies, Fenelon and Furukawa implemented a modified slider-crank actuator that generates four distinct flapping patterns with a DC motor [19]. Their MAV prototype, which measures $200 \times 200 \times 150$ mm and weighs 3.35 g, is capable of constrained hovering and forward flight.

Initial efforts from our group to develop a flapping-wing-mechanism resulted in a large displacement dynamic assessment technique that employed the use of a slider-crank mechanism for driving the forewings in a similar motion to that of *M. sexta* [13]. A moth's inter-wing angle, stroke amplitude and flapping frequency define a few of the major characteristics of the motion of the moth's wings. Measurements of these parameters for a selected subject moth were captured through digitizing high-speed videography and average values of each parameter were used as requirements for design of the flapping-wing mechanism. While this mechanism helped to identify the impact of altering the structural components of the forewing sets, it was not intended to meet the mass and size constraints of a flightworthy vehicle. The desire to substantially reduce the mechanism's size led us to pursue alternate means of actuation.

## 2.2   Scotch Yoke

The Scotch yoke mechanism is another type of actuator for transforming the continuous rotary motion of an electric motor into the oscillatory flapping-like motion of an insect. Although it is a less common approach to driving the wings of a flapping-wing micro aerial vehicle, the Scotch yoke mechanism has been successfully implemented [20–22].

In one instance, this mechanism was used in a slightly altered version referred to as a double spherical Scotch yoke [20]. The double spherical Scotch yoke is capable of recreating the full three-dimensional motion of insect-like flapping wings. This wingtip motion is spherical in nature and is most commonly observed to exhibit a figure-eight-like pattern lending itself to this type of Scotch yoke design. In comparison to a four-bar mechanism, this design produces smoother flapping motion with relatively small inertial loads and non-excessive accelerations.

Nguyen et al. designed a combination linkage system and Scotch yoke mechanism with passive wing rotation that mimics a beetle's flapping frequency and wing kinematics [21]. Results from their force measurement and forward free flight experiments showed that their device could produce an average vertical force of 2 gram-force and reach a maximum forward velocity of 360 mm/s at 17 Hz flapping frequency.

Preliminary work from our group was documented on a Scotch yoke flapping-wing mechanism with the primary goal of achieving insect-scale overall dimensions [22].

This change in dimensionality focused on positioning the flap axis of rotation of the forewings more akin to *M. sexta* and promoting airflow on both the ventral and dorsal sides of the apparatus. In order to accommodate for these adjustments, it was necessary to transition from a slider-crank mechanism to a Scotch yoke. More recently, while the overall concept of the mechanism has remained the same, significant changes to a number of the components have been made. First, the yoke and driving pins are now constructed from Acetal Delrin®, a thermoplastic with a low coefficient of friction and good wear resistance. Furthermore, the two, two degree of freedom shoulder joints are now fabricated using a Formlabs SLA 3D printer permitting a more condensed structure. Lastly, the geometry of both the yoke and shoulder joints has been altered such that the mid-stroke angle on the down stroke and upstroke occurs when the crank rotates 180°. This modification also lessens the likelihood of binding in the drivetrain.

## 3   Methods

### 3.1   Kinematic Models

Kinematic models of the slider-crank and Scotch yoke mechanism are developed and compared to the previously captured hawkmoth data. MATLAB is used to find the angles, angular velocities, and angular accelerations of the wings at each time step of 0.001 s. In comparison, the high-speed video was captured at 500 frames per second therefore having a time step of 0.002 s. A 0.05-second time interval is selected from the hawkmoth data and the average flapping frequency over this interval is calculated to be 25.31 Hz. This flapping frequency (approximately 159 radians/second) along with an initial crank angle of 0 radians is used as the crank angle input to both systems.

**Slider-crank.** The initial design of the actuation mechanism was a slider-crank design as shown in Fig. 1. A governing equation was developed in terms of geometrical constraints in order to calculate the wing angle with respect to the vertical $(\theta_w)$ as a function of the input angle $(\theta_c)$ of the crank with respect to the horizontal. The position of the slider $(y_s)$ can be found by the following Eq. (1).

$$y_s = \overline{L1}\sin(\theta_c) + \sqrt{\left(\overline{L2}^2 - \overline{L1}^2\cos^2(\theta_c)\right)} \tag{1}$$

The orientation of $\overline{L4}$ is determined by setting up a closed vector chain consisting of $\overline{L3}$, $\overline{L4}$, and the vector formed by the slider and flap axis. Once the direction of link $\overline{L4}$ is known, the wing angle (measured from the vertical) is calculated by adding the offset angle A1.

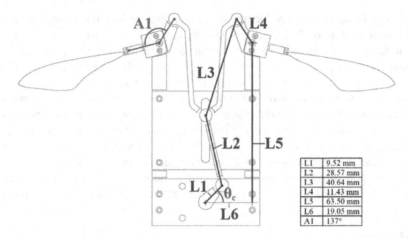

**Fig. 1.** Pictured is a top view of the slider-crank mechanism. Link $\overline{L1}$, the crank, is driven by a DC motor and continuously rotates in the counter-clockwise direction at the desired frequency. At the junction between links $\overline{L2}$, the crankshaft, and $\overline{L3}$ there is a pin that oscillates back and forth within a slot as $\overline{L1}$ rotates. This is known as the slider. The movement of the slider drives $\overline{L3}$ and $\overline{L4}$ thus effectively flapping the wings.

**Scotch yoke.** The design of the Scotch yoke mechanism can be seen in Fig. 2. The wing angle measured from the vertical $(\theta_w)$ is calculated as a function of the crank angle $(\theta_c)$ measured from the horizontal using Eq. (2).

$$\theta_w = \sin^{-1}\left(\frac{\overline{L1}\sin(\theta_c) + \overline{L2} - \overline{L4}}{\overline{L3}}\right) + A1 - \pi/2 \qquad (2)$$

## 3.2   Kinetic Model

The results from the kinematic models (Sect. 4.1) and the size constraints of the flapping wing mechanism suggest that the Scotch yoke is the better candidate for this application. It is therefore chosen for the next step in modeling, which is to incorporate kinetics into the system. The method of Lagrange multipliers is used in order to solve for constraint forces of the multibody system [23]. A representation of the model can be seen in Fig. 3.

Springs are added to the system (in series between the yoke and shoulder pins) as a potential means to aid in stroke reversal. Three generalized coordinates are used to represent the positions of the crank $(\theta_c)$, yoke $(x_y)$, and shoulder $(\theta_s)$. The Lagrangian is shown in (3).

$$L = 1/2\,I_c\dot{\theta}_c^2 + 1/2\,m_y\dot{x}_y^2 + I_{w+s}\dot{\theta}_s^2 - kl_s^2(1 - \cos(\theta_s))^2 \qquad (3)$$

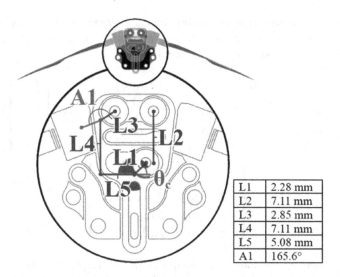

| L1 | 2.28 mm |
|----|---------|
| L2 | 7.11 mm |
| L3 | 2.85 mm |
| L4 | 7.11 mm |
| L5 | 5.08 mm |
| A1 | 165.6° |

**Fig. 2.** A top view of the Scotch yoke mechanism. As link $\overline{L1}$ (the crank) rotates, the yoke is driven back and forth but is constrained to move only in the vertical direction. This vertical displacement of the yoke causes $\overline{L3}$ to rotate about the flap axis (the point at which $\overline{L3}$ and $\overline{L4}$ intersect). The wing is attached to $\overline{L3}$ having an offset angle of A1.

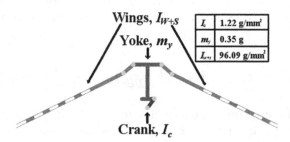

| $I_c$ | 1.22 g/mm$^2$ |
|-------|---------------|
| $m_y$ | 0.35 g |
| $I_{w+s}$ | 96.09 g/mm$^2$ |

**Fig. 3.** Pictured is a depiction of the Scotch yoke kinetic model with inertial terms labeled and a table of their values included.

Where $I_c$ is the moment of inertia of the crank, $I_{w+s}$ is the moment of inertia of the wing and shoulder, $m_y$ is the mass of the yoke, $k$ is the spring constant, and $l_s$ is the length of the shoulder arm (the distance between the shoulder pivot point and driven shoulder pin). Two holonomic constraint equations define the contact surfaces between the crank pin and the yoke, and the yoke and the shoulder pin (4, 5).

$$\phi_1 = x_y - l_c \sin(\theta_c) = 0 \tag{4}$$

$$\phi_2 = x_y - l_s \sin(\theta_s) = 0 \tag{5}$$

Performing the necessary differentiation on the Lagrangian with respect to each of the generalized coordinates and differentiating the constraint equations twice results in a system of equations shown in matrix form (6).

$$
\begin{bmatrix}
I_c & 0 & 0 & l_c\cos(\theta_c) & 0 \\
0 & m_y & 0 & -1 & -1 \\
0 & 0 & 2I_s & 0 & l_s\cos(\theta_s) \\
-l_c\cos(\theta_c) & 1 & 0 & 0 & 0 \\
0 & 1 & -l_s\cos(\theta_s) & 0 & 0
\end{bmatrix}
\begin{Bmatrix}
\ddot{\theta}_c \\
\ddot{x}_y \\
\ddot{\theta}_s \\
\lambda_1 \\
\lambda_2
\end{Bmatrix}
$$
$$
=
\begin{Bmatrix}
T_M \\
0 \\
-2kl_s^2\sin(\theta_s)(1-\cos(\theta_s)) \\
-l_c\dot{\theta}_c^2\sin(\theta_c) \\
-l_s\dot{\theta}_s^2\sin(\theta_s)
\end{Bmatrix}
\tag{6}
$$

Where $\lambda_1$ and $\lambda_2$ are Lagrange multipliers and correspond to the forces at the contact surface between the crank pin and yoke, and the yoke and the shoulder pin, respectively. Additionally, $T_M$ is the motor torque and is an input in to the system.

A Runge-Kutta Fehlberg method with the Cash-Karp coefficients is written in MATLAB and used to solve the system of differential equations [24]. This method is written as opposed to using MATLABs built-in methods (such as ode23 and ode45) in order to allow control over the adaptive step size and implement iteration-based equations in future revisions. The adaptive step size of this method is calculated using Eq. (7).

$$
h_{i+1} = h_i\left(\frac{\epsilon h_i}{2|E|}\right)^{0.25}
\tag{7}
$$

Where $h$ is the step size, $\epsilon$ is the absolute tolerance, and $E$ is the error calculated with the Cash-Karp coefficients from comparing the fourth-order and fifth-order RK methods.

## 4  Results

### 4.1  Kinematic Models

The kinematic models of the slider-crank and Scotch yoke mechanisms were driven at a constant angular velocity of 159 radians/second obtained from averaging the *M. sexta* hawkmoth's flapping frequency over a 0.05-second interval (see Fig. 4). When comparing the real moth and Scotch yoke, a small phase difference is noticed. This is attributed to the moth changing its flapping frequency slightly during flight whereas the simulation is running at a constant angular velocity. Observation of the wing angles indicates a maximum offset between the slider-crank and the Scotch yoke mechanisms of approximately 12° during stroke reversal (around 0.01 and 0.03 s). However, this offset is mostly due to inaccuracies in the linkage lengths and can be remedied easily.

Close inspection of the angular velocities suggests that the Scotch yoke mechanism sustains its maximum velocities for a longer period of time (nearly twice as long during the forward stroke) and transitions between strokes more rapidly similarly to *M. sexta*. We also see this phenomenon when studying the angular accelerations. The Scotch yoke accelerates in the negative direction, transitioning from the backward stroke to the forward stroke near the 0.01-second mark, much more rapidly than the slider-crank. Additionally, the accelerations of the Scotch yoke and hawkmoth level off during midstroke (around 0.02 and 0.04 s) whereas the slider-crank does not. In general, the

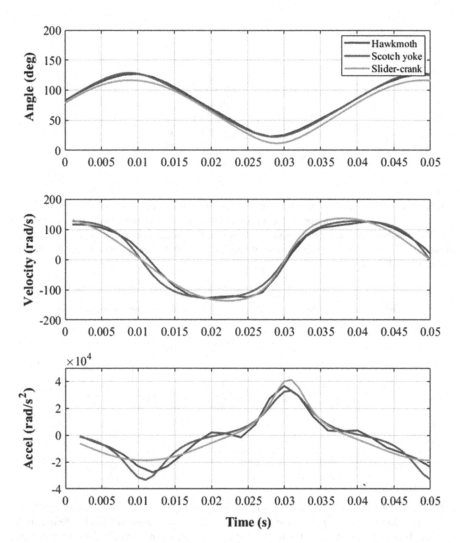

**Fig. 4.** The angle, angular velocity, and angular acceleration of the *M. sexta* hawkmoth data (blue), Scotch yoke model (red), and slider-crank model (yellow) are plotted as a function of time. In all three plots, the Scotch yoke outperforms the slider-crank when compared to the hawkmoth data. (Color figure online)

forward and backward strokes of the slider-crank differ; however, the stroke pattern of the Scotch yoke is symmetric and therefore aligns more closely to the moth.

## 4.2   Kinetic Model

The kinetic model accepts an input of the motor torque as a function of time and produces outputs of the position, velocity, and acceleration of all three generalized coordinates that correspond to the crank, yoke, and the combination of shoulder and wing (Fig. 5).

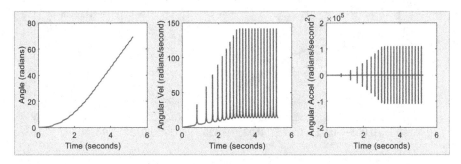

**Fig. 5.** The resultant crank angle, angular velocity, and angular acceleration when the system is subjected to 450 gf•mm of motor torque for 3 s and then allowed to move freely for an additional 2 s. The spikes observed in the angular velocity and angular acceleration plots occur during stroke reversal, just after the crank passes through $n\pi/2$ and the crank pin impacts the alternate side of the yoke's slot.

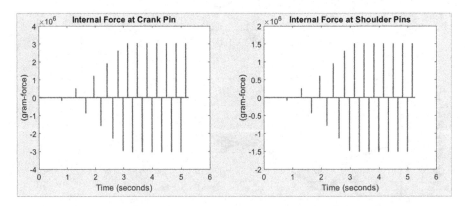

**Fig. 6.** Internal forces for the same 5 s run as shown in Fig. 5. Note that the maximum forces are exaggerated due to the model assuming an instantaneous change in velocity during stroke reversal. However, while the magnitudes of the forces are overestimated, the occurrence and timing of these forces are relevant.

The constraint forces are also calculated and displayed for each run (Fig. 6). These internal forces indicate the potential magnitude of friction forces and thus energy losses within the system. Through observation, it is clear that the internal forces of this system peak during stroke reversal and therefore further refinements to the design of the mechanism will be centered on this phase of the wingbeat cycle.

## 5 Conclusions

The simulations presented in this work lay the groundwork for further development of a flapping wing mechanism capable of efficient hovering. Kinematic models helped to narrow the design scope of the actuator and showed that the Scotch yoke mechanism yields promising initial results. The wing-tip motions of the Scotch yoke more closely resembled *M. sexta* as opposed to the slider-crank, especially when comparing wing angle velocities and accelerations. Additionally, the slider-crank mechanism exhibited asymmetric forward and backward strokes whereas the Scotch yoke and hawkmoth did not. Overall, the Scotch yoke design showed very similar behavior to the biological moth, making it a viable option for the actuation of the robotic moth.

A kinetic model was developed in order to further analyze the Scotch yoke mechanism. The simulation can estimate the internal forces on individual components during the wing's beat cycle. The kinetic model of the Scotch yoke identified crank angles of $\frac{n\pi}{2}$ where $n = 1, 3, 5, \cdots$ as areas throughout the wingbeat cycle in which energy losses are high. These crank angles correspond to the time of stroke reversal. By having a kinetic model, it is now possible to assess the efficiency of the mechanism and estimate the energy consumption as well as develop and apply a controller and observe its performance. With this tool, the mechanism and the controller can be easily modified with the goal of reducing energy losses thus improving its efficiency. The physical geometry and properties of components can be adjusted through model configuration, and the model can be re-run to determine sensitivity of each of the internal forces. This simulation isolates inertial loads from aerodynamic forces in order to assess their impact on the mechanism. In future work, aerodynamic forces will be incorporated into the simulation and the results compared. Subsequently, additional validation will take place by comparing simulation results to empirical results obtained by digitizing high speed videography of the mechanism. Furthermore, the developed model will be used to show that it may be possible to conserve energy during stroke reversal and reduce inefficiencies inherent in flapping wing mechanisms.

## References

1. Sachs, G.: Comparison of power requirements: flapping vs fixed wing vehicles. Aerospace **3** (31), 1–15 (2016)
2. Chen, Y., Gravish, N., Desbiens, A.L., Malka, R., Wood, R.J.: Experimental and computational studies of the aerodynamic performance of a flapping and passively rotating insect wing. J. Fluid Mech. **791**, 1–33 (2016)

3. Bin Abas, M.F., Bin Mohd. Rafie, A.S., Bin Yusoff, H., Bin Ahmad, K.A.: Flapping wing micro-aerial-vehicle: kinematics, membranes, and flapping mechanisms of ornithopter and insect flight. Chin. J. Aeronaut. **29**(5), 1159–1177 (2016)
4. Pesavento, U., Wang, Z.J.: Flapping wing flight can save aerodynamic power compared to steady flight. Phys. Rev. Lett. **103**(11), 1–4 (2009)
5. Hu, H., Gopa Kumar, A., Abate, G., Albertani, R.: An experimental study of flexible membrane wings in flapping flight. In: 47th AIAA Aerospace Sciences Meeting Including the New Horizons Forum and Aerospace Exposition, pp. 1–16 (2009)
6. Combes, S.A., Daniel, T.L.: Into thin air: contributions of aerodynamic and inertial-elastic forces to wing bending in the hawkmoth Manduca sexta. J. Exp. Biol. **206**(Pt 17), 2999–3006 (2003)
7. Ansari, S.A., Zbikowski, R., Knowles, K.: Aerodynamic modelling of insect-like flapping flight for micro air vehicles. Prog. Aerosp. Sci. **42**(2), 129–172 (2006)
8. Combes, S.A.: Materials, structure, and dynamics of insect wings as bioinspiration for MAVs. Encyclopedia of Aerospace Engineering, pp. 1–10 (2010)
9. DeLeón, N.E., Palazotto, A.: The evaluation of a biologically inspired engineered MAV wing compared to the *Manduca Sexta* wing under simulated flapping conditions. Int. J. Micro Air Veh. **3**(3), 149–168 (2011)
10. O'Hara, R.P., Palazotto, A.N.: The morphological characterization of the forewing of the Manduca sexta species for the application of biomimetic flapping wing micro air vehicles. Bioinspir. Biomim. **7**(4), 46011 (2012)
11. Nakata, T., Liu, H.: A fluid-structure interaction model of insect flight with flexible wings. J. Comput. Phys. **231**(4), 1822–1847 (2012)
12. Zheng, L., Hedrick, T., Mittal, R.: A comparative study of the hovering efficiency of flapping and revolving wings. Bioinspir. Biomim. **8**(3), 036001 (2013)
13. Moses, K.C., Michaels, S.C., Willis, M., Quinn, R.D.: Artificial Manduca sexta forewings for flapping-wing micro aerial vehicles: how wing structure affects performance. Bioinspir. Biomim. **12**(5), 055003 (2017)
14. Żbikowski, R., Galiński, C., Pedersen, C.B.: Four-Bar linkage mechanism for insectlike flapping wings in hover: concept and an outline of its realization. J. Mech. Des. **127**(4), 817 (2005)
15. Norris, A.G., Palazotto, A.N., Cobb, R.G.: Structural dynamic characterization of an insect wing, In: 51st AIAA/ASME/ASCE/AHS/ASC Structures, Structural Dynamics, and Materials Conference 18th AIAA/ASME/AHS Adaptive Structures Conference 12th, p. 2790 (2010)
16. Liu, C.H., Chen, C.K.: Kinematic analysis of a flapping-wing micro-aerial-vehicle with watt straight-line linkage. J. Appl. Sci. Eng. **18**(4), 355–362 (2015)
17. Zhang, T., Zhou, C., Wang, C., Zhang, X.: Flapping wing mechanism design based on mechanical creative design theory. In: 2011 International Conference on Mechatronic Science Electronic Engineering and Computer, vol. 3, no. 1, pp. 2237–2240 (2011)
18. Sahai, R., Galloway, K.C., Wood, R.J.: Elastic element integration for improved flapping-wing micro air vehicle performance. IEEE Trans. Robot. **29**(1), 32–41 (2013)
19. Fenelon, M.A.A., Furukawa, T.: Design of an active flapping wing mechanism and a micro aerial vehicle using a rotary actuator. Mech. Mach. Theory **45**(2), 137–146 (2010)
20. Galiński, C., Żbikowski, R.: Insect-like flapping wing mechanism based on a double spherical scotch yoke. J. R. Soc. Interface **2**(3), 223–235 (2005)
21. Nguyen, Q.V., Truong, Q.T., Park, H.C., Goo, N.S., Byun, D.: A motor-driven flapping-wing system mimicking beetle flight. In: 2009 IEEE International Conference on Robotics and Biomimetics, ROBIO 2009, pp. 1087–1092 (2009)

22. Moses, K.C., Michaels, N.I., Hauerwas, J., Willis, M., Quinn, R.D.: An insect-scale bioinspired flapping-wing-mechanism for micro aerial vehicle development. In: Biomimetic and Biohybrid Systems pp. 589–594 (2017)
23. Greenwood, D.T.: Principles of Dynamics, Second. Prentice-Hall, Upper Saddle River (1988)
24. Chapra, S.C., Canale, R.P.: Numerical Methods for Engineers, Fourth. McGraw-Hill, New York (2002)

# A Survival Task for the Design and the Assessment of an Autonomous Agent

Bhargav Teja Nallapu[1,2,3](✉) and Frédéric Alexandre[1,2,3]

[1] INRIA Bordeaux Sud-Ouest, 200 Avenue de la Vieille Tour, 33405 Talence, France
bhargav.teja-nallapu@inria.fr
[2] LaBRI, Université de Bordeaux, Bordeaux INP, CNRS, UMR 5800, Talence, France
[3] IMN, Université de Bordeaux, CNRS, UMR 5293, Bordeaux, France

**Abstract.** Learning to survive in a complex environment is a more relevant task for the design of intelligent autonomous machines than complex problem solving. To establish this statement, we emphasize that autonomy requires emotional- and motivational-like characteristics that are much more straightforward to define in the context of survival tasks than in problem solving which is classically considered with intelligent agents. We also propose that using a simulation platform is a good preliminary step before the design of real machines because it allows to consider another fundamental challenge, related to the association of these emotional and motivational characteristics to higher cognitive functions. These considerations are illustrated by current simulations that we are carrying out with a bio-inspired neuronal model of the cerebral architecture of primates.

**Keywords:** Computational neuroscience · Autonomy
Simulation platform

## 1 Introduction

This paper presents a neuromimetic approach to emulate intelligent behavior in autonomous machines. Lately, striking progresses have been reported in the field of Artificial Intelligence, on hierarchical neuronal models such as Deep Networks applied to specific tasks like playing Go or answering general knowledge questions, setting the focus on dedicated complex problem solving tasks. However, in reference to some characteristics of intelligence in animals, autonomy raises other challenges at least as important as abstract intelligence does. Firstly, in reference to the emotional domain, an autonomous agent should be able to set its own goals by anticipating outcomes and to acquire its preferences by learning. Similarly, motivation should also be considered, to energize potential behaviors according to a level of need felt or to the anticipated cost of an action [Dickinson and Balleine 2002]. As these characteristics have been often associated to bodily

© Springer International Publishing AG, part of Springer Nature 2018
V. Vouloutsi et al. (Eds.): Living Machines 2018, LNAI 10928, pp. 338–347, 2018.
https://doi.org/10.1007/978-3-319-95972-6_36

aspects [Cardinal et al. 2002], these challenges will require further studies about the body and its physiology. Secondly, it has been shown that these embodied aspects play an important role in the most complex aspects of cognition, including decision-making, planning or social skills [Damasio et al. 1996], but the underlying neuronal mechanisms are to be understood in more details.

The above mentioned challenges correspond to two very ambitious research programs of different nature, that are difficult to carry out in tandem, although based on common ground. One issue is to modify the material characteristics of machines to allow them to reflect certain sensory and motor characteristics associated to emotions and motivations, as we observe in the case of animals. The other issue is to understand how these characteristics influence the most elaborate forms of reasoning, particularly allowing to associate subjective and incomparable quantities such as the level of need for a resource and its cost or its social impact.

We present here some elements of a modeling work that bridges the challenges between the above mentioned directions. This work considers the possibility to define an autonomous agent by adapting a well established neuronal model proposed in [Hazy et al. 2006], mimicking the function of major loops in the brain of primates and primarily involving two cerebral structures, the cortex and the basal ganglia. The so-called cortico-basal loops have been associated to the generic function of decision making and action selection and several such loops have been experimentally observed [Alexander et al. 1986]. Based on these observations, we have implemented four loops. Two loops are called sensorimotor and are fed with external spatial and visual information and select actions of orientation and object reaching. The other two loops are called limbic and are fed with internal information carrying emotional and motivational characteristics and make decisions about the need to satisfy and the object to select.

In addition to implementing each of the four loops and their interactions, a major question in our work was to assess the ability of the whole model to emulate an autonomous behavior, by defining what could stand for body and an environment to interact with this model of cerebral architecture and what could be the task to address, to quantify the behavior of the brain+body system, possibly under different dimensions.

In the next section, we propose that learning to survive in a complex environment is a more relevant task than complex problem solving. We define a survival task where the autonomous agent must monitor basic needs such as hunger or thirst to select the resource to be reached in its environment. In the subsequent section, we introduce a simulation platform that simulates the agent, the body as well as its environment, and allows us to control the complexity level of the environment and modify its properties. This also leads to the definition of the emotional and motivational characteristics of the agent and their encoding in the model. We propose that, even if this software platform brings a radical simplification compared to a hardware machine, it is an excellent first step towards building autonomous machines and addresses fundamental questions about embodiment. We then report for illustration the results of the first experiments that we have carried out and finally mention further work that could be considered.

## 2    A Survival Task

Let us first state that, if there is a precise task that characterizes an autonomous agent, it is a task of survival. An autonomous agent has to be able to survive in an unknown environment, being aware of its vital variables and being able to keep those variables in acceptable bounds at any given moment and for the forthcoming moments. Consequently, it has to minimize uncertainty and avoid *surprise* to ensure that it accomplishes the goal of keeping variables in bound. This has been formalized in, e.g., [Friston et al. 2016] and is revisited differently here. A step further, biological systems often fail, e.g. have limited generalization capability or learning performances, and the utopian vision that they are "very general autonomous systems" is questionable: They may more "adapt" than "learn", i.e. change some parameters of some versatile behaviors, instead of "inventing" new behaviors.

To demonstrate this principle, we consider an agent in an environment that has 'objects' that are primarily given an incentive value - their relevance to the amount of hunger they satisfy or the amount of thirst they quench if these needs are considered. The objects also carry a *preference* value with respect to the agent, which could be retrieved from the agent's pre-existing knowledge (or being learned, this very important aspect will not be considered in the present study but see [Carrere and Alexandre 2015] for previous work we made on pavlovian learning, known to contribute to preference learning). The two limbic loops mentioned above that we have implemented are respectively in charge of selecting the need to be considered and the preferred object. We will mention below how they are associated, through the simulation platform, to the internal perception of needs (for motivational aspects) and to the representation of preference as an anticipation of a certain level of pleasure (for emotional aspects).

At any given instant, it is possible that there are no objects perceived by the agent in the vicinity. In this case, the other two loops, the sensorimotor loops, are responsible for the orientation of the agent in space until objects are perceived. If any reveal pertinent to the task, the loops are also responsible for navigation, reaching and consumption of this object. We mention below how the spatial and visual aspects to be processed in the sensorimotor loops are extracted from the simulation platform.

For the moment in our description, the loops are presented independent to each other and each of them respectively carries out a specific function. It is of course necessary to consider some coordination between the loops to emulate a really intelligent and autonomous behavior and we will evoke below several strategies of coordination and how they can be implemented, particularly to give rise to a possibility of different starting points of the survival task. Before all these developments, we describe, in the following section, the generic algorithm implemented for each loop in the model and the Malmo platform we used to create an environment for the task.

# 3    A Model of Cerebral Loops

In the brief description above, each loop has been assigned a very different function, but it is also noticeable to mention that each loop is dynamically computed with the same algorithm, since they are all part of the same circuitry linking the basal ganglia and the sensory and frontal cortical areas.

Firstly, sensory cues, corresponding to actual or desired sensations activate candidate actions in the frontal area. A primitive strategy is to trigger the action most often associated to these sensations. This corresponds to *habits*. Else, a selection process takes place to make a decision based on a deeper contextual analysis. This is attributed as one of the major roles of the basal ganglia.

The basal ganglia is often presented as a competitive system (Go-No Go in [Hazy et al. 2006]), based on several excitatory and inhibitory pathways respectively adding more weight to the selection and the inhibition of each candidate action until one reaches a threshold and is triggered. This dual evaluation is based on the estimated values of the expected sensory consequences of the action and other modulatory contextual information.

There have been computational accounts of such action selection in the basal ganglia using a two-arm bandit task [Pasquereau et al. 2007], that go on to demonstrate how the outcomes of such actions are learned, thereby being able to choose the best rewarding one later [Redgrave et al. 1999, Topalidou and Rougier 2015]. The conflict between two almost equivalent options is resolved by an external noise driving one of them towards selection. Even without a complicated task in context, the same selection between two equivalent stimuli can be demonstrated in a single channel of neural populations. This kind of selection is achieved by implementing the above mentioned complementary pathways in the basal ganglia as neural ensembles with excitatory and inhibitory connections [Leblois et al. 2006].

Each loop described in our model has a respective substrate of the basal ganglia involved for the local selection. Given the space constraints in the paper and the main emphasis being on the high level behaviour, we restrict the description of the dynamics within the basal ganglia in the Eq. 1 as in [Leblois et al. 2006]. Assuming each unit represents an ensemble tuned towards a particular stimulus: $I_{ext}$ is the external input representing the salience of the stimulus, $I_s$ is the input to the unit from its connections (synaptic input) and $\tau$ is the decay time constant of the synaptic input and $m$ is the output of the unit.

$$\tau \frac{dm}{dt} = -m + I_s + I_{ext} \tag{1}$$

The synaptic input to a unit $j, I_s^j$, which is the input as a result of the connections from units of other structures (say $i$), depends on the connections weights $(w_{ij})$ between units $i$ and $j$ , as shown in the Eq. 2. We would like to emphasize that the dynamics given by the Eqs. 1 and 2 are phenomenological and are not constrained to a specific neuronal architecture.

$$I_s^j = \Sigma_i w_{ij} * m_i \tag{2}$$

When an action is triggered, its expected sensory consequences are also activated to a specific desired level, representing the goal of the action. The action will be maintained until the expected sensory consequences (or other conditions for interruption, not developed here) are met.

In some cases, triggering the action is not sufficient to reach the goal (e.g. deciding to eat is not sufficient to get some food) and the desired activity can itself trigger new actions in other loops (e.g. finding some food). This process can recursively trigger other secondary goals, until some goal is immediately achieved, stopping the corresponding action.

This generic algorithm is applied in parallel in the four loops. Among the limbic loops, one is responsible for selecting the need, based on the interoception of internal levels. We refer to this loop as *Why* loop as it corresponds to the motivation behind selecting the need. The other is responsible for selecting perceived items known to satisfy some needs, based on their levels of preference. This loop is referred to as *What* loop as it signifies the qualitative nature of each stimulus owing to its preference level. Among the sensorimotor loops, one is responsible for orienting the agent towards the selected target, which we call *Where* loop. The other, referred to as *How* loop, is responsible for moving to reach the target. The *Why* loop also receives an input from the sensori-motor loops, representing the cost of action involved in reaching a certain stimulus, to be able to compare with the appetitive gain the stimulus might offer. This can be simply implemented using negative connection weights $w_{ij}$ in Eq. 2.

In addition, this selection made locally in a specific loop is also modulated by the selection made in a different loop. For example, the activity strength of selection in *What* loop modulates the activities competing for selection in the *Why* loop. Similarly, the *Why* loop modulates the *Where* loop which in turn modulates the *How* loop. To keep the modulation simple and tractable, we implement a simple biasing factor $b_{ij}$ from unit $i$ to $j$, as a function of the source activity $a_i$ as shown in Eq. 3.

$$b_{ij} = a_i^{\tan \sigma_{IJ} \frac{\pi}{4}} \qquad (3)$$

In Eq. 3, $\sigma_{IJ}$ is a bias strength parameter that is specific between two populations $I$ and $J$. For instance, the bias that the preference-based choice might have on the need-based choice could be less than the bias that the overall limbic choice has on that of any of the sensorimotor loops. This kind of interactions between different cortico-basal ganglial loops in animals (including primates) is a question of wide interest in the field of neuroscience. Here in this work, we stick to a rather simple implementation for the ease of the demonstration of the principle. Therefore, it has to be noted that all the equations given above represent a generalized principle (lateral interactions, modulation etc.) between the neuronal structures and their intra-loop and inter loop dynamics.

## 4   The Malmo Platform

Minecraft is a sandbox video game with a virtual 3D world that can be generated procedurally. With single or multiple agents in it, activities like exploration and resource gathering can be simulated. Malmo is an Artificial Intelligence experimentation platform on the top of Minecraft [Johnson et al. 2016]. Malmo allows to incorporate various models of reinforcement learning, planning and collaborative and competitive strategies into the Minecraft game environment among the agents. Malmo has been used for various kinds of specific experimentations like learning to navigate in the Minecraft world [Matiisen et al. 2017] and computational models of animals living in block world [Strannegård et al. 2017a]. In most of such cases, very specific feature of Malmo is used (either the 3D space in the environment or the block nature of the world or the agent to perform a task. We exploit, simultaneously, various features of Malmo like the agent's internal body attributes, external constraints like vision, and uncertainty that can be induced into the scenario owing to the vast environment and its contents. Furthermore, Malmo provides great convenience to connect our model of generic loops to the Minecraft world, since the model inevitably requires an elaborative environment to study and visualize the behavior in a survival task.

Malmo provides an agent, on which we have a full control on its actions, either through the tool or through our model. The agent by default has an attribute *life* that is affected by the external world (e.g, when in contact with fire or attacked by other agents). Malmo allows to construct a 3D world of the size of choice, in which the agent is present. We can procedurally place certain *items* in the world, in the vicinity of the agent or elsewhere. *Items* can be attributed respective reward values that the agent is able to gain when it collects them. The agent is allowed to execute finely controlled actions like *turn*, *move*, *jump*, etc. At any given time step, the framework provides the *state* of both the agent and the environment with respect to the agent. The *state* includes attributes like agent's life, its position and orientation in absolute coordinates with respect to the world, the items that are present in the chosen accessibility range around the agent and their positions and attributes.

For the survival task we have chosen, attributing bodily and other emotional and motivational characteristics to the agent forms a key aspect of our model. Besides the relevant features of Malmo we use, we augment these characteristics to the agent as well as to the *items* in the task. Agent has two vital variables - *hunger* and *thirst* - which increase with time as well as with the level of efforts (meaning an action *move* or *turn*). Instead of a one dimensional reward, each item carries a motivational index that is relevant to the *hunger* or the *thirst* level it would satisfy, and a level of *preference* with respect to the agent, expressing its emotional value. Also, from a functional point of view, we adapted few aspects like *visibility* of the agent and the information about the *positions* (of items as well as the agent itself). For instance, as the model is desired to be bio-inspired, we consider few bodily, biological constraints to the agent and restrict the agent's field of vision to a plausible value (in our case, $120°$). The information about the objects in the environment is also restricted depending on the distance from the agent within the field of vision. These adaptations were important to add certain biologically plausible restrictions to the task given that we would not model them in detail as they don't fall in the scope of our goals.

## 5    Illustrations

Figure 1 shows several moments from an episode in the task implemented in Malmo, primarily concerned with different questions each loop in the model addresses. In a basic scenario, the agent starts exploring the environment (Fig. 1a) with a *desired* activation for a particular item that (known from previous experience) would satisfy the current major *need* (Fig. 1a, inset). This is a result of the internal state processing in the *Why* loop. When the agent perceives multiple stimuli (Fig. 1b), along with the appetitive relevance of each of the stimuli, the action costs, depending on their positions, are also provided (implemented as a negative signal from the sensory-motor loops). Furthermore, the choice on the pre-existing preferences towards the stimuli corresponding to the selected *need* is made in the *What* loop and it modulates the selection in the *Why* loop.

Once the decision has been made in the *Why* loop and the goal has been set, the execution of goal involves two steps in the two sensorimotor loops. Once a stimulus is chosen, the goal is to orient towards it. The *Where* loop is responsible for the agent to start *turning* towards it (see *apple* in Figure 1c) until the selected stimulus is in the sight of the agent. And finally, owing to the processing in the *How* loop, the agent moves to reach the stimulus that it has oriented towards and *consumes* it (an imaginary action which we equate to the agent reaching the *item* and updates the corresponding *hunger* and *thirst* values).

Sustaining the selection of goal until it is achieved is at the core of the processing in each loop. The *Where* loop, after choosing the orientation to turn, sustains the activity until the object is in sight. And the *How* loop sustains its activity from the point of orienting to the point where it has reached closer to the stimulus, to be able to *consume* it. This would now cascade back to the *limbic* loops which have been sustaining their selected responses. The *Why* loop, which has been active since selecting the current need, is sustained until the need levels are modified by the consumption of the stimulus. Similarly, the *What* loop,

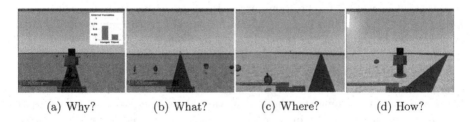

|        (a) Why?        |        (b) What?        |        (c) Where?        |        (d) How?        |

**Fig. 1.** Snapshots at different stages in the task. (a) Internal needs monitored in the *Why* loop (inset). (b) Processing information about the stimuli in the *What* loop. (c) Orienting towards the selected stimulus using the *Where* loop. (d) Reaching the selected stimulus using the *How* loop, once oriented. *Note:* The different third person and first person views in (a) and (b) are only chosen to show the change in proximity of stimuli to the agent, but these views have no effect on the task. They can be switched while watching the task. Similarly, for (c) and (d)

which has been sustaining activity since selecting a preferred stimulus, continues until verifying the consumed stimulus has the expected value.

# 6   Discussion

In the wake of the field of Artificial General Intelligence that advocates intelligent agents should be able to solve general problems, it is rather easy to classify *survival* of an autonomous agent as a general problem. We argue that *survival* of an autonomous agent, in fact, addresses a very specific question, that requires the agent to keep its vital variables within acceptable bounds in the current as well as a future, anticipated state. We emphasize the *body*, which completes a closed-loop of interaction for the agent with the environment, as the key to the process of survival. Consequently, we derive our basis from neuroscience of animal cognition and behavior to build a bio-inspired model that helps an artificial agent survive. The components of our model, representing the cortical and basal ganglia structures in the brain, are inspired to be close to the biological plausibility in their working dynamics. As mentioned earlier, understanding the interactions between these cortico basal-ganglial loops is an active ongoing work in the field of neuroscience and we, through the description and further development of our model, would like to be in a position of useful contribution to that work.

In the field of robotics, there have been accounts of motivation driven robotic systems and a few design frameworks [Strannegård et al. 2017b, Konidaris and Barto 2006]. Most of them address the task of making a choice based on motivation. We derive inspiration from such formalisms and begin to build much more comprehensive scenarios involving the behaviour of agent, in a bio-inspired manner, in which action selection forms a key component. We remain aware that building such scenarios in a bio-inspired manner requires further more understanding of higher level neural mechanisms involved in animal foraging behavior [Kolling et al. 2012, Constantino and Daw 2015]. However, we would like to emphasize that the fundamental basis of demonstrating comprehensive animal behaviours in artificial agent lies in the description of the underlying generic characteristics of the survival task. Therefore, in this work, we contain ourselves to the description of the basic task and required attributes, keeping the developments and performance studies to a much finer study elsewhere. In fact, using the neural structures already involved in certain loops, we account for context-specific preferences of the agent (in the *What* loop) and the action costs involved in choosing a stimulus (in the *Why* loop). In the context of the task that we target to demonstrate, given its complexity, it is considerably difficult to choose the right kind and number of attributes to be encoded in the model. Rightly so, we chose an experimentation platform that inspires our concrete choice of emotional and motivational characteristics of the model.

Different starting points characterize certain scenarios in which agent exhibits a distinct behavior, quite often, that belongs to a set of behaviors extensively studied in neuroscience related to primate cognition. The example scenario illustrated in the section *Illustrations* describes a very prominent animal behavior in neuroscience, called goal-directed behavior [Balleine et al. 2009]. As a part of our ongoing work, we plan to study other key animal behaviors like stimulus-driven behavior where, even in the absence of internal need, the external stimuli in the environment drive the motivation of the animal. We also are interested in extending the model to explain much more interesting, opportunistic behaviors where the agent's chosen current behavior can be interrupted to switch to another, anticipating a higher satisfaction for a future need as opposed to a lower satisfaction of a current need. It is the emergence of such versatile behaviors that helps the animal survive in a dynamic external world. The platform we chose, Malmo, invariantly supports demonstrating various behaviors with no or minimal changes to itself but only from the changes in the state of the agent or the objects in the environment. Unlike other works that used Malmo to interface with Minecraft gaming environment, we utilize its features to have a finer control on the environment and to demonstrate the modulation between the cognitive behaviour and action execution in the environment.

Interestingly enough, understanding the dynamics between such different behaviors is still an open problem in computational neuroscience. That encourages us to strengthen the basis of our model more from biology, exploit the convenient visualization platform like Malmo to demonstrate the model to neuroscientists and gain their insights. After all, we, the intelligent primates, are a perfect example of an autonomous agent trying to survive, only in a real world.

**Acknowledgements.** We would like to acknowledge Thierry Viéville, INRIA Sophia Antipolis, France, for his collaboration.

# References

Alexander, G., DeLong, M., Strick, P.: Parallel organization of functionally segregated circuits linking basal ganglia and cortex. Ann. Rev. Neurosci. **9**, 357–381 (1986)

Balleine, B.W., Liljeholm, M., Ostlund, S.B.: The integrative function of the basal ganglia in instrumental conditioning. Behav. Brain Res. **199**(1), 43–52 (2009)

Cardinal, R.N., Parkinson, J.A., Hall, J., Everitt, B.J.: Emotion and motivation: the role of the amygdala, ventral striatum, and prefrontal cortex. Neurosci. Biobehav. Rev. **26**(3), 321–352 (2002)

Carrere, M., Alexandre, F.: A pavlovian model of the amygdala and its influence within the medial temporal lobe. Front. Syst. Neurosci. **9**(41) (2015)

Constantino, S.M., Daw, N.D.: Learning the opportunity cost of time in a patch-foraging task. Cogn. Affect. Behav. Neurosci. **15**(4), 837–853 (2015)

Damasio, A.R., Everitt, B.J., Bishop, D.: The somatic marker hypothesis and the possible functions of the prefrontal cortex. Philos. Trans. R. Soc. Lond. Ser. B Biol. Sci. **351**(1346), 1413–1420 (1996)

Dickinson, A., Balleine, B.W.: The role of learning in the operation of motivational systems. In: Pashler, H., Gallistel, R. (eds.) Stevens' Handbook of Experimental Psychology, Learning, Motivation and Emotion, vol. 3, 3rd edn, pp. 497–533. Wiley, New York (2002)

Friston, K., FitzGerald, T., Rigoli, F., Schwartenbeck, P., Pezzulo, G., et al.: Active inference and learning. Neurosci. Biobehav. Rev. **68**, 862–879 (2016)

Hazy, T.E., Frank, M.J., O'Reilly, R.C.: Banishing the homunculus: making working memory work. Neuroscience **139**(1), 105–118 (2006)

Johnson, M., Hofmann, K., Hutton, T., Bignell, D.: The malmo platform for artificial intelligence experimentation. In: IJCAI, pp. 4246–4247 (2016)

Kolling, N., Behrens, T.E., Mars, R.B., Rushworth, M.F.: Neural mechanisms of foraging. Science **336**(6077), 95–98 (2012)

Konidaris, G., Barto, A.: An adaptive robot motivational system. In: Nolfi, S., Baldassarre, G., Calabretta, R., Hallam, J.C.T., Marocco, D., Meyer, J.-A., Miglino, O., Parisi, D. (eds.) SAB 2006. LNCS (LNAI), vol. 4095, pp. 346–356. Springer, Heidelberg (2006). https://doi.org/10.1007/11840541_29

Leblois, A., Boraud, T., Meissner, W., Bergman, H., Hansel, D.: Competition between feedback loops underlies normal and pathological dynamics in the basal ganglia. J. Neurosci. **26**(13), 3567–3583 (2006)

Matiisen, T., Oliver, A., Cohen, T., Schulman, J.: Teacher-student curriculum learning (2017). arXiv preprint arXiv:1707.00183

Pasquereau, B., Nadjar, A., Arkadir, D., Bezard, E., Goillandeau, M., Bioulac, B., Gross, C.E., Boraud, T.: Shaping of motor responses by incentive values through the basal ganglia. J. Neurosci. **27**(5), 1176–1183 (2007)

Redgrave, P., Prescott, T.J., Gurney, K.: The basal ganglia: a vertebrate solution to the selection problem? Neuroscience **89**(4), 1009–1023 (1999)

Strannegård, C., Svangård, N., Bach, J., Steunebrink, B.: Generic animats. In: Everitt, T., Goertzel, B., Potapov, A. (eds.) AGI 2017. LNCS (LNAI), vol. 10414, pp. 23–32. Springer, Cham (2017a). https://doi.org/10.1007/978-3-319-63703-7_3

Strannegård, C., Svangård, N., Lindström, D., Bach, J., Steunebrink, B.: The animat path to artificial general intelligence. In: Proceedings of IJCAI-17 Workshop on Architectures for Generality & Autonomy (2017b)

Topalidou, M., Rougier, N.P.: [re] interaction between cognitive and motor corticobasal ganglia loops during decision making: a computational study. ReScience J. **1**(1) (2015)

# Moment Arm Analysis of the Biarticular Actuators in Compliant Robotic Leg CARL

Atabak Nejadfard[1(✉)], Steffen Schütz[1], Krzysztof Mianowski[2], Patrick Vonwirth[1], and Karsten Berns[1]

[1] Robotics Research Lab, Faculty of Computer Science,
University of Kaiserslautern, Kaiserslautern, Germany
{nejadfard,schuetz,vonwirth,berns}@cs.uni-kl.de
[2] Institute of Aeronautics and Applied Mechanics, Faculty of Power
and Aeronautical Engineering, Warsaw University of Technology, Warsaw, Poland
kmianowski@meil.pw.edu.pl
http://agrosy.cs.uni-kl.de

**Abstract.** The biarticular actuators are widely used in the musculoskeletal bipedal robots. We derive the mathematical formulations to explain the static function of the leg muscles. The goal is to report analytical and biological observations to facilitate the design of the anthropomorphic robotic leg. Our analysis indicates that the ratio of the moment arms, in two spanning joints, has the profound influence on the function of the biarticular muscles. Detailed moment arm dataset of the human body is applied to verify the role of the biarticular muscles in various forms of locomotion. Satisfying the technical constraints, we provide a guideline on the structural design of the biarticular actuators based on the associated action directions. Our analyses are investigated using the compliant robotic leg CARL. A vertical jump experiment is performed to demonstrate the action of each actuator and the influence of the moment arm values.

**Keywords:** Biarticular actuators · Musculoskeletal robots
Bipedal robot

## 1 Introduction

In the design of the musculoskeletal robots, it is crucial to understand the mechanical structure and the behavioral role of the biarticular muscles (BiMs). Spanning two neighboring joints, the biarticular elements contribute to the economics of the locomotion by transferring power from large upper muscles to the lower limbs [12,13]. As a consequence, the human leg can achieve better mass distribution with smaller muscles situated at the lower distal limbs. In this work, we derive a mathematical representation that explains the static function of the BiMs. This model is verified with anatomical and physiological dataset of the

© Springer International Publishing AG, part of Springer Nature 2018
V. Vouloutsi et al. (Eds.): Living Machines 2018, LNAI 10928, pp. 348–360, 2018.
https://doi.org/10.1007/978-3-319-95972-6_37

human musculoskeletal system to explore the role of the BiMs in various forms of locomotion.

The advantages of the biarticular actuators (BiAs) are utilized in the design of the musculoskeletal robots [9,17]. The primary principle is to replicate the morphological structure of the human leg; any deviation from the human body structure would introduce a design challenge since the blind replication would not be applicable. We encounter this issue in the design of the BiAs for the compliant robotic leg CARL, see Fig. 1a. CARL utilizes the series elastic actuators that can produce both flexion and extension forces; therefore, one actuator can replace two antagonistic muscles. For example, the action of the two antagonistic BiMs, *Hamstrings* and *Rectus femoris* can be performed by only one actuator. The arising challenge is the structural design of an actuator such that it can closely replicate the function of the substituted antagonistic muscles.

The BiAs in CARL are connected to the corresponding joints using four-bar mechanisms. Hence, the profile of the moment arms depends on the angles of the spanning two joints. The same complex characteristic can be observed in the human muscles. Due to the inherent complexity, few analyses have been reported on the shape of this profile and its influence on the leg movements [4].

In this paper, the geometrical analyses of the BiAs are provided. This static study is the extension of the method introduced in [3]. The formulations indicate that the ratio of the moment arms (RMA) is the primary design parameter. The possible mathematical outcomes for the different values of the RMA are compared and explained by extraction of the biological data of the human geometric model presented in [4]. The relation between RMA values and muscle activities are investigated based on the locomotion data provided in HuMoD database [18]. Our study considers walking, running, continuous jump and squat movements and how the moment arm values influence the activation of BiMs. A practical profile of the moment arms are proposed for the BiAs in CARL that can reproduce the similar action of their biological counterpart. Finally, we present a jump experiment with CARL to demonstrate and conclude the results of the analyses.

## 2    Compliant Robotic Leg (CARL)

The planar robotic leg CARL is designed based on the human morphology [16]. It consists of 5 linear series elastic actuators [14,15] that can replicate the action of the skeletal muscle fibers and tendons. This capable mechatronics benchmark can be used to bring biomechanics knowledge into the realm of robotics.

CARL consists of three conventional mono-articular actuators, denoted as $A_H$, $A_K$ and $A_A$, acting on the hip, knee and ankle joints, respectively. Moreover, there are two BiAs, $A_K^H$, and $A_A^K$. The $A_K^H$ is spanning the hip and the knee joint, reproducing the action of the *Hamstrings* (HAM) and the *Rectus Femoris* (RF) muscles. The biarticular $A_A^K$ is spanning the knee and the ankle joints similar to the *Gastrocnemius* (GA) muscle. The description of the actuators and associated muscles are provided in Table. 1. The shank and thigh links have equal length. The detailed characteristics of CARL are available in [16].

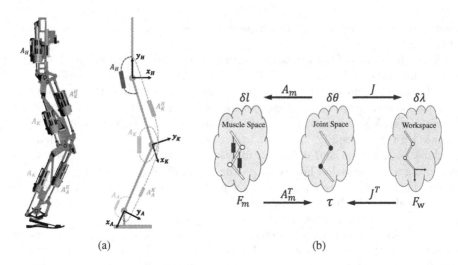

(a)                                        (b)

**Fig. 1.** (a) The schematics of the compliant leg CARL. (b) The kinematic network of the musculoskeletal leg. $\mathbf{A_m}$ is the moment arm matrix of the muscles. $\mathbf{J}$ is the linear Jacobian matrix of the articulated leg. $\delta l$, $\delta \theta$ and $\delta \lambda$ are the displacements of muscle lengths, joint angles and workspace positions, respectively.

**Table 1.** Actuator properties in CARL

| Actuator deployment | Designation | Maximum force [N] | Maximum power [W] | Associated major muscles |
|---|---|---|---|---|
| Hip | $A_H$ | 1500 | 816 | Glutus Maximus/Iliopsoas |
| Knee | $A_K$ | 1500 | 816 | Vasti |
| Ankle | $A_A$ | 700 | 288 | Soleus/Tibialis Anterior |
| Hip-Knee | $A_K^H$ | 1500 | 816 | Hamstrings/Rectus Femoris |
| Knee-Ankle | $A_A^K$ | 700 | 576 | Gastrocnemius |

## 3   Static Analysis of Muscle Forces

In this section, we formulate the mapping from the muscle/actuator force $\mathbf{F_m}$ into the workspace force $\mathbf{F_w}$. This study provides the geometrical explanations on the role of the moment arms. The mapping from the joint to the muscle domain is the moment arm matrix $\mathbf{A_m}$, where

$$\mathbf{V_m} = \mathbf{A_m}\omega \tag{1}$$

$$\tau = \mathbf{A_m^T F_m} \tag{2}$$

In which $\omega$ and $\tau$ are the angular velocity and the torque vectors in the joint space. $\mathbf{V_m}$ and $\mathbf{F_m}$ are the velocity and the force vectors in the muscle space. The velocity and the force of an actuator is positive when it is extending. The positive direction for the joint torques and the angular velocities are presented in Fig. 2a.

For the robot CARL with 5 muscles and 3 joints, the moment arm matrix is

$$\mathbf{A_m} = \begin{bmatrix} a_{11} & 0 & 0 & -a_{14} & 0 \\ 0 & a_{22} & 0 & -a_{24} & -a_{25} \\ 0 & 0 & a_{33} & 0 & -a_{35} \end{bmatrix}^T \tag{3}$$

Where $a_{11}$, $a_{22}$, $a_{33}$ are the lever arms of the mono-articular actuators which exert positive moments on the joints during extension. $a_{14}$ and $a_{24}$ are the lever arms of the biarticular $A_K^H$, acting on the hip and the knee joints, respectively. Similarly, the lever arms of the biarticular $A_A^K$ are $a_{25}$ and $a_{35}$, connected to the knee and the ankle joints. Both the BIAs in CARL generate negative moments during extension; hence, their lever arms are accompanied by the negative sign in (3).

The workspace coordinate is illustrated in Fig. 2b. This coordinate is adopted from [3], where the author provides excellent observations on the role of the BIMs. We use the same method to geometrically derive the linear Jacobian matrix for the planar articulated leg with three joints. The workspace coordinate is assumed to be $F_T - F_R$, illustrated in Fig. 2b. $\mathbf{F_w}$ is decomposed into radial $F_R$ and tangential $F_T$ components. The radial direction $F_R$ is aligned with the hip-ankle line $\overrightarrow{HA}$ and is dependent on the relative location of the hip and the ankle joints. Rotating radial coordinates can indeed simplify formulations as proposed in [6,10] to evaluate the action of BIAs.

By assuming the equal length of thigh and shank, the joint moments can be derived as

$$\tau_H = F_R\, p_t \qquad\quad + F_T\ (p_r + r) \tag{4}$$

$$\tau_K = F_R\ (p_t - q) + F_T\ \left(p_r + \frac{r}{2}\right) \tag{5}$$

$$\tau_A = F_R\, p_t \qquad\quad + F_T\, p_r \tag{6}$$

The above parameters are defined in Fig. 2b. Rearranging the above equations yields

$$F_T = \frac{\tau_H - \tau_A}{r} \tag{7}$$

$$F_R = \frac{1}{q}\left(\frac{\tau_H}{2} - \tau_K + \frac{\tau_A}{2}\right) \tag{8}$$

$$-(2\,q\,p_r + r\,p_t)\,\tau_H + (2\,r\,p_t)\,\tau_K + (2\,q\,p_r - r\,p_t + 2\,r\,q)\,\tau_A = 0 \tag{9}$$

In the following, we extend the above formulation presented in [3] by including the moment arm matrix. Equations (7) and (8) introduce a mapping from the three-dimensional joint space into the two-dimensional workspace which is the pseudo-inverse of the Jacobian matrix $\mathbf{J^+}$ as

$$\mathbf{F_w} = \mathbf{J^{+T}} \tau \tag{10}$$

$$\mathbf{J^+} = \begin{bmatrix} 1/2q & -1/q & 1/2q \\ 1/r & 0 & -1/r \end{bmatrix}^T \tag{11}$$

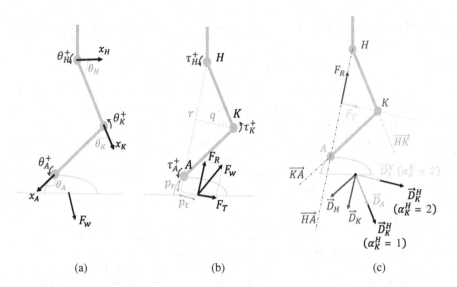

(a)                    (b)                    (c)

**Fig. 2.** (a) The Denavit-Hartenberg definition of joint angles and its positive direction. (b) The geometric illustration for linear Jacobian matrix calculation, adopted from [3]. (c) The principal directions of the muscles derived in (14). For ease of illustrations, the principal directions are depicted downward; they are negative to the direction values presented in (14). Note $\overrightarrow{D_H} \parallel \overrightarrow{KA}$ and $\overrightarrow{D_K} \parallel \overrightarrow{HA}$ and $\overrightarrow{D_A} \parallel \overrightarrow{HK}$. The parallel vectors are depicted in the same color. The influence of $\alpha_K^H$ and $\alpha_A^K$ on principal directions of the biarticular muscles are illustrated.

where $\mathbf{F_w} = [F_R, F_T]^T$ is the external force vector in the workspace. The equality in (10) is fulfilled as long as the joint torques are situated on the torque plane (9). Only, in this case, the static constraints are satisfied.

Substituting (2) for torque vector in (10) yields

$$\mathbf{F_w} = \mathbf{J}^{+T}\mathbf{A_m^T}\mathbf{F_m} \tag{12}$$

The force vector for the actuators is defined as

$$\mathbf{F_m} = \begin{bmatrix} F_H & F_K & F_A & F_K^H & F_A^K \end{bmatrix}^T \tag{13}$$

Where the elements of the force vector correspond to the actuators with the identical indexes. Note that the last two elements are the forces of the BIAs.

The final result can be formulated as

$$\begin{bmatrix} F_R \\ F_T \end{bmatrix} = \begin{bmatrix} 1/2q \\ 1/r \end{bmatrix} a_{11}F_H + \begin{bmatrix} -1/q \\ 0 \end{bmatrix} a_{22}F_K + \begin{bmatrix} 1/2q \\ -1/r \end{bmatrix} a_{33}F_A$$

$$+ \begin{bmatrix} \dfrac{2a_{24} - a_{14}}{2q} \\ \dfrac{-a_{14}}{r} \end{bmatrix} F_K^H + \begin{bmatrix} \dfrac{2a_{25} - a_{35}}{2q} \\ \dfrac{a_{35}}{r} \end{bmatrix} F_A^K \tag{14}$$

For ease of discussion, the principal direction of the actuators are denoted by $\overrightarrow{D}$ where

$$\mathbf{F_w} = a_{11}F_H\overrightarrow{D_H} + a_{22}F_K\overrightarrow{D_K} + a_{33}F_A\overrightarrow{D_A} + F_K^H\overrightarrow{D_K^H} + F_A^K\overrightarrow{D_A^K} \qquad (15)$$

This formulation presents the action direction of the each muscle or actuator in the workspace, see Fig. 2c. In [3], these directions are introduced as the muscle principal directions. It is shown that the principal direction of the $A_H$ is parallel to the shank $\overrightarrow{D_H} \parallel \overrightarrow{KA}$, and the principal direction of $A_A$ actuator is in the direction of the thigh $\overrightarrow{D_A} \parallel \overrightarrow{HK}$, see Fig. 2c. The actuator $A_K$ generates the force in the radial direction aligned with $F_R$. These observations can be easily demonstrated using the formulation in (14).

The focus of this paper is on the study of the moment arm values. In the case of the mono-articular actuators, the moment arms do not affect the associated principal directions. However, the principal directions of the BIAs are directly related to the selection of the moment arms. We introduce the RMA for the BIAs as

$$\alpha_K^H = \frac{a_{14}}{a_{24}} , \qquad \alpha_A^K = \frac{a_{35}}{a_{25}} \qquad (16)$$

The RMA will be used for classifying the role of the BIAs.

## 4    Upper Limb Biarticular Elements

### 4.1    Analytical Results

One popular choice [6,9,17] for the RMA is $\alpha_K^H = 2$. This value would yield

$$\alpha_K^H = 2 \quad \Rightarrow \quad \overrightarrow{D_K^H} = -\frac{a_{14}}{r} \overrightarrow{F_T} \Rightarrow \quad \overrightarrow{D_K^H} \parallel \overrightarrow{F_T} \qquad (17)$$

Choosing this ratio, $A_K^H$ would be able to produce tangential forces, see Fig. 2c. Such a behavior is particularly important since no other mono-articular muscles can generate tangential force, asserting the relative merit of the BIAs in the human balance control [17]. By selecting $\alpha_K^H = 2$, the mechanical advantage of $A_K^H$ for producing radial forces may suffer. Radial forces are essential to provide anti-gravity support for the heavy trunk.

Another plausible choice for $\alpha_K^H$ is

$$\alpha_K^H = 1 \quad \Rightarrow \quad \overrightarrow{D_K^H} = \left[\frac{1}{2q} \quad \frac{-1}{r}\right]^T a_{14} \Rightarrow \quad \overrightarrow{D_K^H} \parallel \overrightarrow{D_A} \qquad (18)$$

Having this ratio, $A_K^H$ generates force in the principal direction of the ankle mono-articular, see Fig. 2c. The larger BIM on the upper part of the leg can help the smaller actuator in the ankle. It improves the ability of the ankle joint in coping with high torque and power requirements in the tasks such as squat jumping and running. In these movements, it is preferable to have $\alpha_K^H = 1$.

## 4.2  Natural Role of Hamstrings and Rectus Femoris

In the human leg, the upper limb BIMs are the HAM and the RF. In CARL, the actuator $A_K^H$ performs the task of these muscles. The positive force simulates the action of the HAM, and the negative force acts as its antagonist RF. In order to design an anthropomorphic actuation, $A_K^H$ should retain the main characteristics of the above-mentioned BIMs. Since CARL is a planar robot, the biological muscles are investigated based on their role in Sagittal plane; therefore, the action of the HAM, RF, and GA are presented based on the flexion/extension axis of the joints.

The geometric model of the human lower extremity has been introduced in [4]. The profile of the moment arms with respect to flexion/extension axis has been reported in detail. In Fig. 3, the ratio $\alpha_K^H$ is depicted for both the HAM and the RF, with respect to the corresponding joint angles. *Biceps Femoris* muscle is selected as the representative of the muscle group HAM. Its $\alpha_K^H$ is at peak value when the knee is fully extended $\theta_K \approx 0°$ and the hip angle is $\theta_H \approx 60°$. The behavior of the RMA is reversed in case of the RF since it reaches the highest point when the knee is totally flexed, see Fig. 3b. By comparing two muscles in Fig. 3, it is clear that the $\alpha_K^H$ of the RF has the smaller range of variations.

We further investigate $\alpha_K^H$ in several types of locomotion. In Fig. 4, the RMA of the BIAs are illustrated related to the corresponding muscle activity or Electromyography (EMG). The locomotion data is adopted from HuMoD benchmark database [18].

The range of fluctuations of $\alpha_K^H$ for HAM is $[0.9, 3.3]$. In contrast, the RF experiences smaller deviations. Only in squat movement, due to the high flexion of the knee, $\alpha_K^H$ takes the peak value of 2.75. In case of the walking and running, when highly activated, the RF experiences $\alpha_K^H \approx 0.9$.

In conclusion, the HAM experiences large variations of the RMA with an average of $\alpha_K^H \approx 2$. However, it is not a correct practice to assume a constant

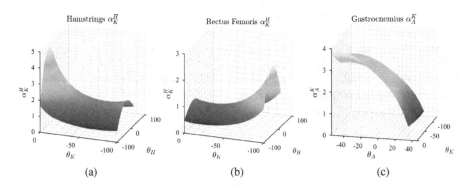

**Fig. 3.** The biological data of the RMA of the human muscles of (a) HAM, (b) RF and (c) GA. The moment arm data is adopted from [4]. The joint angles $\theta_H$, $\theta_K$ and $\theta_A$ are in Degrees and are defined in Fig. 2a. The *Biceps Femoris* is used as the representative of the Hamstrings muscle group.

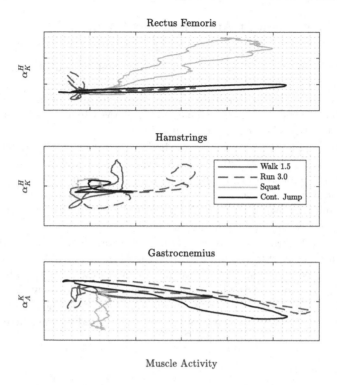

**Fig. 4.** The RMA with respect to muscle activity (EMG) for several forms of loco-motion. Walking and running are performed at $1.5\,\mathrm{ms^{-1}}$ and $3.0\,\mathrm{ms^{-1}}$. The squat and continuous jump is performed akimbo. Muscle activity is multiplied by 10000 for better visibility. The locomotion data is adopted from HuMoD database [18].

$\alpha_K^H$ for this muscle because of its high fluctuations. Considering the principal direction in (17), the HAM has a high tendency to generate tangential forces; therefore, it is highly active in balancing and stabilizing the trunk and the hip for instance in the human walking gait [11].

The action of the RF is entirely different since it experiences the RMA $\alpha_K^H \approx 1$. As shown in (18), the RF tends to help the ankle joint to generate high radial forces. Similar condition can be seen in Fig. 4, where the RF is highly active in running and jumping due to the large ground reaction forces. One crucial implication of $\alpha_K^H \approx 1$ is that the RF generates the same moment in spanning joints. This is ideal to transfer power from hip joint to the lower knee joint, helping the knee mono-articular muscle. Such a behavior is reported in the vertical jump observations [5] and is one of the primary roles of the biarticular elements which should not be ignored in robotic leg design.

### 4.3  Candidate Moment Arm Profile for CARL

The upper limb biarticular actuator $A_K^H$ replaces the HAM and the RF muscles. The moment arm profile of $A_K^H$ should be the combination of Fig. 3a and b. One candidate profile is depicted in Fig. 5b. This candidate is the outcome of selecting a correct configuration for the four-bar linkage transmission depicted in Fig. 5c. The proposed profile behaves as the HAM when the knee is extended and acts as the RF when the knee is fully flexed.

In a robotic platform with high $\alpha_K^H$, the biarticular element generates higher torques at the hip rather than the knee joint; despite the fact that the knee joint commonly experiences the high amount of torque and velocity, demanding powerful and heavy muscles/actuators. *Vasti* muscle group is responsible for this action and together with the RF construct the most powerful muscle group, *quadriceps femoris* muscle, in the human leg [1].

The current technology of series elastic actuator, deployed in CARL, is far behind its human counterpart. Therefore, the high power and torque requirements at the knee joint compel the designer to lower down the $\alpha_K^H$. This way the BIA can help the mono-articular actuator of the knee to cope with demanding scenarios. In our experience, it is recommended to design the moment arm profile in a way that in different movements the ratio is limited to the range $[1.0, 1.7]$. In fact $A_K^H$ would act similar to the RF.

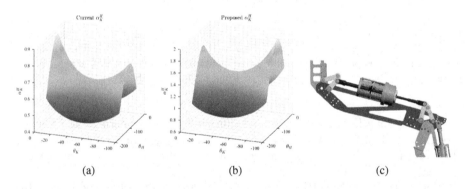

(a)                              (b)                              (c)

**Fig. 5.** The RMA for the biarticular actuator $A_K^H$ in current constructed version of CARL (a) and the proposed candidate profile (b). (c) The connection mechanisms of the $A_K^H$ in CARL. The elements of the four-bar linkage are shown in yellow color. (Color figure online)

## 5  Lower Limb Biarticular Element

The RMA for the $A_A^K$ is defined in (16). This equation can be simplified by assuming the ratio as $\alpha_A^K = 2$, which yields

$$\alpha_A^K = 2 \quad \Rightarrow \quad \overrightarrow{D_A^K} = \frac{a_{35}}{r} \, \overrightarrow{F_T} \quad \Rightarrow \quad \overrightarrow{D_A^K} \parallel \overrightarrow{F_T} \tag{19}$$

As it is mentioned previously, $\alpha_A^K = 2$ results in generating tangential forces. This particular role of $A_A^K$ is also observed in [3].

The analogous muscle in the human body is GA. Its RMA is depicted in Fig. 3c. The ratio achieves its maximum when the ankle is fully plantar flexed, the foot is extended away from the leg.

In different types of locomotion, GA experiences variations of $\alpha_A^K$ in the interval $[1.0, 3.0]$, when activated, see Fig. 4. In natural walking, the ratio has a limited variation approximately around $[2.0, 2.3]$, upon activation. Henceforth; the GA is mainly involved in the constructing tangential forces on the center of mass especially while walking. By selecting $\alpha_A^K = 2$, the biarticular $A_A^K$ generates higher torques at the ankle than the knee joint. Therefore, $A_A^K$ is capable of transferring power from the knee joint to the lower ankle joint [5]. It also helps the actuator $A_A$ to cope with the high torque demand at the ankle joint.

# 6   Jump Experiment

The vertical jump experiment is carried out to demonstrate the influence of the different values of the RMA for the BiA spanning both the hip and the knee joints, see Fig. 6. The robotic leg CARL has performed the jump by producing a vertical ground force of $F_G = 350$ N. The desired joint torques are calculated using Jacobian matrix. The Joint torques are realized using the actuator force distribution based on the normalized minimum force optimization. The further technical information is presented in [8].

The vertical jump experiment provides the measured trajectory of the joint motion and the torques. Actuator force distributions have been compared for two values of RMA of $\alpha_K^H = 1$ and $\alpha_K^H = 2$. In both cases, the RMA for lower BiA is assigned as $\alpha_A^K = 2$, since it is the only plausible choice for the actuator $A_A^K$.

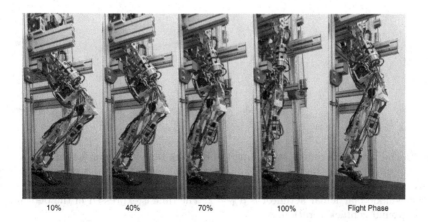

**Fig. 6.** The sequence of the jump experiment. The time is expressed in the percentage of the ground contact duration. Take off occurs in the fourth snapshot.

These evaluations allows us to investigate the role of the RMA on the principal direction of the actuators, illustrated in Fig. 7. Note that the length of the arrows is relative to the amount of force produced by the actuators. According to the minimum force optimization, the actuator with principal direction closer to the direction of $\overrightarrow{F_G}$ would have higher activation. As we discussed earlier, the knee mono-articular actuator $A_K$ is highly activated in both test cases, since its principal direction is radial $\overrightarrow{D_K} \parallel \overrightarrow{HA} \parallel \overrightarrow{F_R}$. By considering the high extension velocity at the knee joint, the $A_K$ is the major power source in the jump experiment.

In the first test, $\alpha_K^H = 1$, $\overrightarrow{D_K^H}$ clearly has the bigger component in the radial direction. It is also aligned with $\overrightarrow{D_A}$, see Fig. 7a, reducing desirably the amount of load on the ankle mono-articular actuator. Due to the higher radial component of $\overrightarrow{D_K^H}$, the BIA helps to reduce the force required at the knee joint. In this experiment, the action of the $A_K^H$ resembles the RF and therefore providing further evidence on the activation of RF in the human vertical jump.

In contrast, with the selection of $\alpha_K^H = 2$ in the second experiment, the $A_K^H$ acts similar to the HAM while providing force in the tangential direction $\overrightarrow{D_K^H} \parallel \overrightarrow{D_A^K} \parallel \overrightarrow{F_T}$, see Fig. 7b. The actuators with tangential forces do not contribute to the production of the vertical force and have a lower activation. In this test case, the knee mono-articular and ankle mono-articular actuators are highly overloaded since they are the only actuators with the vertical principal directions.

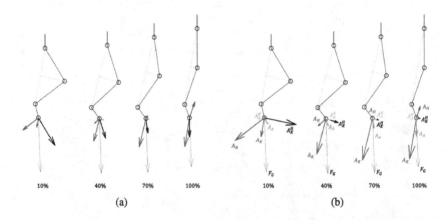

10%     40%     70%     100%          10%     40%     70%     100%

(a)                                    (b)

**Fig. 7.** The jump experiment for testing the RMA in the biarticular actuator $A_K^H$. The principal directions are depicted on the contact point of the foot and the ground. The RMA is selected as in (a) $\alpha_K^H = 1$ and in (b) $\alpha_K^H = 2$. In both test cases, the RMA for the knee-ankle biarticular actuator is $\alpha_A^K = 2$. The time is expressed in the percentage of the ground contact duration.

# 7   Conclusion

In this study, we provided the detailed analyses of the role of the RMA in the action of the biarticular elements. It is demonstrated that the captured data obtained from human motion is consistent with the geometrical results presented here. It is common practice in robotics [9,17] to select a constant RMA for the biarticular hip-knee actuator as $\alpha_K^H = 2$. Our analyses stated that this ratio can be a logical assumption for walking; nevertheless, it would not be advantageous for movements where the RF is highly active such as jumping and running. It is also not favorable from the robotic design perspective since the knee mono-articular actuator, due to the technical restrictions, may not be able to cope with high power demand. The jump experiment with the robotic leg CARL, clearly provided further evidence on how the RMA can influence the activation of different actuators. Our work clarifies the role of the BIAs in several forms of locomotion. The knowledge can be exploited by the reactive muscle control algorithms such as [2,7] to adjust the muscle activities according to the desired tasks.

# References

1. Arnold, E.M., Ward, S.R., Lieber, R.L., Delp, S.L.: A model of the lower limb for analysis of human movement. Ann. Biomed. Eng. **38**(2), 269–279 (2010)
2. Geyer, H., Herr, H.: A Muscle-reflex model that encodes principles of legged mechanics produces human walking dynamics and muscle activities. IEEE Trans. Neural Syst. Rehabil. Eng. **18**(3), 263–273 (2010)
3. Hof, A.: The force resulting from the action of mono-and biarticular muscles in a limb. J. Biomech. **34**(8), 1085–1089 (2001)
4. Horsman, M.K.: The Twente lower extremity model. Consistent dynamic simulation of the human locomotor apparatus. Ph.D. thesis, University of Twente, December 2007
5. Jacobs, R., Bobbert, M.F., van Ingen Schenau, G.J.: Mechanical output from individual muscles during explosive leg extensions: the role of biarticular muscles. J. Biomech. **29**(4), 513–523 (1996)
6. Lakatos, D., Rode, C., Seyfarth, A., Albu-Schäffer, A.: Design and control of compliantly actuated bipedal running robots: Concepts to exploit natural system dynamics. In: 14th IEEE-RAS International Conference on Humanoid Robots (Humanoids), pp. 930–937. IEEE (2014)
7. Luksch, T.: Human-like Control of Dynamically Walking Bipedal Robots. RRLab Dissertations, Verlag Dr. Hut (2010). http://www.dr.hut-verlag.de/978-3-86853-607-2.html
8. Nejadfard, A., Scheutz, S., Mianovski, K., Vonwirth, P., Berns, K.: Coordination of the biarticular actuators based on instant power in an explosive jump experiment. In: IEEE/ASME International Conference on Advanced Intelligent Mechatronics (AIM) (2018)
9. Niiyama, R., Nishikawa, S., Kuniyoshi, Y.: Biomechanical approach to open-loop bipedal running with a musculoskeletal athlete robot. Adv. Robot. **26**(3–4), 383–398 (2012)

10. Oh, S., Kong, K.: Two-degree-of-freedom control of a two-link manipulator in the rotating coordinate system. IEEE Trans. Industr. Electron. **62**(9), 5598–5607 (2015)
11. Perry, J.: Gait analysis: normal and pathological function. SLACK, Thorofare, NJ (1992). oCLC: ocm27816876
12. Prilutsky, B.I., Zatsiorsky, V.M.: Tendon action of two-joint muscles: transfer of mechanical energy between joints during jumping, landing, and running. J. Biomech. **27**(1), 25–34 (1994)
13. Schenau, G.J.V.I.: From rotation to translation: constraints on multi-joint movements and the unique action of bi-articular muscles. Hum. Mov. Sci. **8**(4), 301–337 (1989)
14. Schütz, S., Mianowski, K., Kötting, C., Nejadfard, A., Reichardt, M., Berns, K.: RRLAB SEA - A highly integrated compliant actuator with minimised reflected inertia. In: IEEE International Conference on Advanced Intelligent Mechatronics (AIM) (2016)
15. Schütz, S., Nejadfard, A., Berns, K.: Influence of loads and design parameters on the closed-loop performance of series elastic actuators. In: IEEE International Conference on Robotics and Biomimetics (ROBIO) (2016)
16. Schütz, S., Nejadfard, A., Mianowski, K., Vonwirth, P., Berns, K.: CARL - A compliant robotic leg featuring mono- and biarticular actuation. In: IEEE-RAS International Conference on Humanoid Robots (2017)
17. Sharbafi, M.A., Rode, C., Kurowski, D., Möckel, R., Radkhah, K., Zhao, G., Rashty, A.M., von Stryk, A.: A new biarticular actuator design facilitates control of leg function in biobiped3. Bioinspir. Biomim. **11**(4), 046003 (2016)
18. Wojtusch, J., von Stryk, O.: Humod - a versatile and open database for the investigation, modeling and simulation of human motion dynamics on actuation level. In: Proceedings of the IEEE-RAS International Conference on Humanoid Robots. pp. 74–79. IEEE, Seoul (2015)

# An Adaptive Frequency Central Pattern Generator for Synthetic Nervous Systems

William Nourse(✉)[iD], Roger D. Quinn[iD], and Nicholas S. Szczecinski[iD]

Case Western Reserve University, Cleveland, OH 44106, USA
wrn13@case.edu

## 1 Introduction

For robots using legged locomotion, mathematical models of Central Pattern Generators (CPGs) are being used for controlling the complicated gaits and timing required for stable walking. Traditionally, these models are precisely designed for oscillation at a set of specific frequencies and phase relationships, which while easier to design is not conducive to robust and stable walking.

In recent years, work has been done on designing adaptive models of CPGs. These CPGs are able to exhibit complex behaviors such as learning the resonant dynamics of a system [1] to improve walking stability, as well as using mathematical learning rules to learn arbitrary signals and embed their relationships within the system [2,3].

This work explores the possibility of implementing an adaptive frequency CPG with a similar behavior to these systems, using conductance-based models of dynamic non-spiking neurons connected as a synthetic nervous system (SNS) [4].

## 2 Methods and Results

When designing an adaptive system, it is important to first characterize the existing model. We used conductance-based non-spiking neurons where the membrane voltage varies with a differential equation

$$C_m \frac{dV}{dt} = I_{leak} + I_{syn} + I_{NaP} + I_{app} \tag{1}$$

where

$$I_{leak} = G_m \cdot (E_r - V) \tag{2}$$

$$I_{syn} = \sum_{i=1}^{n} G_{s,i} \cdot (E_{s,i} - V) \tag{3}$$

$$I_{NaP} = G_{Na} \cdot m_\infty(V) \cdot h \cdot (E_{Na} - V) \tag{4}$$

This work was funded by National Science Foundation (NSF) Award #1704366.

V. Vouloutsi et al. (Eds.): Living Machines 2018, LNAI 10928, pp. 361–364, 2018.
https://doi.org/10.1007/978-3-319-95972-6_38

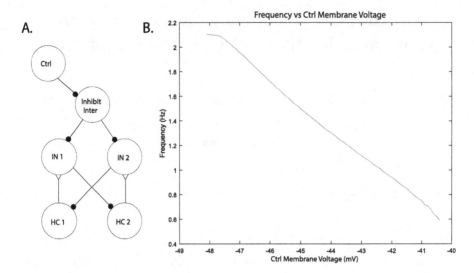

**Fig. 1. (A)** The CPG network consists of two neurons with nonlinear persistent sodium channels (HC 1 and HC 2), which mutually inhibit one another via two nonspiking interneurons (IN 1 and IN 2). A pair of additional neurons can exploit neural dynamics to control the oscillation frequency of the CPG by effectively weakening the strength of mutual inhibition. **(B)** The membrane voltage of the controlling neuron (Ctrl) has a linear relationship with the oscillation frequency of the associated CPG.

and there is an externally applied current $I_{app}$. As shown in Fig. 1, if a pair of inhibiting neurons is added to an SNS model of a CPG, the natural frequency can be linearly controlled by an applied voltage and behaves as a voltage-controlled oscillator. Through the use of previously designed functional subnetworks for arithmetic, integration, and differentiation [4], a larger network can be realized which acts as an arbitrary frequency-to-voltage converter and maps an input signal to the appropriate controlling voltage for the CPG (see Fig. 2). Since these subnetworks have already been successfully tuned for their respective operations, a complicated network can be constructed by combining desired mathematical operations as needed, with minor tuning of the individual neurons and synapses bridging between subnetworks. While the exact topology of this overall network has no direct biological source, the internal subnetworks are all based on results seen from biology [4]. This subnetwork approach may not lead to the most minimal network design for a desired functionality, however it allows the development of very large scale networks where time-intensive optimization need only be performed on a small subset of the network.

In this work, phase information is fed forward from the initial processing of an input signal. Future work could use information from separate sources to control phase, allowing such behavior as inter-leg communication providing frequency control and intra-leg sensory feedback controlling the phase in legged locomotion.

# Network

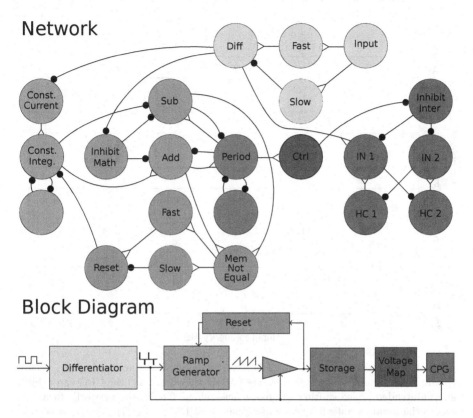

# Block Diagram

**Fig. 2.** A network which uses functional neural subnetworks [4] to alter a CPG's frequency and phase to match that of an incoming signal, as well as a corresponding block diagram. First, a differentiator network subtracts a delayed copy of an input signal to approximate a derivative. An integrator (Const. Integ.) is then supplied with constant current, inducing a ramp which is periodically reset. An addition and subtraction network then equalizes a storage integrator (Period) to the first every input cycle, and resets the original integrator when equalization has occurred. The stored voltage is then mapped to the voltage range demonstrated in Fig. 1 for controlling the frequency of a CPG. Differential spikes from the input are sent to a CPG interneuron, to correct the phase.

Preliminary testing (see Fig. 3) shows that for square wave inputs the system has some slight difficulty adapting to very low frequency signals, but as the frequency increases towards typical walking speeds and up, the system behaves as intended and locks in both frequency and phase with the input. Further work is required to fully characterize the frequency and phase response of this network, including the use of more biologically realistic input signals as well as those with asymmetric phase. Additionally the effects of using more complicated neural models, or the presence of any long-term plasticity could also be analyzed.

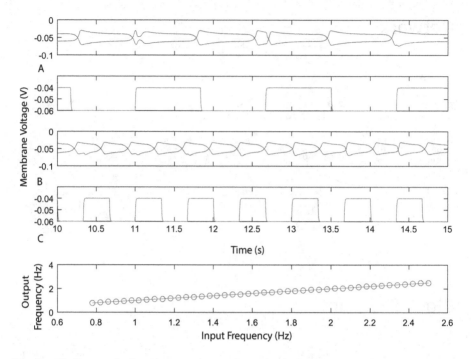

**Fig. 3.** The network shown in Fig. 2 is able to match frequency and phase with a periodic input signal. At lower frequencies (0.6 Hz shown in (**A**)) the CPG can exhibit some unintended phase shifting. At frequencies above 0.8 Hz, the network effectively locks to the input signal's frequency and phase (see 1.5 Hz in (**B**)). As can be seen in (**C**), the frequency of the input square wave and output of the network match once CPG oscillation is stable.

## References

1. Buchli, J., Iida, F., Ijspeert, A.J.: Finding resonance: adaptive frequency oscillators for dynamic legged locomotion. In: IEEE International Conference on Intelligent Robots and Systems, pp. 3903–3909 (2006). https://doi.org/10.1109/IROS.2006.281802
2. Righetti, L., Buchli, J., Ijspeert, A.J.: From dynamic Hebbian learning for oscillators to adaptive central pattern generators. In: Proceedings of 3rd International Symposium on Adaptive Motion in Animals and Machines, AMAM 2005, pp. 1–7 (2005). https://doi.org/record/58529, http://infoscience.epfl.ch/record/58528/files/righetti05b.pdf?version=1
3. Righetti, L., Buchli, J., Ijspeert, A.J.: Dynamic Hebbian learning in adaptive frequency oscillators. Phys. D Nonlinear Phenom. **216**(2), 269–281 (2006). https://doi.org/10.1016/j.physd.2006.02.009
4. Szczecinski, N.S., Hunt, A.J., Quinn, R.D.: A functional subnetwork approach to designing synthetic nervous systems that control legged robot locomotion. Front. Neurorobot. **11**, 1–19 (2017). https://doi.org/10.3389/fnbot.2017.00037. http://journal.frontiersin.org/article/10.3389/fnbot.2017.00037/full

# Texture Perception with a Biomimetic Optical Tactile Sensor

Nicholas Pestell[1,2]([✉]) and Nathan F. Lepora[1,2]

[1] Department of Engineering Mathematics, University of Bristol, Bristol, UK
{nick.pestell,n.lepora}@bristol.ac.uk
[2] Bristol Robotics Laboratory, University of Bristol, Bristol, UK

**Abstract.** In this study we assess the ability of the TacTip to classify a range of 12 textured stimuli with particle sizes ranging from 642 $\mu$m to 15 $\mu$m. We observe stick-slip events at the interface between sensor and stimulus which vary depending on the texture. We compare the use of marker position with marker velocity for encoding texture and found the velocity feature performed substantially better with a RMS error of ∼1.4 stimulus classes compared with ∼2.3 for the position feature. Marker velocity is analogous to rapidly adapting mechanoreceptors, such as Meissner's corpuscles, which are thought to be used for roughness perception, therefore this result may be indicative of the biology of human touch.

**Keywords:** Tactile sensing · Texture perception · Biomimetics

## 1 Introduction

Human tactile perception encompasses sensing a range of stimulation types including texture, hardness and shape [1]. Each stimulation type has unique features for which distinct sub-modalities and corresponding mechanorecptors are specifically responsive to. It is important for roboticists to understand these sub-modalities in order to provide robots with the means for human-like control when interacting physically with their environment.

In the presented study we look at the capabilities of a biomimetic optical tactile sensor, the TacTip, for perception of fine textures. Traditionally, the TacTip has been used for sensing with high spatial acuity [2–5], using static touch. Here we consider dynamic touch, which is how humans perceive fine textures [6].

The TacTip has previously been used for texture analysis [7]; however the finest texture presented in this work had a spatial structure of ∼2 mm. We consider this a macro-structure, which humans can discern with a static touch, motivating our consideration here of fine textures (sandpapers, grit size 30–1200).

© Springer International Publishing AG, part of Springer Nature 2018
V. Vouloutsi et al. (Eds.): Living Machines 2018, LNAI 10928, pp. 365–369, 2018.
https://doi.org/10.1007/978-3-319-95972-6_39

## 2   Methods

**Hardware.** The TacTip is a cheap, 3D-printed optical tactile sensor [2,3]. It works on the principle of transduction from tactile stimulation through a compliant flesh-like structure to an optical signal which is captured via a USB webcam, with a frame-rate of 100 fps defining the sampling frequency. An array of pins is tracked via an image processing algorithm and the pin deflections are mapped to a classification of the contact [4].

The TacTip is mounted as an end effector on a six degree-of-freedom robot arm (UR5, Universal Robotics). The arm can precisely and repeatedly position the sensor (absolute repeatability 0.1 mm) (Fig. 1)

**Experimental Procedure.** The stimuli consisted of 12 sandpapers with average particle size ranging from 642 to 15 $\mu$m (see Fig. 1). We collected four distinct datasets, at differing contact depths, equally spaced over a 0.8 mm range. Each dataset consisted of 12 multi-dimensional, 20-s duration, time-series of pin positions and was recorded whilst sequentially sliding horizontally across each stimulus at 10 mms$^{-1}$.

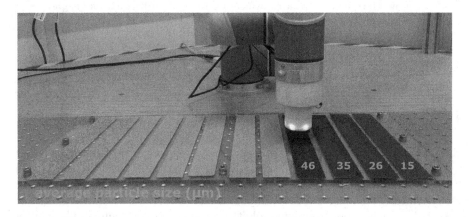

**Fig. 1.** Experimental set-up: TacTip mounted as an end-effector on a 6-DOF robot arm. The 12 stimuli are arranged from roughest on the left to smoothest on the right.

**Perception.** We adopt a bio-inspired perceptual method, where the encoding of sensory data as evidence is learned from training data, considered as a probabilistic model, it has analogues with neural coding. The evidence model is defined by likelihoods for each perceptual hypothesis constructed from histograms of sensor readings. A perceptual decision is made based on a maximum likelihood criterion. For a detailed explanation of this method, we refer the reader to [4].

# 3    Results

Figure 2 shows a truncated section of the raw, unprocessed data for all 127 pins (left column) and the processed pin velocities after taking the mean position across pins at each sample (right column). The top and bottom rows show data collected on the roughest and smoothest stimuli respectively.

The unprocessed pin positions collected on the smoothest stimulus show regular events characterised by a steady increase in pin positions followed by a sharp fall back to the initial position on a frequency of ~5 Hz. We also note that the pins move in a coherent manner, justifying the case for reducing the dimensionality by averaging over pins. In contrast, the unprocessed pin positions collected on the roughest stimulus show fewer noticeable features. The events seen clearly on the smoothest texture are caused by periodic stick-slip at the interface between the TacTip and the textured stimuli.

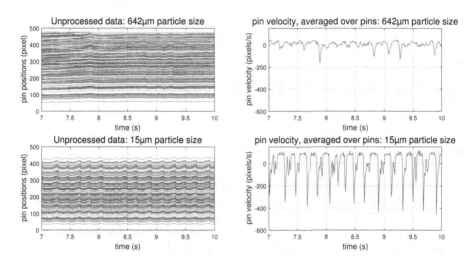

**Fig. 2.** Left column: Section of unprocessed pin positions plotted against time for stimulation on the coarsest (top) and the finest texture (bottom). Right column: Pin velocities averaged over all pins for the corresponding section of data shown to the left.

We compared the performance of using displacement versus velocity as features by building two corresponding models, according to Sect. 2, trained and tested using the two competing features, with a leave-one-out procedure over the four repeated datasets each with a different depth. We used the average over all pins for both feature types.

The RMS error when using the displacement feature was ~2.3 versus ~1.4 stimulus classes when using the velocity. Hence, the velocity component is considered a better feature for perceiving texture. A confusion matrix of results when using the velocity feature is shown in Fig. 3.

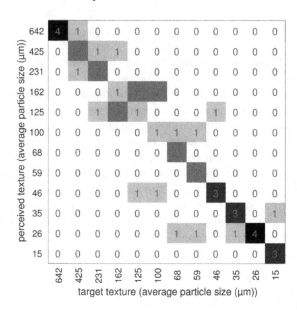

**Fig. 3.** Confusion matrix of results from texture perception experiment using velocity as a feature. Each stimulus was presented four times. Cell values and colours represent instances of perceived texture (y-axis) at the corresponding target texture (x-axis). (Color figure online)

## 4   Conclusions and Further Work

The periodic features (most noticeable on the smoothest texture, Fig. 2) are caused by stick-slip: A static friction force opposes the lateral dragging motion. This causes the sensor contact surface to remain stationary relative to the stimulus (stick), at some point the force exerted by the robot arm exceeds static friction causing the sensor contact surface to slip. The increased rate of stick seen with the smooth texture as compared with the coarse one suggests a higher coefficient of static friction between the TacTip sensing surface and the stimulus.

When comparing the use of pin positions with pin velocities for texture perception, we found that the latter produced significantly better results. This is an interesting finding and may be considered a confirmation of the biology of human touch: Meissner's corpuscles are rapidly adapting mechanoreceptors found in the human fingertip, whose function, it is thought, may include roughness sensing [8]. Rapidly adapting means that these receptors only respond to changes in skin deformation and therefore do not respond to static stimulation. By computing the pin velocities, we have effectively produced a modality which is rapidly adapting, since a velocity response is only produced when the pins are moving in contrast to pin positions which continue to provide a response during static stimulation.

This is an encouraging progression for sensing with the TacTip and, in particular, artificially mimicking the range of tactile modalities available to humans.

# References

1. Klatzky, R.L., Lederman, S.J.: Toward a computational model of constraint-driven exploration and haptic object identification. Perception **22**(5), 597–621 (1993)
2. Chorley, C., Melhuish, C., Pipe T., Rossiter, J.: Development of a tactile sensor based on biologically inspired edge encoding. In: International Conference on Advanced Robotics, pp. 1–6 (2009)
3. Ward-Cherrier, B., Pestell, N., Cramphorn, L., Winstone, B., Elena Giannaccini, M., Rossiter, J., Lepora, N.F.: The TacTip family: soft optical tactile sensors with 3D-printed biomimetic morphologies. Soft Robot. **5**(1), 1–12 (2017)
4. Lepora, N.F., Ward-Cherrier, B.: Superresolution with an optical tactile sensor. In: International Conference on Intelligent Robots and Systems, pp. 2686–2691 (2015)
5. Cramphorn, L., Ward-Cherrier, B., Lepora, N.F.: Addition of a biomimetic fingerprint on an artificial fingertip enhances tactile spatial acuity. IEEE Robot. Autom. Lett. **2**(3), 1336–1343 (2017)
6. Hollins, M., Risner, S.R.: Evidence for the duplex theory of tactile texture perception. Percept. Psychophys. **62**(4), 695–705 (2000)
7. Winstone, B., Griffiths, G., Pipe, T., Melhuish, C., Rossiter, J.: TACTIP - tactile fingertip device, texture analysis through optical tracking of skin features. In: International Conference on Biomimetic and Biohybrid Systems (2013)
8. Dargahi, J., Najarian, S.: Human tactile perception as a standard for artificial tactile sensing-a review. Int. J. Med. Robot. Comput. Assist. Surg. **1**(1), 23–35 (2005)

# Simulation of the Arthropod Central Complex: Moving Towards Bioinspired Robotic Navigation Control

Shanel C. Pickard[✉], Roger D. Quinn, and Nicholas S. Szczecinski

Case Western Reserve University, Cleveland, OH 44106, USA
sxp671@case.edu

**Abstract.** It is imperative that an animal have the ability to track its own motion within its immediate surroundings. It gives the necessary basis for decision making that leads to appropriate behavioral responses. It is our goal to implement insect-like body tracking capabilities into a robotic controller and have this serve as the first step toward adaptive robotic behavior. In an attempt to tackle the first step of body tracking without GPS or other external information, we have turned to arthropod neurophysiology as inspiration. The insect brain structure called the central complex (CX) is thought to be vital for sensory integration and body position tracking. The mechanisms behind sensory integration are immensely complex, but it was found to be done with an elegant neuronal architecture. Based on this architecture, we assembled a dynamical neural model of the functional core of the central complex, two structures called the protocerebral bridge and the ellipsoid body, in a simulation environment. Using non-spiking neuronal dynamics, our simulation was able to recreate *in vivo* behavior such as correlating body rotation direction and speed to activity bump dynamics within the ellipsoid body of the central complex. This model serves as the first step towards using idiothetic cues to track body position and orientation determination, which is critical for homing after exploring new environments and other navigational tasks.

**Keywords:** Sensory integration · Insect central complex · Control

## 1 Introduction

Navigating the world is a vital task for survival, and yet we take the ability to do so for granted. Insects and other arthropods, despite their small size, are capable of incorporating the endless stream of sensory information from their eyes, antennae, and other organs into real-time position and orientation updates in the brain, and use that information to decide where to go next (for reviews,

S. C. Pickard—This work was supported by a GAANN Fellowship and National Science Foundation (Grant Number 1704366).

V. Vouloutsi et al. (Eds.): Living Machines 2018, LNAI 10928, pp. 370–381, 2018.
https://doi.org/10.1007/978-3-319-95972-6_40

see [4,7]). Understanding how the brain is able to seamlessly accomplish such a feat has been at the forefront of insect neurobiology [3,11,12]. The focus of these efforts has been to understand a brain structure known as the central complex (CX), which is thought to be vital for sensory integration and body position tracking.

As roboticists, we are tasked with giving our robots capabilities that we hope can one day be on par with our own. One of the basic necessities that our robots must have is the ability to accurately keep track of their body position relative to objects of interest in the environment. This is a challenge because the current approach to robotic control involves a thorough understanding of the task and environment on the part of the programmer, which must then be implemented as a well thought-out series of "if-then-else" statements. This becomes rather difficult when environments are not globally known, or are ever-changing (e.g. weather devastated locales, extraterrestrial landscapes). Thus, we build robot controllers using dynamical neural structures [10], which we believe will help us mimic animal brain structures and endow robots with animal-like navigation- and decision-making abilities.

## 1.1 Background: Tracking Body Position in the Arthropod CX

How the brain utilizes sensory information to determine body position at any given time and coordinate proper responses is not fully understood. Exciting results from the field of arthropod neurobiology have offered insight into brain substructures that appear to play a pivotal role in this task [3,11]. The central complex is a brain structure found in all arthropods and is comprised, in many species, of four neuropils: the protocerebral bridge (PB), the fan shaped body (FB), the ellipsoid body (EB), and the noduli.

Wolff et al. contributed an excellent survey of central complex connectivity that showed a richly complex network between the PB, FB, and EB. Although this paper does not address functional roles of the cell types, it provides a detailed framework for the "wiring rules" of these neuropils [13]. More recently, physiological work elaborated on the connectivity between the PB and EB and found that these two structures have coordinated activity that correlates to rotational body movement [3,11]. Specifically, a recursive excitatory connectivity between the eight column cells of the PB and the eight wedge cells of the EB maintain activity within these structures that correspond to body rotational location and speed. Three key tenants of CX behavior that our simulation captures in this paper include:

1. The direction of body rotation dictates direction of activity bump movement in the EB layer.
2. The body's rotational speed correlates to bump activity speed in the EB.
3. The activity in the PB leads activity in the EB.

## 1.2    Background: Mathematical Models of the Arthropod CX

Several recent models have sought to reproduce and explain the dynamics of the CX, and how it may give rise to navigational abilities. The work of Webb et al. created an "anatomically constrained" model of the CX, in which they mimicked the connectivity described in the previous subsection, and used the resulting model to control a robot's homing abilities after exploring an environment [8]. They found their model to be robust, with overall functionality not depending strongly on parameter values, as in our work. They constructed their model from static sigmoidal neurons, with recurrent connections added where necessary for memory dynamics. The work of Hirth et al. created a recurrent neural network simulation of the ellipsoid body, and showed that it was capable of aiding in decisions about which direction to go to navigate toward a goal based on its current orientation and simplified visual input [2]. This was accomplished by finding mappings between sensory information and the ellipsoid body that produce the intended goal-seeking behavior in a simulated agent. The result was that this agent could navigate a simple maze toward a goal. Both of these works have used their CX model in a closed-loop way to produce behavior in a simulated or hardware agent, something that we have not yet tested with our model. However, this paper presents a similarly biologically-constrained model, which uses dynamical neural components to reproduce key features of the CX, as listed in the previous subsection. Specifically, our CX model enables the use of idiothetic sensory input to track the body's heading.

## 2    Methods and Results

### 2.1    *In Silico* Model

We constructed a neural model in Animatlab, a 3D graphics environment for neuromechanical simulations [1], using the aforementioned recursive excitatory connectivity between the PB and EB (Fig. 1). This schematic represents the assembly of the processing layers of our simulation while remaining representative of *in vivo* neuronal connectivity. As seen in Fig. 1A, the P-ENs are the column cell projections that originate in the PB and synapse with EB wedge cells (also called E-PGs). Figure 1B shows the returning projections of the EB wedge cells to the PB, thereby completing the recursive loop. Internal to the EB, Fig. 1C shows an example of the inhibition circuit; when an EB wedge is active, the inhibition of connecting wedges is proportional to the activity magnitude.

The neurons themselves were modeled with linear conductance dynamics [10] to represent time dependent electrical properties. The voltage across each neuron's cell membrane, $U$, has the dynamics

$$C_{\text{mem}} \frac{dU}{dt} = I_{\text{ion}} + I_{\text{syn}} + I_{\text{app}}. \tag{1}$$

Equation 1 states that the current across the cell membrane (left hand side of the equation) is equivalent to the incoming, applied current $I_{\text{app}}$, plus the current

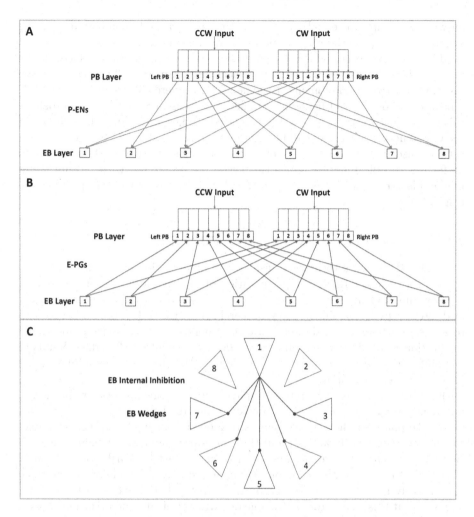

**Fig. 1.** Connectivity of the model. (A) The P-EN excitatory neurons project from PB to EB. Each P-EN connects in a counterclockwise fashion to the EB. (B) The E-PGs, project from the EB to the PB. (C) Internal EB inhibition example. Each wedge internally connects to the other wedges, except for the two immediately adjacent wedges. (Color figure online)

due to ion flux through membrane gates, $I_{\text{ion}}$, plus the current across the synapse (transmitter induced), $I_{\text{syn}}$. Plugging in for the currents, Eq. 1 becomes

$$C_{\text{mem}}\frac{dU}{dt} = g_{\text{mem}} \cdot (U_{\text{rest}} - U) + g_{\text{syn}}(t) \cdot (E_{\text{syn}} - U) + I_{\text{app}}, \qquad (2)$$

where $C_{\text{mem}}$ is the membrane capacitance, $g_{\text{mem}}$ is the membrane conductance constant, $U_{\text{rest}}$ is the equilibrium potential constant (voltage where inward and outward currents are equal), $g(t)_{\mathrm{syn}}$ is the time variable conductance of the synapse, and $E_{\mathrm{syn}}$ is the reversal potential of the synapse.

These equations contain many parameter values that must be tuned. In the past, we have developed methods for selecting parameter values based on the function of network components [10]. Therefore, we were able to directly assemble a network whose overall behavior satisfied our goals in Subsect. 1.1. We believe this is sufficient for two reasons. First, related studies have found the function of the CX structure not to depend heavily on parameter values [8]. Second, without actual sensory input and motor output, it is difficult to tune these values to perform a specific function. Once this system is integrated with sensors and a mobile platform, parameters will be tuned more carefully to correspond to the rest of the system.

## 2.2   Example Process Flow Between PB and EB

The PB and EB work together to use sensory information from head sensors to update the animal's internal representation of its orientation. Incoming motion cues, assumed to already be side-biased prior to reaching the central complex, feed into the preferred side of the protocerebral bridge. When the body starts to rotate, sensory organs sensitive to rotation generate neural activity proportional to rotational speed. This neural activity evenly disinhibits all eight columns of one half of the protocerebral bridge, while the other half remains inhibited due to a lack of sensory input.

Figure 2 illustrates a concrete example to illustrate the process flow of the CX for signal integration and is used to give an idea of the sequence of events that must take place for the activity bumps to move in our model. In this example, the animal is originally at rest, and thus, no input signal is yet being received. However, a memory trace is maintained from the last known body position of $0°$, which corresponds to wedge one being active (Fig. 2A). This memory trace continuously sends a signal bilaterally through the E-PG axons to PB column one cells, but this signal from EB wedge one will not elicit depolarization. This is because at this point, the PB columns are being suppressed by the interneurons. The interneurons will continue to suppress the PB until body motion recommences, at which point the resulting sensory input inhibits the interneurons. It is the combination of receiving a signal from EB wedge one and the sensory input (Fig. 2B) causing disinhibition of the right protocerebral bridge that permits the first column of the right PB to activate (Fig. 2C); the activated first column of the right PB sends a signal via the P-EN axon, which articulates with the counterclockwise wedge eight of the EB, and now the activity bump of the EB has moved from wedge one to wedge eight (Fig. 2D). If the body continues to rotate, the wedge activity is again transmitted, bilaterally, to columns eight of the left and right PB, and the activity bump in the PB now moves from columns one to columns eight on both sides. This sequence of events will continue as long as body motion is present.

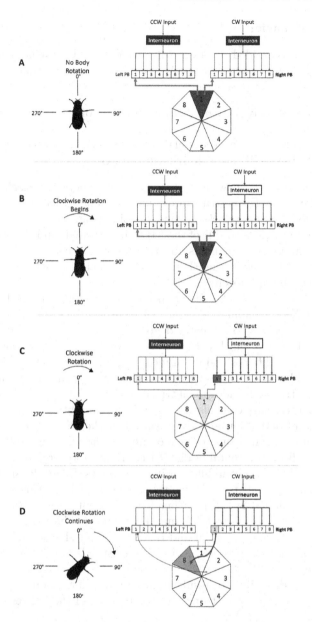

**Fig. 2.** Demonstration of the step-wise process flow of signal transduction within the CX. (A) The body is at rest at a reference point of 0°. The corresponding wedge has sustained voltage activity due to a memory trace of this known position - even while at rest. (B) CW body motion starts which causes a proportional current to feed into the preferred side of the PB, indicated by thicker red input lines. (C) The memory trace activity is passed symmetrically via the E-PG to the first columns of the PB. Because only the right side is disinhibited by sensory feedback, only the right first column of the PB depolarizes, as indicated by the dark green of column one. (D) As the body motion continues, the right PB remains disinhibited, thereby allowing the right PB column one to pass the activity in a counterclockwise fashion to wedge eight. (Color figure online)

## 2.3   Model Behavior

With the model assembled, we tested if our *in silico* CX behaves similarly to the *in vivo* CX. Several key behaviors were seen empirically that we wanted to ensure our model can reproduce:

1. The direction of body rotation dictates direction of activity bump movement in the EB layer.
2. The body's rotational speed correlates to bump activity speed in the EB.
3. The activity in the PB leads activity in the EB.

Experimental studies show that when a fruit fly experiences clockwise motion in the yaw plane, the EB activity bump moves counterclockwise (Fig. 3A); the opposite is true for counterclockwise body motion (Fig. 3B). The connectivity is such that when the preferred side of the PB is disinhibited (and the non preferred side remains inhibited) the signal is able to move up the column (EB to PB) and is passed by the PB back to the EB in a counterclockwise fashion, thus causing counterclockwise bump movement.

When the body rotates at a faster speed, the incoming current from sensory organs to the CX is presumably greater in magnitude. This permits disinhibition of the preferred side PB to a greater degree and as a result, enables the EB to depolarize the PB more quickly. Figure 4A shows the activity of one EB wedge over time, for three different values of incoming sensory current. It is clear that the frequency of bursts increases with increasing sensory current. Figure 4B plots the summary of these, and additional trials, showing that the disinhibitory input to the PB monotonically controls the speed of bump motion in the EB.

The profile of activation and deactivation in the PB and EB also depend on the incoming current from sensory organs to the CX. Figure 4C shows the activity in the left protocerebral bridge (LPB), right protocerebral bridge (RPB), and ellipsoid body (EB) given different input currents. Figure 4C shows that the RPB is disinhibited due to it being the preferred side in this scenario, and that the voltage profile is highly dependent on input speed. In slow rotation (1nA input - corresponding to a 5% max body speed), the PB neurons slightly depolarize above resting potential and take a relatively longer time to do so as indicated by the less steep voltage trace. Faster speeds (10nA and 20nA inputs - corresponding to a 50% and 100% max body speed, respectively) allow for a greater degree of disinhibition, resulting in high depolarization magnitudes and faster rise times. Ultimately, stronger depolarization of the PB results in faster bump hand-off in the EB.

The EB bump profiles of Fig. 4C (bottom) show that these cells will depolarize to roughly the same degree, regardless of speed, but at different rates. Again, a slower rotational speed (i.e. weaker sensory input) results in slower depolarization. Although the synapses in our simulation saturate when the presynaptic voltage is greater than $-40$ mV, the voltage of the EB wedges may surpass this functional range.

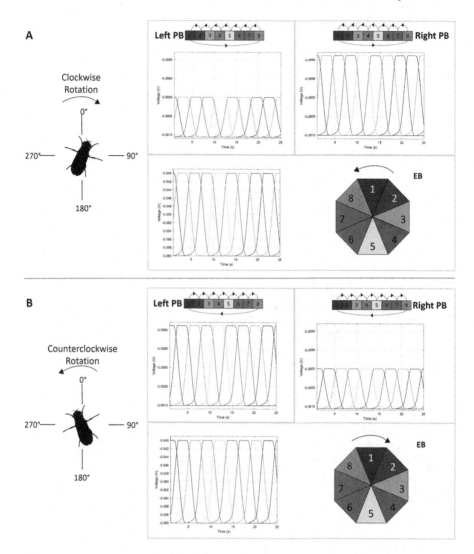

**Fig. 3.** The direction of body rotation dictates the direction of bump activity movement. (A) CW body rotation results in left bump motion in the PB and CCW bump movement in the EB. (B) CCW body rotation results in left bump motion in the PB and CW bump movement in the EB. (Color figure online)

From our signal process flow example (Fig. 2) we hypothesized that an EB wedge (or combination of wedges) must have sustained activity that serves as a memory trace of the last known position after the body motion has stopped. This memory trace serves as a starting point for the activity bump when body motion recommences. Although the memory trace originates in the EB wedge, it is the disinhibition of the PB that permits the bump to start moving to neighboring

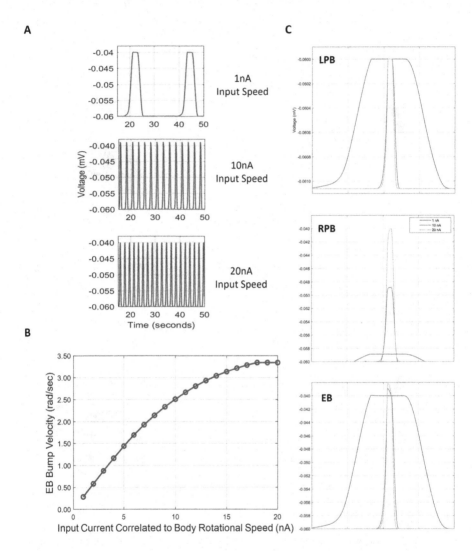

**Fig. 4.** Body rotational speed correlates with the bump speed in the PB and EB, while also correlating depolarization magnitude of the preferred side PB. (A) Fast body rotation (input as current with increasing magnitudes) causes faster bump hand-off in the EB (rad/sec). (B) Bump profiles in the left PB (top), right PB, preferred side (middle), and EB (bottom). Rotational speed effects the depolarization speed of the EB and PB cells, while greatly affecting the depolarization magnitude of the preferred side PB (right, in this case). (C) Example of period between bumps in the EB for slow (1nA), medium speed (10nA) and fast (20nA) rotational speeds. (Color figure online)

wedges. In a sense, the PB serves as a gatekeeper in allowing the bump to be passed and as such, its activity must precede that of the EB. This can be seen in the last step of Fig. 2D, where it is the activation of the PB that permits the EB to pass the bump.

# 3    Discussion

In this paper, we presented a model of the central complex that is able to mimic key neuronal behaviors seen in the brain of the fruit fly. Specifically,

1. The direction of body rotation dictates direction of activity bump movement in the EB layer.
2. The body's rotational speed correlates to bump activity speed in the EB.
3. The activity in the PB leads activity in the EB.

Utilizing the excitatory loop architecture between the PB and EB, we were able to produce a model that appropriately responded to body position and speed.

*Tracking Body Position with Multimodal Sensory Inputs:* Further work will incorporate how environmental stimulation is received by sensory organs and processed upstream to the central complex. More specifically, we wish to explore the interplay between sensory types and how they are prioritized within the central complex or how they may be modulated upstream to the CX. Varga and Ritzmann (2016) reported that units in the CX showed orientation-dependent activity both when a visual landmark was provided, and when it was removed [12]. This suggests that other organs, such as chordotonal organs (COs) in the antennae, sense the motion of the body and also stimulate the CX. In the future, we wish to explore the possible upstream interplay between visual inputs and CO inputs from the antennae. Specifically, how do different environmental conditions (i.e. the presence of visual cues) modulate the CO inputs? How does the total absence of visual input affect the gain of CO input, and thus the strength of these inputs during sensory integration found in the EB? Lastly, how does this inertial pathway (i.e. CO feedback) that feeds into the EB get used in position determination, spatial memory, and coordination of fine movement in downstream networks? Using extracellular CX recordings from cockroaches, we plan to explore how one sensory modality affects the strength of input to the CX, and correlate these sensory signals with CX activity.

*Expanding Model to Include Other CX Neuropils and Brain Structures:* Additionally, we wish to expand our CX model to include more processing layers of the EB, integrate the fan-shaped body (FB), and expand beyond the CX. One cell type we wish to include in future models are the ring cells of the EB. As the name implies, these cells are concentrically organized in four distinct rings at various depths of the EB [9,14,15], and neurophysiology work has shown that they participate in object tracking [15]. In brief, the innervation of these EB cells appears to come from a visual stimulation pathway that feeds through the lateral triangles and into the appropriate EB ring network depending on object location within the visual field. It is our goal to construct a model that simulates the visual activation and the downstream neural dynamics of this pathway. We will then explore how this object tracking pathway, in conjunction to the inertial pathway described above, is used in spatial memory and movement coordination. The FB is thought to be the receiver of these various pathways and serves as the locus of coordination and decision making that may be the key to defining appropriate behavioral responses to experienced stimuli [5].

*Tying It All Together:* In summary, our results show that a simple neuronal architecture can effectively maintain real-time body position updates. This model, and the future work discussed here, serve as a first step in capturing the adaptive capabilities of the arthropod nervous system. With a better understanding of these situational neuronal behaviors seen in arthropods [6,7], our models can be used as a framework for robotic control where we hope to see improved adaptability.

# References

1. Cofer, D., Cymbalyuk, G., Reid, J., Zhu, Y., Heitler, W.J., Edwards, D.H.: AnimatLab: a 3D graphics environment for neuromechanical simulations. J. Neurosci. Methods **187**, 280–288 (2010)
2. Fiore, V.G., Kottler, B., Gu, X., Hirth, F.: In silico interrogation of insect central complex suggests computational roles for the ellipsoid body in spatial navigation. Front. Behav. Neurosci. **11**(142), 1–13 (2017)
3. Green, J., Adachi, A., Shah, K.K., Hirokawa, J.D., Magani, P.S., Maimon, G.: A neural circuit architecture for angular integration in Drosophila. Nature **546**(7656), 101106 (2017)
4. Heinze, S.: Neural coding: bumps on the move. Curr. Biol. **27**(11), R409–R412 (2017)
5. Pfeiffer, K., Homberg, U.: Organization and functional roles of the central complex in the insect brain. Annu. Rev. Entomol. **59**, 165–184 (2014)
6. Ritzmann, R., Harley, C.M., Daltorio, K.A., Tietz, B.R., Pollack, A.J., Bender, J.A., Guo, P., Moromanski, A.L., Kathman, N.D., Nieuwoudt, C., Brown, A.E., Quinn, R.D.: Deciding which way to go: how do insects alter movements to negotiate barriers? Front. Neurosci. **6**, 97 (2012)
7. Varga, A.G., Kathman, N.D., Martin, J.P., Guo, P., Ritzmann, R.E.: Spatial navigation and the central complex: sensory acquisition, orientation, and motor control. Front. Neurosci. **11**, 4 (2017)
8. Stone, T., Webb, B., Adden, A., Weddig, N.B., Honkanen, A., Templin, R., Wcislo, W., Scimea, L., Warrant, E., Heinze, S.: An anatomically constrained model for path integration in the bee brain. Curr. Biol. **27**, 3069–3085
9. Su, T.S., Lee, W.J., Huang, Y.C., Wang, C.T., Lo, C.C.: Coupled symmetric and asymmetric circuits underlying spatial orientation in fruit flies. Nat. Commun. **8**(1), 139 (2017)
10. Szczecinski, N.S., Hunt, A.J., Quinn, R.D.: A functional subnetwork approach to designing synthetic nervous systems that control legged robot locomotion. Front. Neurorobot. **11**, 37 (2017)

11. Turner-Evans, D., et al.: Angular velocity integration in a fly heading circuit. Elife **6**, 139 (2017)
12. Varga, A.G., Ritzmann, R.E.: Cellular basis of head direction and contextual cues in the insect brain. Curr. Biol. **26**, 1816–1828 (2016)
13. Wolff, T., Iyer, N.A., Rubin, G.M.: Neuroarchitecture and neuroanatomy of the Drosophila central complex: a GAL4-based dissection of protocerebral bridge neurons and circuits. J. Comp. Neurol. **523**(7), 997–1037 (2015)
14. Young, J.M., Armstrong, J.D.: Structure of the adult central complex in Drosophila: organization of distinct neuronal subsets. J. Comp. Neurol. **518**(9), 1500–1524 (2010)
15. Seelig, J.D., Jayaraman, V.: Feature detection and orientation tuning in the Drosophila central complex. Nature **503**(7475), 262–266 (2013)

# Challenges of Machine Learning
# for Living Machines

Jordi-Ysard Puigbò[1,2(✉)], Xerxes D. Arsiwalla[1,2,3], and
Paul F. M. J. Verschure[2,3,4]

[1] UPF, Universitat Pompeu Fabra, Barcelona, Spain
jordiysard@gmail.com
[2] IBEC, Institute for BioEngineering of Catalonia, Barcelona, Spain
[3] BIST, Barcelona Institue of Science and Technology, Barcelona, Spain
[4] ICREA, Catalan Institute for Research and Advanced Studies, Barcelona, Spain

**Abstract.** Machine Learning algorithms (and in particular Reinforcement Learning (RL)) have proved very successful in recent years. These have managed to achieve super-human performance in many different tasks, from video-games to board-games and complex cognitive tasks such as path-planning or Theory of Mind (ToM) on artificial agents. Nonetheless, this super-human performance is also super-artificial. Despite some metrics are better than what a human can achieve (i.e. cumulative reward), in less common metrics (i.e. time to learning asymptote) the performance is significantly worse. Moreover, the means by which those are achieved fail to extend our understanding of the human or mammal brain. Moreover, most approaches used are based on black-box optimization, making any comparison beyond performance (e.g. at the architectural level) difficult. In this position paper, we review the origins of reinforcement learning and propose its extension with models of learning derived from fear and avoidance behaviors. We argue that avoidance-based mechanisms are required when training on embodied, situated systems to ensure fast and safe convergence and potentially overcome some of the current limitations of the RL paradigm.

**Keywords:** Reinforcement learning · Neural networks · Avoidance

## 1 Short History of Reinforcement Learning

The growing field of Machine Learning (ML) is attracting the attention, from both, companies and engineers, that see the opportunity to attack automation problems in ways that were unthinkable before; and from biologists, neuroscientists and psychologists, who see a tool to try to understand how primate and non-primate brains are capable of generating the variety of behavior observed in the animal kingdom. Reinforcement learning (RL) currently provides most of the approaches to use ML to address problems typically belonging to the study of the brain, such as navigation, social interaction and theory of mind (to name a few).

© Springer International Publishing AG, part of Springer Nature 2018
V. Vouloutsi et al. (Eds.): Living Machines 2018, LNAI 10928, pp. 382–386, 2018.
https://doi.org/10.1007/978-3-319-95972-6_41

Reinforcement Learning algorithms used in nowadays Machine Learning (ML) are still based on conceptualizations derived from classical conditioning more than 40 years ago [6]. The Rescorla-Wagner model (1) was created as a computational model to explain how in classical conditioning, a neutral stimulus (CS) could be associated to a response when paired to another stimulus (US) that already predicted that same response, indicating that the CS predicted the US.

$$\Delta W_x = r_{CS} R_{US}(\eta - W_{tot}) \tag{1}$$

Must be noted that this model couldn't take into consideration the difference in timing between the CS and the US and required them to be happening at the same time, becoming a correlation-based learning rule. For this reason, the later model of Sutton and Barto, Temporal Difference learning or TD-learning emerged as a solution to this problem [7]. In TD-learning (2), the notion of time is introduced in three ways: first, the temporal sequence of past events and outcomes is stored; second, the objective of learning is to minimize the error that the total outcome at a time $t$ is the same as the total predicted outcome at a next time $t + 1$; and third, this error in value is weighted by a discount factor that devaluates outcomes that are further from the current time point.

$$\Delta W = \eta(V(t + 1) - V(t)) \sum_{k=0}^{t} (\lambda^{t-k} \nabla_w V(k)) \tag{2}$$

This formulation has been used to define the feedback required to solve all kinds tasks, as a mechanism to select how frequently an action should be taken in a given situation. The lack of efficient mechanisms to backpropagate the error of this learning rule through large networks of artificial neurons limited the applicability of these models for 20 years, until computers become fast enough to handle more complex problems in reasonable amounts of time.

While derived from the biologically plausible model of Rescorla-Wagner, the provided solution was not trying to understand biology but to solve a computational problem. Nonetheless, it was in 1993 when Shultz et al. showed that there were some neurons in the mammal brain that where key to learning associations in conditioning [5]. These neurons segregated Dopamine (DA) when Reward Prediction Errors (RPE) where detected, indicating that the brain could be performing some form of TD-learning. Nonetheless, the existence of error backpropagation has not yet been demonstrated in biological systems, highlighting that learning based on RPEs can be just part of a bigger picture.

Advances in computation technology has re-enabled the use of RL algorithms, both showing the range of solutions a good implementation of RL can find and illustrating how RL is not sufficient to explain the complexity of animal behavior. For this reason, it is still difficult to train RL algorithms in the real world.

## 2 Challenges of Reinforcement Learning

Most applications of RL algorithms nowadays are either on simulators or videogames. Despite the huge success of RL algorithms on those environments, it is still difficult to assess when will we be able to transfer these technologies to real-world applications. We identify three of the main problems RL is facing today:

**Continual learning** refers to the training of an ML algorithm over a dataset formed of sequentially obtained data. This means, in continual learning input streams of data are temporally correlated. This is harmful for most ML algorithms because of the phenomenon known as Catastrophic Forgetting (CF): the overwriting of past knowledge with the new one. The most common way to address this problem has been *experience replay*, which proposes to store data in a buffer of past events, partly overcoming CF by training in both past and present data (introduced in [1]). Other approaches propose the use of Bayesian Inference (BI) to identify what memories contribute the most in a set of tasks and retrain in subsequent tasks only on the regions of the network in which the past relies the less [3].

**Exploration** is one of the biggest problems of RL algorithms. Because RL algorithms are based on exploitation of the best possible outcomes, exploration is essential to find the optimal action-state pairs for a specific environment or task. The most common approach is the use of $\epsilon$-greedy approaches: a decaying probability $\epsilon$ of performing a random action instead of the most optimal known action given the current state. This mechanism to slowly converge to exploitation modes lacks a mechanism to assess when exploration and exploitation are really required. The problem of *intrinsic motivation* proposes how empowerment or uncertainty could explain biological systems exploration of the action space. We find worth mentioning a completely different approach proposed in [2] in which the hierarchical concatenation of several RL modules (still with $\epsilon$-greedy exploration) enables a much wider exploration strategy by choosing behaviors instead of single motor commands.

Current RL algorithms are based on computing and learning through RPEs. As suggested in [5] learning through RPEs is mediated by DA in the brain and the reward and addiction circuitries. Nonetheless, only using a mechanism that's meant to learn to repeat a behavior is not sufficiently good for living systems. In situations where unexpected dangerous events occur, quick learning needs to be triggered to rapidly recognize such events and avoid them safely. This problem is particularly evident when training in virtual environments and testing in real ones. One way RL tries to overcome this problem is by training on simulations at faster rates and reduced costs than reality would offer. Nonetheless, there is usually a reality gap (algorithms in simulations tend to perform significantly worse in real environments) that hinders the use of these approaches (although see [8] for recent breakthroughs).

## 3    Biology of Fear, Neuromodulation and Exploration

The learning of avoidance have been also studied through conditioning paradigms. Nonetheless, these models only capture the nature of making associations, independent of the valence (or sign) of the outcome. Studies of fear conditioning in mice and rats, have capitalized on circuitry that largely differs from the dopaminergic system. We differentiate two kinds of studies that highlight different kinds of mechanisms in the biological brain:

- The circuit for *fear* is comprised mostly by the different nuclei in the amygdala. There, an associative process similar to that captured in the Rescorla-Wagner model tries to identify what CSs predict other USs, leading to freezing or startle reflexes. Crucial to form these associations is the neuromodulator Acetylcholine (ACh) which drives plasticity in both, neocortex and amygdala, together with less well understood modulations of the excitatory-inhibitory balance of those areas. Computational models in neuroscience and psychology have proposed Hebbian based systems that use an external error signal to directly bias plasticity and, therefore, associations at the relevant moments. The use of eligibility traces has been proposed for reward [9] but could also be used to associate stimuli to fear responses.
- The circuit for *avoidance* is contained mostly in the cerebellum, where a very unique type of cell (Purkinje Cell) is able to associate the CS with a response triggered by the US with sufficient anticipation to actually avoid the US. Models of anticipatory behavior have already been propose in order to optimize control. In those, a predefined reflex or reactive behavior is triggered in anticipation by the anticipation of the US, triggering the desired behavior at with sufficient time to avoid instead of react [10]. These algorithms capitalize on the convolution of a contextual sensory signal over a set of temporal bases, allowing the learning algorithm to adopt the control signal with sufficient time in advance.

There are other important studies that try to explain other facets of learning and memory, such as how slices of the hippocampus and the cortex in-vitro show learning mechanisms dependent only on the temporal dependencies between spikes or how neuromodulation could mostly be involved in the consolidation of that kind of learning.

## 4   Discussion

We have proposed two directions for the extension of the RL paradigm that accounts for learning from avoidance, one of the 3 key shortcomings faced by RL algorithms. Nonetheless, the solution for the other two could be also hidden within the proposed alternatives: ACh, as well as DA, is a neuromodulator that targets specific regions of the cortex and therefore promotes rapid and phasic learning only on regions where relevant changes are expected. Moreover, it has been suggested that the interactions of ACh with the neocortex may promote the switch between sensory exploitation and exploration modes [4]. Further understanding of how these two mechanisms work, as well as the integration of RL models with models of fear and avoidance learning might promote a significant leap from artificial machine learning to learning for living machines.

**Acknowledgements.** This work is supported by the European Research Councils CDAC project: The Role of Consciousness in Adaptive Behavior: A Combined Empirical, Computational and Robot based Approach, (ERC-2013- ADG341196).

# References

1. Mnih, V., et al.: Human-level control through deep reinforcement learning. Nature **518**(7540), 529 (2015)
2. Kulkarni, T.D., et al.: Hierarchical deep reinforcement learning: Integrating temporal abstraction and intrinsic motivation. In: NIPS (2016)
3. Kirkpatrick, J., et al.: Overcoming catastrophic forgetting in neural networks. Proc. Natl. Acad. Sci. **114**(13), 3521–3526 (2017)
4. Puigbò, J.-Y., et al.: Cholinergic behavior state-dependent mechanisms of neocortical gain control: a neurocomputational study. Mol. Neuro. **55**(1), 249–257 (2018)
5. Schultz, W., Dayan, P., Montague, P.R.: A neural substrate of prediction and reward. Science **275**(5306), 1593–1599 (1997)
6. Rescorla, R.A., Wagner, A.R.: A theory of Pavlovian conditioning: variations in the effectiveness of reinforcement and nonreinforcement. Class. Cond. Curr. Res. Theory **2**, 64–99 (1972)
7. Sutton, R.S.: Learning to predict by the methods of temporal differences. Mach. Learn. **3**(1), 9–44 (1988)
8. Bousmalis, K., et al.: Using simulation and domain adaptation to improve efficiency of deep robotic grasping. arXiv preprint arXiv:1709.07857 (2017)
9. Legenstein, R., Pecevski, D., Maass, W.: A learning theory for reward-modulated spike-timing-dependent plasticity with application to biofeedback. PLoS Comput. Biol. **4**(10), e1000180 (2008)
10. Maffei, G., et al.: The perceptual shaping of anticipatory actions. Proc. R. Soc. B **284**(1869), 20171780 (2017)

# Quad-Morphing: Towards a New Bio-inspired Autonomous Platform for Obstacle Avoidance at High Speed

Valentin Riviere[(✉)] and Stephane Viollet

Institute of Movement Sciences, Biorobotics, CP910, 163, av de Luminy, 13009 Marseille, France
{valentin.riviere,stephane.viollet}@univ-amu.fr

**Abstract.** We developed a new quadrotor robot to pass through narrow gaps that could be smaller than the robot wingspan. To achieve this, we have been inspired by bird's tricks: folding the wings to avoid damages due to contact with obstacles. Based on this observation, we have designed a new mechanism that provides a folding capacity to an aerial quadrotor. This platform, called Quad-Morphing Robot, is able to fold itself and to reduce its wingspan by half. A control strategy was developed to deal with the loss of control in roll axis, making our approach well-suited to high forward velocities ($2.5\,\mathrm{m.s}^{-1}$ in our experiments). In order to provide autonomous capacity to our platform, we placed a light high-speed camera on board to perform visual-based control.

## 1 Introduction

This work describes a new aerial platform and extends a published paper [1].

Several ways have been studied to pass through narrow aperture with quadrotor, in particular strategies based on aggressive maneuvers which consist to reach high angular velocity in roll [2]. This previous work was based on motion capture system for position control but some improvements have been recently made to get a more autonomous system by adding monocular vision system on robots. The robots in [3] performs visual-based gap-passing knowing the size and the shape of the aperture by only using internal sensors, in the same way [4] succeeded to perform narrow gap-passing without any knowledge of the aperture, stereo-vision was provided just to estimate gap orientation and position for trajectory planning.

Thus, in order to reach high angular velocity requirement, robots must have low inertia, which leads to light robots that can only carry small loads. To avoid aggressive maneuvers and light robots, we looked on an alternative strategy: as a bird, our robotic platform can fold up its propellers (as wings for bird) to reduce its wingspan to pass through an aperture that could be narrower than its original wingspan.

We developed a previous platform without embedded camera as a proof of concept, to test our solution, see Fig. 1. To enhance this solution, we designed the

© Springer International Publishing AG, part of Springer Nature 2018
V. Vouloutsi et al. (Eds.): Living Machines 2018, LNAI 10928, pp. 387–390, 2018.
https://doi.org/10.1007/978-3-319-95972-6_42

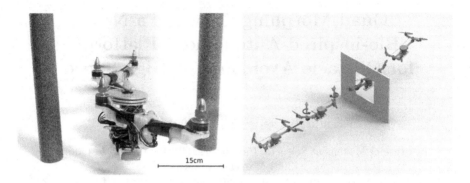

**Fig. 1.** (Left) Photo of the Quad-Morphing platform 1.0 (without camera). (Right) Computer-Aided-Design view of the Quad-Morphing platform flying towards a gap while rotating (folding) the arms supporting its four propellers to reduce its wingspan smoothly and quickly so as to avoid colliding with the gap.

Quad-Morphing 2.0 which is two times heavier and carries a monocular camera. We opted for this solution by considering that most non-predatory birds seems to use only monocular vision for gap-passing, budgerigars have been studied by [5] and it seems that binocular overlap region is too narrow to perform gap-passing task.

We described here the architecture of the platform and the vision-based detection which is implemented on it.

## 2   System Overview

The Quad-Morphing platform is based on a custom-made main board, called RCB2 (Rotor Control Board) which consists of:

- a Gumtix® Overo®'s linux-based (with preemptible kernel) for high-level control (attitude/position/folding control) and communication with the ground station via WiFi.
- a Teensy 3.1 Arduino-based for low-level control (propellers' speed) and sensors acquisition.
- a MPU9250 IMU (9-axis sensor) for attitude estimation.
- a MS5611-01BA03 pressure sensor for altitude estimation.

This board allows to interface the other components on the robot:

- 4 T-motor® F30 propellers with their ESC.
- 4 Hall effect sensors which provide propellers' speed feedback.
- a radio-receiver Spektrum® AR6115e for manual pilot mode and safety.
- a fast servomotor MKS® DS92A+ actuating the folding system.
- an Odroid-XU4 ARM-Cortex A15 linux-based for visual computation.
- a Basler® Dart camera with optical focal length of 6 mm.

We choose to implement visual computation on a dedicated board to keep an efficient real-time controller on the high-level board. The camera weights only 16 g with the S-mount optical lens and can reach a 150FPS (Frames Per Second) frame rate in VGA ($640 \times 480$ pixels). Details of the hardware and software architecture are summarized in Fig. 2.

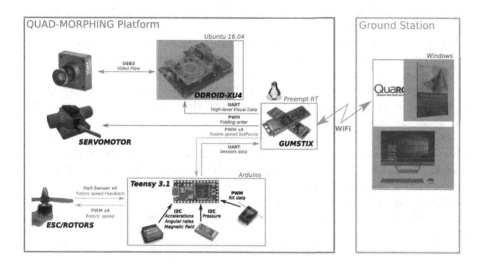

**Fig. 2.** Hardware architecture of the Quad-Morphing platform

## 3   Gap Detection

Several experiments were made in [1] for gap-crossing task. It was shown that our prototype was able to pass through a narrow gap (smaller than the unfolded robot wingspan) by using morphing abilities of the robot.

The implementation of visual gap detection is done by a border following algorithm [6]. This implementation consists in digitizing the image and tracking the borders on it, we chose this algorithm for its low computational time to perform a 100 Hz tracking. Next, the program permits to extract angles of the rectangular gap borders in the camera's field of view. These measures will then feed a controller, which is not described here, to control the robot's position relative to the gap.

## 4   Conclusion

In this paper, a new aerial robotic platform endowed with morphing capabilities and monocular vision is presented. As observed in studies on birds, our robot can suddenly reduce its wingspan to 48% of the unfolded wingspan within a very short time (about 250 ms) in order to pass through a gap such as a small square aperture that can be equal to 54% of the robot's unfolded wingspan. More details about results consideration are examined in recent previous study carried out at our laboratory [1].

This novel morphing structure does not have to make aggressive maneuvers to make the aerial robot cross a gap at high speed. Morphing improves the trade-off between payload and fast dynamics. The same morphing principle could be applied to a bigger and heavier quadrotor, assuming that the rotor folding mechanism shows sufficiently fast dynamics.

In previous experiments, a motion capture system was used but the next generation of the Quad-Morphing platform will carries a monocular vision which could be used to estimate the relative position of the robot to the gap.

Recent studies [7] (in revision) succeeded to pass through an unknown gap at high speed using only monocular vision. Thus, this seems to be very promising for future experiments.

Our new platform QuadMorphing 2.0 carry a monocular vision system to answer to this requirement. Thanks to a new Linux-based board for image processing, we extract the obstacle angles into the camera's field of view and send them to the robot's position controller. In addition to this visual positioning, the robot will have to take the decision to fold up its structure or not on the basis of visual cues, that will be the next challenge to be met by our new Quad-Morphing robot.

# References

1. Riviere, V., Manecy, A., Viollet, S.: Agile robotic fliers: a morphing-based approach. Soft Robot. J. (2018). https://doi.org/10.1089/soro.2017.0120
2. Mellinger, D., Michael, N., Kumar, V.: Trajectory generation and control for precise aggressive maneuvers with quadrotors. Int. J. Robot. Res. 31(5), 664–674 (2012)
3. Falanga, D., Mueggler, E., Faessler, M., Scaramuzza, D.: Aggressive quadrotor flight through narrow gaps with onboard sensing and computing using active vision. In: Proceedings - IEEE International Conference on Robotics and Automation, pp. 5774–5781 (2017)
4. Loianno, G., Brunner, C., McGrath, G., Kumar, V.: Estimation, control, and planning for aggressive flight with a small quadrotor with a single camera and IMU. IEEE Robot. Autom. Lett. 2(2), 404–411 (2017)
5. Schiffner, I., Vo, H.D., Bhagavatula, P.S., Srinivasan, M.V.: Minding the gap: In-flight body awareness in birds. Front. Zool. 11(1), 64–70 (2014)
6. Suzuki, S., Be, K.A.: Topological structural analysis of digitized binary images by border following. Comput. Vis. Graph. Image Process. 30(1), 32–46 (1985)
7. Sanket, N.J., Singh, C.D., Ganguly, K., Fermüller, C., Aloimonos, Y.: GapFlyt: Active Vision Based Minimalist Structure-less Gap Detection For Quadrotor Flight, no. Table I (2018)

# Toward Computing with Spider Webs: Computational Setup Realization

S. M. Hadi Sadati$^{(\boxtimes)}$ and Thomas Williams

Department of Engineering Mathematics, University of Bristol,
Bristol BS8 1TH, U.K.
{s.m.hadi.sadati,t.williams}@bristol.ac.uk

**Abstract.** Spiders are able to extract crucial information, such as the location prey, predators, mates, and even broken threads from propagating web vibrations. The complex structure of the web suggests that the morphology itself might provide computational support in form of a mechanical signal processing system - often referred to as morphological computation. We present preliminary results on identifying these computational aspects in naturally spun webs. A recently presented definition for physical computational systems, consisting of three main elements: (i) a mathematical part, (ii) a computational setup with a theoretical and real part, and (iii) an interpretation, is employed for the first time, to characterize these morphological computation properties. Signal transmission properties of a real spider orb web, as the real part of a morphological computation setup, is investigated in response to step transverse inputs. The parameters of a lumped system model, as the theoretical part of a morphological computation setup, are identified empirically and with the help of an earlier FEM model for the same web. As the possible elements of a computational framework, the web transverse signal filtering, attenuation, delay, memory effect, and deformation modes are briefly discussed based on experimental data and numerical simulations.

**Keywords:** Morphological computation · Spider web · Vibration
Lumped system model · Signal processing

## 1 Introduction

The spider's web is a complex structure created by a dedicated and interactive behavior pattern optimized through evolution over many million years to serve the ultimate purpose of catching prey [1,2]. The efficacy of the web as a trap depends heavily on the correct and robust categorization and localization of various events, including trapped prey, potential mates, broken threads, wind, and others. Somehow spiders are capable of categorizing and locating events robustly based on a very small amount of information that is only locally available. This suggests that the web might not be only a passive catching device, but rather

© Springer International Publishing AG, part of Springer Nature 2018
V. Vouloutsi et al. (Eds.): Living Machines 2018, LNAI 10928, pp. 391–402, 2018.
https://doi.org/10.1007/978-3-319-95972-6_43

contributes to the pattern recognition task. In this research, we propose a theoretical framework toward understanding how spiders may use their web as a computational device for the aforementioned purposes.

The typical spider's orb web consists of a capture spiral which radiates from the center, held by several radial threads (Fig. 2.left) [1]. The radial threads are built using dragline silk, an exceptionally tough material with high tensional strength, which provides the framework of the web [3]. The role of the spiral is to capture prey, benefiting from its sticky thread and large strain elasticity that creates a strong and effective snare, capable of capturing large prey relative to the web [4]. Typically, orb-weaving spiders have poor eyesight and in consequence are heavily dependent on (i) web vibrations, to provide information on current surroundings [4], and (ii) highly sensitive mechanoreceptors on all eight legs [5,6], which together enable the animal to interpret propagating web vibrations [7,8]. The structural [9,10] and vibration properties [5,11,12] of the spider web has been studied extensively. Mortimer et al. have recently studied and summarized the relevant research on the relationship between material properties of the web and its ability to transmit vibrations in experiments and finite element modeling, [7,8]. The following elements are proposed as control mechanisms that the spider employs in order to influence the structure sonic properties such as speed and amplitude [7,8]: super-contraction, web tensioning, and altering longitudinal (along with the threads), lateral (perpendicular to threads in web plan) and transverse (perpendicular to threads and web plan) vibrations. However, modal behavior of a spider orb-web-like, but not quite similar, structure is studied recently for designing an acoustic metamaterial [13].

Taking all this into account the spider web can be perceived as a highly dynamic, morphological computation device. Moreover, an externalized computational resource that the spider is able to build on demand. The concept of outsourcing computation to a physical body (e.g., from the brain to another part of the body) is usually referred to as morphological computation [14–18] and can be observed in biological systems at different scales [19]. Examples of benefiting from structural natural behavior by design for simplifying or improving a task [20], replacing computation units in a traditional computation framework with morphological counterparts [18,21], and emerging adaptive behavior from simple morphological rules [22] are mentioned as candidates for morphological computation. Hauser et al. presented two theoretical frameworks for the concept [17,18], realized in robotic research [15,16,22], where the highly non-linear reservoir in a reservoir computing paradigm is substituted with a complaint body, reducing a complex problem of dynamic filter design or system limit-cycle control to dynamic learning of a set of linear weights. Ghazi-Zahedi et al. have investigated quantitative measures for morphological computation in continuous and discrete systems [23,24]. A summary of the most current state of the art, definitions, and examples of morphological computation is presented by Füchslin et al. [25]. However, a fundamental approach for designing by definition and even identifying instances of morphological computation is not yet presented or agreed upon. However, a good starting point might be employing the methods discussed in the theoretical physics and computer science research on the definition and modeling of a computing physical phenomenon [26,27], despite their differences [25]. For the first time in this study, we try to extend a recently proposed definition for physical computational systems by Giunti [27], (i) to define morphological computational systems, and (ii) to realize the computational capability of a natural structure, i.e. spider webs.

This paper is structured as follows. Materials and methods are presented in Sect. 2. There, the adopted definition for a morphological computation setup is discussed. The experimental procedure used by Mortimer et al. [7,8] is explained. A mathematical lumped mass-spring-damper system model, similar to [9] by using the parameters in [7,8,11], is derived, as the theoretical part for a morphological computation setup. Empirical and numerical results are compared and discussed in Sect. 3. The experimental data set is used to investigate signal processing features such as arrival times (delay), attenuation, frequency filtering, memory effect, and assessing their variation with input location, to realize the web structure behavior, as the real part of a morphological computation setup. A conclusion is presented in Sect. 4.

## 2    Materials and Methods

### 2.1    Morphological Computation System Realization

Giunti [27] has proposed a precise analysis for physical realization of a computational system, by looking at the modeling relation between a dynamic system and phenomena, as a complex object. A computational system contains three parts (Fig. 1.a); (1) a mathematical part in the form of a discrete n-component dynamic system $(DS = (M, (g^t)_{t \in T}))$ with a state space $(M)$, a transition function $(g^t)$ and a time set $(T)$; (2) a computational setup $(H = (F, B_F))$ with a theoretical part $(F)$ and a real (physically feasible) part $(B_F)$; and (3) an interpretation $(I_{DS,H})$ linking the aforementioned parts. Despite the similarity to empirically correct dynamical models for physical phenomena, e.g. modeling a spider orb-web dynamics in this research, a computational system is proved different by characterizing a form of purely theoretical (a-priori) interpretation of the mathematical part on the setup part. This interpretation can be only established empirically (a-posteriori) for models derived to understand phenomena in empirical science. Figure 1.b presents an example of a computational task, consisting of an operation and a memory, calculated with a physical computational setup. The mathematical dynamic system part has two discrete components, a memory, and an operation, interpreted to the theoretical part of the physical computational setup which is an ideal representation of the setup real part. The calculated result by the setup real part is matched with a state of the theoretical physical model, which is then interpreted back to a state in the task mathematical part. We dismiss the exact characteristics and relations of different parts of this definition at the moment to focus on our extension to a morphological computation system.

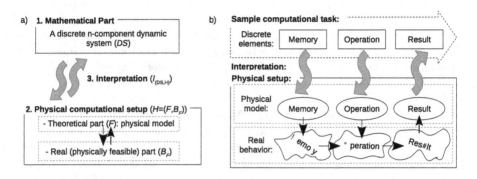

**Fig. 1.** (a) Three elements of a physical computational setup, (b) implementation of a sample computational task, consisting of an operation and a memory element, on a physical computational system.

In a morphological computation system, the setup part $(H)$ has a theoretical model for the physical setup $(F)$, e.g. the lumped system dynamic model for the web, and the real behavior of the web $(B_F)$, which are the physically feasible realizations of the theory. Distinct behaviors observe in the setup empirically, e.g. signal filtering, delay, memory effect, deformation modes, etc., are an $F$-realizer if a close enough theoretical model can be presented for it in $F$. These distinct behaviors indicate that the setup posses discrete behavior, to switch between, as means of discrete programming to be interpreted by a proper dynamic system $DS$. As an example, a signal processing task can be programmed as a discrete sequence of filtering, deformation modes and memory of a few previous time steps, subject to availability and realization of a proper dynamic system $DS$ and an interpretation $I$. Despite a man-made computational device with pre-known systems, computational capabilities of a natural morphological computation setups need to be identified, either in real experiments or based on verifiable predictions from numerical simulations. As a result, not only $I$ and $DS$, but identification and proper formulation of the $H$ is a challenge too.

To realize the spider web as a physical computational setup, we assert that (i) the web structure serves as the real part of a computational setup $(B_F)$, and (ii) the theoretical part of the setup $(F)$ is a mathematical model for the structure dynamics, e.g. the lumped system model presented here. In this study, we try to realize the properties of the web with possible computational capability in experiments and numerical simulations. The possible dynamic system $(DS)$ and interpretation $(I)$ parts are going to be investigated in a future study.

## 2.2   Experiments on Spider Orb-Web

Experimental data were recorded from an orb-web of a Garden Cross Spider Araneus diadematus, which typically positions itself at the hub (Fig. 2.left) [7]. Four points along seven radii of the web were excited, five times each, with a

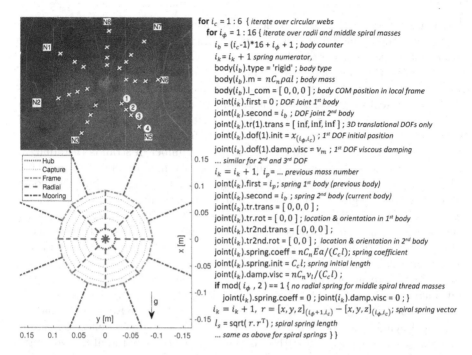

```
for i_c = 1 : 6 { iterate over circular webs
    for i_φ = 1 : 16 { iterate over radii and middle spiral masses
        i_b = (i_c-1)*16 + i_φ + 1 ; body counter
        i_k = i_k + 1 spring numerator,
        body(i_b).type = 'rigid' ; body type
        body(i_b).m = nC_nρal ; body mass
        body(i_b).l_com = [ 0, 0, 0 ] ; body COM position in local frame
        joint(i_k).first = 0 ; DOF Joint 1st body
        joint(i_k).second = i_b ; DOF joint 2nd body
        joint(i_k).tr(1).trans = [ inf, inf, inf ] ; 3D translational DOFs only
        joint(i_k).dof(1).init = x_(i_φ,i_c) ; 1st DOF initial position
        joint(i_k).dof(1).damp.visc = v_m ; 1st DOF viscous damping
        ... similar for 2nd and 3rd DOF
        i_k = i_k + 1, i_p = ... previous mass number
        joint(i_k).first = i_p ; spring 1st body (previous body)
        joint(i_k).second = i_b ; spring 2nd body (current body)
        joint(i_k).tr.trans = [ 0,0,0 ] ;
        joint(i_k).tr.rot = [ 0,0 ] ; location & orientation in 1st body
        joint(i_k).tr2nd.trans = [ 0,0,0 ] ;
        joint(i_k).tr2nd.rot = [ 0,0 ] ; location & orientation in 2nd body
        joint(i_k).spring.coeff = nC_nEa/(C_cl); spring coefficient
        joint(i_k).spring.init = C_cl; spring initial length
        joint(i_k).damp.visc = nC_nv_l/(C_cl) ;
        if mod( i_φ , 2 ) == 1 { no radial spring for middle spiral thread masses
            joint(i_k).spring.coeff = 0 ; joint(i_k).damp.visc = 0 ; }
        i_k = i_k + 1, r = [x,y,z]_(i_φ+1,i_c) − [x,y,z]_(i_φ,i_c); spiral spring vector
        l_s = sqrt( r.r^T ) ; spiral spring length
        ... same as above for spiral springs } }
```

**Fig. 2.** (left) Labeled experimental spider orb-web and top view of 3D Lumped system model. The nodes represent lumped masses and different lines represent the model springs/dampers (right) Sample Matlab code inputs for AutoTMTDyn package as in [28]. The model source code is available from [29].

3 ms duration and 170 μm amplitude square wave input, using a solenoid positioned perpendicular to the structure (transverse direction). Two Laser Doppler vibrometers were used to record both the input signal delivered to the web at four positions along seven radii (Polytec PDV-100) and a unique output response near the hub (Polytec PSV-400), see [7].

## 2.3   Lumped System Model

The web is modeled as a mass-spring-damper network [9] with 8 radii and 6 circular webs to capture all the experimental points (Fig. 2.left). Point masses are assumed at the nodes and middle of the circular webs, to capture the thread second deformation modes and simulate the secondary outer frame as in [10], with Cartesian motion of the masses as generalized coordinates ($q$). AutoTMTDyn Matlab package [28] is used to derive the system constrained Lagrange dynamics in a vector formalism in the form

$$M\ddot{q} + N_m\dot{q} + L_{,q}^T(N_l L_{,q}\dot{q} + K\Delta L) + Mg = \lambda, \; q_{in} = u, \tag{1}$$

where $M$ is the mass matrix, $N_m$ is the lateral damping matrix, $N_l$ is the longitudinal damping matrix, $L$ is the springs' vector, $\Delta L = L_{,q}q - C_c l_0 \hat{L}$ is their deformation vector, $K$ is the stiffness coefficient matrix, $g = 9.81\,\mathrm{m/s}^2$ is the gravity, $u$ is the input signal, $\lambda$ is a Lagrange multiplier resulting from the input constraint, $q_{\mathrm{in}}$ is the generalized coordinate on which the input signal is exerted, $\dot{x} = \partial x / \partial t$ for the time derivatives, and $y_{,x} = \partial y / \partial x$ for the spatial derivatives. $\lambda$, i.e. a constrained dynamic system, is used to match the experiments excitation in numerical simulations since it is hard to measure input force on the web and only the displacement imposed at the excitation location can be observed accurately. Modeling parameters are extracted from the experimental measurements and [7,11]. Threads diameter ($r$-1.2 μm), number of strands ($n$-radial: 3, mooring, hub, outer frame: 4, capture 2), elasticity modulus ($E$-capture: 0.06, others: 4 [GPa]), density ($\rho$-1300 Kg/m$^3$, and web dimensions ($l_0$-hub, free zone: 20, capture zone segments: 11.2, outer frame: 10, mooring 90 mm). The masses ($m = \rho a l$, $a = n\pi r^2$) are calculated based on the adjutant segments initial length ($l = C_c l_0$). The threads elastic coefficient is found from Hook's linear stress-strain relation for axial elongation ($k = Ea/l$ N/m) and the thread average initial stresses (radial: 458, capture: 2.25 μN) reported by Masters [12] are used to calculate supercontraction ratios ($C_c$- radial: 99.7%, capture: 99%) and unloaded thread lengths. The thread lateral damping ($\nu_{\mathrm{m}}$, exerting on masses) is a summation of Stokes' air drag ($\nu_{\mathrm{d}} = 6\pi\nu_{\mathrm{air}}$, $\nu_{\mathrm{air}} = 1.81e{-}5$ Kg/(ms)), valid for very low Reynolds numbers (here $Re \approx 4e{-}3 \ll 1$), and thread deflection damping ($\nu_{\mathrm{thread}} = 1.8e{-}5$ Kg/(m.s))[11], all per unit length. The radial thread longitudinal damping ($\nu_{\mathrm{l_r}}$- exerting on connecting springs.), is the only free parameter which is identified to be 8e-8/$l$ N/m (proportional to thread elastic coefficient with dimension N/m), for the best agreement between the maximum transverse deflection in numerical simulation and experiments. The linear part of the system in Eq. 1 (for $l_0 = 0$) is a proportionally damped system if $\nu_{\mathrm{l_c}}$ for capture thread is proportional with $E$ as $\nu_{\mathrm{l_c}} = \nu_{\mathrm{l_r}} E_c / E_r$. Two corrections coefficients are considered to be multiplied by $n$; $C_n$ which is the ratio of the number of threads in the experiments to that in the model (hub: 7, radial: 4.625, mooring 1.875, capture; 7.75), and $C_\phi = 0.216$, which is due to the reduced angle between the capture and radial threads in the model. Parts of the code used to model the web in AutoTMTDyn package is presented in Fig. 2.right. The discussed parameters in this section are used in the input code too. The model source code is available from [29].

## 3   Results and Discussion

The time series and Fast Fourier Transfer (FFT) of the average of all input signals, plotted in Fig. 3.a, are used in this study. Experimental and simulation time series for N2 (same thread as output, compare Fig. 4.c) and N6 (opposite side of the net) are compared in Fig. 3.b,c. The simulation results for the input response has less accuracy on the opposite side of the web (Fig. 4.c), based on the simulation and experimental signal maximum values. Overall damping is stronger in the simulations where sharper peaks are observed. Smaller variation in maximum signal amplitude of different experiments shows less lateral damping along radial threads. A large hysteresis is observed in some experimental

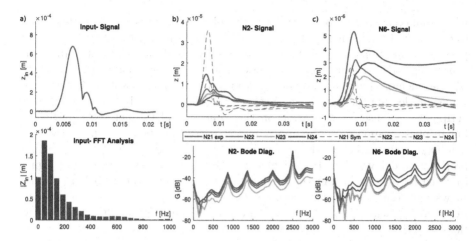

**Fig. 3.** Experimental results: (a) Input signal time series and FFT diagram, experimental and simulation time series and Bode gain diagram results for inputs on (b) N2 and (c) N6. The model thread longitudinal damping ($\nu_{l_r}$) is identified to minimize the max error between the simulation (dash lines) and experimental (solid lines) result time series (b,c- top).

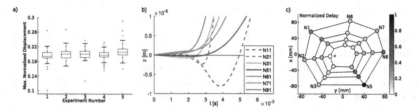

**Fig. 4.** Experimental results: (a) Maximum normalized deformation for different locations along the web in different experimental trials, showing no memory effect between different experiment trials. (b) Arrival output signals from spiral 1, showing antiphase deformation of the hub on the excitation side of the web and in phase deformation on the opposite side of of the web. (c) Normalized signal delay to reach maximum value for different input locations, showing the signal propagation pattern.

results where the output signal settles with an offset from the initial equilibrium point. The web nonlinear damping and structural hysteresis need further investigation in a future study. The experimental signal Bode diagram for input-output gain (Fig. 3.b,c) shows large damping values for low-frequency (1–500 Hz) responses, perhaps to cancel wind and rain disturbances. A smooth response for frequencies more than ≈1000 Hz, perhaps to match the natural frequency of the spider's prey wingbeats [11], is observed that may suggest reduced noise to signal ratio for high-frequency signals. High gain for the bias value (0 Hz) in Bode diagrams shows some overdamped vibration modes (mostly with low frequency), suggesting some memory effect in the continuous signal, meaning that the effect of a low-frequency excitation remains in the structure for some time, while some modes are not filtered out completely, perhaps enabling the spider to exploit useful information from the resultant vibrations. However, the lack of positive correlation between the maximum normalized displacement of different experiment trials at each location shows the elastic behavior of the structure with no memory effect (plastic deformation) in maximum absolute deformation values, neglecting the signal bias, between the trials (Fig. 4.b). Figure 4.b shows antiphase response for excitation on the same side of the net (N11 and N21) but in phase response for the opposite side, that suggests the shape of the web dominant deformation mode for, probably, frequencies of 500–1000 Hz. Signal propagation delay in Fig. 4.c is defined as the time that takes the output signal to reach its maximum, measured from the start of the input signal. Figure 4.c shows high tension pathways along N2, 3, 7 and 8, probably due to the web weight in vertical orientation, have higher wave speed, similar to the observations in [11].

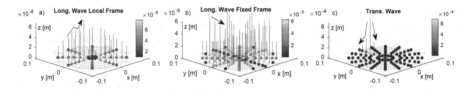

**Fig. 5.** Simulation results for input at N22: Longitudinal wave maximum value (a) amplifies along the threads toward the web hub but (b) looks decaying if measured w.r.t. an external fixed frame. (c) Transverse wave maximum value at the excitation point. Arrows show the values' change trend along a radial thread, bars height and their root point color indicate the deformation values.

Longitudinal waves (Fig. 5.a,b) rather than lateral waves (Fig. 5.c) are arguably the potential key for spider signal processing due to (i) higher signal to noise ratio and (ii) lesser sensitivity to environmental disturbance [7,8]. The longitudinal waves should be measured along the threads (local frame) (Fig. 5.a) rather than along the threads projection on the initial web plan (i.e. w.r.t. an externally fixed reference frame) (Fig. 5.b). This makes their experimental investigation challenging since it is easier to measure the later one with a fixed laser vibrometer, while onboard sensors, i.e. a spider itself, on the structure are needed to measure the former one. Simulations show longitudinal signal amplification toward the free zone (Fig. 5.a), the gap between the hub and the capture zone with no spiral threads, despite lateral waves that are largely damped toward the hub (Fig. 5.c) and prone to noises [7,11].

The discussed model is better in capturing signal maximum amplitudes compared to the FEM model results in [7]; however, the frequency domain responses still presents significant differences compared to the experimental results. We aim to improve our model to capture the actual web spectral behavior and to investigate the Bode diagram differences between the simulation and experimental data (Fig. 6.a), which can be used to investigate the web hysteresis and

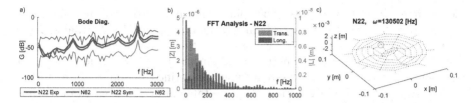

**Fig. 6.** Simulation results for input at N22: (a) Bode gain diagram from simulations and experiments for N22 and N62, showing smoother frequency response with less damping for low frequency domains and along the radial thread in the experiments compared to the simulations. (b) Comparison of FFT analysis results for transverse and longitudinal waves based on simulation results, that shows a highly damped lateral vibration with less contribution of the high frequency modes for the lateral wave, but a distinguishable transfer function with a modal damping pattern for the longitudinal wave frequency response. (c) A mode shape with antiphase deformation of the hub w.r.t. the excitation signal.

damping behavior. This helps with more accurate predictions for the spectral behavior of the longitudinal waves that seem to poses stronger signal filtering capability based on our preliminary results (Fig. 6.b). Besides, our simulations show antiphase deformation mode (Fig. 6.c), similar to the experiments (Fig. 6.a), but for unrealistic high frequencies ($\approx$130 KHz) that needs further investigation. While we try to preserve the theoretical simplicity and clarity of the model, to remain useful as the theoretical part in a computational setup definition, we plan to investigate high fidelity methods such as cyclic symmetric, membrane, and finite element models in the future. An artificial web will be fabricated to further investigate our hypothesis and predictions, and to be used as a morphological computational setup for signal processing with application in designing new vibration and flow sensors.

Our experimental and modeling effort show the possibility of identifying and theoretically realizing the computational properties of the spider web as a morphological computational setup. Preliminary results suggest that we should exploit properties like memory, signal filtering, delay, amplification, and attenuation as computational elements and interpret them ($I$) as meaningful elements of a computational paradigm ($DS$). As a candidate for such computational paradigm ($DS$) and interpretation ($I$), we plan to follow the theoretical foundation for morphological computation presented by Hauser et al. [18]. Their proposed theories established that the nonlinearity and memory effect in a high dimensional (sufficiently rich) dynamic system ($H$- the computational setup), e.g. compliant body robots, can partly characterize a nonlinear, time-invariant filter with fading memory in the form of a Volterra series ($DS$- Dynamic System). The interpretation ($I$) is established since a Volterra series can characterize (i) a nonlinear time-invariant filter with fading memory ($DS$), as well as (ii) any continuous nonlinear dynamic system ($H$). Such morphological filter is able to emulate arbitrary input-output mappings in continuous time by adopting a simple linear readout. In this sense, the spider web may serve as a morphological computational device to generate fading memory response to external signals. Alternatively, Hauser et al. [17] have extended this theory to autonomous generation of a large diversity of periodic movements by providing feedback into the morphological computing system, which is verified in soft robotic studies [16,22]. As a candidate, a generic nonlinear stable limit cycles equation is chosen in [17] as the system target (DS) describing a stable nonlinear limit cycle. The interpretation (I) is established by (i) showing that the computational setup theoretical part (BF) is feedback linearisable (has a feedback equivalent linear system), and (ii) employing a transfer function and a specific feedback to map this feedback equivalent system to our goal system, which can be any sufficiently smooth arbitrary nonlinear function. The former is useful in the current research, as we know that the spider uses the web vibration, i.e. introduces feedback to the system, for structural monitoring and communication. Besides, studying the web deformation modes and web building strategies can give us a framework for designing morphological computational setups.

The theoretical framework and results, discussed in this research, help us with identifying the signal processing properties of spider webs and their possible roles as elements of a morphological computational setup. The identified properties can be used to design new vibration sensors with application in structural health or fluid flow monitoring. The possible morphological computational setup inspires a structural design to outsource the computational burden of signal processing and conditioning, needed to analyze the sensor readings, on the sensor embodiment and morphology. Finally, the relative importance and trade-off between signal processing and pray capturing capabilities of the web structure remain to be investigated further in a future research.

## 4   Conclusion

This paper describes our approach and presents preliminary results for investigating computational properties of the spider web. A naturally spun spider orb web is experimentally and analytically investigated as the real part of a morphological computation setup, based on the definition of a physical computational system, in response to transverse step inputs. A lumped system model is derived based on the parameters of an earlier FEM model as theoretical part of the morphological computation setup. The web transverse and longitudinal signal filtering, attenuation, delay, memory effect, and deformation modes are briefly discussed. Furthermore, the importance of considering the web frequency filtering and the web hub dynamics are elaborated. Our modeling effort aims to identify and theoretically realize possible computational properties of the web for formulating a dynamic system and an interpretation for this interesting structure as a morphological computation setup. Two potential candidates for such interpretation and dynamic system are identified for (i) a nonlinear time-invariant filter with fading memory, and (ii) autonomous generation of adaptive periodic patterns. However, further investigation in these directions will be carried in the future. The goal is to infer design guidelines for novel types of vibration and flow sensors capable of using their morphological features to carry out relevant computations. To this effect, we plan to build prototypes of such sensors and, inspired by spiders, also physical robots that are capable of deploying such sensors on demand.

**Acknowledgment.** This work is supported by the Leverhulme Trust Research Project, "Computing with spiders' web", number RPG-2016-345, granted to H.H. and F.V.; and the Royal Academy of Engineering (research fellowship RF1516/15/11), granted to L.R. With special thanks to Dr. Helmut Hauser, Dr. Ludovic Renson, Dr. Beth Mortimer, Prof. Fritz Vollrth, Dr. S. Elnaz Naghibi and Alan Quille who contribute to this research by helpful discussions, exchanging ideas, proofreading the draft and providing helpful comments.

# References

1. Vollrath, F., Selden, P.: The role of behavior in the evolution of spiders, silks, and webs. Ann. Rev.Ecol.Evol. Syst. **38**(1), 819–846 (2007)
2. Vollrath, F.: Coevolution of behaviour and material in the spiders web. In: Biomechanics in Animal Behaviour, pp. 315–29 (2000)
3. Slotta, U., Hess, S., Spie, K., Stromer, T., Serpell, L., Scheibel, T.: Spider silk and amyloid fibrils: a structural comparison. Macromol. Biosci. **7**(2), 183–188 (2007)
4. Guan, J., Vollrath, F., Porter, D.: Two mechanisms for supercontraction in nephila spider dragline silk. Biomacromolecules **12**, 4030–4035 (2011)
5. Masters, W.M., Markl, H.: Vibration signal transmission in spider orb webs. Science **213**, 363–365 (1981)
6. Barth, F.G., Geethabali: Spider vibration receptors: Threshold curves of individual slits in the metatarsal lyriform organ. J. Comp. Physiol. **148**, 175–185 (1982)
7. Mortimer, B., Soler, A., Siviour, C.R., Zaera, R., Vollrath, F.: Tuning the instrument: sonic properties in the spider's web. J. R. Soc. Interface **13**, 20160341 (2016)
8. Mortimer, B., Soler, A., Siviour, C.R., Vollrath, F.: Remote monitoring of vibrational information in spider webs. Sci. Nature **105**, 37 (2018)
9. Aoyanagi, Y., Okumura, K.: Simple model for the mechanics of spider webs. Phys. Rev. Lett. **104**, 038102 (2010)
10. Soler, A., Zaera, R.: The secondary frame in spider orb webs: the detail that makes the difference. Sci. Rep. **6**, 31265 (2016)
11. Masters, W.M.: Vibrations in the orbwebs of nuctenea sclopetaria (Araneidae): I. Transmission through the web. Behav. Ecol. Sociobiol. **15**(3), 207–215 (1984)
12. Masters, W.M.: Vibrations in the orbwebs of nuctenea sclopetaria (Araneidae): II. Prey and wind signals and the spider's response threshold. Behav. Ecol. Sociobiol. **15**(3), 217–223 (1984)
13. Krushynska, A.O., Bosia, F., Miniaci, M., Pugno, N.M.: Tunable spider-web inspired hybrid labyrinthine acoustic metamaterials for low-frequency sound control. New J. Phys. **19**, 105001 (2017). arXiv:1701.07622
14. Hauser, H., Füchslin, R.M., Pfeifer, R.: Opinions and Outlooks on Morphological Computation. E-Book (2014)
15. Nakajima, K., Li, T., Hauser, H., Pfeifer, R.: Exploiting short-term memory in soft body dynamics as a computational resource. J. R. Soc. Interface **11**, 20140437 (2014)

16. Nakajima, K., Hauser, H., Li, T., Pfeifer, R.: Information processing via physical soft body. Sci. Rep. **5**, 10487 (2015)
17. Hauser, H., Ijspeert, A.J., Füchslin, R.M., Pfeifer, R., Maass, W.: The role of feedback in morphological computation with compliant bodies. Biol. Cybern. **106**, 595–613 (2012)
18. Hauser, H., Ijspeert, A.J., Füchslin, R.M., Pfeifer, R., Maass, W.: Towards a theoretical foundation for morphological computation with compliant bodies. Biol. Cybern. **105**, 355–370 (2011)
19. Pfeifer, R., Bongard, J.: How the Body Shapes the Way We Think: A New View of Intelligence. MIT Press, Cambridge (2006). Google-Books-ID: EHPMv9MfgWwC
20. Sornkarn, N., Howard, M., Nanayakkara, T.: Internal impedance control helps information gain in embodied perception. In: Proceedings - IEEE International Conference on Robotics and Automation, pp. 6685–6690 (2014)
21. Sadati, S., Sullivan, L., Walker, I., Althoefer, K., Nanayakkara, T.: Three-dimensional-printable thermoactive helical interface with decentralized morphological stiffness control for continuum manipulators. IEEE Robot. Autom. Lett. **3**, 2283–2290 (2018)
22. Zhao, Q., Nakajima, K., Sumioka, H., Hauser, H., Pfeifer, R.: Spine dynamics as a computational resource in spine-driven quadruped locomotion. In: 2013 IEEE/RSJ International Conference on Intelligent Robots and Systems, pp. 1445–1451, November 2013
23. Ghazi-Zahedi, K., Haeufle, D.F.B., Montfar, G., Schmitt, S., Ay, N.: Evaluating morphological computation in muscle and DC-motor driven models of hopping movements. Front. Robot. AI **3**, 42 (2016)
24. Ghazi-Zahedi, K., Langer, C., Ay, N.: Morphological computation: synergy of body and brain. Entropy **19**, 456 (2017)
25. Füchslin, R.M., Dzyakanchuk, A., Flumini, D., Hauser, H., Hunt, K.J., Luchsinger, R.H., Reller, B., Scheidegger, S., Walker, R.: Morphological computation and morphological control: steps toward a formal theory and applications. Artif. Life **19**, 9–34 (2012)
26. Giunti, M.: Computation, Dynamics, and Cognition. Oxford University Press, New York (1997)
27. Giunti, M.: What is a physical realization of a computational system? ISONOMIA, 9(Epistemologica Series, Special Issue: Reasoning, Metaphor and Science), 177–192 (2017)
28. Sadati, S., Naghibi, S., Naraghi, M.: An automatic algorithm to derive linear vector form of lagrangian equation of motion with collision and constraint. Procedia Comput. Sci. **76**, 217–222 (2015)
29. Sadati, S.: AutoTMTDyn Software Package, May 2017. https://github.com/hadisdt/AutoTMTDyn

# Whisker-RatSLAM Applied to 6D Object Identification and Spatial Localisation

Mohammed Salman[1,2(✉)] and Martin J. Pearson[1,2]

[1] Bristol Robotics Laboratory, University of the West of England, Bristol, UK
[2] Bristol Robotics Laboratory, University of Bristol, Bristol, UK
ms13417@bristol.ac.uk

**Abstract.** The problem of tactile object identification has a strong connection with the problem of Simultaneous Localization and Mapping (SLAM) in a physical 6-dimensional environment. Here we introduce our preliminary results describing the performance of our RatSLAM-inspired 6D SLAM algorithm dubbed Whisker-RatSLAM, which is used to map and localize a whisker-array relative to the surface of an object. We show that our approach can successfully localize using the physical and simulation data sets taken from an active array of artificial whiskers as they explore a range of household objects. We also demonstrate the ability of Whisker-RatSLAM to be used for object identification.

**Keywords:** Whiskered robotics · Tactile SLAM
6D object identification

## 1 Introduction

Using tactile sensors to identify an object by its shape requires coordinated movement such that the tactile sensor can measure the surface qualities from a range of different poses relative to the object. This coordination between motion and tactile sensing is self-evident as you attempt to blindly identify an object through manipulation between your fingers. For larger objects you may also have to move your hands across the surface or even walk around it's periphery to uniquely identify it. Therefore, the problem of tactile object identification has strong synergies to the mobile robot localization and mapping problems with a number of studies published adhering to this position [1–3].

Here, we propose that such a framework can be neatly extended into a tactile mapping scheme in which uniquely identified local objects can be incorporated as landmarks within a sparsely represented global map for spatial navigation. Inspiration for this work stems from observations of small whiskered mammals as they explore and navigate their environment in complete darkness. It also builds upon previous work that demonstrated the ability of the RatSLAM algorithm [4] to robustly accommodate tactile whisker sensory input for robot localization and mapping [5].

© Springer International Publishing AG, part of Springer Nature 2018
V. Vouloutsi et al. (Eds.): Living Machines 2018, LNAI 10928, pp. 403–414, 2018.
https://doi.org/10.1007/978-3-319-95972-6_44

RatSLAM has been chosen as it performs Bayesian inference using a continuous attractor model of neural dynamics that is particularly well suited for event-driven computing media. As embedded neuromorphic hardware becomes commercially available [6] roboticists should consider the algorithms they choose in order to leverage the considerable power savings that this technology can provide. In this paper we introduce the proposed extension to the overall Whisker-RatSLAM framework for spatial navigation, focusing on the 6D object mapping and localization component of this system.

Using both physically acquired and simulated data sets we present results that demonstrate the ability of the system in localizing relative to the surface of an object as well as uniquely identifying it from a set of candidate objects.

## 2   Extended Whisker-RatSLAM

Land-based mobile robotic platforms are predominantly constrained to moving across a 2-dimensional plane thus reducing localization to a 3-dimensional state estimation problem $(x, y, \theta)$. Uncertainty in the 3D pose estimate of a mobile robot can be reduced through the observation of known landmarks listed in a map. This implies that objects encountered must be uniquely discernible as known landmarks, commonly known as the *correspondence problem.*

Here we are interested in the use of an array of active tactile whisker sensors as the primary sense for navigation which we have demonstrated in prior works using a grid-based particle filter approach [7] and the RatSLAM algorithm [5]. The grid-based mapping approach was limited by the size and resolution of map that could be maintained and updated by the filter using constrained computing resources. The RatSLAM algorithm generated a topological map representing the association of local view and odometry projected as nodes and edges into a 2D plane called the *experience map.* This representation of space requires considerably lower computational cost to update and localize, however, the potential for incorrect re-localizations was high due to ambiguity in local views compounded by the limited sensory information available from the whisker-array.

Whisker sensors are particularly susceptible to the correspondence problem as they sweep across a uniformly textured floor that would be typical in indoor environments, which is why we chose to extend the RatSLAM algorithm to include explicit landmarks within the experience map. This was achieved through the introduction of a mode switch in behavior triggered by the robot's interaction with the environment. As the robot moves across an open space the whiskers sweep the floor updating the state estimate of robot pose and map using the conventional RatSLAM experience map, this behavior will be referred to as *terrain exploration mode.* When the robot encounters an object the algorithm switches into *object exploration mode* which triggers the initialization of a new 6D map referred to as an *object exploration map.*

This *object exploration map* is updated using the 6D Whisker-RatSLAM algorithm (described in the next section) by populating the map with experience nodes similar to a conventional RatSLAM experience map. However, here the experience nodes associate the *feature cells* and *pose-grid cells* that were active at a specific 6D pose of the the whisker array. For this reason we refer to them as *complex experience nodes* to distinguish them from the *simple experience nodes* that populate the *terrain exploration map* (see Fig. 1 for detail).

As the whisker array is freely moved around the object, the *object exploration map* is formed, indeed the map can also be used as a topological 6D map of the object for route planning across its surface. When sufficiently mapped, an *object node* is created and inserted into the *terrain exploration map* at the point at which the object was encountered, i.e., it will replace the previous *simple experience node*. The two types of node differ only in the type of features they reference: an *object node* refers to an *object exploration map* that describes an object at that location; *simple experience nodes* reference the 3D *pose-cell* and *feature cells* that were active during terrain exploration. Therefore, when the robot returns to this region of the environment it can expect to encounter the richly represented tactile landmark from which to robustly update its belief in location. Further, the *object exploration maps* can also be used as a mechanism for tactile object identification by comparing the form of maps against each other as the robot explores an unknown object with its whiskers.

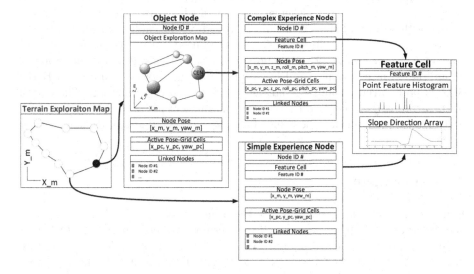

**Fig. 1.** Proposed navigational framework that combines RatSLAM for planar navigation and Whisker-RatSLAM for object recognition to result in a more robust landmark based SLAM algorithm for whisker-tactile sensing. The following work focuses on Whisker-RatSLAM and how an object may be identified during future encounters by first characterizing it's surface's features by generating an *object map*. Characterization involves the mapping of unique geometrical features within a *feature cell* to each region on an objects surface. The *feature cell* includes two vectors: *Point feature histogram* and *slope distribution array*, which describe the contact location and surface slope respectively at a particular whisker-array pose.

## 3   6D Object Exploration Map

The *object map* consists of a collection of *complex experience nodes* that are connected to one another in accordance to their 6-dimensional spatial pose. Each *complex experience node* encapsulates the characteristics of a region of space, including contact features that characterize an object's surface, as well as the set of 6D pose-grid cells that were active at that time. The contact features are stored within a structure referred to as a *feature cell*, which is analogous to a *view cell* in RatSLAM. In our current work we record two geometric features to describe the surface region, a *point feature histogram* and a *slope distribution array*.

The *point feature histogram* (PFH) is generated in accordance to the method described in [8] to produce a statistical signature that characterizes the shape of the region generated from the whisker contact points. The statistics depend upon the geometrical relationship of each contact point relative to one other and is therefore independent of the pose from which the contact points were obtained. The feature provides a convenient metric for comparison as it avoids any need for aligning contact points and being pose and sampling density invariant.

The *slope distribution array* (SDA) describes the slopes of the contacted surface detected at each whisker across the whisker array. The slope or orientation of the object surface is calculated based on the ratios of gradients of the two orthogonal axes of whisker deflection measured during the initial period of contact as described in [9]. SDA provides an additional geometrical property about the surface region that PFH cannot provide, however, unlike PFH the SDA is pose variant making it advantageous for pose localization. The length of the array is equivalent to the number of whiskers in the whisker-array, with each element representing the value of the slope detected at a particular whisker during contact.

## 4   Experiments

Experiments were designed to assess the accuracy of our algorithm to localize across a variety of object shapes and to discriminate between objects. Our data included a set taken using a physical whisker array as it explored the surface of a box shaped object (see panel A of Fig. 2). Five simulated data sets were also generated using ROS/Gazebo for trajectory and odometry, and Matlab for calculating the positions of the whiskers' points of contact as well as their 2D deflection vectors. Our simulation data sets incorporated additive noise in the odometry, contact position and deflection vectors, which were all derived from the statistics of the original physical data set. An overall description of the experimental set up is described further in Fig. 2. To validate the simulation, the virtual box object was explored using the same trajectory as used for exploring the physical box object. All the other simulated objects were explored using the same trajectory but different from that used to explore the box (see Fig. 3 for details).

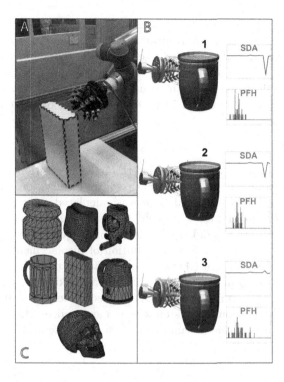

**Fig. 2.** Experimental configuration for physical and simulated data set acquisition. **A**: The physical data set was acquired using a UR-5 arm to move an array of active tactile whiskers around the contours of a plywood box. The whisker-array consists of 18 whisker modules that are able to sense their whisk angle and 2D deflection forces at their base; a detailed description of the sensor array may be found in [10]. The known location of the object was calibrated against the workspace of the UR-5 to serve as a measure of ground truth to whisker contact locations. **B**: The odometry data was generated using ROS/Gazebo which simulated the motion of the UR-5 arm, while the simulated whisker deflection data were calculated using Matlab. The three images were taken from Gazebo at the end of consecutive whisks as the array moved in a downwards direction across the surface of the Kettle. The plots to the right of each image illustrate the two contact features that were used to identify a region. The top is the *slope distribution array* (SDA), a vector whose elements encode the slope of the surface that each whisker has made contact with, while the bottom is the *point feature histogram* (PFH) of the points of contacts detected during the whisk by the whole array. **C**: Several simulated object models were used to test the robustness of the algorithm and to evaluate its ability to discriminate between objects. The average bounding box for all the objects is $20 \times 20 \times 35$ cm. From left to right the objects are named *Top*: Barrel, Blob, Plane. *Middle*: Mug, Box and Kettle. *Bottom*: Skull.

The experimental parameters that were adjusted between runs were: the features used to characterize a surface region (PFH only, SDA only, and both PFH & SDA combined); the introduction of a feature update mechanism that averages matching feature vectors; the approach taken to determine point of whisker-contact (tip-assumption against *support vector regression* (SVR)). The SVR approach was trained to map whisker deflection characteristics and whisker length to a more precise radial distance estimate with an approximate accuracy of 15% relative to the whisker length. Therefore, a total of 12 runs were processed for each object with each run consisting of a unique set of parameters.

## 4.1  Localization

The localization accuracy was determined through the positional and rotational errors measured between the ground truth and re-localization estimates of the whisker-array pose. The positional error was calculated using a Euclidean distance while the rotational error was calculated as the minimum angle required to align the estimated and ground truth orientation in quaternion space following the method described in [11]. The distribution of displacement errors between ground truth pose and integrated raw odometry during the complete exploration of an object are shown in Fig. 3b. We consider a working SLAM algorithm to reduce errors in pose estimates to less than or equal to the minimum step size taken between observations; the step size is measured as the change in pose from one surface region that a sample is taken to the next. The step size used

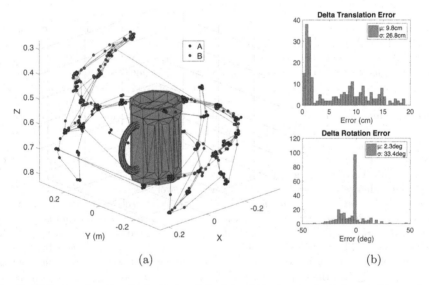

(a)                                        (b)

**Fig. 3.** Object exploration trajectories. **(a)** plots of the two trajectories used to explore the various objects; *Trajectory A,* used for building the Object Maps, and *trajectory B,* a novel trajectory used to gather validation data sets to test the robustness of the system. **(b)** Distribution of displacement errors between those obtained from the ground truth and integrated odometry measurements captured during a complete cycle of *trajectory A*

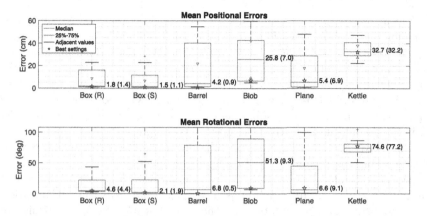

**Fig. 4.** Box plot illustrating the distribution of localization errors (positional and rotational) for each object. Box(R) refers to the physical box data set, while Box(S) the simulation data set. The values within the brackets pertain to star shaped markers, which are the results of the runs using the best set of parameters: SVR based radial distance estimation, Unmerged contact features and Both (PFH and SDA combined) features for region matching. With regards to the notation of the box plot: the blue boxes mark the edges at which 25% or 75% of the data lies below while the adjacent values are used for marking the edges of where the majority of the data distribution lies. The exact formulation for calculating the position of these markers may be found in [12].

for objects other than the box were approximately 11 cm and 12°, while for the Box object the values were approximately 3 cm and 3°.

The aggregated results for all objects used in our experiments are shown in Fig. 4. The lowest errors in re-localization estimates were recorded when using SVR based radial distance estimation, both the PFH and SDA features combined for region matching, and not including the proposed feature merging method. With the exception of the Kettle object, all other objects returned localization errors that were lower than their associated step size. Analysis of the Kettle localization results revealed that the large errors were due to confusion brought on by symmetry. These erroneous localization estimates were eventually corrected following subsequent observations, highlighting a familiar problem for SLAM algorithms failing to localize in symmetrical environments.

Similarly symmetrical objects such as the Barrel and Mug, did not suffer so markedly due to their position in space relative to their associated exploration trajectories. The trajectory around the kettle followed a loosely spheroid outline that shared the same geometric center as the kettle. This resulted in very similar observations from the whisker sensors at a range of array poses.

## 4.2 Object Identification

Our second set of experiments focused on the use of Whisker-RatSLAM for object identification. The object map created by Whisker-RatSLAM is a topological map relating the features of each recorded surface region relative to one another in 6D space. The *object map* thus characterizes an object by its shape and can be used for identifying future encounters with the same object and for determining novel objects. The concept is analogous to treating each object as a room within a building, whereby the agent, in this case the whiskered robot, is switched on and left to explore a particular room with no prior knowledge of its path to that room. A re-localization to a previously explored room, or object in our case, would indicate that the agent has recognized which room it is currently in. Frequent re-localizations on subsequent samples by its whiskers would indicate an increased confidence of room/object identity.

Using this analogy we appended the *experiences* from each *object map* to construct an experience history that assumes sequential visits to multiple objects with no topological connection between them (as shown in Fig. 5). The whiskered robot is then presented with an unknown object and is set to explore its surface using either the same trajectory used for generating the *object maps*, *trajectory A*, or the novel trajectory, *trajectory B*, for testing (see Fig. 3a for details). Figure 5 details a single case in which a previously mapped object (Plane) is explored using *trajectory A* and how the rate of re-localization events (green/red dots) serves as a measure of confidence in classifying object identity.

The complete set of results from all cases are are shown in Fig. 6. For the Skull object, which has not been mapped and therefore does not feature in the experience history, the system exhibits very low confidence levels across all known object identities. It is also clear that when using *trajectory B* the confidence in object identity is much lower than using *trajectory A*. This is understandable since features would inevitably vary due to changes observed features and thus reduce the probability of experiencing consistent observations that lead to re-localizations. The level of activity is however correlated to the correct object identity. It can be seen that in some cases different *object maps* receive somewhat equal activity levels indicating ambiguity in object identity.

## 5    Discussion and Future Work

Using both physical and simulation based experiments we have shown that our RatSLAM inspired Whisker-RatSLAM algorithm is able to successfully localize an array of mobile tactile whiskers in 6D space. Further, we have shown that using the object maps that are generated during object exploration we are able to confidently classify object identity and determine novel objects.

The results illustrate that the algorithm can accommodate novel exploration trajectories for object identification but with significantly reduced confidence. Since the combination of PFH & SDA results in a combined feature-set that would no longer be pose-invariant, the observed features are a given surface region would dependent on the executed trajectory, particularly if the trajectory was generated in an open loop manner like in our experiments. The problem cannot be simply addressed by forgoing the combined feature-set for an only PFH approach since that drastically reduces the localization accuracy as indicated

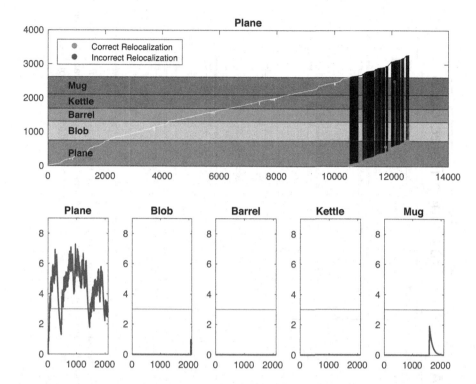

**Fig. 5.** The response of Whisker-RatSLAM as the whisker-array is presented with the previously explored toy Plane object for the purpose of object identification. The **top** panel displays the history of the *experiences* generated through the exploration of all objects (white line). Each individual *experience* has an index (y-axis) and a sample number (x-axis) with the horizontal coloured regions indicating that these *experiences* were generated whilst exploring the object named to the left. The transition between objects has been removed, i.e., the *experiences* representing each object have been sequentially appended in no particular order. The black line of *experiences* outside of the coloured region represent new sample points as the whisker array explores an unknown object. The re-localisations that occur (indicated by green and red dots) indicate that a sample is very close to an existing *experience* which increases the belief in identity of the unknown object. The green markers indicate a re-localization to the correct object identity while the red markers indicate a re-localization to an incorrect object identity. The **lower** panel illustrates the time course of belief in each objects identity during the exploratory phase of the experiment, i.e., sample points >10500 in the experience history plot. The dynamics of belief are governed by a simple leaky integrator which is injected with an impulse when a re-localisation occurs and has a fixed decay constant. A user defined confidence threshold (horizontal red line) marks the desired level in belief required to confidently identify an object. The results in this image belong to the case where the exploration trajectories for the map generation and object identification portions are the same (*trajectory A*). (Color figure online)

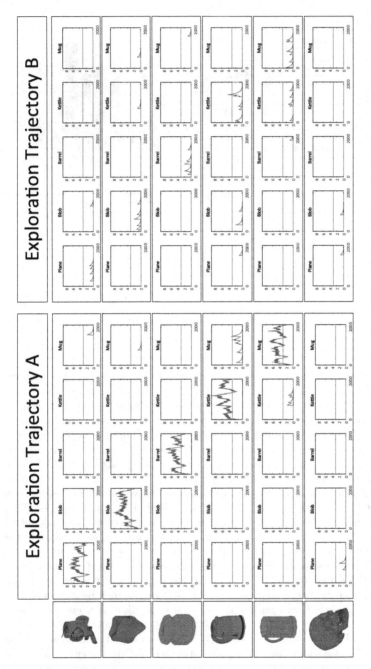

**Fig. 6.** Time course of belief in object identity as the robot explores an unknown object (shown in the images to the left) following the original trajectory used for *object map* generation (A) or the novel trajectory (B). The five columns under each exploration trajectory represent the belief for each previously mapped object (Plane, Blob, Barrel, Kettle and Mug). The Skull object has not been mapped which reflects in the low level in belief in other object identities.

by our results. PFH as described earlier is pose-invariant where as the task of localization would benefit from features that are pose-variant.

To address this issue we plan to investigate an active surface exploration approach, which is described in the work of Mitchinson et al. [13]. The authors present a unified attention model for rat whisking that exhibits an emergent surface following behavior. The implementation of such a model in our system could potentially reduce the variations in trajectories generated during object exploration and thus serve to improve the speed in which we identify objects. Further more the pose of the whisker-array relative to a surface can be limited to ensure a more consistent observation of features when traversing across an objects surface. Ambiguity in object identity could be addressed by exploiting the topological properties of the object maps to determine which region from a set of ambiguous maps are least similar and therefore drive the whisker-array towards it. In the situation where a satisfactory level of confidence still can not be reached then the algorithm can consider the object to be novel and, therefore, generate a new *object map*.

We also plan to integrate the *object maps* into the terrain exploration model as described in Figure 1 such that the platform can navigate efficiently through a sparsely populated landscape defined by richly represented tactile landmarks. Finally, we plan to translate the 6D pose cell network component of the system into an event driven implementation suitable for neuromorphic acceleration.

**Acknowledgement.** This work was partially supported by the EPSRC Center for Doctoral Training in Future Autonomous and Robotic Systems (FARSCOPE) at the Bristol Robotics Laboratory and has received funding from the European Unions Horizon 2020 Research and Innovation Program under Grant Agreement No. 720270 (HBP SGA1).

# References

1. Lee, S., Lee, S., Lee, J., Moon, D., Kim, E., Seo, J.: Robust recognition and pose estimation of 3d objects based on evidence fusion in a sequence of images. In: 2007 IEEE International Conference on Robotics and Automation, pp. 3773–3779. IEEE (2007)
2. Pillai, S., Leonard, J.: Monocular slam supported object recognition. arXiv preprint arXiv:1506.01732 (2015)
3. Strub, C.: A neurodynamic model for haptic spatiotemporal integration, doctoralthesis. Ruhr-Universität Bochum, Universitätsbibliothek (2017)
4. Milford, M., Wyeth, G.: Mapping a suburb with a single camera using a biologically inspired slam system. IEEE Trans. Robot. **24**(5), 1038–1053 (2008)
5. Salman, M., Pearson, M.: Advancing whisker based navigation through the implementation of bio-inspired whisking strategies. In: IEEE International Conference on Robotics and Biomimetics (ROBIO 2016). Institute of Electrical and Electronics Engineers (IEEE) (2016)
6. Furber, S.B., Galluppi, F., Temple, S., Plana, L.A.: The spinnaker project. Proc. IEEE **102**(5), 652–665 (2014)

7. Pearson, M.J., Fox, C., Sullivan, J.C., Prescott, T.J., Pipe, T., Mitchinson, B.: Simultaneous localisation and mapping on a multi-degree of freedom biomimetic whiskered robot. In: 2013 IEEE International Conference on Robotics and Automation (ICRA), pp. 586–592. IEEE (2013)

8. Rusu, R., Marton, Z., Blodow, N., Beetz, M.: Learning informative point classes for the acquisition of object model maps, pp. 643–650, December 2008

9. Kim, D., Möller, R.: Biomimetic whiskers for shape recognition. Robot. Auton. Syst. **55**(3), 229–243 (2007). http://www.sciencedirect.com/science/article/pii/S0921889006001400

10. Sullivan, J.C., Mitchinson, B., Pearson, M.J., Evans, M., Lepora, N.F., Fox, C.W., Melhuish, C., Prescott, T.J.: Tactile discrimination using active whisker sensors. IEEE Sens. J. **12**(2), 350–362 (2012)

11. Hodaň, T., Matas, J., Obdržálek, Š.: On evaluation of 6D object pose estimation. In: Hua, G., Jégou, H. (eds.) ECCV 2016. LNCS, vol. 9915, pp. 606–619. Springer, Cham (2016). https://doi.org/10.1007/978-3-319-49409-8_52

12. Velleman, P.F., Hoaglin, D.C.: Applications, Basics, and Computing of Exploratory Data Analysis. Duxbury Press, Boston (1981)

13. Mitchinson, B., Prescott, T.J.: Whisker movements reveal spatial attention: Unified computational model of active sensing control in the rat. PLoS Comput. Biol. **9**(9), 1003236 (2013)

# Insect Behavioral Evidence of Spatial Memories During Environmental Reconfiguration

Diogo Santos-Pata[1,2(✉)], Alex Escuredo[1,2], Zenon Mathews[2],
and Paul F. M. J. Verschure[1,2,3]

[1] SPECS, Institute for Bioengineering of Catalonia, 08028 Barcelona, Spain
dpata@ibecbarcelona.eu
[2] SPECS, Univesitat Pompeu Fabra, 08018 Barcelona, Spain
[3] Institució Catalana de Recerca i Estudis Avanats (ICREA),
08010 Barcelona, Spain

**Abstract.** Insects are great explorers, able to navigate through long-distance trajectories and successfully find their way back. Their navigational routes cross dynamic environments suggesting adaptation to novel configurations. Arthropods and vertebrates share neural organizational principles and it has been shown that rodents modulate their neural spatial representation accordingly with environmental changes. However, it is unclear whether insects reflexively adapt to environmental changes or retain memory traces of previously explored situations. We sought to disambiguate between insect behavior in environmental novel situations and reconfiguration conditions. An immersive mixed-reality multi-sensory setup was built to replicate multi-sensory cues. We have designed an experimental setup where female crickets Gryllus Bimaculatus were trained to move towards paired auditory and visual cues during primarily phonotactic driven behavior. We hypothesized that insects were capable of identifying sensory modifications in known environments. Our results show that, regardless of the animal's history, novel situation conditions did not compromise the animals performance and navigational directionality towards a new target location. However, in trials where visual and auditory stimuli were spatially decoupled, the animals heading variability towards a previously known position significantly increased. Our findings showed that crickets can behaviorally manifest environmental reconfiguration, suggesting the encoding for spatial representation.

**Keywords:** Insect · Navigation · Memory · Spatial representation

## 1 Introduction

Insects robustly navigate within very dynamic environments with limited resources. At the sensorimotor level, insects need to integrate multi-modal stimuli and continuously adapt their behavioral strategies to survive. Their relatively

V. Vouloutsi et al. (Eds.): Living Machines 2018, LNAI 10928, pp. 415–427, 2018.
https://doi.org/10.1007/978-3-319-95972-6_45

simple nervous system has been subject of research aimed at revealing the mechanisms behind insect navigation, and often their distributed nervous system is described as a stack of simple reflexive loops.

Goal-oriented behavior has been extensively observed in insects such as chemotaxis performed by the silkmoth [1,2] or phonotaxis by female crickets [3]. Earlier research suggests that parallel direct sensory-motor loops are supplemented by specific brain areas that serve to integrate functions related to context, learning and smooth coordination of action [4]. However, if insects would merely perform reactive behaviors, they could not be able to recall hidden target positions [4,5], or to form sensory-action couplets associations [5,6]. Kraft and colleagues [2011] have shown that flying bees are capable of using the polarized-light information to direct their routes towards a food location. Also, experimental work has been conducted to explore the capabilities of flying insects to navigate within distinct maze configurations. In [7], the authors have found that the performance of bees navigating within a maze depends on the regularity of the maze, suggesting a process of spatial abstraction rather than memorizing entire navigational sequences. Such form of context-dependent learning leads to the question of whether insect behavior, as for mammalian behavior, could be described through the main components of operant conditioning paradigms [8].

Operant conditioning implies the ability to build relational maps of contexts, actions and expected outcomes to boost decision-making processes. This form of learning can be observed in insect behavior such as honey-bees representing food locations (waggle dance) [9] or communication suppressing through stop signals by partners who have experienced conspecific attacks at a food source [10]. Furthermore, it has been shown that insects are capable of performing logical operations such as numerical counting [11], pattern recognition [12] or context-dependent learning [13] and most of their behaviors imply successful integration of different sensory modalities signals. These results advocate that insects might be capable of developing higher-level representations of not only their surroundings but also other agents sharing their territories.

In the domain of spatial representation, insects make use of allocentric environmental information to perform homing tasks, and it has been suggested that visual landmarks are used to form cricket place memories [4]. In this context, the emphasis is often placed on the role of the mushroom bodies in the integration of sensory and motor signals. Indeed, neural responses in the mushroom body appear to be related to specific directions of the animal's orientation, which constitutes a type of spatial representation of their body in space [14].

Despite is growing evidence for insect environmental adaptation and place-memory formation during navigational tasks, it remains unclear whether insects form memories of context-specific sensory statistics or merely perform stimulus-stimulus associations. On the one hand, behavioral adaptation could be a reflex derived from environmental reconfiguration. On the other hand, behavioral modulation could be explained by higher level functions such as perceiving contextual modifications.

We sought to find out the behavioral specifics of insects exposed to either environmental novel situations or environmental reconfiguration. Novel situations are characterized by changes in the animals spatial target location while environmental reconfiguration maintains the animals goal location but with induced sensory modifications. We hypothesized that insects can form representations of environmental sensory statistics and display behavioral signatures of environmental sensory reconfiguration. Crickets have a specialized nervous system and behavior repertoire dedicated to sound communication [15], making them ideal for experimental subjects to test modulation of goal-oriented behavior. Male crickets periodically move their wings, rubbing a flexible membrane at the tip of one wing called *plectrum* against a set of *files* placed under the opposite wing [16], generating an attractive species-specific mating sound. Females, on the other hand, possess tympanal membranes in their forelegs allowing them to orient towards the bursting sound of a potential mate, a type of behavior called phonotaxis behavior in which acoustic information is the main component of goal-directed navigation.

To access memory traces of reconfiguration, we tested female crickets during stimulus-stimulus associations tasks, and we have quantified their stereotypical adaptive behavior after stimulus-stimulus dissociation while performing goal-oriented navigation.

## 2   Methods

### 2.1   Experimental Set-Up to Study Insect Navigational Behavior

Besides experimental research to study insect behavior within physical arenas [17–19], many different paradigms have been proposed to analyze animal behavior. On the one hand, compensatory locomotion apparatus have been extensively used to study insect navigation since the 1970's [19–21]. Also, open-loop systems were proposed to analyze cricket antennae movements during visually guided behavior [22,23]. Similar approaches have also been generalized to study neural mechanisms involved in rodents spatial representation [24]. Insect hybrid systems have been deployed to investigate insect behavior in a range of navigational tasks such as phonotaxis behavior [25,26]. Locomotion compensatory apparatus appears to be a plausible tool for investigating animal navigation within controlled environments. In combination with mixed-reality environments, these technologies increase the amount, complexity and ecological validity of possible stimuli to be used during experiments. To study animal behavioral correlates of spatial memories in novel situations and reconfiguration conditions, we have built a virtual reality immersible system (Fig. 1B). The apparatus consists of a polystyrene ball with a diameter of 8 cm floating on an air cushion allowing a tethered insect to move on top of it. The insect is tethered to a rigid beam in such a way that it remains placed on the floating sphere with fixed position and orientation, but perceiving coherent visuomotor responses from the virtual environment. Two two-dimensional optical sensors, located on the horizontal plane and perpendicular to each other, were used to track the sphere's yaw, pitch, and roll transformations triggered by the insects gait. Further, captured animal movements were mapped to navigational displacements within the virtual environment. Three computer screens surrounded the sphere providing 270° visual stimuli to the animals. Computer screens were Samsung SyncMaster 943NW (LCD), $1440 \times 900$ pixels in resolution, 17.3 in. width and 14.5 in. height, with a refresh rate of 75 Hz and 300 cd/m2 of image brightness. A virtual environment was developed using the 3D Object-Oriented Graphics Rendering Engine (OGRE), where landmarks, ambient light or other graphical properties were programmatically manipulated. A sound application (PureData) was integrated into the system to generate insect-specific mating-sounds. Two micro-speakers were placed at a distance of 35 cm from the animal and at $\pm 45°$ azimuth to the front-screen display, providing stereo sound stimuli to the animal tympanal membrane [27]. Visual and auditory sensory modalities together with motor actions were synchronized within the virtual reality environment.

## 2.2 Experimental Design

For the experiments, we acquired female crickets *Gryllus Bimaculatus* with undetermined age bought in colony-boxes from a local store. Animals were fed daily with fruit-based diet, maintained at room temperature and an effort was made to keep the light/dark regime fixed at 12:12-h LD cycle. Animals were food deprived and kept in separated transparent Perspex boxes ($20 \times 35 \times 20$ cm) 24 h before the experiment. The animals were trained with sound and visual stimuli spatially paired. Each trial consisted of navigating from a starting position at the south-center location to the north-west location of the virtual environment (9 trials per animal, Fig. 1A top) and was deemed completed when animals reached at least 80% of the south-north axis length (1.5 * 0.8 m). To induce novel situation or reconfiguration, at the tenth trial one of the stimuli was moved to an unusual position (north-east location of the virtual arena). Because sound is the primary driver of action during phonotactic behavior [3], placing the sound source at a different position (north-east), which implies changing of the goal-location, was considered as the novel situation condition (Fig. 1A, bottom-left). On the other hand, because the visual cue was the stimulus associated to sound but did not affect the target location, moving the visual landmark to a different position (north-east) was considered as environmental reconfiguration (Fig. 1A, bottom-right). With the current setup, we have trained the animals (9 trials each) to move from the starting position towards the north-west location where sound and visual cues were paired (Fig. 1A). At the tenth trial, we have replaced either the sound or the visual cue at the north-east corner of the virtual arena. Animals (n = 10) experiencing a displacement of the sound-source to a new location during the testing trial belonged to the novel situation group, while animals (n = 10) experiencing a displacement of the visual cue to a new position at the testing trial were considered as belonging to the environmental reconfiguration group. In between trials, animals were allowed to rest for approximately 30 s and rewarded with fruit-sucrose, independently of their navigational performance.

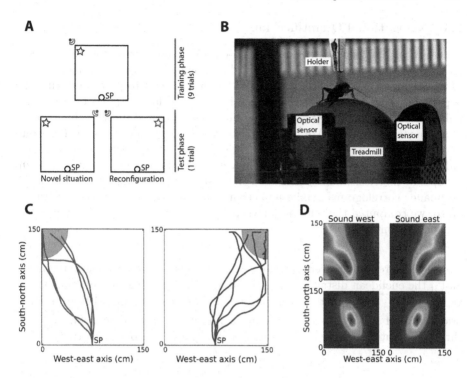

Fig. 1. **Experimental protocol and setup. A** Illustration of the experimental protocol. Trajectories began at starting position (SP) until animals reached the target location (sound). Training trials (top) consisted of paired locations of visual and auditory stimuli. At the testing trial (bottom), either the auditory (novel situation) or the visual stimuli (environmental reconfiguration) was moved to a different position contra-lateral to its testing position. **B** Snapshot of the treadmill setup surrounded by the computer displays. A female cricket runs on a floating sphere's treadmill sustained by a holder. Two optical sensors captured sphere rotations and translated into the virtual reality engine, providing consistent sensory-motor feedback. **C** Phonotaxis behavior with a sound source at the north-west and north-east locations of the virtual environment. **D** Group rate-maps after Gaussian kernel interpolation with 10 pixels standard deviation (top) and occupancy autocorrelograms (bottom) for sound at the north-west and north-east conditions.

In our setup, to motivate female crickets to navigate towards a species-specific mating sound, during each trial, a 4.8 kHz sound tone at a syllable rate of 30 Hz was generated in real-time to mimic male cricket species-specific calling song [16]. The Euclidean distance determined the sound amplitude of each loudspeaker and heading orientation between the animal location and the sound-source location within the virtual environment arena. After the experiment, the animals were released in the open field surrounding the university campus.

## 2.3   Navigational Quantification

Measures of navigational performance focused on both trajectory directionality and angular variability. Trajectory directionality provides a quantification of the expressed goal-directed behavior that insects had to perform during the experiments and was accessed by extracting the angular components of individual trajectory segments. Angular variability was computed through the variance of segments orientation. We have also extracted occupancy measures for group trajectories, which provides a quantification of direction coherence among individual belonging to the same group (Fig. 2C). To quantify for the overall group occupancy metrics, we have extracted the first spatial contour above 10% of the occupancy correlograms maximum activity and calculated their eccentricity. To do so, we computed the semi-major vector between pairs of points found in the occupancy contour as:

$$\overrightarrow{V_{ij_{major}}} = \max ||p_i - p_j|| \tag{1}$$

where $ij$ represent every pair of points along the autocorrelogram contour and $||$ the euclidean distance between $i$ and $j$. After finding the contour longest vector $\overrightarrow{V_{ij_{major}}}$, we applied a projection from its center point with an angular orientation of $\angle \overrightarrow{V_{ij_{major}}} + \frac{\pi}{2}$ obtaining a projection $\overrightarrow{f}$ used to define $\overrightarrow{V_{ij_{minor}}}$ through its intersection with the ratemap occupancy contour, such that:

$$\overrightarrow{V_{ij_{minor}}} = \cap \frac{\overrightarrow{V_{ij_{major}}}}{2} \overrightarrow{f} \tag{2}$$

The occupancy autocorrelogram eccentricity (OAE) which provides a measure of movement directionality was given by:

$$OAE = \frac{||\overrightarrow{V_{ij_{minor}}}||}{||\overrightarrow{V_{ij_{major}}}||} \tag{3}$$

allowing the extraction of the overall group directionality during phonotaxis navigation.

## 3   Results

Before the experiments and to validate induced visual stimuli we quantified the antennae reaction response of 10 female crickets to visual cues traversing within the virtual environment. During testing, animals remained steady on top of the spherical treadmill; however, their automatic motor responses were not translated into motor responses within the virtual environment. Visual cues were presented within ±120 angular degrees of the animal head-orientation and randomly interleaved between the three computer screens surrounding the animal. Antennae responses to visual cues were visually assessed and marked as valid when at least one antennae coherently followed the trajectory of the visual cue. Overall, visual cues appearing in the central computer screen triggered higher responses (95%±4%, mean±std) than lateral computer screens (79%±9%, mean±std). Nonetheless, it suggests that the crickets were able to perceive visual cues within the virtual environment.

To validate the effectiveness of the sound stimulation on guiding the animals' behavior, we conducted a between-groups analysis of their navigational trajectories final locations. Paths of both groups (n = 5 per group) started at the south-center position (SP, Fig. 1A) and, as for the main experiment, were considered as valid when animals reached at least 80% of the south-north axis length. For the first group, the sound-source was placed at the north-west location of the virtual environment, while for the second group the sound-source was placed at the north-east location. Results revealed a significant difference in position along the horizontal axis between the two groups (Wilcoxon rank-sum test: $p = 0.02$), which suggests that the synthesis and mapping of the auditory stimuli were sufficient to modulate animal goal-directed behavior (Fig. 1C, D). Coherently, overall group navigational rate maps and occupancy autocorrelograms suggested effectiveness in modulating the animals goal-location and trajectory directions (Fig. 1D). Given the induced behavioral modulation through the sound stimuli, we next tested cricket navigational behavior in both novel situation and reconfiguration conditions.

To quantify navigational directionality, we have extracted the overall occupancy maps from group trajectories belonging to each condition (Fig. 2C). Visual inspection of occupancy rate maps suggested that animals successfully navigated towards the sound source location. However, despite the fast adaptation to a novel target location during the novel situation condition, the navigational occupancy for environmental reconfiguration condition revealed a higher spreading. Indeed, rate maps autocorrelograms showed differences in their occupancy resolution between novel situation and reconfiguration conditions (Fig. 2C).

Quantification of navigational directionality revealed a lower OAE score for sound-only navigation (north-west $OAE = 0.51$; north-east $OAE = 0.53$) and novel situation group ($OAE = 0.53$) when compared with the environmental reconfiguration group ($OAE = 0.83$) (Fig. 2C). Higher occupancy autocorrelogram eccentricity depicted lower navigation directionality for the reconfiguration group, suggesting a loss in the ratio of directed movements towards the goal-location.

In addition to navigational occupancy and eccentricities measures, we analyzed changes in navigational directionality performed across groups. Because within the presented setup trials could be accomplished through vector-based navigational strategies, we extracted trajectory segments from the last training and testing trials for both groups. Segments extraction was performed through a sliding window with a bin size of 10 data points in the trajectory array and by computing the vector between the first and last position within each bin. Segments with magnitude zero, when animals were quiet, were removed from the analysis. Examples of the head orientation of two animals belonging to different groups can be appreciated in Fig. 2A. For novel situation conditions, the animals heading movements have shifted to the contra-lateral angular quadrant during

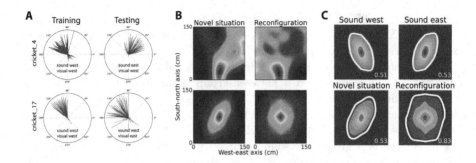

**Fig. 2. Experimental protocol and setup. A** During training (left) both groups exhibited directed movements towards the north-west location of the virtual environment. At testing trials (right), the novel situation group (top-right) shifted their directionality towards the north-east location. **B** Group rate-maps after Gaussian kernel interpolation with 10 pixels standard deviation (top) and occupancy maps (bottom) at novel situation and environmental reconfiguration conditions. **C** Occupancy maps eccentricity measurement. Environmental reconfiguration condition scored lower for directional specific navigation.

the testing trial (e.g., cricket 4), while for environmental reconfiguration the animals directing movements were maintained at the testing trial (e.g., cricket 17), again revealing the effectiveness of the sound stimulation during phonotactic behavior.

To quantify changes in navigational directionality between the last training and testing trials in both groups, we have compared the head-orientation distribution along angular coordinates (Fig. 3A). Following the experimental design, the distribution of segments orientation was more prominent between 54 and 126°, which represents the angular interval to perform vector-based navigation towards a target position placed either at the north-west or north-east corners of the virtual arena. Differences in orientation distribution between last training and testing trials revealed higher changes for the novel situation group than for the reconfiguration group. That was justified by the fact that the sound-source at the testing trial was moved from north-west to the north-east location for novel situation but not for the reconfiguration group.

As expected, the group experiencing novel situation during the testing trial, where the sound-source was moved to a new location, exhibited more significant differences for segments distribution at 54 and 126°. Specifically, animals showed a preference for orientations towards 126° during training (Mann-Whitney U test $p < 0.01$), while during testing animals head directions aligned towards 54° (Mann-Whitney U test $p < 0.01$). On the other hand, movement heading orientation distribution showed no significant differences between training and testing for the environmental reconfiguration condition, where the sound-source but not the visual-stimulus remained at the same location.

We have observed that the occupancy autocorrelogram eccentricity was higher for reconfiguration than for novel situation conditions (Fig. 2C).

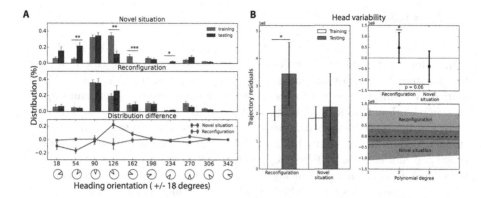

**Fig. 3. Experimental protocol and setup. A** Movement orientation distribution. Comparison between last training and testing trials revealed significant differences for the novel situation group (top panel), but not for the environmental reconfiguration group (middle panel). Each segment encodes the head orientation range of 36°. Angular distribution differences between last training and testing trial for both groups (bottom panel) **B** Trajectory variance. Variability of the trajectory obtained from the sum of squared residuals of the least squares linear fit rank (left and top-right panels). Comparison of residuals between last training and testing trials revealed to be significant for the environmental reconfiguration group (t-test $p = 0.051$). Trajectory residuals were independent of the fit polynomial degree (bottom-right panel), suggesting that variability was not an artifact of vector/non-vector-based navigation type.

Because head orientation differences *per se* are not sufficient to determine if there is lack of perceptual information regarding environmental reconfiguration, we have assessed the animals navigational variability from their trajectories.

To quantify group navigational variability, we performed a linear least-squares fit on the animals paths at both last training and testing trials. Within our setup, optimal performance could be achieved through vector-based trajectories. Thus, the linear fit residuals provided a measurement for trajectory variability (Fig. 3B). As anticipated by the occupancy autocorrelogram eccentricity measures, the trajectory variability at testing trials was significantly different for environmental reconfiguration but not for the novel situation condition (t-test $p = 0.051$), suggesting that movement intentionality was lower when the sensory configuration was altered (Fig. 3B). Normalization to baseline (subtraction of residuals at training trials with the ones at testing trials) revealed a partially significant difference between groups (Ranksum test $p = 0.06$, Fig. 3B top-right panel). Because differences in navigational variability could be an artifact of a linear-fit onto a non-vector-based navigational performance, we have quantified group differences up to 4 polynomial degrees which would reflect arc trajectories. However, group differences were independent of the polynomial degree, suggesting that navigational variability was independent on the type of path performed (Fig. 3 bottom-right).

## 4    Discussion

Insects display striking skills for spatial exploration and are capable of effortless adaptation to dynamic environments. Numerous studies have focused on insect place-memory formation revealing their ability to integrate environmental information. Wessnitzer and colleagues (2008) have shown how crickets can improve their navigational performance in an aversive dry version of the Morris-water maze [28] by considering visual cues to situate themselves in space. Moreover, in the same experimental setup, it was suggested that crickets were able to locate a remapped hidden spot by following previously learned spatial-sensory cues contingencies. Because insects quickly adapt to dynamic environments, one could argue that their reflexive capabilities would be sufficient for surviving in such territories. Another possibility would be that insects are capable of recognizing the environment's dynamics instead of considering each experience as occurring within a unique spatial context. Thus, there is no sufficient evidence of whether insect spatial adaptation is a mnemonic property or a consequence of environmental modifications.

It has been previously shown that rodents modulate the rate of hippocampal neural activity during environmental morphing [29], suggesting that mice constantly update their internal spatial representation [30, 31]. The neural structures of mammals and insects have been compared and suggested to share common organizational principles [32, 33]. Also, it has been suggested that the genetic mechanisms involved in pattern formation of the embryonic body plan and brain development are shared for both insects and mammals [34]. Thus, one could expect that the neural mechanisms underlying insect navigation and spatial representation would resemble the ones of rodents.

Here, we have made an effort to understand whether insects, like rodents, are able to contextualize themselves in space and integrate environmental modifications into their behavioral plans. Within our experimental design, we have focused on insect navigational adaptation during the novel situation and environmental reconfiguration scenarios during goal-oriented behavior. To do so, we have trained female crickets *Gryllus Bimaculatus* to perform phonotaxis behavior within a virtual environment and navigate towards a target location where a visual cue was spatially paired with the sound stimulus. After training trials crickets experiencing the novel situation condition rapidly adapted their navigational plans by reorienting their learned navigational movements towards a new target location. Contrarily, crickets experiencing the environmental reconfiguration condition have maintained their target-location (Fig. 3A). However, their movements orientation variability towards the target location significantly increased when compared to the variability of the novel situation group. Our results suggest that crickets were able to maintain an internal representation of their surroundings and behaviorally expressed environmental modifications through their movements orientation variability (Fig. 3B).

Internal representations of space are supported by multiple neural mechanisms in the rodent brain, such as place-cells, grid-cells and head-direction-cells [30, 31, 35, 36]. Similarly, head-direction-cells have been found in the insect mushroom bodies [37]. However, it is known that insects do not perform only vector-based navigation, raising the possibility that they might also use similar neural mechanisms for spatial representation as rodents do (see [38] for a review).

Insects and rodents perform a common panoply of behaviors, such as homing, foraging and hoarding. Indeed, honey bees perform magnificent hoarding tasks by navigating towards abundant pollen locations and bringing the nectar back to their hives [39,40]. Similarly, desert-hamsters exploit their navigational apparatus to store resources at their home location successfully. However, while the neural circuitry involved in mammalian navigation is relatively well understood and further supported by computational models implementing the neural components necessary for hoarding behavior [41], the computational processes involved in insect navigation is far-less understood. Therefore, how much of those mammalian neural components can be validated into a biologically plausible insect cognitive-architecture, remains an open question. Moreover, cognitive processes thought to be found only in higher order animals, might also have developed in simpler nervous systems animals, such as insects.

**Acknowledgements.** The research leading to these results has received funding from the European Research Council under the European Unions Seventh Framework Programme (FP7/2007-2013)/ERC grant agreement no. [341196] cDAC.

**Author Contributions Statement.** Z.M. and P.V. conceived the experiment, D.S.P. conducted the experiment and analyzed the results. D.S.P, Z.M., and A.E developed the setup. All authors were involved in the revision of the manuscript.

# References

1. Vickers, N.J.: Mechanisms of animal navigation in odor plumes. Biol. Bull. **198**(2), 203–212 (2000)
2. Mathews, Z., Lechón, M., Calvo, J.B., Dhir, A., Duff, A., Verschure, P.F., et al.: Insect-like mapless navigation based on head direction cells and contextual learning using chemo-visual sensors. In: IEEE/RSJ International Conference on Intelligent Robots and Systems, IROS 2009, pp. 2243–2250. IEEE (2009)
3. Thorson, J., Weber, T., Huber, F.: Auditory behavior of the cricket. J. Comp. Physiol. **146**(3), 361–378 (1982)
4. Mizunami, M., Weibrecht, J.M., Strausfeld, N.J.: Mushroom bodies of the cockroach: their participation in place memory. J. Comp. Neurol. **402**(4), 520–537 (1998)
5. Wessnitzer, J., Mangan, M., Webb, B.: Place memory in crickets. Proc. R. Soc. Lond. B Biol. Sci. **275**(1637), 915–921 (2008)
6. Srinivasan, M.V., Poteser, M., Kral, K.: Motion detection in insect orientation and navigation. Vis. Res. **39**(16), 2749–2766 (1999)
7. Zhang, S., Mizutani, A., Srinivasan, M.V.: Maze navigation by honeybees: learning path regularity. Learn. Mem. **7**(6), 363–374 (2000)
8. Skinner, B.F.: The Behavior of Organisms: An Experimental Analysis (1938)
9. Von Frisch, K.: The Dance Language and Orientation of Bees (1967)
10. Nieh, J.C.: A negative feedback signal that is triggered by peril curbs honey bee recruitment. Curr. Biol. **20**(4), 310–315 (2010)

11. Dacke, M., Srinivasan, M.V.: Evidence for counting in insects. Anim. Cogn. **11**(4), 683–689 (2008)
12. Dill, M., Wolf, R., Heisenberg, M.: Visual pattern recognition in drosophila involves retinotopic matching. Nature **365**(6448), 751 (1993)
13. Collett, T., Fauria, K., Dale, K., Baron, J.: Places and patternsa study of context learning in honeybees. J. Comp. Physiol. A **181**(4), 343–353 (1997)
14. Brembs, B., Wiener, J.: Context and occasion setting in drosophila visual learning. Learn. Mem. **13**(5), 618–628 (2006)
15. Horseman, G., Huber, F.: Sound localisation in crickets. J. Comp. Physiol. A **175**(4), 399–413 (1994)
16. Huber, F.: Central nervous control of sound production in crickets and some speculations on its evolution. Evolution **16**, 429–442 (1962)
17. Walker, T.J.: Specificity in the response of female tree crickets (orthoptera, gryllidae, oecanthinae) to calling songs of the males. Ann. Entomol. Soc. Am. **50**(6), 626–636 (1957)
18. Latimer, W., Lewis, D.: Song harmonic content as a parameter determining acoustic orientation behaviour in the cricketteleogryllus oceanicus (le guillou). J. Comp. Physiol. A **158**(4), 583–591 (1986)
19. Wendler, G., Dambach, M., Schmitz, B., Scharstein, H.: Analysis of the acoustic orientation behavior in crickets (gryllus campestris l.). Naturwissenschaften **67**(2), 99–101 (1980)
20. Kramer, E.: Orientation of the male silkmoth to the sex attractant bombykol. Olfaction Taste **5**, 329–335 (1975)
21. Weber, T., Thorson, J., Huber, F.: Auditory behavior of the cricket. J. Comp. Physiol. **141**(2), 215–232 (1981)
22. Honegger, H.-W.: A preliminary note on a new optomotor response in crickets: antennal tracking of moving targets. J. Comp. Physiol. **142**(3), 419–421 (1981)
23. Kammerer, R., Bauer, W., Honegger, H.: On-line analysis of rapid motion with a microcomputer. J. Neurosci. Methods **19**(2), 89–94 (1987)
24. Domnisoru, C., Kinkhabwala, A.A., Tank, D.W.: Membrane potential dynamics of grid cells. Nature **495**(7440), 199–204 (2013)
25. Emoto, S., Ando, N., Takahashi, H., Kanzaki, R.: Insect-controlled robotevaluation of adaptation ability. J. Robot. Mechatron. **19**(4), 436 (2007)
26. Shiramatsu, D., Ando, N., Takahashi, H., Kanzaki, R., Fujita, S., Sano, Y., Andoh, T.: Target selection mechanism for collision-free navigation of robots based on antennal tracking strategies of crickets. In: 2010 3rd IEEE RAS and EMBS International Conference on Biomedical Robotics and Biomechatronics (BioRob), pp. 259–264. IEEE (2010)
27. Kleindienst, H.-U., Wohlers, D.W., Larsen, O.N.: Tympanal membrane motion is necessary for hearing in crickets. J. Comp. Physiol. **151**(4), 397–400 (1983)
28. Morris, R.: Developments of a water-maze procedure for studying spatial learning in the rat. J. Neurosci. Methods **11**(1), 47–60 (1984)
29. Leutgeb, J.K., Leutgeb, S., Moser, M.-B., Moser, E.I.: Pattern separation in the dentate gyrus and ca3 of the hippocampus. Science **315**(5814), 961–966 (2007)
30. Tolman, E.C.: Cognitive maps in rats and men. Psychol. Rev. **55**(4), 189 (1948)
31. O'keefe, J., Nadel, L.: The Hippocampus as a Cognitive Map, vol. 3. Clarendon Press, Oxford (1978)
32. Strausfeld, F., Nicholas, J., Hirth, F.: Deep homology of arthropod central complex and vertebrate basal ganglia. Science **340**(6129), 157–161 (2013)

33. Tomer, R., Denes, A.S., Tessmar-Raible, K., Arendt, D.: Profiling by image registration reveals common origin of annelid mushroom bodies and vertebrate pallium. Cell **142**(5), 800–809 (2010)
34. Hirth, F., Reichert, H.: BioEssays
35. Hafting, T., Fyhn, M., Molden, S., Moser, M.-B., Moser, E.I.: Microstructure of a spatial map in the entorhinal cortex. Nature **436**(7052), 801–806 (2005)
36. Taube, J.S.: Head direction cells recorded in the anterior thalamic nuclei of freely moving rats. J. Neurosci. **15**(1), 70–86 (1995)
37. Homberg, U.: In search of the sky compass in the insect brain. Naturwissenschaften **91**(5), 199–208 (2004)
38. Mathews, Z., et al.: Generic neuromorphic principles of cognition and attention for ants, humans and real-world artefacts: a comparative computational approach (2011)
39. Rinderer, T.E., Baxter, J.R.: Honey bee hoarding behaviour: effects of previous stimulation by empty comb. Anim. Behav. **27**, 426–428 (1979)
40. Wang, Y., Kocher, S.D., Linksvayer, T.A., Grozinger, C.M., Page, R.E., Amdam, G.V.: Regulation of behaviorally associated gene networks in worker honey bee ovaries. J. Exp. Biol. **215**(1), 124–134 (2012)
41. Maffei, G., Santos-Pata, D., Marcos, E., Sánchez-Fibla, M., Verschure, P.F.: An embodied biologically constrained model of foraging: from classical and operant conditioning to adaptive real-world behavior in DAC-X. Neural Netw. **72**, 88–108 (2015)

# Object Localisation with a Highly Compliant Tactile Sensory Probe via Distributed Strain Sensors

Marco Schultz[1] and Volker Dürr[1,2(✉)]

[1] Department of Biological Cybernetics, Bielefeld University,
Bielefeld, Germany
volker.duerr@uni-bielefeld.de
[2] Cognitive Interaction Technology – Center of Excellence,
Bielefeld University, Bielefeld, Germany

**Abstract.** Insect antennae have been repeatedly proposed as paragons of active tactile sensors for biomimetic robots. A challenging aspect of using insect-like feelers for tactile localisation concerns the compliance of the long and slender structure of insect antennae. Other than in a rigid sensory probe, where the contact location in space may be estimated from the pointing direction and contact distance along the probe (polar coordinates), the strong compliance of insect antennae during contact events raises the question how insects can localise contact positions in space. Here we study the stick insect antenna to address this question. Our main objective was to test whether and how the bending properties of the insect antenna may allow reliable estimation of spatial contact locations through an array of bending sensors. During walking and climbing, the stick insect *Carausius morosus* executes cyclic antennal movements to explore the ambient space ahead. When the antenna touches an obstacle, it often bends strongly. Nevertheless, the insect can reliably reach for the contacted obstacle. Here, we systematically deflected insect antennae with an industrial robot to mimic an array of static contact locations. Then, we measured the resulting curvature of the flagellum, assuming that campanifom sensilla distributed along the flagellum could encode the corresponding bending profile. We found that we could train an artificial neural network to estimate the contact positions in 3D space with an accuracy of 0.5 mm or less from a given set of curvature data. This suggests that the bending characteristics of a tactile sensory probe could be tuned to aid spatial localisation by contact-site-dependent, compliant deformation.

**Keywords:** Insect antenna · Tactile localisation · Flagellum · Passive bending
Curvature · Artificial neural network

## 1 Introduction

Active tactile exploration of the near-range environment is a common aspect of autonomous behaviour in animals (e.g.: [1]). For example in insects, the information transfer among antennae (feelers) and legs and vice versa highlights the intimate

© Springer International Publishing AG, part of Springer Nature 2018
V. Vouloutsi et al. (Eds.): Living Machines 2018, LNAI 10928, pp. 428–438, 2018.
https://doi.org/10.1007/978-3-319-95972-6_46

relationship of active exploration and spatial coordination of the whole body [2]. To date, several biomimetic approaches have proposed insect-inspired tactile sensors for near-range exploration. Given a reasonably stiff antenna, the location of an obstacle relative to the head may be inferred from the pointing direction of the sensory probe and a suitable distance estimate. Whereas early approaches used actuated, un-sensorised beams to estimate contact distance from the torque [3] or vibration spectrum [4] measured at the base, more recent approaches have proposed different types of sensorised probes. For example, distance estimates could be extracted from the vibration spectrum measured at the tip [5, 6].

All of these systems have the disadvantage that the antenna has to be stiff, meaning it cannot sweep past object but has to move around it. Moreover, serious problems occur if the tip jams with an obstacle ahead. In insects and other arthropods, the antennae are compliant and flexible, allowing very strong deformation without breaking [7] and damped return to the resting posture after deflection [8, 9]. A technical system that exploits elastic deformation for spatial measurements in the horizontal plane has been proposed by Demir et al. [10]: It uses multiple actuated and sensorised segments to measure the lateral distance of a wall as it slides along. Other than that, insects can exploit the high compliance of their antennae during active exploration of the 3D environment. Here, we claim that if an insect was to infer the spatial location of a contact site during strong deformation of its antenna, it would likely have to take into account the curvature of the flagellum (the passive distal part of the antenna). Assuming that local bending of the flagellum may be encoded by a set of strain-sensitive mechanoreceptors (campaniform sensilla) that are embedded in the cuticle, we test the hypothesis that such a sensory array could encode antennal curvature for reliable estimation of tactile contact location in 3D.

To do so, we use experimental data of the stick insect *Carausius morosus*. Its antennae are very compliant, with a length:diameter ratio of 100:1 [8]. As all antennae of higher insects, it consists of three functional segments (Fig. 1, top). The two proximal segments, scapus and pedicellus, are actuated by muscles and can be moved actively by rotation about true joints. The junction between the flagellum and the pedicellus, and the flagellum do not contain actuated joints and can be bent passively only [11]. During walking and climbing, *C. morosus* constantly moves its antennae so as to search the near-range space ahead. As the flagellum is pulled past an object, it often bends strongly as shown in Fig. 1.

In situations similar to those shown in Fig. 1, stick insects can reach for objects that they previously touched with their antenna [12]. Given the presence of strain sensing campaniform sensilla on the flagellum of the stick insect antenna (Fig. 2) and the finding that pedicellar campaniform sensilla encode bending direction of the flagellum in locusts [13], we expect that the population of campaniform sensilla on the stick insect flagellum could provide sufficient information about the curvature profile of the flagellum, and that this may be taken into account by the animal. Here, we test whether tactile contact locations in 3D can be inferred reliably from static bending of a stick insect antenna. To do so, we measured the static curvature of the flagellum during controlled deflections by a robot manipulator. Assuming that local strain in the flag-ellum cuticle is proportional to local curvature, we then trained an artificial neural network to estimate tactile contact location in 3D from empirical curvature data.

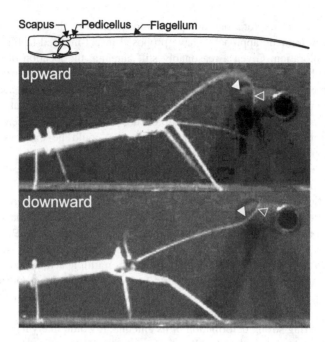

**Fig. 1. The flagellum of the stick insect antenna bends when touching an obstacle. Top:** Schematic of the antenna, showing the two basal segments, scapus and pedicellus, and the long and thin flagellum. **Bottom:** Single frames from side view videos of a blindfolded stick insect that touches a horizontal rod during walking. In the two trials shown, the flagellum touches the rod either during an upward or a downward sweep of the antenna. During both contact events, the flagellum bends considerably (filled arrow heads point at location of maximum curvature). The contact points are indicated by open arrow heads.

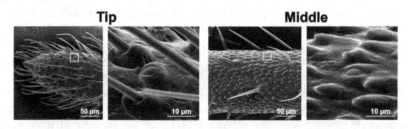

**Fig. 2. Scanning electron micrographs of campaniform sensilla.** Two examples of campaniform sensilla are shown, one near the tip (left) and one in the middle (right) of the flagellum. Locations of close-ups are marked by white squares in the overview images. Campaniform sensilla occur along the entire length of the flagellum. Typically, they are oval-shaped with their long axis aligned with the axis of the flagellum. Images by Annelie Exter.

# 2   Materials and Methods

## 2.1   Animals

A total of fourteen antennae from seven adult female individuals of the species *Carausius morosus* (de Sinéty, 1901) were studied in the experiments described here. All animals originated from the breeding stock of the Department for Biological Cybernetics at Bielefeld University, where they were kept at 24 °C at a 12/12h light-dark cycle. The length of the 14 intact flagella ranged from 27.3 mm to 34.1 mm with a mean of 31.6 mm.

## 2.2   Experimental Setup

In the interest of precision and repeatability between animals, curvature measurements were done with a semi-automated setup, where the antennae could be deflected by an industrial Cartesian robot (Yamaha SXYx with a cubic workspace volume of 42.9 dm$^3$ and an RCX240S controller). The robot was mounted above a table that carried the animal holder (Fig. 3, Top). The robot manipulator was moved along a standard 'deflection path' with 23 hold points distributed across the entire static bending range of the flagellum. Beyond this range, the flagellum slipped past the manipulator and returned to its resting posture. For each one of four deflection directions (dorsal, ventral, medial and lateral) a total of 16 postures were photographed by a digital video camera (Basler acA1920 155 μm) that was mounted below the table. The remaining seven hold positions yielded baseline estimates at each column of the deflection path, i.e., images without induced bending of the flagellum.

After taping the animal to the holder, the two joints of one antenna were immobilised with dental cement (3M ESPE, Protemp). The contralateral antenna was either bent out of sight or, in case it had been glued and measured previously, cut off. Before the measurement, the flagellum was aligned with the horizontal axis of the camera image (equivalent to one axis of the robot) and the manipulator was positioned at the pedicellus-flagellum junction. During a computer-controlled measurement sequence, the manipulator followed the deflection path, stopped at every point of the deflection pattern for a period of seven seconds (to ensure static bending), and a photo was taken by the camera (Fig. 3, Middle). After each measurement sequence, the roll angle of the animal (and the antenna) was changed in steps of 90° and the measurement repeated.

## 2.3   Image Processing

Acquired images were further processed using Matlab (The Mathworks). First, the image was undistorted using the camera calibration toolbox from Matlab. Next, a circular Hough transformation was applied to track and remove the image of the manipulator tip. After remapping of the grayscale palette to remove background influences, a ball dilation operation was applied to remove the effects of sclerotised, dark rings on the flagellum. Finally, the grayscale image was converted into black-and-white, and the flagellum was extracted by tracing the border between the black and the white pixels (Fig. 3, bottom). The resulting contour was smoothed by use of a

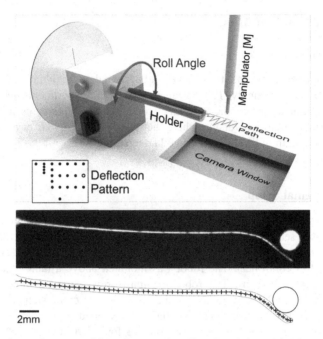

**Fig. 3. Experimental setup and image processing. Top:** Rendering of the setup. A stick insect was fixed to a holder with tape. We used a linear robot to move the manipulator along the indicated deflection path with a total of 23 hold points, as shown by the circles of the deflection pattern (insert). At each hold point, a camera took a photo of the bent flagellum from below, through the camera window in the table. **Middle:** Representative raw image of a bent flagellum. The white circle is the manipulator. The corresponding position in the deflection pattern is indicated by an open circle in the insert. **Bottom:** Image processing extracts the relevant features, i.e., the manipulator, the contour and midline of the flagellum.

Butterworth filter, and subsequently divided into 40 equidistant sections on both sides. From these sections, the midline was calculated. After smoothing the midline points by means of a Gaussian kernel of width 5, the curvature was calculated from the angles between the 40 equidistant midline sections. The curvature is equivalent to the inverse of the radius of the outer bounding circle for every triplet of midline points. Representative curvature data are shown in Fig. 4, plotted over the length of the flagellum.

In the curvature plots of Fig. 4 and in all further analyses, the baseline curvature without induced bending was subtracted, thus yielding the contact-induced change in curvature for each contact point of the deflection pattern. A comparison of the curvature graphs between the left and right flagellum showed no significant difference between the right and the left flagellum. Therefore, they were pooled for all further analysis.

## 2.4   Artificial Neural Network

To test whether the curvature data of the flagellum are sufficient to estimate the spatial location of the contact point with reasonable accuracy, an artificial neural network was

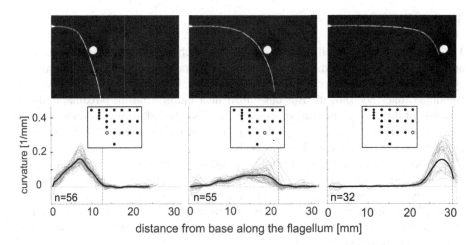

**Fig. 4. Flagellum curvature is unique for different contact positions.** Representative images for three contact positions (inserts show position within deflection pattern) and corresponding curvature graphs. Grey lines show individual measurements; bold black line shows the mean.

trained and tested. For this we used the neural network toolbox from Matlab®. Since the neurophysiology of the neuropils of the deutocerebrum that process afferent information from campaniform sensilla is not well understood, we do not attempt to model the computational properties of the real neural networks here. Instead, we investigate how well a mapping of local bending to contact position in 3D can be. To do so, we trained a feed-forward network with labeled curvature data derived from the images, using the 'scaled conjugate gradient backpropagation' algorithm. All hidden layers had a sigmoid transfer function, the transfer function of the output layer was linear.

**Data Preparation.** When the flagellum was strongly bent by manipulator contacts close to the head, its tip reached beyond the captured frame (for example, Fig. 4, Top left). Therefore, the maximum flagellum length logged for all contact positions was curtailed from a mean of 31 mm to exactly 20 mm. As a consequence, the most distal parts of the flagellum were removed from the training data. To ensure consistent input, the curvature data was divided into 40 query points via interpolation of the first 20 mm of the flagellum midline. This resulted in a sampling distance of 0.5 mm, without exceeding the mean length of the midline sections of ~0.3 mm.

**Network Architecture.** To find the optimal number of layers and neurons for the neural network, several architectures were trained and tested. The root mean square error between measured and estimated contact points was calculated to assess the quality of each fully trained network. Each network architecture was trained in 20 repetitions, and the mean error per architecture was calculated. A total of 617 architectures were tested, ranging from no hidden layer to three hidden layers. A five-layered network architecture with hidden layer sizes of 50-35-5 neurons was selected for the main experiment.

# 3  Results

The static curvature of the flagellum showed several characteristics that indicated non-uniform mechanical properties along its length. As would be expected from a uniform cylindrical beam, the overall peak curvature increased with increasing deflection amplitude (data not shown). But other than in a uniform beam, proximal-to-distal variation of the deflection location caused a corresponding shift of the curvature peak (Fig. 4). Whereas in a uniform rod the curvature peak would remain at its proximal fixing point, the curvature peak was near the base for proximal manipulator positions (Fig. 4, left) but shifted towards the tip for distal manipulator positions (Fig. 4, right). Also, deflection in the mid-range of the flagellum caused lower curvature peaks with a much broader range of bending (compare mid panel of Fig. 4 with left and right panels). These differences to a uniform beam indicate that the biomechanical properties of the flagellum vary from base to tip, with a stiffer proximal region and much more compliant distal region.

With regard to the sensory encoding of curvature, our measurements suggested characteristic curvature profiles for different manipulator positions. Accordingly, it was likely that individual curvature profiles be could mapped to particular contact locations in 3D. To test this, we trained a five-layered feed-forward artificial network (ANN) to output Cartesian coordinates of the manipulator position given an input set of 80 local curvature values (40 query points corresponding to the current bending direction and 40 mapping to the orthogonal direction set to 0). An example of the mapping learned by this ANN is shown in Fig. 5. Here the contact point estimates made by the ANN are plotted next to the corresponding measured positions. Since the test dataset was drawn at random, the number of data points per manipulator position varied. Moreover, the actual contact positions could vary for identical manipulator positions, owing to different curvatures among animals and consequent slipping around the manipulator. To account for potentially non-uniform distributions of estimation errors, we used the mean absolute error (MAE) to determine the accuracy of the position estimates obtained.

The MAE was 0.5 mm along the proximal-to-distal axis (X direction), equivalent to was 2.5% of the total length considered. Along the medial-to-lateral (Y direction) and ventral-to-dorsal axes (Z direction) the accuracy was 2.91% (MAE:0.35) and 3.75% (MAE:0.45) of the tested deflection range ($\pm$12 mm), respectively. The linear regressions of estimated position on target position explained more than 98% of the total variance along any of the three dimensions. The regression functions were very close to unity with slopes always exceeding 0.99, and the intercept always being smaller than 0.1 mm, i.e., less than the tip diameter of the flagellum. In summary, biomechanical bending properties of the stick insect antenna resulted in characteristic static curvature profiles for different contact locations in 3D. These curvature profiles could be mapped to the corresponding contact location in 3D with a MAE of 0.5 mm.

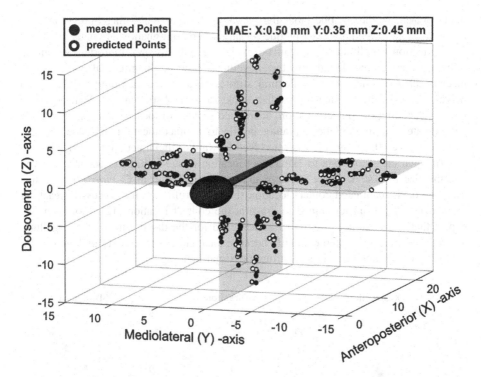

**Fig. 5. Overview over all measured and predicted contact positions.** Measured contact positions are shown as full circles, the corresponding predicted positions are shown as open circles. The mean absolute errors of all data points indicates the accuracy of the predicted points in the different directions.

## 4 Discussion

### 4.1 Unique Curvature Profiles for Different Contact Locations

Given the compliant deformation of arthropod antennae during tactile exploration (Fig. 1; see also [7, 9]), we wondered whether it could be possible to exploit the bending characteristics of the flagellum for tactile localisation of the contact site. In case of a cylindrical beam of uniform material, passive deflection at any site along the beam would always cause maximal bending at the base of the beam. Though the beam will bend along the entire length from the base to the contact location, the magnitude of bending will decrease strongly from base to tip. Accordingly, a given torque measured at the base can be caused by contact-induced, static deflection for different combinations of contact distance and deflection amplitude. As a consequence, contact distance could be estimated only from rotational compliance, e.g., during active movement of the antenna while maintaining contact [3], but not during static deflection. Our curvature measurements (Fig. 4) show that the bending characteristics of the stick insect antenna deviate strongly from what would be expected from a mechanically uniform cylindrical beam. Our finding that both position and spread of the curvature peak vary with contact distance implies that the curvature profile of the flagellum is at least distinctive and potentially even unique for any given combination of contact distance and deflection amplitude. This can be explained only by non-uniform mechanical properties along the length of the flagellum. Indeed, longitudinal variation of mechanical properties such as flexural stiffness [7, 9] and damping [8] has been demonstrated for the antennae of crayfish, cockroaches and stick insects. With regard to sensory decoding of contact location, distributed sensing of local bending should allow an accurate mapping of the curvature profile to contact location in space. Indeed, Figs. 5 and 6 confirm that a five-layered feed-forward artificial neural network can map experimental curvature data to 3D contact location at sub-millimeter accuracy. Given that the size of a stick insect tarsus is approximately 5 mm in *C. morosus* [14], this accuracy of the estimated contact location should be sufficient for successful reaching movements of a front leg aimed to grasp at the contact location [12]. Moreover, we expect that this accuracy could also be achieved for the distal third of the flagellum, although this was not tested explicitly because local curvature data at the flagellum tip could not be obtained in cases of strong proximal bending.

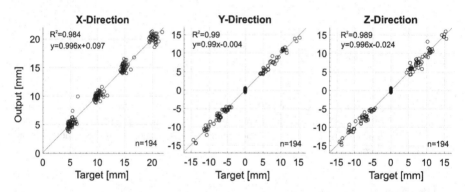

**Fig. 6. Regression plots of the test dataset for the different directions.** The position output of the ANN is plotted over to the true distance of the contact point. Since the fitted lines fitted to the data are very close to the diagonals, the prediction can be considered near to optimal.

## 4.2 Distributed Proprioception of Antennal Bending

The pedicellus and flagellum of the antenna are known to carry campaniform sensilla (Fig. 2; [11]), strain-sensitive mechanoreceptors embedded in the cuticle [15]. To date, bending sensitivity and directional tuning of antennal campaniform sensilla has only been measured for the Hicks' organ of the locust, a ring of campaniform sensilla located on the distal pedicellus [13]. There, individual campaniform sensilla were found to be directionally tuned to flagellar bending away from the sensillum. The abundance and distribution of campaniform sensilla on an insect flagellum have not been published yet, but it is reasonable to assume that they are distributed along the entire length of the flagellum. If so, this population should encode flagellar bending with each sensillum encoding the locally acting, bending-induced shear force. In our ANN model, we assumed (i) that bending force is proportional to local curvature, and

(ii) that 40 sensilla per 20 mm were equally spaced along the flagellum. Future studies will need to validate these assumptions, e.g., by mapping the position, shape and orientation of campaniform sensilla along the flagellum. Also, the model may be expanded further with input data mimicking real sensor data, either neural spikes, for example with proprioceptor models as used by [16], or the output of technical bend sensors (as used in [17]).

Additionally to campaniform sensilla, different types of tactile hairs can be found along the flagellum [18, 19] with increasing density towards the tip [8].These hairs might supply accurate estimates of the contact site along the flagellum and thus improve the accuracy spatial localisation of the contact in 3D. Alternatively, they could provide information on surface roughness or the texture of the encountered obstacle (e.g., see [20, 21]).

Additional mechanosensory information may be particularly relevant for the dissociation of passively versus actively induced bending of the flagellum. Walking stick insects continuously move their antennae [2, 11]. At present our model accurately estimates contact location with respect to the antennal base but it does not care whether the contact cue was generated by its own action or rather (as in our experiments) by passive deflection. Future extensions may include postural and motion cues from other antennal mechanoreceptors.

### 4.3    Potential Use in Biomimetic Tactile Exploration

Our results suggest that an array of bending sensors on a mechanically non-uniform probe could be used to measure contact locations in 3D. On a mobile robotic platform such a sensorised probe could be used for active exploration of the near-range environment, e.g. to allow obstacle avoidance in the dark. For example, a system as proposed by Hoinville et al. [6], with the probe mounted to a position-controlled pan-tilt unit on a wheeled robot could execute rhythmic searching movements and determine the pointing direction. The array of bending sensors could then monitor the contact location relative to base of the probe. The proposed application also has only two degrees of freedom, therefore avoiding common positioning redundancy issues. A mobile robot with an insect-inspired, sensorised and compliant feeler has been tested successfully in a wall-following paradigm [17], but there the feeler was not actively moved during the behaviour. Nevertheless, the array of flex sensors used in that study should be appropriate for an actively moved probe as well. The mechanical tuning of a suitable light-weight probe, however, remains a challenge.

## References

1. Prescott, T.J., Diamond, M.E., Wing, A.M.: Active touch sensing. Philos. Trans. R. Soc. Lond. Ser. B Biol. Sci. **366**, 2989–2995 (2011)
2. Dürr, V., Theunissen, L.M., Dallmann, C.J., Hoinville, T., Schmitz, J.: Motor flexibility in insects: adaptive coordination of limbs in locomotion and near-range exploration. Behav. Ecol. Sociobiol. **72**, 379 (2018)
3. Kaneko, M., Kanayama, N., Tsuji, T.: Active antenna for contact sensing. IEEE Trans. Robot. Autom. **14**, 278–291 (1998)

4. Ueno, N., Svinin, M.M., Kaneko, M.: Dynamic contact sensing by flexible beam. IEEE/ASME Trans. Mechatron. **3**, 254–264 (1998)

5. Patanè, L., Hellbach, S., Krause, A.F., Arena, P., Dürr, V.: An insect-inspired bionic sensor for tactile localization and material classification with state-dependent modulation. Front. Neurorobotics **6**, 1–18 (2012)

6. Hoinville, T., Harischandra, N., Krause, A.F., Dürr, V.: Insect-inspired tactile contour sampling using vibration-based robotic antennae. In: Duff, A., Lepora, N.F., Mura, A., Prescott, T.J., Verschure, P.F.M.J. (eds.) Living Machines 2014. LNCS (LNAI), vol. 8608, pp. 118–129. Springer, Cham (2014). https://doi.org/10.1007/978-3-319-09435-9_11

7. Sandeman, D.C.: Physical properties, sensory receptors and tactile reflexes of the antenna of the australian freshwater crayfish Cherax destructor. J. Exp. Biol. **141**, 197–217 (1989)

8. Dirks, J.-H., Dürr, V.: Biomechanics of the stick insect antenna. Damping properties and structural correlates of the cuticle. J. Mech. Behav. Biomed. Mater. **4**, 2031–2042 (2011)

9. Mongeau, J.-M., Demir, A., Dallmann, C.J., Jayaram, K., Cowan, N.J., Full, R.J.: Mechanical processing via passive dynamic properties of the cockroach antenna can facilitate control during rapid running. J. Exp. Biol. **217**, 3333–3345 (2014)

10. Demir, A., Samson, E.W., Cowan, N.J.: A tunable physical model of arthropod antennae. In: 2010 IEEE International Conference on Robotics and Automation, pp. 3793–3798. IEEE (2010)

11. Staudacher, E.M., Gebhardt, M., Dürr, V.: Antennal movements and mechanoreception. Neurobiology of active tactile sensors. In: Advances in Insect Physiology, vol. 32, pp. 49–205. Elsevier (2005)

12. Schütz, C., Dürr, V.: Active tactile exploration for adaptive locomotion in the stick insect. Philos. Trans. R. Soc. Lond. B Biol. Sci. **366**, 2996–3005 (2011)

13. Heinzel, H.-G., Gewecke, M.: Directional sensitivity of the antennal campaniform sensilla in locusts. Naturwissenschaften **66**, 212–213 (1979)

14. Bässler, U.: Neural Basis Of Elementary Behavior in Stick Insects. Springer, Berlin (1983)

15. Chapman, K.M., Duckrow, R.B., Moran, D.T.: Form and role of deformation in excitation of an insect mechanoreceptor. Nature **244**, 453–454 (1973)

16. Gollin, A., Dürr, V.: Estimating body pitch from distributed proprioception in a hexapod. In: Vasiliki, V., et al. (eds.) Living Machines 2018. LNAI, vol. 10928, pp. 187–199. Springer, AG (2018).

17. Lee, J., Sponberg, S.N., Loh, O.Y., Lamperski, A.G., Full, R.J., Cowan, N.J.: Templates and anchors for antenna-based wall following in cockroaches and robots. IEEE Trans. Robot. **24**, 130–143 (2008)

18. Slifer, E.H.: Sense organs on the antennal flagellum of a walkingstick Carausius morosus Brünner (Phasmida). J. Morphol. **120**, 189–201 (1966)

19. Monteforti, G., Angeli, S., Petacchi, R., Minnocci, A.: Ultrastructural characterization of antennal sensilla and immunocytochemical localization of a chemosensory protein in Carausius morosus Brünner (Phasmida. Phasmatidae). Arthropod Struct. Dev. **30**, 195–205 (2002)

20. Comer, C., Baba, Y.: Active touch in orthopteroid insects: behaviours, multisensory substrates and evolution. Philos. Trans. R. Soc. Lond. Ser. B Biol. Sci. **366**, 3006–3015 (2011)

21. Okada, J., Akamine, S.: Behavioral response to antennal tactile stimulation in the field cricket Gryllus bimaculatus. J. Comp. Physiol. A Neuroethol. Sens. Neural Behav. Physiol. **198**, 557–565 (2012)

# How the Sandfish Lizard Filters Particles and What We May Learn from It

Anna Theresia Stadler[1]([✉]), Michael Krieger[2], and Werner Baumgartner[1]

[1] Institute of Biomedical Mechatronics, Johannes Kepler University Linz,
Altenberger Str. 69, 4040 Linz, Austria
anna.stadler@jku.at

[2] Institute of Fluid Mechanics and Heat Transfer, Johannes Kepler University Linz,
Altenberger Str. 69, 4040 Linz, Austria

**Abstract.** The sandfish lizard *Scincus scincus* spends its life in the aeolian dune deserts. To prevent sand grains from entering its lungs, it is hypothesized that the particles are aerodynamically filtered when they enter the nasal cavity: The vestibulum is a narrow rounded channel leading to a kind of »chamber«, where cilia and mucus are present. In this chamber the particles get caught by mucus during a slow, long-lasting inhalation (2 s) due to the air flow induced by the characteristic morphology in this area, and eventually get exhaled because of an intense, cough-like exhalation that lasts only 40 ms. To verify this theory we studied the filtering system by integrating experiments and computational fluid dynamic simulations of fluid and particle flow. The simulations show that the flow profile anterior to and in the chamber is characterized by a strong cross-flow velocity that moves the sand grains towards the mucus-covered wall; particles usually remain close to the lower wall of the vestibulum and subsequently get trapped. Due to the air flow profile particles would get trapped even if they reached the central region of the nasal cavity. In this context we explore the possibility to optimize state of the art filtering systems.

## 1 Introduction

The sandfish lizard *Scincus scincus* lives in the aeolian sand dunes of North Africa and the Middle East [1]. It adjusts its body temperature by moving between layers of loose sand, and only comes to the surface during the mating season, for foraging and defecating. The locomotory apparatus, subsurface locomotion and the low-abrasive skin have been described and studied previously [2–9]. Vihar et al. [10] studied the respiratory physiology of the sandfish and the physical properties of its natural habitat; they discovered that the sandfish can remain in sand for prolonged periods of time due to interstitial air-filled pockets created by irregular shapes of the sand particles. In our previously published work [11] we integrated biological studies, analytical calculations and physical experiments to understand how the sandfish lizard prevents sand particles from entering its lungs. A 3-dimensional model of one part of the bilateral structure

© Springer International Publishing AG, part of Springer Nature 2018
V. Vouloutsi et al. (Eds.): Living Machines 2018, LNAI 10928, pp. 439–449, 2018.
https://doi.org/10.1007/978-3-319-95972-6_47

of the entire upper respiratory system was created from a detailed histology (see Fig. 1) to experimentally study particle movements and to analytically estimate air flow profiles. Based on these results, the following hypothesis was formulated: When particles enter the respiratory tract during inhalation, they stay in the area superior to the vomero-nasal organ owing to a great drop in velocity, where they are »caught« by the mucus. The cilia transport the particles either towards the naris or towards the palatine cleft. Because of the rapid cough-like exhalation, some of the particles are coughed out through the naris. The rest may be transported into the oral chamber through the palatine cleft and swallowed.

The purpose of the present study was to verify the hypothesis by investigating the 3D-model by means of computational fluid dynamics (CFD). We therefore simulated (i) the fluid flow in the nasal cavity during inhalation and exhalation, and (ii) the trajectory of single particles with different diameters during inhalation. Special attention was payed to the area, where the particles are trapped. We furthermore discuss the possible advantages of an aerodynamic filtering system that mimics the nasal organ of the sandfish lizard.

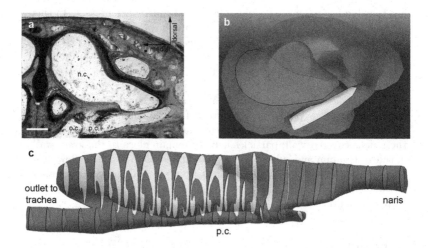

**Fig. 1.** A representative section of the upper respiratory tract (a) histology, (b) model; the palatine cleft (p.c.) is the connection between nasal (n.c.) and oral cavity (o.c.); scale bar, 200 μm. (c) 3-dimensional model with sectioning for a better visualization. Color code: the main air flow goes through the red area; the yellow channel represents the olfactory chamber. (Color figure online)

## 2    Methods

Fluid flow is generally described by the Navier-Stokes equations, which is a set of non-linear partial differential equations. ANSYS Fluent (18.0, ANSYS Inc., USA), a general purpose finite-volume Navier-Stokes solver, was used to obtain a numerical solution. This requires the discretization of the computational domain, the definition of boundary conditions and further modelling assumptions.

The 3-dimensional model of the upper respiratory organ was imported into ANSYS IcemCFD (18.0, ANSYS Inc., USA) to create an unstructured tetrahedral mesh consisting of approximately 40,0000 cells. The meshed geometry was subsequently transferred to ANSYS Fluent.

Flow boundary conditions were defined as follows: A constant pressure was applied at the naris (inlet) and a time dependent outflow velocity (simulating the respiration patterns) was set at the outlet to the trachea. The fluid was air with material parameters set according to the International Standard Atmosphere at sea level. Maximum Reynolds-number during exhalation was determined to be approximately 500, the flow was therefore modeled as laminar.

Sand grains were approximated to be of spherical shape and modeled as single Lagrangian particles. They were injected at a central position at the naris with a starting velocity of $v_s = 0.02$ m/s. Four particles of different diameters were introduced: 0.1, 0.15, 0.2 and 0.3 mm respectively [1]. For each particle the flow rate ($dm = m/dT$), time of injection (at the beginning of the inhalation) and the material were defined. We approximated the density of the sand particles by applying the density of quartz ($SiO_2$, $\rho_Q = 2,652$ kg/m$^3$).

### 2.1 Respiration Pattern Simulation

To simulate the respiration patterns (discussed in Sect. 3.1), a user defined function (UDF) was used. Each phase of the ventilation cycle (exhalation, inhalation, relaxation and pause) was integrated and interpolated by quadratic and cubic spline functions (Fig. 2) in MATLAB (R2016a, MathWorks, USA).

### 2.2 Particle Trajectories

The capabilities of ANSYS Fluent to predict the trajectories of discrete Lagrangian particles are described in the ANSYS Fluent Theory Guide [12]. The particle trajectories are calculated by integrating the following force balance (Newton's second principle):

$$\frac{du_p}{dt} = F_D + F_G + F_P, \tag{1}$$

where $u_p$ is the particle velocity, $F_D$ the particle drag force per unit mass, $F_G$ the gravity force and $F_P$ can represent additional forces (like virtual mass, Saffman force, etc.). In the current case the additional forces could be neglected, since the density difference between sand particles and air is high, the particle size is relatively large, etc. [12]. The drag force per unit mass is given by

$$F_D = \frac{u - u_p}{\tau_r}, \tag{2}$$

with $\tau_r$ being the particle relaxation time

$$\tau_r = \frac{\rho_p d_p^2}{18\mu} \frac{24}{C_d Re_p}. \tag{3}$$

Here, $\mu$ denotes the molecular viscosity of the fluid, $\rho$ the fluid density, $\rho_p$ the density of the particle, and $d_p$ denotes the particle diameter. $Re_p$ denotes the particle Reynolds-number, which is defined as

$$Re_p = \frac{\rho d_p |\boldsymbol{u_p} - \boldsymbol{u}|}{\mu}. \tag{4}$$

Highest particle Reynolds-numbers were estimated to be approximately 10 during inhalation. $C_d$ denotes the particle's drag coefficient. For spherical particles the relationships provided by Morsi and Alexander [13] can be applied. Since the particles are relatively large, we included the particle torque balance in our simulation. The rotational lift force was taken into account; this lift is caused by a pressure differential along a particle's surface. To determine the rotational lift coefficient the Oesterle and Bui Dinh formulation was used (see [12]); it agrees well with experiments for $Re_p < 2,000$.

Additionally, the gravitational force, i.e. the magnitude ($g = 9.81 \, \text{m/s}$) and direction of the gravity vector, was included.

At the walls of the respiratory tract the particles are reflected. ANSYS Fluent provides a reflection model that can account for wall friction and particle rotation. The standard friction coefficient of 0.2 was applied. The reader should refer to the ANSYS Theory Guide [12] and references therein for further information regarding this model.

## 3    Results and Discussion

### 3.1    Underlying Basics

For a comprehensive understanding of the entire project, in the following the results of biological studies and fluid mechanics experiments of our previous work are shortly outlined. For a more detailed description, we refer to our recent work [11].

**Histology of the Upper Respiratory Tract.** A detailed histology of the upper respiratory tract from the nostrils to trachea was conducted. The digitized histological samples were merged to build a three-dimensional model of one side of the bilateral structure of the entire upper respiratory system. The model was geometrically analyzed, and the data was used to import the model into IcemCFD (see Fig. 1).

The upper respiratory tract consists of nasal and olfactory chamber. Most of the inhaled and exhaled air bypasses the olfactory chamber and flows directly through the nasal tract.

The palatine cleft connects the nasal and oral cavities. It begins posterior to the vomero-nasal organ and ends at the choana. It seems though that the connection between nasal and oral cavity is blocked by mucous secretion. In the CFD simulations it was therefore assumed that the palatine cleft is permanently closed.

Sand grains of the sandfish' natural habitat have a diameter ranging from approximately 0.1 to 0.5 mm; the nasal opening has a diameter of 0.84 mm, and the cavity is narrowest at the outlet to the trachea (0.73 mm).

**Respiration Patterns.** The ventilation cycle of the sandfish is triphasic, consisting of exhalation, inhalation and relaxation. Below sand, the exhalation lasts approximately 45 ms and is 60% more intense than above sand. The inhalation lasts approximately 2,036 ms, more than twice as long as above sand. Below sand, the relaxation lasts as long as the exhalation. According to Vihar et al. [10] the average tidal volume inhaled by one upper respiratory tract during one respiration cycle is 113.5 μL (Fig. 2).

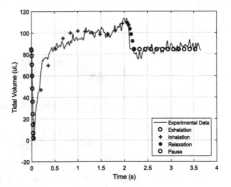

**Fig. 2.** Tidal volume of one respiratory cycle in sand.

**Fluid Mechanics Experiments.** The model of the upper respiratory tract was 3D-printed to experimentally mimic the lizard's respiration. The 3D-model was connected to a little pump to simulate the lungs and buried in sand. With the pump we imitated the ventilation cycles. In all conducted experiments, particles, if present, were found anterior to the area, where the organ separates into olfactory and respiratory channel.

### 3.2   CFD Simulations

**Flow Simulation.** Some important aspects of the air flow are visualized in Figs. 3, 4 and 5. Figures 3 and 4 show contour plots of the velocity magnitude during exhalation and inhalation in the model of the nasal cavity; both midplanes through the inlet (naris) and the outlet (to trachea) are shown. The simulation demonstrated that the flow velocities remain close to zero in the olfactory chamber during each phase. The air flow goes directly from the naris to the trachea outlet or vice versa during inhalation and exhalation, respectively.

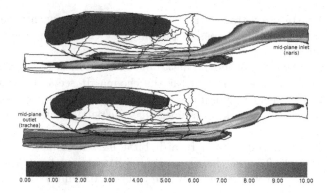

**Fig. 3.** Contour plots of the exhalation velocity after 4 ms (exhalation lasts approximately 40 ms); To visualize the velocities at the inlet and the outlet, mid-planes of both inlet and outlet were created.

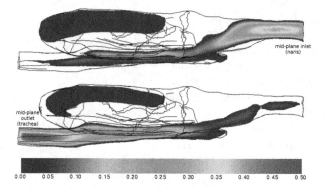

**Fig. 4.** Contour plots of the inhalation velocity after 110 ms (inhalation lasts approximately 2,000 ms); To visualize the velocities at the inlet and the outlet, mid-planes of both inlet and outlet were created.

The vector plots in Fig. 5 show the development of the cross-flow velocity during inhalation in different cross-sections with increasing distance from the inlet. Due to the characteristic shape of the nasal cavity a strong cross-flow develops. At first the direction of the cross-flow is predominantly lateral; as the shape of the nasal tract changes from spherical to sickle-shaped, the cross-flow slowly begins to change its direction. Finally, the vectors point directly into the »chamber«, where mucus and cilia are present. This flow behavior is essential for the filtering mechanisms of the respiratory tract, because it forces the particles towards the wall, where they adhere to mucus.

**Particle Simulation.** Particle trajectories were calculated for each of the four particle diameters (shown in Fig. 6). All particles follow a similar path towards the »chamber«. At first the particles move towards the lower wall of the nasal tract due to gravitational acceleration. The trajectory remains close to the wall until the particles reach the lower chamber, where mucus and cilia are present. Previous experiments indicate that particles are trapped there. To show that the particles would still be trapped if they somehow moved further towards the center of the respiratory tract, we simulated particle trajectories without including the gravitational force.

Figure 7 displays one representative particle path (0.15 mm diameter) in varying velocities). The resulting particle trajectory is surprisingly linear. In the section close to the inlet the laminar flow profile accelerates the particles in z-direction. This initial momentum is enough for the particles to reach the posterior end of the vestibulum following a nearly straight path-line while they continuously decelerate. Finally they reach the region in the respiratory tract where the lateral and downward velocity starts to develop, as has been illustrated in Fig. 5. This prevents the particles from reaching the olfactory tract since they get accelerated towards the »chamber«. The particle trajectory reaches the »chamber« on a posterior position as compared to the particle trajectories calculated with gravitational acceleration. However, even at this position mucus and cilia are

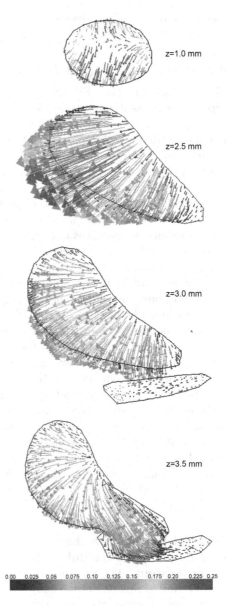

**Fig. 5.** Cross-flow velocity vectors colored by velocity magnitude during inhalation in four different cross-sections. The variable z denotes the distance from the inlet.

present and the particles may be trapped there. During exhalation high velocities are reached in this region of the »chamber« and particles are very likely to be coughed out. Particle trajectories never reach the olfactory tract since velocities remain close to zero there during the entire respiratory cycle.

## 3.3   The Aerodynamic Filtering System

**Description of the Filtering Principle.** The nasal cavity of the sandfish lizard has the ability to filter sand particles without a physiological filtering system that would hinder particles from entering the lungs. Instead the animal filters particles with an aerodynamic filtering system. The morphology of the upper nasal cavity in combination with characteristic respiration patterns is designed to aerodynamically filter particles of a certain size.

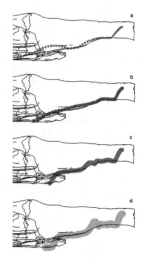

The filtering system of the sandfish lizard not only prevents sand particles from reaching the trachea but also from reaching the olfactory tract. On the one hand, the geometric properties of the respiratory tract produce a flow-field which hinders particles from entering the olfactory tract. On the other hand, the filtering mechanism comprises a combination of various factors: size and shape of the nasal cavity and the corresponding flow-field, the properties of thin layers of mucus and the respiration pattern. This enables trapping sand grains when flow velocities are low during inhalation and coughing them out during a fast and intense exhalation.

**Fig. 6.** Particle trajectories of four particles, with (a) 0.1 mm, (b) 0.15 mm, (c) 0.2 mm and (d) 0.3 mm diameter. They all describe a similar path until they are moved towards the wall due to the characteristic air flow in the »chamber«.

**Minimal Particle Size Estimation for an Aerodynamic Filtering System.** The sandfish filters all sand grains (0.1 to 0.5 mm) of its natural habitat. We estimated the minimal particle size that the lizard could still filter with its aerodynamic filtering system.

The numerical results reveal that both buoyancy and inertial forces are relevant in order to trap sand particles on a sticky, mucuscovered surface. Both mechanisms

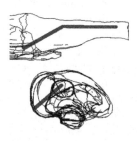

**Fig. 7.** Pathline of one representative particle simulated without gravitational acceleration. It shows that even if particles moved towards the main air stream with highest velocities, they would get trapped at the »chamber«.

depend on particle size and density. Smaller and lighter particles would closely follow the flow streamlines into the trachea. A rough estimate of the critical size of captured particles can be performed using the relationships presented in [14]. For buoyancy-dominated separation a particle drift velocity can be calculated by equating the buoyancy and the particle drag forces. Considering the area of the mucus-covered surface of the sandfish, the critical diameter of the sand grains is approximately 50 µm. For an estimate of inertia-dominated separation, the particle-relaxation time must be evaluated. This is a characteristic timescale for particles to respond to changes in the flow velocity, which allows for an estimate of the streamline deviation of particles. Considering the flow channel diameter and the mean air velocity during inhalation, the critical diameter for the sandfish is roughly 20 µm. Both estimates are of a similar order of magnitude, demonstrating that the sandfish possesses a redundant aerodynamic filtering system for typical sand grain sizes.

**Possible Applications.** Surveys like [15] show that most homes are underventilated, which leads to higher health risk. Therefore, whole house ventilation systems have become a standard technology when new buildings are planned and constructed [16]. The filtering units in these systems, though, may even worsen air quality due to lacking in maintenance, contamination, poor filter fit or duct leakage [17]. The consequences are an increased risk of asthma and other allergic respiratory symptoms for the occupants [18].

A biomimetic aerodynamic filtering system would not need a filtering membrane, and hence eliminate the current problems. Due to the absence of this membrane the system would be low-maintenance, energy-efficient and quiet, because lower air flow velocities would be possible; in consequence the system would be economical and sustainable. The filtered particles could be collected temporary and frequently blown out (simulating the exhalation of the sandfish lizard).

## 4   Conclusion and Outlook

The air flow and the trajectories of single Lagrangian particles were simulated using CFD. Simulation results tend to confirm the hypothesis developed based on the previous experimental investigations. Fluid flow simulations demonstrate that the characteristic shape of the nasal cavity produces a flow field that aerodynamically filter sand particles. The particles are forced towards the walls, where they are trapped by mucus. Further studies are however necessary to establish concepts for an aerodynamic filtering system. These studies should comprise CFD simulations with higher spacial resolution, improved modeling of the sand particle movement, and of the particle wall adhesion. Sand grains are relatively large compared to the dimensions of the respiratory tract; modeling them as a discrete phase is hence not accurate enough. Significant improvement can be achieved by applying moving and deforming meshes. Also, the wall properties should be adapted to imitate mucus and the interaction between sand particles and mucus. In subsequent steps it would be interesting to inject particles into the »chamber« at the beginning of the exhalation to see if particles are indeed coughed out of the respiratory tract. Experimental investigations concerning the wall adhesion of sand particles residing on a mucus covered surface are being prepared. The possible practical applications certainly justify further research.

# References

1. Hartmann, U.-K.: Beitrag zur Biologie des Apothekerskinks Scincus scincus (Linnaeus, 1758): Teil 1: Taxonomie, Verbreitung, Morphologie und Ökologie. Mag. Herpetol. Herpetoculture **11**(59), 17–25 (1989)
2. Baumgartner, W., Fidler, F., Weth, A., Habbecke, M., Jakob, P., Butenweg, C., Böhme, W.: Investigating the locomotion of the sandfish in desert sand using NMR-imaging. PLoS ONE **3**(10), e3309 (2008)
3. Maladen, R.D., Ding, Y., Li, C., Goldman, D.I.: Undulatory swimming in sand: subsurface locomotion of the sandfish lizard. Science **325**(5938), 314–318 (2009)
4. Knight, K.: Sandfish swim effortlessly to burrow. J. Exp. Biol. **216**(2), i–ii (2012)
5. Sharpe, S.S., Ding, Y., Goldman, D.I.: Environmental interaction influences muscle activation strategy during sand-swimming in the sandfish lizard *Scincus scincus*. J. Exp. Biol. **216**(Pt 2), 260–274 (2013)
6. Sharpe, S.S., Koehler, S.A., Kuckuk, R.M., Serrano, M., Vela, P.A., Mendelson, J., Goldman, D.I.: Locomotor benefits of being a slender and slick sand swimmer. J. Exp. Biol. **218**(Pt 3), 440–450 (2015)
7. Dorgan, K.M.: The biomechanics of burrowing and boring. J. Exp. Biol. **218** (Pt 2), 176–183 (2015)
8. Baumgartner, W., Saxe, F., Weth, A., Hajas, D., Sigumonrong, D., Emmerlich, J., Singheiser, M., Böhme, W., Schneider, J.M.: The sandfish's skin: morphology, chemistry and reconstruction. J. Bionic Eng. **4**(1), 1–9 (2007)
9. Staudt, K., Saxe, F., Schmied, H., Böhme, W., Baumgartner, W.: Sandfish inspires engineering. In: Martín-Palma, R.J., Lakhtakia, A. (eds.) SPIE Smart Structures and Materials + Nondestructive Evaluation and Health Monitoring, SPIE Proceedings, pp. 79751B–79751B-9. SPIE (2011)
10. Vihar, B., Wolf, C., Böhme, W., Fiedler, F., Baumgartner, W.: Respiratory physiology of the sandfish (Squamata: Scincidae: *Scincus scincus*) with special reference to subharenal breathing. Salamandra **51**(2) (2015)
11. Stadler, A.T., Vihar, B., Günther, M., Huemer, M., Riedl, M., Shamiyeh, S., Mayrhofer, B., Böhme, W., Baumgartner, W.: Adaptation to life in aeolian sand: how the sandfish lizard, *Scincus scincus*, prevents sand particles from entering its lungs. J. Exp. Biol. **219**(Pt 22), 3597–3604 (2016)
12. ANSYS Inc.: ANSYS Fluent Theory Guide: Release 18.0
13. Morsi, S.A., Alexander, A.J.: An investigation of particle trajectories in two-phase flow systems. J. Fluid Mech. **55**(02), 193 (1972)
14. Kaufmann, B., Niedermayr, A., Sattler, H., Preuer, A.: Separation of nonmetallic particles in tundishes. Steel Res. **64**(4), 203–209 (1993)
15. Dimitroulopoulou, C.: Ventilation in European dwellings: a review. Build. Environ. **47**, 109–125 (2012)
16. Schild, P.G.: Contributed Report 07: State-of-the-art of low-energy residential ventilation. International Energy Agency (2007)

17. Sublett, J.L.: Effectiveness of air filters and air cleaners in allergic respiratory diseases: a review of the recent literature. Curr. Allergy Asthma Rep. **11**(5), 395–402 (2011)

18. Zock, J.-P., Jarvis, D., Luczynska, C., Sunyer, J., Burney, P.: Housing characteristics, reported mold exposure, and asthma in the European Community Respiratory Health Survey. J. Allergy Clin. Immunol. **110**(2), 285–292 (2002)

# Braided Pneumatic Actuators as a Variable Stiffness Approximation of Synovial Joints

Alexander G. Steele$^{(\boxtimes)}$ and Alexander J. Hunt

Department of Mechanical Engineering,
Portland State University (PSU), Portland, OR, USA
{ajmar,ajh26}@pdx.edu

**Abstract.** This paper presents the design of a novel adjustably damped hip and ankle joint using braided pneumatic actuators. These joints provide a wide range of motion and exhibit the same change in stiffness as flexion increases that human joints exhibit, which should also increase bipedal stability, adaptability, and controllability. The theoretical behaviors of the joint make them desirable for use in mobile robotics and should provide a lightweight yet mechanically strong connection that is resistant to unexpected perturbations and catastrophic failure. The joints also bridge the gap between completely soft robotics and completely rigid robotics.

**Keywords:** Ball joint · Robotics · Biomimetics · Synovial joint
Hip · Ankle · Pneumatic actuator · Artificial muscle
McKibben artificial muscles

## 1 Introduction

Currently most robot designs use the same rigid connecting joints that are used in industrial robots. These joints are ideal when dealing with the high precision requirements needed for most industrial robots. In such cases, rigid connections are preferred because the job being done is repetitive and rarely changes, such as the industrial robots used in automotive assembly lines. These rigid connections are also optimal for surgical robots because of the high precision and robust control they provide. However, rigid connections are highly susceptible to damage from impact loads [1].

The same stiff connections that give these previous examples their high precision also causes the artificial way mobile robot platforms move [2]. Mobile robots that use these rigid connections need to minimize the impact loading from the walking motions they are trying to mimic. When these rigid joints are used for mobile robotic platforms, they create an entirely set of new problems that limit robot mobility, speed, and adaptability [3]. To overcome this, there needs to be compliant connecting joints specifically for mobile robots.

Compliant joints reduce the damage from the high stress cyclical loading conditions caused from walking [4, 5]. A compliant joint sacrifices some of the high precision stiff joints offer; however, mobile robots seldom need this high precision. Moreover, adding compliance to joints improves control and create a more natural walking gait [5].

© Springer International Publishing AG, part of Springer Nature 2018
V. Vouloutsi et al. (Eds.): Living Machines 2018, LNAI 10928, pp. 450–458, 2018.
https://doi.org/10.1007/978-3-319-95972-6_48

Current designs typically rely on material properties to augment impact forces on rigid connections [6]. This is not ideal because it still requires rigid joints to sustain some of the impact forces. However, drawing inspiration from the way the human body connects bones, we create a solution that reduces the risk of catastrophic failure and increases the life of the joint.

Synovial joints are the most common and most flexible type of joint in the human body [7]. The joint joins bones with a fibrous capsule that is filled with synovial fluid or synovia. Synovia is a non-Newtonian fluid, which has the consistency of the white of an egg. This fluid acts as lubrication between the cartilage of the joint during movement [8].

While there are six different classifications of synovial joints, the focus of this work is on the ball and socket type, such as the hip or shoulder and the hinge type, such as the ankle or the carpals of the wrist. Both of these joint types have distinct movement characteristics that are primarily defined by the articulating surfaces of the bones. The ball and socket type joint allows for all types of movement with the exception of gliding (flexion/extension, abduction/adduction, and lateral/medial rotation), while hinge type joints only allow for flexion and extension in one plane [8–10].

While the ankle joint is thought to have 3 degrees of freedom, modeling the joint is typically done as a hinge joint due to the instability that the other degrees of freedom introduce into the human joint (i.e. an ankle sprain). Because we simplify the geometry of the joint for use in robotics, we will approximate both the hip and ankle joints as ball and socket type joints. This approximation will help remove some of the instability of the ankle joint and give the joint increased range of motion.

Figure 1 is a cutaway view of a synovial joint structure and shows how the structure connects each side of the joint. The joints are all made up of a synovial cavity, a joint capsule, and articular cartilage. The synovial cavity is the space between the bones that is filled with synovia. The joint capsule is then further broken up into the outer layer and inner layer, the inner layer is made up of the synovial membrane, which secretes synovia, while the outer layer is a fibrous membrane that sometimes contains ligaments. Finally, the articular cartilage functions to reduce friction during movement and protects the joint from impact forces [8, 11, 12].

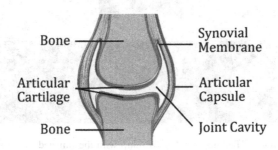

**Fig. 1.** Structure of a synovial joint

While there are typically two different design processes for robots, they will be either completely rigid, or completely soft, they are two extremes of design processes.

In contrast, the human body is neither completely soft, nor rigid, so by designing a semi-soft robot we not only better model the human body, but also we also design robots that have movements that are more natural with increased adaptability and improved controllability.

## 2 Design Methods

### 2.1 Medical Scans to 3D Model

To design the two joints, CT and MRI scans of the lower extremities were used to create 3D models of the joints using an open-source software called 3D Slicer, as shown in Fig. 2. This program organizes the Digital Imaging and Communications in Medicine (DICOM) files so they are manipulatable in a 3D environment. The software selects specific portions of each layer and by applying an extrusion operation corresponding to the layer thickness of the medical scan, creates a 3D model. Once these layers are extruded, a tangent smooth operation is applied to the model to eliminate the stepping artifacts from the extrusion operation. Using this process, we recreate the structures from the medical scan into a high fidelity 3D model. From these models, the initial articulating surfaces of the designed joint are created and sized similarly to the corresponding joints in the body. The files used to create our hip model were obtained from an open source biomedical 3D printing community called embodi3d [13].

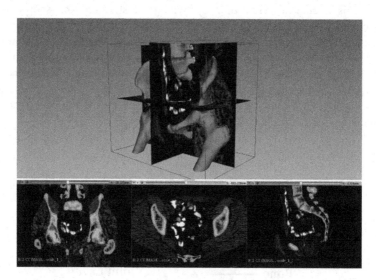

**Fig. 2.** Assembled CT scans of the human hip with the finished 3D model overlaid

The hip joint is a ball and socket type synovial joint which has several different geometric considerations that need to be taken into consideration in order to maximize the life of the designed joint [14, 15]. These geometric parameters, shown in Fig. 3, are the femoral neck length, the narrow neck width, and the neck-shaft angle. The neck of the femur is especially at risk of fracture from loading. The joint geometry in the design comes from the median values of the accepted range for an adult male and not the medical scans since these are considered the ideal values [16]. However, the overall shape of the contacting surfaces is based on the medical scan models.

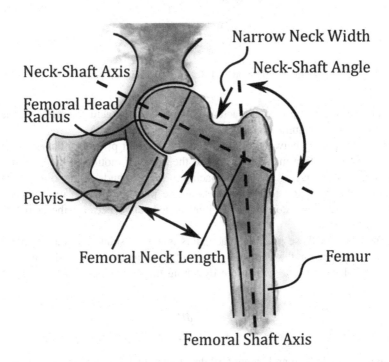

**Fig. 3.** Geometry of the human hip used to determine the femoral neck length, the narrow neck width, and the neck-shaft angle

Figure 4 shows the 3D model of the proposed femoral head design using the median measured values of the human femur. A way to attach the pneumatic actuator securely to each side of the joint needed to be included into the design process because the braided pneumatic actuators are going to need to resist some of the applied load. Adjustable steel hose clamps secure the actuator to either side of the joint; a recess on both ends of the links keeps the actuator firmly secured when tension is applied to the joint. Unlike the hip, the ankle joint is not as dependent on the geometry of the bones and uses the same design process laid out above, so we will not cover the design explicitly.

## 2.2  Range of Motion

Once the hip was designed, the length of the pneumatic actuator needed to be determined in order to maximize the range of motion, because it is dependent upon the

**Fig. 4.** 3D model of the proposed femoral head

stiffness of the braided pneumatic actuator, the pneumatic actuator pressure, the joint gap, and the empty volume inside the pneumatic actuator.

The initial spacing between the two ends of the joint prior to inflation is set such that the range of motion matches closely to the range of motion of the corresponding human joint. By increasing the initial spacing of the two ends of the joint, the braided pneumatic actuator is forced to compress as the joint end comes into contact. This compression of the actuator gives the joint added range because the actuator is no longer fully extended.

Stiffness (k) for these pneumatic actuators is not constant and is a function of the length and pressure of the actuator. This stiffness function is found using a model created by Colbrunn et al. [17] where by taking the derivative of actuator force with respect to length

$$k = \frac{dF}{dL} \tag{1}$$

then using a model Chou and Hannaford developed for BPA latex pneumatic actuators [18] to determine force expressed in terms of gauge pressure ($P_g$) and length (L)

$$F = \frac{P_g b^2}{4\pi n^2}\left(\frac{3L^2}{b^2} - 1\right) \tag{2}$$

and if we differentiate (2) with respect to L,

$$k = \frac{b^2}{4\pi n^2}\left(\frac{3L^2}{b^2} - 1\right)\frac{dP_g}{dL} + \frac{3P_g L}{2\pi n^2} \tag{3}$$

where b is the thread length of braided sleeve and n is the number of turns for a single thread in the length of the braided sleeve seen in Fig. 5.

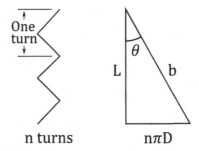

**Fig. 5.** Parameters for determining the single thread length of the braided sleeve and the number of turns for that thread.

Colbrunn et al. [17] assumes that the actuator is a membrane such that the pressure inside the actuator stays constant throughout the range of motion of the actuator. This assumption means

$$\frac{dP_g}{dL} \approx 0 \tag{4}$$

making this assumption and applying it to (3) we now have

$$k = \frac{3P_gL}{2\pi n^2} \tag{5}$$

which gives the theoretical stiffness in terms of gauge pressure ($P_g$), actuator length (L) and single thread length (b). This approximation is then used to determine the axial stiffness.

However, to determine radial stiffness, the beam model, where the actuator is treated as a slender member and loaded in a single plane is used. This formula relates the curvature of the beam ($\varphi$), the applied moment (M), the internal pressure (P) and the beam radius (r) such that

$$M = Pr^3 \frac{\frac{\pi}{2}[(\pi - \varphi) + \sin\varphi\,\cos\varphi] - v[(\pi - \varphi)^2 - (\pi - \varphi)\sin\varphi\,\cos\varphi - \left(2\sin\varphi\right)^2]}{\sin\varphi + (\pi - \varphi)\cos\varphi} \tag{6}$$

where v is the Poisson's ratio of the actuator, Eq. (6) is used to determine the stiffness as the joint angle changes. Figure 6 shows how variations in angle cause a change in stiffness with an initial pressure of 25 psi based on this model. Unfortunately, this model is only valid when the joint surfaces inside the air muscle do not make contact because once the surfaces make contact we need to take into consideration the restoring forces the joint adds to the model and is no longer be assumed to be zero. The restorative force of the joint links created by the compression force of the actuator along with the added friction, increase the joint stiffness and this change needs to be taken into account.

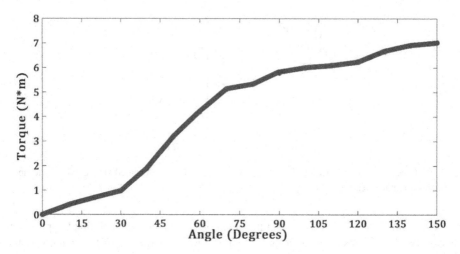

**Fig. 6.** Theoretical change in stiffness as it relates to joint angle at an initial pressure of 25 psi based on the model we have outlined.

The empty volume remaining inside the actuator has significant effects on the range of motion and stability of the joint. As a bending moment is applied to the joint, the contact surface inside the actuator moves along the ball surface, similar to the joints of the human body and is held in place by the actuator. Therefore, the empty volume inside the joint creates a mechanical limit to the amount of motion that the joint achieves. Table 1 shows the range of motion for the hip and ankle joints of the average adult male [19–21], the variables that impact the range of motion should be adjusted to match closely to these values while attempting to maintain maximum joint stability.

**Table 1.** Range of motion of the hip and ankle joint for average adult males in the US [19–21]

|  | Motion | Range (degrees) |
|---|---|---|
| Hip joint |  |  |
|  | Flexion/Extension | 32–88 |
|  | Adduction/Abduction | 51–61 |
|  | Internal/External rotation | 79–99 |
| Ankle joint |  |  |
|  | Planter Flexion/Dorsiflexion | 59–71 |
|  | Inversion/Eversion | 42–56 |

## 2.3   Damping

Reynolds et al. [22] using a sudden reduction in load with constant pressure experimentally determined the independent estimates for the spring coefficient (k) and the damping coefficient (B) of braided pneumatic actuators. They determined that both increase linearly with the change in pressure and that B and k could be functions of loading. This means that as the applied load increases, the damping of the system increases causing the system to become overdamped, conversely when the load decreases the system acts closer to a critically damped system.

This behavior should help increase the controllability of the system because the system will not oscillate due to perturbations. This also means that damping is expected to increase as the joint angle increases, which should further help stabilize the system.

## 3  Discussion

Both joint stiffness and damping is expected to change as the angle of the joint changes, due to the increase in the curvature of the pneumatic actuator and the associated change in pressure, this change mimics the observed behavior of the human ankle [23–26]. This behavior should help stabilize a bipedal robot just as it helps stabilize humans.

Additionally, the joints should exhibit increased stability as the angle of the joint increases because the stiffness of the joint is expected to increase as a result of bending. This means the joint is expected to behave closer to a rigid joint as the angle increases; this too should be beneficial in robotic control.

Because braided pneumatic actuators have a protective fiber braid around the air bladder, should the air bladder puncture or become damaged, if the joint is in tension, the fiber braid should support the load which should help limit damage to the system as a whole. Conversely, if the air bladder fails and the joints are in tension, the fiber wrapping should mechanically limit the joint movement and while the system dynamics of the joint have changed, as long as the load applied to the fiber braid does not exceed its tensile strength the joint should remain semi-functional.

Future work should include experimentally testing the relationship between the length of the actuator, the joint gap after pressurization, initial pressure of the actuator, and the remaining volume inside the actuator to create a more complete model of the joint.

**Acknowledgments.** The authors acknowledge the support of the Mechanical and Materials Engineering Department in the Maseeh College of Engineering at Portland State University.

## References

1. Pratt, G.A., Williamson, M.M., Dillworth, P., Pratt, J., Wright, A.: Stiffness isn't everything. In: Khatib, O., Salisbury, J.K. (eds.) Experimental Robotics IV, pp. 253–262. Springer, Heidelberg (1997). https://doi.org/10.1007/BFb0035216
2. Collins, S.H., Ruina, A.: A bipedal walking robot with efficient and human-like gait. In: Proceedings of the 2005 IEEE International Conference on Robotics and Automation, pp. 1983–1988 (2005)
3. Pratt, G.A.: Low impedance walking robots. Integr. Comp. Biol. **42**, 174–181 (2002)
4. Kim, B.-H.: Work analysis of compliant leg mechanisms for bipedal walking robots. Int. J. Adv. Robot. Syst. **10**(9), 334 (2013)
5. Iida, F., Minekawa, Y., Rummel, J., Seyfarth, A.: Toward a human-like biped robot with compliant legs. Robot. Auton. Syst. **57**, 139–144 (2009)

6. Zhou, X., Bi, S.: A survey of bio-inspired compliant legged robot designs. Bioinspir. Biomim. **7**, 041001 (2012)
7. Standring, S.: Gray's Anatomy. Elsevier (2015)
8. Levangie, P.K., Norkin, C.C.: Joint Structure and Function: A Comprehensive Analysis, 5th edn. F. A. Davis Company, Philadelphia (2011)
9. Hewitt, J., Guilak, F., Glisson, R., Vail, T.P.: Regional material properties of the human hip joint capsule ligaments. J. Orthop. Res. **19**, 359–364 (2001)
10. van Arkel, R.J., Amis, A.A., Cobb, J.P., Jeffers, J.R.T.: The capsular ligaments provide more hip rotational restraint than the acetabular labrum and the ligamentum teres: an experimental study. Bone Jt. J. **97-B**, 484–491 (2015)
11. Mansour, J.M.: Biomechanics of cartilage. In: Biomechanical Principles (2013)
12. Halonen, K.S., Mononen, M.E., Jurvelin, J.S., Töyräs, J., Kłodowski, A., Kulmala, J.-P., Korhonen, R.K.: Importance of patella, quadriceps forces, and depthwise cartilage structure on knee joint motion and cartilage response during gait. J. Biomech. Eng. **138**, 071002-1–071002-11 (2016)
13. Pelvis and Hip - CT Scan. https://www.embodi3d.com/files/file/11745-pelvis-and-hip-ct-scan/
14. Kazemi, S.M., Qoreishy, M., Keipourfard, A., Sajjadi, M.M., Shokraneh, S.: Effects of hip geometry on fracture patterns of proximal femur. Arch. Bone Jt. Surg. **4**, 248–252 (2016)
15. Wu, H.-H., Wang, D., Ma, A.-B., Gu, D.-Y.: Hip joint geometry effects on cartilage contact stresses during a gait cycle. In: Annual International Conference of the IEEE Engineering in Medicine and Biology Society, pp. 6038–6041 (2016)
16. Hartel, M.J., Petersik, A., Schmidt, A., Kendoff, D., Nüchtern, J., Rueger, J.M., Lehmann, W., Grossterlinden, L.G.: Determination of femoral neck angle and torsion angle utilizing a novel three-dimensional modeling and analytical technology based on CT datasets. PLoS ONE **11**, e0149480 (2016)
17. Colbrunn, R.W., Nelson, G.M., Quinn, R.D.: Modeling of braided pneumatic actuators for robotic control. In: Proceedings of the 2001 IEEE/RSJ International Conference on Intelligent Robots and Systems. Expanding the Societal Role of Robotics in the Next Millennium (Cat. No. 01CH37180), vol. 4, pp. 1964–1970 (2001)
18. Chou, C.-P., Hannaford, B.: Measurement and modeling of McKibben pneumatic artificial muscles. IEEE Trans. Robot. Autom. **12**, 90–102 (1996)
19. Soucie, J.M., Wang, C., Forsyth, A., Funk, S., Denny, M., Roach, K.E., Boone, D.: Range of motion measurements: reference values and a database for comparison studies. Haemophilia **17**(3), 500–507 (2011)
20. Roaas, A., Andersson, G.B.J.: Normal range of motion of the hip, knee and ankle joints in male subjects, 30–40 years of age. Acta Orthop. Scand. **53**, 205–208 (1982)
21. Kouyoumdjian, P., Coulomb, R., Sanchez, T., Asencio, G.: Clinical evaluation of hip joint rotation range of motion in adults. Orthop. Traumatol. Surg. Res. **98**, 17–23 (2012)
22. Reynolds, D.B., Repperger, D.W., Phillips, C.A., Bandry, G.: Modeling the dynamic characteristics of pneumatic muscle. Ann. Biomed. Eng. **31**, 310–317 (2003)
23. Amiri, P., Kearney, R.E.: Ankle intrinsic stiffness is modulated by postural sway, July 2017
24. Misgeld, B.J.E., Zhang, T., Lüken, M.J., Leonhardt, S.: Model-based estimation of ankle joint stiffness (2017)
25. Guarin, D.L., Kearney, R.E.: Time-varying identification of ankle dynamic joint stiffness during movement with constant muscle activation, August 2015
26. Hettich, G., Assländer, L., Gollhofer, A., Mergner, T.: Human hip–ankle coordination emerging from multisensory feedback control. Hum. Mov. Sci. **37**, 123–146 (2014)

# An Analysis of a Ring Attractor Model for Cue Integration

Xuelong Sun[1]([✉]), Michael Mangan[2], and Shigang Yue[1]

[1] Computational Intelligence Lab, School of Computer Science,
University of Lincoln, Lincoln, UK
15612083@students.lincoln.ac.uk
[2] Sheffield Robotics, Department of Computer Science,
The University of Sheffield, Sheffield S1 4DP, UK
http://www.ciluk.org/

**Abstract.** Animals and robots must constantly combine multiple streams of noisy information from their senses to guide their actions. Recently, it has been proposed that animals may combine cues optimally using a ring attractor neural network architecture inspired by the head direction system of rats augmented with a dynamic re-weighting mechanism. In this work we report that an older and simpler ring attractor network architecture, requiring no re-weighting property combines cues according to their certainty for moderate cue conflicts but converges on the most certain cue for larger conflicts. These results are consistent with observations in animal experiments that show sub-optimal cue integration and switching from cue integration to cue selection strategies. This work therefore demonstrates an alternative architecture for those seeking neural correlates of sensory integration in animals. In addition, performance is shown robust to noise and miniaturization and thus provides an efficient solution for artificial systems.

**Keywords:** Ring attractor · Cue integration · Sensor fusion
Optimal · Bayesian integration · Head direction cells

## 1 Introduction

A fundamental principle underlying animal intelligence is the capacity to appropriately combine redundant sensory information (e.g. vision, olfactory and haptic) of the same percept (e.g. location of a sensory source) to achieve a more accurate and robust estimate [1,2]. For example, both mammals and insects constantly track their pose using head-direction cells which combine information from external cues (e.g. from surrounding visual features) with self-motion cues (from path integration) to maintain a precise estimate of their current orientation [3,4] (Fig. 1). Yet, as all sensory information is subject to errors which can change drastically depending on the situation (e.g. relying on visual cues in

---

M. Mangan and S. Yue—Joint last authors.

© Springer International Publishing AG, part of Springer Nature 2018
V. Vouloutsi et al. (Eds.): Living Machines 2018, LNAI 10928, pp. 459–470, 2018.
https://doi.org/10.1007/978-3-319-95972-6_49

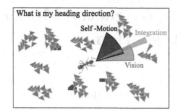 

**Fig. 1. The cue integration problem.** Left: An example of an animal maintaining an estimate of it's current pose (green area) using different cues of varying certainty (Self-motion, black area, and vision, red area). Right: cues can be represented by conflicting Gaussian functions with the width describing the uncertainty of each and the optimal solution (green) given by weighting each cue according to their known variance as described by Bayes' rule. (Color figure online)

a darkened room) animals must employ an adaptive cue combination strategy reflecting the known errors (variance) in the different sensory signals to achieve the optimal estimate of the desired environmental property.

Bayes' theorem (1) provides a mathematical framework describing the optimal way in which information from different sources should be combined, and it has been argued that animals have Bayesian brains [2,5–7]. According to Bayes' Rule, the posterior probability $P(x_{true}|x_{cue})$ (the probability of event $x$ will happen when the cue about $x$ is sensed) is proportional to the product of the prior probability $P(x_{true})$ (the probability of event $x$ happening based on prior knowledge) and the likelihood function $P(x_{cue}|x_{true})$ (the probability of the cue when $x$ truly happened, which represents the reliability of this cue). Assuming that the prior probability $P(x_{true})$ is uniform and $x_{cue}$ is corrupted by Gaussian noise with variance $\sigma^2$, then the posterior probability is proportional to $1/\sigma^2$. Therefore, when there are $n$ cues all concerning $x$ event and corrupted by Gaussian noise with variance $\sigma_i^2, i = 1, 2, ...n$, the optimal way to reduce the uncertainty of estimating $x$ (i.e., the maximum the posteriori probability) is averaging the cues weighted by their reciprocal variances $1/\sigma^2$, as indicated by (2), which is identical with results calculated by the maximum-likelihood estimate (MLE) [6,8]. The theorem asserts that cues with low variance (i.e more reliable) should be weighted more than those with high variance (i.e less reliable) as demonstrated in Fig. 1.

$$P(x_{true}|x_{cue}) = P(x_{cue}|x_{true}) P(x_{true}) / P(x_{cue}) \qquad (1)$$

$$\hat{X} = \sum_{i}^{n} W_i X_i, W_i = \left(1/\sigma_i^2\right) / \left(\sum_{j}^{n} 1/\sigma_j^2\right) \qquad (2)$$

Artificial systems must also solve the same problem although in robotics it is commonly known as sensor fusion. Sensor fusion for mobile robot navigation is a long standing issue and many statistical methods based on maximum *a posteriori* and maximum-likelihood estimation have been applied to solve it [9].

Recent advances in deployment of robot systems such as cars with their suite of GPS, radar, cameras, and laser scanning sensors to estimate precise lane position, owe much to adoption of probabilistic integration of cues in line with the Bayesian formulation described above [10]. Yet, current SLAM methods [11], tend to be computationally expensive and unsuitable for application on small, cheap robot platforms. Learning from biology may bring significant benefits for solving these problems in artificial systems.

We therefore take a bio-inspired approach to firstly understand how animals resolve this task, which in turn may offer inspiration to engineers seeking efficient solutions. As a starting point, we use a classic neural network architecture known as a ring attractor network. Ring attractors can be constructed such that the output activity resembles a Gaussian profile that is maintained even in the absence of sensory input. When new sensory input is presented, the activity profile will shift towards and stabilize at the new location. If this sensory input is driven by orientation cues such as path integration or visual features then the Gaussian mean will naturally track the animal orientation. Such networks have been proposed to underpin the head-direction cells in animals [12,13]. Further when more than one input signal is presented ring attractors can be constructed such that the output settles on the weighted average of the combined cues as required for optimal cue integration [14]. In a recent review, Jeffery et al. [15] proposed that ring-attractor networks may provide a general architecture for optimal cue integration. Their biomimetic model (constrained by physiological data from rats) used a re-weighting mechanism to achieve optimal integration. Specifically, in the region where conflicting cues overlap, Hebbian learning rapidly strengthens local sysnapses causing peak activity to shift towards the position consistent with optimal integration.

In this study, we revisit the Touretsky [14] ring attractor network and assess its ability to combine conflicting cues of different strengths. Specifically we seek to assess how this network performs when given cues of different strengths and with different levels of conflict. Further, we wish to document if and when the network optimally integrates cues or if it adheres to a winner-takes-all (WTA) solution, or switches strategy depending on the situation.

Our results suggest that a Touretsky ring attractor network can integrate cues in a manner approaching optimal (i.e, consistent with MLE) for small conflicts. For larger conflicts the network switches to WTA mode, mirroring results of ethological experiments [16]. Performance is shown to be robust to noise and significant reduction in the network size, and thus provides a simple (no re-weighting mechanism required), compact ring attractor solution to cue integration that can provide inspiration for those seeking similar integration networks in animals or act as a bio-inspired method for optimal sensor fusion in robots.

## 2   Models and Methods

### 2.1   Touretsky Ring Attractor Model

**Artificial Neurons.** The network is constructed using two populations of CTRNN (continuous time recurrent neural network) neurons which are simple nonlinear and continuous dynamical neurons suitable for simulating the subset of real numbers as required for our ring attractor model [17]. The average membrane potential $c_i$ of a CTRNN $i^{th}$ neuron is updated by the differential equation (3), where $\tau$ is the positive time constant and $I_i$ is the total number of inputs into the neuron which equals the weighted sum of other neurons' outputs $O_j, j = 1, 2, ...n$ and the external inputs, as shown in (4), where $W_{ji}$ is the weight matrix representing the connection strength from $j^{th}$ to $i^{th}$ neuron, $g$ is the activation function and $X_i$ is the external input. To acquire the nonlinear property of the network, the activation function of $g$ should be a nonlinear function. Here we simply applied a semi-linear threshold function with a threshold defined by $\theta$ as indicated in (5).

$$\tau \frac{c_i}{dt} = -c_i + I_i \tag{3}$$

$$I_i = \sum_{j=1}^{n} W_{ji}O_j + X_i = \sum_{j=1}^{n} W_{ji}g(c_j) + X_i \tag{4}$$

$$g(c) = max(0, \theta + c) \tag{5}$$

**Network Geometry.** We implemented a variant of the classic ring attractor network [12] (Fig. 2(a)) which replaces the inhibitory interneurons with a single global inhibitory (uniform inhibitory) neuron making the network easier to tune while giving the same performance [14]. Each excitatory neuron in the network has recurrent excitatory connections to all other neurons in the ring with weights decreasing with distance which is crucial for generating the bell-shape activation profile in stable state, as revealed in (6), where $d_{ij}$ is the distance between the $i^{th}$ and $j^{th}$ neuron. Our network posses a single dynamic inhibitory neuron that sums inputs from the excitatory neurons and then proportionally inhibits the entire network. Note, for ease of understanding the recurrent connections from a single excitatory cell are shown in Fig. 2(a) but in reality each neuron has the same set of recurrent connections.

$$W_{ji}^{E \rightarrow E} = e^{\frac{-d_{ji}^2}{2\sigma^2}} \tag{6}$$

Figure 2(b) shows the process by which the network combines input from multiple cues. We simulate cues of different strengths using Gaussian functions (see Eq. (7) where $K$ is the scale factor, $\mu$ defines the peak position of the Gaussian curve (estimation of the certain property based on the cue) and $\sigma^2$ is the variance of the Gaussian function determining the reliability of the signal). To have a corresponding connection with the integration neurons in the attractor,

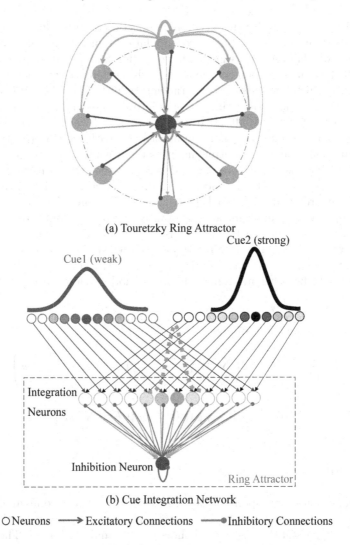

(a) Touretzky Ring Attractor

(b) Cue Integration Network

○ Neurons    ⟶ Excitatory Connections    ⟶● Inhibitory Connections

**Fig. 2. The implemented Touretzky ring attractor network.** (a) Excitatory neurons are shown by green circles, and the global inhibitory neuron depicted by the blue circle. The recurrent excitatory interneurons are shown by orange arrows with connection strength decreasing with distance between neurons. Excitatory and inhibitory connections between the global inhibitory neuron are also shown in blue and green respectively. (b) The full integration network shown in unwrapped form (minus recurrent connections for ease of reading) with example inputs and optimal output overlaid. (Color figure online)

the cues are represented by the activation profile of $N$ neurons with their preference $p_i$, and so the Gaussian curve is sampled by $N$ points at intervals. This input is then passed to the integration population which is shown in unwrapped form in Fig. 2(b), and with the recurrent connections omitted for ease of reading. The integration population (and also population representing cue 1 and cue 2) has $N$ neurons labeled with their preferences (for example, if these neurons represent the heading directions of the animal, the preferences will be the preferred directions evenly distributed around the entire 360° of possible directions). The inhibitory population has a single dynamic postulated inhibition neuron summing the activations from all integration neurons and which recurrently inhibits all integration neurons. Therefore, in accordance with Eqs. (3)–(5), the average membrane potential of the output neurons (neurons in integration population) is computed by Eq. (8), where $X1$ and $X2$ represent the activation vectors of cue 1 and cue 2 respectively and $u$ is the membrane potential of the uniform inhibitory neuron (calculated by Eq. (9)). Note that in order to maintain the nonlinear property and simultaneously guarantee the positive output of the model, we tuned the total input $I$ to $c$ and $u$ using function $g$ according to [14].

Note that in this paper, as an example, we use the ring attractor to represent the heading direction system so all the values have the unit-degree. But generally the unit could be other meanings when this model is applied to other specific contexts.

$$F(i) = \frac{K}{\sqrt{2\pi}\sigma} e^{-\frac{(p_i - \mu)^2}{2\sigma^2}} + \xi N(0,1), i = 1, 2, ...N \tag{7}$$

$$\tau \frac{dc_i}{dt} = -c_i + g\left(\sum_{j=1}^{n} W_{ji}^{E \to E} c_j + X1_i + X2_i + W^{I \to E} u\right) \tag{8}$$

$$\tau \frac{du}{dt} = -u + g\left(W^{I \to I} u + W^{E \to I} \sum_{k=1}^{n} c_k\right) \tag{9}$$

## 3    Results

Figure 3(a) shows the response of our ring attractor network configured with 100 neurons when stimulated with two conflicting cues (65° apart) with different variances ($\sigma_{cue1} = 40°, \sigma_{cue2} = 35°$) shown by red and black lines. The response of the network (green line) approaches the MLE, i.e., the optimal integration (blue dashed line) rather than following the WTA solution. Figure 3(b) shows that the network response is robust to noise with each cue corrupted by Gaussian white noise ((7) with $\xi = 0.01$). Finally, inspired by recent anatomical results showing that insects encode their heading direction using populations of only 8 directional neurons in each hemisphere of the central complex [18,19] we reduced the number of neurons in our integration network from 100 to 8. Figure 3(c) demonstrates that the cue integration properties of the network remained stable despite the obvious loss of resolution in the Gaussian functions.

To assess the performance of the network across likely scenarios we performed two more experiments using the noise free network with 100 neurons. Firstly, we assessed the performance of the network when presented with cues that were increasingly disparate. Cue 1 ($\mu_{cue1} = 0°, \sigma_{cue1} = 40°$) was presented at the

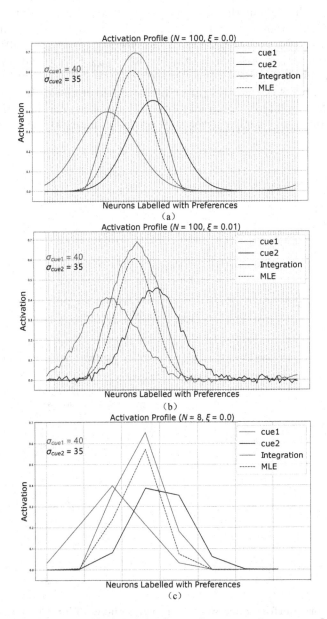

**Fig. 3. Integration of conflicting cues by a ring attractor network.** Activation profiles of cues are shown by the red and black curves, the output profile of RA (the ring attractor) by the green line, and the MLE by the blue dashed line. (a) shows the results for a noise-free network with 100 neurons, (b) shows the results of the same network with added white noise, and (c) show the results when the number of neurons is reduced to 8. (Color figure online)

same position throughout the tests, while Cue 2 was presented at increasingly distant positions (from 0° to 180° in 5° steps). We performed this analysis under three conditions: (a) cues with identical variance ($\sigma_{cue1} = \sigma_{cue2} = 40°$); (b) cues with slight differences in variance ($\sigma_{cue1} = 40°, \sigma_{cue2} = 35°$); and (c) cues with significantly different variance ($\sigma_{cue1} = 40°, \sigma_{cue2} = 20°$). Figure 4(a–c) shows the peak response of the network (green line) overlaid on the MLE (blue line) and WTA (red line) solutions. With cues of equal variance (Fig. 4(a)) the network response approaches (though never very precisely matches) the MLE solution

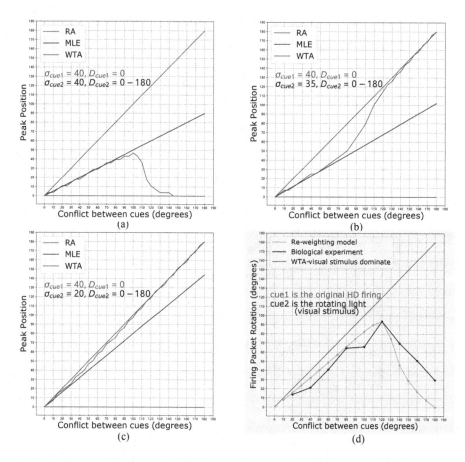

**Fig. 4. Network performance with increasing cue conflict.** Cue 1 was presented in the same location while cue 2 was presented at increasing distances. For (a), (b) and (c), the response of the RA (ring attractor) is shown by the green line, the WTA prediction by the red line, and the MLE by the blue line. (a) Cues of equal variance (b) Cue 1 with slightly higher variance than Cue 1, (c) Cue 1 with significantly higher variance than cue 1. (d) data from similar cue combination study in rats (black line) [16] and alternative re-weighting model (orange line) [20] (data provided with thanks by Dr. Hector Page and Prof. Kate Jeffery). (Color figure online)

but changes to WTA-like responses when cue-conflict exceeded approximately 100°. With small differences in variance (Fig. 4(b)), the network again weights cue in an approximately optimal manner but shifts to a WTA response at higher values (>110°). In contrast when more significant differences in variance were presented (Fig. 4(c)), the network changes from the MLE to WTA response at much smaller conflicts (>60°).

Figure 4(d) shows data from a previous cue-combination experiment in rats [16] (black line) overlaid with the biologically constrained ring attractor network with re-weighting mechanism [20] (orange line) as the cue conflict is increased as in our experiment. We note that our model response (Fig. 4(a)) adheres closely to the animal data.

Secondly we assessed the performance of the network when the certainty of one cue was altered while the other was held constant. Specifically, cue 1 and cue 2 were presented 90° apart. While cue 2 variance was held at 40°, the variance of cue 1 was increased from 5° to 200°. Figure 5 shows the peak position of the activation profile of the network changes from a WTA state for uncertainty of cue 1 below 15° and above 160° but performs a weighted average when uncertainty of cue 1 in the range 20° to 155°. Thus, although not acting in a truly optimal manner the switch from WTA to weighted-average and back again follows the general profile of the MLE prediction.

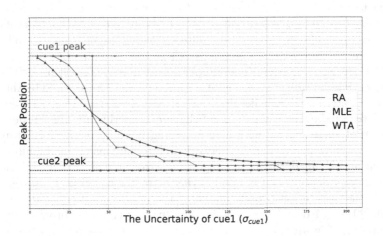

**Fig. 5. Network performance with changes in cue variance.** Cue 1 and cue 2 were presented at the same location 90° apart. The variance of cue 2 was kept at 40° while cue 1 changed from 5° to 200° in intervals of 5°. The position the peaks of activation profile of cues 1 and 2 are shown by the dashed red and black lines respectively; the WTA response by the solid red line; the MLE by the blue line; and the RA (ring attractor) output by the green line. (Color figure online)

# 4   Discussion

In this work, we re-visited the classic ring-attractor network described by Touretsky [14] to assess if it could be configured for optimal cue integration, and if so whether this might give inspiration for those seeking such networks in animals or provide a biologically-inspired solution for robotics.

We report that our implementation of the classic Touretsky ring attractor network perform optimal-like cue integration when presented with conflicting cues rather than tending to a winner-takes-all solution as often cited. The network output is also shown to be robust to noise on the sensory input and to reduction to 8 neurons encoding direction (as in insects). Our sweep tests showed that both the variance and distance between conflicting cues strongly affect the network properties. With equal or small differences in variance of cues the network performs a weighted average for small cue conflicts, but switches to a WTA response for larger conflicts. For larger differences the network switches to WTA responses at much small conflicts. This changing of response is akin to meta-Bayesian decision making where it is highly sub-optimal to integrate two hugely conflicting cues e.g. one should not go West, when one cue states North and the other South. Instead one should choose the best single option, but how does the agent know when to apply each strategy? We show that the [14] ring attractor network inherently possesses this capacity.

Over two decades ago the ring attractor network was proposed as a possible solution underpinning the head direction cells in mammals that integrate directional cues from different sensory modalities to maintain an accurate read-out of their current orientation [12]. Recent models of the head direction cells of mammals have moved away from the original ring attractor architecture because the physiology does not mirror the excitatory interconnections required by the original model [20,21], and the belief that ring attractors will tend to a WTA outcome over the weighted-average observed in behavioral experiments [15]. Through augmentation of these models with a re-weighting mechanism (Hebbian learning) [20] it has been proposed that this network architecture may be a ubiquitous neural circuit underlying optimal cue integration across many functions [15]. Here we provide new evidence that the original ring attractor network can also perform weighted cue integration (closely matching the performance of the re-weighting network [20] Fig. 4(d)), or cue selection in a manner closely approximating data from rats [16] (Fig. 4(d)).

Direction cells have recently been revealed in insects (*Drosophila*) with so-called E-PG neurons forming a bump of activity that moves in response to both rotation of vision cues and self-motion and combines in both cue selection or cue integration like a averaged weighted [4]. These E-PG neurons have also been shown to have ring attractor dynamics [22]. Biomimetic models constrained by the anatomy of the animal have successfully recreated the activation phenomena of behavioral experiments [23,24] but have not, as yet, been extended to the broader cue integration problem discussed here and in [15]. We note that [23] showed that fixed connection weights are sufficient to track the self-motion and visual cues well with the dynamic re-weighting with slower learning rates giving improved performance describing a trade-off between computational complexity and required robustness.

By analyzing the Touretzky ring attractor network, we show that it should still be considered a biologically plausible mechanism to achieve cue integration of the animals. Although not well suited to describe the head-direction system of mammals due to physiological constraints, it is an open question whether other areas of animal brains that perform cue integration may use this ring attractor architecture. For instance, the lateral accessory lobe (LAL) of insects brain, which is a converging point of sensory information and has inputs from sensory lobes, mushroom body and the central complex [25, 26] provides a candidate to search for such network architectures. To date, we know little about how different cues (like vision memory from mushroom body and path integration from central complex) might be integrated in this area and wherein ring attractors may also play crucial roles. As a bio-inspired neural network, the ring attractor is a compact but efficient model to solve the similar problems in sensor fusion and its anti-noise and stable performance with only 8 neurons endow it the advantage of implementation on robots with limited computation resources.

**Acknowledgments.** This work was supported by EU FP7 projects HAZCEPT (318907), HORIZON 2020 project STEP2DYNA (691154). We also thank Prof. Kate Jeffery and Dr. Hector Page for provision of data shown in Fig. 4(d).

# References

1. Shettleworth, S.J.: Cognition, Evolution, and Behavior. Oxford University Press, Oxford (2010)
2. Ernst, M.O., Knoblich, G.: A Bayesian view on multimodal cue integration. In: Human Body Perception from the Inside Out, vol. 131, pp. 105–131 (2006)
3. Blair, H.T., Sharp, P.E.: Visual and vestibular influences on head-direction cells in the anterior thalamus of the rat. Behav. Neurosci. **110**(4), 643 (1996)
4. Seelig, J.D., Jayaraman, V.: Neural dynamics for landmark orientation and angular path integration. Nature **521**, 186–191 (2015). https://doi.org/10.1038/nature14446
5. Cheng, K., Shettleworth, S.J., Huttenlocher, J., Rieser, J.J.: Bayesian integration of spatial information. Psychol. Bull. **133**(4), 625 (2007)
6. Kording, K.P., Wolpert, D.M.: Bayesian integration in sensorimotor learning. Nature **427**(6971), 244 (2004)
7. Kording, K.P.: Bayesian statistics: relevant for the brain? Curr. Opin. Neurobiol. **25**, 130–133 (2014)
8. Ernst, M.O., Banks, M.S.: Humans integrate visual and haptic information in a statistically optimal fashion. Nature **415**(6870), 429 (2002)
9. Kam, M., Zhu, X., Kalata, P.: Sensor fusion for mobile robot navigation. Proc. IEEE **85**(1), 108–119 (1997)
10. Thrun, S., Burgard, W., Fox, D.: Probabilistic Robotics. MIT press, Cambridge (2005)
11. Fuentes-Pacheco, J., Ruiz-Ascencio, J., Rendón-Mancha, J.M.: Visual simultaneous localization and mapping: a survey. Artif. Intell. Rev. **43**(1), 55–81 (2015)

12. Zhang, K.: Representation of spatial orientation by the intrinsic dynamics of the head-direction cell ensemble: a theory. J. Neurosci. **16**(6), 2112–2126 (1996)
13. Skaggs, W.E., Knierim, J.J., Kudrimoti, H.S., McNaughton, B.L.: A model of the neural basis of the rat's sense of direction. In: Advances in Neural Information Processing Systems, pp. 173–180 (1995)
14. Touretzky, D.S.: Attractor network models of head direction cells. In: Head Direction Cells and the Neural Mechanisms of Spatial Orientation, pp. 411–432 (2005)
15. Jeffery, K.J., Page, H.J., Stringer, S.M.: Optimal cue combination and landmark-stability learning in the head direction system. J. Physiol. **594**(22), 6527–6534 (2016)
16. Knight, R., Piette, C.E., Page, H., Walters, D., Marozzi, E., Nardini, M., Jeffery, K.J.: Weighted cue integration in the rodent head direction system. Philos. Trans. R. Soc. Lond. B Biol. Sci. **369**(1635) (2014). https://doi.org/10.1098/rstb.2012.0512
17. Beer, R.D.: On the dynamics of small continuous-time recurrent neural networks. Adapt. Behav. **3**(4), 469–509 (1995)
18. Pfeiffer, K., Homberg, U.: Organization and functional roles of the central complex in the insect brain. Annu. Rev. Entomol. **59**, 165–184 (2014)
19. Heinze, S.: Unraveling the neural basis of insect navigation. Curr. Opin. Insect Sci. **24**, 58–67 (2017)
20. Page, H.J., Walters, D.M., Knight, R., Piette, C.E., Jeffery, K.J., Stringer, S.M.: A theoretical account of cue averaging in the rodent head direction system. Philos. Trans. R. Soc. B Biol. Sci. **369**(1635), 20130283 (2014)
21. Page, H.J., Walters, D., Stringer, S.M.: Architectural constraints are a major factor reducing path integration accuracy in the rat head direction cell system. Front. Comput. Neurosci. **9**, 10 (2015)
22. Kim, S.S., Rouault, H., Druckmann, S., Jayaraman, V.: Ring attractor dynamics in the Drosophila central brain. Science **356**(6340), 849–853 (2017)
23. Cope, A.J., Sabo, C., Vasilaki, E., Barron, A.B., Marshall, J.A.: A computational model of the integration of landmarks and motion in the insect central complex. PLoS ONE **12**(2), e0172325 (2017)
24. Kakaria, K.S., de Bivort, B.L.: Ring attractor dynamics emerge from a spiking model of the entire protocerebral bridge. Front. Behav. Neurosci. **11**, 8 (2017)
25. Homberg, U.: Flight-correlated activity changes in neurons of the lateral accessory lobes in the brain of the locust Schistocerca gregaria. J. Comp. Physiol. A **175**(5), 597–610 (1994)
26. Barron, A.B., Klein, C.: What insects can tell us about the origins of consciousness. Proc. Natl. Acad. Sci. **113**(18), 4900–4908 (2016)

# Hide and Seek: Knowledge Search in Biomimicry

Sun-Joong Kim[(⊠)] [iD]

HomoMimicus Co., Ltd, Yooseong, Daejeon 34051, Republic of Korea
sun@mimic.us

**Abstract.** Conceptual designs from nature can effectively solve complex design problems confronting mankind. Inspiration from nature helps us to generate creative and novel solutions, with numerous references and even naturally existing systems and sustainable solutions on various scales. In this research, an analogical reasoning engine for a design support system is suggested to increase the probability of success of biomimicry.

**Keywords:** Biomimicry · Design process · Analogical reasoning
Design creativity

## 1 Introduction

### 1.1 Hidden Knowledge

By what mechanisms do breakthrough innovations occur during the design process? How can we demonstrate the *creativity* of designers? Where can we apply past design experiences to future breakthrough innovations?

Generally, the secret of creative problem solving is said to be the innovative *combination of knowledge* (Herstatt and Kalogerakis 2005). In other words, when connecting a piece of knowledge to hidden knowledge in a manner never done before, the possibility of deriving a creative output becomes very high (Sternberg 1977; Sternberg and Rifkin 1979; Gick and Holyoak 1980; Herstatt and Kalogerakis 2005; Ozkan and Dogan 2013; Chai et al. 2015). At such a moment, technically, the designer who solves a problem may use an *analogical reasoning* strategy to search for the piece of the knowledge to be combined and build a network of knowledge to derive new design concepts or solutions.

Likewise, an innovative solution to a design problem can be created when knowledge pairs within a *close relationship* are newly connected via *analogical reasoning* (Herstatt and Kalogerakis 2005; Ozkan and Dogan 2013). Of course, the *close relationship* here indicates not only knowledge pairs in *synonymous relationships* but also knowledge pairs in *antonymous relationships*. When utilizing an analogical reasoning strategy such as *anomaly*, it is possible to combine antonymous knowledge pairs to generate brand new solutions (Gentner and Markman 1997).

However, when thinking conventionally, consciously attempting to renew a method of knowledge combination is clearly not easy. Specifically, searching for hidden

V. Vouloutsi et al. (Eds.): Living Machines 2018, LNAI 10928, pp. 471–476, 2018.
https://doi.org/10.1007/978-3-319-95972-6_50

knowledge of outside of one's own knowledge is virtually impossible, and pairing new with conventional knowledge can be too risky (Terninko et al. 1998).

## 1.2    Seek Knowledge from Nature

As a design method, biomimicry provides toolkits by which to apply hidden knowledge to devise a design solution (Carroll et al. 2005; Sartori et al. 2010; Shu et al. 2011). This process is iterative and involves convergent and divergent design thinking processes, similar to many other design methods (Nagel et al. 2017). However, the most important method when searching for highly suitable analogues as part of the biomimicry design process has yet to be discovered. Nonetheless, many seekers (designers) must find hidden knowledge with their own skills. In other words, unfortunately, the design method (biomimicry) appears to guarantee the application of hidden knowledge from nature, but biomimicry itself cannot guarantee that one will be successful when seeking knowledge. In the real world, this knowledge-seeking task heavily relies upon the knowledge space of the design team (Herstatt and Kalogerakis 2005; Goel et al. 2012). As a natural consequence, a small knowledge space in nature will only offer a slim chance of successful knowledge finding (Dickinson 1999). This limitation seriously invokes solution-driven biomimicry and not problem-driven biomimicry (Fig. 1).

**Fig. 1.**  Difference between problem-driven biomimicry and solution-driven biomimicry

A systematic tool by which to reduce the reliance on designers has been suggested to expand the solution space of biomimicry. Computational support is expected to increase the knowledge space used in biomimicry dramatically, which currently remains at 0.2% of the total knowledge of nature, as determined by the percentage of the number of species which have been applied to biomimicry (Jacobs et al. 2014). In this manner, the suggested computational supporting mechanisms seek to increase the success rate of biomimicry (Kim and Lee 2017). However, computational support still cannot meet the needs, as it cannot fully support the analogical reasoning process of designers.

## 2   Methodology

### 2.1   Computational Supports for Knowledge Seeking in Biomimicry

The needs of the problem-driven biomimicry and the development of computational support have arisen from the engineering design domain to reduce the reliance to the knowledge space of an individual designer or advisor. Specifically, these computational supporting systems have the goal of revealing undiscovered or hidden knowledge incubated by nature (Kindlein and Guanabara 2005). Most knowledge seeking scenarios involving computational tools encompass the theoretical background of analogical reasoning, which is fundamental for biomimicry. This explains why many of these tools recommend knowledge pieces using the explicitly defined functionality for a design problem. Hence, the knowledge seeking process for a biomimicry design can be modeled as a process of building a proposition of an analogy: (A:B::C:D) (Fig. 2).

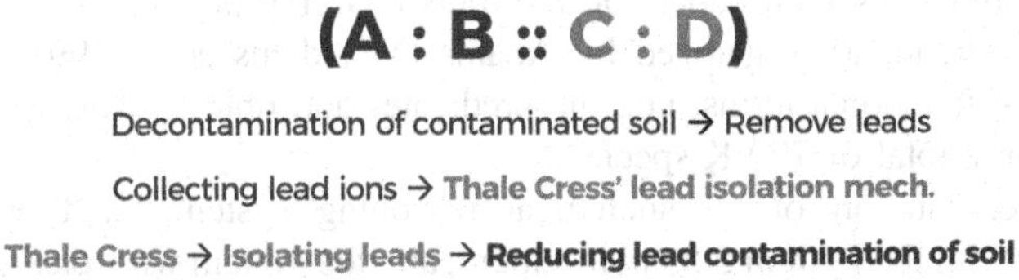

## (A : B :: C : D)

Decontamination of contaminated soil → Remove leads

Collecting lead ions → Thale Cress' lead isolation mech.

Thale Cress → Isolating leads → **Reducing lead contamination of soil**

**Fig. 2.** Proposition example of the knowledge seeking process in biomimicry

### 2.2   Systematic Analogical Reasoning and Biomimicry

However, not all knowledge search systems sophisticatedly support analogical reasoning. Mostly, the functionality of a system is limited to accepting a query in the style of functional decomposition. Examples include "*collect lead ions*" or "*remove leads*" in the style of a combination of a predicate and an object. Moreover, these systems cannot

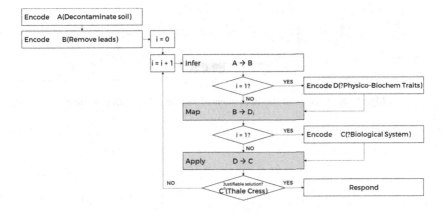

**Fig. 3.** Algorithm for analogical reasoning in biomimicry

provide reasoning for related functions pertaining to, for instance, the "*decontamination of contaminated soil*" (a design problem) or biological system related to the desired functions, such as "*thale cress*" (a biological system) (Fig. 3).

## 2.3   Data Collection and Implementation

Building an expert system to support the analogical reasoning process for biomimicry can resolve both the reliance problem which arises during the knowledge seeking process and the biased tendencies associated with solution-driven biomimicry. This system is expected to have the functionalities of (1) decomposing a design problem into several related functions, and (2) recommending physico-biochemical traits and their biological systems.

A knowledgebase which operates with these types of logic must contain an index of functional jargon containing the predicates and objects as well as the physical, biological, and chemical traits of biological systems as well. The system presented here contains 20 million research papers on the traits of living organisms. In addition, the function word dictionary organized by Adams (McAdams et al. 1999) was used to standardize the functional terms, i.e., the predicates and objects. The system contains information on a total of 700 K species.

The implementation of an analogical reasoning system for biomimicry was accomplished with the Python 3.5 environment, and the system was released to the web using the AWS serverless service (Fig. 4).

**Fig. 4.** Screenshot of the implemented analogical reasoning system

# 3   Conclusion

In this research, an analogical reasoning process for the biomimicry was suggested. This system is expected to resolve several problems of current computational toolkits. With the proposed systematic algorithm for analogical reasoning, an expert system could be designed and implemented as a web service.

As future research, the ecological traits of species will be indexed to explain qualitatively the reasoning result printed out by this system (Ptacek and Hankinson 2009). Regarding the actual use of this system, the functionality of case reuse must be implemented in the system. This is left for future research.

# References

Carroll, S.B., Greineir, J.K., Weatherbee, S.D.: From DNA to Diversity. Blackwell Publishings, Oxford (2005)

Chai, C., Cen, F., Ruan, W., Yang, C., Li, H.: Behavioral analysis of analogical reasoning in design: differences among designers with different expertise levels. Des. Stud. **36**, 3–30 (2015)

Dickinson, M.H.: Bionics: Biological insight into mechanical design. Proc. Nat. Acad. Sci. Unit. States Am. **96**(25), 14208–14209 (1999)

Gentner, D., Markman, A.B.: Structure mapping in analogy and similarity. Am. Psychol. **52**(1), 45–56 (1997)

Gick, M.L., Holyoak, K.J.: Analogical problem solving. Cogn. Psychol. **12**, 306–355 (1980)

Goel, A.K., Vattam, S., Wiltgen, B., Helms, M.: Cognitive, collaborative, conceptual and creative – four characteristics of the next generation of knowledge-based CAD systems: a study in biologically inspired design. Comput. Aided Des. **44**(10), 879–900 (2012)

Herstatt, C., Kalogerakis, K.: How to use analogies for breakthrough innovations. Int. J. Innov. Technol. Manag. **2**(3), 331–347 (2005)

Jacobs, S.R., Nichol, E.C., Helms, M.E.: "Where are we now and where are we going?" The BioM innovation database. J. Mech. Des. **136**(11), 10 (2014)

Kim, S.-J., Lee, J.-H.: A study on metadata structure and recommenders of biological systems to support bio-inspired design. Eng. Appl. Artif. Intell. **57**, 16–37 (2017)

Kindlein, W., Guanabara, A.S.: Methodology for product design based on the study of bionics. Mater. Des. **26**(2), 149–155 (2005)

Nagel, J.K.S., Rose, C.S., Pidaparti, R., Beverly, C.L., Pittman, P.L.: Teaching Bio-Inspired Design Using C-K Theory. American Society for Engineering Education (2017)

McAdams, D.A., Stone, R.B., Wood, K.L.: Functional interdependence and product similarity based on customer needs. Res. Eng. Des. **11**, 1–19 (1999)

Ozkan, O., Dogan, F.: Cognitive strategies of analogical reasoning in design: differences between expert and novice designers. Des. Stud. **34**, 161–192 (2013)

Ptacek, M.B., Hankinson, S.J.: The Pattern and process of speciation. In: Evolution. The Belknap Press of Harvard University Press, Cambridge (2009)

Sartori, J., Pal, U., Chakrabarti, A.: A methodology for supporting 'Transfer' in biomimetic design. Artif. Intell. Eng. Des. Anal. Manuf. **24**(4), 483–506 (2010)

Shu, L.H., Ueda, K., Chiu, I., Cheong, H.: Biologically inspired design. CIRP Annal.: Manuf. Technol. **60**(2), 673–693 (2011)

Sternberg, R.J.: Component processes in analogical reasoning. Psychol. Rev. **84**(4), 353–378 (1977)

Sternberg, R.J., Rifkin, B.: The development of analogical reasoning processes. J. Exper. Child Psychol. **27**, 195–232 (1979)

Terninko, J., Zusman, A., Zlotin, B.: Systematic Innovation: An Introduction to TRIZ. St. Lucie Press, Boca Raton (1998)

# Direction-Specific Footpaths Can Be Predicted by the Motion of a Single Point on the Body of the Fruit Fly *Drosophila Melanogaster*

Nicholas S. Szczecinski[(✉)], Ansgar Büschges, and Till Bockemühl

University of Cologne, Cologne, Germany
nszczeci@uni-koeln.de

**Abstract.** This work presents a probabilistic mathematical model for generating footpaths in an insect's frame of reference, based on its body's (i.e. thorax's) motion in the ground frame of reference. This model uses digitized video data of fruit flies walking freely on a transparent surface to track the location of each foot and the motion of the body while in stance phase. We use this data to tune a rigid body kinematic model that predicts the motion of the feet, given the body's motion. The result is a model that can be used to study other aspects of insect locomotion, or used to generate stepping motions for an insect-like robot.

**Keywords:** *Drosophila melanogaster* · Walking · Kinematics

## 1 Introduction

Insects encode walking direction in the central complex, and these signals modulate reflexes in the thoracic ganglia to change walking direction ([1], for a review see [2]). While the brain has an internal representation of how the *body* is moving in space, it is not known how these signals are converted into *foot* motion during walking. Models suggest that local networks could interpret walking speed and direction to generate foot trajectories [3]. Experiments with tethered curve-walking animals on a slippery surface support this hypothesis, because the legs in each segment clearly produce directional steps, even though proprioceptive coupling between the feet via the ground is absent [4, 5]. During these experiments, however, it is difficult to know the animal's intended direction of locomotion, because the body is held stationary. Therefore, to better understand how the motion of the body correlates with footpaths during walking, we conducted experiments with freely-walking fruit flies, and observed how footpaths depend on body motion.

The fruit fly *Drosophila* is a good model for exploring the control of animal locomotion. Previous studies have shown that fruit flies exhibit a speed-dependent continuum of interleg coordination [6], just like other insect species [7]. Their walking direction can be controlled by signals transmitted through sparse descending connectives [8], consistent with what is known about locomotion control in other insects.

One can also study the descending control of locomotion via neuromechanical simulations [5] and robots [9]. Such a model or robot would need to control the motion of the feet given the agent's intended body motion. Of course, legs that are simultaneously

© Springer International Publishing AG, part of Springer Nature 2018
V. Vouloutsi et al. (Eds.): Living Machines 2018, LNAI 10928, pp. 477–489, 2018.
https://doi.org/10.1007/978-3-319-95972-6_51

in stance phase must follow kinematic constraints dictated by rigid body kinematics [10], and likely use sensory feedback to solve the problem of reducing internal forces between the legs [7]. However, this leaves many questions unanswered, such as where the feet are placed in each step, and if the insect has a specific frame of reference in which it specifies such placement.

In this work, we filmed fruit flies walking freely in an arena, and quantified their footpaths in the fly's frame of reference (FFR) for a continuum of walking speeds and directions. Then, we constructed a kinematic model that relates the motion of the body to the motion of the feet in the FFR. This model only has one parameter to tune, $Q$, a point on the fly's body in the FFR that has no lateral velocity. Thus, the forward speed of this point and angular velocity of the body fully describe the animal's motion in the plane of the substrate. We show that this model captures the animal footpaths well, and demonstrate how it may be used to generate a probability distribution of animal-like stance paths. In general, our data shows that the body's motion is an excellent predictor of footpaths during free walking, and may be used to enhance models and robots in the future.

## 2  Methods

### 2.1  Animal Experiments

Here, we used *Drosophila melanogaster* of the wildtype strain Berlin and the mutant strain $w^{1118}$, $Tbh^{nM18}$ [11]. The Tbh mutant has strongly reduced levels of octopamine, a noradrenaline-analogue in invertebrates; consequently, Tbh mutants walk more slowly [6], thus extending the observable range of walking speeds. Flies were reared under normal conditions, with a 12 h/12 h light/dark cycle and were kept on standard food. Flies used in experiments were between 3 and 10 days old. To increase the tendency for spontaneous walking we starved fruit flies for one day prior to an experiment but provided water. The arena (80 mm diameter) consisted of an inverted petri dish onto which the fly was placed. To prevent escape we covered the arena with a watch glass. Walking flies were recorded with a high-speed video camera (Vieworks, model VC-2MC-M340E0-CM) at 200 Hz via a surface mirror in an area of approximately 30 by 30 mm in the center of the arena. A ring of IR LEDs (870 nm) illuminated the arena and was synced to video acquisition. To elicit curve walking we made use of the optomotor response in insects and presented two rotating vertical bars on an LED display (160 by 40 LEDs, wavelength 470 nm) that surrounded the arena [12]. Videos frames were acquired continuously into a ring buffer of several seconds duration. Data acquisition was triggered automatically after a fly produced a sufficiently long walking track (approx. 10 body lengths). Each track recorded in this way constituted a single trial for subsequent data analysis.

### 2.2  Experimental Data Annotation

For each frame of each trial, we used custom-written routines in Matlab that first located the fly and then rotated and translated the frame to center and orient the fly.

Manual annotation on a frame-by-frame basis provided the anterior extreme positions (AEP) of each step in body-centered as well as arena-centered coordinates, establishing the time and location of touch-down. During the stance phase, the leg tips are rigidly attached to the ground; therefore, we were able to extrapolate the complete footpaths based on the first touch-down location. User input is only required to determine the time of lift-off at the posterior extreme position (PEP). Note that the complete tarsus is not entirely rigid and bends very slightly. These movements were neglected here, since they did not have any influence on the actual position of contact.

Using the time and location of the AEPs and PEPs of each step, as well as the position and orientation of the fly, subsequent routines extracted each step of each leg and computed the foot's path during that step, the step's duration, and the translation and rotation of the body throughout that step. Then, steps from each leg of the same individual (across multiple trials) were combined.

## 2.3    Mathematical Model

Our model is based on rigid body kinematics [10]. The underlying idea is that when the body of the animal moves relative to the ground, all of the feet in stance phase must have velocities of 0 relative to one another and the ground. It would be simple to control the feet from the global frame of reference, simply requiring that all stance phase feet stay in place. However, the animal must control the motion of its feet *in its own frame of reference*, which gives rise to non-obvious, nonlinear relationships between the motion of the body and the motion of the feet. In this section, we use the kinematics of the body to derive the nonlinear, asymmetrical mapping between body motion and foot motion.

Figure 1 shows a schematic of a fly, with three legs drawn in stance phase (the others are omitted). The ground coordinate axes are labeled with the subscript "G". This frame of reference does not translate or rotate. The FFR axes are labeled with the subscript "$F_i$". This coordinate system translates and rotates with the animal's body. Our video data records each step in $n + 1$ frames, and the subscript "i" indicates that the measurements corresponds to the $i^{th}$ frame.

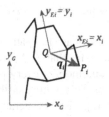

**Fig. 1.** A simplified schematic showing a fly (hexagon) with three legs in contact with the ground. Two coordinate axes are drawn: the ground frame (subscript G), and the fly's frame of reference at video frame i (subscript F, i).

**Model Parameters.** The model assumes that the body has one point, $Q$, attached to the FFR, which has no lateral velocity in the FFR (i.e. $\dot{Q} \cdot x_i = 0$). This implies that the velocity of the body relative to the ground is determined by the forward speed of $Q$, and the rotation of the body about $Q$. A particular foot's location, $P_i$, does not change in the ground frame of reference when it is in stance. However, it *does* change in the FFR as the body translates and rotates throughout a step. We assume that the body translates distance $r$ in the $y_F$ direction and rotates $\psi$ in the $z_F$ direction over the course of one step, at a constant rate. This is a simplification, because the animal does rock side-to-side as it walks [7]. However, we will show that this simplification does not reduce the model's utility. In this case, the vector $q_i = P_i - Q$ (i.e. the position of the foot relative to the body, in the FFR) can be transformed from frame $i$ to frame $i + 1$ with the rigid body transformation:

$$q_{i+1} = R(-\psi/n) \cdot q_i - \frac{r}{n} \cdot y_{i+1},  \tag{1}$$

where $n + 1$ is the number of frames per step, where frame $n/2$ is the PEP, frame $-n/2$ is the AEP, and

$$R(-\psi/n) = \begin{bmatrix} cos\frac{-\psi}{n} & -sin\frac{-\psi}{n} \\ sin\frac{-\psi}{n} & cos\frac{-\psi}{n} \end{bmatrix}.  \tag{2}$$

Thus, if the position of a foot is known at any point throughout stance phase, the body's motion throughout that stance phase can be used to calculate the trajectory of the foot in the FFR. This calculation implicitly assumes that each leg steps at the same frequency; previous studies have shown this to be the case in *Drosophila*, e.g. [6].

This calculation can be simplified if it is known that every stance phase trajectory passes through a particular point, $P_0$, no matter the body's motion. Our model assumes that this point is halfway between the AEP and PEP, along the stance trajectory. Figure 2A shows that the halfway point between the AEP and PEP forms tight clusters, with standard deviations of these clusters along the major axis of the distribution typically between 20% and 25% of the step amplitude (here defined as the distance between AEP and PEP in body-centered coordinates). This is tight considering that it includes data from the animal moving with a diverse mix of step amplitudes and path curvatures (Fig. 2B).

We can calculate the entire stance phase footpath when $r, \psi$, and $P_0$ are known, and we choose a value for $Q$. We assume that $Q$ lies along the midline of the body, although, like the rear axle of an automobile, every point on the $x$ axis has no lateral velocity. Choosing $Q$ represents the only tuning in this model, which effectively has only one parameter. Then, we use Eqs. 1 and 2 iteratively to compute $q_{\frac{n}{2}} = P_{PEP} - Q$:

$$q_{\frac{n}{2}} = [R(-\psi/n)]^{\frac{n}{2}} \cdot q_0 - \sum_{i=1}^{\frac{n}{2}} [R(-\psi/n)]^i \cdot r/n \cdot \hat{J}_i.  \tag{3}$$

## Despite a diversity of $r$ and $\psi$ values, $P_0$ is consistent for each leg.

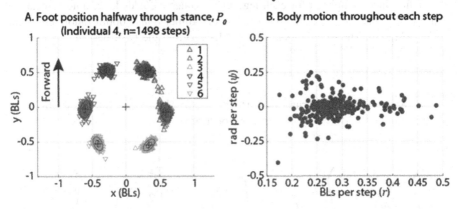

**A.** Foot position halfway through stance, $P_0$ (Individual 4, n=1498 steps)

**B.** Body motion throughout each step

**Fig. 2.** A. Each foot's path passes through a very small region in the FFR, regardless of the step amplitude or direction of walking. B. A scatter plot of the body's motion throughout each step shown in (A). Note that there is a wide diversity of body motion.

To find $q_{-\frac{n}{2}} = P_{AEP} - Q$, we must first rearrange Eq. 1 to find $q_i$ in terms of $q_{i+1}$:

$$q_i = R^{-1}(-\psi/n) \cdot \left( q_{i+1} + \frac{r}{n} \cdot y_{i+1} \right) \tag{4}$$

Using this equation iteratively yields the expression for the AEP:

$$q_{-\frac{n}{2}} = \left[ R^{-1}(-\psi/n) \right]^{\frac{n}{2}} \cdot q_0 - \sum_{i=1}^{\frac{n}{2}} \left[ R^{-1}(-\psi/n) \right]^i \cdot r/n \cdot \hat{J}_i. \tag{5}$$

Figure 3 illustrates the process of calculating the footpaths based on $r, \psi, P_0$, and $Q$ with a simple, fabricated example. In this example, $n = 4$. For the animals, however, $n$ was usually about 14. The top row shows the state of the model at five frames throughout stance phase. Note that while $P$ does not change in the ground frame of reference, it does change in the FFR. The bottom row shows the transition between each pair of frames, applying a portion of the body's total transformation throughout this step. Note that this transformation is applied in the FFR.

To select the $Q$ of best fit, we follow the process illustrated in Fig. 4. Given a particular value of $Q$, the distribution of all possible $P_0$, and the body's motion $(r, \psi)$, a distribution of possible footpaths is generated. The shape of these footpaths depends strongly on the value of $Q$. These footpaths are mapped into the step amplitude (i.e. the distance the foot travels during stance phase relative to the thorax, abbreviated $M$) and stride angle ($\phi$) space. These values are used to plot surface mappings $f_M : (r, \psi) \to M$ and $f_\phi : (r, \psi) \to \phi$. Because $P_0$ is a distribution of points, not a single point, this surface mapping has a location-dependent variation. Then, the coefficient of determination, $r^2$, between these surface mappings and the animal data *outside the variation of the surface mappings* are calculated, to quantify the goodness of it. It should be noted that the coefficient of determination for a nonlinear fit can be smaller than 0, unlike for a linear fit. Once completed for each leg, all $r^2$ values are added, yielding a scalar to maximize to find the best fit. We used a one-dimensional optimization program, *fminbnd* (Matlab, The Mathworks, Natick, MA), to find the $Q$ of best fit.

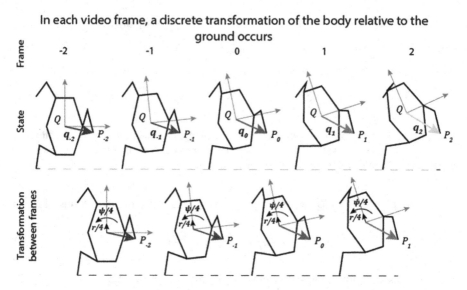

**Fig. 3.** As the body moves in each video frame, it not only changes $q = P - Q$, but also the position and orientation of the FFR. Each step can be split into a number of discrete transformations between frames, enabling the calculation of the AEP and PEP given an estimation of $r$, $\psi$, and $P_0$.

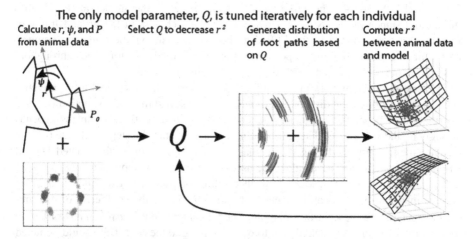

**Fig. 4.** Illustration of the tuning process for $Q$. See the text for a description.

## 3   Results

Raw data from the animal reveals clear changes in footpaths as the body's motion changes. Figure 5 shows footpaths in the FFR from one animal trial. The footpaths are color coded by $\psi$, the body rotation per step (scale on the right). Feet on the inside of turns (red on right, blue on left) make short, strongly directional motions to pull the animal in the intended direction. Feet on the outside of turns (blue on right, red on left) make longer, less directional motions to push the body faster on that side. The hind legs do not show much variation in length or direction.

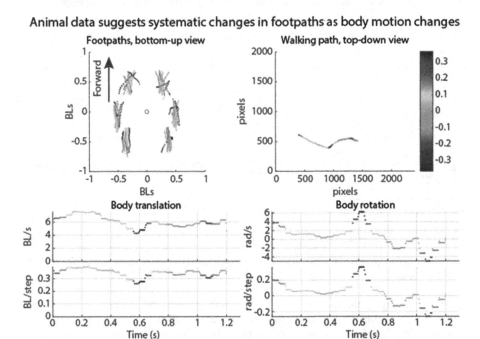

**Fig. 5.** Raw data from the animal suggests that body motion may enable one to predict footpaths based on body motion and measurements of the animal. All traces are color coded by the body rotation, measured in radians per step. (Color figure online)

The animal data supports our decision to use spatial parameters to describe body motion. The body translation is displayed both in terms of the body lengths per second and the body lengths per step. These traces are nearly identical (aside from scale), suggesting that using the spatial parameter accurately captures the animal's motion, without requiring us to explicitly consider time in our model. The same can be said for the body rotation plots.

Our model enables us to produce a distribution of stance phase foot trajectories given the body's motion. Figure 6 shows example traces for a particular individual and specific values of $(r, \psi)$. Figure 6A shows that the value of $Q$ has a strong effect on the shape of the footpaths. Figure 6B shows how $M$ and $\phi$ change as a function of $\psi$, given a particular value for $r$. Examining this transformation of the data is useful because previous studies of insect locomotion have summarized footpaths with these metrics [4, 5]. One should note that these curves have very specific nonlinear characteristics, which $Q$ strongly influences. Specifically, one can observe that as $Q$ is moved to the rear of the animal: 1. the variation in $M$ increases in the front legs; 2. both $M$ and $\phi$ become more asymmetrical in the middle legs; and 3. the variation in $M$ decreases in the hind legs.

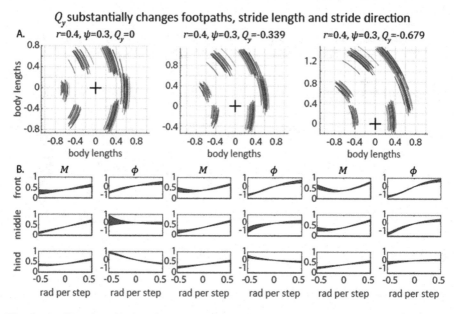

**Fig. 6.** A. Changing the location of $Q$ on the body changes the footpaths required for a particular body motion. The same body motion is produced in all three plots, but the foot motions are distinct. B. Changing the location of $Q$ on the body changes how the step amplitude, $M$, and the stride direction, $\phi$, vary with the body rotation per step, $\psi$.

Our nonlinear model captures much of the variation in the animal's data (i.e. $M$ and $\psi$). Figure 7 shows three-dimensional scatter plots of animal data, with the surfaces of best fit based on our model. The goal is not for the reader to compare the data and the surface, as much as for the reader to gain an intuitive understanding of how our model predicts $M$ and $\phi$ should change with $r$ and $\psi$. Specifically, the model produces highly nonlinear surfaces, not based on splining data points from the animal, but because of the kinematic constraints that exist within a closed-chain system of an animal with multiple legs on the ground.

## Nonlinear model captures variation in animal data, with only one free parameter.

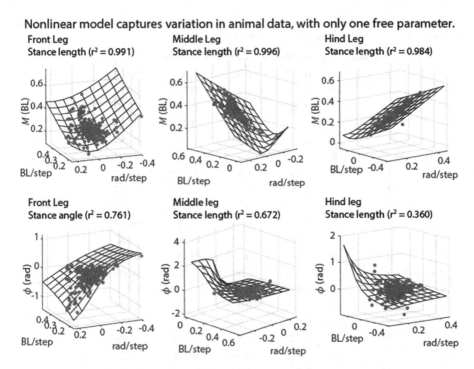

**Fig. 7.** Example surfaces from our model (meshes) and data from an individual fruit fly (points) relating the body motion to the step amplitude, $M$, and the stride angle, $\phi$. The nonlinear shapes are not due to fitting a spline to the data; instead, the nonlinear shapes arise from the kinematics of the fruit fly.

To quantitatively compare the data and the surface, Table 1 shows the $r^2$ value for the fit for each leg of each individual. Our model generates a highly constrained, nonlinear relationship between the body motion and footpaths, whose parameters have physical meaning for the animal. To compare our model to a simpler approach, Table 1 also shows the $R^2$ for a plane of best fit, computed via linear least squares minimization. In general, our model predicts the footpaths as accurately as or more accurately than the linear least squares fit. In addition, our model does not simply quantify correlation, like the linear fit; instead, it is a generative and predictive model, enabling us to measure quantities from the animal, and produce a distribution of possible footpaths when walking in any direction. Each individual shows idiosyncratic values of $Q$. Table 2 shows this value for each individual. In general, $Q$ is between the middle and hind legs.

**Table 1.** Coefficient of determination ($r^2$) of model fits. Columns that correspond to the nonlinear model presented in this paper are shaded.

| Individual | Leg | $M$, Nonlin. | $M$, Planar | $\phi$, Nonlin. | $\phi$, Planar |
|---|---|---|---|---|---|
| 1 | 1 | 0.977 | 0.960 | 0.583 | 0.502 |
| 1 | 2 | 0.990 | 0.984 | 0.233 | 0.131 |
| 1 | 3 | 0.985 | 0.962 | 0.259 | 0.103 |
| 1 | 4 | 0.984 | 0.954 | 0.472 | 0.456 |
| 1 | 5 | 0.995 | 0.983 | 0.311 | 0.180 |
| 1 | 6 | 0.980 | 0.970 | 0.207 | 0.087 |
| 2 | 1 | 0.997 | 0.987 | 0.682 | 0.616 |
| 2 | 2 | 0.980 | 0.978 | 0.405 | 0.027 |
| 2 | 3 | 0.973 | 0.987 | 0.576 | 0.458 |
| 2 | 4 | 0.990 | 0.951 | 0.899 | 0.845 |
| 2 | 5 | 0.996 | 0.990 | 0.590 | 0.382 |
| 2 | 6 | 0.972 | 0.963 | 0.753 | 0.614 |
| 3 | 1 | 0.971 | 0.951 | 0.627 | 0.602 |
| 3 | 2 | 0.988 | 0.994 | 0.410 | 0.476 |
| 3 | 3 | 0.948 | 0.972 | 0.361 | 0.239 |
| 3 | 4 | 0.973 | 0.982 | 0.694 | 0.659 |
| 3 | 5 | 0.989 | 0.992 | 0.093 | 0.098 |
| 3 | 6 | 0.942 | 0.989 | 0.318 | 0.239 |
| 4 | 1 | 0.991 | 0.893 | 0.761 | 0.685 |
| 4 | 2 | 0.996 | 0.992 | 0.562 | 0.439 |
| 4 | 3 | 0.984 | 0.975 | 0.360 | 0.236 |
| 4 | 4 | 0.985 | 0.895 | 0.788 | 0.755 |
| 4 | 5 | 0.996 | 0.983 | 0.672 | 0.228 |
| 4 | 6 | 0.990 | 0.985 | 0.257 | 0.058 |
| 5 | 1 | 0.897 | 0.730 | 0.946 | 0.685 |
| 5 | 2 | 0.996 | 0.963 | 0.877 | 0.439 |
| 5 | 3 | 0.974 | 0.867 | 0.918 | 0.236 |
| 5 | 4 | 0.993 | 0.906 | 0.880 | 0.755 |
| 5 | 5 | 0.991 | 0.992 | 0.685 | 0.228 |
| 5 | 6 | 0.929 | 0.927 | 0.351 | 0.058 |
| 6 | 1 | 0.966 | 0.933 | 0.767 | 0.767 |
| 6 | 2 | 0.959 | 0.945 | 0.779 | 0.562 |
| 6 | 3 | 0.864 | 0.975 | 0.159 | 0.366 |
| 6 | 4 | 0.940 | 0.932 | 0.608 | 0.595 |
| 6 | 5 | 0.906 | 0.984 | 0.474 | 0.159 |
| 6 | 6 | 0.800 | 0.902 | 0.260 | 0.096 |

**Table 2.** Location of $Q$ for each individual.

| Individual | $Q$ (BLs) |
|---|---|
| 1 | −0.242 |
| 2 | −0.188 |
| 3 | −0.198 |
| 4 | −0.339 |
| 5 | −0.336 |
| 6 | −0.370 |

## 4 Discussion

In this work, we present a model for generating footpaths in an animal's frame of reference based on the body's motion in the ground frame of reference. This calculation is based on the kinematics of the body, and assumes that the animal has one point, $Q$, that has no lateral velocity in its own frame of reference. This calculation also assumes that each leg has some point, $P_0$, that the foot passes through in every step, no matter the body's motion throughout the step. Using digitized animal data, we can calculate the locations of these points that minimize the prediction error of the model. This one-parameter, nonlinear model captures more variability than an 18-parameter, linear model. Our model can then be used to generate a distribution of possible footpaths, given the body's motion.

Such a model is important because the animal must control its motion in the ground frame of reference to forage, escape predators, and find mates, but can only control motion within its own frame of reference. Recordings from the central complex of insects suggest that the animal can encode its motion in the ground frame of reference, that is, its speed and direction of travel [1, 2]. Measurements of insects' footpaths while they walk on a slippery surface suggests that each leg significantly changes its motion to move the body in different directions [4, 5]. Therefore, somewhere in the nervous system the animal must make a transformation between its location and orientation in the world, and how it moves its legs relative to its own body.

Given the relatively low number of neurons in insects and even lower number of descending neurons between the brain and ventral nerve cord that are potentially able to control low level motor output it seems plausible, that these transformations rely on sparse and compact parameters similar to $Q$. Understanding the relationship between current position and orientation, intended changes, and the necessary motor commands enables mathematical modelers to explore what considerations the animal must make during this transform, such as the timing between steps with different legs. It is also useful to robot controllers, although the authors do not intend this model to generate robotic footpaths in real-time; instead, it is meant to aid in parameter tuning of other walking controllers, for instance in [3].

In spite of the initial success of this model, there are still improvements to be made. In general, the model predicts the stance direction of the hind legs less accurately. The reason for this is unclear, but we have several possible explanations. $Q$ was located towards the posterior end of every animal. Geometrically, a small change in the location of $Q$ would have a larger effect on the stride direction $\phi$ of the hind legs than the front. This suggests that the control of the middle and hind legs may need to be more precise than that of the front legs. Another possibility is that our assumption that the point $Q$ is in a constant location on the body is insufficient. Indeed, an animal may wish to change this point depending on its current behavior (e.g. *Drosophila* courtship behavior, during which males extensively strafe side to side). In the future, we will expand this model to consider more general movement conditions of the body.

The fruit fly's small size makes this experiment relatively easy to run, because a static camera can capture a comparatively large walking area for the animal without extreme magnification or moving the camera. However, its small size prevents measuring the individual joint angles during locomotion. What is needed in the future is an experimental setup that will enable the same experiments to be performed in larger insects, whom can be easily marked for limb tracking [13, 14]. Such a method would enable the experimenter to simultaneously measure the motion of the body, feet, and leg joints, elucidating changes that take place at the joint level during curve walking.

Previous studies have suggested that there is a discontinuous, left-right dichotomy to the control of turning in insects [5, 15]. However, the continuous nature of the data and the model in this work suggest that the nervous system could accomplish such locomotion with a continuous, but highly nonlinear system. It is difficult to answer whether the nervous system controls turning in a side-specific manner without more invasive experiments. However, future experiments with tethered insects might make use of the method in this paper to estimate the animal's intended body motion, thus connecting changes in neural activity to the animal's precise direction of locomotion.

# References

1. Martin, J.P., Guo, P., Mu, L., Harley, C.M., Ritzmann, R.E.: Central-complex control of movement in the freely walking cockroach. Curr. Biol. **25**, 2795–2803 (2015)
2. Varga, A.G., Kathman, N.D., Martin, J.P., Guo, P., Ritzmann, R.E.: Spatial navigation and the central complex: sensory acquisition, orientation, and motor control. Front. Behav. Neurosci. **11**, 4 (2017)
3. Szczecinski, N.S., Quinn, R.D.: Template for the neural control of directed walking generalized to all legs of mantisbot. Bioinspir. Biom. **12**(4), 045001 (2017)
4. Gruhn, M., Zehl, L., Buschges, A.: Straight walking and turning on a slippery surface. J. Exp. Biol. **212**, 194–209 (2009)
5. Szczecinski, N.S., Brown, A.E., Bender, J.A., Quinn, R.D., Ritzmann, R.E.: A neuromechanical simulation of insect walking and transition to turning of the cockroach Blaberus discoidalis. Biol. Cybern. **108**, 1–21 (2014)
6. Wosnitza, A., Bockemühl, T., Dübbert, M., Scholz, H., Büschges, A.: Inter-leg coordination in the control of walking speed in drosophila. J. Exp. Biol. **216**, 480–491 (2013)
7. Dürr, V., Theunissen, L.M., Dallmann, C.J., Hoinville, T., Schmitz, J.: Motor flexibility in insects: adaptive coordination of limbs in locomotion and near-range exploration. Behav. Ecol. Sociobiol. **72**, 1–21 (2018)
8. Bidaye, S.S., Machacek, C., Wu, Y., Dickson, B.J.: Neuronal control of drosophila walking direction. Science **344**, 97–101 (2014)

9. Szczecinski, N.S., Getsy, A.P., Martin, J.P., Ritzmann, R.E., Quinn, R.D.: MantisBot is a robotic model of visually guided motion in the praying mantis. Arthropod Struct. Dev. **46**(5), 736–751 (2017)

10. Murray, R.M., Li, Z., Sastry, S.S.: A Mathematical Introduction to Robotic Manipulation. CRC Press, Boca Raton (1994)

11. Monastirioti, M., Linn, C.E., White, K.: Characterization of Drosophila tyramine beta-hydroxylase gene and isolation of mutant flies lacking octopamine. J. Neurosci. **16**, 3900–3911 (1996)

12. Reiser, M.B., Dickinson, M.H.: A modular display system for insect behavioral neuroscience. J. Neurosci. Meth. **167**, 127–139 (2008)

13. Bender, J.A., Simpson, E.M., Ritzmann, R.E.: Computer-assisted 3D kinematic analysis of all leg joints in walking insects. PLoS ONE **5**, e13617 (2010)

14. Dallmann, C.J., Dürr, V., Schmitz, J.: Joint torques in a freely walking insect reveal distinct functions of leg joints in propulsion and posture control. Proc. Biol. Sci. **283**, 20151708 (2016)

15. Gruhn, M., Rosenbaum, P., Bockemühl, T., Büschges, A.: Body side-specific control of motor activity during turning in a walking animal. eLife **5**, e13799 (2016)

# A Novel Spatially Resolved 3D Force Sensor for Animal Biomechanics and Robotic Grasping Hands

Séverine Toussaint[1,2(✉)] ⓘ and Artémis Llamosi[3] ⓘ

[1] UFR Sciences du Vivant, Université Paris Diderot,
Sorbonne Universités, Paris, France
[2] CR2P, UMR 7207, CNRS/MNHN/UPMC, Paris, France
severine.toussaint@mnhn.fr
[3] Laboratoire Matière et Systèmes Complexes, UMR 7057,
Université Paris Diderot, CNRS, Paris, France
artemis.llamosi@gmail.com

**Abstract.** Possessing a sense of touch is fundamental for robots to grasp and operate in unknown environments. Nevertheless, force sensing technologies adapted for manipulative abilities are still less mature than vision in commercial robots. Here we present a novel spatially-resolved force sensor allowing the dynamic measurement of both the intensity and the direction of forces exerted on a custom-shaped surface. Originally designed for the study of grasping biomechanics in arboreal primates, this sensor meets several challenges in engineering robotic skin. Importantly, the sensor's ability to measure friction forces would be instrumental for robotic hands to grasp deformable and unknown objects. This sensor is composed of independent measuring points made in soft, biocompatible, weather resistant and EMI resistant material. Based on optical measurements of deformations, this sensor array presents an adaptable architecture where one to hundreds of force measurement points can be handled simultaneously. We present two prototypes, a flat one and a cylindrical one, designed to demonstrates the performance of this sensor in reconstructing normal and tangential forces. Mimicking the grasping properties of our small primate models, we created these prototypes for forces under 3N, with a spatial resolution of 4 points per cm². We will discuss the numerous adaptation options of this system along with its potential applications for dexterous robotic hands.

**Keywords:** 3D force sensor · Grasping · Biomechanics · Robotic hand

## 1 Extended Abstract

Grasping capabilities play an essential role for locomotion, feeding and social interaction in a wide variety of tetrapod vertebrates [1]. In primates, grasping hands and feet are also crucial in manipulative behaviors and are central for understanding their origins and evolution. Indeed, the ability to oppose the thumb from the other individualized digits and the possession of nails instead of claws constitute defining characters of the whole order of Primates. Yet, the evolutive history of these morphological features is still poorly understood and is under active research. For instance, it is still

© Springer International Publishing AG, part of Springer Nature 2018
V. Vouloutsi et al. (Eds.): Living Machines 2018, LNAI 10928, pp. 490–493, 2018.
https://doi.org/10.1007/978-3-319-95972-6_52

unclear how and why did nails appeared and with which function. Two possible explanations are that it confers a better sensitivity and/or permits to apply stronger forces on the fingertips [2]. Therefore, investigating primate hand and foot biomechanics, such as forces applied by the fingers while grasping, connects to fundamental questions concerning primate origins.

Here we present a novel spatially-resolved force sensor which allows the dynamic measurement of both the intensity and the direction of forces exerted on a custom-shaped surface. This technology was developed specifically for measuring small arboreal primate grasping and particularly for measuring dynamically the repartition of both intensity and direction of contact forces on hands and feet. This sensor makes it possible to measure friction forces. These are crucial in arboreal locomotion since hands and feet need to develop tangential forces while grasping branches to stabilize the body. Importantly pressure information is insufficient to capture friction forces, which limits the use of commercially available pressure sensors.

Based on optical measurements of deformations, our sensor is composed of an array of sensing units. It has a soft, biocompatible, weather resistant and EMI resistant body. Each sensing unit, or cell, consists of a soft hemisphere which deforms when a contact force is applied (made in Polydimethylsiloxane). The applied force is reconstructed through the measurement of the cell's deformation. To this end, an optical tracer is embedded within the cell elastic and transparent material, moving when the cell deforms. Tracer displacement is measured by optical triangulation. For each cell, an optical fiber illuminates the tracer and 3 optical fibers collect light which intensity depends upon the tracer position. All collecting optical fibers are imaged together at the same time by a single CMOS sensor. This allows to build arrays of hundreds to thousands of sensing cells. In our experiments, force reconstruction from images took less than 30 ms.

This project was supported by a technological transfer company and the technology has been patented (IFBL15SLTFOS). Here, we report the results and performance in reconstructing both normal and tangential components of various forces on a flat prototype (Fig. 1). A cylindrical prototype mimicking a branch (20 cm long and 4 cm in diameter) was also made but won't be described here.

Although biomechanics motivated the development of this sensor, measuring the repartition of normal and tangential forces opens promising perspectives for other research fields, such as robotics. Indeed, characterizing animal grasping entails many similar challenges with the design of robotic grasping hands. Many design choices, such as having soft and sensitive digits for robots, which enables grasping objects with precision, come from the study of animal grasping mechanisms and permit to create efficient and functionally analogous robots. Moreover, friction forces are also central for manipulation. For example, mapping friction forces during manipulation provides valuable insights on haptic exploration where forces prevail over geometry in human haptic ability [3]. Symmetrically, our sensor would be instrumental in improving robotic grasping capabilities. Although pressure or contact information can be sufficient for a wide array of functions, when it comes to grasping, having access to both normal and tangential components of contact force is fundamental. This is particularly true for grasping deformable and unknown objects, as it has been demonstrated on several robotic hands [4–6]. Yet, except a few noticeable exceptions [7, 8], existing touch sensor are all pressure or contact sensors [9].

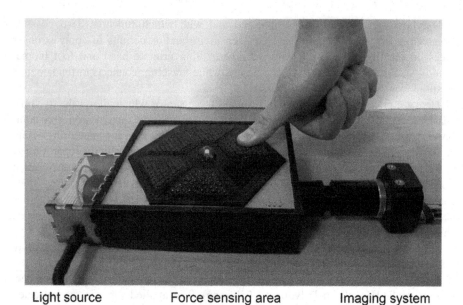

Light source            Force sensing area            Imaging system

**Fig. 1.** Flat prototype showing the 3 main components of the 3D force sensor. At the center, an enlarged uncoated cell shows a tracer. Each triangular sector contains 49 measurement cells.

Adding senses to robots, such as a precise feedback of forces applied by the digits, allows them to service outside controlled environments by apprehending autonomously novel situations and objects. However, robotic skin filled with tactile sensors are not a mature field yet. Similarly to the natural animal skin, an efficient robotic skin would probably features a mixture of sensing elements [10]. Mirroring the upcoming characterization of primate hands and feet, it would be informative to equip a robotic hand with our force sensors at its fingertips in a similar way as in previous works [5, 6], (Fig. 2). The sensor architecture is designed to have many sensing cells and is therefore well adapted to multi-fingered robotic hands, having a single deported image acquisition and processing unit for all cells. The cell's hemispherical shape, made of soft and deformable material, mimics the manual finger pads structure and function. Sensor characteristics presented here are adapted for primate biomechanics and precision grasp in robotics with a spatial resolution of 4 points per cm$^2$ and a force measurement range of 0–3N at 80 Hz. It was designed to be adaptable as the cell size, measuring range or density on a given surface can be customized for instance. Much smaller sensing cells, possibly under a millimeter, could be made using soft lithography techniques. This allows building a collection of sensors which is similar to human skin with different sensing units with distinct properties being present in various proportions and densities depending on the body location [11]. Therefore, embedding this sensor in robotic hands would permit to improve their prehensile adjustment, making them more efficient in complex grasping tasks and in robot-human interactions. At last, studying grasping with force feedback in robots would provide an objective assessment of the impact of the sense of touch on the performance of grasping and haptic exploration which is of interest for biomechanics and primatology as well.

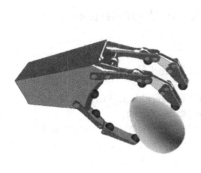

**Fig. 2.** Mirrored use of 3D force sensors for robotics and biomechanics

# References

1. Sustaita, D., Pouydebat, E., Manzano, A., Abdala, V., Hertel, F., Herrel, A.: Getting a grip on tetrapod grasping: form, function, and evolution. Biol. Rev. **88**, 380–405 (2013)
2. Hamrick, M.W.: Functional and adaptive significance of primate pads and claws: evidence from New World anthropoids. Am. J. Phys. Anthropol. **106**(2), 113–127 (1998)
3. Robles-De-La-Torre, G., Hayward, V.: Force can overcome object geometry in the perception of shape through active touch. Nature **412**, 445–448 (2001)
4. Ascari, L., Bertocchi, U., Corradi, P., Laschi, C., Dario, P.: Bio-inspired grasp control in a robotic hand with massive sensorial input. Biol. Cybern. **100**, 109–128 (2009)
5. Zaidi, L., Corrales, J.A., Bouzgarrou, B.C., Mezouar, Y., Sabourin, L.: Model-based strategy for grasping 3D deformable objects using a multi-fingered robotic hand. Rob. Auton. Syst. **95**, 196–206 (2017)
6. Kaboli, M., Yao, K., Cheng, G.: Tactile-based manipulation of deformable objects with dynamic center of mass. In: IEEE-RAS International Conference on Humanoid Robot, pp. 752–757 (2016)
7. Park, J., Lee, Y., Hong, J., Lee, Y., Ha, M., Jung, Y., Lim, H., Kim, S.Y., Ko, H.: Tactile-direction-sensitive and stretchable electronic skins based on human-skin-inspired interlocked microstructures. ACS Nano **8**, 12020–12029 (2014)
8. Tar, Á., Cserey, G.: Development of a low cost 3D optical compliant tactile force sensor. In: IEEE/ASME International Conference on Advanced Intelligent Mechatronics, AIM, pp. 236–240 (2011)
9. Núñez, C.G., Navaraj, W.T., Polat, E.O., Dahiya, R.: Energy-autonomous, flexible, and transparent tactile skin. Adv. Funct. Mater. **27**, 1606287 (2017)
10. Bartolozzi, C., Natale, L., Nori, F., Metta, G.: Robots with a sense of touch. Nat. Mater. **15**, 921–925 (2016)
11. Macefield, V.G.: Physiological characteristics of low-threshold mechanoreceptors in joints, muscle and skin in human subjects. Clin. Exp. Pharmacol. Physiol. **32**, 135–144 (2005)

# Aquatic Swimming of a Multi-functional Pedundulatory Bio-Robotic Locomotor

Dimitris P. Tsakiris[1,2]([⊠]), Theodoros Evdaimon[1], and Emmanouil Papadakis[1]

[1] Institute of Computer Science, FORTH, Heraklion, Greece
{tsakiris,evdemon,manospapad}@ics.forth.gr
[2] Department of Computer Science, Aberystwyth University, Aberystwyth, UK

**Abstract.** This paper considers aquatic swimming of a *pedundulatory* bio-robotic system, inspired by the outstanding aquatic and terrestrial locomotion capabilities of the *polychaete annelid* marine worms. The robot employs lateral undulations of its elongated body, augmented by the oscillation of active lateral appendages (*parapodia*), to propel itself. The efficient propulsion and terrain adaptability of such robots on unstructured terrestrial substrates have been demonstrated in previous work. Here, we explore *gait generation* for underwater propulsion by *direct* (tail-to-head) lateral body waves, either alone (*undulatory modes*) or combined with appropriately coordinated parapodial motion (*pedundulatory modes*). A three-segment compliant-body robotic prototype is used, whose body was fabricated by molding polyurethane elastomers. This robot was tested in a laboratory water tank, to demonstrate the advantage gained from the exploitation of both tail-to-head body undulations and parapodia for underwater swimming. The forward speed may more than double and the propulsive force may increase ten-fold, compared to the case where only undulations are used.

**Keywords:** Biologically inspired systems · Robotics
Undulatory robotics · Soft robotics · Underwater locomotion

## 1 Introduction

The possibility of developing advanced reduced-size amphibious bio-robotic vehicles, with an agility and efficiency approaching that of living organisms, could enable a host of significant applications in unstructured environments, which are challenging present-day robotic systems [1–6]. Such environments may be the sea-shore, the intertidal zone, lakes, swamps or river estuaries, even analogous extraterrestrial environments. The inspection of man-made structures, search-and-rescue operations, or monitoring and exploration of ecosystems in environments like the above, using multi-purpose robotic systems which do not significantly perturb their surroundings, are prime examples of such applications.

The biological paradigm of organisms like the *polychaete annelid* worms (Fig. 1a), which are able to adapt robustly to a wide variety of terrains and

© Springer International Publishing AG, part of Springer Nature 2018
V. Vouloutsi et al. (Eds.): Living Machines 2018, LNAI 10928, pp. 494–506, 2018.
https://doi.org/10.1007/978-3-319-95972-6_53

environmental conditions, is particularly relevant to investigations of amphibious robotic systems [7–10]. The outstanding behavioral adaptability of these segmented worms, ranging from crawling and burrowing at the seashore or at the depths of the oceans, to swimming near the surface, is supported by substantial morphological and neuromuscular variability. Their *rapid crawling* and *swimming* behaviors are characterized by a unique form of *direct* body undulations, propagating from the posterior towards the anterior of the organism, i.e. in the opposite direction than body waves of eels and snakes. These undulations are coordinated with the motion of lateral paddle-like appendages, called *parapodia*, so that their *power* (resp. *recovery*) stroke occurs when the parapodia are at the crest (resp. trough) of the body wave [10–17]. This locomotion mode has been termed *polychaete-like pedundulatory* mode, and previous work by our group, emulating it on elongated modular robotic systems, has demonstrated the locomotor advantage it affords over pure undulatory locomotion by lateral waves, when crawling on irregular granular terrains [18–24].

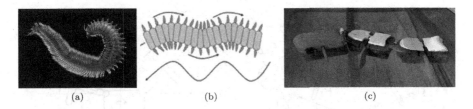

(a)                           (b)                           (c)

**Fig. 1.** Polychaete annelids: (a) *Nereis pelagica* [25], (b) Coordination between body undulations and parapodial oscillations. (c) The pedundulatory bio-robotic prototype in a water tank.

In contrast to these previous works, which explored terrestrial locomotion, the present study explores, for the first time, the *aquatic* locomotion of *pedundulatory bio-robotic swimmers* (Fig. 1c), establishing that: (i) such a swimming mode is feasible and advantageous over just undulatory swimming, (ii) the polychaete-like pedundulatory mode generates forward swimming propulsion, when each segment's longitudinal and transverse drag coefficients are approximately equal, and (iii) the movement of the parapodia affects considerably the velocity and propulsive force of the robot. Experiments inside a water tank, in a laboratory setting, coupled with an appropriate velocity and force measurement setup, are used in these aquatic locomotion studies.

Section 2 of the paper outlines the modeling of underwater pedundulatory robotic systems and the generation of undulatory and pedundulatory gaits. Section 3 depicts briefly the development of the compliant-body pedundulatory robot, and describes the related experimental setups for measuring velocity, segment drag and propulsive force in water. Section 4 presents experimental studies and results of swimming of the robot in a water tank, focusing on the effect of parapodia on propulsive velocity and forces. Section 5 discusses further the results and the possible extensions of this work.

## 2  Gait Generation

### 2.1  Mechanical Model

A simplified planar mechanical model of the compliant-body pedundulatory bio-robot is shown in Fig. 2. It is composed of a planar serial arrangement of three identical segments (designated as $B_j$, where $j = 1..3$) of length $l_b$, interconnected by planar rotary joints, where $\phi_i$, $i = 1, 2$ are actively-controlled joint angles. On each segment, a pair of laterally placed parapodial links of length $l_p$ is mounted at a distance $b$ from the segment's rear edge. The parapodia (designated as $P_j$, where $j = 1..6$) are connected to the segment via planar single-degree-of-freedom rotary joints, allowing them to move on a vertical plane (dorsoventrally). When all parapodia are removed, the mechanism is reduced to an undulatory system. In pedundulatory modes, the desired "paddling" action of the parapodia emerges when their up-down movements are combined with body undulations. More details, and the modeling of compliant joint elements, are presented in [24].

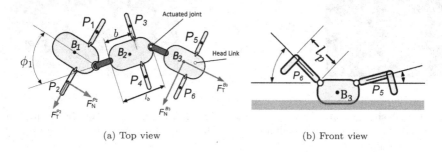

(a) Top view                    (b) Front view

**Fig. 2.** Mechanical model of the 3-segment pendundulatory bio-robotic prototype.

**Interaction with the Environment:** Locomotion of an undulating body results from the coupling of its internal shape changes to external motion constraints, which are usually due to external forces, resisting the motion of the links and applied through the interaction with the locomotion environment. A *fluid drag model* can be used to emulate swimming, where the force on a body segment is assumed to depend on its velocity, not on its acceleration. This model is a first approximation of the hydrodynamics involved [26–29], assuming that: the fluid forces are mainly inertial; the fluid is stationary, so that its force on a single link is due only to the motion of that link; the tangential ($F_T$) and normal ($F_N$) components of the fluid force are decoupled (Fig. 2), as described in [30], a notion used extensively in the robotics literature (e.g., [20,31–33]) despite ignoring secondary effects of water movement. These forces are, then, calculated, for individual links, as $F_T^{B_i} = -\lambda_T \mathrm{sgn}(v_T^i) \cdot (v_T^i)^2$ and $F_N^{B_i} = -\lambda_N \mathrm{sgn}(v_N^i) \cdot (v_N^i)^2$, where $v_T^i$ and $v_N^i$ are the tangential and normal components of the velocity of the $i$th link. Estimates for the associated drag coefficients $\lambda_T$ and $\lambda_N$ may be obtained as $\lambda = \frac{1}{2}\rho C S$, where $S$ is the link's effective area, $\rho$ is the fluid density and $C$ is a shape coefficient. However, in this case, these coefficients are estimated from the above drag force model, by measuring the corresponding drag force and link velocity, as described in Sect. 4. The same approach is adopted for the drag force components $F_T^{P_i}$ and $F_N^{P_i}$ on the parapodia.

The ratio $\lambda_N/\lambda_T$ of the drag coefficients is a key parameter in undulatory locomotion. The elongated body of eel-like animals is smooth and of elliptical cross-section, so that $\lambda_T \ll \lambda_N$, and the overall locomotion direction is *opposite* to that of the wave direction. Thus, forward propulsion is achieved by body waves propagating from head to tail (*retrograde* wave), while reversing the propulsive wave enables backwards swimming. If the body is not smooth, as in the case of the polychaete annelids [10, 30], the tangential component of the propulsive force may be greater than or approximately equal to the normal one, corresponding to $\lambda_N < \lambda_T$ or $\lambda_N \approx \lambda_T$. For such rough-body conditions, locomotion is *along* the direction of wave propagation, i.e. forward motion is achieved by a tail-to-head wave (*direct* wave). Related simulation studies appear in [20, 21].

## 2.2  Gait Generation

The motion control strategies, which give rise to the undulatory and pedundulatory swimming modes under investigation, are as follows (Fig. 3):

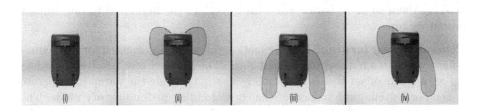

**Fig. 3.** The swimming gaits considered (CAD drawings: body segments shown in brown, parapodia in green): (i) Undulatory (UG), (ii) Undulatory with parapodia up (UG-up), (iii) Undulatory with parapodia down (UG-down), (iv) Pedundulatory (PedUG).

*Undulatory gait (UG):* In the purely undulatory mode, when all parapodia are removed, locomotion is obtained through the coupling of the mechanism's shape changes to the drag forces applied through the interaction with the aquatic environment (for details, see [20] and refs. therein). Assuming full position control of the mechanism's joint angles, the implementation of this gait is based on a *tail-to-head* body wave (opposite than eels and snakes) of uniform amplitude, by specifying the desired trajectories of the body joints according to the equation:

$$\phi_i(t) = A\sin(2\pi ft + (3 - i)\varphi_0) + \psi, \ i = 1, 2, \tag{1}$$

where $A$, $f$ and $\psi$ denote, respectively, the amplitude, frequency and angular offset of the joint sinusoidal motion, while $\varphi_0 > 0$ is the phase shift between consecutive joints. This equation can be easily extended to more body joints, or to different oscillation characteristics for each joint. A lower-level control loop ensures faithful tracking of these trajectories in the presence of perturbations.

*Undulatory gait with parapodia up (UG-up):* A second undulatory gait is considered, where the parapodia are not removed, but are fully retracted and remain immobile, in this retracted position, during the whole body undulation.

*Undulatory gait with parapodia down (UG-down):* A third undulatory gait is considered, where the parapodia are fully extended and remain immobile, in this extended position, during the whole body undulation.

*Pedundulatory gait (PedUG):* In the pedundulatory mode, body undulations are combined with the periodic activation of the lateral parapodial appendages, which occurs in waves propagating in the same direction as the body undulations. Appropriate coordination is required, in order to ensure the positive contribution of the parapodia in thrust generation during each locomotion cycle. Two main such pedundulatory modes have been developed [18, 19, 23], which are inspired by the locomotion of centipedes (for retrograde wave propagation) and of polychaete marine worms (for direct wave propagation, Fig. 1b). Only the second such gait (polychaete) is considered in the present study. The robotic system of Figs. 1c and 2 cannot propel itself by the simple dorso-ventral parapodial movements alone; it is the traveling body wave that effectively positions the parapodia, allowing them to move backwards with respect to the fluid, and to thus impart propulsive forces.

*Pedundulatory turning:* Turning motions may be implemented for the pedundulatory gait in a number of different ways. The simplest one, involves introducing an angular offset $\psi \neq 0$ in the body wave (1), while the parapodia operate in the normal bilateral fashion of the corresponding pedundulatory mode. The path curves in the clockwise or counter-clockwise direction, depending on the sign of $\psi$ and the body wave direction. Other possibilities on pedundulatory turning strategies are discussed in [19, 23].

## 3 Robot Prototype and Experimental Setup

### 3.1 Bio-Robotic Prototype Development

In the present paper, we are using a three-segment compliant-body pedundulatory robotic prototype (Fig. 1), weighing 1960 g, measuring 380 mm in length, and able to propel itself submerged in water.

Each segment (Fig. 4d) is composed of a compliant shell (Fig. 4c), a coupling joint element, the electronics' case, an upper lid of the shell, two lateral parapodia (Fig. 4b), two waterproof servomotors (Hitec HS-5086WP) actuating the parapodia, and a third waterproof servomotor (Hitec HS-5646WP), actuating the segment joint. Each segment has dimensions 120 mm × 74 mm × 74 mm, with a wall thickness of 2.5 mm. Its front part has a semi-ellipsoidal shape, to facilitate aquatic locomotion. The joint elements, interconnecting successive

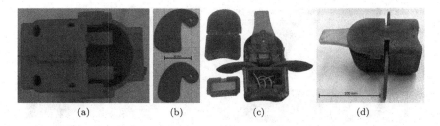

(a)                (b)                (c)                (d)

**Fig. 4.** Pedundulatory compliant-body bio-robotic prototype components: (a) 3dp-rinted cast for fabrication of a segment shell, (b) two types of parapodia (large - up, small - down), (c) a segment with the lids removed, (d) a complete segment.

segments, can influence the overall rigidity of the robot. Both rigid and compliant joint elements were developed, measuring 88 mm x 48 mm x 6.5 mm in length, maximum width and thickness, respectively. The parapodia are driven by dedicated servomotors, which move each parapodium independently, in a plane perpendicular to the direction of the robot's motion. Various parapodia designs have been fabricated, with the smaller variants being 70 mm x 40 mm x 5 mm (weight 7.6 g) and the larger ones 75 mm x 50 mm x 5 mm (weight 9.2 g). Each segments' weight is 550 g, while the head segment weighs 860 g.

**Prototype Fabrication:** The exploitation of compliant materials for the fabrication of the robot's body presents considerable technical challenges, as it involves the design of castable elastomeric body parts and their interlocking assembly to form a single unit.The material used for the fabrication of the prototype is a two-component polyurethane (PMC-746, Smooth-On) cast in 3D-printed ABSplus molds fabricated for each compliant component of the robot, to host the polyurethane mixture. The final mixture results in an amorphous polymer that exhibits viscoelastic behavior. The fabrication process and the material properties are detailed in [24].

**Electronics:** Mounted on the robot's head segment is a Teensy 3.1 platform, based on the ARM Cortex M4 microcontroller, which generates the PWM signals for the RC servos according to the desired motion profiles of the selected locomotion mode. Power to the various electronic components is provided by an on-board 7.4 V LiPo battery through a series of voltage regulators. The robot also integrates an RF module that allows for wireless data exchange with an external PC. Gel is used for the waterproofing of electronics.

### 3.2   Experimental Setup

The prototype was tested inside a laboratory water tank with dimensions 200 cm x 70 cm x 60 cm, filled with freshwater. The $x$-axis of the experimental setup is along the longitudinal direction of the water tank, with its positive direction from left to right; the $y$-axis is along the vertical direction of the water tank,

**Fig. 5.** (a) Laboratory water tank and coordinate frame of reference, (b) Experimental setup for body segment drag force measurements, view from above the tank, (c) Experimental setup for robot propulsive force measurements.

with its positive direction opposite the direction of gravity; the $z$-axis is along the lateral direction of the water tank.

**Position and Velocity Measurement:** The position and orientation of the robot were tracked with a high-definition camera fixed at one side of the tank, and looking inwards, via computer vision methods, exploiting the viewing of a checkerboard marker of known size, placed on the rear side of the head (Fig. 5a).

**Segment Drag Force Measurement:** To measure the drag forces induced by the movement of each body segment of the robot, the experimental setup of Fig. 5b was used, employing a high-precision digital dynamometer (Alluris FMI-210A5). The linear stage pulled the robot segment that was fixed to it, in either its tangential or normal direction, with an accurately-controlled velocity, while the dynamometer measured the corresponding drag force component. The force measurements were performed for displacement velocities of 4.6 and 9.2 mm/sec.

**Propulsive Force Measurement:** The measurements of the propulsive force generated by the robot in its axial direction, for locomotion in freshwater, were performed via the experimental setup of Fig. 5c. This also employs the above digital dynamometer, which, this time, is being pulled by the swimming robot via the cable and pulley configuration shown.

## 4    Experimental Results

In this Section, we present experimental results with the three-segment pedundulatory bio-robotic prototype on freshwater[1].

**Segment Drag Force:** The drag coefficient, in the tangential or normal direction of the segment, was calculated as $\lambda = F/v^2$, where $F$ is the measured drag force component and $v$ is the corresponding speed of the segment relative to the fluid. Indicative force results are shown in Fig. 6a. From these measurements, the tangential and normal drag coefficients were estimated, for the UG-down gait, as $\lambda_N = 3,774 \text{ Ns}^2/\text{m}^2$ and $\lambda_T = 3,483 \text{ Ns}^2/\text{m}^2$, so that $\lambda_N/\lambda_T \approx 1.08$. The two drag force coefficients, when the papapodia are fully deployed, are, then, approximately equal. Similarly, when the parapodia are removed (UG gait).

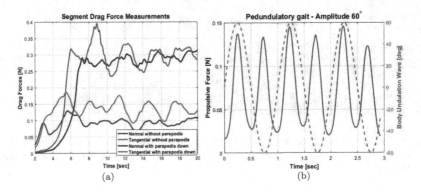

**Fig. 6.** Measurements of (a) the body segment drag force for the UG and UG-down gaits, and (b) the robot propulsive force for the PedUG gait over 3 periods of undulation.

**Robot Propulsive Force:** Measurements of the propulsive force generated by the robot in the axial direction, for locomotion in freshwater, were performed with the experimental setup of Fig. 5c. Figure 6b shows a typical force profile, containing two force peaks in each period of undulation. Figure 7 presents the average of the peak propulsive forces, as a function of the amplitude $A$, for each gait considered (two measurements per mean point in the graph). The generated propulsive force, which can be seen to increase with $A$, is noticeably higher for the pedundulatory gait (PedUG), than for any of the undulatory gaits (UG, UD-up, UG-down). In particular, the maximum mean force corresponding to the PedUG gait is more than ten times that corresponding to the UG gait.

---

[1] A supplementary video with footage from these experiments can be downloaded from http://tinyurl.com/LM18-forth.

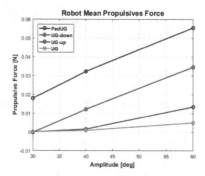

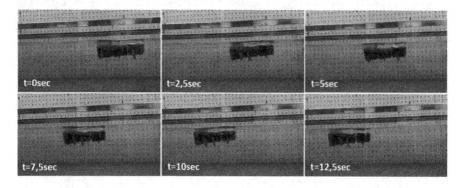

**Fig. 7.** Measurement of the mean propulsives forces of the robot, for all gaits considered.

**Fig. 8.** Experimental results: Forward swimming by the PedUG gait, from right to left along the x-axis for 12.5 periods of undulation (2.5 periods between snapshots, $f = 1\text{Hz}, A = 60°, \psi = 0°$).

**Aquatic Locomotion Velocity:** A series of experiments were conducted for undulatory and pedundulatory locomotion in freshwater, using the experimental setup presented in Sect. 3.2. A series of snapshots of forward swimming for the PedUG gait are shown in Fig. 8, where the time instant, that each one was taken, is indicated. Indicative trajectories for gait UG-down is shown in Fig. 9a. Figure 9b shows the average velocities attained for the different gaits by the swimming bio-robotic prototype (two measurements per mean point in the graph). We observe, that, as in the case of the propulsive forces, these velocities can be seen to increase with the body wave amplitude $A$. Moreover, they are noticeably higher in the case of the pedundulatory gait (PedUG), than in the case of any of the undulatory gaits (UG, UD-up or UG-down). In particular, the maximum velocity for the PedUG gait is more than double that of the UG gait, reaching 30.4 mm/s (0.08 body-lenths/s). Preliminary evidence indicates an even more substantial velocity increase when the large parapodia are used.

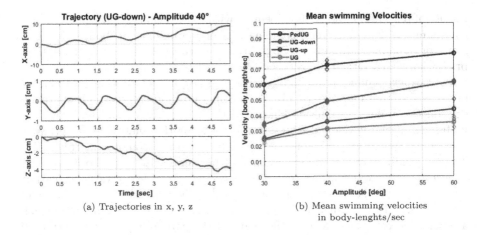

(a) Trajectories in x, y, z

(b) Mean swimming velocities in body-lenghts/sec

**Fig. 9.** Swimming trajectories and velocities attained for various forward gaits.

**Turning:** To determine the capability of the robot to make a turn in water, experiments were performed with numerous offset values $\psi$ for the body wave, and with the various gaits considered. The most effective turns were performed with non-zero offset values $\psi$ for the body wave, and the parapodia operating in their normal manner during the PedUG gait. Figure 10 presents indicative snapshots from these tests, for a counterclockwise 90° turn.

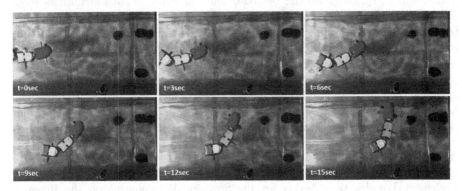

**Fig. 10.** Experimental results: Turning counterclockwise by the pedundulatory gait for 15 periods (3 periods between snapshots, $f = 1\text{Hz}, A = 52°, \psi = 8°$). The robot moves to the right. View from above the tank.

## 5 Discussion and Conclusions

In this paper, we study experimentally, for the first time, the *aquatic swimming* behavior of *pedundulatory* robots. The use of lateral appendages (*parapodia*) noticeably increases the speed and propulsive force of the system, compared to the use of pure undulations, in agreement with our previous studies in terrestrial environments [23,24]. Several combinations of the undulatory body wave with static or dynamic parapodial configurations are considered, to investigate their propulsion characteristics in terms of speed and generated force.

Our experimental studies highlight the complex and interdependent influence of various system parameters, like the locomotion mode or the body morphology, on the aquatic propulsion characteristics of the robot, and underline the usefulness of the developed experimental tools for the analysis and optimization of the design and control of complex bio-robotic locomotor morphologies. The key findings of the present study can be summarized as follows: *(i)* The *polycheate-like pedundulatory swimming mode* via *direct* body waves, is feasible for a multi-segment bio-robot in the inviscid regime, where the drag forces of each segment in the tangential and normal direction are approximately equal, although the robot design (e.g., the shape of the parapodia) was not optimized for aquatic swimming. *(ii)* Coordinating the parapodia with the body undulation in the manner suggested by the polychaete-like pedundulatory mode, namely by extending (resp. retracting) the parapodia when these are at the crest (resp. trough) of the body wave, increases the robot velocity and propulsive force, compared to just employing body undulations for propulsion, or body undulations combined with only static parapodia. *(iii)* Increasing the undulation amplitude of the body also increases both the velocity and the propulsive force.

Further related issues to be investigated include the effect of the number of segments, of the use of chaetae-like structures or of variations in the segment and parapodial morphology on the behavior and efficiency of such swimmers (e.g., obtain forward propulsion also by retrograde waves). Also, the combination of terrestrial and aquatic propulsive modes towards the generation of amphibious robotic systems. Moreover, issues to be further investigated include a more accurate study by CFD methods of the hydrodynamic forces and vortical patterns produced by such underwater swimmers, and specification of parameters that optimize their hydrodynamic characteristics (e.g., via the high-fidelity immersed boundary method [34] to capture the required large deformations of the robot body, as in our previous work [35]).

**Acknowledgement.** This work was supported in part by the project "Advanced Research Activities in Biomedical & Agroalimentary Technologies" (MIS 5002469) implemented under the "Action for the Strategic Development on the Research & Technological Sector", funded by the Operational Programme "Competitiveness, Entrepreneurship & Innovation" (NSRF 2014–2020), co-financed by Greece and the European Union (European Regional Development Fund).

# References

1. Yang, G.Z., Bellingham, J., Dupont, P.E., Fischer, P., Floridi, L., Full, R., Jacobstein, N., Kumar, V., McNutt, M., Merrifield, R., Nelson, B., Scassellati, B., Taddeo, M., Taylor, R., Veloso, M., Lin Wang, Z., Wood, R.: The grand challenges of science robotics. Sci. Robot. **3**, eaar7650 (2018)
2. Cho, K.-J., Wood, R.: Biomimetic robots. In: Siciliano, B., Khatib, O. (eds.) Springer Handbook of Robotics, pp. 543–574. Springer, Cham (2016). https:// doi.org/10.1007/978-3-319-32552-1_23
3. Iida, F., Ijspeert, A.J.: Biologically inspired robotics. In: Siciliano, B., Khatib, O. (eds.) Springer Handbook of Robotics, pp. 2015–2034. Springer, Cham (2016). https://doi.org/10.1007/978-3-319-32552-1_75
4. Liljebäck, P., Pettersen, K., Stavdahl, Ø., Gravdahl, J.: A review on modelling, implementation, and control of snake robots. Robot. Auton. Syst. **60**, 29–40 (2012)
5. Crespi, A., Karakasiliotis, K., Guignard, A., Ijspeert, A.J.: Salamandra robotica ii: an amphibious robot to study salamander-like swimming and walking gaits. IEEE T-RO **29**(2), 308–320 (2013)
6. Yamada, H., Takaoka, S., Hirose, S.: A snake-like robot for realworld inspection applications (the design and control of a practical active cord mechanism). Adv. Robot. **27**, 47–60 (2013)
7. Gray, J.: Annelids. In: Animal Locomotion, Weidenfeld & Nicolson, pp. 377–410 (1968)
8. Gray, J.: Studies in animal locomotion. JEB **13**(2), 192–199 (1936)
9. Brusca, R., Brusca, G.: Invertebrates. Sinauer Associates, Sunderland (1990)
10. Clark, R.B., Tritton, D.J.: Swimming mechanisms in nereidiform polychaetes. J. Zool. **161**, 257–271 (1970)
11. Clark, R.B., Hermans, C.: Kinetics of swimming in some smooth-bodied polychaetes. J. Zool. **178**, 145–159 (1976)
12. Hesselberg, T.: Biomimetics and the case of the remarkable ragworms. Naturwissenschaften **94**(8), 613 (2007)
13. Wootton, R.: Invertebrate paraxial locomotory appendages: design, deformation and control. JEB **202**(23), 3333–3345 (1999)
14. Clark, R.B.: Undulatory swimming in polychaetes. In: Perspectives in Experimental Biology, pp. 437–446 (1976)
15. Mettam, C.: Segmental musculature and parapodial movement of Nereis diversicolor and Nephthys hombergi (Annelida: Polychaeta). J. Zool. **153**(2), 245–275 (1967). The Linnean Society of New South Wales
16. Mettam, C.: Functional morphology of locomotion in Chloeia (Polychaeta; Amphinomidae). In: Huchings, P.A. (ed.) Proceedings First International Polychaete Conference, pp. 390–400. The Linnean Society of New South Wales (1984)
17. Lawry Jr., J.V.: Mechanisms of locomotion in the polychaete, Harmothoë. Comp. Biochem. Phys. **37**(2), 167–179 (1970)
18. Sfakiotakis, M., Tsakiris, D.P., Karakasiliotis, K.: Polychaete-like pedundulatory robotic locomotion. In: Proceedings of the IEEE International Conference on Robotics and Automation, (ICRA 2007), pp. 269–274 (2007)
19. Sfakiotakis, M., Tsakiris, D.P.: Pedundulatory robotic locomotion: centipede and polychaete modes in unstructured substrates. In: Proceedings of the International Conference on Robotics and Biomimetics (ROBIO 2008), pp. 651–658 (2009)
20. La Spina, G., Sfakiotakis, M., Tsakiris, D.P., Menciassi, A., Dario, P.: Polychaete-like undulatory robotic locomotion in unstructured substrates. IEEE T-RO **6**, 1200–1212 (2007)

21. Sfakiotakis, M., Tsakiris, D.P.: SIMUUN: a simulation environment for undulatory locomotion. Int. J. Model. Simul. **26**(4), 350–358 (2006). Taylor & Francis

22. Sfakiotakis, M., Tsakiris, D.P.: A biomimetic centering behavior for undulatory robots. IJRR **26**(11–12), 1267–1282 (2007)

23. Sfakiotakis, M., Tsakiris, D.P.: Undulatory and pedundulatory robotic locomotion via direct and retrograde body waves. In: Proceedings of the IEEE International Conference on Robotics and Automation (ICRA 2009), pp. 3457–3463 (2009)

24. Sfakiotakis, M., Chatzidaki, A., Evdaimon, T., Kazakidi, A., Tsakiris, D.P.: Effects of compliance in pedundulatory locomotion over granular substrates. In: Proceedings of the 24th Mediterranean Conference on Control and Automation (MED), pp. 532–538, June 2016

25. Semenov, A.: Metallic snake-nereis pellagica (2008). https://www.flickr.com/photos/a_semenov/3099126862

26. Vogel, S.: Modes and scaling in aquatic locomotion. Integr. Comp. Biol. **48**(6), 702–712 (2008)

27. Nachtigall, W.: Hydromechanics and biology. Biophys. Struct. Mech. **8**(1), 1–22 (1981)

28. Porez, M., Boyer, F., Ijspeert, A.J.: Improved lighthill fish swimming model for bio-inspired robots: modeling, computational aspects and experimental comparisons. IJRR **33**(10), 1322–1341 (2014)

29. Gazzola, M., Argentina, M., Mahadevan, L.: Gait and speed selection in slender inertial swimmers. PNAS **112**(13), 3874–3879 (2015)

30. Taylor, G.: Analysis of the swimming of long and narrow animals. Proc. R. Soc. Lond. A: Math. Phys. Eng. Sci. **214**(1117), 158–183 (1952)

31. McIsaac, K.A., Ostrowski, J.P.: Motion planning for anguilliform locomotion. IEEE Trans. Robot. Autom. **19**(4), 637–652 (2003)

32. Ekeberg, Ö.: A combined neuronal and mechanical model of fish swimming. Biol. Cybern. **69**(5–6), 363–374 (1993)

33. Ijspeert, A.J.: A connectionist central pattern generator for the aquatic and terrestrial gaits of a simulated salamander. Biol. Cybern. **85**(5), 331–348 (2001)

34. Ge, L., Sotiropoulos, F.: A numerical method for solving the 3D unsteady incompressible navier-stokes equations in curvilinear domains with complex immersed boundaries. J. Comput. Phys. **225**, 1782–1809 (2007)

35. Kazakidi, A., Tsakiris, D.P., Ekaterinaris, J.A.: Propulsive efficiency in drag-based locomotion of a reduced-size swimmer with various types of appendages. Comput. Fluids **167**, 241–248 (2018)

# Evolution of Neural Networks for Physically Simulated Evolved Virtual Quadruped Creatures

Neil Vaughan[1,2(✉)]

[1] University of Chester, Chester, UK
n.vaughan@chester.ac.uk
[2] Royal Academy of Engineering, London, UK

**Abstract.** This work develops evolved virtual creatures (EVCs) using neuroevolution as the controller for movement and decisions within a 3D physics simulated environment. Previous work on EVCs has displayed various behaviour such as following a light source. This work is focused on complexifying the range of behaviours available to EVCs. This work uses neuroevolution for learning specific actions combined with other controllers for making higher level decisions about which action to take in a given scenario. Results include analysis of performance of the EVCs in simulated physics environment. Various controllers are compared including a hard coded benchmark, a fixed topology feed forward artificial neural network and an evolving ANN subjected to neuroevolution by applying mutations in both topology and weights. The findings showed that both fixed topology ANNs and neuroevolution did successfully control the evolved virtual creatures in the distance travelling task.

**Keywords:** Evolved creatures · Neuroevolution · Quadruped gait

## 1 Introduction

Since the pioneering work of a computer artist Karl Sims (1994), Evolved Virtual Creatures (EVCs) have been a significant area of research. Sims work showed 3D physics simulated creatures were able to produce various complex behaviors. These behaviors included travelling a distance in a physics simulated 3D landscape, following a light source, competing directly against each other in a block ownership task, moving on both land and in water.

After Sims (1994) research, increases in the complexity of the behaviours exhibited by evolved virtual creatures has slowed or stopped to a standstill. Some variations on EVC research had emerged, such as Framsticks (Komosinski 2000) which involves creatures made of flexible sticks, connected by joints and controlled with neural network. However the physics are simplified and there is limited interaction between agents.

Neural networks were proposed as a method of connecting the sensor inputs of an EVC to their motor outputs. Input signals can include sensors of the surrounding

© Springer International Publishing AG, part of Springer Nature 2018
V. Vouloutsi et al. (Eds.): Living Machines 2018, LNAI 10928, pp. 507–516, 2018.
https://doi.org/10.1007/978-3-319-95972-6_54

environment such as light distance to objects and perhaps other EVCs. Other sensors can be related to monitoring the EVC's own body to give feedback on motion.

Many initial EVC models used a fixed topology neural network which was limited is size and complexity which in turn limited behavioral complexity. To avoid this problem, Stanley and Miikkulainen (2002) proposed the NEAT method which uses a neural network in the same way but applies neuroevolution to enable the brain structure to grow in complexity over time to match requirements of the task by modifying both the weights and topology of links between neurons in the ANN.

## 1.1 Related Work

Recently a few areas of research have begun to exhibit EVCs with a wider range of complex behaviors. There have been developments in the body, the brain controller and resulting behaviour. Robinson et al. (2000) have shown deliberative behaviours on tasks such as river crossing, by combining the evolved ANNs with shunting models and other approaches. This enabled creatures to collect building materials and construct a bridge across the river. However the shunting model could provide the EVC with an internal map of the environment, whereas biological creatures have to discover the map themselves from scratch and memorize the routes which lead to rewards.

Further advances in EVCs producing more complex behavior was produced by the Encapsulation, Syllabus, Pandemonium (ESP) method (Lessin 2014; Lessin et al. 2014a). Encapsulation captures and separates skills once they have evolved, which prevents them from being un-learnt or forgotten and enables new skills to be learnt without interference. Syllabus is a series of training steps defined by the human to guide the learning process. Pandemonium is preventing learned skills from working against or conflicting with each other. One disadvantage with ESP is that human input is required to define the syllabus.

Conventional EVCs model muscles as uniform drives between rigid sections controlled by a 'brain', however a recent developent implemented muscle density, orientation, attachment points, and size to control the muscles (Lessin et al. 2014b), which helps decrease required complexity.

Rather than humans having to painstakingly design the morphology and control of agile autonomous machines, evolutionary algorithms can be used to search for robotic designs and behaviours without presupposing what those designs and behaviours may be (Cheney et al. 2017). It can yield machines that do not resemble any animals currently found on earth (Langton et al. 1989).

Recently in 2016 soft bodies model robots were evolved with dual CPPNs (Cheney et al. 2016) one CPPN is for the morphology as a $7 \times 7 \times 7$ cube where an output represents presence of material and an output represents type of material. The second CPPN is for control of muscle tissues describing phase offset from a sinusoidal wave input. A limitation to many voxel based soft robot EVC simulations appears to be the limitation of resources, since most currently implement maximum size of $20 \times 20 \times 20$ which could limit how meaningful the analogy is between EVCs and biological animal morphology.

Also online simulations of evolving virtual creatures are available (Moore 2018) and Novelty search has also been applied (Lehman and Stanley 2011).

## 1.2 State of Outstanding Problems

Legged robots are playing an increasingly important role in our daily lives plus are increasingly used in industry and military. There are commercial consumer walking biped or quadruped robots like Asimo and the dog aibo. They can potentially out perform wheels when on rugged terrain but the disadvantage is the complexity required for their controllers. (Clune et al. 2009b).

Quadruped robot bodies are a popular experiment for evolutionary algorithms. Many scientists report that the algorithms struggle when a large number of parameters need to be configured. They may succeed evolving a controller for one leg but fail once evolution is challenged with evolving a controller from many inputs and outputs from separate legs (Clune et al. 2009b). This is actually how octopuses work. They have a separate brain to control each leg independently.

Most EVC developments separate the body from the brain. The brain receives input from sensors on the body which as mentioned can sense the environment, other EVCs or parts of the EVC itself such as joint angles. The brain then sends it's decisions to the parts of the body which are required to move. This has resulted in a beautiful and unexpected ability to walk, swim, even move towards a light. Future work could focus on combining brain and body into one, both evolving together.

Future EVC work could aim towards building upon recent advances by Jolley and Channon (2017) which has used HyperNEAT for deliberative motion planning which can impressively switch between different modes to perform sequences of tasks such as moving back and forth to collect separate stones when building a bridge to cross a river.

Future EVC work should be inspired hybrid neurocontrollers. It was shown by Clune et al. (2009a) that for quadruped gait task HyperNEAT is best used only for the first part of evolution and then it can switch to FTNEAT which is fixed topology to optimise the solution found by HyperNEAT with up to 40% improvement. This was particularly good at irregular problems where quadruped leg joint angles had an angle of error artificially introduced. This demonstrated that indirect and direct encodings can be used together for the first time, although the advantages of both had been previously noted.

## 2 The Machine Learning Task

The given inputs and expected outputs were kept strictly equal for all tested controllers. Therefore here we can formally define the machine learning task based on the relationship between inputs and outputs of the controller. This is critical step because small changes to the representations of input and output can make big changes to the difficulty of the task for the controller to learn.

In total the EVC has five input sensors: (1) a sine wave which is useful to induce rhythmic motion, (2) 4 join angle sensors. (3) There is one random number input. This is independent so that EVCs can randomly determine an action or movement to take.

# 3  Benchmark Algorithm

The developed system included designing a custom developed hard-coded benchmark algorithm for generating a forward movement by controlling the angles of the joints directly from the sin wave input.

This results in some forward movement, but is not optimised in any way. This can be used for a comparison between the hard-coded benchmark and the evolved controllers. The benchmark algorithm was used in this research as a comparison or gold standard to assess the performance of the fixed topology and evolving ANN algorithms.

# 4  Developed Physics Environment

A pre-existing 3D simulated physics library called Open Dynamics Engine was used to ensure the complete range of physics interactions were implemented. This was combined with a custom designed C programmed OpenGL Graphics implementation.

An algorithm was created to randomly generate EVCs of various morphology from within a fixed size range. All 4 legs could be different lengths and the body could also be of different sizes and weights. Every generated EVC was a different size. Figure 1 shows various sizes of EVC which were generated and subsequently simulated in the physics environment, being controlled by random fixed topology ANNs.

# 5  Fixed Neural Network Training

Initially a fixed topology ANN was used. The ANN topology had 8 inputs, including 4 joint angle sensors (one for each leg), a sin input, cosine input and two biases. The one hidden layer had 8 fully connected nodes and 4 outputs, with only feed forward connections, no recurrence. The weights were randomly assigned to produce a succession of randomly tuned fixed topology ANNs. This produced some working movement behaviour although it was not producing elegant movement.

In total 5042 randomly generated ANNs were tested. Of these, 4562 (90.4%) travelled less than 5 units. Only 480 ANNs (9.6%) travelled over 5 units, 86 ANNs (1.7%) travelled over 10 units, 30 ANNs (0.5%) were over 15 units, only 4 ANNs (0.08%) travelled more than 20 units. The champion travelled 24.5 units. This distribution is shown in Fig. 2.

This simulation model is interesting since a high performance cannot be obtained only by a well-tuned ANN controller alone, nor only a well-proportioned EVC body, but in fact a combination of these two factors together is required for top performance.

All of the 5042 simulated random EVCs including the best performing were recorded into a comma separated value (csv) file, storing the sizes of all legs and body, plus the values of all ANN connection weights. This feature enables the best performing EVCs to be reloaded on demand into the physics simulator, for examination to identify the features which caused the best EVCs to perform highly.

**Fig. 1.** Various sizes of quadruped EVCs were algorithmically generated with unique ANN controllers. One EVC has jumped upside down (2nd from top) and another EVC is in the process of jumping (bottom). A walking strategy evolved (top and 2nd from bottom).

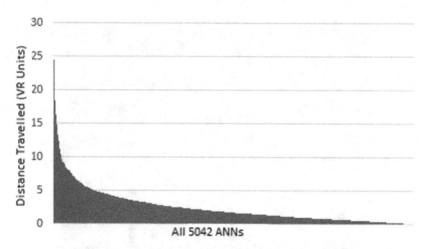

**Fig. 2.** Assessment of fitness (distance travelled) by 5042 EVCs with randomly generated ANNs, the champion travelled 24.5 units but 90.4% travelled less than 5 units (ordered by fitness, not by evolutionary generations).

The best EVCs had an ANN which caused all four legs to move in synchronisation, with the back and front legs moving in a way to produce forward movement. The best EVC bodies was usually long which was more stable and less prone to the problem of flipping over (Fig. 1b).

Some of the best and fastest walking behaviors appeared to be very efficient. One technique used a trailing leg to prevent overbalancing. Some techniques used diagonal legs in synchronization (similar to galloping) whereas the fastest running techniques used all four legs, including the two front legs together to push forwards (Figs. 3 and 4).

**Fig. 3.** A running EVC uses a trailing rear leg to prevent overturning.

**Fig. 4.** The EVC uses both front and rear legs together effectively to launch forwards multiple times.

## 6  Evolving ANN Controllers

Neuroevolution was applied to evolve neural networks which were then applied as the controller for EVCs. Between generations, the controller was subject to genetic change, by modifying the ANN both in terms of the weights and the topological structure, including the number and location of connections.

Initially, the ANNs were set blank, with no hidden layer nodes. The additional nodes are added by evolution over time.

The fitness function was set to 1 point for each VR unit of distance travelled from the central starting point.

A comprehensive set of tests was done with EVCs left to run for a fixed length of time. The ANN controllers were subject to neuroevolution in populations of size 15 organisms over 100 generations and this was repeated 10 times. Afterwards a further 5 repetitions of 100 generations was completed, this time with populations of 150 organisms which is a more conventional population size for neuroevolutionary algorithms.

In all runs there were some useful movement strategies evolving. By the 10th generation organisms often had increased their fitness.

In later experiments the body of the EVC was also subject to genetic change over time, so that an EVC body could evolve to be optimized for the ANN controller, or vice versa.

In the initial experiment, all ANN controllers were tested with the same EVC body shape and size to ensure that furthest movement was due to the ANN and not due to changes in body shape or size.

Initially the most outstanding solution evolved by neuroevolution was to take a large jump in the air (Fig. 5). This satisfied the fitness criteria by travelling a long distance, but often resulted in the EVC landing upside down and it was unable to continue further. Soon it had evolved to land upright so that it could jump a second time. The jumping strategy outperformed walking strategy and became a local optimum as the evolution process tended to select jumping techniques in subsequent generations, preventing further evolution of walking strategies.

The benefits of jumping over walking could also have been influenced by the time that each EVC was left to run before recording it's fitness which was set to a limit of 5 s.

**Fig. 5.** The neural network controller has evolved a jumping technique, the EVC travels a large distance quickly.

In this short time, a running or walking EVC may not have had enough time to catch up with a jumping EVC.

Over time, the fitness increased up to a maximum distance travelled of around 13 VR units, shown in the graph in Fig. 6. Fitness reached various plateaus early on during evolution. After around 1200 EVCs had evolved, the majority of EVCs obtained a fitness of between 8 and 13.

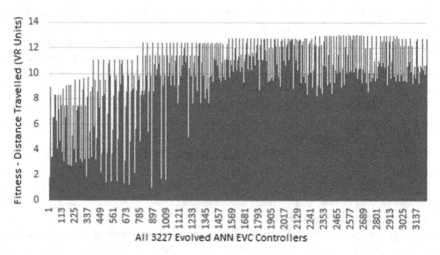

**Fig. 6.** The fitness over time of each EVC controller during the evolution process (ordered by evolutionary generations).

The distribution of fitness of all EVCs that evolved is shown in Fig. 7. This shows that there are fewer EVCs with fitness below 8, because after the first 1200 EVCs, the majority had fitness over 8. This can be directly compared to the same graph for the fixed topology ANNs (Fig. 2).

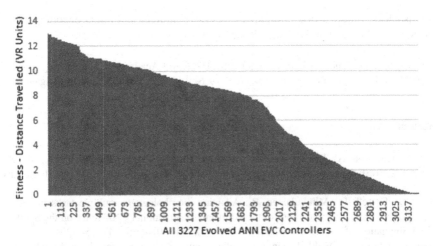

**Fig. 7.** The fitness of all EVC controllers during the neuroevolutionary process (ordered by fitness).

Neuroevolution produced medium to high fitness much more reliably and often than with fixed ANNs, shown by the comparison between graphs in Figs. 2 and 5. The highest fitness in neuroevolution was less of a chance occurrence and more of a gradual, iterative process reflecting the constructive and selective behavior of natural selection.

## 7 Conclusions and Future Work

This paper has investigated the benefits of neuroevolution compared to fixed topology ANN by testing how EVC behaviour can evolve to travel a distance within a physics simulated environment compared to a benchmark algorithm and a fixed ANN.

This research applied evolutionary algorithms to evolve the ANN topology and weights.

Some of the best and fastest walking behaviors appeared to be very efficient. One technique used a trailing leg to prevent overbalancing. Some techniques used diagonal legs in synchronization (similar to galloping) whereas the fastest running techniques used all four legs, including the two front legs together to push forwards.

Future EVC work could aim towards building deliberative motion planning which can switch between different modes to perform sequences of tasks such as moving back and forth to collect food and return it to a central nest.

Future EVC work should be inspired by hybrid neurocontrollers. For a quadruped gait task such as this, ANN topology evolution could be used only for the first part of evolution and then a fixed topology could be used to optimize the solution found during topology evolution, as this approach was shown by Clune et al. (2009a) to give 40% improvement. This could be particularly good at irregular problems where quadruped leg joint angles need to overcome obstacles or behave differently in other circumstances. Future work could also investigate indirect and direct encodings being used together during this EVC quadruped gait task.

**Acknowledgment.** The research was funded by The Royal Academy of Engineering (RAEng) as part of the Research Fellowship awarded to Dr Neil Vaughan as Principle Investigator.

# References

Jolley, B., Channon, A.: Toward evolving robust, deliberate motion planning with HyperNEAT. In: 2017 IEEE Symposium Series on Computational Intelligence (SSCI), pp. 1–8. IEEE, November 2017

Lessin, D., Fussell, D., Miikkulainen, R.: Adapting morphology to multiple tasks in evolved virtual creatures. In: Proceedings of the Fourteenth International Conference on the Synthesis and Simulation of Living Systems (ALIFE 2014), vol. 2014, pp. 247–254 (2014a)

Lessin, D., Fussell, D., Miikkulainen, R.: Trading control intelligence for physical intelligence:-muscle drives in evolved virtual creatures. In: Proceedings of the 2014 Conference on Genetic and Evolutionary Computation, pp. 705–712. ACM (2014b)

Lessin, D.: Evolved Virtual Creatures as Content: Increasing Behavioral and Morphological Complexity, Dissertation (2014)

Moore, J.: Evolve-A-Robot. http://jaredmmoore.com/EvoEnv/evo_main.html. Accessed 4 Feb 2018

Lehman, J., Stanley, K.O.: Evolving a diversity of creatures through novelty search and local competition. In: Proceedings of the Genetic and Evolutionary Computation Conference (GECCO 2011) (2011)

Komosinski, M.: The World of framsticks: simulation, evolution, interaction. In: Heudin, J.-C. (ed.) VW 2000. LNCS (LNAI), vol. 1834, pp. 214–224. Springer, Heidelberg (2000). https://doi.org/10.1007/3-540-45016-5_20

Clune, J., Beckmann, B.E., Pennock, R.T., Ofria, C.: HybrID: A hybridization of indirect and direct encodings for evolutionary computation. In: Kampis, G., Karsai, I., Szathmáry, E. (eds.) ECAL 2009, Part II. LNCS, vol. 5778, pp. 134–141. Springer, Heidelberg (2009a)

Clune, J., Beckmann, B. E., Ofria, C., Pennock, R. T.: Evolving coordinated quadruped gaits with the HyperNEAT generative encoding. In: 2009 IEEE Congress on Evolutionary Computation. CEC 2009. pp. 2764–2771. IEEE (2009b)

Cheney et al.: On the Difficulty of Co-Optimizing Morphology and Control in Evolved Virtual Creatures (2016)

Cheney, N., Bongard, J., SunSpiral, V., Lipson, H.: Scalable Co-Optimization of Morphology and Control in Embodied Machines. arXiv preprint arXiv:1706.06133 (2017)

Langton, C.G., et al.: Artificial Life. Addison-Wesley Publishing Company, Redwood City, CA (1989)

Robinson, E., Ellis, T., Channon, A.: Neuroevolution of agents capable of reactive and deliberative behaviours in novel and dynamic environments. In: Almeida e Costa, F., Rocha, L.M., Costa, E., Harvey, I., Coutinho, A. (eds.) ECAL 2007, pp. 345–354. Springer, Heidelberg (2007). https://doi.org/10.1007/978-3-540-74913-4_35

Sims, K.: Evolving 3D morphology and behavior by competition. Artif. Life 1(4), 353–372 (1994)

Stanley, K.O., Miikkulainen, R.: Evolving neural networks through augmenting topologies. Evol. Comput. 10(2), 99–127 (2002)

# Evolutionary Robot Swarm
# Cooperative Retrieval

Neil Vaughan[1,2(✉)]

[1] University of Chester, Chester, UK
n.vaughan@chester.ac.uk
[2] Royal Academy of Engineering, London, UK

**Abstract.** In nature bees and leaf-cutter ants communicate to improve cooperation during food retrieval. This research aims to model communication in a swarm of autonomous robots. When food is identified robot communication is emitted within a limited range. Other robots within the range receive the communication and learn of the location and size of the food source. The simulation revealed that communication improved the rate of cooperative food retrieval tasks. However a counter-productive chain reaction can occur when robots repeat communications from other robots causing cooperation errors. This can lead to a large number of robots travelling towards the same food source at the same time. The food becomes depleted, before some robots have arrived. Several robots continue to communicate food presence, before arriving at the food source to find it gone. Nature-inspired communication can enhance swarm behaviour without requiring a central controller and may be useful in autonomous drones or vehicles.

**Keywords:** Swarm communication · Agents based modelling
Cooperative retrieval · Robot simulation

## 1 Introduction

Various animals including ants and bees communicate the location of food sources within groups. Leaf cutter ants generate multimodal communication signals in form of vibrations when cutting leaves which act as recruitment signals to other ants. Simulated models of insect navigation have been developed (Wystrach et al. 2016). Mammals such as mole rats use vocalization to communicate food presence.

For general purpose animal evolution, numerous evolutionary framework platforms were recently developed to enable study of virtual creature evolution to produce complex features combining previously evolved building blocks such as Avida (Lenski et al. 2003), (Devosoft 2009) and Darwin Pond (Ventrella and Dodd 2005). Noble Ape, 3DVCE, Tierra and Framsticks, Virtual models of living systems and artificial life evolution are growing in popularity within autonomous navigation research. Evolved virtual creatures (EVCs) within virtual reality environments provide an ideal platform for producing and testing methods of navigation and evolution (Sims 1994), (Olson 2013). Navigation in quadrupeds has recently been tackled (Coros et al. 2011).

© Springer International Publishing AG, part of Springer Nature 2018
V. Vouloutsi et al. (Eds.): Living Machines 2018, LNAI 10928, pp. 517–521, 2018.
https://doi.org/10.1007/978-3-319-95972-6_55

Nature inspired algorithms led to recent multi-agent reinforcement learning. Image processing has been shown as useful for visual navigation (Vaughan 2015).

Other recent multi-agent reinforcement learning research simulating communication of swarm agents applied neuroevolution controllers for swarm agents (Vaughan 2018).

## 2 Methods

For simplicity and speed, robots were modelled in 2D. Many available 3D robot robotic simulator tools currently model in 3D however the benefits of 3D are limited if the robots navigate on a flat ground. The robots were free to autonomously navigate. Each robot has numerous properties. Temporary properties include: x, y, angle, current state (see FSM) and quantity of food being carried. Other properties which can evolve over generations using a genetic algorithm are size, speed and colour. The robots had one memory location for location and size of food. The behaviour of each robot can be in one of a finite number of states within a finite state machine (FSM) (Fig. 1). The FSM diagram shows the states and transitions between states.

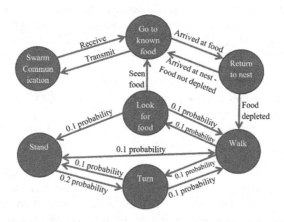

**Fig. 1.** Finite state machine controls autonomous navigation.

For swarm cooperation, when a robot identified food, the robot emitted a communication within a limited range. If any other robots are within the range they receive the communication. In this way the swarm can become aware of the location and size of the food source. The food location is stored in robot memory, overwriting memory of any smaller food (Fig. 2).

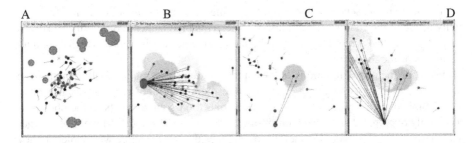

**Fig. 2.** Custom developed FSM cooperative swarm retrieval simulation. (A) shows no communication, the agents locate food individually. (B–D) shows with communication. (B) All agents within distance $x$ converge on largest food, (C) a purple agent found a small food, returned to the center to communicate, then (D), agents within distance $x$ converge.

## 3   Finite State Machine (FSM) Navigation

Finite state machine was developed to define the changes between six different states: (1) walking, (2) standing, (3) turning, (4) looking for food, (5) going to a known food source and (6) returning to nest. Probabilities were defined as the chance of changing from one state to another (Fig. 1).

For collision detection, at each display time step, the screen is reloaded after each robot has been moved according to their current speed in their current direction. If a robot's new position would make it collide or overlap with the edge of the screen, or with another robot, they do not get moved and their position stays in the previous position. When robots and obstacles are circular, collision detection becomes a simple comparison of the distance between two robots compared to the sum of the robot radius. Collision detection was switched off during the communication simulation because it led to excessive congestion in larger swarms.

## 4   Results

The simulation revealed that individual non-communicating food retrieval (Fig. 2A) was out-performed by communicating agent retrieval (Fig. 2B–D). This was beneficial to increase the rate of cooperative tasks such as collecting and retrieving food to the nest when compared to. Fitness was measured as number of food collected over time.

Agent communications only propagate distance $x$ from the agent (Fig. 2C). Higher values of $x$ represent louder speech or better eyesight in audio or visual communication.

A video of the running simulation can be seen online at youtu.be/RKrceeOyykQ.

There can be re-communication problem as counter-productive chain reactions occur when robots repeat the communications they heard from other robots. This chain reaction effect reduced efficiency of cooperation. When a large number of robots travel towards the same food source at the same time, other potentially lucrative food sources are left and forgotten. In this case, the food source is used up quickly, yet some slower robots still had not arrived yet and believed that the food would still exist. They continued to communicate its presence erroneously, triggering other robots to follow, only to eventually arrive at the food source, to find it gone. This predicament could only be solved once all robots had arrived together at the food source to find it empty, which erased all memories of the food source.

Effect of memory limitations led to another finding that robots could benefit from having larger memory enabling them to store more than one food source at a time. In the limited memory situation where only one food source can be remembered, it commonly occurred that robots would forget a known food source in favour of a larger one communicated to them by another robot. Once the larger source was depleted, they had already forgotten about the original smaller source, which remained un-eaten for some further time, whilst the robot reverted to searching for food. If the robot had remembered the previous food in addition, it could have returned to get the first food after finishing the larger second food. A recursive approach could be proposed for food retrieval. However having extra memory could also cause longer delays between initially learning of a food source and eventually returning to it, which increases chances that the food may no longer exist due to other robots having heard the initial communications and already finished retrieving it.

## 5  Conclusions

Autonomous navigation research continues to rapidly increase with investments from many beneficiaries including autonomous vehicles, augmented smartphones, autonomous drones and autopilot technologies, autonomous robotics and computer game engines. Novel aspect of this research is a proposal for a new approach using simulated swarm communication within a virtual environment combined with finite state machine (FSM). This simulator approach provides a platform to develop and test algorithms for autonomous navigation which appropriately respond to sensory information in real-time. The study has revealed potential problems with unconstrained communication in swarms leading to inefficient cooperation in retrieval tasks. This could be remedied by adjustments to the structure of robots such as increasing memory.

**Acknowledgment.** The research was funded by The Royal Academy of Engineering (RAEng) as part of the Research Fellowship awarded to Dr Neil Vaughan as Principle Investigator.

The OpenGL source code in c and the compiled executable for windows are available to download: http://dec.bmth.ac.uk/∼nvaughan/robot.

## References

Coros, S., et al.: Locomotion skills for simulated quadrupeds. ACM Trans. Graphics (TOG) **30**(4), 1–11 (2011)
Devosoft: Avida (2009). http://avida.devosoft.org
Ventrella, J., Dodd, B.: Darwin Pond (2005). http://www.ventrella.com/darwin/darwin.html
Lenski, R.E.: The evolutionary origin of complex features. Nature **423**, 139–144 (2003)
Olson, R., et al.: Evolved digital ecosystems: dynamic steady state, not optimal fixed point. In: Advances in ALife, ECAL, vol. 12, pp. 126–133 (2013)

Sims, K.: Evolving 3D morphology and behavior by competition. Artif. Life **1**(4), 353–372 (1994)

Vaughan, N.: Simulated robotic autonomous agents with motion evolution. In: European Conference on Artificial Life ECAL (2015)

Vaughan, N.: Swarm communication by evolutionary algorithms. In: IEEE Evolving and Adaptive Intelligent Systems (EAIS). IEEE (2018)

Wystrach, A., Dewar, A.D.M., Philippides, A., Graham, P.: How do field of view and resolution affect the information content of panoramic scenes for visual navigation? A computational investigation. J. Comp. Physiol. A **202**(2), 87–95 (2016)

# Multi-agent Reinforcement Learning for Swarm Retrieval with Evolving Neural Network

Neil Vaughan[1,2(✉)]

[1] University of Chester, Chester, UK
n.vaughan@chester.ac.uk
[2] Royal Academy of Engineering, London, UK

**Abstract.** This research investigates methods for evolving swarm communication in a simulated colony of ants using pheromone when foraging for food. This research implemented neuroevolution and obtained the capability to learn pheromone communication autonomously. Building on previous literature on pheromone communication, this research applies evolution to adjust the topology and weights of an artificial neural network (ANN) which controls the ant behaviour. Comparison of performance is made between a hard-coded benchmark algorithm (BM1), a fixed topology ANN and neuroevolution of the ANN topology and weights. The resulting neuroevolution produced a neural network which was successfully evolved to achieve the task objective, to collect food and return it to a location.

**Keywords:** Artificial ants · Neuroevolution · Swarm communication

## 1 Introduction

This research has developed a model of ant colony swarm intelligence behaviour. The novel aspect is that behaviour of pheromone navigation was not hard coded, as in most implementations, but has evolved using ANNs and an implementation of neurovevolution. Compared to previous research which failed to evolve standard and fixed topology ANNs for ant behaviour (Collins and Jefferson 1990), this research produces successful evolution and applies a more comprehensive neuroevolution methodology including complexification and augmentation of ANN topology and weights, as described by NEAT (Stanley 2004).

Inspired by biological ants, this research aims to provide insights to advance understanding of how pheromone communication evolved in biological organisms. Application of neuroevolutionary computational modelling provides a useful analogy to how brains may have evolved to produce biological organism behaviours. Nature inspired algorithms largely enabled recent advances in multi-agent reinforcement learning.

© Springer International Publishing AG, part of Springer Nature 2018
V. Vouloutsi et al. (Eds.): Living Machines 2018, LNAI 10928, pp. 522–526, 2018.
https://doi.org/10.1007/978-3-319-95972-6_56

### 1.1 Background of Swarm Communication Systems

The core interest of this work is how ant pheromone communication can be evolved in a computational model. There have been some interesting works attempting to evolve ant pheromone communication, and evolving swarm communication in general. Literature on pheromone communication is described by various key words: ant evolution, pheromone simulation, central-place foraging algorithm (CPFA), pheromone recruitment (Letendre and Moses 2013).

A milestone early attempt to use a computer simulation to evolve ant foraging strategies using pheromones which resemble behaviours of biological ants was AntFarm (Collins and Jefferson 1990). AntFarm implemented an early form of neuroevolution, which was used to evolve the ANNs which learn behaviour for effective ant pheromone communication (Collins and Jefferson 1990). Neuroevolution methods in AntFarm evolved both the ANN connectivity pattern (topology) and weights of the ANN which were under genetic control in a genotype. Limitations were that: (1) AntFarm did not successful evolve any cooperative foraging which was the main objective. (2) A basic, conventional ANN was used, when compared to the wider range of operators, sigmoids and activation functions with complexification as used in more recent neuroevolution models such as NEAT (Stanley 2004). (3) The number of neurons and connections were not under genetic control. That feature is possible in this new research.

The first research to evolve Ant pheromone foraging was by Panait and Luke (2004). Previous research showed that 3D physical simulated robots can evolve longer legs and better eyesight by natural selection when in competition (Vaughan 2015).

## 2 Implementation of Swarm Reinforcement Learning

Amongst foraging behaviours, signals can 'evaporate over time' simulated by decrementing the artificial pheromone – a global rather than local update. Ants have 13 input sensors: (1, 2) the location within the 9 adjacent cells (Moore neighbourhood) of the highest pheromone, (3, 4) the location within Moore neighbourhood which is closest to the nest, given by a 'compass sensor'. (5, 6) location within Moore neighbourhood of food. (7, 8) the direction of the ant's previous move, (9, 10) a direction picked at random, (11) a Boolean indicating whether the ant is currently carrying food, (12) a random number, (13) a fixed value of 1 (Bias). These are referred to as the pre-computed inputs and they remain the same even when the controller is changed (BM1, ANNs, NEAT).

The controller is a 'black box' brain which decides the animal behaviour at timestep $t$, based on the pre-computed inputs from the ant's sensors. The experiments were repeated using different controllers: a hard-coded benchmark (BM1), a fixed topology neural network and neuroevolution by adjusting the topology and weights of an ANN.

The resulting output of the controller determines the direction in which the ant moves. After each ant has moved, a number of post-move local updates are automatically applied. (1) If the ant is now standing on food and isn't carrying any, it automatically picks food up. (2) If the ant is carrying food, pheromone is deposited with strength inversely proportional to the time since collection. (3) If an ant is already carrying food and is now standing on a nest, it automatically drops the food. This representation realistically assumes that biological ants already could pick up and drop food before they evolved pheromone communication. These tasks are regarded as automatic responses which we assume have been learnt previously. After a full iteration, when all ants have finished making a move, a global update is triggered in which all pheromone is evaporated (decremented). A number of different evaporation rates including decrementing and various percentage reductions were tested to identify how evaporation rate affects the ability to evolve navigation controllers.

## 3   Custom Designed Benchmark Algorithm

A hard-coded benchmark foraging algorithm was developed and tested with 10 random levels of food and obstacles generated in a 500 × 300 grid. The benchmark was run for 5000 timesteps and the number of food collected to the nest was recorded. Each run took approximately 19 s. Some of the 10 levels resulted in food being returned very rapidly, due to random positioning close to the nest (Fig. 1).

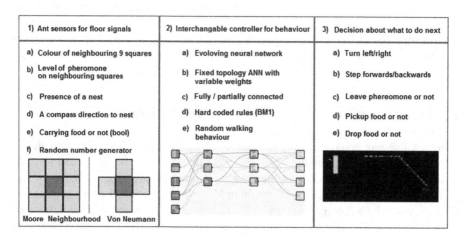

**Fig. 1.** The three main components of the developed evolving ant pheromone system.

Every food square has 30 foods so it requires 30 collections either by the same or different ants. Food squares are in clusters or around 10–15 on each cluster (Fig. 2).

A scenario was tested in which there was no compass, to identify whether a benchmark locate the nest direction, using only pheromone. The algorithm did not locate the nest, ants moved randomly, leaving pheromone everywhere, attracting other ants in the wrong directions (Fig. 3). Also obstacles (yellow) cause blockages (Fig. 4b).

Food distance from nest has various effects. With closer food, the pheromone trail will be stronger and it takes less time to get back to the nest. But longer trails have

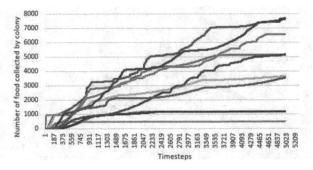

**Fig. 2.** Food collected over time during ten runs applying BM1 for pheromone foriaging.

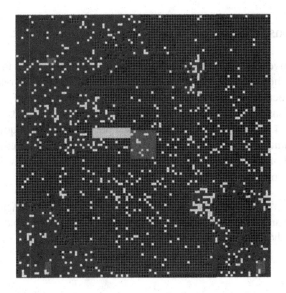

**Fig. 3.** The BM1 algorithm running without a compass sensor – ants have no way of finding the nest once food is discovered and pheromone is scattered randomly. (Color figure online)

greater chance of other ants walking into them by accident, so further food may attract more ants that way (Fig. 4a). Two foods were discovered: a small food in the upper right is favoured compared to a larger food in the bottom left, because it is closer, the pheromone is stronger and all ants abandon the larger food until the pheromone evaporates and knowledge of its location is lost to the swarm.

Each decision that an ant times is subject to probability so that it is always possible for an ant to do something unpredictable at any time. The effect of introducing a probability of random decisions.

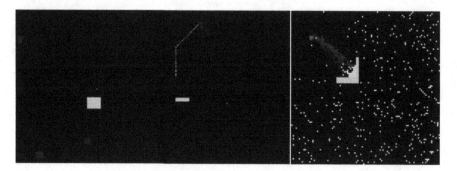

**Fig. 4.** (a) A large food supply (lower left) is abandoned in favour of a small food (upper right), closer to the nest with stronger pheromone. (b) a V shaped obstacle. (Color figure online)

## 4   Conclusions

This paper has investigated the benefits of neuroevolution compared to fixed topology ANN by testing how pheromone behaviour can evolve in both, in relation to a hard coded designed benchmark (BM1).

This paper has demonstrated neuroevolution applied to evolve pheromonome communication in simulated ant colonies. The core intelligence required to perform pheromone communication was summarised in form of the hard coded benchmark BM1, comprised of an IF block with 5 conditions and this behaviour was demonstrated to be effectively mimicked by the evolving ANN.

**Acknowledgment.** The research was funded by The Royal Academy of Engineering (RAEng) as part of the Research Fellowship awarded to Dr Neil Vaughan as Principle Investigator, and was supported by the University and Chester.

## References

Collins, R.J., Jefferson, D.: Antfarm: towards simulated evolution. Computer Science Department, University of California (1990)

Vaughan, N.: Simulated robotic autonomous agents with motion evolution. In: European Conference on Artificial Life ECAL, p. 27. MIT Press (2015). http://www.cs.york.ac.uk/nature/ecal2015/late-breaking/ecal2015-late-breaking-proceedings.pdf

Stanley, K.O.: Efficient evolution of neural networks through complexification (Doctoral dissertation) (2004)

Letendre, K., Moses, M.E.: Synergy in ant foraging strategies: memory and communication alone and in combination. In: Proceedings of the 15th Annual Conference Companion on Genetic and Evolutionary Computation (GECCO 2013 Companion), pp. 41–48. ACM, New York (2013)

Panait, L., Luke, S.: Learning ant foraging behaviors. In: Proceedings of the Ninth International Conference on the Simulation and Synthesis of Living Systems (ALIFE9), pp. 575–580 (2004)

# A Neuromechanical Rat Model
# with a Complete Set of Hind Limb Muscles

Fletcher Young[1(✉)], Alexander J. Hunt[2], and Roger D. Quinn[1]

[1] Department of Mechanical and Aerospace Engineering,
Case Western Reserve University, Cleveland, OH 44106-7222, USA
{fry2, rdq}@case.edu
[2] Department of Mechanical and Materials Engineering,
Portland State University, Portland, OR 97207, USA
ajh26@pdx.edu

**Abstract.** To accomplish many useful tasks, robots must be capable of navigating complex, dynamic environments. For this reason, robots often take inspiration from the adaptive responsiveness inherent to living organisms. Our existing model of rat neuromechanics [1] has provided insight into neuromuscular control structures that can generate quadruped locomotion. However, that model is limited by only using a single antagonistic muscle pair per hind limb joint. This work demonstrates a neuromuscular rat hind leg model of a complete muscle set with biologically derived attachment points as reported in the literature. The redundant nature of the muscle architecture provides new challenges for coordinating walking, including the need to account for synergistic muscle contractions. A linear decomposition of generalized muscle activation is applied to functional muscle groups responsible for actuating hind limb actuation. Functional group activation signals are then combined to recreate the generalized inputs previously determined to coordinate motion indicating a possible method of representing muscle synergy in the expanded model. This expanded hind limb model is fundamental to the analysis of three-dimensional motion as well as the impact of more sophisticated muscle synergy decompositions.

**Keywords:** Robot · Biomechanics · Muscle · Muscle synergy

## 1 Introduction

More and more, robots must be able to navigate complex, real-world environments. Sufficient muscle, limb, and gait coordination methods must be developed in parallel with dynamic control systems to create machines capable of functioning in unforeseen circumstances. Nature provides a framework for living creatures to navigate unfamiliar environments with relative ease. Living organisms benefit from a highly coupled neurological and biomechanical (neuromechanical) control system that is difficult to replicate with existing synthetic resources. Designing agile robots while simultaneously considering the impacts of both of these aspects of the neuromechanical system could hold the key to robotic innovation.

© Springer International Publishing AG, part of Springer Nature 2018
V. Vouloutsi et al. (Eds.): Living Machines 2018, LNAI 10928, pp. 527–537, 2018.
https://doi.org/10.1007/978-3-319-95972-6_57

Biologically inspired, legged robots have been developed to model organisms from small insects [6, 15] to large humanoid robots [17, 21]. These robots include mechanical and control systems, in some ways modeling the neuromechanical system in their animal counterparts. Control systems for robotic movement range from relatively simple finite state machines [2] to more complex control algorithms [13]. These control systems may be well suited for predetermined environments in which the robot must carry out defined tasks. However, animals rely on a deeply interconnected set of neural pathways to modulate their activity and respond to a diverse range of conditions, all while maintaining the ability to carry out vital tasks.

Quadruped locomotion has been extensively studied in small animals such as rats [9, 10, 12] and cats [5, 14, 16]. Our previous model of rat locomotion, shown in Fig. 1, demonstrated stable walking patterns produced by generalized extensor and flexor muscles located in the hind limbs [8, 9]. Muscle contractions are generated by motor neuron activations and coordinated by pattern formation layers at each joint.

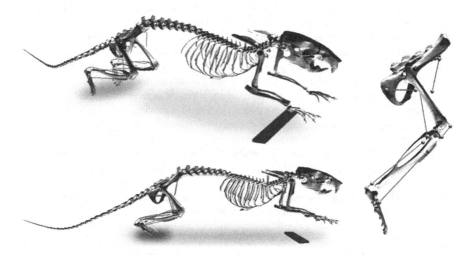

**Fig. 1.** The previous rat model includes a complete rat skeleton actuated by a set of generalized antagonistic muscle pairs (red lines). Muscle attachment points (yellow) are derived from biological data [12]. (Color figure online)

A muscle synergy describes the spatial and temporal combination of multiple muscles to coordinate movement as a possible method for the body to reduce the complexity of motor control [1]. Modeling the redundancy of muscular control is a complex challenge as there exist an infinite combination of muscle activations that result in the overall action of the group. Additionally, many muscles are activated in multiple synergies, making the classification of functional groups difficult.

Prior generalized muscle analysis provides insight into the necessary actions of a complete muscle synergy. We hypothesized that this generalized signal could be decomposed into individual muscle activation signals to simulate the effects of synergy-based actuation. Prior work has demonstrated the capability of generalized signals to generate stepping motion. Ultimately, muscle synergy groups will need to produce similar aggregate signals for comparable stepping motion.

## 2  Modeling Animal Locomotion

### 2.1  Model Description

A model of rat locomotion was developed in Animatlab [4], a neuromechanical simulation program. The model utilizes 3D-rendered bone meshes of a statically fused rat skeleton with hinge joints located in the hind limbs at the hip, knee, and ankle. These joints constrain motion to the sagittal plane, allowing connected bone meshes to be driven by a set of antagonist muscles. The rat forelimbs are suspended 5 cm above a bar that moves along the ground with a small coefficient of friction. One muscle of a generalized extensor/flexor antagonistic pair generates torque about each hind limb joint, creating walking patterns as motor neuron stimulation is applied via a model neural system [7].

Twelve pairs of generalized muscles control the hind limb joints. All muscles are represented as linear Hill muscles (Fig. 2), modeling both passive and active elements of natural muscle [18]. The Hill model represents muscle stiffness, tendon compliance, and viscoelastic damping. A single active component represents the tension-generating, contractile unit of the muscle.

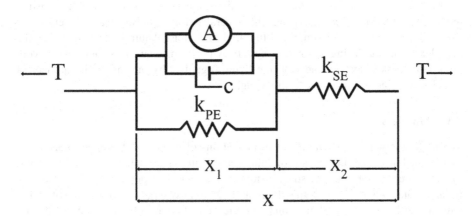

**Fig. 2.** Linear Hill muscle model

Toe force recordings were used to calculate joint torque from inverse kinematics [22]. All motion torque is generated by the antagonist muscle pair at each joint. Whole-muscle torque calculations were used to determine muscle tension in the generalized extensor and flexor.

Once the tension for the entire muscle was determined, individual muscle activation levels (the active unit of the Hill model) were calculated using the following equation:

$$\frac{dT}{dt} = \frac{k_{SE}}{c} \left( k_{PE}x + c\dot{x} - \left( 1 + \frac{k_{PE}}{k_{SE}} \right) T + A \right)$$

where T is the tension in the whole muscle, x is the muscle length, c is the damping, $k_{pe}$ is the parallel element stiffness, $k_{se}$ is the series element stiffness, and A is the activation of the contractile element.

Using the Hill stimulus-tension equation, the activation was mapped to the motor neuron activation voltage necessary to generate appropriate contractions in the muscle using the following equation.

$$A = \left( 1 - \frac{(x - x_{REST})^2}{x_{WIDTH}^2} \right) \cdot \frac{A_{MAX}}{1 + \exp(-S \cdot (E_{MID} - V_{MN}))}$$

where $A_{max}$ is the maximum active force the muscle can apply, S is the maximal slope of the activation curve, and $E_{mid}$ shifts the sigmoid along the V axis. This equation represents both the length-tension and stimulus-tension curves of the Hill muscle model [4].

## 2.2    Expanding the Muscle System

In order to account for more complex leg motions, it is necessary to expand the existing model to include more muscles than the generalized antagonistic pairs currently utilized. The previous model simplified the hind limb musculature system to reduce the complexity of interfacing the neural system with the mechanical system. This work brings the model more in line with the living organism by increasing the number of muscles per hind leg from six to thirty-eight.

## 2.3    Muscle Synergy

Leg motion is not simply the result of activations of pairs of antagonistic muscles at each joint but a coordinated set of individual contractions called muscle synergies. Muscle synergies describe the spatial and temporal muscle group activations necessary for an organism to carry out a specific motion. Muscle synergies have been explored in humans [20] and cats [19] in which muscle activation profiles are combined with varying weights to produce limb motion. A more thorough neuromechanical model of the rat hind limb needs a more complete musculature and a neural model that activates those muscles to form complete synergies for efficient limb motion and force production.

Expanding out model to include the complete hind limb muscle system of the rat and understanding its muscle synergies will allow us to develop a neural system for its control that should better match that of the rat. The long term goal is to develop a neuromechanical model that mimics the rat's abilities to walk, rapidly respond to perturbations, and intentionally place its limbs for stability. The work reported here examines a simple muscle synergy method in which the generalized extensor/flexor activation levels and motor neuron activations are equally divided between muscles in their respective functional groups.

## 3   Methods

Muscles attachment points from the literature [11] were transformed from bone-centric coordinate systems to Animatlab local coordinate systems. Attachments points allowed for the addition of thirty-eight muscles to the hind limb. Muscles were categorized into functional groups depending on which joint they primarily actuated. Generalized extensor and flexor activation levels were calculated for each joint. The generalized signals were then linearly decomposed into individual muscle activations split evenly among all muscles within the associated extensor or flexor group.

### 3.1   Attachments

Muscle attachment coordinates for proximal, intermediate, and distal connections of thirty-eight documented muscles in the rat hind limb [11] were used to determine the attachment locations on the Animatlab model. In the literature, attachment coordinates were measured with respect to a bone coordinate system defined by bony landmarks that differed from the local reference frame associated with bone meshes used by the simulation.

Approximate positions of the bony landmarks were manually added to each bone mesh. Bone coordinate system unit vectors were created with respect to the bony landmarks as defined by Johnson [11]. A coordinate transform was applied to the bone coordinate system positions, providing local reference frame positions for each muscle attachment. Figure 3 demonstrates the coordinate system orientation and subsequent attachment point map.

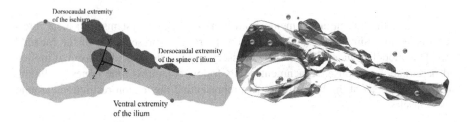

**Fig. 3.** Left, three dimensional positions of bony landmarks were approximated in Animatlab. Bone coordinate systems were positioned relative to the bony landmarks of the structure. Right, a completed rendering of the pelvis with muscle attachment points in the local reference frame.

Transformed attachment points were mapped onto individual bone structures separately to verify the accuracy of the coordinate transform. Independent bone structure point maps were then applied to a full hind limb model. Hind limb muscles were then attached to the relevant muscle attachment points. Some muscles were connected by an intermediate point to represent constrained muscle movement due to support structures such as tendinous bands at the ankle. This full muscle leg represents a more thorough hind limb model well-suited for 3D motion and muscle synergy analysis.

While the coordinates of the muscle attachments themselves were very clear, the bony landmarks were approximated. Additionally, coordinate system directions in dorsal and caudal directions had to be fine-tuned to determine a viable point configuration.

### 3.2    Muscle Synergy

Each muscle was sorted into muscle synergy groups based on their insertion points and the joint for which the muscle would generate the greatest range of motion. Many muscles act across multiple joints, making definitive classification of specific functional groups difficult. For example, the set of muscles connecting the pelvis to the tibia generate extension of the hip but also flexion of the knee. Functional group classifications of other rodent functional groups [3] were considered when categorizing the muscle synergy groups for this work. Synergy group activation levels were developed using the aforementioned muscle activation technique and divided evenly between each muscle in the group.

### 3.3    Muscle Activation Levels

A program that analyzed the force activation levels of generalized antagonistic muscles in the rat hind limb [8] was modified to activate muscle synergies instead of individual muscles. Theta and torque data from videos of a walking rat were evaluated by the program to determine muscle activation levels for the generalized extensor and flexor at each joint. The resulting generalized activations signals were then divided equally between all extensor and flexor muscles of the synergy group.

## 4    Results

Transforming the muscle attachments from bone coordinate systems to a local reference frames in Animatlab resulted in a more thorough representation of the rat hind limb. This model includes all muscles necessary to generate three dimensional motion and perturbation response. Attachment points follow contours of the bones, including intermediate points at the base of the tibia representing the tendon restrictions around those muscles.

The generalized activation signals were divided into the number of muscles in each extensor flexor group for the hind limb joints. In the case of the hip extensor group, for example, the overall muscle activation signal was divided equally between the ten muscles. With the decomposed activation, no individual muscle is capable of replicating the generalized muscle response. However, when the entire synergistic muscle group is activated the group is able to achieve the same activation response as the generalized extensor (Figs. 4 and 5).

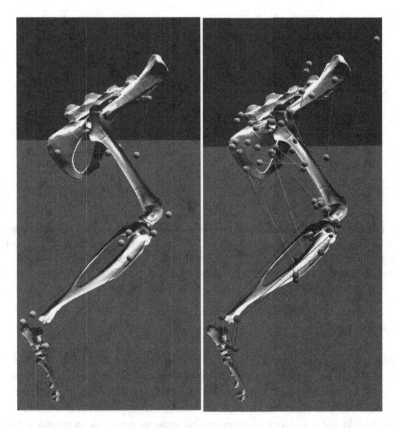

**Fig. 4.** Left, the previous hind limb model for the rat. Each red line represents a generalized muscle. Right, the complete hind limb model. Colors represent muscles of the same synergy group but do not directly affect function. The full list of muscles and their associated functional group are listed in Table 1. (Color figure online)

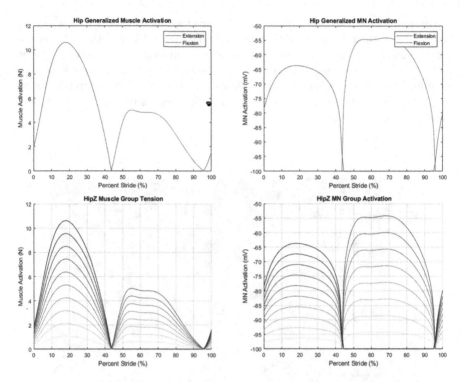

**Fig. 5.** Top, the generalized muscle responses of the extensor and flexor of the hip. Bottom, the effect of adding synergistic muscle responses. The increasing color saturation represents the addition of muscle contributions to the functional group. As more muscles are added to the functional group, the activation response resembles the generalized activations previously generated. (Color figure online)

## 5    Discussion

This work has expanded upon a simplified version of the rat hind limb model utilizing biologically relevant muscle attachment points. A more complete set of muscles is fundamental to analyzing the coordination of muscle synergies in future model analysis. Additionally, a previous method for determining generalized activations was modified to add the capability of representing muscle synergies in neural activation. Both the biomechanical and neural developments presented in this work demonstrate the capability of the revised model to represent a more complete picture of the animal's biological activity.

A method of parsing up an existing generalized signal into individual muscle activation has been presented. While this work adds nuance to the generalized representations of the previous model, it is unlikely that individual muscle responses will be divided equally between individual components of the synergy group. Synergy responses are largely task-specific and also depend upon individual muscle parameters. In the future, a more sophisticated method will provide further insight into how cooperative muscle activation can generate a comprehensive signal comparable to the generalized activations presented previously.

Increasing the complexity of the hind limb acts as a gateway to future work. Abstracted models of the rat hind limb prevent comprehensive exploration of 3D motion and the impact of muscle synergies on leg action. In striving for a more biologically relevant model, these key factors must be addressed. A leg model with biologically relevant muscle attachments is fundamental to a complete rat model.

As the project moves forward, a more refined muscle stimulation protocol must be implemented to determine exactly which synergies are activated, what the muscular composition of those synergies are, and how they are coordinated with a neural control system.

**Acknowledgements.** This work was supported by NSF IIS160811 and a GAANN Fellowship (Grant No. P200A150316).

# Appendix

See Table 1.

**Table 1.** List of muscles included in the revised rat hind limb model and associated muscle synergy group

| Muscle | Functional Group |
|---|---|
| Adductor brevis | Hip Ext |
| Adductor longus | Hip Ext |
| Adductor magnus | Hip Ext |
| Biceps femoris anterior | Hip Ext |
| Caudofemoralis | Hip Ext |
| Gemellus inferior | Hip Ext |
| Gemellus superior | Hip Ext |
| Obturator externus | Hip Ext |
| Obturator internus | Hip Ext |
| Quadratus femoris | Hip Ext |
| Gluteus maximus | Hip Flx |
| Gluteus medius | Hip Flx |
| Gluteus minimus | Hip Flx |
| Illiopsoas | Hip Flx |
| Pectineus | Hip Flx |
| Piriformis | Hip Flx |
| Rectus femoris | Hip Flx |
| Tensor fascia latae | Hip Flx |
| Vastus intermedius | Knee Ext |

(*continued*)

**Table 1.** (*continued*)

| Muscle | Functional Group |
|---|---|
| Vastus lateralis | Knee Ext |
| Vastus medialis | Knee Ext |
| Biceps femoris posterior | Knee Flx |
| Gracilis anticus | Knee Flx |
| Gracilis posticus | Knee Flx |
| Semimembranosus | Knee Flx |
| Semitendinosus accessory | Knee Flx |
| Semitendinosus primary | Knee Flx |
| Flexor digitalis longus | Ankle Ext |
| Flexor hallicus longus | Ankle Ext |
| Lateral gastrocnemius | Ankle Ext |
| Medial gastrocnemius | Ankle Ext |
| Peronei | Ankle Ext |
| Plantaris | Ankle Ext |
| Popliteus | Ankle Ext |
| Soleus | Ankle Ext |
| Tibialis posterior | Ankle Ext |
| Extensor digitorum longus | Ankle Flx |
| Tibialis anterior | Ankle Flx |

# References

1. Bernstein, N.: The Coordination and Regulation of Movement. Pergamon Press, London (1967)
2. Brooks, R.: A robot that walks; emergent behaviors from a carefully evolved network. Neural Comput. **1**(2), 253–262 (1989)
3. Charles, J.: Musculoskeletal geometry, muscle architecture and functional specialisations of the mouse hindlimb. PLoS ONE **11**(4), e0147669 (2016)
4. Cofer, D.: AnimatLab: a 3D graphics environment for neuromechanical simulations. J. Neurosci. Meth. **187**(2), 280–288 (2010)
5. Conway, B., Hultborn, H., Kiehn, O.: Proprioceptive input resets central locomotor rhythm in the spinal cat. Exper. Brain Res. **68**(3), 643–656 (1987)
6. Goldberg, B., Zufferey, R., Doshi, N., Helbling, E.F., Whittredge, G., Kovac, M., Wood, R.: Power and control autonomy for high-speed locomotion with an insect-scale legged robot. IEEE Robot. Autom. Lett. **3**(2), 987–993 (2018)
7. Hooper, S.: Neural control of unloaded leg posture and of leg swing in stick insect, cockroach, and mouse differs from that in larger animals. J. Neurosci. **29**(13), 4109–4119 (2009)
8. Hunt, A.J., Szczecinski, N.S., Andrada, E., Fischer, M., Quinn, R.D.: Using animal data and neural dynamics to reverse engineer a neuromechanical rat model. In: Wilson, S.P., Verschure, P.F.M.J., Mura, A., Prescott, T.J. (eds.) LIVINGMACHINES 2015. LNCS (LNAI), vol. 9222, pp. 211–222. Springer, Cham (2015). https://doi.org/10.1007/978-3-319-22979-9_21

9. Hunt, A., Schmidt, M., Fischer, M., Quinn, R.D.: Neuromechanical simulation of an inter-leg controller for tetrapod coordination. In: Duff, A., Lepora, N.F., Mura, A., Prescott, T.J., Verschure, P.F.M.J. (eds.) Living Machines 2014. LNCS (LNAI), vol. 8608, pp. 142–153. Springer, Cham (2014). https://doi.org/10.1007/978-3-319-09435-9_13

10. Joãoa, F.: Anatomical reference frame versus planar analysis: implications for the kinematics of the rat hindlimb during locomotion. Rev. Neurosci. **21**(6), 469–486 (2010)

11. Johnson, W.: A three-dimensional model of the rat hindlimb: musculoskeletal geometry and muscle moment arms. J. Biomech. **41**(3), 610–619 (2008)

12. Johnson, W.: Application of a rat hindlimb model: a prediction of force spaces reachable through stimulation of nerve fascicles. IEEE Trans. Biomed. Eng. **58**(12), 3328–3338 (2011)

13. Kim, J., Park, I., Oh, J.: Walking control algorithm of biped humanoid robot on uneven and inclined floor. J. Intell. Robot. Syst. **48**(4), 457–484 (2007)

14. McCrea, D., Rybak, I.: Organization of mammalian locomotor rhythm and pattern generation. Brain Res. Rev. **57**(1), 134–146 (2008)

15. Minati, L.: Versatile locomotion control of a hexapod robot using a hierarchical network of nonlinear oscillator circuits. IEEE Access **6**, 8042–8065 (2018)

16. Pearson, K.: Role of sensory feedback in the control of stance duration in walking cats. Brain Res. Rev. **57**(1), 222–227 (2008)

17. Ramezani, A., Hurst, J., Hamed, K., Grizzle, J.: Performance analysis and feedback control of ATRIAS, a three-dimensional bipedal robot. J. Dyn. Syst. Measur. Control **136**(2), 021012-021012-12 (2014)

18. Shadmehr, R., Wise, S.: Computational Neurobiology of Reaching and Pointing: a Foundation for Motor Learning. MIT Press, Cambridge, MA (2005)

19. Ting, L., Macpherson, J.: A limited set of muscle synergies for force control during a postural task. J. Neurophysiol. **93**(1), 609–613 (2005)

20. Torres-Oviedo, G., Ting, L.: Muscle synergies characterizing human postural responses. J. Neurophysiol. **98**(4), 2144–2156 (2007)

21. Van der Noot, N., Ijspeert, A., Ronsse, R.: Bio-inspired controller achieving forward speed modulation with a 3D bipedal walker. Int. J. Robot. Res. **37**(1), 168–196 (2018)

22. Witte, H., Biltzinger, J., Hackert, R., Schilling, N., Schmidt, M., Reich, C., Fischer, M.: Torque patterns of the limbs of small therian mammals during locomotion on flat ground. J. Exper. Biol. **205**(9), 1339–1353 (2002)

# Guided Growth of Bacterial Cellulose Biofilms

Katia Zolotovsky[1,2(✉)], Merav Gazit[2], and Christine Ortiz[3]

[1] Department of Biological Engineering,
Massachusetts Institute of Technology, Cambridge, USA
zolka@mit.edu
[2] Department of Architecture,
Massachusetts Institute of Technology, Cambridge, USA
[3] Department of Materials Science and Engineering,
Massachusetts Institute of Technology, Cambridge, USA

**Abstract.** Biofilm, a colony of microorganisms embedded in a polymeric substance, is a bio-hybrid material system that naturally integrates the sensing-actuating capabilities of living cells with the mechanical properties of an organic material. To realize the potential of designing novel biologically active materials from natural biofilms, we propose here a Guided Growth design process, as an example, using the cellulose-producing bacterium *Gluconacetobacter xylinus*. The Guided Growth process employs three design strategies: *information* (programming living cells), *growth* (growing biomaterials that inhabit cells), and *flow* (regulating growth environment). This combination of programming bacteria and regulating the biofilm growth promotes the development of future living materials and devices, for applications such as responsive robotic skins, solar cells, or even photosynthetic building envelopes.

**Keywords:** Biohybrid materials · Living materials · Synthetic biology
Material patterning · Biofilms · Multiscale design · Guided growth
Bio-computational interface · 3D Printing

## 1 Introduction

Natural multicellular assemblies such as biofilms and skeletal tissues have distinctive characteristics that would be useful for materials production and patterning [1–7]. They can respond to their environment and tune material structure and properties in the process of hierarchical self-assembly [7–9]. Furthermore, as the cells stay biologically-active within the material, they can continuously perform functions of sensing, actuating, self-healing [9, 10]. In this work, we use one such material system - a biofilm of bacterial cellulose - directly rather than as an inspiration, to design novel living materials that can be further developed for applications in the field of robotics, medicine, and sustainable products. We design workflows to grow, pattern, edit structure and properties of bacterial cellulose biofilms, and shape them into three-dimensional components. Furthermore, we build a device to guide the process of growth into three-dimensional components with tunable structure and properties by regulating the flow of nutrients, additives, and air.

© Springer International Publishing AG, part of Springer Nature 2018
V. Vouloutsi et al. (Eds.): Living Machines 2018, LNAI 10928, pp. 538–548, 2018.
https://doi.org/10.1007/978-3-319-95972-6_58

A biofilm of bacterial cellulose is a coordinated population of *G. xylinus* embedded in a structural layer of cellulose. As one of its basic functions, *G. xylinus* cells polymerize glucose into long chains of cellulose. These chains then self-assemble on the cell membrane into cellulose fibers that mesh together to create structural cellulose where bacteria cells stay embedded (Fig. 1).

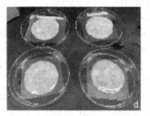

**Fig. 1.** Bacterial cellulose biofilm.

Bacterial cellulose (BC) has recently received extensive attention from researchers due to its unique material properties, such as high water capacity, high crystallinity, ultrafine fiber networks with a diameter of 20–100 nm, high purity, and Young's modulus [11–13]. The Young's modulus of BC sheet is about 30 GPa [14, 15], while the modulus of isolated BC fiber is 130 GPa which is comparable to Kevlar and steel [14, 16]. Due to its unique properties, BC holds excellent potential for a range of applications, such as textiles [12], biomedical applications (e.g., drug delivery, tissue engineering scaffolds) [12, 13], and sustainable building components [17].

We see the potential of BC to become a living material. By pairing genetic regulation of cellulose production by *G. xylinus* cells with the regulation of biofilm growth, we produce self-assembling biologically active biofilms with tunable structure, properties, and function.

In the scope of this paper, we present initial results in genetically engineering *G. xylinus*. In parallel, we present novel workflows for culturing, adding substances *in-situ*, and post-processing 3D components from bacterial cellulose. We combine tools of materials science and digital fabrication to shape bacterial cellulose into three-dimensional components as it grows, add substances to it to create bio-composites, and modify its properties. We built custom-made microcontrollers and designed computational scripts to control physicochemical conditions and regulate the shape and properties of bacterial cellulose biofilms in each growth vessel.

## 2   Materials and Methods

### 2.1   Culturing *G. Xylinus*

Bacterial cellulose biofilm was obtained by statically culturing *G. xylinus* (ATCC 53582) in Hestrin–Schramm (HS) medium at 27 °C for seven days. The growth rate was 10 mm of biofilm in 5–7days [18]. The harvested BC pellicle was soaked in 1N NaOH and heated to 90 °C for 20 min followed by washing thoroughly with deionized (DI) water three times and washing until neutral pH was achieved. The rest of chemicals were analytical grade and used without any further treatment.

## 2.2    Genetic Transformation of *G. Xylinus*

Plasmids were introduced into G. xylinus cells via a conjugation process with E. coli WM6026, defected in death associated gene (DAP), received from Lina Gonzalez from the Voigt lab, MIT. A plasmid of interest was first introduced to *E. coli* WM6026 via electroporation [19]. Both bacteria cultures were grown in 50 ml of corresponding media (HS media for G. *xylinus* and DAP enriched LB media for *E. coli* WM6026).

For *G. xylinus*, the culture was vortexed to release the cells from the cellulose matrix, and the supernatant was transferred into 50 ml Falcon tube. *G. xylinus* was centrifuged for 10 min at maximum speed and suspended in 5 ml HS media. *E. coli* WM6026 was washed twice with DAP enriched media to remove all the antibiotics from the overnight culture, and then resuspended again in 5 mL DAP enriched LB without antibiotics.

150 uL of *G. xylinus* and 50 uL of *E. coli* WM6026 were added into a 1.5 mL tube. The mixture of cells was plated on HS glucose agar with no antibiotics and the mating reaction takes place for 8 h. After this, the transformed colonies were grown in 5 mL HS media without antibiotics overnight, vortexed to release cells from the cellulose matrix, plated on HS agar with antibiotics at 30 °C for 3–5 days until the transformed colonies appear.

## 2.3    Growth Vessels Fabrication

Molds for silicone casting were modeled in Rhinoceros and 3D printed on Makerbot Replicator+ Desktop 3D Printer using flexible filament (NinjaFlex TPU 3D Printing Filament) for easy demolding. Silpot 184 silicone casting resin (Dow Corning) was used for the growth vessels. The elastomer and curing agent (Parts A & B) were mixed in 10:1 ratio. The mixture was then placed in a vacuum chamber for 10 min to avoid air bubbles. After degassing, the mixture was poured into the 3D printed molds and baked for 20 min at 125 °C in an oven until cured. Special features were integrated into the growth vessels design: inlet and outlet for incoming and outgoing tubing and ridges for growing edges (Fig. 5).

## 2.4    Bio Composites Preparation

The preparation of the BC with polyvinyl alcohol (PVA) composites was made by modifying protocol [20] as follows: BC membranes, grown for seven days, with a thickness of ∼3 mm were washed from the growth medium with distilled water and purified by immersing in NaOH. PVA solution was prepared by mixing PVA and distilled water for 30 min at 80 °C. The samples were then immersed in PVA solution with a concentration of 6% or 10% for 18 h in ∼35 °C, followed by 14 h in ∼90 °C. The samples were then frozen for 17 h in −20 °C and thawed for 6 h in room temp. After thawing, the samples were reheated in the oven at ∼65 °C to remove excess PVA. They were then frozen again at −20 °C followed by −80 °C in preparation for freeze-drying. The samples were then freeze-dried for six days. The BC-Magnetite ($Fe_3O_4$) composite was prepared by adding magnetite particles into the culture medium.

## 2.5  Mechanical Testing

G. *xylius* was incubated as a static culture for seven days at 30C. After that BC biofilm was harvested from the growth culture, washed in distilled water, purified by boiling in 0.1M NaOH for 30 min, and washed again with water. The BC biofilm was sealed in plastic and placed in a stove 70C for 48 h to dry. The dried material was laser cut using 120 W Epilog machine, with parameters of speed 40, power 3, into dogbone geometries (ASTM D638 TypeV) for tensile testing. The weight of each sample was ~0.02 g. The samples were loaded in uniaxial tension until failure on a Zwick mechanical tester (Zwick Z010, Zwick Roelle, Germany) under displacement controlled loading at a strain rate of 0.5 mm/min using a 2.5 kN load cell.

## 2.6  Bioreactor Components

The bioreactor device consists of 21 hexagon growth vessels, 4 types of growth medium for variation in in-situ growth conditions, PVA solution and $Fe_3O_4$ powder for post-growth bio-composites, reserve containers for renewable waste, 10 miniature solenoid valves, 6 liquid and air pumps, custom-made MOSFET circuits, and Arduino microcontroller connected to a laptop in order to actuate, monitor and receive feedback from the system.

# 3  *Information*: Programming Living Cells

In the bacterial cellulose system, the processes of biochemical transformations and molecular self-assembly of cellulose biofilm from sugar molecules are encoded in the DNA. Therefore, macro-scale material structure and properties emerge from and are

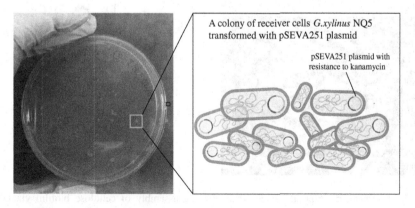

**Fig. 2.** DNA-level programming of cellulose-producing bacteria. (left) G. *xylinus* NQ5 colonies transformed with pSEVA251 plasmid acquire new property of antibiotic resistance. (right) Schematic description of a transformed colony of cells containing the plasmid.

dependent on the DNA-encoded information and the response of living cells to their environment.

We introduce synthetic gene networks, engineered DNA circuits for a genetic design of living components (cells), to pattern cellulose fibers through the intake of substances in response to signals in their environment (such as small chemicals, UV light). As a first step, we develop a transformation method and introduce synthetic DNA molecule (pSEVA251 plasmid) with new information (antibiotic resistance) into *G. xylinus* cells (See 2.2 in *Methods,* Fig. 2).

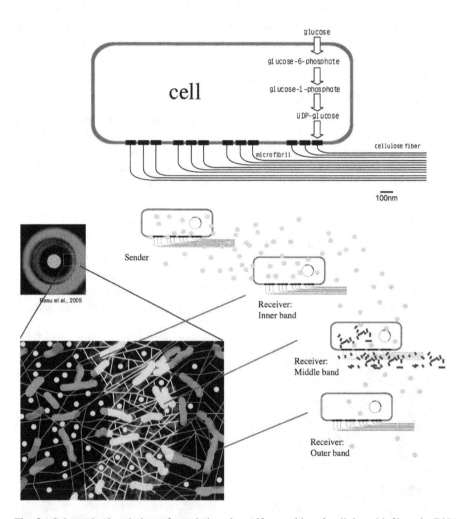

**Fig. 3.** Schematic description of regulating the self-assembly of cellulose biofilm via DNA design. (top) Schematic description of the multi-step metabolic process of cellulose production. (bottom) Schematic description of a density gradient pattern within the cellulose biofilm.

In our ongoing project, we design a synthetic gene network to detect center and edge and produce a gradient of material properties within cellulose biofilm (Fig. 3). The main innovation of this ongoing work is to implement the pattern-forming cell-to-cell communication device within the structural material to modify material structure and properties. The design in Fig. 3 below shows bull-eye pattern previously developed in our laboratory for E. coli cell lawn [19], implemented here within cellulose biofilm, demonstrating a band of higher density by localizing activation of cross-linking proteins production.

To generate this pattern, we program three types of computational constructs (or plasmids):

(a) the sender plasmids that are placed in the middle and are responsible for sending the signal and creating the spatial orientation gradient;
(b) the high-detect plasmids that produce fusion proteins with high sensitivity to the signal concentration;
(c) the low-detect plasmids that produce fusion proteins with low sensitivity to the signal concentration;

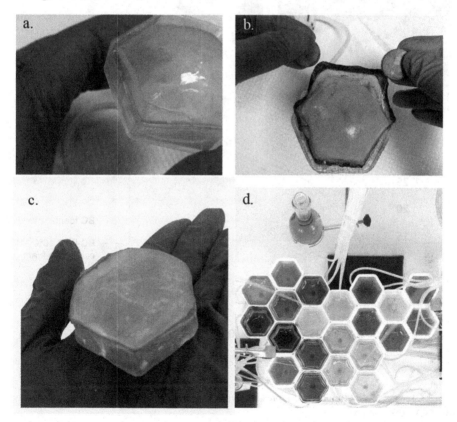

**Fig. 4.** Guided growth of cellulose biofilms. (a) Biofilm grows on the interface of nutrient-rich liquid and air. (b) In-situ biocomposite with magnetite to create 3D shaped magnetic biofilms. (c) Liquids were pumped out and replaced with air to stabilize 3D biofilm. (d) Multiple growth vessels within 3D printed frame routed with silicone tubing. (Color figure online)

The specific range and the intensity and type of the middle band response can be user-specified and engineered. We can design, computationally predict, and experimentally tune the location, type of response, its intensity, and duration [9]. The results from this portion of the project will be published as a separate paper.

## 4 *Growth*: Growing Biofilms that Inhabit Cells

We regulate the physical and chemical parameters of the growth environment to shape biofilms as they grow and tune their mechanical properties. We design growth vessels that allow permeability to oxygen and not to liquid to shape biofilms into three-dimensional components (Fig. 4a, b). We successfully fabricate three-dimensional shapes from bacterial cellulose.

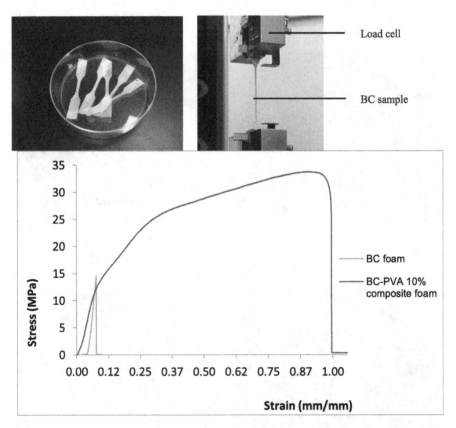

**Fig. 5.** Tensile testing (upper) and representative stress-strain curves (bottom) of BC sheets and BC-PVA 10% composite.

To demonstrate the effect of chemical conditions on the mechanical properties of cellulose biofilms, we create *in-situ* composites of magnetite to produce magnetic biofilms and polyvinyl alcohol (depicted black and blue respectively in Fig. 4d). We use tensile testing to characterize the mechanical properties of resulting. We observed that BC samples broke very sharply, without plastic deformation, in a brittle failure. However, the BC-PVA 10% composites were much more ductile and experienced plastic deformation and necking before fracture. Representative stress-strain curves for tested samples are plotted in Fig. 5.

## 5 *Flow*: Regulating Growth Environment

We automate the production of three-dimensional components from bacterial cellulose with a desired shape and material properties, according to a predefined composition of parameters generated into the system. We design and fabricate a device to vary physicochemical conditions in multiple growth vessels. We built custom-made microcontrollers and designed computational scripts to regulate the flow of nutrients, added substances, and air in and out the growth vessels. Scripts allow the adjustment of medium composition, *in-situ* substance addition (see 2.4 in *Methods*), and replacement of fluids with air to stabilize biofilms' three-dimensional shape (Fig. 4a, b, c).

Each cell has an inlet and outlet, and the entire system is routed by silicone tubes (Fig. 6). Multiple components control the flow of air and liquids in and out of growth

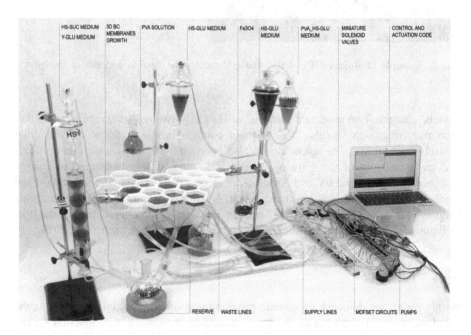

**Fig. 6.** Regulating the flow of nutrients, liquids, and air in and out multiple growth vessels via computational scripts (food coloring detects variation in medium composition). (Color figure online)

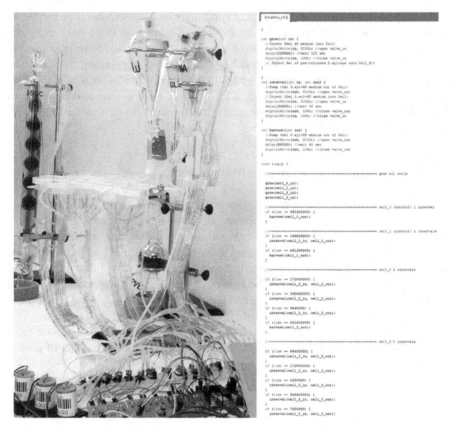

**Fig. 7.** Example of Arduino IDE script that orchestrates the flow in and out of the growth vessels.

vessels' clusters. Two miniature solenoid valves (X-Valve by Parker) are connected to each pair of growth vessels. One solenoid controls incoming flows and the other controls waste flows. The solenoids are also connected to pumps which pump fluids and air in and out of the growth vessels. The solenoids are connected to custom designed electronic circuits, and Arduino microcontrollers enable communication and feedback with the programming environment. A script in Arduino IDE, a programming language for Arduino open-source electronics platform, actuates and controls the flow of liquids and air through the silicone tubing to and from the growth vessels (Fig. 7).

## 6  Conclusions

In this paper, we demonstrate genetic programming of microorganisms, such as the cellulose-producing bacteria *G. xylinus*, and guiding their material production for the formation of shapes, composites, and patterns. We also demonstrate how digital fabrication and computation can be integrated with biological growth.

The work presented here suggests the future of biological integration not as an attempt to emulate nature, but to integrate biological systems—their matter, computations, and metabolisms—into materials. The applications currently proposed for cellulose and its composites include medical applications, textiles, and high-performance acoustic materials [9, 11, 15]. However, by combining genetic regulation of this material with the physicochemical environment that supports biological growth, we can preserve the biological responsiveness of these materials, and develop future living materials and devices, for applications such as responsive robotic skins, solar cells, or even photosynthetic building envelopes.

**Acknowledgements.** The authors would like to acknowledge Dr. Eric Arndt for his valuable advice and feedback. We thank undergraduate researchers Trinh Nguyen and Hang Le Thi Nguyet for their work on this project. We thank Lina M. González from the Voigt Lab at MIT for *E. coli* WM6026 and the conjugation protocol. We thank Prof. De Lorenzo and the SEVA collection for the plasmids used in this project. This research was funded by the National Science Foundation Division of Materials Research (NSF DMR) under the grant #1508072 named "Material and morphometric control of bacterial cellulose via genetic engineering post-processing and 3D printed molding".

# References

1. Epstein, A.K., Pokroy, B., Seminara, A., Aizenberg, J.: Bacterial biofilm shows persistent resistance to liquid wetting and gas penetration. Proc. Natl. Acad. Sci. **108**(3), 995–1000 (2011)
2. O'Toole, G., Kaplan, H.B., Kolter, R.: Biofilm formation as microbial development. Annu. Rev. Microbiol. **54**(1), 49–79 (2000)
3. Blouin, S., et al.: Mapping dynamical mechanical properties of osteonal bone by scanning acoustic microscopy in time-of-flight mode. Microsc. Microanal. **20**(3), 924–936 (2014)
4. Aizenberg, J., Weaver, J.C., Thanawala, M.S., Sundar, V.C., Morse, D.E., Fratzl, P.: Skeleton of Euplectella sp.: structural hierarchy from the nanoscale to the macroscale. Science **309**(5732), 275–278 (2005)
5. Ortiz, C., Boyce, M.C.: Bioinspired structural materials. Science **319**(5866), 1053–1054 (2008)
6. Meyers, M.A., Chen, P.-Y., Lin, A.Y.-M., Seki, Y.: Biological materials: structure and mechanical properties. Prog. Mater Sci. **53**(1), 1–206 (2008)
7. Cartwright, J.H.E., Checa, A.G.: The dynamics of nacre self-assembly. J. R. Soc. Interface **4**(14), 491–504 (2007)
8. Davies, J.: Mechanisms of Morphogenesis. Academic Press, Cambridge (2013)
9. Chen, A.Y., et al.: Synthesis and patterning of tunable multiscale materials with engineered cells. Nat. Mater. **13**(5), 515–523 (2014)
10. Qin, G., Panilaitis, B.J., Kaplan, Z.S.D.L.: A cellulosic responsive 'living' membrane. Carbohydr. Polym. **100**, 40–45 (2014)
11. Yamanaka, S., et al.: The structure and mechanical properties of sheets prepared from bacterial cellulose. J. Mater. Sci. **24**(9), 3141–3145 (1989)
12. Svensson, A., et al.: Bacterial cellulose as a potential scaffold for tissue engineering of cartilage. Biomaterials **26**(4), 419–431 (2005)

13. Bäckdahl, H., et al.: Mechanical properties of bacterial cellulose and interactions with smooth muscle cells. Biomaterials **27**(9), 2141–2149 (2006)
14. Brown, R.M.: Cellulose microfibril assembly and orientation: recent developments. J. Cell Sci. **1985**(Suppl. 2), 13–32 (1985)
15. Johnson, D.C., Neogi, A.N.: Sheeted products formed from reticulated microbial cellulose. US4863565 A, 05 September 1989
16. Lin, S.-P., Calvar, I.L., Catchmark, J.M., Liu, J.-R., Demirci, A., Cheng, K.-C.: Biosynthesis, production and applications of bacterial. Cellulose **20**(5), 2191–2219 (2013)
17. Long, J.W., Rolison, D.R.: Architectural design, interior decoration, and three-dimensional plumbing en route to multifunctional nanoarchitectures. Acc. Chem. Res. **40**(9), 854–862 (2007)
18. Araya, S., Zolotovsky, K., Gidekel, M.: Living architecture micro performances of bio fabrication. ECAADe - vol. Prod. (2012)
19. Basu, S., Gerchman, Y., Collins, C.H., Arnold, F.H., Weiss, R.: A synthetic multicellular system for programmed pattern formation. Nature **434**(7037), 1130–1134 (2005)
20. Wang, J., Gao, C., Zhang, Y., Wan, Y.: Preparation and in vitro characterization of BC/PVA hydrogel composite for its potential use as artificial cornea biomaterial. Mater. Sci. Eng., C **30**(1), 214–218 (2010)

# Author Index

Affeld, Klaus   110
Aicardi, Christine   129
Akiyama, Kyoichi   1
Alexandre, Frédéric   338
Andersen, Kayla B.   6
Andrada, Emanuel   134
Arnold, Dirk   134
Arreguit, Jonathan   1
Arsiwalla, Xerxes D.   11, 179, 382
Aubin, Lise   16
Audu, Musa L.   276

Bachmann, Richard J.   326
Bailly, François   28
Barceló, Xavier   316
Baumgartner, Werner   439
Bels, Vincent   28
Berns, Karsten   348
Blanchard, Arnaud   40
Bockemühl, Till   477
Bonnet, Frank   73
Bračun, Drago   52
Bredeche, Nicolas   73, 85
Burnus, Niels   263
Burton, Saheli Datta   129
Büschges, Ansgar   477

Camilleri, Daniel   64
Casas, Jerome   115
Cazenille, Leo   73, 85
Chayaamor-Heil, Natasha   97
Chemtob, Yohann   73
Chiel, Hillel J.   6, 236
Cho, Moonsung   110
Cianchetti, Matteo   288
Cramphorn, Luke   263

Dalgaty, Thomas   115
Daltorio, Kathryn A.   6, 236
De Salvo, Barbara   115

Del Dottore, Emanuela   288
Deng, Kaiyu   134
Dupeyroux, Julien   145
Dürr, Volker   187, 428

Escuredo, Alex   415
Esser, Falk   157
Evdaimon, Theodoros   494

Filippeschi, Carlo   168
Fiorello, Isabella   168
Fischer, Martin   134
Freire, Ismael T.   11, 179

Gazit, Merav   538
Girard, Benoît   16
Gollin, Arne   187
Gribovskiy, Alexey   73

Halloy, José   73, 85
Hayasaka, Tomoaki   321
Hilts, Wade W.   200
Hosoda, Koh   255
Huang, Jiaqi V.   213
Hunt, Alexander J.   52, 134, 200, 450, 527

Ijspeert, Auke Jan   1
Indiveri, Giacomo   115
Ishiguro, Akio   1, 249, 304
Ishikawa, Masato   304
Iza, M.   223

James, Jasper W.   232
Jayachandran, Prithvi R.   236

Kandhari, Akhil   6, 236
Kano, Takeshi   1, 249
Kawashima, Hiroki   255
Khamassi, Mehdi   16

Kim, Sun-Joong   471
Krapp, Holger G.   213
Krieger, Michael   439
Krüger, Friederike   157

Lepora, Nathan F.   232, 263, 365
Liu, Chujun   276
Llamosi, Artémis   490
Lonsberry, Andrew G.   276
Lunni, Dario   288
Ly, Denys   115

Mahfoud, Tara   129
Mangan, Michael   459
Marshall, Lauren   300
Masselter, Tom   157
Masuda, Yoichi   304
Mathews, Zenon   415
Mazzolai, Barbara   168, 288
Mebarki, Djamel   40
Melo, Kamilo   1
Mestre, Rafael   316
Mianowski, Krzysztof   348
Mishra, Anand Kumar   168
Mizuno, Fumio   321
Mondada, Francesco   73
Moses, Kenneth C.   326

Nallapu, Bhargav Teja   338
Nandor, Mark J.   276
Nejadfard, Atabak   348
Neubauer, Peter   110
Nourse, William   361
Nowak, Etienne   115

Ortiz, Christine   538

Paez, Laura   1
Papadakis, Emmanouil   494
Patiño, Tania   316
Pearson, Martin J.   403
Pestell, Nicholas   365
Pickard, Shanel C.   370
Pouydebat, Emmanuelle   28
Prescott, Tony   64
Prigg, David   326
Puigbò, Jordi-Ysard   11, 179, 382

Quinn, Roger D.   6, 52, 134, 200, 236, 276,
    326, 361, 370, 527

Rechenberg, Ingo   110
Riviere, Valentin   387
Rollins, Alexander   236
Rose, Nikolas   129

Sadati, S. M. Hadi   391
Sadeghi, Ali   288
Sajnani, Umakshi   255
Salman, Mohammed   403
Sanchez, Samuel   316
Santos-Pata, Diogo   415
Schroeder, Adam   300
Schultz, Marco   428
Schütz, Steffen   348
Serres, Julien   145
Shimizu, Masahiro   255
Signorelli, Camilo M.   11
Sinibaldi, Edoardo   288
Škulj, Gašper   52
Souères, Philippe   28
Speck, Thomas   157
Stadler, Anna Theresia   439
Steele, Alexander G.   450
Stover, Matthew C.   236
Sun, Xuelong   459
Szczecinski, Nicholas S.   52, 134, 200, 361,
    370, 477

Tao, Yilin   263
Toussaint, Séverine   490
Tramacere, Francesca   168
Trease, Brian   300
Tricinci, Omar   168
Tsakiris, Dimitris P.   494

Vaughan, Neil   507, 517, 522
Verschure, Paul F. M. J.   11, 179, 382, 415
Vianello, Elisa   115
Viollet, Stéphane   145, 387
Vonwirth, Patrick   348

Watier, Bruno   28
Wei, Yiran   213
Weisfeld, Matthias   326

Williams, Thomas   391
Willis, Mark   326

Yamaguchi, Takami   321
Yasui, Kotaro   1

Yoshizawa, Ryo   249
Young, Fletcher   527
Yue, Shigang   459

Zolotovsky, Katia   538

Printed in the United States
By Bookmasters